50 ¢

Next Quiz —
9,10,11 —
Q.t.M.

a-15

QUESTIONS THAT MATTER

AN INVITATION TO PHILOSOPHY

E D. L. MILLER

Professor of Philosophy
University of Colorado

McGRAW-HILL BOOK COMPANY

New York   St. Louis   San Francisco   Auckland   Bogotá   Hamburg   Johannesburg
London   Madrid   Mexico   Montreal   New Delhi   Panama
Paris   São Paulo   Singapore   Sydney   Tokyo   Toronto

For the Fair Cynthia

QUESTIONS
THAT
MATTER

AN INVITATION
TO PHILOSOPHY

34567890 DOCDOC 898765

ISBN 0-07-042175-7

See Acknowledgments on pages 487–490.
Copyrights included on this page by reference.

This book was set in Goudy Old Style by University Graphics, Inc.
The editors were Kaye Pace, Anne Murphy, and Barry Benjamin;
the designer was Anne Canevari Green;
the production supervisor was Phil Galea.
The cover art was by Hans Erni.
The drawings were done by Burmar.
R. R. Donnelley & Sons Company was printer and binder.

Library of Congress Cataloging in Publication Data

Miller, Ed. L. (Ed. LeRoy), date
    Questions that matter.

    Includes index.
    1. Philosophy—Introductions. I. Title.
BD21.M46 1984   100   83-13596
ISBN 0-07-042175-7

CONTENTS

PART ONE
THE QUESTION OF REALITY

**PART TWO
THE QUESTION OF KNOWLEDGE**

**PART FIVE
THE QUESTION OF SOCIETY**

P R E F A C E

This book is intended as an introductory text for students whose college experience may not include a subsequent course in philosophy. I have endeavored to make lucid a very difficult and often confusing subject and, at the same time, to do justice to its history and importance. It is hoped that the integrity of the subject has survived my efforts at simplification and abbreviation.

In the pursuit of this goal I have been mindful of the classroom setting: (a) *The instructor's task.* The best way of showing respect and concern for the goals and methods of the individual instructor is to provide a text that is not confining or burdensome. Instead, it provides instructors with a point of departure that will enhance and strengthen their personal approaches to the subject and their goals for their students. (b) *The student's task.* Most of the students using this text will have no background in philosophy and are likely to be baffled by their first encounter with the subject's language, distinctions, concepts, etc. This first encounter is likely to be the student's best (and for many, only) opportunity to master a subject which really does pose the questions that matter. A student can be cheated of that mastery but can never avoid the questions. Thus I have been guided throughout by a concern to represent and discuss the issues in a coherent, readable, and stimulating style. Furthermore, I have attempted to organize the content so that the students will be able to appreciate for themselves that there really is coherence and direction amid the twists and turns. I have also been guided by a conviction that explanatory aids can be utilized to promote understanding in an often difficult subject.

My attempts to present the material in a way that will most profit the student and the classroom is evident in the following:

- Major historical thinkers have been discussed, but not to the exclusion of contemporary contributions.
- Appropriate and extended selections from primary sources have been included, interspersed throughout the discussions, making it possible for students to read the major thinkers for themselves.
- Major fields in philosophy have been included, as well as the major issues and traditions in those fields.
- No topic or issue has been excluded on the grounds that it was too difficult.

- The book seeks to accommodate the instructor's creative use of the primary materials, thus allowing him or her to develop self-designed exchange with the students.
- Fields and issues have been chosen that are most likely to be relevant to the student's mastery of elementary philosophy.

Each part of the book represents a major topic in philosophy, though instructors are encouraged to consider these topics in whatever order they deem appropriate. Each chapter contains a discussion of the relevant issues, plus a variety of supplemental material. The discussion is presented in as logical and historical a manner as possible, showing connections, roots, and influences. The issues and positions are documented with frequent and usually copious quotations from philosophers, woven into the text. The rather generous margins contain running summaries of the adjoining section. These serve the student not only as an indexing device, but also as a method for quick review of the most important ideas. At those points where basic terms, concepts, or positions need to be explained, summarized, or emphasized, the section is interrupted with a boxed insert. Still other insertions contain relevant information—for example, biographical sketches. Illustrations have been included so as to provide, on occasion, visual relief and reinforcement. Each chapter concludes with a review section which includes a brief summary, a list of basic ideas, a self-test, and questions for reflection and possible discussion, to assist students in their mastery of the material in that chapter.

A two-chapter introduction has been prefixed to the whole. The first chapter explains the nature of philosophy, and includes various definitions and conceptions, as well as discussion of issues and problems involved in the philosophical enterprise itself, and its relation to other fields. The second chapter provides an introductory discussion of logic for the use of those instructors (a growing number) who believe that such an overview is important in introductory philosophy courses.

With respect to the broad outline of the book, it was felt that the more or less standard way of organizing and presenting philosophical material is, after all, the best. The reader will find here a much more restrained approach than may be found in some texts, which verge on the flamboyant and far-flung, and at the same time an attempt to provide, nonetheless, a visually arresting format. Furthermore, the interest in treating (whenever possible) *historical* contexts, connections, and developments can only benefit both the study and the teaching of philosophy.

> For us who have undertaken the toil of abbreviating, it is no light matter, but calls for sweat and loss of sleep.
>
> —II Macc. 2:26 (Revised Standard Version)

This book has grown out of many years of teaching beginning philosophy courses to innumerable students. I have tried to pay attention to what works and what doesn't in the attempt to confront, engage, and instruct. Beyond that, I have been much helped at every stage by my editors at McGraw-Hill, chiefly Kaye Pace, but also Anne Murphy and Barry Benjamin, and by those who reviewed the material: Professor Frank W. Derringh (New York City Technical College, Brooklyn, N.Y.); Professor Desmond FitzGerald (University of San Francisco, San Francisco, Calif.); Professor Richard L. Oliver (San Antonio College, San Antonio, Tex.); Professor Clarence M. Parker (Central State University, Edmund, Okla.); Professor George Cronk (Bergen Community College, Paramus, N.J.); Professor Frederick R. Struckmeyer (West Chester State College, West Chester, Pa.); Professor Edward H. Bloomfield (Cerritos College, Norwalk, Calif.); and Professor Leonard O'Brien (Elgin Community College, Elgin, Ill.). Closer to home, I wish to thank my own colleagues at the University of Colorado, including Professor Wes Morriston, who read the entire manuscript, and Professor William Prior, who read parts of it, and my philosopher-friend, Lee Speer, who made invaluable contributions regarding the basic concept of the book and provided excellent counsel all along the way. With respect to manuscript preparation, much thanks goes to several assistants: Craig Hubbard, Dan Handschy, Michael Thompson, Paul Awald, but above all to John S. Meyer, who provided constant and unfailing support and assistance in all matters. I also wish to thank my wife who read through the proofs from a student's perspective, and to whom it is dedicated.

Ed. L. Miller

INTRODUCTION

THE NATURE OF PHILOSOPHY

"Philosophical reflection is not an activity indulged in only by specialists called philosophers who allegedly live in architectural monstrosities known as ivory towers. Just as each of us at times engages casually in horticulture or medicine or carpentry without special training, so practically all of us on certain occasions spontaneously occupy ourselves with philosophical questions.

"We may, for example, read in the newspapers of a child born hopelessly malformed and defective, but who, if operated upon at once, might nonetheless be kept alive. And we may read further that the physician in charge, realizing that the child's life could not be other than a grievous burden to himself, to his parents, and to society, refrained from operating and allowed the child to die. Then, in letters from readers to the editors of newspapers all over the country, controversy rages about whether the physician's action was morally right or morally wrong. And even if we do not ourselves take active part in them, we too form opinions on the question.

"In such a controversy the participants do not merely state their moral appraisal of the physician's course. They also give reasons of one kind or another to support the validity of their judgment. And if these reasons are in turn challenged, each participant brings forth considerations he believes adequate to vindicate the validity of his reasons.

"The reasons, and the reasons for the reasons, that are thus appealed to as grounds for endorsing or condemning the physician's action, constitute a moral philosophy, or at least a fragment of one. And the mental activity of searching for those reasons, and of then so editing them as to purge them of the inconsistencies of exaggerations or errors that opponents were able to point out, constitute philosophizing, or philosophical reflection.

"In this example the issue is a moral one, and the philosophy constructed on the spur of the occasion by a participant is therefore, as far as it goes, a moral philosophy: that is, a theory of the nature of the difference between moral right and wrong, and of the nature of the situations to which appraisal in terms of morality and immorality is congruous. But similar controversies, or indeed doubts within one person's mind, arise about issues of other kinds: about the merits of certain works of art, for example, or about educational issues, or about the sufficiency of the evidence offered as basis for a given assertion, and so on. The fragmentary philosophies similarly improvised on such occasions are then a philosophy of art, a philosophy of education, or a philosophy of knowledge. And there can be no doubt that, on the occasions impelling us to engage in such reflection, a judgment shaped by the conclusions reached in that reflective manner is likely to be wiser than would be one made without it."

C. J. Ducasse, *The Key Reporter*, 23 (1958), p. 3.

CHAPTER 1

WHAT IS PHILOSOPHY?

Inasmuch as this text seeks to introduce the reader to philosophy, it may seem appropriate to begin by defining the term. We will indeed try to define and characterize philosophy, but the reader should have no illusions that this is how one really comes to understand it. The real way to understand what philosophy is about is to *participate* in it. This means to be confronted with philosophical questions, to use philosophical language, to become acquainted with differing philosophical positions and maneuvers, to read the philosophers themselves, and to grapple with the issues for oneself. Therefore it is not at the beginning but rather at the *end* of such a book as this that one might really understand something of philosophy. Nevertheless, we must begin somewhere, and it may be useful to have at least *some* idea of the subject before us, right at the start.

THE WORD ITSELF

Four ways of getting at the meaning and nature of philosophy may be proposed. *First*, let us look at the word itself. "Philosophy" comes from a Greek word which means "love of wisdom." It was first used by the ancient Greek thinker Pythagoras (about 600 B.C.), who likened philosophers—pursuers of wisdom—to spectators at ancient games:

Philosophy: The love of wisdom

> . . . when Leon the tyrant of Phlius asked him who he was, he said, "A philosopher," and that he compared life to the Great Games, where some went to compete for the prize and others went with wares to sell, but the best as spectators; for similarly, in

3

life, some grow up with servile natures, greedy for fame and gain, but the philosopher seeks for truth.[1]

To be sure, something of the spirit and character of philosophy is suggested in this way by the very meaning of the word—but not much. We must know more about this "pursuit of wisdom."

> "Philosophy is like the measles. It must be caught from someone who is already infected. To learn to philosophize, you must try your luck arguing with a live philosopher."
>
> Elmer Sprague, *What Is Philosophy?* (New York: Oxford University Press, 1961), p. 3.

Pythagoras, the first to call himself a "philosopher"

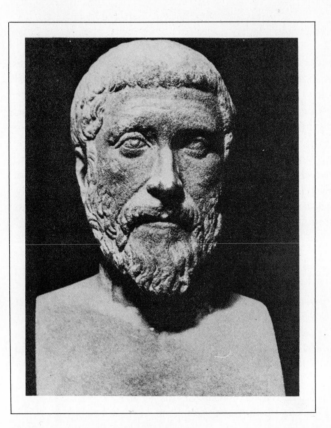

[1]Diogenes Laertius, *Lives of Eminent Philosophers*, VIII, 8, tr. R. D. Hicks (Cambridge, Mass.: Harvard University Press, 1925), II.

THE FIELDS OF PHILOSOPHY

Let us then, *second*, approach the meaning of philosophy from a different standpoint, namely, from the standpoint of its several fields or areas of investigation. Not all lists of the fields of philosophy would agree, but most of them would almost certainly include six: *metaphysics, epistemology, value-theory, ethics, aesthetics,* and *logic.* Some of these terms may seem to be taken from a foreign language, but they are not as difficult as they sound.

Metaphysics means, usually, the study or theory of reality. The question of metaphysics is: What is reality? What is real? This involves, of course, many related questions, such as, Is reality some kind of "thing"? Is it one or is it many? If it is one, then how is it related to the many things around us? Can ultimate reality be grasped by the five senses, or is it supernatural or transcendent? And so on. It should be mentioned that sometimes the word "metaphysics" is used in a narrower way to concern only *transcendent* reality, that is, reality which lies beyond the physical world and cannot therefore be grasped by means of the senses. Therefore, supernaturalists do metaphysics in the first sense because they raise the question of reality, and they do metaphysics also in the narrower sense because they believe in supernatural or transcendent reality, say, God. On the other hand, materialists do metaphysics in the first sense because they too raise the question of reality, but their belief is not metaphysical in the narrower sense because they deny that anything is real except matter.

Epistemology is the study or theory of knowledge. The question of epistemology is: What is knowledge? What does it mean "to know"? This too implies many other questions, such as, How is knowledge acquired? What, if anything, do the senses contribute to knowledge? What does reason contribute? Can we be really certain of anything? What is truth? Some philosophers think that the fields of metaphysics and epistemology are, in a way, the pillars of all the rest. Why would one say this? Are the questions, What is real? And how can I know it? in some

Metaphysics

Epistemology

As a philosophical concept, metaphysics originated in the first century B.C. when Andronicus, a scholar in Rhodes, was editing Aristotle's works. He found it difficult to classify one of these works and simply placed it *meta ta physika*, which in Greek meant "after the physical [works]." By a happy coincidence the *Metaphysics* of Aristotle did in fact concern primarily the "first principles" of things, the ultimate causes that lie after or beyond (*meta*) the physical (*physika*).

sense the most basic questions of all? Is it possible that how you answer these questions will determine your whole philosophical outlook?

Value-theory

Value-theory is, obviously, the study of value. The question here is: What is value? It should be noted that this question does not involve any particular sort of value, but of value of *all* sorts—the value of tables, steaks, political ideologies, laws,

Ethics

actions—with value in any and all of its manifestations. *Ethics,* on the other hand, is concerned with a *particular* sort of value, namely, value as it applies to personal actions, decisions, and relations; it is concerned with *moral* value. It raises the question, What is morally good? What is right? Here again a whole cluster of questions suggest themselves, such as, Are there any absolute or universal moral principles?

Aesthetics

Does the end ever justify the means? Am I my brother's keeper? *Aesthetics* is also the study of a particular sort of value, namely, the values involved in art and our experience of beauty. It raises the question, What is art? It addresses such issues as the relation of beauty to art, whether there can be any objective standards by which artistic works may be judged (or is beauty in the eye of the beholder?), and the connection between art, reality, and truth. (It should be noted that ethics, which studies moral value, and aesthetics, which studies aesthetic values, are properly subfields of value-theory, which raises the question of value as such.)

Logic

Logic is the formulation of the principles of right reasoning. We have saved logic for last, since traditionally it stands in a somewhat different relation to the philosopher than the other fields do. The other fields suggest something that is studied by the philosopher—reality, knowledge, value, etc. Logic is a *tool* which philosophers employ as they set about to investigate these issues. This was recognized already in antiquity. Aristotle was the first to formulate in a systematic way the principle of right reasoning, and the writings in which he did this (his "logical" writings) came to be called the *Organon,* which in Greek means "instrument" or "tool." This view of logic as a tool has, however, changed somewhat in recent years. With the rise of mathematical and symbolic logic, logic itself has become for many a proper *object* of philosophical study.

The unity of philosophical questions

When we distinguish in this way the several fields of philosophy we suggest something of the diversity of philosophical questions: The question of reality, the question of knowledge, the question of morality, etc. But the questions posed by these various fields cannot, after all, be so neatly separated. In many ways these questions (and their answers) rise and fall together. Do not the questions of value-theory bear directly upon ethics, aesthetics, and metaphysics itself? Would not one's theory of reality (for example one's affirmation or denial of God) probably hold implications for one's view of morality, knowledge, and reality? Would not the opinion that there is no certain knowledge whatsoever cast a certain light—or darkness—over all questions of reality, value, or anything else? In this way we must emphasize also the *unity* of philosophical questions.

The "philosophy of ———" areas

In addition to the standard fields of philosophy some further areas should be mentioned, namely, where philosophical concern relates itself to other disciplines: The "philosophy *of* ———" category. Examples are the philosophy of religion,

---

THE FIELDS OF PHILOSOPHY

- *Metaphysics:* The study of reality (sometimes also the study of transcedent reality).
- *Epistemology:* The study of knowledge.
  Value-theory: The study of value.
- *Ethics:* The study of moral value, right and wrong.
- *Aesthetics:* The study of beauty and art.
- *Logic:* The principles of right reasoning.

---

philosophy of science, philosophy of education, and philosophy of law. Here a particular discipline is viewed and treated *philosophically*; the philosopher is concerned with such issues as the nature of that discipline's subject matter, the adequacy of its methodology, the meaning and clarification of its concepts, its logical coherence, and its relation to and implications for other fields. In the "philosophy of ————" studies, it is sometimes difficult to separate the *primary* subject (religion, science, education, law) from the *secondary* questions raised by the philosopher (questions concerning methodology, concepts, logic, relations). Nonetheless, it

---

SECOND-ORDER INQUIRIES

An ordinary question, such as "What is *X*?", is called a *first-order* question. A question about a first-order question is called a *second-order* question, for example, "What is the meaning of the question, 'What is *X*?'?" Second-order questions are also called *meta-* questions, or "talk about talk." Sometimes whole studies can be oriented in the direction of second-order concerns. Thus *meta-*ethics is talk about ethical talk. Philosophical areas such as philosophy of religion, philosophy of science, philosophy of law, and philosophy of education, tend to be second-order inquiries. On the other hand, it is often difficult to separate talking about talk from the primary talking itself. Why would you raise a second-order issue unless you were interested in the primary issue in the first place?

Second-order studies

should be clear that the "philosophy of ————" studies are largely "second-order" studies, that is, studies *about* studies. If, for example, you ever take a course in the philosophy of science, you won't light any bunsen-burners, collect any specimens, or dissect any frogs. What you will do is think and talk *about* science. That is, you will analyze the meaning of science, scientific language and concepts, scientific procedures, conclusions, and implications.

It should be noted, though, that in actual usage the distinction between the fields of philosophy and the "philosophy of ————" areas is not hard and fast. Aesthetics, for example, could accurately be represented as the philosophy of art, whereas philosophy of religion would certainly raise, say, the metaphysical issue of God's existence and nature.

A RATIONAL, CRITICAL ENTERPRISE

In our *third* attempt to characterize philosophy we propose something more illuminating than giving the root meaning of the word, and something less cumbersome than spelling out its several fields. And we come to the heart of the matter when we suggest that whatever else it may be, philosophy is a *rational* and *critical* enterprise.

Rationalism

The word "rational" is important. Sometimes in philosophical discussion the words "rational," "rationalist," and "rationalism" are used with a rather technical meaning, as we shall see later. But here we intend these words in a more ordinary and loose sense. They have to do with *reason* and *reasonableness*. A rational argument, for example, is one that makes sense, is coherent, and is well-founded. A rationalist is a person who is given to argument, investigation, and evaluation. And rationalism is the position which affirms reason as one of the highest authorities — maybe even *the* highest authority — in matters of belief and conduct. There is, in all of this, a certain *critical* activity that must not be missed. In being a *rational* enterprise, philosophy seeks to eradicate from our perspectives every taint and vestige of ignorance, superstition, prejudice, blind acceptance of ideas, and any other form of irrationality. It challenges our ideas, analyzes them, and tests them in light

Philosophy involves reason, criticism, examination, analysis

RATIONALISM (THE LOOSE SENSE)

The view which affirms reason, with its interest in evidence, examination, and evaluation, as authoritative in all matters of belief and conduct.

> "... it is owing to their wonder that men both now begin and at first began to philosophize; they wondered originally at the obvious difficulties, then advanced little by little and stated difficulties about the greater matters."
>
> —ARISTOTLE

of evidence and arguments. It presses us to coherent and valid expressions of our ideas.

The early Greek philosopher Socrates (ca. 470–399 B.C.) has always been regarded as a kind of *symbol* of philosophical activity, especially its rational and critical nature. It is no wonder. Socrates was constantly pressing himself and everyone else for clarity and answers. His method was to engage someone over the meaning of some term or idea, usually a moral concept, and then to cross-examine his opponent mercilessly until some progress or clarity was achieved. According to Plato's *Apology* (an account of Socrates' defense at his trial), Socrates likens himself to a gadfly which incessantly stings and disturbs and challenges the citizenry:

Socrates: the symbol of philosophical activity

> If you put me to death, you will not easily find anyone to take my place. It is literally true, even if it sounds rather comical, that God has specially appointed me to this city, as though it were a large thoroughbred horse which because of its great size is inclined to be lazy and needs the stimulation of some stinging fly. It seems to me that God has attached me to this city to perform the office of such a fly, and all day long I never cease to settle here, there, and everywhere, rousing, persuading, reproving every one of you. You will not easily find another like me, gentlemen, and if you take my advice you will spare my life. I suspect, however, that before long you will awake from your drowsing, and in your annoyance you will take Anytus' advice and finish me off with a single slap, and then you will go on sleeping till the end of your days, unless God in his care for you sends someone to take my place. . . .[2]

It is from this same context that perhaps the most famous line of all philosophical literature comes: "The unexamined life is not worth living":

"The unexamined life is not worth living."

> I tell you that to let no day pass without discussing goodness and all the other subjects about which you hear me talking and examining both myself and others is really the very best thing that a man can do, and that life without this sort of examination is not worth living. . . .[3]

[2]Plato, *Apology*, 29D–31A, 33B–C, tr. Hugh Tredennick, in *Plato: The Collected Dialogues*, ed. Edith Hamilton and Huntington Cairns (New York: Pantheon Books, 1961).

[3]Ibid., 38A.

SOCRATES

Socrates was born in Athens about 470 B.C. He must have come from a fairly well-to-do family (there is some evidence that his father was a stonecutter), since as a young man he was a fully armed hoplite in the army.

His appearance and character are notorious. He is said to have resembled a satyr, we know that he had a pug nose, and the comic dramatist Aristophanes represented him as strutting like a waterfowl and rolling his eyes. We also know that he was a man of considerable physical endurance: He could spend long hours in meditation (once, a whole day and night) uninterrupted by the need for food; he once went barefoot on a wintry military expedition; and he could consume vast amounts of wine without becoming the least tipsy. More than once he distinguished himself for bravery during the Peloponnesian War, during which time he married Xanthippe, who according to tradition was one of the world's outstanding shrews.

In the *Apology* (Plato's account of Socrates' trial) Socrates relates the origin of his philosophical mission: Once a friend of Socrates asked the Delphic Oracle who the wisest of men was, to which the Oracle responded, "Socrates." Socrates himself was much perplexed by this answer and concluded that if indeed he was wisest it could only be because he was so aware of his *ignorance*. Much turned off by the Sophists, who seemed to him to be more interested in the appearance of truth than in truth itself (and even charged for their instruction), Socrates pursued abiding and fixed truth. In fact, Aristotle credits him with being the first to seek *definitions*, especially of moral ideas such as justice and piety. Socrates utilized *dialogue* as the method of this pursuit, confronting, interrogating, and wheedling his adversaries into clearer thinking.

Eventually, he was found on the wrong side politically and was tried and found guilty of trumped-up charges of teaching strange gods and corrupting the youth. He scorned the opportunity of escaping prison and willingly drank the poisonous hemlock. The year was 399 B.C.

Although universally regarded as the model of the philosophic spirit, and in some ways as the founder of Western philosophy, Socrates never published a word—and thus today would have been denied tenure at any major university.

As in Socrates, the accent in all philosophy clearly falls on reason and criticism. But can *everything* be reasoned? Must *every* proposition, idea, and belief be exposed to the searchlight of critical reflection? Some philosophers would answer with a loud Yes. Others would not be so optimistic, insisting that there are *limits* to the rational and critical enterprise. If true, then this in itself is an important fact about philosophy and must be reckoned with constantly. Many philosophers do in fact recognize that reality and our experience of it is, after all, bigger than philosophy: Not everything can be grasped intellectually; not everything can be reduced to an argument; not everything can be expressed in language. But what happens at the point where reason gives out? Do we simply draw a blank? Some would say that it is at this point that the *nonrational* too plays a role, and even an inevitable role. But it is important here that we do not confuse "nonrational" with

The limits of reason

Nonrational and irrational

NONRATIONAL AND IRRATIONAL

It is important not to confuse what is *nonrational* with what is *irrational*. A nonrational claim is one that is justified, if at all, through an appeal to something *other* than or *different* from reason: authority, feeling, intuition, religious illumination, mystical experience, and the like. For better or for worse, everyone makes nonrational claims at some time or other. An irrational claim, on the other hand, is one which is *contrary* to reason. This can take two forms. *First*, such a claim may be irrational in the sense that it flies in the face of everything we would expect from history, experience, and nature. An example of this would be the claim,

(1) Herds of giraffes are presently roaming the White House.

Such a claim is highly improbable and absurd. But it is at least *logically* possible: It could conceivably be true. Not so with the *second* kind of irrational claim,

(2) Jupiter is populated by four-sided triangles.

This sort of claim is impossible from the start. It involves a self-contradiction and is therefore *logically* impossible: It could not conceivably be true. One *might* venture an irrational claim in the first, and lesser, sense; but one *could not possibly* venture an irrational claim in the second, and stricter, sense—at least not without being thought a philosophical fool.

"irrational." That which is *irrational* is incompatible with general experience or reason itself, whereas that which is *non*rational is simply different from and maybe even higher than experience or reason.

If we *do* believe in nonrational knowledge, what forms might it take? Certainly philosophers disagree among themselves about the possible significance of the claims of intuition in the sense of an immediate and direct apprehension of truth, mystical experience as a transcendent and ecstatic union with ultimate reality, various forms of religious and inner illumination, poetic visions or feelings, and the like. On the other hand, many would agree at least on the inevitable presence of *ultimate presuppositions* (also called basic assumptions, faith assertions, etc.) which are known with certainty as the foundations of all of our other ideas but which

Foundationalism themselves cannot be proved. This view is known as *foundationalism*. Probably the most common defense of this view is the claim that from a purely logical standpoint not everything can be argued or there would never be an end to the arguing. A long time ago Aristotle pointed out that every argument finally rests on something that cannot be proved, and that it is the mark of an uneducated person not to realize that. There must be, as it were, a last outpost or final court of appeal. Do you believe with the foundationalists that every philosophical system or position or argument necessarily rests at some point or other on some idea or ideas which are certain and basic and undemonstrable? If so, then you must believe that here, if no place else, the *non*rational too makes a contribution.

FOUNDATIONALISM

Some philosophers believe that all knowledge rests ultimately on fundamental truths. These truths, which are themselves not subject to any proof, are the foundations of all other truths. Hence, "foundationalism."

DIFFERING CONCEPTIONS

So far, so good. Nearly everyone would agree with what has been said here about the meaning and origin of the word "philosophy," about the several standard fields and areas of philosophy, and about its rational and critical nature. Beyond that it is not so easy to say what philosophy is. In fact, the definition and meaning of philosophy is itself one of the big issues in contemporary philosophy! In our *fourth* way of getting at the meaning and nature of philosophy, it will be useful to suggest something of the very different forms which philosophy as a rational and critical enterprise has taken. We will limit ourselves to three: The speculative, the analytic, and the existential conceptions of philosophy.

The *speculative* approach is probably the most familiar. On this view, philosophy is the grandest of all disciplines. The speculative philosopher raises and tries to answer the most ultimate and far-ranging questions of all (what is reality? what is the ultimate good? what is the total meaning of things?) and to make sense of reality and experience as a whole. Advocates of this conception of philosophy insist that it is faithful to the broad sweep and character of our philosophical tradition and to what the giants of that tradition were really up to. In the beginning, Plato had, in fact, described the philosopher as a "spectator of time and eternity," and many philosophers since (such as Aristotle, St. Thomas, Descartes, Spinoza, Kant, Hegel) saw their philosophical task as a sort of cosmic one. The American philosopher Alfred North Whitehead (1861–1947) is a modern example of this view. Whitehead himself employed the expression "speculative philosophy" and defined it as

> the endeavor to frame a coherent, logical, necessary system of general ideas in terms of which every element of our experience can be interpreted. By this notion of "interpretation" I mean that everything of which we are conscious, as enjoyed, perceived, willed, or thought, shall have the character of a particular instance of the general scheme.[4]

Certainly less flamboyant is the *analytic* approach to philosophizing. This view of philosophy (which is not called "analytic" for nothing) takes *linguistic analysis*, or the analysis of language, as the proper and legitimate task of the philosopher. Although these philosophers also see their forerunners among the traditional philosophers, analytic philosophy as a clearly defined approach to philosophical issues is essentially a recent and contemporary movement. What is the driving conviction behind this approach? These thinkers, or at least the "ordinary language" analysts, lay the muddles, mistakes, and dead ends which characterize the history of philosophy to *linguistic confusion*. The proper task of the philosopher, at least for now, is therefore to unravel and to clarify philosophical language. When this is done, it will be seen that many or most of the traditional problems of philosophy turn out to be not real problems at all, but *pseudo*problems, problems not of reality but of language. One of the best-known of these philosophers is the English philosopher G. E. Moore (1873–1958), who provides an excellent statement of the analytic view of philosophy:

> It appears to me that in Ethics, as in all other philosophical studies, the difficulties and disagreements, of which its history is full, are mainly due to a very simple cause:

Three views of the philosopher's task

The speculative approach

The analytic approach

---

[4]Alfred North Whitehead, *Process and Reality* (New York: Macmillan, 1929), p. 4.

Alfred North Whitehead, an example of the speculative approach

namely to the attempt to answer questions, without first discovering precisely what question it is which you desire to answer. I do not know how far this source of error would be done away, if philosophers would try to discover what question they were asking, before they set about to answer it. . . . But I am inclined to think that in many cases a resolute attempt would be sufficient to assure success; so that, if only this attempt were made, many of the most glaring difficulties and disagreements in philosophy would disappear.[5]

The existential approach

With the *existential* approach the pendulum swings back in the opposite direction. For the existentialist philosopher, traditional philosophy has been too occupied with abstractions and trivialities. The primary object of philosophical reflection is, rather, the human being as a concretely existing reality—this approach isn't called "existentialism" for nothing. Authentic philosophizing will, for these thinkers, reflect the sense of urgency and crisis of contemporary human existence and experience. A good example of this view of the philosophical enterprise is the late French writer and thinker Albert Camus (1913–1960), who focuses the existentialists' understanding of the most fundamental question of philosophy:

[5]George Edward Moore, *Principia Ethica* (Cambridge: Cambridge University Press, 1903), p. vii.

Judging whether life is or is not worth living amounts to answering the fundamental question of philosophy. All the rest—whether or not the world has three dimensions, whether the mind has nine or twelve categories—come afterwards. These are games. . . . I have never seen anyone die for the ontological argument. . . . the meaning of life is the most urgent of questions.[6]

A WORKING DEFINITION

Perhaps, finally, we may pose a working definition of philosophy, one that does some justice to what we have seen to be both its theme and its variations: *Philosophy is the attempt to think rationally and critically about the most important questions.*

Philosophy defined

The *theme* is that philosophy is a rational and critical activity. Philosophizing in all forms seeks to think and to think hard about something. But about what? Here we have the *variations.* Our references to the speculative, analytic, and existential approaches in philosophy should provide sufficient evidence that there are quite differing ideas as to what philosophy should be rational and critical *about.* Still, even here philosophers have in common that they see themselves as addressing the really important questions, questions which are fundamental to everything.

Variations on a theme

PHILOSOPHY: A WORKING DEFINITION

Philosophy is the attempt to think rationally and critically about the most important questions.

PHILOSOPHY, RELIGION, AND SCIENCE

If this is what philosophy is, then how does it stand in relation to those two other great enterprises, *religion* and *science*?

As if we did not already have enough problems, "religion" is a slippery word indeed, as is evident from looking in any dictionary. But two things are clear. First, religion has to do with many of the same things philosophy has to do with: ulti-

What is religion?

[6]Albert Camus, *The Myth of Sisyphus and Other Essays,* tr. Justin O'Brien (New York: Knopf, 1955), pp. 3–4.

mate reality, the meaning of life, good and evil, immortality, human nature, and so on. In fact, religion usually involves *beliefs* about such things and beliefs that are worked out and adhered to in a fairly systematic and fixed manner, though perhaps not in as critical a manner as in philosophy. But, second, in addition to this intellectual aspect of religion is a more important one, one that concerns not so much the thinking as the *willing* side of our being. What is really distinctive of religion is the *commitment* it involves.

It may be helpful to note that this latter aspect of religion is true to the very origin of the word: "Religion" comes from the Latin *religio*, which means "to bind one thing to another." The religious individual is someone who is personally *bound* to something. This something is usually understood to be God, and the worship of God and active participation in rituals, ceremonies, and proclamation is further evidence for the existential rather than intellectual character of religion. We might ask, however, whether the object of such commitment must be *God*. Perhaps the object of such commitment need only be something *ultimate*—as the German-American theologian Paul Tillich said, one's "ultimate concern." Could this something as easily be a political cause? the pursuit of pleasure? the acquisition of wealth? But then again, Tillich reminds us that some things may be perceived as being ultimate which really are not. Is it possible to be bound "religiously" to something that is not ultimate, to have an *idolatrous* faith, to be worshipping an idol instead of the real thing? Be that as it may, religion would appear to have mainly to do not so much with our intellects as with our decision, action, worship, and love. Not so much with what we think as with what we do.

Religion as ultimate concern

What is science?

But science brings us back to the *study* of something. In fact our word "science" comes from the Latin *scientia*, which means simply "knowledge." It was in this sense of the word that it was held (and still is by some) that "theology is the queen of the sciences and philosophy is her hand-maid." For most people the word has lost this original meaning and is now used sometimes to refer to the *social* sciences (such as sociology, psychology, anthropology, etc.), but even more often to the *natural* sciences (such as physics, biology, chemistry, astronomy, etc.). Almost always the words "science" or "scientist" are associated with such things as test tubes, dissections, microscopes, telescopes, periodic charts, nuclear fission chambers, and laboratories occupied by people wearing white jackets.

Science: the study of the natural world

Taken in this usual sense it is not hard to relate science to philosophy. *Like* philosophy science is the pursuit of knowledge: It is an intellectual activity and it *studies* something. *Unlike* philosophy, however, its focus is much more restricted. Specifically, it narrows its focus to the study of the *natural world alone*, whereas our experience of nature may be but one aspect of the total reality that interests philosophers. Likewise the scientific *method* is more restricted than the philosopher's method may be. Inasmuch as scientists are interested in the world of nature they naturally employ primarily the tools of *observation* and *experimentation*: the test-tubes, dissections, microscopes, and telescopes mentioned above.

SOME DIFFERING CONCEPTIONS OF RELIGION

William James
> Religion . . . shall mean for us the feelings, acts, and experiences of individual men in their solitude, so far as they apprehend themselves to stand in relation to whatever they may consider the divine.[1]

Paul Tillich
> Religion is the aspect of depth in the totality of the human spirit . . . What does the metaphor *depth* mean? It means that the religious aspect points to that which is ultimate, infinite, unconditional in man's spiritual life. Religion, in the largest and most basic sense of the word, is ultimate concern. And ultimate concern is manifest in all creative functions of the human spirit.[2]

James 1:27
> Religion that is pure and undefiled before God and the Father is this: to visit orphans and widows in their affliction, and to keep oneself unstained from the world.

Random House Dictionary
> Religion: A set of beliefs concerning the cause, nature, and purpose of the universe, esp. when considered as the creation of a superhuman agency or agencies, usually involving devotional and ritual observances and often having a moral code for the conduct of human affairs.[3]

Rudolf Otto
> Desiring to give it [the essential element in religious feeling] a name of its own, I propose to call it "creature-consciousness" or creature-feeling. It is the emotion of a creature, abased and overwhelmed by its own nothingness in contrast to that which is supreme above all creatures.[4]

[1]William James, *The Varieties of Religious Experience* (New York: Mentor, 1958), p. 42.

[2]Paul Tillich, "Religion," in *Man's Right to Knowledge*, 2d series (New York: Muschel, 1954), p. 81.

[3]*Random House Dictionary of the English Language*, College Edition (1968).

[4]Rudolf Otto, *The Idea of the Holy*, tr. by John W. Harvey, 2d ed. (New York: Oxford University Press, 1950), pp. 9–10.

OF BEARDS AND BREAD

"The beard does not the philosopher make"

But back to philosophy. A few further observations may be useful for understanding its nature. For one thing, *Barba philosophum non facit,* "The beard does not the philosopher make."

Philosophy: a universal enterprise

In some sense we are *all* philosophers. We all think and reflect in our own critical way about the questions that matter most to us. Naturally, there are good philosophers and there are bad philosophers—some reason and reflect more critically than others, some are oblivious to the fallacies and mistakes in their reasoning, some are more coherent than others in their philosophical expression, some can give it more time than others, some are professionals while most are amateurs. But *everyone* asks the important questions and tries, however feebly, to formulate meaningful answers. Everyone participates, more or less, in the philosophical enterprise.

Is everyone a philosopher by nature?

Some would even take philosophical awareness and activity as being constitutive of human nature; that is, philosophical activity is part of what it means to be a human being, or at least a full and healthy human being. Mind you, it is not just thinking that makes us philosophers, but thinking critically about the biggest things. Aristotle expressed it better than anyone in the very first words of his *Metaphysics:* "All men by nature desire to know."[7] And it is clear from what followed that he meant knowing about the biggest things, about the questions that really matter.

"Philosophy bakes no bread"

Another important point: *Philosophia panem non torrit,* "Philosophy bakes no bread." Sometimes this saying is intended to express the perception (often true enough) that there is little money in the philosophy business. More often, it is a way of expressing the apparent irrelevance or impracticality or *uselessness* of philosophy.

It has seemed to many that philosophical concerns are far removed from the everyday world of work, political parties, abortion, love, death, automobiles,

"Life without philosophy is inconceivable."
—Socrates

"Philosophy is a silent dialogue between the soul and itself."
—Plato

"All men by nature desire to know."
—Aristotle

[7]Aristotle, *Metaphysics,* 980a, tr. W. D. Ross, in *The Basic Works of Aristotle,* ed. Richard McKeon (New York: Random House, 1941).

euthanasia, radios, capital punishment, bank loans, and the draft. This impression is understandable. Questions about the eternity of the world, the nature of the highest good, whether tables and chairs continue to exist when we leave the room, whether a runner can pass through an infinite number of points in a finite amount of time, how the mind interacts with the body, and how many angels can dance on the head of a pin, certainly appear abstract, academic, and remote from the real world. The impression is also very old. Plato tells that Thales, the first philosopher of the Western tradition, was once strolling along while gazing into the sky and

Is philosophy really useful?

THALES' LAST LAUGH

Thales, traditionally called the first philosopher, has always been the butt of jokes about philosophers who are so preoccupied with things above them that they have little idea of what is going on in the real world. It all began with a story reported by Plato about

> a Thracian maidservant who exercised her wit at the expense of Thales, when he was looking up to study the stars and tumbled down a well. She scoffed at him for being so eager to know what was happening in the sky that he could not see what lay at his feet.[1]

On the other hand, Aristotle relates a story of what happened when Thales

> was reproached for his poverty which was supposed to show the uselessness of philosophy. According to the story, Thales knew by his skill in the stars while it was yet winter that there would be a great harvest of olives in the coming year; so, having a little money, he gave deposits for the use of all the olive-presses in Chios and Miletus, which he hired at a low price because no one bid against him. When the harvest-time came, and many were wanted all at once and of a sudden, he let them out at any rate which he pleased, and made a quantity of money. Thus he showed the world that philosophers can easily be rich if they like, but that their ambition is of another sort.[2]

[1]Plato, *Theatetus*, 174A, tr. F. M. Cornford, in *Plato: The Collected Dialogues*.
[2]Aristotle, *Politics*, 1259a, tr. Benjamin Jowett, in *Basic Works of Aristotle*.

making certain astronomical observations—and fell into a well. Ever since, people have poked fun at philosophers who seem to be so preoccupied with what is above their heads that they have little idea of what is at their feet.

Philosophical issues as the basic ones

But the idea that philosophers merely think about the world while others live in it obviously involves a misunderstanding of the real nature of philosophy. A moment's thought would reveal that the questions that may seem to be the most remote are also the most important. What we think about our own selves, God, the physical universe, value, and the like—and, as we just insisted, we all *do* think about these things—determines how we actually live in the world, and what we think about things like abortion, politics, euthanasia, capital punishment, death, and the draft. Everything else in our practical lives is dictated in some way by our views about those "remote" things.[8] If you doubt this, a little reflection on your activities, commitments, aspirations, and decisions this very day will probably prove it. Or consider your view on some important or controversial issue, such as abortion or war. Do you not discover there some fundamental philosophical principles or ideas at work? And why are you reading this book, anyway?

In some sense, then, everyone is a philosopher, and philosophical questions are, in spite of their appearance, the most basic and most important of all. In a well-known lecture, "The Present Dilemma in Philosophy," the American philosopher William James (1842-1910) summarized both of these points in his own way:

> I know that you, ladies and gentlemen, have a philosophy, each and all of you, and that the most interesting and important thing about you is the way in which it determines the perspective in your several worlds. You know the same of me. And yet I confess to a certain tremor at the audacity of the enterprise which I am about to begin. For the philosophy which is so important in each of us is not a technical matter; it is our more or less dumb sense of what life honestly and deeply means. It is only partly got from books; it is our individual way of just seeing and feeling the total push and pressure of the cosmos. . . .
>
> . . . There is, it must be confessed, a curious fascination in hearing deep things talked about, even though neither we nor the disputants understand them. We get the problematic thrill, we feel the presence of the vastness. Let a controversy begin in a smoking-room anywhere, about free-will or God's omniscience, of good and evil, and see how every one in the place pricks up his ears. Philosophy's results concern us all most vitally, and philosophy's queerest arguments tickle agreeably our sense of subtlety and ingenuity.
>
> Philosophy is at once the most sublime and the most trivial of human pursuits. It works in the minutest crannies and it opens out the widest vistas. It "bakes no bread," as has been said, but it can inspire our souls with courage; and repugnant

---

[8]Sometimes the question "How many angels can dance on the head of a pin?" is cited jokingly as an example of the irrelevance of philosophical issues. But even this question (whether or not it was ever actually posed in this way) can be shown to involve an issue which, in its medieval and scholastic context, held important implications.

as its manners, its doubting and challenging, its quibbling and dialectics, often are to common people, no one of us can get along without the far-flashing beams of light it sends over the world's perspectives. These illuminations at least, and the contrast-effects of darkness and mystery that accompany them, give to what it says an interest that is much more than professional.[9]

THE INEVITABILITY OF PHILOSOPHY

In his *A Preface to Philosophy*, Mark B. Woodhouse provides a nice set of examples of the inescapability of philosophical issues:[1]

1. A neurophysiologist, while establishing correlations between certain brain functions and the feeling of pain, begins to wonder whether the "mind" is distinct from the brain.

2. A nuclear physicist, having determined that matter is mostly empty space containing colorless energy transformations, begins to wonder to what extent the solid, extended, colored world we perceive corresponds to what actually exists, and which world is the more "real."

3. A behavioral psychologist, having increasing success in predicting human behavior, questions whether any human actions can be called "free."

4. Supreme Court justices, when framing a law to distinguish obscene and nonobscene art forms, are drawn into questions about the nature and function of art.

5. A theologian, in a losing battle with science over literal descriptions of the universe (or "reality"), is forced to redefine the whole purpose and scope of traditional theology.

6. An anthropologist, noting that all societies have some conception of a moral code, begins to wonder just what distinguishes a moral from a nonmoral point of view.

7. A linguist, in examining the various ways language shapes our view of the world, declares that there is no one "true reality" because all views of reality are conditioned and qualified by the language in which they are expressed.

8. A perennial skeptic, accustomed to demanding and not

---

[9]William James, "The Present Dilemma in Philosophy," in *Pragmatism* (New York: Longmans, Green & Co., 1907), pp. 3–6.

receiving absolute proof for every view encountered, declares that it is impossible to know anything.

9. A county commissioner, while developing new zoning ordinances, begins to wonder whether the *effect* or the *intent* (or both) of zoning laws makes them discriminatory.

10. An IRS director, in determining which (religious) organizations should be exempted from tax, is forced to define what counts as a "religion" or "religious group."

11. A concerned mother, having decided to convert her Communist son, is forced to read the *Communist Manifesto* and to do some thinking about Marxist and capitalist ideologies.

[1]Mark B. Woodhouse, *A Preface to Philosophy* (Belmont, Calif.: Wadsworth, 1980), pp. 25–26.

Tender- and tough-minded philosophers

In "The Present Dilemma in Philosophy," James also suggested that philosophers (that is, all of us) tend to fall into one of two camps, the "tender-minded" and the "tough-minded," and he drew up two tables, indicating the very different philosophical inclinations.[10]

The tender-minded	*The tough-minded*
Rationalistic	Empiricist
Intellectualistic	Sensationalistic
Idealistic	Materialistic
Optimistic	Pessimistic
Religious	Irreligious
Free-willist	Fatalistic
Monistic	Pluralistic
Dogmatical	Skeptical

The tender-minded philosopher looks primarily to the reason as the source of knowledge, whereas the tough-minded looks primarily to the five senses. Closely related, the tender-minded is rather given to the life of the intellect and ideas, whereas the tough-minded is oriented toward the world of science and facts. The tender-minded tends to view mind as the underlying reality of all things, whereas the tough-minded finds in matter the ultimate reality. The tender-minded views the world and history as meaningful and purposeful, whereas the tough-minded

[10]Ibid., p. 12.

views them as devoid of any ultimate point. The tender-minded reckons seriously with the spiritual dimension of existence, while the tough-minded finds no evidence for the "spiritual." The tender-minded believes that the will is not completely enslaved to antecedent and mechanical causes, whereas the tough-minded believes that it is. The tender-minded sees all things as essentially unified, whereas the tough-minded emphasizes the disparateness of things. The tender-minded tends to be a person of conviction and belief, whereas the tough-minded suspends judgment and waits for more evidence.

It should be seen that James' lists reflect broad emphases, and that while some of the terms are mutually exclusive (for example, you could not be both an idealist and a materialist), it would be possible to be part "tender" and part "tough" (for example, one might be rationalistic, idealistic, dogmatical, but pessimistic). On the other hand, one who is pretty much half-tender and half-tough is no doubt philosophically schizophrenic! What kind of a philosopher are *you*? Tender or tough? This book will help you find out.

WHERE DO WE BEGIN?

So then, we want to philosophize, and we must even if we don't want to. But where do we begin? Here again James may be helpful. In still another well-known essay, "The Will to Believe," James introduced the colorful idea of "living options." To each of us some things are clearly believable while others are not. Some ideas are more or less familiar, they just sort of fit in with the rest of our ideas and experience, and we can imagine ourselves actually affirming and believing these ideas if we do not already. Other ideas, though, just somehow do *not* fit, and it is difficult imagining ourselves actually believing them. The former of these ideas James called "living options," while the latter he called "dead options."[11]

The distinction between living and dead options can be usefully adapted to our present question: Where do we begin? Each of us confronts living and dead options every day. But living and dead options are seldom (if ever) the same from one person to the next. Here we must be clear that the distinction between *living* and *dead* options is not the same as that between *true* and *false* ones. What makes an idea true or false has nothing to do with the individual—

Living and dead options

> It fortifies my soul to know
> That, though I perish, Truth is so.

But what makes it living or dead has *very* much to do with the individual, such as the circumstances of birth, education, upbringing, and so on. For those reared in

[11]William James, "The Will to Believe," in *The Will to Believe and Other Essays* (New York: Longmans, Green & Co., 1897), p. 3.

the Judeo-Christian tradition, the idea that Jesus was the Son of God, for example, might be a living option: It fits in more or less with their other ideas, and, well, one just might believe it. But that Krishna was an incarnation of Vishnu may strike the same individual as an utterly alien idea, one that has no place in his or her general understanding of things, and that person simply cannot believe it. What makes an option living or dead is, then, *relative* to the individual.

Now we may respond to this situation in one of two ways. The first might be called the *whimpering* response. It consists in a kind of whimper: "Well, if I had been born at a different time and place, and brought up in a different way, well, then I would see things very differently." This approach must be rejected. For one thing, it tends to confuse living and dead options with *true* and *false* ones, and for another thing, it tends to degenerate into a dead-end and indifferent, "So what? Nothing matters." Very different is the second possible approach, which we may call the *practical* response. It begins self-consciously and deliberately with living options as *the only tools available*, and moves out from there, testing and challenging and scrutinizing these ideas in the interest of being *right* about what we believe. In the course of this "moving out" with one's living options, some living options will die off, some dead ones will come to life, and, in a word, some philosophical *progress* will be made.

This, then, is where we begin: with the ideas, perspectives, and experiences which we happen already to enjoy—the only place we *can* begin if we want to get anywhere at all.

The whimpering response

The practical response

Chapter 1 in Review

SUMMARY

The best way to appreciate what philosophy is about is to *philosophize*. This book will make it possible to be actually confronted with basic philosophical issues and to engage many important philosophers on their own ground.

In the meantime, though, something important can be learned about philosophy through a consideration of the word itself (the "love of wisdom"), its several branches (metaphysics, epistemology, ethics, etc.), and differing styles of philosophizing (such as the speculative, analytic, and existential). In an attempt to emphasize both the essence and the breadth of philosophical activity, we proposed a working definition: Philosophy is the attempt to think rationally and critically about the most important questions. One should always remember Socrates and his challenge, "The unexamined life is not worth living," as embodying the ultimate philosophical concern. On the other hand, it must be admitted that reason has its limits, and what role is to be played by the nonrational (say, ultimate presuppositions) is itself a good philosophical question.

Everyone is more or less engaged in the philosophical enterprise, and though philosophical issues may seem at times rather remote, a moment's reflection will reveal that they really are basic and, whether one realizes it or not, they deeply affect our daily lives. Let us, then, make the most of our philosophical impulses by beginning where we are and, by critical reflection, analysis, and clarification, progress if possible to someplace even better.

BASIC IDEAS

- The problem of understanding philosophy
- "Philosophy": the love of wisdom
- The fields of philosophy
  Metaphysics
  Epistemology
  Ethics
  Value theory
  Aesthetics
  Logic
- The unity of philosophical questions
- The nature of the "philosophy of ———" areas
- Second-order studies
- Rationalism (the loose sense)
- Socrates as a model of the philosophical spirit
- The limits of reason
- The nonrational and the irrational
- Foundationalism
- Three conceptions of philosophy
  The speculative
  The analytic
  The existential
- Philosophy: a working definition
- Philosophy and religion
- Philosophy and science
- Philosophy as a universal enterprise
- The importance of philosophy
- "Tender-minded" and "tough-minded" philosophers
- Living and dead options
- Two responses to the relativity of options

TEST YOURSELF

1. What is characteristic of the existential conception of philosophy?
2. Why is Socrates regarded as a symbol of philosophizing?
3. True or false: A "tough-minded" philosopher is apt to be monistic.
4. ———— was a good example of a "speculative" philosopher.

5. What are two ways in which science differs from philosophy?

6. A "living option" is an idea that is (a) scientifically demonstrable, (b) believable at the time, (c) known in a nonrational way.

7. Ethics and aesthetics can be construed as subfields of _____. Why?

8. Why is philosophy "rationalistic" (in the loose sense)?

9. What is the working definition of philosophy suggested in this chapter?

10. What did William James contribute to the discussions in this chapter?

QUESTIONS FOR
REFLECTION

- In spite of their stress on the use of reason, some philosophers readily concede that reason has its limits. Do you believe that it is possible, nonetheless, to know something in a *non*rational way? Why do some even maintain that this is crucial to philosophizing itself? How might the appeal to the nonrational be abused?

- Is the ideal of reasoning in a purely objective way (that is, uninfluenced by biases and the like) really possible? If not, then what? And what about the difference in intellectual "temperaments"? Is that good or bad? What's to be done about it?

- How might it be argued that the borderlines between philosophy and *all* other disciplines may often be very blurred? Why might philosophers look upon their own discipline as the biggest and best?

C H A P T E R 2

A L I T T L E L O G I C

We have seen that philosophers, more than most people, strive to make their arguments, positions, and pronouncements *rational,* that is, well-conceived, well-evidenced, well-stated, and persuasive. To ensure this goal philosophers pay attention to the philosophical discipline of *logic,* which we have already defined as the study of right reasoning. Not that there is any choice about it. The philosopher can no more do without logic than the physicist can do without mathematics. It is the tool or, as someone has suggested, the "key" to philosophizing.

From the traditional logic first formulated by Aristotle to the various forms of contemporary symbolic and mathematical logic (which would seem to many like a foreign language), the science of logic has become a very complicated and sophisticated business. A real course in logic would have to take up many matters: the nature and uses of language, problems of definition, types of propositions, types of arguments, the construction and use of symbolic languages, probability theory, the nature of hypotheses and theories, etc. We cannot do much in the space of a single chapter, but a beginner in philosophy should be introduced at least to some of the bare elements of logic. An acquaintance with these is not only relevant for our thinking about the ideas and positions represented in this book, but also for our thinking about everything, everyday.

THE THREE LAWS OF THOUGHT

We might appropriately begin with the Three Laws of Thought, for in a sense they are the beginning of all thinking. Traditionally, these principles have been perceived as the rock-bottom principles of all thought and discourse, the principles that make thought and discourse even *possible*. It is important, therefore, to pay attention to these laws. They are:

1. *The Law of Non-Contradiction*
   Nothing can both be and not be at the same time
   and in the same respect.
2. *The Law of the Excluded Middle*
   Something either is or it is not.
3. *The Law of Identity*
   Something is what it is.

It is important to see that if these principles are not accepted as true, then nothing we think or say makes any sense, not even this very sentence. They make our ideas and words and language *stand still*, as it were, while we deal with them. Try to imagine making any claim about anything if any one of these principles did not hold. Go ahead, try!

Some Comments   Some comments on the Three Laws. First, at a technical level these principles actually turn out to be identical. Even so, you should try to appreciate that at the level of ordinary and practical discourse they get at very different issues. Next, as stated above these principles have a kind of metaphysical cast, expressing as they do what can or cannot *be*. They could just as easily be given an epistemological cast, expressing what can or cannot *be true*: A statement cannot be both true and false at the same time and in the same respect; a statement is either true or false; a true statement is true. Also, concerning the Law of Non-Contradiction the qualifying phrase "at the same time and in the same respect" must be emphasized. A table, for example, may indeed be red and not red at *different* times; or it may be rectangular and not be four-legged at the same time in these *different* respects; but it cannot both be and not be (anything) at the *same* time and in the *same* respect.

The Three Laws as Basic   Further, as *fundamental* principles these cannot be shown to be true, since they are the principles by which all *other* claims may be shown to be true. It was, in fact, the Law of Non-Contradiction that Aristotle was speaking of when he said that it is the mark of an uneducated person not to realize that some things cannot be proved, otherwise *nothing* could be proved.

> *Some, indeed, demand to have the law proved, but this is because they lack education; for it shows lack of education not to know of what we should require proof, and of what we should not. For it is quite impossible that everything should have a proof; the process would go on to infinity, so that even so there would be no proof.*[1]

---

[1]Aristotle, *Metaphysics*, 1006a, tr. W. D. Ross, in *Basic Works of Aristotle*, ed. Richard McKeon (New York: Random House, 1941).

Do you see that there must be some "anchors" for our thinking and discoursing if our thinking and discoursing are to be ultimately meaningful? And that these anchors must be undemonstrable? Think of geometry. All its reasoning depends finally on its axioms. But there is no way to prove the axioms.

Finally, various objections to the Three Laws are inevitably raised, but they usually involve misunderstandings. *Against the Law of Non-Contradiction:* Aren't there situations which involve inherently self-contradictory factors? Answer: No. Factors in a situation may stand in *tension* with one another or in *opposition* with one another, but such conflicts do not constitute *self-contradictory* situations in which one and the same thing both is and is-not at the same time and in the same respect. *Against the Law of the Excluded Middle:* Is everything either black or white with nothing in between? Answer: That isn't a good example, for something may be *neither* black nor white; it may be gray. What the principle states is that either something is X or it is not-X, white or not-white, gray or not-gray, etc. *Against the Law of Identity:* Things change, don't they? Answer: Yes, but the principle has reference to *whole* ideas, including any change they might involve. Thus the fact that tables are always changing doesn't detract a bit from the truth that a table is a table.

Some misunderstandings

Contemporary logicians sometimes question the exalted position that in the past has been bestowed on the Three Laws of Thought. It is now seen, for example, that the logical territory mapped out by these principles is only a part of the total territory. Nonetheless, they may be accepted as basic to the world of everyday discourse that most of us live in, and often crucial to philosophical reasoning as well. They still stand as important anchors of thought and discourse.

WHAT IS AN ARGUMENT?

When you see the word "argument" you might think of disagreements or quarrels, often accompanied by shouting, clenched fists, tears, and the like. Well, an argument might or might not involve these things. Consider the following interchange:

> A: Abortion is immoral.
> B: No it isn't!
> A: Yes it is!
> B: Well, what do *you* know about it?!
> A: I know more than it than you do!
> B: Oh yeah? You're an idiot!

There is plenty of disagreement and lots of noise here but no *argument*. An argument is an attempt to show that something is true by providing evidence for it. More technically, it is a group of propositions in which one is said to follow from at least one other. The proposition which follows from the others, that is, the

Argument: premises, conclusion . . .

"something to be shown," is called the *conclusion*; the propositions from which the conclusion follows, that is, the evidence, are called *premises*. Thus we have the argument

> It is immoral to kill persons.
> Abortion is the killing of persons.
> ─────────────────────────────────
> Therefore, abortion is immoral.

in which the first two propositions are the premises of the argument and the third is the conclusion. Naturally, in an argument not just any old propositions can serve as premises and conclusion, as in

> In fourteen-hundred-and-ninety-two,
>   Columbus sailed the ocean blue.
> Switzerland exports many cuckoo-clocks.
> ─────────────────────────────────────
> Therefore, abortion is immoral.

. . . and inference   but there must be some *connection* between them. This connection, by which the conclusion is said "to follow" from the premises, is called an inference.

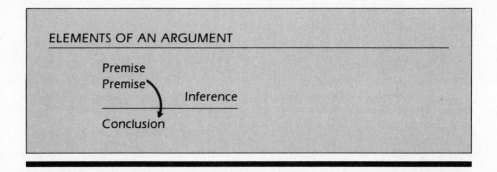

ELEMENTS OF AN ARGUMENT

Premise
Premise
            Inference
─────────────
Conclusion

In ordinary discourse, arguments may be presented in a variety of ways. Usually, though, there are certain words or expressions that introduce premises, and another set of words that introduce conclusions. We list here just a few of them:

Premise-signals   Since, because, for, as, inasmuch
                       as, otherwise, in view of the fact
                       that, for the reason that.

Conclusion-signals   Therefore, thus, accordingly, we
                       may infer, which shows that,
                       points to the conclusion that, as a
                       result.

Can you separate the premises from the conclusion in the following argument?

. . . for a producer to convince the institutions which finance movies that his film will be profitable, he has to line up a "bankable" star; and if he has a project for a political movie, the star is unlikely to sign on if he doesn't agree with the film's politics. Which means that the political movies the public is getting from Hollywood today represent, by and large, the political thinking of actors.

Richard Grenier, "Jane Fonda & Other Political Thinkers," *Commentary,*
June 1979

What is the nature of the connection between premises and conclusion—the inference—that results in arguments? Here the important distinction between *deductive* and *inductive* arguments come₀ into play. It is sometimes said that deductive arguments reason from the whole to the part, or from the general to the specific, as in

Deductive and inductive arguments

> All humans are mortal. —————————— universal proposition
> Socrates is a human.
> ————————————
> Therefore, Socrates is mortal. —————— particular proposition

whereas inductive arguments reason from the part to the whole, or from the specific to the general, as in

> Socrates is mortal.
> Plato is mortal.
> Aristotle is mortal. —————————— particular propositions
> Vivaldi is mortal.
> Tim is mortal.
> ⋮
> ————————————
> Therefore, all humans are mortal. —————— universal proposition

While this is certainly true of *some* deductive and inductive arguments, it fails to express their real nature. What is more important, again, is the kind of connection that exists between premises and conclusion in deductive and inductive arguments. In a valid deductive argument the premises ensure, or *guarantee,* the conclusion: If the premises are true, the conclusion *must* be true also. It is a matter of necessity. In a good inductive argument, on the other hand, the premises *suggest* the conclusion ("to induce" means "to influence" or "to persuade"): If the premises are true, the conclusion is *probably* true. It is a matter of *probability.*

DEDUCTIVE REASONING

Let us consider deductive arguments a little further. What is this necessity we spoke of when we said that if the premises are true, the conclusion *must* be true? Why *must* the conclusion be true? Answer: By virtue of a relation of *entailment,* or logical

Logical entailment

Aristotle

Aristotle is credited as the first to formulate systematically the principles of reasoning. His "logical works" were eventually collected and issued under the title Canon, *a Greek word which means "standard" or "rule."*

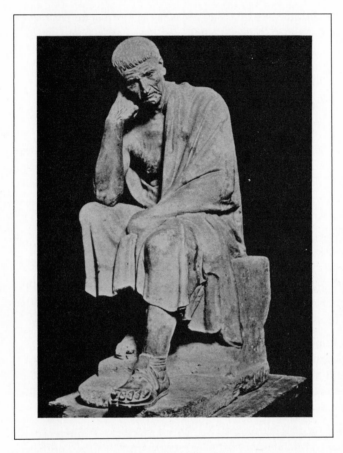

implication, between terms or propositions in the premises. "To entail" means "to include" or "to involve." Thus deductive entailment has to do with the way in which a term or proposition may be included in another. And the way in which *this* may be done so as to result in a valid argument is specified by *valid argument forms.*

The syllogism

The most traditional and even yet one of the most common forms of a deductive argument is the *syllogism.* This is a type of argument consisting of two premises and a conclusion ("syllogism" comes from a Greek word meaning "propositions considered together").

The syllogism provides an excellent introduction to the essential nature of deductive reasoning. There are three different kinds of syllogism. First, we have the *categorical* syllogism, so-called because both of the premises are categorical propositions, that is, propositions about *classes* of things, and which affirm or deny that

The categorical syllogism

one class is included in another class. An example of a valid categorical syllogism, or at least the *form* of one, is:

> All X are Y.
> All Y are Z.
> _____
> Therefore, all X are Z.

A possible translation, or substitution for the symbols, might be:

> All politicians are liars.
> All liars are despicable.
> _____
> Therefore, all politicians are despicable.

Next, there are four, and only four, forms of categorical propositions:

1. All X are Y (All politicians are liars).
2. No X are Y (No politicians are liars).
3. Some X are Y (Some politicians are liars).
4. Some X are not Y (Some politicians are not liars).

And there are rules, six of them, according to which categorical syllogisms may be judged valid or invalid; none of them may be violated.

Rules for the categorical syllogism

Rule 1. A valid categorical syllogism must contain exactly three terms, each of which is used in the same sense throughout the argument.

Rule 2. In a valid categorical syllogism, the middle term (the term present to both premises and absent to the conclusion) must be distributed, or refer to all members of the class, in at least one premise.

Rule 3. In a valid categorical syllogism, if either term is distributed in the conclusion, then it must be distributed in the premises.

Rule 4. No categorical syllogism is valid which has two negative premises.

Rule 5. If either premise of a valid categorical syllogism is negative, the conclusion must be negative.

Rule 6. No valid categorical syllogism with a particular conclusion can have two universal premises

Thus, some valid forms of the categorical syllogism are:

> No X are Y.
> All Z are X.
> _____
> Therefore, no Z are Y.

Some X are Z.
All X are Y.

Therefore, some Y are Z.

Some X are not Z.
All X are Y.

Therefore, some Y are not Z.

Some *invalid* forms are:

All X are Y.
All Z are Y.

Therefore, all Z are X.

All X are Y.
Some Z are not X.

Therefore, some Z are not Y.

No X is Y.
No Z is Y.

Therefore, no X is Z.

Do you see what makes these argument forms invalid? The first one violates *Rule 2*; the second violates *Rule 3*; and the third violates *Rule 4*. Study these examples until you see the fallacies (mistakes in reasoning) involved.

The disjunctive syllogism

Second, we have the *disjunctive* syllogism. As with the categorical syllogism, the disjunctive syllogism takes its name from the kind of proposition it contains, namely, a disjunctive proposition. This is a proposition which poses alternatives— the alternatives, or "disjuncts," being indicated by the words "either ... or." For example, "Either it rained last night or a street cleaner went by." Unlike a categorical proposition, a disjunctive proposition doesn't "categorically" assert the truth of either of the alternatives; rather, it asserts that at least one of them is true, and possibly both. Thus we have the form of any valid disjunctive syllogism:

Either X or Y.
Not X.

Therefore, Y.

or

Either X or Y.
Not Y.

Therefore, X.

Possible translation:

> Either it rained last night or a street cleaner went by.
> It did not rain last night.
> _____
> Therefore, a street cleaner went by.

There is only one rule that governs valid disjunctive syllogisms:

Rule for the
disjunctive
syllogism

> *Rule.* A valid disjunctive syllogism must contain in the premises a denial of
> one alternative while the conclusion affirms the other.

It is obvious how breaking this rule results in an invalid argument form:

> Either X or Y.
> X.
> _____
> Therefore, not Y.

INVALID

Here, for all we know, X might be the case and Y too. The affirmation of one
disjunct does not imply the denial of the other. Note that the argument

> Either Terryl is in Istanbul or he is in Bangkok.
> Terryl is in Istanbul.
> _____
> Therefore, Terryl is not in Bangkok.

which certainly appears to be valid, is no exception to this. For there is the implicit
or hidden premise assumed here: "It is not possible for Terryl to be both in Istanbul
and Bangkok at the same time." One must always be on the lookout for unex-
pressed premises.

The third form of the syllogism is the *hypothetical* syllogism, so named because
the premises contain a hypothetical or *conditional* proposition. This is a proposition
that involves an antecedent and a consequent, signaled by the words "if … then."
For example, "If it rained last night {antecedent}, then the streets are wet
{consequent}." If both premises are conditional propositions, we have a *pure* hypothetical syllogism:

The hypothetical
syllogism

> If X, then Y.
> If Y, then Z.
> _____
> Therefore, if X, then Z.

Possible translation:

> If you water the lawn, then it will grow.
> If the lawn grows, then you will have to mow it.
> _____
> Therefore, if you water the lawn, then you will have to mow it.

> *Rule.* Any pure hypothetical syllogism is valid in which the first premise and
> the conclusion have the same antecedent, the second premise and the

Rule for the pure
hypothetical
syllogism

conclusion have the same consequent, and the consequent of the first premise is the same as the antecedent of the second premise.

If one premise is conditional and one categorical, then we have a *mixed* hypothetical syllogism. One valid form of the mixed hypothetical syllogism is:

> If X, then Y.
> X.
> _____
> Therefore, Y.

Possible translation:

> If it rained last night, then the streets are wet.
> It rained last night.
> _____
> Therefore, the streets are wet.

Rule 1 for the mixed hypothetical syllogism

Rule 1. Any mixed hypothetical syllogism is valid in which the categorical premise affirms the antecedent of the conditional premise, and the conclusion affirms its consequent.

One must be careful of confusing a valid argument-form with the clearly invalid

> If X, then Y.
> Y.   INVALID
> _____
> Therefore, X.

The fallacy is apparent in the possible translation:

> If it rained last night, then the streets are wet.
> The streets are wet.
> _____
> Therefore, it rained last night.

It takes no great intelligence to see immediately that the streets might be wet even if it didn't rain last night—maybe a street cleaner went by. This is called the *Fallacy of Affirming the Consequent.*

Another valid form of the hypothetical syllogism is:

> If X, then Y.
> Not Y.
> _____
> Therefore, not X.

Possible translation:

> If it rained last night, then the streets are wet.
> The streets are not wet.
> _____
> Therefore, it did not rain last night.

Rule 2 for the
mixed
hypothetical
syllogism

Rule 2. Any mixed hypothetical syllogism is valid in which the categorical premise denies the consequent of the conditional premise, and the conclusion denies its antecedent.

Again, one must be on guard against confusing this valid argument form with the clearly invalid

If X, then Y.
Not X.
INVALID
─────────────
Therefore, not X.

And, again, the fallacy is obvious in the possible translation:

If it rained last night, then the streets are wet.
It did not rain last night.
INVALID
─────────────
Therefore, the streets are not wet.

As before, a street cleaner might have gone by, leaving the streets wet anyway. The argument commits the *Fallacy of Denying the Antecedent.*

In these pages we have tried to display the nature of deductive arguments. Focusing on the syllogism, we presented some of the most obvious of the valid argument forms and *in*valid argument forms. These must be taken as samples, but useful ones inasmuch as they figure prominently in philosophical arguments.

> "A syllogism is a reasoning in which something different emerges with necessity from what has been laid down."
>
> —Aristotle

One of the most important things to appreciate here is that deductive validity has to do with *form*, and form *alone*. What makes an argument valid is that it con-forms to a valid argument *form*, either one of the above or some other. But there is a big difference between *validity* and *truth*. An argument may be absolutely valid even though every proposition in it is false:

Truth and validity

All politicians are Communists.
Babe Ruth is a politician.
─────────────
Therefore, Babe Ruth is a Communist.

It goes without saying that every proposition, including the conclusion, in an argument might be true, and the argument be invalid nonetheless:

> All U.S. Presidents have been males.
> Abraham Lincoln was a male.
> _____
> Therefore, Abraham Lincoln was a U.S. President.

Obviously, what we are interested in is *both* validity and truth. We may call a deductive argument that is valid *and* whose premises are true a "sound" argument.

A "SOUND" ARGUMENT

A deductive argument that is valid and whose premises are true.

INDUCTIVE REASONING

The example of Sherlock Holmes

It is hardly possible to give a better example of the essential nature of inductive reasoning than that provided by the master sleuth himself, Sherlock Holmes, whose "powers of deduction" were actually powers of *induction*. Look at the procedure and kinds of evidence he employs in *The Hound of the Baskervilles*:

"So far as I can follow you, then, Mr. Holmes," said Sir Henry Baskerville, "someone cut out this message with a scissors———"

"Nail-scissors," said Holmes. "You can see that it was a very short-bladed scissors, since the cutter had to take two snips over 'keep away.'"

"That is so. Someone, then, cut out the message with a pair of short-bladed scissors, pasted it with paste———"

"Gum," said Holmes.

"With gum on to the paper. But I want to know why the word 'moor' should have been written?"

"Because he could not find it in print. The other words were all simple and might be found in any issue, but 'moor' would be less common."

"Why, of course, that would explain it. Have you read anything else in this message, Mr. Holmes?"

"There are one or two indications, and yet the utmost pains have been taken to remove all clues. The address, you observe, is printed in rough characters. But the Times is a paper which is seldom found in any hands but those of the highly educated. We may take it, therefore, that the letter was composed by an educated man who wished to pose as an uneducated one, and his effort to conceal his own writing

suggests that that writing might be known, or come to be known, by you. Again, you will observe that the words are not gummed on in an accurate line, but that some are much higher than others. 'Life,' for example, is quite out of its proper place. That may point to carelessness or it may point to agitation and hurry upon the part of the cutter. On the whole I incline to the latter view, since the matter was evidently important, and it is unlikely that the composer of such a letter would be careless. If he were in a hurry it opens up the interesting question why he should be in a hurry, since any letter posted up to early morning would reach Sir Henry before he would leave his hotel. Did the composer fear an interruption—and from whom?"

"We are coming now rather into the region of guess work," said Dr. Mortimer.

"Say, rather, into the region where we balance probabilities and choose the most likely. It is the scientific use of the imagination, but we have always some material basis on which to start our speculations. Now, you would call it a guess, no doubt, but I am almost certain that this address has been written in an hotel."

"How in the world can you say that?"

"If you examine it carefully you will see that both the pen and the ink have given the writer trouble. The pen has spluttered twice in a single word, and has run dry three times in a short address, showing that there was very little ink in the bottle. Now, a private pen or ink-bottle is seldom allowed to be in such a state, and the combination of the two must be quite rare. But you know the hotel ink and the hotel pen, where it is rare to get anything else. Yes, I have very little hesitation in saying that could we examine the waste-paper baskets of the hotels round Charing Cross until we found the remains of the mutilated Times *leader we could lay our hands straight upon the person who sent this singular message.[2]*

This is an excellent illustration of what goes on in inductive arguments: moving from particular facts here, analogies there, common threads and connections everywhere, to a conclusion that is suggested by all of that evidence.

We have seen above that in deductive arguments validity in the form results in a necessity of the conclusion. In the case of inductive arguments, however, it is not a question of validity at all, and therefore no logical necessity in the conclusion can be expected. What *is* aimed at is truth in the premises and probability in the conclusion. It cannot be stressed too strongly that no inductive argument can deliver a conclusion that is demonstratively certain. The most that can be hoped for is a degree of probability, though the more supportive the premises, the more reasonable and the higher the probability of the conclusion. Thus, as with deductive arguments, not just any old premises will do. Here too there must be an inference between premises and conclusion, just as in deductive arguments. On the other hand, whereas in deductive arguments the inference is a strictly *logical* one resulting in a *necessary* conclusion, in inductive arguments the inference is a *supportive* one resulting in a *probable* conclusion.

Not necessity but probability

[2]A. Conan Doyle, *The Hound of the Baskervilles* (New York: McClure, Phillips & Co., 1902), pp. 46–48.

DEDUCTION AND INDUCTION

- *In a valid deductive argument:* If the premises are true the conclusion must be true, by virtue of a logically necessary inference.
- *In a strong inductive argument:* If the premises are true the conclusion is probably true, by virtue of a supportive inference.

What is the connection, this "supportive inference," between premises and conclusion in an inductive argument that makes the conclusion at least reasonable and probable? We note here just two of the ways in which inductive arguments can take shape.

The method of generalization

The first and most obvious form of inductive reasoning is to *generalize* on the basis of particular instances. The simplest of this kind of argument is called *universal generalization,* and has the form

> Instance 1 of A is observed to be X.
> Instance 2 of A is observed to be X.
> Instance 3 of A is observed to be X.
> Instance 4 of A is observed to be X.
> Instance 5 of A is observed to be X.
> $\vdots$
> _____
> Therefore, all A is X.

The method of analogy

Quite different from the inductive methods of generalization is the method of *analogy*. This kind of reasoning can take many different forms, but its essential nature is indicated by

> A is observed to be X and Y.
> B is observed to be X and Y.
> C is observed to be X and Y.
> D is observed to be X and Y.
> $\vdots$
> M is observed to be X.
> _____
> Therefore, M is Y.

That is, if M is analogous, or similar, to A, B, C, D ... in being X, it is probably also similar in being Y.

Naturally, one can make mistakes in inductive reasoning. But unlike mistakes in deductive reasoning, which have to do with the *form* of the argument, inductive mistakes are of a different character, as is apparent from these samples:

Some inductive
mistakes

- *Hasty Induction:* Basing a conclusion on an insufficient number of premises or observations.
- *Lazy Induction:* Not drawing a conclusion as strong as the evidence suggests.
- *Forgetful Induction:* Neglecting some known data which, if recalled, would cast the total reasoning in a different light.

And, of course, one may be mistaken in his or her inductive reasoning even though the reasoning is done well. Consider the following argument:

Limitations of
induction

> This swan is white.
> That swan is white.
> Every swan we've ever seen is white.
> We've never heard of any swans that aren't white.
> _____
> Therefore, all swans are white.

Based on the premises, the conclusion is surely a reasonable one. The generalization is overwhelmingly supported by the evidence. Knowing only what is given in the premises it would be foolish to reject the conclusion. Nonetheless, it is false. However great inductive evidence may be, it is always by its nature limited to the *actual* experience, observations, field trips, microscopes, and telescopes of a *limited* number of individuals. And a yet wider experience has revealed that there are, in fact, black swans. And who knows what will turn-up next? Thus we return to an earlier point: No inductive arguments can be demonstratively certain.

   Still, we must be careful not to overdo the limitations of inductive reasoning. To be sure, we must be attentive to its inherent limitations, but we can hardly do without it. Reasoning on the basis, say, of generalizations and analogies from our experience is one of the most obvious and powerful intellectual tools we possess. We employ it constantly in all spheres of our thinking. Where would Sherlock Holmes be without it? And where would *science* be without it?

THE DRAWBACK OF INDUCTION

All inductive reasoning is based on *particular* and *limited* observations. By its nature, therefore, it can never deliver *certain* and *universal* knowledge.

INFORMAL FALLACIES

We have already encountered logical fallacies. Those were *formal* fallacies, or mistakes in reasoning which resulted from breaking some rule of validity: a mistake with respect to the *form* of an argument. Informal fallacies are quite different. They are mistakes which arise from carelessness with respect to the relevance of ideas, or carelessness with respect to the clarity and consistency of our language. In fact, informal fallacies are usually classified as *fallacies of relevance* and *fallacies of ambiguity*. There are many such fallacies. We give here only some of the most common ones of each type. Mastery of them will not only provide a chance to review a little Latin, but will prevent many unnecessary blunders in philosophical discussion, and, for that matter, any discussion whatsoever.

Fallacies of relevance

Twelve fallacies of relevance

1. *Argumentum ad Baculum* (appeal to force) employs threat, intimidation, pressure, etc., as tools of persuasion.
2. *Argumentum ad Hominem: Abusive* (argument which directs abuse at the individual) irrelevantly attacks the person making a claim rather than attacking the claim itself.
3. *Argumentum ad Hominem: Circumstantial* (argument which appeals to the circumstances of the individual) seeks to undermine a claim by calling attention to the (irrelevant) circumstances of the one making the claim. When it specifically cites the origins or causes of someone's opinion ("You believe in God because you were raised as a Catholic") it is known as the *Genetic Fallacy*.

LOGICAL FALLACIES

Formal	*Informal*
Mistakes in reasoning due to a failure in following the rules for the formal structure of valid arguments. These fallacies do not concern truth or falsity but validity.	Mistakes in reasoning due to carelessness regarding relevance and clarity of language. These fallacies bear directly on issues of truth and falsity.

4. *Argumentum ad Ignorantiam* (argument from ignorance) affirms the truth of something on the basis of the lack of evidence to the contrary: X must be the case, since it has not or cannot be shown to be false.

5. *Argumentum ad Populum* (appeal to popular opinion, or appeal to the "gallery") seeks to strengthen a claim by an emotional appeal to the passions and prejudices of the listeners.

6. *Argumentum ad Misericordiam* (appeal to pity) is a special form of *Argumentum ad Populum,* directing attention from relevant evidence by arousing pity and sympathy for the plight of someone.

7. *Argumentum ad Verecundiam* (appeal to authority) is an appeal to an unqualified expert or irrelevant authority.

8. *Petitio Principii* (begging the question) occurs when the conclusion of an argument is already present, usually disguised, in one of its premises. Circular reasoning ("What he claims must be true, because he always speaks the truth") is a good example of *Petitio Principii.*

9. *Accident* is the fallacy of applying a general rule to a specific situation in which some accidental condition makes it an exception to the rule.

10. *Converse Accident* or *Hasty Generalization* consists in generalizing on the basis of an inadequate number of instances or on the basis of atypical instances, and thus moves in the opposite direction from the Fallacy of Accident.

11. *False Cause* is the fallacy consisting either in (a) confusing an effect or feature of a condition with the cause of the condition (*non causa pro causa,* "taking what is not the cause for the cause") or (b) identifying X as the cause of Y merely on the grounds that X occurs before Y (*post hoc ergo propter hoc,* "after this, therefore because of this").

12. *Complex Question* consists of posing a question which can only be answered on the basis of an answer to a prior and unasked question: "Where did you hide the money you stole?" clearly assumes an affirmative answer to the question, "Did you steal the money?"

Fallacies of ambiguity

1. *Equivocation* occurs when a word or expression changes its meaning in the course of an argument.

2. *Amphiboly* (literally, "thrown on both sides") is an ambiguous grammatical construction that can be understood in two ways: "The Duke yet lives that Henry shall depose." The fallacy occurs when something is concluded on the basis of the unintended meaning of the amphibolous expression.

3. *Misplaced Accent* consists of so emphasizing a word or expression, or omitting relevant information, as to yield a misleading sense.

Five fallacies of ambiguity

SOME INFORMAL FALLACIES

Fallacies of relevance

Argumentum ad Baculum
Argumentum ad Hominem:
   Abusive
Argumentum ad Hominem:
   Circumstantial
Argumentum ad Ignoratiam
Argumentum ad Populum
Argumentum ad Misericordiam
Argumentum ad Verecundiam
Petitio Principii
Accident
Converse Accident
False Cause
Complex Question

Fallacies of ambiguity

Equivocation
Amphiboly
Misplaced Accent
Composition
Division

4. *Composition* results from attributing the characteristics of the parts of a whole to the whole itself: "If every player on the team is good, then it's a good team."

5. *Division* (the reverse of the Fallacy of Composition) attributes the characteristics of the whole to its parts: "The team is good, so each of its players is good."

Find the fallacy!   Here are some examples of reasoning which involve informal fallacies. Can you identify them?

"I'm all for women having equal rights," said Bullfight Association president Paco Camino. "But I repeat, women shouldn't fight bulls because a bullfighter is and should be a man."

San Francisco Chronicle, March 28, 1972.

In that melancholy book The Future of an Illusion, *Dr. Freud, himself one of the last great theorists of the European capitalist class, has stated with simple clarity the impossibility of religious belief for the educated man of today.*

John Strachey, *The Coming Struggle for Power*

The Moral Majority's Rev. Jerry Falwell . . . claims that Jesus Christ favored the death penalty. On the Cross, Falwell says, He could have spoken up: "If ever there was a platform for our Lord to condemn capital punishment, that was it. He did not."

Time, January 24, 1983

Mysticism is one of the great forces of the world's history. For religion is nearly the most important thing in the world, and religion never remains for long altogether untouched by mysticism.

John McTaggart and Ellis McTaggart, "Mysticism," *Philosophical Studies*

I also admit that there are people for whom even the reality of the external world and the identification leading to it constitute a grave problem. My answer is that I do not address them, but that I presuppose a minimum of reason in my readers.

Paul Feyerabend, "Materialism and the Mind-Body Problem," *Review of Metaphysics*, 1963

According to R. Grunberger, author of A Social History of the Third Reich, *published in Britain, the Nazis used to send the following notice to German readers who let their subscriptions lapse: "Our paper certainly deserves the support of every German. We shall continue to forward copies of it to you, and hope that you will not want to expose yourself to unfortunate consequences in the case of cancellation."*

Parade, May 9, 1971

"Who did you pass on the road?" the King went on, holding his hand out to the messenger for some hay.

"Nobody," said the messenger.

"Quite right," said the King: "this young lady saw him too. So of course Nobody walks slower than you."

Lewis Carroll, *Through the Looking-Glass*

We have listed above seventeen informal fallacies, but there are many more. In fact, someone has distinguished *over a hundred*. The important thing, of course, is to be able to identify them even though we may not be able to name them. The following letters to the editor in *Newsweek* (Oct. 11, 1982) contain informal fallacies not listed above. Can you identify them?

The Israelis leaned on their machine guns and did nothing to prevent the massacre of men, women and children in Lebanon. . . . These same Israelis condemn the Germans who, while living in a police state, were expected to speak up to Hitler about his atrocities. Lest Americans of any persuasion become smug in their condemnations, however, one remembrance of Vietnam or Hiroshima should restore a sense of perspective.

The massacre in Beirut was the work of Lebanese Christian militiamen supported and armed by Israel—which is supported and armed by the United States. Every American taxpayer shares the blame.

And what sorts of informal fallacies and abuses of language do you find in the following report of electioneering rhetoric (*Rocky Mountain News*, Oct. 30, 1982)?

SCHROEDER VS. DECKER

    On the day he began his campaign against Rep. Patricia Schroeder in April, Republican Arch Decker said he was sure most Denver voters shared his "values," not Schroeder's.

    Decker didn't define those values. But he kept that "moral" question simmering in the 1st District campaign.

    It wasn't the only issue, of course. President Reagan's policies were always an issue—Decker pro, Schroeder con.

    Decker said balanced budgets were the issue. Schroeder deplored the nuclear arms race and the dismantling of "necessary" welfare programs.

    Decker, more than most of Schroeder's previous rivals, tried to appeal to key elements of her political base: elderly, minority and blue-collar voters.

    Schroeder, in turn, aimed appeals at Decker's conservative base, advocating pay-as-you-go budgeting and a balance between military and other spending. She also opposed congressional tax breaks.

    Underneath, the "moral" issue was always there.

    A Denver magazine published by Decker said his backers want leaders "in tune with biblical principles of morality."

    Later, Decker addressed the congregation of a large Denver church, and (according to witnesses who called Schroeder's office) questioned her religious convictions. (Schroeder has said she believes in God and considers herself "very religious.")

    Last week the "moral" issue boiled over. In a TV debate, Decker charged that she voted to allow continued medical "butchery" of live fetuses.

    Schroeder protested that such experimentation is illegal and isn't being done. Her backers called Decker's charge an act of desperation.

    Decker said he only wanted to set Schroeder's voting record straight. His later "documentation" of the charge, at a press conference, consisted of unauthenticated statements by congressmen in the Congressional Record.

Chapter 2 in Review

SUMMARY   Traditionally, logic has been regarded as the primary tool or "key" of philosophizing. This is understandable inasmuch as philosophy aims at critical, coherent, and persuasive reasoning, and logic is the formulation of the principles of correct reasoning.

For a long time the Three Laws of Thought (Non-Contradiction, Excluded Middle, Identity) were regarded as the ultimate principles of all being and thinking. These principles do not now usually enjoy such an exalted status, but they still serve as important guides for ordinary as well as philosophical discourse. Is it not the case that failure to honor them would result in the greatest confusion? Can you imagine holding a meaningful conversation with someone who will not honor any one of them?

Still more relevant is the nature of *arguments*. If philosophers aren't good at arguing, what *are* they good at? A real argument is a carefully devised piece of reasoning involving premises (what is reasoned *from*), a conclusion (what is reasoned *to*), and an inference (the connection which yields the conclusion from the premises). But does the conclusion follow from the premises necessarily or probably? This is the difference between a valid *deductive* argument, where the conclusion is *guaranteed* by the premises, and an *inductive* argument, where the conclusion is *supported* by the premises.

The classic example of deductive reasoning is the *syllogism*, a type of argument which comes in different forms and is governed by several rules, but always involves two premises and a conclusion. It is important to see that the power of deductive arguments—such as syllogisms—depends solely on their *form* and their ability to deliver *conclusions which follow validly*. Whether the conclusion of such an argument is *true* is an entirely different, but certainly a no less important, question. Of course we are interested in conclusions that follow validly *and* are true. Arguments which deliver such conclusions we have called "sound" arguments.

Very different from deductive reasoning is inductive reasoning. Here, as was just said, the conclusion is *supported* rather than guaranteed by the premises. The premises contain information derived from facts, observation, collection of data, and the like, and pass this along to the conclusion, which will be only as strong as the premises. The limitation of inductive reasoning is obvious: the premises, and therefore the conclusion, can never be certain. This, however, should not blind us to the importance and pervasiveness of this kind of reasoning.

Among the most important things to be learned from an introduction to logic are the informal fallacies. As opposed to *formal* fallacies, mistakes with respect to the formal structure of an argument, *informal* fallacies arise from inattention to the relevance or clarity of language. In fact, the several specific informal fallacies divide into the *fallacies of relevance* and the *fallacies of ambiguity*. Mastery of the informal fallacies will prove rewarding time and time again.

BASIC IDEAS

- Logic as the tool or key to philosophizing
- The Three Laws of Thought
    - Non-Contradiction
    - Excluded Middle
    - Identity

- The nature and elements of an argument
- Deductive reasoning
- Logical entailment
- Syllogism
- Categorical syllogism
- Rules for the categorical syllogism
- Disjunctive syllogism
- Rule for the disjunctive syllogism
- Hypothetical syllogism: pure and mixed
- Rules for the hypothetical syllogism
- Two formal fallacies
    Affirming the Consequent
    Denying the Antecedent
- The distinction between truth and validity
- Inductive reasoning
- The method of generalization
- Analogical reasoning
- Mistakes in inductive reasoning
    Hasty Induction
    Lazy Induction
    Forgetful induction
- The limitations of inductive reasoning
- The distinction between formal and informal fallacies
- Informal fallacies
    Fallacies of relevance (twelve of them)
    Fallacies of ambiguity (five of them)

TEST YOURSELF

1. What is an argument?
2. What is the relation of premises and conclusion in a deductive argument? In an inductive argument?
3. True or false: Syllogisms can yield conclusions which are only probably true.
4. What is the difference between a formal fallacy and an informal fallacy?
5. If either premise of a valid categorical syllogism is negative, the conclusion must be _____.
6. Evaluate the following. Is it an argument? Deductive or inductive? Is it a syllogism? If so, what kind? Or is it invalid? If so, what fallacy does it commit?

We know that if the music is played too loudly Tim will surely get a headache. He always does. And he does have a headache, so the music must be too loud.

7. State exactly what is involved in *logical necessity*. Consider the statement, "All barking dogs bark."

8. True or false: The Fallacy of Composition is a fallacy of ambiguity. Why or why not?

9. What is the difference between truth and validity? Why is it important to have both?

10. What kind of logician was Sherlock Holmes? Why?

- Why is it often said that logic is the primary tool of philosophers? Why has it been called the "key" to philosophizing?

- Even though we have distinguished between deductive and inductive reasoning, how might they both play a part in a single argument? The conclusion may follow validly from the premises, but how might we come by the premises?

- Everyday talk is sometimes replete with fallacies, especially informal fallacies. Can you spot and identify any in today's newspaper? You might pay special attention to the editorial pages and letters to the editor.

QUESTIONS FOR
REFLECTION

P A R T

1

T H E   Q U E S T I O N   O F   R E A L I T Y

What is reality? What are things made of? What is ultimate? What is it that everything depends on for its existence? What is *really real?*

There are many ways of posing the question of reality. However you pose the question, you *do* have an answer—don't you? Your idea of reality may be only half-conscious (and it may be only half-baked), but you do have some answer of your own to the question: What is really real? The point is to have a *good* answer, an answer that is well-conceived and well-evidenced. Why is this so important?

Some philosophers would say that in some ways the metaphysical question, or the question of reality, is the basis of all the other questions that matter. Whether or not this is strictly true, no one would deny that the metaphysical question is at least a *basic* one. Will not what you believe about reality determine to some degree what you believe about all sorts of other things? If, for example, someone told you that he or she believes that all that exists is matter in motion, governed by fixed and unalterable laws, then couldn't you predict pretty much what that person thinks about some other important things? If, on the other hand, you were informed that he or she believes in a supernatural and absolute being, couldn't you immediately guess that his or her views on those matters would probably be quite different?

In this way, then, the question of reality is a fundamental one. How we answer it will determine in a big way our perspectives on many issues, as well as our perspective on the universe and our experience *generally.* Let us, then, have a care with respect to the question of reality.

CHAPTER 3

THE FIRST METAPHYSICIANS

Aristotle said that philosophy began (and always begins) with "wonder," and the Pre-Socratic philosophers (those philosophers who lived before Socrates) wondered mainly about *reality*. They asked the biggest question of all: What is reality? What is the essential nature of things? What is the *underlying* reality which is revealed in the many things about us? And how is this underlying, essential reality related to these many things? How are the many things about us *derived* from this underlying reality? This is the *problem of the One and the Many*. As one can see, it actually involves two questions:

The Problem of the One and the Many

- What is the ultimate reality (the One)?
- How is everything else (the Many) related to it?

It is important to appreciate this problem because philosophers grappled with it from the very beginning and still do.

THE PROBLEM OF THE ONE AND THE MANY

The problem of identifying the ultimate reality (the One) that underlies all things (the Many), and of explaining the relation between them or how the Many derives from the One.

THE FIRST THEORY OF REALITY

Thales, the first philosopher

Western philosophy came to birth about 600 B.C. More specifically, it came to birth in the city of Miletus on the western coast of Ionia (now Turkey) in the person of Thales, traditionally called the first philosopher. To the question, "What is ultimate reality?", Thales seems to have answered, first, that reality is *one* thing. He and his followers in Miletus have therefore been called the Milesian monists. As a meta-physical theory, monism (literally, "one-ism") emphasizes in some way or other the *unity* of reality. Usually, it is the doctrine that everything is reducible to or is an expression of a single essence or nature.

The Principle of Simplicity

Why these earliest philosophers were bent upon reducing all things to *one* reality is not easy to explain. Perhaps it was a carry-over from the mythological period when everything was derived from the gods, who were themselves traced back through a genealogy of the gods to the divine Parents—and indeed Parent—of all. Be that as it may, the desire to reduce everything to *one* is not peculiar to these earliest philosophers. All of us take simplicity, economy, and unity as principles of explanation. In this way a scientific theory, for example, may be judged preferable to others by virtue of the fact that it encompasses and unifies the others.

MONISM

As a metaphysical term, monism (from the Greek *monos*, "one") is the belief that reality is in some sense *one*, usually one in essence or nature.

OCKHAM'S RAZOR

We all have an instinctive appreciation for "Ockham's Razor," a principle formulated by William of Ockham (d. 1349?) for the purpose of cutting away superfluous or unnecessary ideas: *Entia non sunt multiplicanda praeter necessitatem*, "Entities are not to be multiplied without necessity."

To the question, "What is ultimate reality?", Thales answered, second, that it is *water*. Understandably, one might be amused at this view of ultimate reality. But it may not be as silly as it seems at first, and you could probably imagine why Thales said this. First, water is a necessity for all living things. Second, water, or moisture, seems to be present in most things. Third, water seems to be everywhere: It bubbles up out of the ground, it comes down from the sky, and it collects on windshields. Fourth, as we peer out over the vast expanses of the ocean it might seem (as in fact is the case) that there is more of this "stuff" than anything else in the world. This may have been especially relevant for Thales who lived on the edge of the Great Sea (the Mediterranean) and who inherited the belief that the world was surrounded by the great River Oceanus. Fifth, it should be noted that water, more obviously than other common substances, can exist in different forms; it exists usually in liquid form, but it can be frozen solid, and it can exist as a gas.

The first metaphysical theory: Water is reality

Why water?

Aristotle gives us a brief account of the first philosopher's search for an underlying reality, and also some speculations of his own as to why Thales identified it with water.

Aristotle on Thales' claim

> Of the first philosophers, . . . most thought the principles which were of the nature of matter were the only principles of all things. That of which all things that are consist, the first from which they come to be, the last into which they are resolved (the substance remaining, but changing in its modifications), this they say is the element and this the principle of things, and therefore they think nothing is either generated or destroyed, since this sort of entity is always conserved, as we say Socrates neither comes to be absolutely when he comes to be beautiful or musical, nor ceases to be when he loses these characteristics, because the substratum, Socrates himself, remains. Just so they say nothing else comes to be or ceases to be; for there must be some entity— either one or more than one—from which all other things come to be, it being conserved.
>
> Yet they do not all agree as to the number and the nature of these principles. Thales, the founder of this type of philosophy, says the principle is water (for which reason he declared that the earth rests on water), getting the notion perhaps from seeing that the nutriment of all things is moist, and that heat itself is generated from the moist and kept alive by it (and that from which they come to be is a principle of all things). He got his notion from this fact, and from the fact that the seeds of all things have a moist nature, and that water is the origin of the nature of moist things.[1]

In any event, this was the first metaphysical theory. Reality is *one*, and it is *water*. It was the first metaphysical theory, but it was hardly the last. Thales' successors had their own theories about ultimate reality.

[1]Aristotle, *Metaphysics*, 983b, tr. W. D. Ross, in *Basic Works of Aristotle*, ed. Richard McKeon (New York: Random House, 1941).

TWO PYTHAGOREAN VIEWS ON HOW THE WORLD BEGAN

Some say that the solid body is constructed from one point. For this point, by fluxion, creates the line, and the line, by fluxion makes the plane, and this, by moving in depth, generates the three-dimensional body. But this position of the Pythagoreans differ from the earlier.[1]

The first principle of all things is the One. From the One came the Indefinite Dyad as material substance for the One, which is cause. From the One and the Indefinite Dyad came numbers; from numbers, points; from points, lines; from lines, plane figures; from plane figures, solid figures, from solid figures, sensible bodies, of which the elements are four: fire, water, earth, air. Changing and transforming themselves completely, there arises out of them a cosmos, animate, intelligent, spherical, surrounding the earth which is at the center and which itself is spherical and inhabited.[2]

Comment: The first of these accounts, with its image of a point flowing into a line, a line into a plane, etc., is the later and more sophisticated.

The point flows into a line;   _____

the line flows into a square;

the square flows into a cube.

In the second account, the One, the ultimate reality, generates the "Idefinite Dyad" or "Two," which represents a sort of indeterminate matter out of which the One fashions numbers, the building blocks of the cosmos. In both accounts it is difficult to know where, if at all, the gulf between *incorporeal* and *corporeal* reality is bridged. It is often observed that this distinction did not even clearly exist at the time of the Pre-Socratics.

[1]From Sextus Empiricus, *Against the Mathematicians*, X, 281, tr. Ed. L. Miller.
[2]From Alexander Polyhistor, quoted in Diogenes Laertius, *Lives of Eminent Philosophers*, VIII, 25, tr. Ed. L. Miller.

THREE PRE-SOCRATIC
TRADITIONS

We cannot go into detail on all the Pre-Socratic theories. We may, however, distinguish three broad traditions: the Ionian, the Italian, and the Pluralist. It was characteristic of the early philosophers living in Ionia to identify reality with some *sensible* substance, that is, with some substance we can see, touch, hear, and smell. Thales said *water*. Others in the Ionian tradition advanced other candidates. Anaximander, for example, proposed an *indeterminate* substance, perhaps a kind of mixture which the sensible qualities (hot, cold, moist, dry) have been sorted out of. Anaximenes proposed *air,* which, through thickening and thinning, produces the different things about us and holds all things together as a sort of life-principle. Xenophanes opted for both water and earth. Heraclitus stressed the fluctuating or ever-changing character of things and championed *fire* as the underlying reality, which, though continually transformed into and out of the other elements, always displays a divinely appointed balance and order.

The thinkers in the Italian tradition, however, inclined in a different direction. Pythagoras and the Pythagoreans believed that everything is essentially *number*. It sounds strange, of course, to say that the underlying reality is number, and it is not perfectly clear, in fact, what Pythagoras and his followers meant by this. It *is* clear, though, that this idea points us away from the ordinary sensible elements in the physical world and in the direction, rather, of the nonsensible, or incorporeal, *structure* of things. Even more extreme in this regard were the philosophers from Elea. Parmenides, for example, insisted that only *Being* is, and that Being must

---

A GUIDE TO PRE-SOCRATIC PRONUNCIATION

Thales	Thā'-lēz
Anaximander	A-naks-i-man'-der
Anaximenes	An-aks-im'-e-nēz
Xenophanes	Ze-nof'-a-nēz
Heraclitus	Her-a-klī'-tus
Pythagoras	Pi-thag'-o-rus
Parmenides	Par-men'-i-dēz
Empedocles	Em-ped'-o-klēz
Anaxagoras	An-aks-ag'-o-ras
Leucippus	Loo-ki'-pus
Democritus	Di-mok'-ri-tus

be *one* and *immutable*; with this he denied utterly the reality of the sensible world along with all plurality and motion.

The Pluralists

The Pluralists, as may be guessed from the name, sought to identify reality with a plurality of substances while maintaining that each of these, at least, is a Being and thus one and immutable. Of the Pluralists, Empedocles was the first to posit the four traditional elements as principles of all things: *earth, air, fire,* and *water.* In addition he posited Love and Strife which, respectively, draw the elements together and separate them in an endless cycle. A world, such as ours, results when the four elements are unified under the attraction of Love. Anaxagoras taught that all things are constituted by a mixture of an infinite number of infinitely divisible particles or *seeds* (each seed being dominated by a certain quality, and a given thing

Thales, the first philosopher, who believed that water is the underlying reality of all things.

being determined by the kind of seeds that dominate it), but that pure *Mind* controls the whole. Leucippus and Democritus advocated the first atomic theory, explaining that everything arises mechanically out of a sort of coagulation of an infinite number of irreducible *atoms* (the Greek word *atomos* means, literally, "uncuttable" and therefore something irreducible).

The historian of philosophy F. C. Copleston has provided a statement of the importance of the Pre-Socratics with respect both to (1) their formulation of the Problem of the One and the Many and (2) their more distinctive roles as the first cosmologists, the first to advance rational theories about the nature of the *kosmos* or world.

> It is often said that Greek philosophy centres round the problem of the One and the Many. Already in the very earliest stages of Greek philosophy we find the notion of unity: things change into one another—therefore there must be some common substratum, some ultimate principle, some unity underlying diversity. Thales declares that water is that common principle, Anaximenes air, Heraclitus fire: they choose different principles, but they all three believe in one ultimate principle. But although the fact of change—what Aristotle called "substantial" change—may have suggested to the early Cosmologists the notion of an underlying unity in the universe, it would be a mistake to reduce this notion to a conclusion of physical science. As far as strict scientific proof goes, they had not sufficient data to warrant their assertion of unity, still less to warrant the assertion of any particular ultimate principle, whether water, fire or air. The fact is, that the early Cosmologists leapt beyond the data to the intuition of universal unity: they possessed what we might call the power of metaphysical intuition, and this constitutes their glory and their claim to a place in the history of philosophy. If Thales had contented himself with saying that out of water earth is evolved, "we should," as Nietzsche observes, "only have a scientific hypothesis: a false one, though nevertheless difficult to refute." But Thales went beyond a

---

COSMOS

Although the Pre-Socratics grappled in different ways with the problem of reality and change, they always maintained a respect for the world as *ordered* and *rational.* In fact, the Greek word for "world" was *kosmos,* which meant, originally, a "decoration" or "ornament," a thing of beauty. This overtone was eventually lost, but for the earliest philosophers *kosmos* could best be translated as "world-system."

mere scientific hypothesis: he reached out to a metaphysical doctrine, expressed in the metaphysical doctrine, that Everything is One.

Let me quote Nietzsche again. "Greek philosophy seems to begin with a preposterous fancy, with the proposition that water is the origin and mother-womb of all things. Is it really necessary to stop there and become serious? Yes, and for three reasons: Firstly, because the proposition does enunciate something about the origin of things; secondly, because it does so without figure and fable; thirdly and lastly, because in it is contained, although only in the chrysalis state, the idea—Everything is one. The first-mentioned reason leaves Thales still in the company of religious and superstitious people; the second, however, takes him out of this company and shows him to us as a natural philosopher; but by virtue of the third, Thales becomes the first Greek philosopher." This holds true of the other early Cosmologists; men like Anaximenes and Heraclitus also took wing and flew above and beyond what could be verified by mere empirical observation. At the same time they were not content with any mythological assumption, for they sought a real principle of unity, the ultimate substrate of change: what they asserted, they asserted in all seriousness. They had the notion of a world that was a whole, a system, of a world governed by law. Their assertions were dictated by reason or thought, not by mere imagination or mythology; and so they deserve to count as philosophers, the first philosophers of Europe.

But though the early Cosmologists were inspired by the idea of cosmic unity, they were faced by the fact of the Many, of multiplicity, of diversity, and they had to attempt the theoretical reconciliation of this evident plurality with the postulated unity—in other words, they had to account for the world as we know it. While Anaximenes, for example, had recourse to the principle of condensation and rarefaction, Parmenides, in the grip of his great theory that Being is one and changeless, roundly denied the facts of change and motion and multiplicity as illusions of the senses. Empedocles postulated four ultimate elements, out of which all things are built up under the action of Love and Strife, and Anaxagoras maintained the ultimate character of the atomic theory and the quantitative explanation of qualitative difference, thus doing justice to plurality, to the many, while tending to relinquish the earlier vision of unity, in spite of the fact that each atom represents the Parmenidean One.

We may say, therefore, that while the Pre-Socratics struggled with the problem of the One and the Many, they did not succeed in solving it. The Heraclitean philosophy contains, indeed, the profound notion of unity in diversity, but it is bound up with an over-assertion of Becoming and the difficulties consequent on the doctrine of Fire. The Pre-Socratics accordingly failed to solve the problem, and it was taken up again by Plato and Aristotle, who brought to bear on it their outstanding talent and genius.

But if the problem of the One and the Many continued to exercise Greek philosophy in the Post-Socratic period, and received much more satisfactory solutions at the hands of Plato and Aristotle, it is obvious that we cannot characterise Pre-Socratic philosophy by reference to that problem: we require some other note of character-

isation and distinction. Where is it to be found? We may say that Pre-Socratic philosophy centres round the external world, the Object, the not-self. Man, the Subject, the self, is of course not excluded from consideration, but the interest in the not-self is predominant. This can be seen from the question which the successive Pre-Socratic thinkers set themselves to answer: "Of what is the world ultimately composed?" In their answers to this question the early Ionian philosophers certainly went beyond what the empirical data warranted, but, as already remarked, they tackled the question in a philosophic spirit and not in the spirit of weavers of mythological fancies. They had not differentiated between physical science and philosophy, and combined "scientific" observations of a purely practical character with philosophic speculations; but it must be remembered that a differentiation between physical science and philosophy was hardly possible at that early stage—men wanted to know something more about the world, and it was but natural that scientific questions and philosophical questions should be mingled together. Since they were concerned with the ultimate nature of the world, their theories rank as philosophical; but since they had not yet formed any clear distinction between spirit and matter, and since their question was largely prompted by the fact of material change, their answer was couched for the most part in terms and concepts taken from matter. They found the ultimate "stuff" of the universe to be some kind of matter—naturally enough—whether the water of Thales, the Indeterminate of Anaximander, the air of Anaximenes, the fire of Heraclitus, or the atoms of Leucippus, and so a large part of their subject-matter would be claimed by physical scientists of to-day as belonging to their province.

The early Greek philosophers are then rightly called Cosmologists, for they were concerned with the nature of the Cosmos, the object of our knowledge, and man himself is considered in his objective aspect, as one item in the Cosmos, rather than in his subjective aspect, as the subject of knowledge or as the morally willing and acting subject. In their consideration of the Cosmos, they did not reach any final conclusion accounting for all the factors involved; and this apparent bankruptcy of Cosmology, together with other causes to be considered presently, naturally led to a swing-over of interest from Object to Subject, from the Cosmos to Man himself. . . .

Although it is true that Pre-Socratic philosophy centres round the Cosmos, the external world, and that this cosmological interest is the distinguishing mark of Pre-Socratic as contrasted with Socratic philosophy, it must also be remarked that one problem at any rate connected with man as the knowing subject was raised in Pre-Socratic philosophy, that of the relation between sense-experience and reason. Thus Parmenides, starting with the notion of the One, and finding himself unable to explain coming-to-be and passing-away—which are given in sense-experience—set aside the evidence of the senses as illusion, and proclaimed the sole validity of reason, which alone is able to attain the Real and Abiding. But the problem was not treated in any full or adequate manner, and when Parmenides denied the validity of sense-perception, he did so because of a metaphysical doctrine or assumption, rather than from any prolonged consideration of the nature of sense-perception and the nature of non-sensuous thought.

Since the early Greek thinkers may justly be termed philosophers, and since they proceeded largely by way of action and reaction, or thesis and antithesis (e.g. Heraclitus over-emphasising Becoming and Parmenides over-stressing Being), it was only to be expected that the germs of later philosophical tendencies and Schools would already be discernible in Pre-Socratic philosophy. Thus in the Parmenidean doctrine of the One, when coupled with the exaltation of Reason at the expense of sense-perception, we can see the germs of later idealism; while in the introduction of Nous by Anaxagoras—however restricted his actual use of Nous may have been—we may see the germs of later philosophical theism; and in the atomism of Leucippus and Democritus we may see an anticipation of later materialistic and mechanistic philosophies which would endeavor to explain all quality by quantity and to reduce everything in the universe to matter and its products.

From what has been said, it should be clear that Pre-Socratic philosophy is not simply a pre-philosophic stage which can be discounted in a study of Greek thought—so that we should be justified in starting immediately with Socrates and Plato. The Pre-Socratic philosophy is not a pre-philosophic stage, but is the first stage of Greek philosophy: it may not be pure and unmixed philosophy, but it is philosophy, and it deserves to be studied for the sake of its own intrinsic interest as the first Greek attempt to attain a rational understanding of the world. Moreover, it is not a self-contained unit, shut off from succeeding philosophic thought in a watertight compartment; rather is it preparatory to the succeeding period, for in it we see problems raised which were to occupy the greatest of Greek philosophers. Greek thought develops, and though we can hardly over-estimate the native genius of men like Plato and Aristotle, it would be wrong to imagine that they were uninfluenced by the past. Plato was profoundly influenced by Pre-Socratic thought, by the Heraclitean, Eleatic and Pythagorean systems; Aristotle regarded his philosophy as the heir and crown of the past; and both thinkers took up philosophic problems from the hands of their predecessors, giving, it is true, original solutions, but at the same time tackling the problems in their historic setting.[2]

THE DISCOVERY OF FORM

It is true, in spite of their obscurity and fragmentary nature, that the speculations of the earliest philosophers are not only fascinating but important. For here lie the roots of the first major philosophies. And in this respect yet another point must be made, namely, the progress of the Pre-Socratics toward "the discovery of form," as it is called by a noted historian of Greek philosophy, W. K. C. Guthrie:

The Egyptians had thought of geometry as a matter of individual rectangular or triangular fields. The Greek lifts it from the plane of the concrete and material and begins to think about rectangles and triangles themselves, which have the same prop-

[2]Frederick Copleston, A History of Philosophy, I, (Westminster, Md.: Newman Press, 1946), pp. 76–80.

SOME PRE-SOCRATIC PRONOUNCEMENTS[1]

"As our soul, being air, holds us together, so also spirit and air encompasses the whole world."

—Anaximenes

"You cannot step twice into the same river."

—Heraclitus

"It is necessary to say and to think what *is*. For Being is, and Non-Being is not."

—Parmenides

"In everything there is a portion of everything else, except for Mind. And in some things there is Mind also."

—Anaxagoras

". . . the four roots of all things: Shining Zeus, life-bearing Hera, Aidoneus, and Nestis who with tears fills the springs of mortals with water."

—Empedocles

"Nothing happens at random, but all things from reason and by necessity."

—Leucippus

[1]Tr. Ed. L. Miller

---

erties whether they are embodied in fields of several acres or in pieces of wood or cloth a few inches long, or simply represented by lines drawn in the sand. In fact their material embodiment ceases to be of any importance, and we have made the discovery which above all others stands to the especial credit of the Greeks: the discovery of form. The Greek sense of form impresses itself on every manifestation of their activity, on literature and the graphic and plastic arts as much as on their philosophy. It marks the advance from percepts to concepts, from the individual examples perceived by sight or touch to the universal notion which we conceive in our minds—in sculpture no longer an individual man but the ideal of humanity; in geometry, no longer triangles but the nature of triangularity and the consequences which logically and necessarily flow from being a triangle.[3]

But it remained for Socrates, Plato, and Aristotle to bring the discovery to full light, and to draw out its full philosophical implications.

[3]W. K. C. Guthrie, *A History of Greek Philosophy*, I (Cambridge: Cambridge University Press, 1962), pp. 36–37.

Chapter 3 in Review

SUMMARY

Something happened about 600 B.C. which marked the beginning of our own philosophical tradition. What happened was that the human intellect took a quantum leap in *critical* thinking. According to Aristotle, what sparked this leap was a new and wide-eyed wonder at the world and a search for its underlying nature.

All of the early philosophers were guided by the Principle of Simplicity, and

---

THE MOST FUNDAMENTAL QUESTION OF ALL: "WHY IS THERE ANYTHING?"

". . . each of us is grazed at least once, perhaps more than once, by the hidden power of this question, even if he is not aware of what is happening to him. The question looms in moments of great despair, when things tend to lose all their weight and all meaning becomes obscured. Perhaps it will strike but once like a muffled bell that rings into our life and gradually dies away. It is present in moments of rejoicing, when all the things around us are transfigured and seem to be there for the first time, as if it might be easier to think they are not than to understand that they are and are as they are. The question is upon us in boredom, when we are equally removed from despair and joy, and everything about us seems so hopelessly commonplace that we no longer care whether anything is or is not—and with this question "Why is there anything rather than nothing?" is evoked in a particular form.

"But this question may be asked expressly, or, unrecognized as a question, it may merely pass through our lives like a brief gust of wind; it may press hard upon us, or, under one pretext or another, we may thrust it away from us and silence it. In any case it is never the question that we ask first in point of time.

"But it is the first question in another sense—in regard to rank. This may be clarified in three ways. The question "Why is there anything rather than nothing?" is first in rank for us first because it is the most far reaching, second because it is the deepest, and finally because it is the most fundamental of all questions."

Martin Heidegger, *An Introduction to Metaphysics*, tr. Ralph Manheim (Garden City, N.Y.: Anchor Books, 1961), pp. 1–2 (with slight editing).

sought to understand the world in terms of some *one* reality, or as few as possible. They differed, though, as to the character and number of the underlying reality. The Ionian, Italian, and Pluralist traditions reflect the widely different courses taken by the Pre-Socratics. Always, however, it was the twofold Problem of the One and the Many: (1) What is the underlying nature or reality of all things? and (2) How is the multiplicity of things around us derived from this reality, or how do we *get* from the One to the Many?

Already in the Pre-Socratics the idea of Form, or the ideal essence which is imperfectly represented in the Many, was emerging. As we will see in the next chapter, this was the dominating idea of Socrates, Plato, and Aristotle, and the whole continuing tradition stemming from these thinkers. We will also see that two Pre-Socratic philosophers, namely Heraclitus and Parmenides, exerted a special influence on the subsequent thinkers.

BASIC IDEAS

- The problem of the One and the Many
- Monism
- The Principle of Simplicity
- The first theory of reality: water
- Three Pre-Socratic traditions
    The Ionians
    The Italians
    The Pluralists
- The emergence of "Form"

TEST YOURSELF

1. The problem of the One and the Many is really *two* problems. What are they?
2. The philosopher of Becoming was _____, and the philosopher of Being was _____.
3. True or false: The Italian tradition was more abstract in its conception of reality than the Ionian tradition.
4. Give a few reasons why Thales might have identified water as the ultimate reality.
5. What did the discovery of "Form" consist in?

QUESTIONS FOR REFLECTION

- Were the Pre-Socratics so odd in seeking a *simple* explanation for the nature of things? What is meant, exactly, by the claim that simplicity has *always* been a principle of explanation?
- It is always easy *when looking back* to judge an idea or theory as naive. What might be said *on behalf* of the earliest theories of reality as being well-conceived, critical, and persuasive at the time?

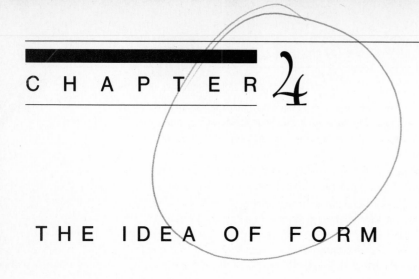

CHAPTER 4

THE IDEA OF FORM

Plato, the first "systematic" philosopher

Philosophy really came of age with Plato (427–347 B.C.). Here we encounter the first full-fledged philosophical *system*. By a philosophical system we mean a fundamental idea or theory that is worked out for all aspects of experience. Thus Plato's philosophy addresses everything from reality, to knowledge, to ethics, to art, to religion, to cosmology, etc. So encompassing and magnificent is Plato's philosophy that one philosopher has observed that all subsequent philosophy is but a series of footnotes to it!

PLATO AND SOCRATES

Platonic dialogues

Plato, who is sometimes called the finest writer of ancient Greece, expressed his philosophy in numerous "dialogues." In the earlier of these dialogues Plato develops the ideas of his teacher Socrates through portrayals of Socrates' discussions with his contemporaries, discussions which proceed by questions and answers. Socrates is usually represented as asking in one way or another, "What is X?" His respondent's answer is then subjected to a searching analysis which generates still more and better answers. A representative passage from one of these early dialogues is the following from the *Euthyphro*:

> EUTHYPHRO: . . . *I would indeed affirm that holiness is what the gods all love, and its opposite is what the gods all hate, unholiness.*

SOCRATES: *Are we to examine this position also, Euthyphro, to see if it is sound? Or shall we let it through, and thus accept our own and others' statement, and agree to an assertion simply when somebody says that a thing is so? Must we not look into what the speaker says?*

EUTHYPHRO: *We must. And yet, for my part, I regard the present statement as correct.*

SOCRATES: *We shall soon know better about that, my friend. Now think of this. Is what is holy holy because the gods approve it, or do they approve it because it is holy?*

EUTHYPHRO: *I do not get your meaning.*

SOCRATES: *Well, I will try to make it clearer. We speak of what is carried and the carrier, do we not, of led and leader, of the seen and that which sees? And you understand that in all such cases the things are different, and how they differ?*

EUTHYPHRO: *Yes, I think I understand.*

SOCRATES: *In the same way what is loved is one thing, and what loves is another?*

EUTHYPHRO: *Of course.*

SOCRATES: *Tell me now, is what is carried "carried" because something carries it, or is it for some other reason.*

EUTHYPHRO: *No, but for that reason.*

SOCRATES: *And what is led, because something leads it? And what is seen, because something sees it?*

EUTHYPHRO: *Yes, certainly.*

SOCRATES: *Then it is not because a thing is seen that something sees it, but just the opposite—because something sees it, therefore it is seen. Nor because it is led, that something leads it, but because something leads it, therefore it is led. Nor because it is carried, that something carries it, but because something carries it, therefore it is carried. Do you see what I wish to say, Euthyphro? It is this. Whenever an effect occurs, or something is effected, it is not the thing effected that gives rise to the effect; no, there is a cause, and then comes this effect. Nor is it because a thing is acted on that there is this effect; no, there is a cause for what it undergoes, and then comes this effect. Don't you agree?*

EUTHYPHRO: *I do.*

SOCRATES: *Well then, when a thing is loved, is it not in process of becoming something, or of undergoing something, by some other thing?*

EUTHYPHRO: *Yes, certainly.*

SOCRATES: *Then the same is true here as in the previous cases. It is not because a thing is loved that they who love it love it, but it is loved because they love it.*

EUTHYPHRO: *Necessarily.*

SOCRATES: *Then what are we to say about the holy, Euthyphro? According to your argument, is it not loved by all the gods?*

EUTHYPHRO: *Yes.*

SOCRATES: *Because it is holy, or for some other reason?*

EUTHYPHRO: *No, it is for that reason.*

SOCRATES: *And so it is because it is holy that it is loved; it is not holy because it is loved.*

EUTHYPHRO: *So it seems.*

SOCRATES: *On the other hand, it is beloved and pleasing to the gods just because they love it?*

EUTHYPHRO: *No doubt of that.*

SOCRATES: *So what is pleasing to the gods is not the same as what is holy, Euthyphro, nor, according to your statement, is the holy the same as what is pleasing to the gods. They are two different things.*

EUTHYPHRO: *How may that be, Socrates?*

SOCRATES: *Because we are agreed that the holy is loved because it is holy, and is not holy because it is loved. Isn't it so?*

EUTHYPHRO: *Yes.*

SOCRATES: *Whereas what is pleasing to the gods is pleasing to them just because they love it, such being its nature and its cause. Its being loved of the gods is not the reason of its being loved.*

EUTHYPHRO: *You are right.*

SOCRATES: *But suppose, dear Euthyphro, that what is pleasing to the gods and what is holy were not two separate things. In that case if holiness were loved because it was holy, then also what was pleasing to the gods would be loved because it pleased them. And, on the other hand, if what was pleasing to them pleased because they loved it, then also the holy would be holy because they loved it. But now you see that it is just the opposite, because the two are absolutely different from each other, for the one {what is pleasing to the gods} is of a sort to be loved because it is loved, whereas the other {what is holy} is loved because it is of a sort to be loved. Consequently, Euthyphro, it looks as if you had not given me my answer—as if when you were asked to tell the nature of the holy, you did not wish to explain the essence of it. You merely tell an attribute of it, namely, that it appertains to holiness to be loved by all the gods. What it is, as yet you have not said. So, if you please, do not conceal this from me. No, begin again. Say what the holy is, and never mind if gods do love it, nor if it has some other attribute; on that we shall not split. Come, speak out. Explain the nature of the holy and unholy.*

EUTHYPHRO: *Now, Socrates, I simply don't know how to tell you what I think. Somehow everything that we put forward keeps moving about us in a circle, and nothing will stay where we put it.*[1]

---

[1]Plato, *Euthyphro*, 9E–11B, tr. Lane Cooper, in *Plato: The Collected Dialogues*, ed. Edith Hamilton and Huntington Cairns (New York: Pantheon Books, 1961).

In the *Dialogues,* which were composed over many years, Plato gradually introduced his own (and more developed) ideas in place of those of the historical Socrates, though he continued to employ Socrates as the mouthpiece of these ideas. It is, of course, a problem to know where the real Socrates leaves off and Plato's own ideas begin. This is called the Socratic Problem. For the purpose of our discussion here we will not concern ourselves with this problem and will simply speak of the philosophy embodied in the *Dialogues* as Plato's philosophy.

The Socratic Problem

PLATONIC DIALOGUE

"Plato presented philosophy in an entirely spontaneous form, not as ponderous treatises but in dramatic dialogues between friends, in which Socrates figured as the presiding genius. He invented the form to make his concepts intelligible to the layman, and never was philosophy graced with more beauty; this first attempt to humanize knowledge was warm, personal, fresh, and frequently humorous, an intoxicating mixture of poetry and hard thought."

Felix Marti-Ibanez, *Tales of Philosophy* (New York: Potter, 1964), p. 31.

THE TWO WORLDS: APPEARANCE AND REALITY

Many philosophers have found it necessary to conceive of reality in two spheres or levels: what *appears* to be real, and what *is* real. Already in the beginning stages of the history of philosophy Plato introduced this two-layer view of reality. For Plato, too, it is the difference between Appearance and Reality, though he expressed it also by means of the terms Becoming and Being. With such talk Plato affirms his conviction that in addition to the ever-changing world around us (Becoming), there is another world, an eternal and unchanging reality (Being). Why would one believe in an *additional* world such as this?

The two-layer view of reality

Plato had many reasons for believing in a transcendent world, that is, a reality lying beyond space and time. We will limit ourselves to two of these reasons, but perhaps the two most important.

First, Plato's view of reality is a reaction to his predecessor, Protagoras. Protagoras, a Sophist[2] who was active about 425 B.C., was responsible for one of the most famous lines ever uttered: "Man is the measure of all things." His meaning is clear from a more accurate and complete quotation:

Protagoras: "A man is the measure of all things"

A man is the measure of all things; of the things that are, that they are, and of the things that are not, that they are not.[3]

This means that the individual—each and every person—is the criterion unto himself or herself as to what exists and what doesn't. The thought was expanded, of course, to include truth and morality. Whatever you perceive as true or false *is* true or false, and whatever you think is good or bad *is* good or bad. This is known as relativism or subjectivism because it makes the most important things *relative* to and dependent upon the individual (or community, society, etc.), or because it asserts that the subject (either an individual, community, society, etc.) is the source and standard of being, truth, and goodness.

For Plato (and for most philosophers since) it was absurd to say that being,

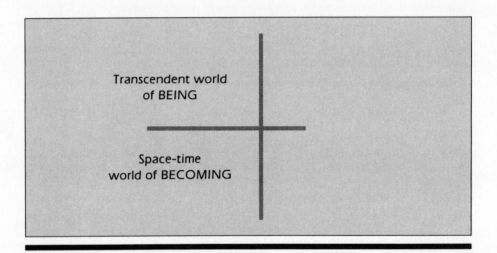

Transcendent world
of BEING

Space-time
world of BECOMING

---

[2]The Sophists (literally, "wise men") were the first to teach wisdom for a fee, something that irked Socrates. Actually, the Sophists may not have been as wise as they were clever with words, and they were accused of "making the stronger argument appear to be the weaker, and the weaker argument appear to be the stronger." But in the days of the Athenian democracy, when an individual was required to defend himself in the law courts, the Sophists' "wisdom" was, understandably, much in demand!

[3]Protagoras, *Fragment 1*, tr. Ed. L. Miller.

TRANSCENDENT REALITY

. . . in philosophy usually means reality which transcends or lies beyond *space* and *time*. Thus God, as he is represented in classical theology, is a transcendent being, and true Reality, for Plato, is transcendent. Can you *imagine* a transcendent being in the sense of forming a mental image of him? The answer is No, for images are bound by spatio-temporal conditions, such as size, color, shape, motion, etc. Can you *conceive* of a transcendent being? The answer is Yes, if by that you mean that you can have an idea or concept of that being. Thus you cannot *imagine* God, though you may have an *idea* of him.

truth, and morality are "up for grabs" and can be or mean whatever an individual wishes! This would mean the immediate collapse not only of all serious talk about what's real and unreal, and what's true and false, but also all talk about moral responsibility, praise, blame, punishment, and so on. No, says Plato. Our understanding of being, truth, and goodness must—if it is to be really meaningful—be anchored in some *objective* (that is, it exists outside of our own minds), *independent* (it is not dependent on anything else for its existence), and *absolute* (it does not come or go or otherwise change) Reality. There must then exist above our minds and beyond this world another world, a world of Reality and Being.

Plato's rejection of subjectivism

Second, Plato's view of reality is a reaction to still another of his predecessors, the Pre-Socratic philosopher Heraclitus. Heraclitus went about saying things like, "The sun is new every day," and "We are and we are not." These are ways in which Heraclitus expressed his view—a very famous view—that everything is constantly changing, nothing stands still for a moment, the world and everything in it is in a ceaseless movement, activity, coming and going, ebbing and flowing. In fact, "All things flow" caught on as a Heraclitean slogan, and Heraclitus himself appears to have likened the fluctuating universe to a river: "You can't step twice into the same river." The idea is that by the time you have put foot into the water, different water is flowing there.

Heraclitus: "All things flow"

What did this colorful and dynamic view of the world have to do with the development of Plato's conception of reality? Just as Protagoras' relativism, says Plato, leads to impossible conclusions, so does Heraclitus' doctrine of flux: If all reality is constantly changing, then all discourse is impossible, and the same is true for knowledge itself. Why is this? For the answer, read on.

HOW TO AVOID PAYING YOUR DEBTS

It appears that the playwright Epicharmus, a contemporary of
Heraclitus, spoofed Heraclitus' doctrine of the ever-changing nature
of things: You will have difficulty making me pay back money I
borrowed from you because everything changes and I am no longer
the one who borrowed it!

Plato inherited from still another Pre-Socratic philosopher, Parmenides, the
idea that genuine knowledge and discourse must be about what *is*, not what *is not*—
after all, you can't think about, talk about, or have any knowledge of what *isn't*,
can you? (The word "nothing" does not denote something, but rather the negation
or absence of something.) Furthermore, what *is* (Being) must be *one* and *unchanging*.
Do you see why being must be one and unchanging? Do not multiplicity and
change involve difference, absence, relativity, and degrees? And do not these in
turn involve various sorts of nonbeing? Now since a thing cannot both be and not
be (the Law of Non-Contradiction), it is *logically* impossible that what *is* could also
be what *is not*. How then could that which *is* involve multiplicity and change? True
Being is therefore one and unchanging. And only this can be an object of knowledge and discourse.

**The implications of
Heraclitean flux**
Now consider again Heraclitus' world of flux. What is it that you refer to
when you comment on that table over there in the corner? "Why," you say, "just
that table over there in the corner." But on the Heraclitean view there *is* no table
over there in the corner: By the time you say "that table" it is no longer *that* table,
but has already become a *different* table. Likewise for everything in the Heraclitean
world of flux. If then, says Plato, knowledge and talk about tables, chairs, dogs, cats,
justice, and anything else, is about anything *real*, it must be because there is more
to reality than the sensible world of multiplicity and change. There must be a world
of *Being* in addition to the world of *Becoming*.

In his dialogue *Timaeus*, Plato himself poses the distinction between the two
worlds, the worlds of Being and Becoming, and the corresponding difference
between knowledge and opinion, as clearly as one could hope for:

> . . . *we must make a distinction and ask, What is that which always is and has no
> becoming, and what is that which is always becoming and never is? That which is
> apprehended by intelligence and reason is always in the same state, but that which*

is conceived by opinion with the help of sensation and without reason is always in a process of becoming and perishing and never really is.[4]

The same distinction is strikingly posed in the *Republic*, where Plato clearly represents the world of Becoming as a "twilight" zone or "half-way region" between reality and unreality:

. . . we have discovered that the many conventional notions of the mass of mankind about what is beautiful or honourable or just and so on are adrift in a sort of twilight between pure reality and pure unreality.

We have.

And we agreed earlier that, if any such object were discovered, it should be called the object of belief and not of knowledge. Fluctuating in that half-way region, it would be seized upon by the intermediate faculty.

Yes.

So when people have an eye for the multitude of beautiful things or of just actions or whatever it may be, but can neither behold Beauty or Justice itself nor follow a guide who would lead them to it, we shall say that all they have is beliefs, without any real knowledge of the objects of their belief.

That follows.

But what of those who contemplate the realities themselves as they are for ever in the same unchanging state? Shall we not say that they have, not mere belief, but knowledge?

That too follows.

And, further, that their affection goes out to the objects of knowledge, whereas the others set their affections on the objects of belief; for it was they, you remember, who had a passion for the spectacle of beautiful colours and sounds, but would not hear of Beauty itself being a real thing.

I remember.

So we may fairly call them lovers of belief rather than of wisdom—not philosophical, in fact, but philodoxical. Will they be seriously annoyed by that description?

Not if they will listen to my advice. No one ought to take offence at the truth.

The name of philosopher, then, will be reserved for those whose affections are set, in every case, on the reality.

By all means.[5]

[4]Plato, *Timaeus*, 27D–28A, tr. Benjamin Jowett, in *Plato: The Collected Dialogues*.

[5]Plato, *The Republic*, 479D–480A, tr. Francis MacDonald Cornford (New York: Oxford University Press, 1941).

PLATO

Plato was born in Athens in 428 B.C. According to one tradition he was originally named Aristocles but came to be called Plato (from the Greek *platus*, "wide") because of his broad shoulders. He came from an aristocratic family and no doubt received a very cultured education. He was at first bent upon a career in politics, but was soon captivated by Socrates and his philosophy, and the fate of Socrates at the hands of the Athenian democracy (he was present at Socrates' trial) further sealed Plato's revulsion at such politics. From Socrates Plato learned to fix his attention not on the fluctuating objects of sense experience, but on the fixed and abiding *essence* of things as the only possible objects of true knowledge.

When he was about 40, Plato visited Italy, possibly to engage the Pythagoreans there and to see the volcanoes. In Italy he became friends with Dion, the brother-in-law of Dionysus I, tyrant of Syracuse. Dionysus I, however, disliked Plato and had him sold as a slave. He was recognized by an acquaintance who ransomed him and had him sent back to Athens. There, in 388 B.C., he founded his school, the Academy, sometimes called the first European university. At the Academy Plato produced many elegant Dialogues and lectured on many different topics (the lectures are lost), including rhetoric, biology, mathematics, astronomy, and, of course, philosophy—the pursuit of the highest reality and truth. Plato was intensely interested in political philosophy, and it was his desire to experiment with his ideal of the Philosopher-King that led him to return to Syracuse, where Dionysus I had been succeeded by his nephew, Dionysus II. Intrigues within the court spoiled Plato's philosophical education of Dionysus II, and the project was a failure.

Plato presided over the Academy until his death in 348 B.C. In the meantime, however, a pupil had matriculated at the Academy by the name of Aristotle.

Plato is universally regarded as one of the finest writers of Greek literature. His numerous and polished Dialogues include the *Apology, Euthyphro, Phaedo, Phaedrus, Meno, Republic, Symposium, Theaetetus, Sophist, Timaeus, Statesman,* and *Laws*.

THE THEORY OF THE FORMS

Grasping the distinction between the two worlds is the first step toward an understanding of Plato's theory of reality. The next step is to grasp that for Plato the transcendent world, the world of Being, is populated by realities called Forms, which are the causes of the particular things that exist beneath them, like tables, chairs, dogs, cats, circles, human beings, instances of beauty, examples of justice, and so on for every different kind of thing there is.

We are ready, then, to consider Plato's *theory of the Forms*. At least that is what it is usually called. It is also sometimes called the *theory of Ideas*. But here we must be on guard not to confuse *these* Ideas (capital *I*) with the ideas (small *i*) that exist merely in our minds. It will be seen that while our ideas have no existence apart from our minds, the Platonic Ideas exist objectively and absolutely: They would exist even if everything else were to disappear. In any case, it is useful to employ a capital *F* and *I* to remind us of the unique status of the Platonic Forms or Ideas.

Forms or Ideas

Why the word "Form"? It translates the Greek word *eidos*, which does, in fact, mean "form" in the ordinary, usual sense: shape, structure, appearance. As will shortly be seen, Plato certainly does *not* mean something visible. Still, it is easy to see why Plato took over this word for his own purpose. After all, a Platonic Form does have everything to do with what a thing *is*, and thus even with its physical structure, shape, or appearance. But if it helps, there are many expressions one could substitute for the word "Form": essence, nature, essential structure, object of a definition, etc. Again, what they all designate is what a thing *is*, its "whatness."

Why the word "Form"?

It may be helpful, further, to outline the main features of Forms. They may be characterized as:

Six features of Forms

- *Objective.* They exist "out there" as objects, independently of our minds or wills.
- *Transcendent.* Though they exist "out there," they do not exist in space and time; they lie, as it were, above or beyond space and time.
- *Eternal.* As transcendent realities they are not subject to time and therefore not subject to motion or change.
- *Intelligible.* As transcendent realities they cannot be grasped by the senses but only by the intellect.
- *Archetypal.* They are the models for every kind of thing that does or could exist.
- *Perfect.* They include absolutely and perfectly all the features of the things of which they are the models.

Perhaps now we are ready for a more explicit statement of the theory of the Forms: It is the belief in a transcendent world of eternal and absolute beings, corresponding to every kind of thing that there is, and causing in particular things their essential nature.

Summary of the theory of Forms

PLATO'S CONCEPTION OF FORMS AND THINGS

FORMS in the world of **BEING**	transcendent eternal intelligible archetypal perfect
THINGS in the world of **BECOMING**	spatio-temporal changeable sensible copied imperfect

---

More generally: For every particular and imperfect thing in the world of Becoming (a table, a chair, an instance of justice, an example of beauty, a circle) there is a corresponding reality which is its absolute and perfect essence or Form in the world of Being (Table, Chair, Justice, Beauty, Circle). The particular and imperfect thing, though imperfect, is what it is by virtue of its corresponding Form, which imparts to it, or causes in it, its essence or general nature. Because something has an essence or general nature it is an imperfect *something*. On the other hand, it is an *imperfect* something because while it reflects Being from above, it is invaded and contaminated by Nonbeing from below: The changeless is set in motion, the one is multiplied into many, the absolute is relativized, the universal is particularized.

In view of all of this, the following passage form Plato's *Euthyphro* should make a lot of sense. Here Socrates has asked Euthyphro about the meaning of holiness. Euthyphro responded with *examples* of holiness.

> SOCRATES: . . . *try to tell me more clearly what I asked you a little while ago, for, my friend, you were not explicit enough before when I put the question. What is holiness? You merely said that what you are now doing is a holy deed—namely, prosecuting your father on a charge of murder.*
>
> EUTHYPHRO: *And, Socrates, I told the truth.*
>
> SOCRATES: *Possibly. But, Euthyphro, there are many other things that you will say are holy.*

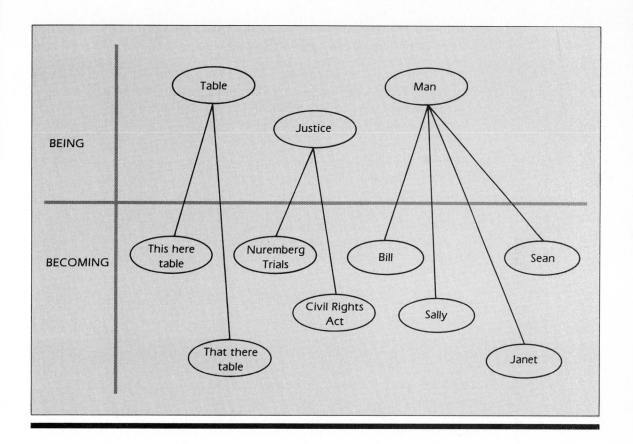

THE THEORY OF THE FORMS

. . . is the belief in a transcendent world of eternal and absolute beings, corresponding to every kind of thing that there is, and causing in particular things their essential natures.

EUTHYPHRO: *Because they are.*

SOCRATES: *Well, bear in mind that what I asked of you was not to tell me one or two out of all the numerous actions that are holy; I wanted you to tell me what is the essential form of holiness which makes all holy actions holy. I believe you held that there is one ideal form by which unholy things are all unholy, and by which all holy things are holy. Do you remember that?*

EUTHYPHRO: *I do.*

SOCRATES: *Well then, show me what, precisely, this ideal is, so that, with my eye on it, and using it as a standard, I can say that any action done by you or anybody else is holy if it resembles this ideal, or, if it does not, can deny that it is holy.*[6]

This brief passage expresses or embodies many of the things we have just explained. Notice for example, (1) Plato's use of words or phrases like "essential form" and "ideal" for the essence in the world of Being; (2) the contrast between the *one* essence in the world of Being (in this case Holiness) and the *many* instances of it in the world of Becoming (numerous holy acts); (3) the way in which the Form is said to be the cause of its many sensible instances; (4) the Form referred to as a standard for judgment; and (5) the way in which the particular instance is said to resemble the model.

This last point leads us further. We have said above that particular things have a nature or essence because they stand in some sort of relation to their Forms. But what, exactly, is this relation? How does the Form impart essence to the particular thing? This is a troublesome question, and Plato seems to have been bothered by it, though he never resolved it. Until now, we have been representing the Form as the model, and the sensible instance of the Form as a copy or imitation of it. This is the most common way of representing Plato's theory at this point. But Plato actually resorts to *two* explanations (really, *metaphors*) of how the Form gives essence to particular things. Sometimes, as in the above passage in the *Euthyphro*, he talks as if sensible things are *copies* or *imitations* of the Forms, and at other times he talks of a *participation* of the sensible thing in its Form. Thus a table is a table because it imperfectly reflects or is an imperfect copy of its pattern or model, the Form Tableness, or it is a table because it participates in the Form Tableness. The following passage from the *Phaedo* is useful not only because it makes explicit (though ambiguous) reference to a Form's relation to its sensible instances—he speaks of the Form's "presence in it" or "association with it"—but also because it shows that Plato did not concern himself with a rigorous explanation of this point:

. . . It seems to me that whatever else is beautiful apart from absolute beauty is beautiful because it partakes of that absolute beauty, and for no other reason. Do you accept this kind of causality?

Yes, I do.

Well, now, that is as far as my mind goes; I cannot understand these other ingenious theories of causation. If someone tells me that the reason why a given object is beautiful is that it has a gorgeous color or shape or any other such attribute, I

---

[6]Plato, *Euthyphro*, 6C–E.

disregard all these other explanations—I find them all confusing—and I cling simply and straightforwardly and no doubt foolishly to the explanation that the one thing that makes that object beautiful is the presence in it or association with it, in whatever way the relation comes about, of absolute beauty. I do not go so far as to insist upon the precise details—only upon the fact that it is by beauty that beautiful things are beautiful. This, I feel, is the safest answer for me or for anyone else to give, and I believe that while I hold fast to this I cannot fall; it is safe for me or for anyone else to answer that it is by beauty that beautiful things are beautiful. Don't you agree?[7]

We will see later that Plato's failure to be precise on the nature of the Form's relation to the particular is exactly what Aristotle seized as the Achilles' heel of Plato's whole theory.

Another important matter: Things can participate in more than one Form. This can happen in two ways. *First*, Forms themselves "blend" with one another, so that by imitating or participating in one Form a thing may actually be sharing

The "blending" of Forms

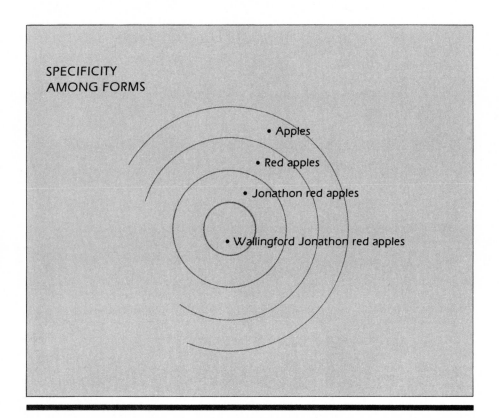

SPECIFICITY
AMONG FORMS

• Apples

• Red apples

• Jonathon red apples

• Wallingford Jonathon red apples

---

[7]Plato, *Phaedo*, 100C–E, tr. Hugh Tredennick, in *Plato: The Collected Dialogues.*

in many Forms. Is this not necessary, since the Forms both of X and Y may hold some essential feature in common? For example, if it is the essence of trees, dogs, cats, and humans to live, then however their Forms may otherwise differ they must at least all blend with the Form Life; if apples, cherries, bananas, and oranges are all by nature sweet, then whatever else each of their Forms involves they must all encompass Sweetness. Plato does not, however, believe that blending can go on forever as if we could just keep throwing in new ingredients to explain more and more specialized kinds of things. There must be a last, most specific definition in order to account for the ultimate difference of things.

Accidental features

But what about a feature which is not properly part of a thing's essence? Ink does not have to be blue in order to be ink, does it? This brings us to the *second* way things can imitate or participate in more than one Form. The Form Ink involves whatever it means to be *ink,* including having color. Now if this happens to be blue, then in addition to imitating or participating in the essential Form of Ink, including color, this ink must also participate in the Form Blue. Ask yourself: Is a certain feature of a thing part of that thing's very essence? If so, then that feature is one of the Forms that blend to make up the Form of that thing. If not, then that thing participates in this particular feature or Form accidentally or "on its own," as it were.

DEGREES OF REALITY AND KNOWLEDGE

So far we have been speaking as if Plato distinguished between two layers or levels of reality: *Being* and *Becoming,* Forms and their sensible copies. But Plato's theory of reality is somewhat more complicated than that. Here his famous image of the

The Divided Line

Divided Line, from the *Republic,* is helpful—Plato must have known that a picture is worth a thousand words.

> . . . take a line divided into two unequal parts, one to represent the visible order, the other the intelligible; and divide each part again in the same proportion, symbolizing degrees of comparative clearness or obscurity. Then (A) one of the two sections in the visible world will stand for images. By images I mean first shadows, and then reflections in water or in close-grained, polished surfaces, and everything of that kind, if you understand.
>
> Yes, I understand.
>
> Let the second section (B) stand for the actual things of which the first are likenesses, the living creatures about us and all the works of nature or of human hands.
>
> So be it.
>
> Will you also take the proportion in which the visible world has been divided as corresponding to degrees of reality and truth, so that the likeness shall stand to the

original in the same ratio as the sphere of appearances and belief to the sphere of knowledge?

Certainly.

Now consider how we are to divide the part which stands for the intelligible world. There are two sections. In the first (C) the mind uses as images those actual things which themselves had images in the visible world; and it is compelled to pursue its inquiry by starting from assumptions and travelling, not up to a principle, but down to a conclusion. In the second (D) the mind moves in the other direction, from an assumption up towards a principle which is not hypothetical; and it makes no use of the images employed in the other section, but only of Forms, and conducts its inquiry solely by their means.

I don't quite understand what you mean.

Then we will try again; what I have just said will help you to understand. (C) You know, of course, how students of subjects like geometry and arithmetic begin by postulating odd and even numbers, or the various figures and the three kinds of angle, and other such data in each subject. These data they take as known; and, having adopted them as assumptions, they do not feel called upon to give any account of them to themselves or to anyone else, but treat them as self-evident. Then, starting from these assumptions, they go on until they arrive, by a series of consistent steps, at all the conclusions they set out to investigate.

Yes, I know that.

You also know how they make use of visible figures and discourse about them, though what they really have in mind is the originals of which these figures are images: they are not reasoning, for instance, about this particular square and diagonal which they have drawn, but about the *Square* and the *Diagonal*; and so in all cases. The diagrams they draw and the models they make are actual things, which may have their shadows or images in water; but now they serve in their turn as images, while the student is seeking to behold those realities which only thought can apprehend.

True.

This, then, is the class of things that I spoke of as intelligible, but with two qualifications: first, that the mind, in studying them, is compelled to employ assumptions, and, because it cannot rise above these, does not travel upwards to a first principle; and second, that it uses as images those actual things which have images of their own in the section below them and which, in comparision with those shadows and reflections, are reputed to be more palpable and valued accordingly.

I understand: you mean the subject-matter of geometry and of the kindred arts.

(D) Then by the second section of the intelligible world you may understand me to mean all that unaided reasoning apprehends by the power of dialectic, when it treats its assumptions, not as first principles, but as hypotheses in the literal sense, things "laid down" like a flight of steps up which it may mount all the way to something that is not hypothetical, the first principle of all; and having grasped this, may turn back and, holding on to the consequences which depend upon it, descend at last *to a conclusion, never making use of any sensible object, but only of Forms, moving through Forms from one to another, and ending with Forms.*

I understand, he said, though not perfectly; for the procedure you describe sounds like an enormous undertaking. But I see that you mean to distinguish the field of intelligible reality studied by dialectic as having a greater certainty and truth than the subject-matter of the "arts," as they are called, which treat their assumptions as first principles. The students of these arts are, it is true, compelled to exercise thought in contemplating objects which the senses cannot perceive; but because they start from assumptions without going back to a first principle, you do not regard them as gaining true understanding about those objects, although the objects themselves, when connected with a first principle, are intelligible. And I think you would call the state of mind of the students of geometry and other such arts, not intelligence, but thinking, as being something between intelligence and mere acceptance of appearances.

You have understood me quite well enough, I replied. And now you may take, as corresponding to the four sections, these four states of mind: intelligence for the highest, thinking for the second, belief for the third, and for the last imagining. These you may arrange as the terms in a proportion, assigning to each a degree of clearness and certainty corresponding to the measure in which their objects possess truth and reality.

I understand and agree with you. I will arrange them as you say.[8]

There is no end to what could be said about Plato's philosophy on the basis of the Line. Here we will summarize the most important points.

To begin with, note that the Line is not divided into equal parts but *unequal* parts, and likewise the bottom and top segments of the Line are divided in the same ratio. This is Plato's way of suggesting that as we proceed from the bottom to the top of the Line we attain greater and greater degrees of reality and certainty. The first and major division of the Line represents, obviously, the distinction between the world of Being and the world of Becoming. By now we are certainly familiar with this distinction. But now each of the resulting lines, below and above, is in turn divided. This results in a sort of ladder of reality (on the metaphysical side of the Line) and a ladder of knowledge (on the epistemological side). The ladder of reality extends from mere images of sensible things (reflections in pools of water, photographs, paintings, memories, etc.) to the sensible things themselves (actual tables, chairs, humans, instances of justice or beauty, etc.), to the Forms which these sensible things copy. If the Form or essence includes a specific and concrete physical embodiment (Table, Circle, Human), then the Form is a "lower Form"; if the Form has no specific and concrete physical embodiment (Justice, Beauty), then it is a "higher Form." Corresponding to this ladder of reality is the ladder of knowledge. This extends from mere imagination (which grasps images) to perception (which grasps actual sensible things) to reason (which is a rational

[8]Plato, *The Republic*, 509D–511E.

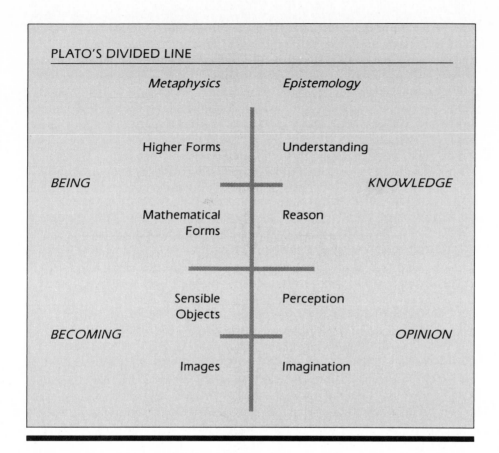

PLATO'S DIVIDED LINE

Metaphysics   *Epistemology*

Higher Forms   Understanding

BEING   *KNOWLEDGE*

Mathematical   Reason
Forms

Sensible   Perception
Objects

BECOMING   *OPINION*

Images   Imagination

and deductive way of grasping the lower Forms) to understanding (which grasps the higher Forms in a direct and intuitive way).

THE GOOD, THE SUN, AND THE CAVE

But there is more. It turns out that there is something above even the Forms themselves, something which we must situate at the very top of the Line. In the *Republic* Plato calls it the "essential Form of the Good."[9] Why must we believe in something

The Good: Form of the Forms

[9]According to a later form of Platonism, Neo-Platonism, Plato calls this Supreme Reality by various names, depending on the context. In the *Symposium,* where Plato is talking about the soul's quest for the beautiful, it is called *Beauty*; elsewhere, when Plato considers reality in a kind of mathematical light, he appears to have called it the *One*. But in the *Republic* it is called by its most familiar name: the *essential Form of the Good.*

even above the Forms, a sort of Form of the Forms? The answer is this: Just as the many images, say in a pool of water, must derive their relative being from some one thing above them, like an actual table, and actual tables must derive their relative being from some one thing above *them*, the Form Table, so must the Forms (both lower and higher) derive *their* being from a source which is above *them*: the Form of the Good. And just as it is above all realities and is their ultimate source, so it is above all knowledge and is its ultimate source. Of course, in order to be the *source* of being and knowledge, it itself cannot be *a* being or *a* thing known. That is why Plato says of the Good that it is *beyond being and knowledge*.

In a well-known analogy, Plato likens the essential Form of Goodness to the sun. The Good is to the intelligible world, or world of Being, as the sun is to the visible world, or world of Becoming:

The Analogy of the Sun

> First we must come to an understanding. Let me remind you of the distinction we drew earlier and have often drawn on other occasions, between the multiplicity of things that we call good or beautiful or whatever it may be and, on the other hand, Goodness itself or Beauty itself and so on. Corresponding to each of these sets of many things, we postulate a single Form or real essence, as we call it.
>
> Yes, that is so.
>
> Further, the many things, we say, can be seen, but are not objects of rational thought; whereas the Forms are objects of thought, but invisible.
>
> Yes, certainly.
>
> And we see things with our eyesight, just as we hear sounds with our ears and, to speak generally, perceive any sensible things with our sense-faculties.
>
> Of course.
>
> Have you noticed, then, that the artificer who designed the senses has been exceptionally lavish of his materials in making the eyes able to see and their objects visible?
>
> That never occurred to me.
>
> Well, look at it in this way. Hearing and sound do not stand in need of any third thing, without which the ear will not hear nor sound be heard; and I think the same is true of most, not to say all, of the other senses. Can you think of one that does require anything of the sort?
>
> No, I cannot.
>
> But there is this need in the case of sight and its objects. You may have the power of vision in your eyes and try to use it, and colour may be there in the objects; but sight will see nothing and the colours will remain invisible in the absence of a third thing peculiarly constituted to serve this very purpose.
>
> By which you mean—?
>
> Naturally I mean what you call light; and if light is a thing of value, the sense of sight and the power of being visible are linked together by a very precious bond, such as unites no other sense with its object.

No one could say that light is not a precious thing.

And of all the divinities in the skies is there one whose light, above all the rest, is responsible for making our eyes see perfectly and making objects perfectly visible?

There can be no two opinions: of course you mean the Sun.

And how is sight related to this deity? Neither sight nor the eye which contains it is the Sun, but of all the sense-organs it is the most sun-like; and further, the power it possesses is dispensed by the Sun, like a stream flooding the eye. And again, the Sun is not vision, but it is the cause of vision and also is seen by the vision it causes.

Yes.

It was the Sun, then, that I meant when I spoke of that offspring which the Good has created in the visible world, to stand there in the same relation to vision and visible things as that which the Good itself bears in the intelligible world to intelligence and to intelligible objects.

How is that? You must explain further.

You know what happens when the colours of things are no longer irradiated by the daylight, but only by the fainter luminaries of the night: when you look at them, the eyes are dim and seem almost blind, as if there were no unclouded vision in them. But when you look at things on which the Sun is shining, the same eyes see distinctly and it becomes evident that they do contain the power of vision.

Certainly.

Apply this comparison, then, to the soul. When its gaze is fixed upon an object irradiated by truth and reality, the soul gains understanding and knowledge and is manifestly in possession of intelligence. But when it looks towards that twilight world of things that come into existence and pass away, its sight is dim and it has only opinions and beliefs which shift to and fro, and now it seems like a thing that has no intelligence.

That is true.

This, then, which gives to the objects of knowledge their truth and to him who knows them his power of knowing, is the Form or essential nature of Goodness. It is the cause of knowledge and truth; and so, while you may think of it as an object of knowledge, you will do well to regard it as something beyond truth and knowledge and, precious as these both are, of still higher worth. And, just as in our analogy light and vision were to be thought of as like the Sun, but not identical with it, so here both knowledge and truth are to be regarded as like the Good, but to identify either with the Good is wrong. The Good must hold a yet higher place of honour.

You are giving it a position of extraordinary splendour, if it is the source of knowledge and truth and itself surpasses them in worth. You surely cannot mean that it is pleasure.

Heaven forbid, I exclaimed. But I want to follow up our analogy still further. You will agree that the Sun not only makes the things we see visible, but also brings them into existence and gives them growth and nourishment; yet he is not the same thing as existence. And so with the objects of knowledge: these derive from the Good not only their power of being known, but their very being and reality; and Goodness is not the same thing as being, but even beyond being, surpassing it in dignity and power.[10]

It may be useful to spell out exactly the various elements in the analogy: The sun is analogous to the Form of the Good; the visible world is analogous to the intelligible world (the world of Forms); Light is analogous to Truth; the objects of sight are analogous to the objects of knowledge (the Forms); and sight is analogous to knowledge. Or perhaps the more visual summary in this box will help:[11]

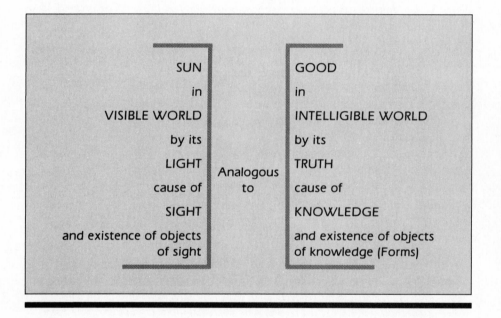

SUN	Analogous to	GOOD
in		in
VISIBLE WORLD		INTELLIGIBLE WORLD
by its		by its
LIGHT		TRUTH
cause of		cause of
SIGHT		KNOWLEDGE
and existence of objects of sight		and existence of objects of knowledge (Forms)

The two main points of the analogy are: *First*, just as the sun lights up the world and makes physical objects visible to our eyes so does the Good illuminate intelligible objects (Forms) and render them knowable by the mind. *Second*, and closely related, just as the sun actually causes things in the world to exist and sustains them—without the light of the sun, the world would wither away—so does the Good cause in the Forms their very being and truth.

[10]Plato, *The Republic*, 507A–509B.

[11]The following table is based on R. C. Cross and A. D. Woosley, *Plato's Republic: A Philosophical Commentary* (London: Macmillan, 1966), pp. 202, 231.

In Plato's theory of reality, the Good is, then, the ultimate principle of reality and truth. Any degree or instance of being, truth, unity, harmony, beauty, or intelligibility found anywhere, either in the world of Becoming or in the world of Being, is traceable finally to the Good. This is, some would say, the closest thing in Plato to traditional conceptions of God, both Western and Eastern.

The Good is also the ultimate object of the soul's progress. And now we are ready for the Allegory of the Cave, one of the most famous passages in all literature. In this allegory Plato asks us to picture men imprisoned in an underground cavern who mistake the shadowy figures and echoes reflected on the wall facing them for reality. But how deluded they are! It is only by forcing them (and that is what it would take to dislodge them from their comfortable and familiar setting) out of the cave and into the upper world that, though temporarily dazzled and blinded by the true light, they would eventually recognize their former delusion. But read it for yourself.

The Allegory of the Cave

. . . here is a parable to illustrate the degrees in which our nature may be enlightened or unenlightened. Imagine the condition of men living in a sort of cavernous chamber underground, with an entrance open to the light and a long passage all down the cave. Here they have been from childhood, chained by the leg and also by the neck, so that they cannot move and can see only what is in front of them, because the chains will not let them turn their heads. At some distance higher up is the light of a fire burning behind them; and between the prisoners and the fire is a track with a parapet built along it, like the screen at a puppet-show, which hides the performers while they show their puppets over the top.

I see, said he.

Now behind this parapet imagine persons carrying along various artificial objects, including figures of men and animals in wood or stone or other materials, which project above the parapet. Naturally, some of these persons will be talking, others silent.

It is a strange picture, he said, and a strange sort of prisoners.

Like ourselves, I replied; for in the first place prisoners so confined would have seen nothing of themselves or of any other, except the shadows thrown by the fire-light on the wall of the Cave facing them, would they?

Not if all their lives they had been prevented from moving their heads.

And they would have seen as little of the objects carried past.

Of course.

Now, if they could talk to one another, would they not suppose that their words referred only to those passing shadows which they saw?

Necessarily.

And suppose their prison had an echo from the wall facing them? When one of the people crossing behind them spoke, they could only suppose that the sound came from the shadow passing before their eyes.

No doubt.

In every way, then, such prisoners would recognize as reality nothing but the shadows of those artificial objects.

Inevitably.

Now consider what would happen if their release from the chains and the healing of their unwisdom should come about in this way. Suppose one of them set free and forced suddenly to stand up, turn his head, and walk with eyes lifted to the light; all these movements would be painful, and he would be too dazzled to make out the objects whose shadows he had been used to see. What do you think he would say, if someone told him that what he had formerly seen was meaningless illusion, but now, being somewhat nearer to reality and turned towards more real objects, he was getting a truer view? Suppose further that he were shown the various objects being carried by and were made to say, in reply to questions, what each of them was. Would he not be perplexed and believe the objects now shown him to be not so real as what he formerly saw?

Yes, not nearly so real.

And if he were forced to look at the fire-light itself, would not his eyes ache, so that he would try to escape and turn back to the things which he could see distinctly, convinced that they really were clearer than these other objects now being shown to him?

Yes.

And suppose someone were to drag him away forcibly up the steep and rugged ascent and not let him go until he had hauled him out into the sunlight, would he not suffer pain and vexation at such treatment, and, when he had come out into the light, find his eyes so full of its radiance that he could not see a single one of the things that he was now told were real?

Certainly he would not see them all at once.

He would need, then, to grow accustomed before he could see things in that upper world. At first it would be easiest to make out shadows, and then the images of men and things reflected in water, and later on the things themselves. After that, it would be easier to watch the heavenly bodies and the sky itself by night, looking at the light of the moon and stars rather than the Sun and the Sun's light in the day-time.

Yes, surely.

Last of all, he would be able to look at the Sun and contemplate its nature, not as it appears when reflected in water or any alien medium, but as it is in itself in its own domain.

No doubt.

And now he would begin to draw the conclusion that it is the Sun that produces the seasons and the course of the year and controls everything in the visible world, and moreover is in a way the cause of all that he and his companions used to see.

Clearly he would come at last to that conclusion.[12]

[12]Plato, The Republic, 514A-516C.

The point of the story should be obvious. We, like the prisoners in the cave, are deluded about reality. We mistake the unreal for the real, and only with the greatest difficulty can we be turned, and indeed we might have to be *forced*, in the direction of truth and reality. But we *must* be turned in that direction, and we *must* ascend into the upper regions of truth and reality. Why? Because rationality is the essence of man. Thus our nature is fulfilled in the contemplation and knowledge of reality. And this means happiness or well-being. Even in this life, as much as possible we must be liberated and detached from the darkness of the sensible world of Becoming and opinion and live as much as possible in the enjoyment of Being and Knowledge. At death, however, the soul will be freed forever from the distractions and imperfections of Becoming and can enjoy absolutely and without interruption the knowledge of Being. That is why, says Plato, the real philosopher—lover of wisdom—looks forward to death.

ARISTOTLE'S CRITICISM OF PLATO

As Plato was a student of Socrates and developed his ideas, so Aristotle was the student of Plato and developed *his* ideas. Less charitably, Aristotle ruthlessly criticized his master's theory of the Forms, and propounded a quite different one.

Toward the beginning of his *Metaphysics*, Aristotle provides his own summary of the Socratic-Platonic theory:

> . . . [Plato], having in his youth first become familiar with Cratylus[13] and with the Heraclitean doctrines (that all sensible things are ever in a state of flux and there is no knowledge about them), these views he held even in later years. Socrates, however, was busying himself about ethical matters and neglecting the world of nature as a whole but seeking the universal in these ethical matters, and fixed thought for the first time on definitions; Plato accepted his teaching, but held that the problem applied not to sensible things but to entities of another kind—for this reason, that the common definition could not be a definition of any sensible thing, as they were always changing. Things of this other sort, then, he called Ideas, and sensible things, he said, were all named after these, and in virtue of a relation of these; for the many existed by participation in the Ideas that have the same name as they.[14]

Aristotle on Plato

Later he criticizes this view with a long string of objections; in fact, some have counted as many as twenty-five or more. Not all of Aristotle's objections are as

[13]Cratylus was a follower of Heraclitus but pushed the teaching of his master even further, for he said that one could not step into the same river even *once!*

[14]Aristotle, *Metaphysics*, 987a–b, tr. W. D. Ross, in *Basic Works of Aristotle*, ed. Richard McKeon (New York: Random House, 1941).

important as others, as when he twits Plato for creating an additional world of things, as if we did not already have enough to explain!

The Third-man Argument

More important is Aristotle's so-called Third-man Argument. It goes like this. In order to explain the similarity between (1) a first man and (2) a second man, we must posit (3) a third man, the Ideal Man or Form. But then there will have to be a similarity between (1) the first two men and (2) the third man posited, the Form of Man. How do we now explain this similarity? We must again posit (3) a third and "higher" man. But then there will be a similarity between (1) all the previous men and (2) *this* third man. How do we explain *this* similarity? According to Aristotle, the process of positing a "third man" will have to go on forever, but in that case, the original similarity is never explained. Is this a fair argument against Plato? Some have countered that the argument will only work if you think the original third man, the Form of Man, is itself actually a *man* and possessing the features which particular men possess. Would Plato agree to this? Is the Form of Man *itself* two-legged and rational? This is a difficult question, and much ink has been spilt trying to explain just how Plato viewed the Forms in this respect. Be that as it may, this is still not Aristotle's main objection to Plato.

The problem of the *chōrismos*

The main problem, for Aristotle, is the problem of the *chōrismos*, a Greek word which means "separation." Aristotle correctly represents Plato as having placed the ultimate causes of things (the Forms) in a transcendent world and thus *separated* from the things they are supposed to be the causes of. But this gives rise immediately to two very big questions, as Aristotle shows in the following:

> *Above all one might discuss the question what on earth the Forms contribute to sensible things, either to those that are eternal or to those that come into being and cease to be. For they cause neither movement nor any change in them. But again they help in no wise either towards the knowledge of the other things (for they are not even the substance of these, else they would have been in them), or towards their being, if they are not in the particulars which share in them; though if they were, they might be thought to be causes, as white causes whiteness in a white object by entering into its composition. . . .*
>
> *But, further, all other things cannot come from the Forms in any of the usual senses of "from." And to say that they are patterns and the other things share in them is to use empty words and poetical metaphors. . . .*
>
> *Again, it would seem impossible that the substance and that of which it is the substance should exist apart; how therefore, could the Ideas, being the substances of things, exist apart? In the Phaedo the case is stated in this way—that the Forms are causes both of being and of becoming; yet when the Forms exist, still the things that share in them do not come into being, unless there is something to originate movement.*[15]

[15]Ibid., 991a–b.

One question Aristotle poses is, How can the Forms be the causes of the natures or "whatnesses" of things without being *in* those things? His answer: They can't. *Another* question which Aristotle poses is, How do Plato's transcendent and unchanging Forms account for the most evident fact about the things around us, namely, their coming into being and their motion and change? His answer: They don't. In sum, the *chōrismos*, or separation, between the Forms and particular sensible things, like a great gulf fixed, makes it impossible for the Forms to *do* anything for those things at the most critical points. That is bad enough. What is worse, when Plato attempts to explain how the Forms are related to sensible things he provides no really rigorous philosophical explanation but resorts to "empty words and poetical metaphors," such as *participation* and *imitation.*

In fairness to Plato, it should be noted that many of Aristotle's specific criticisms (for example, the Third-man Argument) were anticipated and discussed by Plato himself. More generally, in the *Timaeus* Plato did account for motion and change in the world, and as for his attempt to bridge the two worlds with "empty words and poetical metaphors," we saw in an earlier passage from the *Phaedo* that Plato freely granted the difficulty of language at this point.

ARISTOTLE'S VIEW OF FORM

One must not conclude from the above that Aristotle rejected Plato's theory of reality for a radically different one. Aristotle too believed absolutely in Forms. As with Plato, so with Aristotle: Only by means of Forms, the objective essences of things, can we account for the order around us, both in nature and in morality, and only because of Forms is knowledge of anything possible. The *difference* lies in their views of how the Forms are related to particular things.

It should be clear from the above quotation that Aristotle rejected Plato's idea of *transcendent* Forms in favor of an idea of *immanent* Forms, that is, a view of Forms as existing *within* particular sensible things. He overcomes Plato's unbridgeable chasm between Forms and sensible things by asserting that Forms can only be causes of things if they are *in* those things. But understand: There is no abstract "tableness" out there any more than there is any unimaginable formless matter or formless "stuff." What *is* out there are particular *tables*—this table, that table, and other tables. The Form or essence Table exists only as individualized or particularized (that is, turned into a concrete, particular thing) by some wood, glue, and varnish. And likewise with everything. The Form (which accounts for the essence or whatness of a thing) combined with matter (which gives that essence a concrete and particular expression) is what is *real*. As one slogan puts it, "No form without matter, and no matter without form." For those who prefer a more technical expression, this view or idea is called *hylomorphic composition* (from the Greek *hylē*, "matter," and *morphē*, "form"): Everything in the natural world is composed of both

Aristotle: Forms must be in things

"No form without matter, no matter without form"

*Plato and Aristotle,
from "The School of
Athens" by Raphael.
Plato, holding a copy of
the* Timaeus, *is
pointing upward, thus
signifying his belief in
Forms as transcendent
and separate from the
sensible world.
Aristotle, holding a
copy of his* Ethics,
*signifies by his gesture
his belief that Forms
are immanent in
sensible things.*

form and matter; there can be no instances of unformed matter or "unmattered" form.

God: Pure Form

Thus it is with everything in the *natural* world. With respect to God, the situation is quite different. The matter in a thing provides for its changeability and movement, since matter is the potential in a thing to change or become something different. Think of a table. It can be chopped into bits, burned into ashes, or dismantled and turned into a chair, only because there is *wood* there. But there can

---

HYLOMORPHIC COMPOSITION

Although Aristotle himself never used this expression it was eventually coined to represent the Aristotelian emphasis on the necessary twofold composition, material and formal, of everything in the natural world.

---

be no matter, or potential for change and motion, in God, who is the Unmoved Mover. God, the immutable source of all motion, must himself be utterly devoid of matter. He is Pure Form.

The real difference between Plato's idea of *transcendent* Forms and Aristotle's idea of *immanent* Forms shows up very vividly in their discussions of art. In the last parts of the *Republic*, Plato argued that art is "thrice removed" from reality: A painting is an imperfect representation or copy of a man who himself is an imperfect copy of the real thing, Man; likewise a drama imperfectly represents people and things which are themselves imperfect copies of their Forms. For these reasons Plato advocated banishing the arts—at least the *representative* arts—from the ideal society. Aristotle, with his view of immanent Forms, draws exactly the opposite conclusion. It is because the essence and ideal of things are embodied *in* those things that the artistic representation brings us *closer* to reality. As Aristotle says in a helpful passage in his *Poetics*, what the artist does is represent things in their *universality*, to use Aristotle's term, and that is why the artist's work is more philosophical than, say, the historian's work which represents things merely in their *particularity*.

> *. . . the poet's function is to describe, not the thing that has happened, but a kind of thing that might happen, i.e. what is possible as being probable or necessary. The distinction between historian and poet is not in the one writing prose and the other verse—you might put the work of Herodotus into verse, and it would still be a species of history; it consists really in this, that the one describes the thing that has been, and the other a kind of thing that might be. Hence poetry is something more philosophic and of graver import than history, since its statements are of the nature rather of universals, whereas those of history are singulars. By a universal statement I mean one as to what such or such a kind of man will probably or necessarily say or do— which is the aim of poetry, though it affixes proper names to the characters; by a singular statement, one as to what, say, Alcibiades did or had done to him.*[16]

[16]Aristotle, *Poetics*, 1451a–b, tr. Ingram Bywater, in *Basic Works of Aristotle*.

Aristotle vs. Plato on art

**Aristotle's Four
Causes**

Two final points. First, although we have dwelt upon form and matter, according to Aristotle there are actually *four* principles, or "causes," which are necessarily involved in the constitution or explanation of a thing:

- Material Cause
- Formal Cause
- Efficient Cause
- Final Cause

The *Material Cause* is the matter, or "stuff," something is made out of; the *Formal Cause* is its essence, or whatness; the *Efficient* or *Moving Cause* is what brings the thing into being; and the *Final Cause* is the end, or purpose, of the thing. Can you identify the four causes of, say, a table? It may be noticed that the last three causes are closely related, and Aristotle himself suggests that they may be lumped together under the formal cause, leaving us with the general twofold distinction: Material Cause/Formal Cause. Thus the key terms in the constitution and explanation of things are matter and form. Second, Aristotle stressed even more strongly than Plato the difference between "substantial" Forms and "accidental" Forms. Fido *necessarily* involves the Form Dog; it is of Fido's very nature or substance to be a dog. But it is only an accident that Fido involves the Forms Shaggy, Brown, and Short-legged; it is not part of Fido's essence that he possesses these features—he might or might not, and still be a *dog*.

**Substantial and
accidental Forms**

AFTER PLATO AND ARISTOTLE

Aristotle provides, thus, a criticism of Plato's theory of reality. But his own theory, after all, is not really all that different. For both Plato and Aristotle the true reality of something is identified with its Form. And this general view, often called *realism*, was propagated throughout subsequent centuries, mainly through the Christian thinkers St. Augustine (d. 430), who taught more or less the Platonic version, and St. Thomas Aquinas (d. 1275), who taught more or less the Aristotelian version.

**Ockham's Razor
again**

Obviously, this kind of philosophy is radically different from all those approaches which reject Form as sort of spooky or philosophically superstitious. It was, in fact, against this very idea that William of Ockham (d. 1349?) formulated the principle, which we encountered in the last chapter, known as Ockham's Razor, in an attempt to cut away all unnecessary principles and realities: *Entia non est multiplicanda praeter necessitatem*, "Entities are not to be multiplied without necessity." The resulting view was known as *nominalism* (from the Latin *nomen*, "name"), the view that Forms or universals (such as Animal, Whiteness, etc.) have no external or independent existence, but are merely names or words by which we group together things which possess similar features.

Nominalism

REALISM VS. NOMINALISM

- *Realism:* The doctrine that Forms, or essences, possess objective reality.
- *Nominalism:* The doctrine that Forms, or universals, are merely universal names by which we group together things which possess similar features.

Nominalism will perhaps appear to you as a very simple and clean approach: Away with all that silly and needless talk about substantial forms, accidental forms, metaphysical causes, and the like! On the other hand, we must not forget about the problems that spawned the belief in Forms in the first place: Without objective Forms, or essences, how, for example, are real knowledge, rational discourse, and moral judgment possible?

Chapter 4 in Review

"Form" is one of the most important words in the history of philosophy. In fact, when the first full-blown philosophies came on the scene, those of Plato and Aristotle, they were built almost entirely around this concept.

 SUMMARY

In an important sense, the idea of Form is an answer to any philosophy, such as that of Heraclitus (as Plato understood him) and Protagoras, which dissolves everything into a flux of relativity. According to Plato and other Form-philosophers, we must believe in an objective basis for the things existing around us, for knowledge, and for value judgments. This basis is the Form, or essence, which constitutes the real *Being* of a thing. As Being, the Form must be one, immutable, ideal, transcendent, etc., and this Being is imperfectly represented in particular, sensible things by "participation" or "imitation." Plato conceives all reality as a ladder or scale and, corresponding to this, knowledge too (the image of the Divided Line). But the basic distinction is between the sensible world of Becoming and the transcendent or intelligible world of Being, with the essential Form of Goodness ranging over all (the Analogy of the Sun). The practical point is to make our way, as much as possible in this life, into the higher realm of the intelligible and to enjoy the illumination of reality and truth (the Allegory of the Cave).

Aristotle belongs to this philosophical tradition too, but represents an important variation. He criticized Plato's theory of the Forms in several ways, but mainly because of the gap it leaves between the Forms and the things they are the Forms *of*: the problem of the *chōrismos*. Instead, Aristotle insisted that, while we must believe in the Forms or objective essences of things, they cannot be separated from those things. This is Aristotle's doctrine of *immanent* (rather than transcendent) Forms: The Forms must be *in* things. His conception of matter as potentiality and therefore providing for change, and his doctrine of the Four Causes are also important features of his thought.

In subsequent centuries the realist metaphysics of Plato and Aristotle received Christian reinterpretations and restatements, most notably at the hands of St. Augustine and St. Thomas Aquinas. On the other hand, it was also *attacked* by nominalist philosophers, such as Ockham, for whom the Forms were merely general or universal terms which lump similar things into classes. The debate between realism (Forms have objective reality) and nominalism (Forms are universal terms) is a fundamental and continuing one.

BASIC IDEAS

- "Systematic" philosophy
- The nature of a Platonic Dialogue
- The Socratic Problem
- The problem with Protagorean subjectivism
- The problem with Heraclitean flux
- The distinction between the worlds of Becoming and Being
- The meaning of "Form"
- Six features of Platonic Forms; they are
    Objective
    Transcendent
    Eternal
    Intelligible
    Archetypal
    Perfect
- Two explanations for the Form's relation to the particular
    Imitation
    Participation
- Two ways in which something can share in more than one Form
- The Divided Line: Degrees of reality and knowledge
- The Good as the Form of Forms
- The Analogy of the Sun
- The Allegory of the Cave
- Aristotle's main criticism of Plato's theory: The problem of the *chōrismos*, "separation"

- Aristotle's Four Causes
    Material
    Formal
    Efficient
    Final
- Aristotle's conception of immanent Forms
- Hylomorphic composition
- Substantial and accidental Forms
- Ockham's Razor
- Realism vs. nominalism

1. True or false: Plato believed that "a man is the measure of all things."
2. According to Plato, the sun is to the _____ as the Good is to the _____.
3. What did Heraclitus and Parmenides contribute to Plato's theory of the Forms?
4. Who was Protagoras?
5. True or false: Aristotle's Efficient Cause is the agent through which something comes into being.
6. What is the point of the Allegory of the Cave?
7. Aristotle believed not in transcendent Forms but _____ Forms.
8. Plato taught that Forms are related to particular things by means of (a) the Final Cause, (b) participation, (c) hylomorphic composition, (d) imitation.
9. True or false: Aristotle was a nominalist.
10. In the medieval and Scholastic periods Plato's and Aristotle's theories of reality were preserved, in a Christian version, by _____ and _____ respectively.

- Plato's philosophy is sometimes called a rather "poetic" one. What does this mean? Is it good or bad? What is to be made of the fact that Plato anticipated Aristotle's criticisms but did not regard them as decisive? (You might recall the distinction between "tender-minded" and "tough-minded" philosophers in Chapter 1.)
- If one rejects every philosophy of Forms, such as that of Plato or Aristotle, what then? What about the initial problems that sparked such philosophies in the first place?

CHAPTER 5

MIND AND MATTER

If you were to meet someone on the street and ask what he or she thinks reality is, you might get a response something like this:

> Well, I know that I have a mind (or soul, or whatever you want to call it), and I know that in addition to my mind—and presumably other minds too— there is a world of material things like my own body, and tables and chairs, and all the other things "out there." And, well, I guess there is a real difference between mind and matter such that my mind might exist even *apart* from matter.

A common theory of reality

This view of reality, *mind-matter dualism,* is a very common one, held by many who have never heard its name or have never even heard of metaphysics. It is called a dualism because it reduces everything to two basic realities, in this case, mind and matter. As a genuine philosophical position, however, it is considerably more complex than the opinion expressed by our friend on the street. For its most forceful expression we turn to the French thinker René Descartes[1] (1596–1650).

DUALISM

The metaphysical view that all things are reducible to two essentially different realities.

---

[1]Pronounced *Day-cart'*.

DESCARTES: THE FATHER OF
MODERN PHILOSOPHY

In addition to being a mathematician and scientist (he discovered analytic geometry and made numerous contributions to physics) Descartes was also a philosopher and has been called, in fact, the father of modern philosophy. Everything changed with Descartes, and nearly all modern philosophies may be traced back, in one way or another, to his.

In a sense, modern philosophy originated in a dream, or a series of dreams, in which a new approach to knowledge was revealed to Descartes. It is not known exactly what "came" to Descartes in these dreams, but it appears that it had something to do with the unity of all branches of knowledge and perhaps the method of achieving this unity. In his *Discourse on Method,* Descartes tells of his disillusionment with traditional philosophy:

> . . . *seeing that it has been cultivated for many centuries by the best minds that have ever lived, and that nevertheless no single thing is to be found in it which is not subject of dispute, and in consequence which is not dubious, I had not enough presumption to hope to fare better there than other men had done. And also, considering how many conflicting opinions there may be regarding the self-same matter, all supported by learned people, while there can never be more than one which is true, I esteemed as well-nigh false all that only went as far as being probable.*[2]

On the other hand, he was much struck by the certainty of mathematical procedures:

Descartes' "geometrical" method

> *Most of all was I delighted with mathematics because of the certainty of its demonstration and the evidence of its reasoning.*[3]

He determined that if philosophy too was to be successful it must annex to itself something like a "geometrical method" so that its starting-points and conclusions might be as certain as those of geometry.

It will be best to consider Descartes' conception of philosophical knowledge in Part II, "The Question of Knowledge." Here it should be enough to say only that Descartes turned his back on the doubtful truths delivered through the senses, and turned rather to what could be known with certainty through *reason alone.* In the intellect he found, as in geometry, two fundamental, foolproof operations: intuition and deduction. Through intuition he could know certain basic and undoubtable truths, and through deduction he could draw from these basic truths still fur-

Intuition and deduction

[2]René Descartes, *Discourse on Method,* in *The Philosophical Works of Descartes,* tr. Elizabeth S. Haldane and G. R. T. Ross (Cambridge: Cambridge University Press, 1911), I, 85–86.
[3]Ibid., I, 85.

René Descartes

In addition to his contributions to mathematics, physics, and physiology, Descartes' contributions to philosophy have earned him the title of "father of modern philosophy." He is the most famous advocate of mind-matter dualism.

ther truths. Through both of them together he believed that he could construct a whole philosophy.

Armed with his geometrical method, Descartes set out to formulate a new and certain and definitive philosophy. The best expressions of this philosophy may be found in Descartes' *Discourse on Method* (especially Part Four), and his *Meditations on First Philosophy*. It may be helpful to anticipate a bit by saying that Descartes' philosophy unfolds in three major stages: First, the knowledge of the *mind*; second, the knowledge of *God*; and third, the knowledge of *matter*.

"WHAT CAN I KNOW FOR CERTAIN?"

We have already noted that Descartes was disillusioned with previous philosophies because of their contradictions and muddledness. This distress was genuine (one may even detect an element of personal crisis in it) and probably reflected certain recent upheavals in the medieval view of the world. We can imagine him peering out his window and exclaiming, "If I cannot be certain that the sun moves across the sky—something I can see with my own eyes—then of what *can* I be certain?!" Descartes thus resolved, first, to doubt anything and everything that was doubtable, in hopes of discovering something, even one thing, that was not doubtable, something certain, something unshakable, some indubitable truth that might serve as a secure foundation of his philosophy. In this respect, Descartes likened himself to the ancient Archimedes who said in relation to his newly discovered principle of the fulcrum, "Give me a place to stand, and I will move the world!" Descartes said, in effect, "Give me just one certain truth, and I will build upon it an entire philosophy!"

Thus, Descartes embarked on his process of *systematic doubt*, that is, the process of doubting everything that can be doubted to see if there is anything that *cannot* be doubted. Since our senses sometimes deceive us, Descartes supposed that perhaps the world of sense experience was not at all as it seems to be. Since people make the simplest mistakes in reasoning, he rejected as false all the demonstrations he had previously accepted. And noticing the similarities between waking life and dreams, he even ventured that nothing was more real than dreams. And noticing that even when dreaming, two plus three equals five, he went so far as to devise the hypothesis of an "evil genius" bent upon his constant deception even about mathematical truths. Descartes documents his progress in the *Meditations*:

Systematic doubt

> *I shall proceed by setting aside all that in which the least doubt could be supposed to exist—just as if I had discovered that it was absolutely false; and I shall ever follow in this road until I have met with something which is certain, or at least, if I can do nothing else, until I have learned for certain that there is nothing in the world that is certain. Archimedes, in order that he might draw the terrestrial globe out of its place, and transport it elsewhere, demanded only that one point should be fixed and immoveable; in the same way I shall have the right to conceive high hopes if I am happy enough to discover one thing only which is certain and indubitable.*
>
> *I suppose, then, that all the things that I see are false; I persuade myself that nothing has ever existed of all that my fallacious memory represents to me. I consider that I possess no senses; I imagine that body, figure, extension, movement and place are but the fictions of my mind. What, then, can be esteemed as true? Perhaps nothing at all, unless that there is nothing in the world that is certain.[4]*

THE INTUITION OF MIND

In this way Descartes sought to erase, as it were, everything from the chalkboard of human knowledge. Finally, he found himself exactly opposite of the naive realist

---

[4]Descartes, *Meditations on First Philosophy*, in *Philosophical Works of Descartes*, I, 149.

Cogito ergo sum:
"I think, therefore
I am."

who thinks that things are exactly as they appear. Descartes could doubt *every-thing*—except for one. In all of this doubting and erasing, one thing finally presented itself as *undoubtable* and *unerasable*. As he expressed it in the famous line from the *Discourse, Cogito ergo sum,* "I think, therefore I am." After all, if I am mistaken about this, then there is no "I" to be mistaken!

> *. . . whilst I thus wished to think all things false, it was absolutely essential that the "I" who thought this should be somewhat, and remarking that this truth "I think, therefore I am" was so certain and so assured that all the most extravagant suppositions brought forward by the sceptics were incapable of shaking it, I came to the conclusion that I could receive it without scruple as the first principle of the Philosophy for which I was seeking.[5]*

Here, then, is rock-bottom certitude, unshakable even by the most radical doubt, a place for Descartes to stand as he sought to build a philosophy.

Mind: A substance
the essence of
which is to think

"I think, therefore I am." But *what* am I? What *is* mind? What *is* soul? What *is* my spirit? (Descartes uses all of these terms interchangeably.) Descartes' answer in the *Discourse:* It is "a substance the whole essence or nature of which is to think,"[6] or for short, a *thinking substance.* But here we must make our terms clear. We have a good idea what Descartes means by "thinking"; it means all the intellectual operations, such as affirming, denying, imagining, doubting, reflecting, inferring, and the like. We may have more trouble with the word "substance." Some readers may find themselves almost hopelessly afflicted with the idea that substance means some concrete, physical thing. But the word itself (from the Latin *substantia*) means, literally, "that which stands under," or "that which upholds" something. To use Descartes' own example, consider a ball of wax. It may be hard, soft, have a certain color, odor, and texture, and these may change from time to time, but then there is the wax *itself,* the substance of these qualities. Can you imagine texture or shape existing without something that *is* textured and shaped? Can you imagine thinking without something that *does* the thinking? Just as in grammar there could be no predicates without a subject, so in the world of sensible things there could be no qualities without a material substance, and in the intellectual world no thinking activities without a mental substance. But it is not just that there is no thinking apart from mind—mind *is* thinking, a thinking substance. It *may* affirm, deny, doubt, reflect, imagine, infer, etc., but it *must* think.

In the *Meditations,* Descartes provides a summary of this first stage of his reasoning: (1) It is certain that I exist, and (2) I am a mind or thinking substance.

> *. . . I was persuaded that there was nothing in all the world, that there was no heaven, no earth, that there were no minds, nor any bodies: was I not then likewise persuaded that I did not exist? Not at all; of a surety I myself did exist since I persuaded myself*

[5]Descartes, *Discourse on Method,* I, 101.
[6]Ibid.

SUBSTANCE

"Substance" is popularly thought to be a *physical thing*. But the term was used by Descartes and subsequent thinkers in quite a different way, and with its original sense of "that which stands under" and thus "upholds" something (from the Latin *substantia*). In Descartes and others, mind is the substance which underlies mental activities, as matter is the substance underlying and upholding physical qualities.

---

of something [or merely because I thought of something]. But there is some deceiver or other, very powerful and very cunning, who ever employs his ingenuity in deceiving me. Then without doubt I exist also if he deceives me, and let him deceive me as much as he will, he can never cause me to be nothing so long as I think that I am something. So that after having reflected well and carefully examined all things, we must come to the definite conclusion that this proposition: I am, I exist, is necessarily true each time that I pronounce it, or that I mentally conceive it. . . .

But what am I, now that I suppose that there is a certain genius which is extremely powerful, and, if I may say so, malicious, who employs all his powers in deceiving me? Can I affirm that I possess the least of all those things which . . . pertain to the nature of body? I pause to consider, I revolve all these things in my mind, and I find none of which I can say that it pertains to me. It would be tedious to stop to enumerate them. Let us pass to the attributes of soul and see if there is any one which is in me? What of nutrition or walking . . . ? But if it is so that I have no body it is also true that I can neither walk nor take nourishment. Another attribute is sensation. But one cannot feel without body, and besides I have thought I perceived many things during sleep that I recognised in my waking moments as not having been experienced at all. What of thinking? I find here that thought is an attribute that belongs to me; it alone cannot be separated from me. I am, I exist, that is certain. But how often? Just when I think; for it might possibly be the case if I ceased entirely to think, that I should likewise cease altogether to exist. I do not now admit anything which is not necessarily true: to speak accurately I am not more than a thing which thinks, that is to say a mind or a soul, or an understanding, or a reason, which are terms whose significance was formerly unknown to me. I am, however, a real thing and really exist; but what thing? I have answered: a thing which thinks.[7]

Thus we are led to the first of Descartes' three major metaphysical conclusions: *There is mind.*

Descartes' first conclusion: Mind

---

[7]Descartes, *Meditations on First Philosophy*, I, 150, 151–152.

RENÉ DESCARTES

René Descartes was born in Touraine, France, in 1596. His mother died in giving him birth, and from her he appears to have inherited a frail constitution. At 8 years he was enrolled in the Jesuit school at La Flèche, where his poor health won for him certain privileges, including sleeping late, a habit that Descartes cherished throughout his life. At La Flèche, he displayed the inclination for mathematics and geometry which later exerted such an influence over his whole philosophy.

At 16, Descartes left La Flèche and journeyed to Paris, where, provided by his father with a valet and money, he especially enjoyed gambling—his friends attributed his gambling successes to the fact that he bet according to his unusual knowledge of mathematics rather than to chance. In Paris, he made the acquaintance of the celebrated mathematician Mydorge. A certain restlessness and eagerness to learn from "the book of the world," as he put it, caused Descartes, in 1617, to go to Holland where he enlisted as a volunteer without pay in the army of Prince Maurice of Nassau. He was not much of a soldier, though it was during this stint that he discovered analytic geometry, thus insuring his niche in the history of mathematics. In 1619, the Thirty Years War broke out, and Descartes joined the Catholic forces and found himself eventually in Prague. On November 10, 1619, Descartes had his famous three dreams in which a way of unifying all knowledge was revealed to him. Tired of soldiering, he returned to Paris (which he found too hectic), and then, in 1628, he went to the Netherlands where his serious philosophical and scientific activity and writing got under way, as well as other things: Here he had a mistress who bore him a daughter. It was during this period that Descartes published his major philosophical works, though, noting the fate of Galileo, he suspended the publication of a book on cosmology.

In time he was repeatedly entreated by Queen Christina of Sweden (a robust and masculine woman) to tutor her in his philosophy. Because of his physical condition he hesitated, but eventually accepted the invitation in 1649. Upon his arrival he learned to his horror that the queen insisted on receiving philosophy lessons at five o'clock in the morning! This first winter was especially severe, and Descartes quickly took pneumonia and died. To the end of his life he professed the Catholic faith. He is buried in Ste. Geneviève du Mont in Paris.

Some of Descartes' more important works are: *Rules for the Direction of the Mind, Discourse on Method, Meditations on First Philosophy, Optics, Geometry, Meteorology, Principles of Philosophy.*

But that is not the only important thing that has been learned. Through reflection on the character of this primary certainty—I exist—Descartes has discovered what he can take as the hallmark or criterion of *any* indubitable and certain idea: *clarity* and *distinctness*.

Clear and distinct ideas as the foundation of further knowledge

> *After this I considered generally what in a proposition is requisite in order to be true and certain; for since I had just discovered one which I knew to be such, I thought that I ought also to know in what this certainty consisted. And having remarked that there was nothing at all in the statement "I think, therefore I am" which assures me of having thereby made a true assertion, excepting that I see very clearly that to think it is necessary to be, I came to the conclusion that I might assume, as a general rule, that the things which we conceive very clearly and distinctly are all true— remembering, however, that there is some difficulty in ascertaining which are those that we distinctly conceive.[8]*

THE DEDUCTION OF GOD

On the basis of mind as a thinking substance, along with the criterion of clear and distinct ideas, Descartes leads us to a further consideration: God. He provides two proofs for the existence of God, both of them rooted in the thinking self, both of them employing clear and distinct premises, and both of them involving the idea of perfection.

The first of these two proofs has no particular name, so we may propose for convenience the label Eidological Argument for God, from the Greek word for "idea." Descartes' reasoning is that God must exist in order to account for our *idea of perfection*. Descartes discovered in his mind the idea of a being more perfect than himself—after all, he doubted, and it is a greater perfection to know than to

Descartes' Eidological Argument for God

DESCARTES' EIDOLOGICAL PROOF FOR GOD*

If I have an idea of perfection, then there must actually exist a perfect being as its cause.
I have an idea of perfection.

Therefore, there must actually exist a perfect being.

*In the form of a mixed hypothetical syllogism.

---

[8]Ibid., I, 101–102.

doubt—but where did this idea of something more perfect come from? Now it is absurd that this idea might have come from nothing, for I have a clear and distinct notion that nothing comes from nothing. Nor could it have come from myself, since it is no less absurd that the more perfect should come from the less perfect than that something should come from nothing. We are driven rationally to the only conclusion: The idea of perfection has been placed in our minds by a perfect being. This proof comes out best in the *Discourse*:

> *Following upon this, and reflecting on the fact that I doubted, and that consequently my existence was not quite perfect (for I saw clearly that it was a greater perfection to know than to doubt), I resolved to inquire whence I had learnt to think of anything more perfect than I myself was; and I recognised very clearly that this conception must proceed from some nature which was really more perfect. As to the thoughts which I had of many other things outside of me, like the heavens, the earth, light, heat, and a thousand others, I had not so much difficulty in knowing whence they came, because, remarking nothing in them which seemed to render them superior to me, I could believe that, if they were true, they were dependencies upon my nature, in so far as it possessed some perfection; and if they were not true, that I held them from nought, that is to say, that they were in me because I had something lacking in my nature. But this could not apply to the idea of a Being more perfect than my own, for to hold it from nought would be manifestly impossible; and because it is no less contradictory to say of the more perfect that it is what results from and depends on the less perfect, than to say that there is something which proceeds from nothing, it was equally impossible that I should hold it from myself. In this way it could but follow that it had been placed in me by a Nature which was really more perfect than mine could be, and which even had within itself all the perfections of which I could form any idea—that is to say, to put it in a word, which was God.*[9]

It should be noted that this is a *causal* argument for God; that is, it argues that God must exist as the only adequate cause of something, in this case, the cause of the idea of perfection. We are reminded, though, how seriously Descartes takes mind and ideas. Even an idea is some sort of reality or *thing* (though obviously not a physical thing), and a thing the existence of which needs explaining no less than tables or chairs or worlds or galaxies.

Descartes' second proof for God is a version of the Ontological Argument. As with the first, this one too is stated in the *Discourse*, though it is developed further in the *Meditations*. And like the first, it begins with the idea of perfection or the idea of a most perfect being. Descartes observed that the very concept of God implies his real existence. For what does "God" mean? It means a being who is a supremely perfect being, and who therefore possesses the sum of all possible perfections. Thus, God must be—to name a few—omniscient (for that is a perfec-

**Descartes'
Ontological
Argument for God**

[9]Descartes, *Discourse on Method*, I, 102.

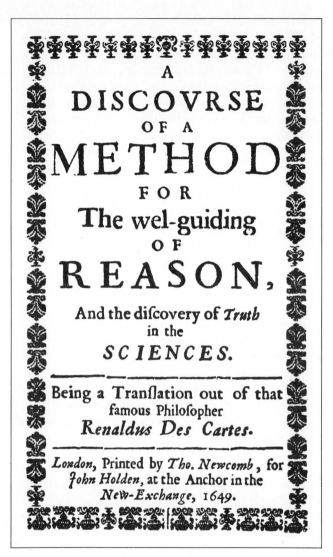

A
DISCOVRSE
OF A
METHOD
FOR
The wel-guiding
OF
REASON,
And the diſcovery of *Truth*
in the
SCIENCES.

Being a Tranſlation out of that
famous Philoſopher
Renaldus Des Cartes.

London, Printed by *Tho. Newcomb,* for
John Holden, at the Anchor in the
New-Exchange, 1649.

*Title page of the
English translation of
the* Discourse on
Method

tion), God must be omnibenevolent (for that is a perfection), and God must *exist* (for that *too* is a perfection). Is not real existence just as necessary to a supremely perfect being as any other of these perfections? Could God be the absolutely perfect being if he was not omnipotent? Could God be the absolutely perfect being if he did not even *exist?* Of course it does not follow from the fact that you cannot separate the idea of a mountain from the idea of a valley that there *are* any mountains or valleys. But that is because existence is not part of what it means to be a mountain or valley. But it *is* part of what it means to be God. On this reasoning, as soon as you get hold of the idea of God as a supremely perfect being you get hold of a God who exists. When we come to Part III, "The Question of God," we will have to consider the Ontological Argument more carefully, and there we will give Descartes' own statement of it. For now we simply let it stand, along with his first argument for God, as bringing us to Descartes' second main conclusion: *There is a God.*

Descartes' second conclusion: God

THE DEDUCTION OF MATTER

On the basis of God, and some other clear and distinct ideas, Descartes leads us to a further consideration: the world of material objects.

According to Descartes, it is only on the belief in God that we may be assured of the existence of the external world and the things in it: tables, chairs, dogs, cats, the earth, stars, our own bodies, and so on. How does Descartes arrive at this thesis? Surely, says Descartes, we can doubt the existence of such things. Aside from the inevitable distortions and misrepresentations of our senses, is it not at least *possible* that we are now dreaming, and that the world "out there" is not at all as we perceive it, or even that it *is* not at all—period? Apart from God, it is possible. But *with* God, it is not possible. Why not? Because everything in us, including our clear and distinct ideas, has come from God, and God, a supremely perfect being and the author of all good, is by his divine nature incapable of creating in us false or misleading ideas. And even if he could, he *wouldn't*, since deception is clearly a moral defect, whereas God is the supremely perfect being—can you imagine God being a deceiver?!

God, the guarantor of clear and distinct ideas

How errors occur

To be sure, many of our ideas may be confused, obscure, or false, but that is because they have become contaminated with nothingness, "from below," as it were, whereas as created and implanted in us by God, "from above," they cannot fail to be true. And, to be sure, many of our judgments are mistaken. But that is because of a misuse of our will (also given by God) whereby because of passion, prejudice, or haste, we affirm as true or deny as false an idea that is not clear and distinct. If you look at the sun and judge it to be about two feet across, your decision has overstepped the boundaries of your clear and distinct ideas, and that is your problem, not God's. Descartes summarizes:

> . . . as often as I so restrain my will within the limits of my knowledge that it forms no judgment except on matters which are clearly and distinctly represented to it by the understanding, I can never be deceived; for every clear and distinct conception is without doubt something, and hence cannot derive its origin from what is nought, but must of necessity have God as its author—God, I say, who being supremely perfect,

cannot be the cause of any error; and consequently we must conclude that such a conception {or such a judgment} is true.[10]

Thus God is the guarantor of our knowledge:

. . . so I very clearly recognise that the certainty and truth of all knowledge depends alone on the knowledge of the true God, in so much that, before I knew Him, I could not have a perfect knowledge of any other thing. And now that I know Him I have the means of acquiring a perfect knowledge of an infinitude of things, not only of those which relate to God Himself and other intellectual matters, but also of those which pertain to corporeal nature. . . .[11]

And we are now in a position to reintroduce into our picture of reality what Descartes originally found it necessary to exclude: the external world of material objects.

Do we not have a clear and distinct idea of an external world? A world of tables, chairs, dogs, cats, the earth, stars, and our own bodies existing outside our minds and independently of us? Is not the "externality" of such a world and such things clearly and distinctly evident from the passivity of our sense perceptions? That is, we do not wish or imagine or dream up this world. It is just *there*, imposing itself on us, independently of our wills. Furthermore, is it not evident that just as it was required in the world of mind to believe in a *substance* which upholds and supports the various intellectual activities, so also in the external world there must be a *substance* which upholds and supports the various physical qualities which we experience—colors, tastes, shapes, and the like? We will call this substance *material* substance. And is it not evident that extension (to use Descartes' expression), or the ability to occupy space or possess dimensions (to use our own), is the very essence of material substance? We observed earlier that minds (or thinking substances) may deny, affirm, imagine, remember, and so on, but *think* they *must*. Likewise, we may say of material objects that they may be red, or blue, or rectangular, or hard, or sweet, and so on, but *extended* they *must* be. Of course, says Descartes, the things "out there" may not be entirely as they are represented to us by our senses, but they must at least possess the geometrical features which we clearly and distinctly perceive (such as length, breadth, and depth).

How many of the ideas in the above paragraph can you find substantiated in the following paragraph from the *Meditations*?

I further find in myself faculties employing modes of thinking peculiar to themselves, to wit, the faculties of imagination and feeling, without which I can easily conceive myself clearly and distinctly as a complete being; while, on the other hand, they

> **Knowledge of the external world**

> **Matter: A substance the essence of which is to be extended**

---

[10]Descartes, *Meditations on First Philosophy*, I, 178.

[11]Ibid., I, 185.

cannot be so conceived apart from me, that is without an intelligent substance in which they reside, for [in the notion we have of these faculties, or, to use the language of the Schools] in their formal concept, some kind of intellection is comprised, from which I infer that they are distinct from me as its modes are from a thing. I observe also in me some other faculties such as that of change of position, the assumption of different figures and such like, which cannot be conceived, any more than can the preceding, apart from some substance to which they are attached, and consequently cannot exist without it; but it is very clear that these faculties, if it be true that they exist, must be attached to some corporeal or extended substance, and not to an intelligent substance, since in the clear and distinct conception of these there is some sort of extension found to be present, but no intellection at all. There is certainly further in me a certain passive faculty of perception, that is, of receiving and recognising the ideas of sensible things, but this would be useless to me [and I could in no way avail myself of it], if there were not either in me or in some other thing another active faculty capable of forming and producing these ideas. But this active faculty cannot exist in me [inasmuch as I am a thing that thinks] seeing that it does not presuppose thought, and also that those ideas are often produced in me without my contributing in any way to the same, and often even against my will; it is thus necessarily the case that the faculty resides in some substance different from me in which all the reality which is objectively in the ideas that are produced by this faculty is formally or eminently contained, as I remarked before. And this substance is either a body, that is, a corporeal nature in which there is contained formally [and really] all that which is objectively [and by representation] in those ideas, or it is God Himself, or some other creature more noble than body in which that same is contained eminently. But, since God is no deceiver, it is very manifest that He does not communicate to me these ideas immediately and by Himself, nor yet by the intervention of some creature in which their reality is not formally, but only eminently, contained. For since He has given me no faculty to recognise that this is the case, but, on the other hand, a very great inclination to believe [that they are sent to me or] that they are conveyed to me by corporeal objects, I do not see how He could be defended from the accusation of deceit if these ideas were produced by causes other than corporeal objects. Hence we must allow that corporeal things exist. However, they are perhaps not exactly what we perceive by the senses, since this comprehension by the senses is in many instances very obscure and confused; but we must at least admit that all things which I conceive in them clearly and distinctly, that is to say, all things which, speaking generally, are comprehended in the object of pure mathematics, are truly to be recognised as external objects.[12]

Descartes' third conclusion: Matter Thus we have arrived at Descartes' third conclusion: *There is matter.* And we have progressed from our knowledge of mind to a knowledge of God, and from our knowledge of God to a knowledge of matter.

[12]Ibid., I, 190–191.

SOME OBJECTIONS

For all its importance and influence, Descartes' theory of reality has hardly escaped criticism. We may mention a few of these, first some lesser ones and then one very big one.

First of all, there is the question of Descartes' method. Few philosophers would align themselves with such a rigorous exclusion of sense experience as a legitimate means of acquiring knowledge; indeed many, quite opposite to Descartes, have admitted *only* sense experience as the source of knowledge, and with the result that they have arrived at quite different conclusions about reality. We will speak of this again in Part II. Here it must suffice to say that there are more ways to begin a philosophy than with a *cogito.* And, speaking of the *cogito,* are we very sure that thinking requires a thinker? What would result if we simply denied the necessity of mental substance, or *any* substance? Why not let there be simply intellectual activities and physical qualities? We will see that some have in fact argued for just this view. Also, it has often been charged that Descartes has committed the informal fallacy of *Petitio Principii* or circular reasoning. Upon his reflection on the *Cogito ergo sum,* Descartes is willing to accept any clear and distinct idea as indubitable; he uses such ideas in his proofs for God, but then insists that it is God who ensures the reliability of these clear and distinct ideas.

And regarding Descartes' proofs for God: In his first proof, some have stumbled over the notion that ideas are *things,* that they possess some sort of objective reality, and thus that they must be caused in a way similar to tables and chairs. And are we sure that the idea of God could not be devised without God actually existing? This, however, brings us to the Ontological Argument for God, and that will be best treated in Chapter 13.

THE MIND-BODY PROBLEM

But now we must address the really big problem posed by Descartes' philosophy. If we leave God aside and focus our attention just on the natural world (including ourselves as part of it), then Descartes' view of reality may appropriately be called *dualistic:* There are *two* essentially different substances, mind and matter, which constitute the "stuff" of this world. This is, in fact, how Descartes' theory of reality is usually represented, and as such it poses one of the most vexing problems in the history of philosophy: *the mind-body problem.*

The mind-body problem simply stated is this: Once we define mind and matter as essentially different substances, which means that they can have nothing in common, no bridge between them, no causal connection, then *how do we get them back together again?* And we *must* get them back together again, for there clearly *is* some sort of connection between them. Obviously, our bodily states can affect our mental states. We are familiar with all sorts of ways in which physics and chemistry can affect the mind. Just think of the mental effects of caffeine, drugs, old age, the alteration of brain states, etc., and if someone beats you over the head long enough, you will become *depressed!* On the other hand, it is also obvious that mental states can give rise to bodily states. Psychosomatic medicine, with its mentally induced sicknesses, is evidence enough, and have you ever felt physically ill because of some idea—like the prospect of failing a course? That the mind and body stand in a causal relation to one another appears to be a fact. The question is *how*, if they are absolutely different in nature from one another.

THE MIND-BODY PROBLEM

If the mind and body are essentially different substances, then how can there by any causal connection between them?

**Descartes'
solution:
Interactionism**

Descartes himself was not oblivious to the problem. The solution he proposed has been called *interactionism*. It is simply the view that there is, after all, some kind of interaction between the two essentially different substances.

> *Nature also teaches me by these sensations of pain, hunger, thirst, etc., that I am not only lodged in my body as a pilot in a vessel, but that I am very closely united to it, and so to speak so intermingled with it that I seem to compose with it one whole. For if that were not the case, when my body is hurt, I, who am merely a thinking thing, should not feel pain, for I should perceive this wound by the understanding only, just as the sailor perceives by sight when something is damaged in his vessel; and when my body has need of drink or food, I should clearly understand the fact without being warned of it by confused feelings of hunger and thirst. For all these sensations of hunger, thirst, pain, etc. are in truth none other than certain confused modes of thought which are produced by the union and apparent intermingling of mind and body.*[13]

Where does this "union" and "intermingling" of mind and body take place? Descartes' answer: the pineal gland in the center of the brain. Apparently he thought that the pineal gland was a likely candidate for this honor because it is the most inward part of the brain, and perhaps, too, because it appeared to Descartes to be the only thing in the body without a double or counterpart. (It is reported that Descartes would secure discarded carcasses from the local butcher for the purpose of dissection and examination.)

[13]Ibid., I, p. 192.

Diagrams from a work on physiology by Descartes showing the brain and the pineal gland. Descartes believed this gland to be the locus of the soul and its point of contact, or interaction, with the body.

It has seemed to many that Descartes' solution was, of course, no solution at all. It only moved the question one step further back, and the question now becomes, *How* do mind and matter interact in the pineal gland? Nonetheless, interactionism as a solution to the mind-body problem is here to stay. After all, what constitutes a causal connection even between *like* substances is no easy matter. And who is to say outright what substances can or cannot do? Further, talk of an unbridgeable "gap" between mind and matter is strange inasmuch as mind is not conceived as spatial at all. On the other hand, mind *is* in space and time in *some* sense: Does not your mind exist right *here* and right *now?* At least in some way, then, mind and matter *do* occupy a common ground.

There have been other proposed solutions. Before mentioning two radical solutions, we may mention three traditional ones. No sooner had Descartes presented the world with the mind-body problem than the French thinker Malebranche (1638–1715) proposed *occasionalism* as a solution: On the occasion of bodily stimuli or impressions, God creates the appropriate idea and response in the mind. The German philosopher Leibniz (1646–1716) proposed a *preestablished harmony*, according to which bodily and physical states have been preordained by God to correspond at every point with appropriate mental states, like two clocks synchronized and set to ticking at the same time. The Dutch philosopher Spinoza proposed what has been called the *double-aspect theory*. On this view there is only

Occasionalism

Preestablished harmony

The double-aspect theory

PHILOSOPHERS: MEN OF MANY FIELDS (SOMETIMES)

Many of the greatest philosophers have been geniuses in more than one field. Descartes is a good example. Besides his philosophical contributions, Descartes contributed many valuable mathematical and scientific insights, theories, and discoveries.

In addition to Descartes' discovery of *analytic geometry* (the most important advance in mathematics since the Greeks), one scholar has summarized his achievements in *optics* as: the statement of the wave theory of light; the vector analysis of motion; the law of sines in refraction; the first theoretical account of far-sightedness and nearsightedness; the first adequate account of space perception; the first adequate account of the theory of lenses; the first recognition of spherical aberration and of the method of correcting it; the determination of light-gathering power in a telescope; the principle of the iris diaphragm; the draw-tube; the telescopic finder; the use of illuminating equipment in conjunction with the microscope; and the parabolic mirror.

Likewise, his contributions to the field of *meteorology* may be summarized as: the rejection of divine intervention as the explanation of events; the kinetic theory of heat, and the concept of specific heat; the first outline of a scientific meteorology in his treatment of winds, clouds, and precipitation; a correct and accurate description and explanation of the primary, secondary, and reflection rainbows; a description of the division of white light into colors by a prism; and the apparatus of the slit spectroscope.[1]

[1]Cf. Laurence J. Lafleur, Introduction to *René Descartes: Discourse on Method,* 2d ed., tr. Laurence J. Lafleur (Indianapolis: Bobbs -Merrill, 1956), pp. xvii f.

---

one reality, unknown to us except through its attributes of mind and matter, two of the infinite number of aspects of this one reality.

The more radical solution

There is, however, a much more radical approach to the mind-body problem. Like some forms of radical surgery, which cut out the disease by cutting out the organ, this approach cuts out the problem by cutting out one or the other of the substances. But which has to go? How you answer that may determine whether you go the way of *idealism* or the way of *materialism,* the topics of our next two chapters.

Gottfried Wilhelm Leibniz, who solved the mind-body problem with his theory of "preestablished harmony"

RYLE: IS MIND A MYTH?

In the meantime, however, consider an altogether different way of looking at the issue.

Perhaps the whole approach is misguided. This is the view of the contemporary British philosopher Gilbert Ryle and many thinkers after him. In a very important book, *The Concept of Mind*, Ryle said that the mind-body problem, like so many philosophical problems, is not a *real* problem, but results rather from *linguistic and conceptual confusion*. That is, it is a problem that results from our misunderstanding and misuse of *language* and *concepts*. (Ryle is a good example of an "analytic" philosopher, such as we mentioned in Chapter 1.)

Ryle begins by sketching the "official doctrine":

There is a doctrine about the nature and place of minds which is so prevalent among theorists and even among laymen that it deserves to be described as the official theory. Most philosophers, psychologists and religious teachers subscribe, with minor reservations, to its main articles and, although they admit certain theoretical difficulties in it, they tend to assume that these can be overcome without serious modifications being made to the architecture of the theory. It will be argued here that the central principles of the doctrine are unsound and conflict with the whole body of what we know about minds when we are not speculating about them.

The official doctrine, which hails chiefly from Descartes, is something like this. With the doubtful exceptions of idiots and infants in arms every human being has both a body and a mind. Some would prefer to say that every human being is both a body and a mind. His body and his mind are ordinary harnessed together, but after the death of the body his mind may continue to exist and function.

Human bodies are in space and are subject to the mechanical laws which govern all other bodies in space. Bodily processes and states can be inspected by external observers. So a man's bodily life is as much a public affair as are the lives of animals and reptiles and even as the careers of trees, crystals and planets.

But minds are not in space, nor are their operations subject to mechanical laws. The workings of one mind are not witnessable by other observers; its career is private. Only I can take direct cognisance of the states and processes of my own mind. A person therefore lives through two collateral histories, one consisting of what happens in and to his body, the other consisting of what happens in and to his mind. The first is public, the second private. The events in the first history are events in the physical world, those in the second are events in the mental world.[14]

The Category Mistake

But what, exactly, is the confusion that Ryle sees in this "official doctrine"? Ryle said that Descartes, and most people after him, were guilty of a *Category Mistake*, as he called it. This is the mistake of treating a concept as if it belonged to one system or category of ideas when, in fact, it belongs to another. An example will help. Imagine yourself showing a visitor around the campus. Your friend asks you to point out the library, and you point at a building and say, "Over there." He then asks to see the Student Union, and you take him to another building. He then asks to be shown the humanities building, and you show it to him. Then he asks to see the *college*. But you are puzzled by this request because your friend appears to think that the college is something you can *see*. You might say to him: "What do you mean, 'Show me the college'? The college is not a building or a *thing*, it is an organization of various departments and faculties. You have confused the idea of a college with *things*, such as buildings." Ryle makes the application:

I shall often speak of [the "official doctrine"] with deliberate abusiveness, as "the dogma of the Ghost in the Machine." . . . It is not merely an assemblage of particular mistakes. It is one big mistake and a mistake of a special kind. It is, namely, a category-mistake. It represents the facts of mental life as if they belonged to one logical type or category (or range of types or categories), when they actually belong to another. The dogma is therefore a philosopher's myth.[15]

[14]Gilbert Ryle, *The Concept of Mind* (London: Hutchinson, 1949), pp. 11–12.
[15]Ibid., p. 16.

Where did Descartes (and all the other proponents of the "official doctrine") go wrong? Right at the start, when he began thinking about the mental world in terms that were only appropriate for the physical world: "thing," "stuff," "attribute," "state," "process," "change," "cause," and "effect." We cannot here give a full account of Ryle's more positive theory of mind. But is not mind more like a college than a building? Is it not, rather, a way of representing the organization, interrelationships, and activities of faculties—in this case *mental* faculties?

Chapter 5 in Review

SUMMARY

Although the metaphysical theory known as mind-matter dualism has been widely held, it has nowhere received a more powerful expression than in Descartes, the father of modern philosophy.

Descartes believed that it was possible to unfold a complete philosophy by reason alone (we will have more to say about his theory of knowledge in Part II) and to arrive, specifically, at a certain knowledge of the essentially different substances, mind ("a substance the essence of which is to think") and matter ("a substance the essence of which is to be extended"), with considerable help from his idea of God. He found that it was impossible to doubt the existence of the self—otherwise the very activity of doubting would be impossible. Thus, one of the best-known pronouncements in the history of philosophy: "I think, therefore I am." Armed with this fundamental certitude, Descartes then proceeded to demonstrate the existence of God from the presence in our minds of the idea of a perfect being (most notably, the Ontological Argument). On the basis of both our passivity to what must be external objects and the impossibility that God, the perfect being, should deceive us with respect to our faculty of clear and distinct ideas, we may also rest assured as to the existence and at least relative nature of the radically different world of material substances outside us. The main moves may be represented simply as: Mind → God → Matter.

However, any version of mind-matter dualism which portrays mind and matter as *essentially* different faces a tremendous problem: If they are so *different,* how can they relate to one another (as they obviously do) and therefore be in some necessary way the *same?* Traditionally, solutions were proposed in the form of interactionism, occasionalism, a preestablished harmony, and the double-aspect theory. More recently, however, it has been suggested that the whole problem stems from a mistaken concept of the mind. Ryle, for example, has argued that viewing mind as if it were a substance underlying various activities is to import an inappropriate model: a Category Mistake.

BASIC IDEAS

- Dualism
- Descartes' method

- Two fundamental operations of the intellect
   Intuition
   Deduction
- Descartes' procedure of systematic doubt
- *Cogito ergo sum*
- Descartes' conception of mind
- Substance
- The nature and role of clear and distinct ideas
- Descartes' arguments for God
   Eidological Argument
   Ontological Argument
- God as the source of clear and distinct ideas
- How errors occur
- How we acquire knowledge of the external world
- Descartes' conception of matter
- Various objections to Descartes' philosophy
- The mind-body problem
- Some traditional solutions to the mind-body problem
   Interactionism
   Occasionalism
   Preestablished harmony
   Double-aspect theory
- Radical solutions to the mind-body problem: materialism and idealism
- The Category Mistake

TEST YOURSELF
1. Why is Descartes' method called a "geometrical" method?
2. In Descartes' view, mind is to doubting as matter is to (a) God, (b) color, (c) the pineal gland, (d) substance.
3. What is so important in Descartes' philosophy about *Cogito ergo sum*?
4. True or false: Descartes says that we have an immediate intuition of the external world.
5. What is Descartes' definition of mind? of matter?
6. True or false: Descartes' arguments for God are not based in any way on the sensible world.
7. What has the German philosopher Leibniz to do with the mind-body problem?
8. Descartes' own solution to the mind-body problem is called _____.
9. What did Gilbert Ryle contribute to the discussion in this chapter?
10. True or false: Descartes is a good example of a "tough-minded" philosopher.

- At the beginning of the chapter it was asserted that mind-matter dualism is a very common metaphysical theory. Do you think so? Would you have answered the question of reality along these lines? What *would* have been your answer?

- It is sometimes observed that Descartes' way of viewing *mind* and its *activities* was too easily influenced by a prevailing way of talking about things in the external world in terms of *substance* and *qualities:* Would this in itself make Descartes' view of mind wrong? Might this be the origin of the Category Mistake that Ryle talks about?

- If you *do* maintain the mind-matter dualist position, what do *you* do about the mind-body problem?

IDEALISM

Idealism as a radical solution to the mind-body problem

One way—a very radical way—of solving the mind-body problem is simply to deny the reality of matter. If all there is is mind, then there can hardly be a problem of relating it to something essentially different, for there *isn't* anything different. It is just a matter of doing away with one-half of Descartes' mind-matter dualism (matter) and exalting the other half (mind) as the *sole* reality.

From mind-matter dualism two radically different theories of reality may be hatched, depending on which idea is suppressed. If the idea of matter is suppressed, then idealism may be hatched.

Mind-Matter Dualism

Idealism   Materialism

WHAT IS IDEALISM?

To a beginner in philosophy it must sound remarkably strange to say that reality is *mind*. But this thesis is one of the most important in the history of philosophy and has had many advocates. In fact, there is a whole tradition in philosophy called *idealism*. As with so many other philosophical terms, this one too needs some explaining. By "idealism" we do not mean, as is often meant, a sort of utopianism or optimism about things. As used here "idealism" is a metaphysical theory, a theory of reality, a theory about the ultimate nature of things. As a general definition we may say that idealism is the metaphysical view that mind (in some sense) is ultimate and that all things are thus reducible to mind and ideas. (If it helps, think of idealism as "idea-ism.")

"Idealism": Its popular and technical meanings

   As was said above, idealism has had many advocates. It has also had many variations. In the interest of simplicity, though, we will divide all idealists into two camps: the *objective* idealists and the *subjective* idealists. An objective idealist believes that all things are made out of mind and ideas, but that things exist nonetheless *objectively,* that is, "out there," independently of our perceiving or knowing them—they would continue to exist even if we did not. A subjective idealist, on

Objective and subjective idealism

IDEALISM

The metaphysical theory that all things are constituted by mind and its ideas.

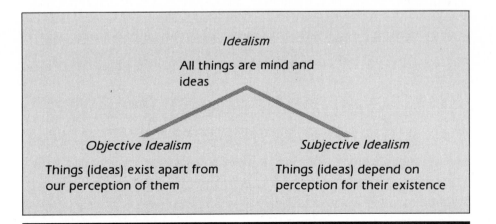

Idealism
All things are mind and ideas

Objective Idealism
Things (ideas) exist apart from our perception of them

Subjective Idealism
Things (ideas) depend on perception for their existence

the other hand, believes that all things are made out of mind and ideas, but that
these things have no existence apart from perception of them—they would cease
to exist if all perceivers did. One way of getting a hold on this idea is to think again
of Plato. Do you see that in a sense Plato was an objective idealist? He believed that
reality was *intelligible* (that is, of the nature of ideas, and apprehensible only by the
mind) but also that it existed *outside* our minds. But in this chapter it is not objective but *subjective* idealism that interests us. Surely it is one of the most fascinating
views in the whole history of philosophy.

BERKELEY AND LOCKE

To many it will surely sound crazy to be told that things exist if and only if[1] they
are *perceived,* that things cease to exist if they are not being at that moment experienced! We are all familiar with the question whether a tree falling over on an
uninhabited desert island would make any noise. But could we doubt that the tree
itself and the whole island would disappear if no one were there to observe it? The
English philosopher Bishop George Berkeley[2] (1685–1753) *did* doubt it. In fact, he
was certain of it. And his arguments for it are not to be laughed off.

As with most other philosophies, it is hardly possible to grasp Berkeley's theory of reality except against the background of what had gone before. Certainly
Descartes lies in this background, but more important is the English philosopher
John Locke, Berkeley's immediate predecessor. Here we must emphasize three features of Locke's philosophy, all of which had everything to do with Berkeley's radically new view.

First. Locke, like Descartes, believed in *substance.* This was conceived as an
underlying *something* which upholds the physical qualities of sensible things (such
as size, shape, color, position, sound, and movement), and a *something* which likewise underlies and upholds intellectual activities (such as thinking, willing, denying, and doubting). In the first case the something is *matter,* and in the second case
it is *mind.* And since he believed that these are the only substances, at least in the
natural world, he was, like Descartes, a *mind-matter dualist.*

Second. Locke expressed better than anyone else the view that has sometimes
been called *epistemological dualism,* a view we will encounter again in Chapter 11.
As you can guess from the label, it had to do with knowledge ("epistemological")
and with two things ("dualism"). Specifically, it is the view that two main things
are involved in the act of knowing: the knower and the known. But do not be
misled here. While it is obvious that the thing that knows is the mind, the thing
known is not the object "out there" in the external world such as a table. What is

**Three features of
Locke's
philosophy:**

**(1) Two
substances, mind
and matter**

**(2) Ideas as the
objects of
knowledge**

---

[1]Philosophers are fond of insisting on distinctions that would never occur to normal people. Thus philosophers often find it important to distinguish between "if," "only if," and "if, and only if." These do,
in fact, involve three quite different meanings. Think about these expressions until you see the
differences.

[2]Pronounced *Barkly.*

actually known must be something akin to the mind and *in* the mind. And what is in the mind and known by the mind is certainly not the table itself—that exists *out there*—but rather a mental representation or *idea* of the table: brown, rectangular, smooth, flat, and four-legged. What is important here is that according to Locke what is directly known by the mind are ideas which themselves correspond to things in the external world.

Third. We mentioned above that Locke believed in matter as an underlying "something" which upholds the sensible qualities of a thing. Now what about these sensible qualities? Like many before him, Locke says that we must divide these qualities into two kinds: primary and secondary qualities. This will take a bit of explaining. A *primary quality* is a quality which exists independently of a perceiver; that is, it would exist even if no perceiver were present. Examples of primary qualities would include size, position, shape, and movement. A *secondary quality* is a quality which depends for its existence on a perceiver; that is, it would cease to exist were no perceiver present. Examples of secondary qualities would be color, sound, texture, and taste. Generally, we could say that primary qualities of things are *objective* (they exist in the object), whereas secondary qualities are *subjective* (they exist in the knowing or perceiving subject).

The distinction between primary and secondary qualities is an important one and has figured recurringly in philosophical discussions. Why would one draw this distinction? What is the evidence for it? The evidence takes two forms. (1) Our perceptions, or ideas, of primary qualities *resemble* those qualities. For example, our perception or idea of triangularity resembles the shape of a triangle; our idea of motion resembles something in motion. But colors, sounds, and tastes do not resemble anything "out there": Red *is* the perception, loud *is* the perception, sweet *is* the perception. (2) Secondary qualities, unlike primary qualities, vary with perceivers and are therefore *relative*. What color is the beachball? Well, it depends on whether you are color-blind, the way the sunlight and shadows are striking it, how

> **(3) The distinction between primary and secondary qualities**
>
> **The basis for the distinction:**
>
> **Primary qualities resemble something "out there"**
>
> **Secondary qualities are relative to the perceiver**

PRIMARY AND SECONDARY QUALITIES

- *Primary qualities:* Those qualities of a thing which exist *independently* of a perceiver. They have *objective* existence. Examples: shape, size, position, and motion.
- *Secondary qualities:* Those qualities of a thing which *depend* for their existence on a perceiver. They have only *subjective* existence. Examples: color, sound, and taste.

What is the basis of this distinction? Why should one accept it?

far you are from it, and your sun-glasses. Is the lemonade sweet enough for you? It depends on whether you have been sucking on a green persimmon. Was the thunderclap loud? It depends on how close you were and the condition of your ears. In the case of secondary qualities everything is *relative to* and thus *dependent on* the subject: the status of one's sense organs, one's perspective, one's position, and so on. No perceiver—no perception. Not so with primary qualities. Shape, motion, and extension, for example, are what they are irrespective of perceivers.

We are back to the tree falling over on a desert island. Do you see that it can make no sound and have no color or taste (secondary qualities), though it must have size, shape, and motion (primary qualities)?[3]

BERKELEY'S VIEW: *ESSE EST PERCIPI*

Esse est percipi:
"To be is to be perceived"

Berkeley himself focussed his theory of reality in a three-word Latin sentence: *Esse est percipi,* "to be is to be perceived." We just saw that Locke and others accepted this principle as applied to *secondary qualities* of things, but Berkeley means it *absolutely.* To be is to be perceived, period. *Everything* is dependent for its existence upon perception, and apart from a perceiving or knowing subject, *nothing* exists. In the absence of a perceiver, not only the tree's sound, color, taste, etc., but also its sound *waves,* color *frequencies,* shape, motion, extension, coconuts, the sand, mountains, and the *entire island* cease to exist!

Berkeley summarizes his strange-sounding view in the following:

Summary of
Berkeley's position

Wood, stone, fire, water, flesh, iron, and the like things which I name and discourse of are things that I know. And I should not have known them, but that I perceived them by my senses; and things perceived by the sense are immediately perceived; and things immediately perceived are ideas; and ideas cannot exist without the mind; their existence therefore consists in being perceived; when therefore they are actually perceived, there can be no doubt of their existence.[4]

Do you see the argument contained here? We may recast it as a simple categorical syllogism:

Ideas exist only in minds.
All things are ideas.

Therefore, all things exist only in minds.

[3]Of course, it depends on what you mean, for example, by "color" or "sound." But here these obviously refer to *perceptions,* which exist in the perceiver, and not to color frequencies or sound waves, which exist in the external world. The tree falling over on a desert island emits no noise, though it does emit sound waves.

[4]George Berkeley, *Three Dialogues Between Hylas and Philonous,* ed. Colin M. Turbayne (Indianapolis: Bobbs-Merrill, 1954), p. 76.

BISHOP GEORGE BERKELEY

George Berkeley was born in 1685 in the habitable part of the ruins of Dysert Castle, not far from Kilkenny, Ireland. He studied mathematics and classics at Trinity College, Dublin, where he was also instructed in the philosophies of Descartes and Locke. Berkeley conceived his subjective idealism when he was 22. Apparently its basic principles burst upon him in a sort of revelatory manner, not unlike Descartes' discovery of analytic geometry.

In 1707, he became a tutor at Trinity and later junior lecturer. About this time too he embarked upon his career as an Anglican churchman, being ordained as a deacon and then a priest. From this period comes his *Essay Towards a New Theory of Vision* and his *Treatise Concerning the Principles of Human Knowledge.*

The year 1713 found Berkeley in London. The years following included writing (most notably, the *Dialogues*) and traveling. During this time he visited the French philosopher Malebranche who may have suffered a premature death on account of Berkeley. The story goes that Malebranche, ill with pneumonia, argued with Berkeley so violently and loudly as to cause an inflammation of the lungs resulting in his death!

In 1720, Berkeley returned to Dublin. There he was awarded the B.D. and D.D. degrees by Trinity College and was made senior lecturer and university preacher. During this period he inherited a handsome sum and had a sort of vision of a better society. He obtained a charter from King George I and set out for Bermuda to found a college for educating the clergy and converting Indians. In September 1728 he set sail for the new world along with his bride. A navigational error brought them instead to Newport, Rhode Island. He remained there for two years, but the failure of promised funds to materialize made it impossible for him to realize his dream.

Back in Ireland, in 1734 Berkeley was made bishop of Cloyne in County Cork. Twenty years were now spent in episcopal duties. In poor health he moved in 1752 to be near his son who had matriculated in Oxford. He suffered from gallstones, and died suddenly in January 1753.

Berkeley conceived of his theory of reality, as contained in the *Principles* and the *Dialogues,* as the first part of a plan including, second, psychology and ethics, third, physics, and fourth, mathematics. He made headway only as far as into the second, and even this was lost.

Berkeley's three most important works are: *Essay Towards a New Theory of Vision, Treatise Concerning the Principles of Human Knowledge,* and *Three Dialogues Between Hylas and Philonous.*

You will note that this reasoning is perfectly valid; that is, if the premises are true the conclusion must be true. The question is whether the premises *are* true.

Everything here depends on what Berkeley means by the word "idea." In fact, though, Berkeley means by "idea" what most everyone means, including probably you yourself and John Locke: the mental representation of something in the external world, say, a table, composed of all the qualities that make up that thing, such as brown, rectangular, smooth, flat, and four-legged. If so, then we can hardly object to Berkeley's first premise, *ideas exist only in minds.* It is, in fact, true by its very conception—that is, it *must* be true by virtue of the very meaning of the terms involved. Well, what about the second premise? Must we accept that *all things are ideas?* With this claim Berkeley clearly rejects his predecessors' view that ideas represent or correspond to material objects in the external world: Those realities *are* ideas. Surely it is *this* premise that raises the real problems—in fact, we tend instinctively to reject it as fantastic and absurd.

We will see, though, that Berkeley himself regarded his subjective idealism as the most *commonsensical* view. He develops it in both his *Treatise Concerning the Principles of Human Knowledge* and his *Three Dialogues Between Hylus and Philonous.*

Berkeley's first premise

Berkeley's second premise

George Berkeley

Berkeley's principle that "to be is to be perceived" resulted in one of the most astonishing and controversial philosophies ever devised.

GEORGE BERKELY,
BISHOP of CLOYNE.

BERKELEY'S ARGUMENT*
Ideas exist only in minds.
All things are ideas.
Therefore, all things exist only in minds.
*In the form of a categorical syllogism

FIVE PROOFS FOR SUBJECTIVE IDEALISM

Berkeley's often ingenious defense of his thesis may be reduced to five distinct lines of reasoning.[5]

First Proof: The Discontinuity of Dualism. The first argument brings us back to the mind-body problem and some comments we made at the beginning of this chapter. Berkeley inherited from Locke, who inherited it from Descartes, the view that all reality (at least in the natural world) is reducible to two essentially different substances, mind and matter. But, as we have now observed repeatedly, such a view of reality gives rise to the metaphysical problem of explaining how these two essentially different substances can relate to one another. Obviously, Berkeley's idealism overcomes this problem by simply denying the existence of material substance: There is *one* reality, mind and its ideas.

Likewise, mind-matter dualism gave rise to an epistemological problem: How can mind know reality if reality is utterly unlike mind and its ideas? If the external world and the things in it are essentially unlike our ideas of them, how can our ideas represent or be *like* them? Again, with one stroke Berkeley cuts away the problem, for reality *is* ideas and is therefore of the same nature as mind. Closely related to this, Berkeley's idealism overcomes the skepticism, or doubt, about the external world implicit in epistemological dualism. On that view, how could we ever know that our ideas correctly represent or correspond to the external world? Are we not forever bound to our *ideas* of it? For Berkeley, such doubts could never arise because there *is* no difference between our ideas and reality. *Esse est percipi.*

Second Proof: Matter as a Meaningless Idea. A second argument directs our attention to the very idea of a material substance and asks whether it is even meaningful.

Mind and matter again

---

[5]The following fivefold way of organizing Berkeley's arguments, as well as some of the terminology, is suggested by the useful outline in John Herman Randall, Jr., and Justus Buchler, *Philosophy: An Introduction* (New York: Barnes & Noble, 1942), pp. 210–212.

"Berkeley brought the manuscript of the *Dialogues* with him to London in January, 1713. Three years earlier he had published in Dublin *The Principles of Human Knowledge*. It had been most unfavorably received. In London, particularly, it had been immediately ridiculed. A physician argued that its author must be mad. A bishop pitied Berkeley for seeking notoriety by trying to start something new. A third critic said that Berkeley was not as far gone as another thinker who denied not only the existence of matter, but of persons. Many factors may have led to the failure of the *Principles*. To read it through required a great deal of intellectual effort. Moreover, the paradox that matter does not exist, which Berkeley advanced was a bold one."

Turbayne, *Three Dialogues*, pp. viif.

Is "matter" a meaningless word?

It could be asked, first, whether "matter" does not turn out to be an empty and meaningless word. Philosophers such as Descartes and Locke felt compelled to posit a substance underlying and upholding physical qualities, but what could they really say about it? In this respect, Locke likened himself to the Indian who was asked what held up the earth and answered that it was supported by a great elephant who stood on the back of an ancient tortoise. But when asked what held up the tortoise he answered: "Something I know not what." This, in fact, was the best that Locke could say about the nature of material substance: "It is something I know not what." In this way, those who talk big about some underlying material substance in the end do not know what they are talking about!

But it is not just that they *don't* know what they're talking about—they *can't* know what they're talking about. For the very idea of matter is an *inconsistent* one. This is Berkeley's real point here. It is not even possible to frame a meaningful *idea* of matter, because matter itself is devoid of any qualities (since it is said to *underlie* all qualities), and it is only by means of the qualities of something that we can have an idea of it, and we cannot know or talk about something we have no idea of. *Esse est percipi.*

Third Proof: The Unexperienced as Inconceivable. This last point can be broadened. It is true not only in the case of matter, but in the case of *anything*, that it cannot be conceived except as experienced. If you doubt this, try to think of something that is not experienced. Can you? No. This is because the second you frame an idea of something (with its various qualities, such as red, circular, rough, loud, and bitter) you are thereby *experiencing* it. To say this in another way: You cannot

Can the unexperienced be thought?

A

TREATISE

Concerning the

PRINCIPLES

OF

Human Knowlege.

PART I.

Wherein the chief Causes of Error and Difficulty in the *Sciences*, with the Grounds of *Scepticism*, *Atheism*, and *Irreligion*, are inquir'd into.

By *George Berkeley*, M. A. Fellow of *Trinity-College*, *Dublin*.

DUBLIN:

Printed by AARON RHAMES, for JEREMY PEPYAT, Bookfeller in *Skinner-Row*, 1712

think of something without thinking of its qualities, and to think of qualities is to perceive or experience them. *Esse est percipi.*

Fourth Proof: The Inseparability of Primary and Secondary Qualities. In the fourth argument we return to the distinction between primary and secondary qualities.

It will be recalled that everyone accepts the subjectivity of secondary qualities.

Can primary and secondary qualities be separated?

That is not in question. But consider now that primary qualities can no more be separated from secondary qualities than secondary qualities can be separated from primary qualities. They rise and fall together. The proof of this is simple. Try to conceive of primary qualities apart from secondary qualities. Try to think of a colorless shape. Imagine, for example, a beachball. Of course it possesses a shape—it is round. And what color is it? Red, yellow, blue, alternating green and orange bands? Now in your imagination try to remove all color from the shape. It is impossible. Even a vague, dull gray is a color! And if some wiseacre announces that his beachball is *transparent,* we would only ask him to tell us what are the colors of the things that he sees *through* the transparent sphere of the beachball and thus fill the shape with colors. Similarly with other primary qualities. They cannot be conceived except as inseparably bound up with secondary qualities.

Are primary qualities relative too?

So what has this to do with *esse est percipi?* The answer is that since secondary qualities *are* accepted as subjective and requiring a perceiver, and since primary qualities must go the same way as secondary qualities, primary qualities *too* must be subjective. With respect, then, to *all* we can know about a table (its shape, texture, sound, weight, motion, color, etc.) *esse est percipi.*

Fifth Proof: The Relativity of all Qualities. The last argument also depends on the distinction between primary and secondary qualities. But whereas the previous argument reasoned that primary qualities must be subjective because secondary qualities are, here the argument is that primary qualities considered *in themselves* must be subjective.

We saw earlier that a decisive argument for the subjectivity of secondary qualities, or that they exist in the perceiver, is that they are *relative to perceivers.* This is the only way to account for the fact that colors, tastes, sounds, and the like, vary with perceivers, or are perceived differently by different perceivers. But now Berkeley asks whether it is not the same with primary qualities. Are they not every bit as relative to perceivers?

We have a natural tendency to think that though colors, sounds, and tastes disappear with the perceiver, qualities like shape, size, and motion continue even when unperceived. But take shape, for example. Is there really anything such as a perception of a rectangle? In fact, do two people ever perceive the same shape? Is not every shape relative to and dependent upon the perceiver's perspective? Consider a large rectangle drawn on a chalkboard or the rectangular surface of a table in the front of the room.

You *think* it's a rectangle. You *call* it a rectangle. But you do not actually *perceive* a rectangle. What *do* you perceive? Well, depending on your perspective, you may

actually perceive this,

or this,

or this,

or any one of an infinite number of other shapes, since there is an infinite number of viewpoints or perspectives. Even if you were to suspend yourself from the ceiling, centered directly over the surface of the table, you would perceive not a rectangle but something like this:

As for the other primary qualities, like size, position, and motion, just a moment's reflection should reveal that these too are relative to the perceiver, and that makes them *perceptions* or *ideas*. There is, then, no difference between primary and secondary qualities: *All* qualities are ideas in the mind of the perceiver. *Esse est percipi.*

HYLAS AND PHILONOUS

You will be able to appreciate some of the above points in the following extracts from the *Three Dialogues Between Hylas and Philonous.* Hylas (from the Greek *hyle,* "matter") argues for the reality of material substance, whereas Philonous (from *philos* and *nous*) is the "friend of mind" and thus represents Berkeley's position.

PHILONOUS: *You are still then of opinion that extension and figures are inherent in external unthinking substances?*

HYLAS: *I am.*

PHILONOUS: *But what if the same arguments which are brought against secondary qualities will hold good against these also?*

HYLAS: *Why then I shall be obliged to think they too exist only in the mind.*

PHILONOUS: *Is it your opinion the very figure and extension which you perceive by sense exist in the outward object or material substance?*

HYLAS: *It is.*

PHILONOUS: *Have all other animals as good grounds to think the same of the figure and extension which they see and feel?*

HYLAS: *Without doubt, if they have any thought at all.*

PHILONOUS: *Answer me, Hylas. Think you the senses were bestowed upon all animals for their preservation and well-being in life? Or were they given to men alone for this end?*

HYLAS: *I make no question but they have the same use in all other animals.*

PHILONOUS: *If so, is it not necessary they should be enabled by them to perceive their own limbs and those bodies which are capable of harming them?*

HYLAS: *Certainly.*

PHILONOUS: *A mite therefore must be supposed to see his own foot, and things equal or even less than it, as bodies of some considerable dimension, though at the same time they appear to you scarce discernible or at best as so many visible points?*

HYLAS: *I cannot deny it.*

PHILONOUS: *And to creatures less than the mite they will seem yet larger?*

HYLAS: *They will.*

PHILONOUS: *Insomuch that what you can hardly discern will to another extremely minute animal appear as some huge mountain?*

HYLAS: *All this I grant.*

PHILONOUS: *Can one and the same thing be at the same time in itself of different dimensions?*

HYLAS: *That were absurd to imagine.*

PHILONOUS: *But from what you have laid down it follows that both the extension by you perceived and that perceived by the mite itself, as likewise all those perceived by lesser animals, are each of them the true extension of the mite's foot; that is to say, by your own principles you are led into an absurdity.*

HYLAS: *There seems to be some difficulty in the point.*

PHILONOUS: *Again, have you not acknowledged that no real inherent property of any object can be changed without some change in the thing itself?*

HYLAS: *I have.*

PHILONOUS: *But, as we approach to or recede from an object the visible exten-*

sion varies, being at one distance ten or a hundred times greater than at another. Does it not therefore follow from hence likewise that it is not really inherent in the object?

HYLAS: *I own I am at a loss what to think.*

PHILONOUS: *Your judgment will soon be determined if you will venture to think as freely concerning this quality as you have done concerning the rest. Was it not admitted as a good argument that neither heat nor cold was in the water because it seemed warm to one hand and cold to the other?*

HYLAS: *It was.*

PHILONOUS: *Is it not the very same reasoning to conclude there is no extension or figure in an object because to one eye it shall seem little, smooth, and round, when at the same time it appears to the other great, uneven, and angular?*

HYLAS: *The very same. . . .*

PHILONOUS: *"Material substratum" call you it? Pray, by which of your senses came you acquainted with that being?*

HYLAS: *It is not itself sensible; its modes and qualities only being perceived by the senses.*

PHILONOUS: *I presume then it was by reflection and reason you obtained the idea of it?*

HYLAS: *I do not pretend to any proper positive idea of it. However, I conclude it exists because qualities cannot be conceived to exist without a support.*

PHILONOUS: *It seems then you have only a relative notion of it, or that you conceive it not otherwise than by conceiving the relation it bears to sensible qualities?*

HYLAS: *Right.*

PHILONOUS: *Be pleased, therefore, to let me know wherein that relation consists.*

HYLAS: *Is it not sufficiently expressed in the term "substratum" or "substance?"*

PHILONOUS: *If so, the word "substratum" should import that it is spread under the sensible qualities or accidents?*

HYLAS: *True.*

PHILONOUS: *And consequently under extension?*

HYLAS: *I own it.*

PHILONOUS: *It is therefore somewhat in its own nature entirely distinct from extension?*

HYLAS: *I tell you extension is only a mode, and matter is something that supports modes. And is it not evident the thing supported is different from the thing supporting?*

PHILONOUS: *So that something distinct from, and exclusive of, extension is supposed to be the substratum of extension?*

HYLAS: *Just so.*

PHILONOUS: *Answer me, Hylas, can a thing be spread without extension, or is not the idea of extension necessarily included in spreading?*

HYLAS: *It is.*

PHILONOUS: *Whatsoever therefore you suppose spread under anything must have in itself an extension distinct from the extension of that thing under which it is spread?*

HYLAS: *It must.*

PHILONOUS: *Consequently, every corporeal substance being the substratum of extension must have in itself another extension by which it is qualified to be a substratum, and so on to infinity? And I ask whether this be not absurd in itself and repugnant to what you granted just now, to wit, that the* substratum *was something distinct from and exclusive of extension?*

HYLAS: *Aye, but, Philonous, you take me wrong. I do not mean that matter is spread in a gross literal sense under extension. The word "substratum" is used only to express in general the same thing with "substance."*

PHILONOUS: *Well then, let us examine the relation implied in the term "substance." Is it not that it stands under accidents?*

HYLAS: *The very same.*

PHILONOUS: *But that one thing may stand under or support another, must it not be extended?*

HYLAS: *It must.*

PHILONOUS: *Is not therefore this supposition liable to the same absurdity with the former?*

HYLAS: *You still take things in a strict literal sense; that is not fair, Philonous.*

PHILONOUS: *I am not for imposing any sense on your words; you are at liberty to explain them as you please. Only, I beseech you, make me understand something by them. You tell me matter supports or stands under accidents. How! is it as your legs support your body?*

HYLAS: *No; that is the literal sense.*

PHILONOUS: *Pray let me know any sense, literal or not literal, that you understand it in.—— How long must I wait for an answer, Hylas?*

HYLAS: *I declare I know not what to say. I once thought I understood well enough what was meant by matter's supporting accidents. But now, the more I think on it, the less can I comprehend it; in short, I find that I know nothing of it.*

PHILONOUS: *It seems then you have no idea at all, neither relative nor positive, of matter; you know neither what it is in itself nor what relation it bears to accidents?*

HYLAS: *I acknowledge it.*

PHILONOUS: *And yet you asserted that you could not conceive how qualities or accidents should really exist without conceiving at the same time a material support of them?*

HYLAS: *I did.*

PHILONOUS: *That is to say, when you conceive the real existence of qualities, you do withal conceive something which you cannot conceive?*

HYLAS: *It was wrong I own. . . .*

PHILONOUS: *. . . if I understand you rightly, you say our ideas do not exist* *without the mind, but that they are copies, images, or representations of certain originals that do?*

HYLAS: *You take me right.*

PHILONOUS: *They are then like external things?*

HYLAS: *They are.*

PHILONOUS: *Have those things a stable and permanent nature, independent of our senses, or are they in a perpetual change, upon our producing any motions in our bodies, suspending, exerting, or altering our faculties or organs of sense?*

HYLAS: *Real things, it is plain, have a fixed and real nature, which remains the same notwithstanding any change in our senses or in the posture and motion of our bodies; which indeed may affect the ideas in our minds, but it were absurd to think they had the same effect on things existing without the mind.*

PHILONOUS: *How then is it possible that things perpetually fleeting and variable as our ideas should be copies or images of anything fixed and constant? Or, in other words, since all sensible qualities, as size, figure, color, etc., that is, our ideas, are continually changing upon every alteration in the distance, medium, or instruments of sensation—how can any determinate material objects be properly represented or painted forth by several distinct things each of which is so different from and unlike the rest? Or, if you say it resembles some one only of our ideas, how shall we be able to distinguish the true copy from all the false ones?*

HYLAS: *I profess, Philonous, I am at a loss. I know not what to say to this.*

PHILONOUS: *But neither is this all. Which are material objects in themselves—perceptible or imperceptible?*

HYLAS: *Properly and immediately nothing can be perceived but ideas. All material things, therefore, are in themselves insensible and to be perceived only by their ideas.*

PHILONOUS: *Ideas then are sensible, and their archetypes or originals insensible?*

HYLAS: *Right.*

PHILONOUS: *But how can that which is sensible be like that which is insensible? Can a real thing, in itself* invisible, *be like a* color, *or a real thing which is not* audible *be like a* sound? *In a word, can anything be like a sensation or idea, but another sensation or idea?*

HYLAS: *I must own, I think not.*[6]

Along such lines as these, then, Berkeley defends his thesis that all things are ideas. What he says of a cherry he could say of *all* things: It is nothing more than a collection of perceptions:

PHILONOUS: *. . . I see this cherry, I feel it, I taste it, and I am sure nothing cannot be seen or felt or tasted; it is therefore real. Take away the sensations of*

---

[6]Berkeley, *Three Dialogues Between Hylas and Philonous*, pp. 28–30, 38–41, 47–48.

softness, moisture, redness, tartness, and you take away the cherry. Since it is not a being distinct from sensations, a cherry, I say, is nothing but a congeries of sensible impressions, or ideas perceived by various senses, which ideas are united into one thing (or have one name given them) by the mind because they are observed to attend each other. Thus, when the palate is affected with such a particular taste, the sight is affected with a red color, the touch with roundness, softness, etc. Hence, when I see and feel and taste in sundry certain manners, I am sure the cherry exists or is real, its reality being in my opinion nothing abstracted from those sensations. But if by the word "cherry" you mean an unknown nature distinct from all those sensible qualities, and by its "existence" something distinct from its being perceived, then, indeed, I own neither you nor I, nor anyone else, can be sure it exists.[7]

What is the upshot of all this? Berkeley strains to get you to accept the *simplicity* of his claim. Consider the table again. What is it that you are considering? Well, the perceptions of brown, rectangularity, smooth surface, four-legged, at rest, five feet long, etc. Why not just let the table *be* those things? Why insist on some mysterious, unknowable, and, indeed, incoherent notion of a material "something" beyond those perceptions? Why not allow the table to be just what it is perceived to be, namely, a bundle of different perceptions or *ideas*? Berkeley believed that such a view would immediately strike one as the most *commonsensical*, once the reasoning is followed and our built-in prejudices about "matter" are laid aside.

SOLIPSISM OR GOD?

Solipsism

It will appear to some readers that Berkeley must be a solipsist. Solipsism is the belief that only one thing exists, the solipsist himself. Everything else, including other people, exists only in his mind. One wonders, of course, what would happen if two solipsists were introduced to one another! It would be something like the gingham dog and the calico cat who got into a fight and left only scraps of themselves behind since they ate each other up.

Berkeley certainly was *not* a solipsist. Like all other people in their right minds, Berkeley acknowledged the reality of things outside the mind. The simple and sole and sufficient evidence for the reality of things outside ourselves is the *passivity of perception.* Leaving our imagination out of it (by which in an instant we

Evidence for external reality: The passivity of perception

can create castles and fortunes) it is obvious that our senses respond passively to things outside us. For example, when you enter a room you do not *conjure up* blackboards, chairs, people, and light fixtures, you do not *will* them into existence, you do not say, "Let there be blackboards ..." *They are simply there.* What you wish or will or say has nothing to do with it. (We encountered this idea in Chapter 5.)

But, now, does not Berkeley have a tremendous problem on his hands? Has

[7]Ibid., p. 97.

SOLIPSISM

Solipsism (from the Latin *solus,* "alone") is the belief in one reality, the solipsist himself, upon whose thoughts and perceptions all other things depend for their existence. It has been observed that if you ever meet a solipsist you had better take good care of him, for when he goes we all go!

---

he not maintained two incompatible theses? He argues on the one hand that all things are ideas existing only in minds, but he argues also that things do in fact exist outside our minds. How can he possibly reconcile these two incompatible and mutually exclusive claims?

Two incompatible claims

A clue to the answer lies in noting that Berkeley has not said that all things exist in *our* minds but only that they exist in *some* mind. A further clue lies in the full title of his *Dialogues: Three Dialogues Between Hylas and Philonous, in Opposition to Skeptics and Atheists.* For those who still cannot guess the answer, the following verses (of unknown authorship) will remove all doubt:

> *I have always thought that God*
> *Must find it exceedingly odd*
> *To think that his tree*
> *Won't continue to be*
> *When there's no one about in the quad.*

> *Dear Sir:*
> *Your astonishment's odd.*
> *For I am always about in the quad.*
> *And so my tree will continue to be,*
> *Since observed by*
> *Yours faithfully,*
> *God.*

In fact, Berkeley's entire reasoning is, in a sense, a gigantic proof for the existence of God. For only on the hypothesis of God as an infinite Mind which constantly perceives all things can we believe *both* that all things are ideas existing in mind, *and* that they continue to exist even when unperceived *by us.* Berkeley puts the matter thus:

God: The absolute mind and grand perceiver of all things

> PHILONOUS: . . . *You indeed said the reality of sensible things consisted in an absolute existence out of the minds of spirits, or distinct from their being perceived.*

*And, pursuant to this notion of reality, you are obliged to deny sensible things any
real existence; that is, according to your own definition, you profess yourself a skeptic.
But I neither said nor thought the reality of sensible things was to be defined after
that manner. To me it is evident, for the reasons you allow of, that sensible things
cannot exist otherwise than in a mind or spirit. Whence I conclude, not that they have
no real existence, but that, seeing they depend not on my thought and have an existence distinct from being perceived by me,* there must be some other mind
wherein they exist. As sure, therefore, as the sensible world really exists, so sure is
there an infinite omnipresent Spirit, who contains and supports it.*

HYLAS: *What! this is no more than I and all Christians hold; nay, and all
others, too, who believe there is a God and that He knows and comprehends all things.*

PHILONOUS: *Aye, but here lies the difference. Men commonly believe that all
things are known or perceived by God, because they believe the being of a God;
whereas I, on the other side, immediately and necessarily conclude the being of a God,
because all sensible things must be perceived by him.*

HYLAS: *But so long as we all believe the same thing, what matter is it how we
come by that belief?*

PHILONOUS: *But neither do we agree in the same opinion. For philosophers,
though they acknowledge all corporeal beings to be perceived by God, yet they attribute to them an absolute subsistence distinct from their being perceived by any mind
whatever, which I do not. Besides, is there no difference between saying,* there is a
God, therefore He perceives all things, *and saying,* sensible things do really
exist; and if they really exist, they are necessarily perceived by an infinite
mind: therefore there is an infinite mind, or God? *This furnishes you with a
direct and immediate demonstration, from a most evident principle, of the* being of
a God.[8]

Again, it may be helpful to formulate this part of Berkeley's philosophy as a simple
argument (what kind of argument is it?):

> The sensible world exists if, and only if, it is perceived by a
> mind;
> The sensible world exists unperceived by human minds;
> _____
> Therefore, the sensible world must be perceived by an infinite
> mind.[9]

**Berkeley's idea of
creation**
      It should be noted that Berkeley's view of God and the world involves a quite
different notion of creation than the usual one. On the popular view, God created
the world (bang!) so many years ago. But on Berkeley's view, creation is something
that goes on constantly. *At this moment,* as at every moment, God is creating and

[8]Ibid., pp. 55–56.
[9]Cf. Turbayne, in ibid., p. xx.

sustaining the world by his continuing perception of it. Most theologians have not shared Berkeley's view of *esse est percipi* with its peculiar implications for God's existence. But they have, usually, shared the idea that God's creation of the world is such that the world depends at every moment upon the creative act of God.

We have tried to show throughout this chapter why and how Berkeley denies the reality of material substance (or matter) and claims that there is only one kind of reality: mental substance (mind) and ideas. But now we are in a position to understand the full meaning of Berkeley's claim. *Esse est percipi* commits us to a belief in (1) sensible things as ideas, (2) minds which are finite and created mental substances and which might or might not perceive those sensible things, and (3) a Mind which is an infinite mental substance and which perceives all sensible things at all times and creates finite minds to perceive them too. As with Descartes, we know our own finite minds through introspection and an immediate self-intuition. But peculiar to Berkeley is the belief that we know the infinite and absolute Mind as a necessary condition for the continued existence of sensible things unexperienced by finite minds.

SOME OBJECTIONS

In spite of Berkeley's insistence that his idealist theory of reality is really the most commonsensical, it has always struck most people as fantastic, to say the least. As was noted above, during his own lifetime Berkeley was thought by some to be mad, and nearly every one since has had a built-in resistance to his theory. You yourself probably instinctively object: "This just can't be true!"

Before we comment on possible criticisms of Berkeley, a word of caution. To what degree is the acceptance or rejection of a philosophical view a matter of *psychology*? William James said that the history of philosophy is "a clash of temperaments," which of course involves differing tastes, styles, inclinations, and desires. This is no doubt inevitable, and it may even be helpful to the philosophical enterprise. But, again, it is the job of the philosopher (which means you, too) not to confuse temperament with reason. And how much more must we be on guard against blind and uncritical *prejudice*. It is probably truer in the case of Berkeley's philosophy than most others that it runs almost exactly counter to our *deeply rooted biases* and *preconceived notions* concerning the way things must be. But this is hardly grounds for its rejection. If you do reject Berkeley's philosophy, make sure that it is, as much as possible, a *philosophical* rejection.

Even though Berkeley (especially in the third *Dialogue*) anticipated and treated nearly all objections to his view, they persist: Berkeley denies the reality of sensible things; he abuses the ordinary meanings of language; he destroys the distinction between real things and ideas of them; he makes God the author of immoral and evil acts; he fails to account for the nature of illusory ideas; he makes it impossible for more than one person to experience the same thing; etc. Surely

Are your objections philosophically or psychologically rooted?

Common criticisms

the most famous refutation of Berkeley—and geared especially to his appeal to common sense—was that of Samuel Johnson who repeatedly kicked against a stone and, rebounding from the thuds, exclaimed: "I refute him *thus!*"

Has Berkeley denied the reality of things?

Many, or even most, objections of this kind misfire. They sometimes involve an inattentive reading of Berkeley, or a failure really to *listen* and to *hear* what Berkeley says. For example, no one who really understood Berkeley's theory could really believe that the hardness of a stone is a contradiction to it. Do you see this? And do you see how Berkeley would answer some of the other criticisms too? In evaluating criticisms of Berkeley's theory we must above all keep in mind that Berkeley did not deny the *reality* of things, but their *materiality*. He insists over and over:

> The question . . . is not whether things have a real existence out of the mind of this or that person, but, whether they have an absolute existence, distinct from being perceived by God, and exterior to all minds.[10]

Three further issues

Still, three further lines of criticism may be mentioned.

First, what about imagining and conceiving? Does Berkeley do justice to this distinction? He says that you cannot conceive the unexperienced. But surely we can conceive many things which we cannot experience. For to conceive something is to define it without contradiction. Thus we can define infinity, a thousand-sided figure, and even God, though we cannot *picture* any of them. Such conceptualizations, or pure concepts, would seem to be absolutely necessary to our thinking and knowing, but they are excluded by Berkeley's "sensationalist" view of ideas. This in turn raises the question whether knowledge and ideas can so simply be equated with sensations. What if one simply began with a quite different view of knowledge—such as Plato's, or Descartes'?

Second, we can raise here an objection that we raised against Descartes. For Berkeley, though he denied the reality of material substance, nevertheless continued to affirm the reality of *mental* substance. But why not simply dissolve mind itself into a bundle of ideas? We will see in Chapter 10 that this is exactly what the philosopher Hume did, taking some of Berkeley's arguments against the reality of matter and applying them also to mind.

Third, the objections posed by Ryle against Descartes' idea of mental substance may be raised here too. Is it even meaningful to talk about mind as if it were a sort of *blob* of something or a *thing?* Would it be, again, a *Category Mistake* to view mind as a *substance* and having attributes, causing things, being in certain states, etc.? Would it be like confusing a building on the campus with the university?

As you may guess, though, the most radical rejection of any idealist philosophy turns it exactly on its head: It denies the reality of mind and exalts *matter* as the essential "stuff" of all things and this brings us to Chapter 7.

---

[10]Ibid., pp. 81–82.

Chapter 6 in Review

Idealism is the monist view that all reality is, in some way or another, mind. The most striking version of idealism is subjective idealism, and the most influential subjective idealist was Berkeley.

Berkeley propounded what to most ears would seem to be a preposterous idea: *Esse est percipi*, "to be is to be perceived." On this principle, nothing exists except as an object of perception or experience, and that means that everything that exists is an idea in the mind and that nothing exists outside mind. Berkeley defended this thesis with several considerations: (1) the impossibility of having ideas that are similar to realities which are essentially different from ideas; (2) the impossibility of framing any meaningful idea of material substance; (3) the impossibility of thinking of something that is unexperienced; (4) the impossibility of separating primary qualities from secondary qualities, which makes primary as well as secondary qualities subjective, or "idea-istic"; (5) the impossibility of absolutizing even primary qualities, which thus turn out to be as relative as secondary qualities.

However, Berkeley, no less than others, had to reckon with the *passivity* of our perceptions, which leads us to posit objects that are, after all, outside us and independent of us. He thus introduced God, an infinite Mind, who perceives all things at all times. This preserves *both* the reality of the world external to us (passivity of perception) but internal to God (*esse est percipi*).

In spite of Berkeley's insistence that subjective idealism is the most common-sensical of philosophies, many objections are bound to be raised. One of these should *not* be that Berkeley has denied the *reality* of things; his concern is, rather, for the *nature* of things, specifically, the mental nature of things.

- Idealism (popular sense)
- Idealism (metaphysical sense)
  Objective idealism
  Subjective idealism
- Epistemological dualism
- Primary and secondary qualities
- *Esse est percipi*
- Berkeley's basic argument
- The discontinuity of dualism
- Matter as a meaningless idea
- The unexperienced as inconceivable
- The inseparability of primary and secondary qualities
- The relativity of all qualities
- Solipsism
- The passivity of perception

- The necessity of God as a perceiver of all things
- Berkeley's idea of creation
- The difference between psychologically and philosophically grounded criticisms

TEST YOURSELF

1. What is the difference between an objective idealist and a subjective idealist?
2. Who are Hylas and Philonous?
3. True or false: Colors, sounds, tastes, shapes, and sizes are, for *Berkeley*, all examples of subjective qualities.
4. What is the simple argument that expresses Berkeley's subjective idealism?
5. One of Berkeley's proofs for the subjectivity of perceived all is based on the inseparability of _____ and _____.
6. Is Berkeley a monist? Why or why not?
7. Solipsism is the belief in (a) one God, (b) one mind, (c) material substance, (d) continual creation.
8. According to Berkeley, how big is a mite's foot?
9. According to Berkeley, the existence of an all-knowing God solves what very big problem?
10. True or false: Berkeley says that the concept of matter is empty and useless.

QUESTIONS FOR REFLECTION

- As a theory of reality Berkeley's subjective idealism certainly is a radical departure from the ordinary view of things. But what *practical* difference does it make? Can you think of any sphere of actual life and practice that would be much altered (if at all) by the adoption of this theory?
- In spite of its apparent radicalness, Berkeley views his theory of reality as the most *commonsensical*. How would you defend this claim in your own words? In the end, is it *really* commonsensical?
- As in Descartes' philosophy, God plays a central role in Berkeley's. What exactly is the role? Is it a more crucial role than in Descartes' philosophy? Could Berkeley's theory of reality be construed as a gigantic proof for the existence of God?

CHAPTER 7

MATERIALISM

Materialism is actually a form of *naturalism,* and it might be best first to get an idea of this larger metaphysical perspective. All naturalisms share a repudiation of any supernatural or spiritual reality, and claim that only that exists which can, at least in principle, be investigated scientifically. And just as believers in the supernatural or the spiritual are often given to faith, dogma, intuition, authority, and the like, so naturalists are generally given to observation, experimentation, and healthy doses of skepticism. In a word, and recalling a point from Chapter 1, naturalists tend to be "tough-minded" philosophers.

> But we must distinguish between a narrower and a wider naturalism, corresponding to a narrower and a wider view of nature itself. The narrower view defines nature as the physical world, and may be called *materialism.* The wider naturalism, on the other hand, defines nature more broadly so as to include matter as but one of *many* dimensions or aspects of nature. In this chapter we will focus our attention on materialism.

Materialism and naturalism

WHAT IS MATERIALISM?

As with the word "idealism," the word "materialism" also has a popular and a more technical sense. In popular usage materialism means a preoccupation with earthly goods (such as money, ski chalets, and sailboats), and a materialist in this sense is one whose life revolves around the pursuit of such things. But here we intend "materialism" in its more technical and metaphysical sense: Matter with its motions and qualities is the ultimate reality of all things. More generally, what this means

"Materialism": Its popular and technical meanings

is that everything in the universe—from subatomic particles, to tables, chairs, dogs, and cats, to thoughts, feelings, perceptions, and ideals—*everything* is reducible to matter with its motions and qualities, to physical states, to a position in space and time, to what can be quantified.

MATERIALISM

The metaphysical doctrine that matter with its motions and qualities is the ultimate reality of all things.

Materialism as a radical solution to the mind-body problem

There are few forks on the philosophical road that are more unmistakable than the one where idealism and materialism veer off from each other. We saw in our last chapter that one radical solution to the mind-body problem is simply to do away with matter. The result is *idealism*, the view that there is only one reality, and that is mind and its ideas. Materialism takes exactly the opposite course and denies the reality of mind, or at least reduces it (along with everything else) to matter. As a radical solution to the mind-body problem materialism is certainly as effective as idealism, for it too overcomes entirely the old problem of relating two essentially different substances, for there *is* no other substance, only matter. In the same way that Descartes, with his mind-matter dualism, unwittingly spawned modern idealism, so did he spawn modern materialism. This is not to say that the only reason for adopting materialism is that it is a way of avoiding the mind-body prob-

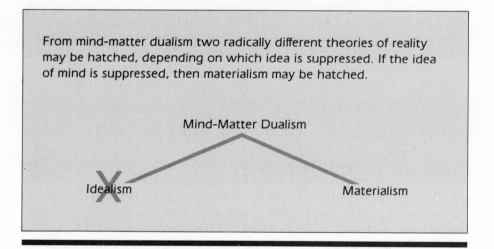

From mind-matter dualism two radically different theories of reality may be hatched, depending on which idea is suppressed. If the idea of mind is suppressed, then materialism may be hatched.

Mind-Matter Dualism

Idealism   Materialism

lem. As with idealism, materialism too has still other advantages. Advantages aside, certainly as a theory of reality it is in some respects the starkest and the most hard-headed.

Materialism is actually a very old philosophy. Already among the Pre-Socratics, Democritus and Leucippus taught that all things, including the soul, are made of indivisible particles or atoms. This idea was adopted by the Greek philosopher Epicurus (about 300 B.C.). He concluded from the materialistic nature of the soul that upon death its parts disperse, and therefore there can be no life after death — so eat, drink, and be merry! After Epicurus, the Roman poet Lucretius (about 60 B.C.) wrote as if he himself were even then providing a materialist (and atomistic) response to Descartes' mind-body problem:

Materialism, an old philosophy

> I now declare that mind and soul are joined
> together, and form one single entity,
> but the head so to speak, that rules in all the body,
> is counsel, mind, and intellect, as we say,
> and this is placed midway within the breast.
> For here leap terror and panic, this spot feels
> sweet joy; here, then, are intellect and mind.
> The rest of the soul, dispersed through all the body,
> obeys the mind and moves to its command.
> For mind thinks its own thoughts, knows its own pleasures,
> when nothing has stimulated soul or body.
> And as when injury attacks our head
> or eye, they hurt, but we're not agonized
> all over, thus the mind sometimes feels pain
> or joy and strength, and when other parts of soul
> in limb and joint have felt no novel impulse.
> But when the mind is deeply stirred by terror,
> all through the body we see the soul affected;
> we pale, and over all the body sweat
> pours out, the tongue stumbles, voice goes awry,
> eyes are befogged, ears ring, the knees give way,
> yes, from sheer terror of mind we often see
> men fall in a faint; thus readily we perceive
> the union of soul and mind, for soul, when struck
> by mind, in turn strikes body and makes it move.
> This argument also proves that soul and mind
> are physical things. Clearly, they move our limbs,
> arouse the body from sleep, change our expression,
> and guide and govern the man in all his being.
> Yet without touch, we see, such things can't happen,
> nor touch without matter; must we not then admit

the soul and mind in act are physical things?
Besides, we see that in our bodies, soul
and body act and react in sympathy.
If a bristling spear has driven deep, exposing
sinew and bone, and yet not taking life,
still faintness follows and sweet swooning down
to earth, and there a sense of rocking motion,
sometimes with vaguely felt desire to rise.
And so the soul must be a physical thing,
since physical weapon and wound can make it suffer.
   I'll now proceed to argument and proof
of what makes up the soul, and what its substance.
To begin, I say the soul is subtly built
of infinitesimal atoms. You may see
and learn that this is so from what's to come.
Nothing whatever, we see, can move as fast
as the mind when it conceives and starts an action;
thus nothing whose nature clearly lies within
our range of vision moves faster than the mind.
But whatever is so mobile must be made
of very round and very tiny atoms,
so that the slightest impulse starts them moving.
Yes, just a touch makes water move and flow:
it's made, you see, of small-sized shapes that roll.
But the nature of honey tends to be more stable;
its fluid is thicker and less disposed to move.
For all the atoms of its substance cling
more closely, being of particles less smooth,
you see, and not so delicate or so round.
Take poppyseed: a gentle puff of air
at the top will blow a tall heap helter-skelter,
but not, on the other hand, a heap of stones
or grain. According, then, as particles
are smallest and smoothest, they will move with ease.
But on the other hand, as some are found
rougher and heavier, so are they more stable.
Now since the soul has been revealed to be
uncommonly mobile, we must grant it made
of atoms very tiny, smooth, and round.
Take this to heart, good friend; in many ways
you'll find it a useful, helpful thing to know.
This fact, too, tells the nature of the soul,
how fine its fabric, and in how small a space

it could be held, if it were all rolled up:
when once the carefree peace of death has seized
a man, and the substance of soul and mind has left him,
from his whole body you'd see nothing lost
in appearance or in weight; death leaves him all
but the humid heat and sentience that mean life.
The entire soul, then, must consist of tiny
atoms, strung out through sinews, vitals, veins,
since, when it all has gone from all the body,
the outer dimensions of body-parts remain
unaltered, and not an ounce of weight is lost.
It's such as when bouquet of wine floats off,
or breath of perfume is wafted to the winds,
or when from a substance flavor dies away;
to the eye, the physical thing appears no smaller
for all of that, and suffers no loss of weight.
Why? Because many minuscule atoms make
flavors and scents throughout the range of things.
Thus you may know the substance of the mind
and soul, I insist, is formed of most minute
atoms, for slipping away, it steals no weight.[1]

In the modern period, the eighteenth-century English philosopher Thomas **A modern**
Hobbes expressed the materialist thesis with a theistic twist: The notion of *spirit*, as **statement**
opposed to *matter* or *body*, should be reserved for God alone.

From these Metaphysics, which are mingled with the Scripture to make School Divin-
ity, we are told, there be in the world certain Essences separated from Bodies, which
they call Abstract Essences, and Substantial Forms: For the Interpreting of which
Jargon, there is need of somewhat more than ordinary attention in this place. Also I
ask pardon of those that are not used to this kind of Discourse, for applying my self
to those that are. The World, (I mean not the Earth only, that denominates the Lovers
of it Worldly men, but the Universe, that is, the whole mass of all things that are)
is Coporeal, that is to say, Body; and hath the dimensions of Magnitude, namely,
Length, Breadth, and Depth: also every part of Body, is likewise Body, and hath the
like dimensions; and consequently every part of the Universe, is Body; and that which
is not Body, is no part of the Universe: And because the Universe is All, that which
is no part of it, is Nothing; and consequently no where. Nor does it follow from
hence, that Spirits are nothing: for they have dimensions, and are therefore really
Bodies; though that name in common Speech be given to such Bodies only, as are

[1]Lucretius, *The Nature of Things*, III, 136–230, tr. Frank O. Copley (New York: Norton, 1977).

visible, or palpable; that is, that have some degree of Opacity: But for Spirits, they call them Incorporeal; which is a name of more honour, and may therefore with more piety be attributed to God himself; in whom we consider not what Attribute expresseth best his Nature, which is Incomprehensible; but what best expresseth our desire to honour Him.[2]

Such a view of reality has taken several forms. Perhaps the harshest is *mechanistic materialism.*

MAN A MACHINE

The key to understanding mechanistic materialism lies in the word "mechanistic," which means "machinelike." According to this theory of reality, not only are all things reducible to matter and motion and locatable in space and time, but all

Thomas Hobbes, a modern materialist

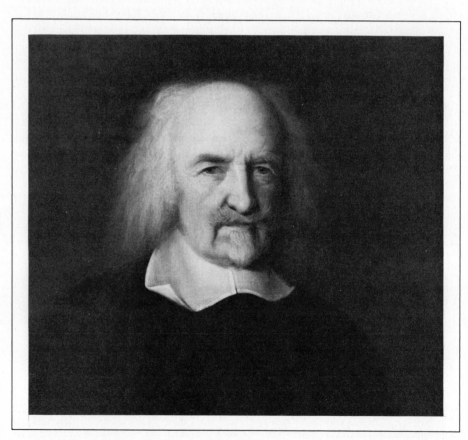

[2]Thomas Hobbes, *Leviathan*, chap. 46, ed. A. D. Lindsay (New York: Dutton, 1950) (slightly edited).

things happen and have their particular features according to a finite number of fixed physical laws. That is to say, the world and everything in it is a *machine*.

Mechanistic materialism really took shape as a philosophical position (and in some ways even as a philosophical movement) soon after Descartes. The thinkers advocating this idea were very much influenced by the "new science," and were especially captivated by Sir Isaac Newton's Three Laws of Motion, the basis of Newtonian mechanics. They were also influenced by Descartes himself, who believed that—at least with respect to the *matter* part of his dualism—the world is ordered by fixed laws, and that animals, like everything else in the external world, are mechanisms.

Mechanistic materialism

Some roots of the mechanistic view

---

mech·a·nism (mek′ə·niz′əm) *n.* **1.** The parts or arrangement of parts of a machine: the *mechanism* of a watch. **2.** Something similar to a machine in the arrangement and working of its parts: The human body is a magnificent *mechanism*. **3.** The process or technique by which something works or produces an action or effect: the complicated *mechanism* of democracy. **4.** The technique or the mechanical method of execution of an artist, writer, etc. **5.** A theory that all natural phenomena can be explained by the laws of chemistry and physics. **6.** *Psychol.* The mental processes, conscious or unconscious, by which certain actions or results are effected. Abbr. *mech.*
mech·a·nist (mek′ə·nist) *n.* **1.** A mechanician. **2.** A believer in mechanism (def. 5). —*adj.* Mechanistic.
mech·a·nis·tic (mek′ə·nis′tik) *adj.* **1.** Of, pertaining to, or of the nature of mechanics. **2.** Pertaining to or based on mechanism (def. 5). **—mech′a·nis′ti·cal·ly** *adv.*

NEWTON'S THREE LAWS OF MOTION

1. A body remains at rest or in motion with a constant velocity unless acted on by an outside force.
2. The sum of the forces acting on a body is equal to the product of its mass and acceleration.
3. For every action there is an equal and opposite reaction.

It is important not to miss the full force of the claim that the universe is a machine. It is not just that all things (and everything *about* all things) are caused. We all believe that. It is, rather, that everything is caused in such a way that *it could not have been otherwise*. This pen, this desk, that paperclip in just that position, the smoke curling upwards from this pipe, everything that *is* and is going on in this room, in all rooms, in all the world, in all worlds—everything in the universe down to the minutest detail is, on this view, *exhaustively predetermined* by infinitely long and converging chains of blind, irrational antecedent causes. One of the most concise expressions of this mechanist point of view was provided by the French astronomer and mathematician Laplace:

Are all things predetermined?

> *We ought then to regard the present state of the universe as the effect of its anterior state and as the cause of the one which is to follow. Given for one instant an intelligence which could comprehend all the forces by which nature is animated and the respective situation of the beings who compose it—an intelligence sufficiently vast to submit these data to analysis—it would embrace in the same formula the movements of the greatest bodies of the universe and those of the lightest atom; for it, nothing would be uncertain and the future, as the past, would be present to its eyes.*[3]

That is, on the mechanistic view of things, if you could somehow know the exact status of every detail in the universe at one point, then you could know perfectly every detail in the universe at any point in the past or the future.

Sir Isaac Newton

One cannot overestimate Newton's influence on subsequent science and philosophy. It is not difficult to see how Newtonian mechanics, specifically, played into the hands of materialistic philosophy.

[3]Pierre Simon de Laplace, *A Philosophical Essay on Probabilities*, tr. Frederick Wilson Truscott and Frederick Lincoln Emory (New York: Dover, 1951), p. 4.

> ### MECHANISM
>
> The view which conceives of the universe and everything in it as a machine, that is, as governed by a fixed and finite number of laws.

Even so, it is *still* possible that some may fail to note the full implications of the mechanistic claim. If *everything* in the universe is matter in motion and is governed by mechanistic laws, then so is man. And then so is his thinking, feeling, purposing, valuing, and willing. Man too, through and through, is a machine.

Is man a machine?

"Man a machine" was in fact the title of a remarkable little volume published in 1748 by the French physician and agnostic La Mettrie. (He has been called "the scapegoat of eighteenth-century materialism.") Like many others before and after him, La Mettrie argued for a purely materialistic basis of human consciousness. Thoughts, sensations, and emotions are all a matter of organs, nerves, impulses, reflex movements, pumping blood, and the like. These in turn are physiological counterparts of springs, cogs, wheels, wire, and so on, so it all reduces to physics and chemistry. On such a view, as someone has said, the brain secretes thought in the same way that the liver secretes bile! A few passages from La Mettrie:

> *Man is so complicated a machine that it is impossible to get a clear idea of the machine beforehand, and hence impossible to define it. . . .*
>
> *But since all the faculties of the soul depend to such a degree on the proper organization of the brain and of the whole body, that apparently they are but this organization itself, the soul is clearly an enlightened machine. . . .*
>
> *The soul is therefore but an empty word, of which no one has any idea, and which an enlightened man should use only to signify the part in us that thinks. Given the least principle of motion, animated bodies will have all that is necessary for moving, feeling, thinking, repenting, or in a word for conducting themselves in the physical realm, and in the moral realm which depends upon it. . . .*
>
> *Grant only that organized matter is endowed with a principle of motion, which alone differentiates it from the inorganic (and can one deny this in the face of the most incontestable observation?) and that among animals, as I have sufficiently proved, everything depends upon the diversity of this organization: these admissions suffice for guessing the riddle of substances and of man. It {thus} appears that there is but one {type of organization} in the universe, and that man is the most perfect {example}. . . .*
>
> *Let us then conclude boldly that man is a machine, and that in the whole universe there is but a single substance differently modified. This is no hypothesis set forth by dint of a number of postulates and assumptions; it is not the work of prej-*

L'HOMME

MACHINE.

Eſt-ce là ce Raion de l'Eſſence ſuprème,
    Que l'on nous peint ſi lumineux?
Eſt-ce là cet Eſprit ſurvivant à nous mème?
Il naît avec nos ſens, croit, s'affoiblit
        comme eux.
Helas! il périra de mème.
                    VOLTAIRE.

À LEYDE,
DE L'IMP. D'ELIE LUZAC, FILS.
MDCCXLVIII.

udice, nor even of my reason alone; I should have disdained a guide which I think to be so untrustworthy, had not my senses, bearing a torch, so to speak, induced me to follow reason by lighting the way themselves. Experience has thus spoken to me in behalf of reason; and in this way I have combined the two.

    . . . Need I say that I refer to the empty and trivial notions, to the pitiable and trite arguments that will be urged (as long as the shadow of prejudice or of superstition remains on earth) for the supposed incompatibility of two substances which meet and move each other unceasingly? Such is my system, or rather the truth, unless I am much deceived. It is short and simple. Dispute it now who will.[4]

[4]Julien Offray de La Mettrie, *Man a Machine*, tr. Gertrude C. Bussey et al. (La Salle, Ill.: Open Court, 1912), pp. 89, 18, 140–141.

MAN, A COMPUTER?

Especially with the rise of computer technology the temptation to create man in the image of a computer has sometimes been irresistible.

"Each human being is a superbly constructed, astonishingly compact, self-ambulatory computer. . . ."

—Carl Sagan

If you have the impression that the conception of man as a machine is just an idle piece displayed in the historical museum of philosophical ideas, your impression is quite wrong. It is true that the La Mettrie and pre–La Mettrie type of mechanism was based on the "billiard-ball" model of the universe (everything happens according to strict laws and direct or indirect physical contacts), and that the billiard-ball model is now "out." And even the classical Newtonian mechanics has now been succeeded by complicated things like *quantum* mechanics and Heisenberg's Uncertainty Principle according to which there is no causal determinism at the level of subatomic particles. How this latter involves a "dematerialization" of matter is described by the scientist and philosopher N. R. Hanson:

The "demateriali-zation" of matter

> *Matter has been dematerialized, not just as a concept of the philosophically real, but now as an idea of modern physics. Matter can be analyzed down to the level of fundamental particles. But at that depth the direction of the analysis changes, and this constitutes a major conceptual surprise in the history of science. The things which for Newton typified matter—e.g., an exactly determinable state, a point shape, absolute solidity—these are now the properties electrons do not, because theoretically they cannot, have. . . .*
>
> *The dematerialization of matter . . . has rocked mechanics at its foundations. . . . The 20th century's dematerialization of matter has made it conceptually impossible to accept a Newtonian picture of the properties of matter and still do a consistent physics.[5]*

Nonetheless, the materialistic perspective thrives. Consider, for example, the materialism of the Australian philosopher J. J. C. Smart. Under the sway of contemporary physics he rejects complete causal determinism, but asserts, nevertheless, a purely physicalistic theory of mind. More specifically, he asserts what is called the Identity Thesis.

A new materialism

[5]N. R. Hanson, "The Dematerialization of Matter," in *The Concept of Matter*, ed. Ernan McMillin (Notre Dame, Ind.: University of Notre Dame Press, 1963), pp. 556-557.

First of all let me try to explain what I mean by "materialism." I shall then go on to try to defend the doctrine. By "materialism" I mean the theory that there is nothing in the world over and above those entities which are postulated by physics (or, of course, those entities which will be postulated by future and more adequate physical theories). Thus I do not hold materialism to be wedded to the billiard-ball physics of the nineteenth century. The less visualizable particles of modern physics count as matter. Note that energy counts as matter for my purposes: indeed in modern physics energy and matter are not sharply distinguishable. Nor do I hold that materialism implies determinism. If physics is indeterministic on the micro-level, so must be the materialist's theory. I regard materialism as compatible with a wide range of conceptions of the nature of matter and energy. For example, if matter and energy consist of regions of special curvature of an absolute space-time, with "worm holes" and what not, this is still compatible with materialism: we can still argue that in the last resort the world is made up entirely of the ultimate entities of physics, namely space-time points.

. . . [M]y definition will in some respects be narrower than those of some who have called themselves "materialists." I wish to lay down that it is incompatible with materialism that there should be any irreducibly "emergent" laws or properties, say in biology or psychology. According to the view I propose to defend, there are no irreducible laws or properties in biology, any more than there are in electronics. Given the "natural history" of a superheterodyne (its wiring diagram), a physicist is able to explain, using only laws of physics, its mode of behavior and its properties (for example, the property of being able to receive such and such a radio station which broadcasts on 25 megacycles). Just as electronics gives the physical explanation of the workings of superheterodynes, etc., so biology gives (or approximates to giving) physical and chemical explanations of the workings of organisms or parts of organisms. The biologist needs natural history just as the engineer needs wiring diagrams, but neither needs nonphysical laws.

It will now become clear why I define materialism in the way I have done above. I am concerned to deny that in the world there are nonphysical entities and nonphysical laws. In particular I wish to deny the doctrine of psychophysical dualism. (I also want to deny any theory of "emergent properties," since irreducibly nonphysical properties are just about as repugnant to me as are irreducibly nonphysical entities.)

Popular theologians sometimes argue against materialism by saying that "you can't put love in a test tube." Well you can't put a gravitational field in a test tube (except in some rather strained sense of these words), but there is nothing incompatible with materialism, as I have defined it, in the notion of a gravitational field.

Similarly, even though love may elude test tubes, it does not elude materialistic metaphysics, since it can be analyzed as a pattern of bodily behavior or, perhaps better, as the internal state of the human organism that accounts for this behavior. (A dualist who analyzes love as an internal state will perhaps say that it is a soul state, whereas the materialist will say that it is a brain state. It seems to me that much of our ordinary language about the mental is neither dualistic nor materialist but is neutral between the two. Thus, to say that a locution is not materialistic is not to say that it is immaterialistic.)

But what about consciousness? Can we interpret the having of an after-image or of a painful sensation as something material, namely, a brain state or brain process? We seem to be immediately aware of pains and after-images, and we seem to be immediately aware of them as something different from a neurophysiological state or process. For example, the after-image may be green speckled with red, whereas the neurophysiologist looking into our brains would be unlikely to see something green speckled with red. However, if we object to materialism in this way we are victims of a confusion which U. T. Place has called "the phenomenological fallacy." To say that an image or sense datum is green is not to say that the conscious experience of having the image or sense datum is green. It is to say that it is the sort of experience we have when in normal conditions we look at a green apple, for example. Apples and unripe bananas can be green, but not the experiences of seeing them. An image or a sense datum can be green in a derivative sense, but this need not cause any worry, because, on the view I am defending, images and sense data are not constituents of the world, though the processes of having an image or a sense datum are actual processes in the world. The experience of having a green sense datum is not itself green; it is a process occurring in grey matter. The world contains plumbers, but does not contain the average plumber; it also contains the having of a sense datum, but does not contain the sense datum. . . .

It may be asked why I should demand of a tenable philosophy of mind that it should be compatible with materialism, in the sense in which I have defined it. One reason is as follows. How could a nonphysical property or entity suddenly arise in the course of animal evolution? A change in a gene is a change in a complex molecule which causes a change in the biochemistry of the cell. This may lead to changes in the shape or organization of the developing embryo. But what sort of chemical process could lead to the springing into existence of something nonphysical? No enzyme can catalyze the production of a spook! Perhaps it will be said that the nonphysical comes into existence as a by-product: that whenever there is a certain complex physical structure, then, by an irreducible extraphysical law, there is also a nonphysical entity. Such laws would be quite outside normal scientific conceptions and quite inexplicable: they would be, in Herbert Feigl's phrase, "nomological danglers." To say the very least, we can vastly simplify our cosmological outlook if we can defend a materialistic philosophy of mind.[6]

ARE THE MIND AND BODY
IDENTICAL?

Two major criticisms of materialism center around (1) the claimed identity of mind and body, and (2) the claimed universality of strict determinism. A little later, in

[6]J. J. C. Smart, "Materialism," *Journal of Philosophy*, 22 (October 1963), pp. 651–653, 660.

our discussion of B. F. Skinner, we will have occasion to address the second of these. For the moment, consider the first.

All forms of materialism involve a physicalistic interpretation of mind. In the case of Smart, we have just seen that this takes the form of the Identity Thesis, so-called because it views the mind (including thoughts, perceptions, emotions, etc.) as identical with brain states (nerve cells, electrical impulses, etc.). One of the most common objections to this view has already been anticipated by Smart. Are not the differences between mental states and brain states so great that no amount of empirical or scientific analysis can bridge them? For example, consider a surgeon who completes his last delicate and precise penetration into an innermost recess of the brain. What does he see there—*red* or *affection?* No. He sees more muscle, brain tissue, blood, cells, and so on. It's a serious question: Do the sensations of red, the idea of a table, the feeling of repulsion, and the desire for food sit right there in the brain alongside veins and synapses, waiting to be exposed?

Some are not satisfied that Smart and others have successfully laid this objection to rest. The American philosopher Richard Taylor presses the difference between mind and body by raising *logical* problems with identity-talk: I can be blamed, but can my *body* be blamed? I can be religious, but can my *body* be religious? My thoughts can be true or false, but can my *brain* be true or false?

By "identity" the materialist must mean a strict and total identity of himself and his body, nothing less. Now to say of anything, X, and anything, Y, that X and Y are identical, or that they are really one and the same thing, one must be willing to assert of X anything whatever that he asserts of Y, and vice versa. This is simply a consequence of their identity, for if there is anything whatever that can be truly asserted of any object X, but cannot be truly asserted of some object Y, then it logically follows that X and Y are two different things, and not the same thing. In saying, for instance, that the British wartime prime minister and Winston Churchill are one and the same person, one commits himself to saying of either whatever he is willing to say of the other—such as, that he lived to a great age, smoked cigars, was a resolute leader, was born at Blenheim, and so on. If there were any statement whatever that was true of, say, Mr. Churchill, but not true of the wartime prime minister, then it would follow that Mr. Churchill was not the wartime prime minister, that we are here referring to two different men, and not one.

The question can now be asked, then, whether there is anything true of me that is not true of my body, and vice versa. There are, of course, ever so many things that can be asserted indifferently of both me and my body without absurdity. For instance, we can say that I was born at such and such place and time, and it is not the least odd to say this of my body as well. Or we can say that my body now weighs exactly so many pounds, and it would be just as correct to give this as my weight; and so on.

But now consider more problematical assertions. It might, for instance, be true of me at a certain time that I am morally blameworthy or praiseworthy. Can we then say that my body or some part of it, such as my brain, is in exactly the same sense blameworthy or praiseworthy? Can moral predicates be applied without gross incongruity to any physical object at all? Or suppose I have some profound wish or desire, or some thought—the desire, say, to be in some foreign land at a given moment, or thoughts of the Homeric gods. It seems at least odd to assert that my body, or some part of it, wishes that it were elsewhere, or has thoughts of the gods. How, indeed, can any purely physical state of any purely physical object ever be a state that is for something, or of something, in the way that my desires and thoughts are such? And how, in particular, could a purely physical state be in this sense for or of something that is not real? Or again, suppose that I am religious, and can truly say that I love God and neighbor, for instance. Can I without absurdity say that my body or some part of it, such as my foot or brain, is religious, and loves God and neighbor? Or can one suppose that my being religious, or having such love, consists simply in my body's being in a certain state, or behaving in a certain way? If I claim the identity of myself with my body, I must say all these odd things; that is, I must be willing to assert of my body, or some part of it, everything I assert of myself. There is perhaps no logical absurdity or clear falsity in speaking thus of one's corporeal frame, but such assertions as these are at least strange, and it can be questioned whether, as applied to the body, they are even still meaningful.

The disparity between bodily and personal predicates becomes even more apparent, however, if we consider epistemological predicates, involved in statements about belief and knowledge. Thus, if I believe something—believe, for instance, that today is February 31—then I am in a certain state; the state, namely, of having a certain belief which is in this case necessarily a false one. Now how can a physical state of any physical object be identical with that? And how, in particular, can anything be a false physical state of an object? The physical states of things, it would seem, just are, and one cannot even think of anything that could ever distinguish one such state from another as being either true or false. A physiologist might give a complete physical description of a brain and nervous system at a particular time, but he could never distinguish some of those states as true and others as false, nor would he have any idea what to look for if he were asked to do this. At least, so it would certainly seem.[7]

BEYOND FREEDOM AND
DIGNITY: SKINNER

Probably the best recent example of one who asserts both a physicalistic view of mind along with a pervasive causal determinism is not a philosopher but the behaviorist psychologist B. F. Skinner.

What is *behaviorism?* Generally, behaviorism is a school of psychology which emphasizes observable human behavior as the proper object of psychological study.

Behaviorism: Soft and hard

[7]Richard Taylor, *Metaphysics*, 2d ed. (Englewood Cliffs, N.J.: Prentice-Hall, 1974), pp. 13–15.

The metaphysics of hard behaviorism

Now here we have to draw a distinction. For there is a big difference between (1) the view that the description of observable behavior is the psychologist's task, which we may call descriptive or *soft* behaviorism, and (2) the view that observable behavior *is all there is,* which we may call *hard* behaviorism. Obviously, soft behaviorism is not our concern here inasmuch as it makes no claim at all about reality or human nature itself. Hard behaviorism, however, most certainly does involve a claim about reality—specifically a claim about the nature of human nature itself. This form of behaviorism is, therefore, at a certain level inseparable from a metaphysical perspective, and the perspective is a materialistic and mechanistic one. It is therefore appropriate to consider this form of behaviorism in a chapter on materialism, especially since, through Skinner's book *Beyond Freedom and Dignity,* it has enjoyed a renewed and far-reaching impact in recent years.

Behaviorism

The school of psychology which emphasizes observable behavior as the proper object of psychological study.

Soft Behaviorism

The form of Behaviorism which limits itself to the description of observable behavior.

Hard Behaviorism

The form of Behaviorism which extends itself beyond the task of describing behavior to the claim that there *is* nothing beyond behavior.

There can be no doubt about the physicalistic and mechanistic character of Skinner's appraisal of the human person. Though Skinner's physicalism, or reduction of the total person to physical states, underlies and pervades Skinner's work everywhere, it is nowhere really argued, at least not with any rigor. Rather, it is treated as an assumption that any enlightened twentieth-century person would surely embrace, in contrast to earlier and "prescientific" notions which uncritically employ ideas such as mind, transcendence, free will, and the like. Our interest in Skinner is not, therefore, so much with his defense of physicalism (because he gives none) but with what he does with it as the foundation of his proposed "technology of behavior," a program of psychological engineering, or manipulation of human nature in the interest of the improvement and progress of the species.

Almost all our major problems involve human behavior, and they cannot be solved by physical and biological technology alone. What is needed is a technology of behavior, but we have been slow to develop the science from which such a technology might be drawn. One difficulty is that almost all of what is called behavioral science continues to trace behavior to states of mind, feelings, traits of character, human nature, and so on. Physics and biology once followed similar practices and advanced only when they discarded them. The behavioral sciences have been slow to change partly because the explanatory entities often seem to be directly observed and partly because other kinds of explanations have been hard to find. The environment is obviously important, but its role has remained obscure. It does not push or pull, it selects, and this function is difficult to discover and analyze. The role of natural selection in evolution was formulated only a little more than a hundred years ago, and the selective role of the environment in shaping and maintaining the behavior of the individual is only beginning to be recognized and studied. As the interaction between organism and environment has come to be understood, however, effects once assigned to states of mind, feelings, and traits are beginning to be traced to accessible conditions, and a technology of behavior may therefore become available. It will not solve our problems, however, until it replaces traditional prescientific views, and these are strongly entrenched. Freedom and dignity illustrate the difficulty. They are the possessions of the autonomous man of traditional theory, and they are essential to practices in which a person is held responsible for his conduct and given credit for his achievements. A scientific analysis shifts both the responsibility and the achievement to the environment. It also raises questions concerning "values." Who will use a technology and to what ends? Until these issues are resolved, a technology of behavior will continue to be rejected, and with it possibly the only way to solve our problems. . . .

A child is born a member of the human species, with a genetic endowment showing many idiosyncratic features, and he begins at once to acquire a repertoire of behavior under the contingencies of reinforcement to which he is exposed as an individual. Most of these contingencies are arranged by other people. They are, in fact, what is called a culture, although the term is usually defined in other ways. Two eminent anthropologists have said, for example, that "the essential core of culture consists of traditional (i.e., historically derived and selected) ideas and especially their attached values." But those who observe cultures do not see ideas or values. They see how people live, how they raise their children, how they gather or cultivate food, what kinds of dwellings they live in, what they wear, what games they play, how they treat each other, how they govern themselves, and so on. These are the customs, the customary behaviors, of a people. To explain them we must turn to the contingencies which generate them.

Some contingencies are part of the physical environment, but they usually work in combination with social contingencies, and the latter are naturally emphasized by those who study cultures. The social contingencies, or the behaviors they generate, are the "ideas" of a culture; the reinforcers that appear in the contingencies are its "values."

A person is not only exposed to the contingencies that constitute a culture, he helps to maintain them, and to the extent that the contingencies induce him to do so the culture is self-perpetuating. The effective reinforcers are a matter of observation and cannot be disputed. What a given group of people calls good is a fact: it is what members of the group find reinforcing as the result of their genetic endowment and the natural and social contingencies to which they have been exposed. Each culture has its own set of goods, and what is good in one culture may not be good in another. To recognize this is to take the position of "cultural relativism." What is good for the Trobriand Islander is good for the Trobriand Islander, and that is that. Anthropologists have often emphasized relativism as a tolerant alternative to missionary zeal in converting all cultures to a single set of ethical, governmental, religious, or economic values. . . .

It is in the nature of an experimental analysis of human behavior that it should strip away the functions previously assigned to autonomous man and transfer them one by one to the controlling environment. The analysis leaves less and less for autonomous man to do. But what about man himself? Is there not something about a person which is more than a living body? Unless something called a self survives, how can we speak of self-knowledge or self-control? To whom is the injunction "Know thyself" addressed?

It is an important part of the contingencies to which a young child is exposed that his own body is the only part of his environment which remains the same (idem) from moment to moment and day to day. We say that he discovers his identity as he learns to distinguish between his body and the rest of the world. He does this long before the community teaches him to call things by name and to distinguish "me" from "it" or "you."

A self is a repertoire of behavior appropriate to a given set of contingencies. A substantial part of the conditions to which a person is exposed may play a dominant role, and under other conditions a person may report, "I'm not myself today," or, "I couldn't have done what you said I did, because that's not like me." The identity conferred upon a self arises from the contingencies responsible for the behavior. Two or more repertoires generated by different sets of contingencies compose two or more selves. A person possesses one repertoire appropriate to his life with his friends and another appropriate to his life with his family, and a friend may find him a very different person if he sees him with his family or his family if they see him with his friends. The problem of identity arises when situations are intermingled, as when a person finds himself with both his family and his friends at the same time.

Self-knowledge and self-control imply two selves in this sense. The self-knower is almost always a product of social contingencies, but the self that is known may come from other sources. The controlling self (the conscience or superego) is of social origin, but the controlled self is more likely to be the product of genetic susceptibilities to reinforcement (the id, or the Old Adam). The controlling self generally represents the interests of others, the controlled self the interests of the individual.

The picture which emerges from a scientific analysis is not of a body with a *person inside, but of a body which is a person in the sense that it displays a complex repertoire of behavior. The picture is, of course, unfamiliar. The man thus portrayed is a stranger, and from the traditional point of view he may not seem to be a man at all. "For at least one hundred years," said Joseph Wood Krutch, "we have been prejudiced in every theory, including economic determinism, mechanistic behaviorism, and relativism, that reduces the stature of man until he ceases to be man at all in any sense that the humanists of an earlier generation would recognize." Matson has argued that "the empirical behavioral scientist . . . denies, if only by implication, that a unique being, called Man, exists." "What is now under attack," said Maslow, "is the 'being' of man." C. S. Lewis put it quite bluntly: Man is being abolished.*

There is clearly some difficulty in identifying the man to whom these expressions refer. Lewis cannot have meant the human species, for not only is it not being abolished, it is filling the earth. (As a result it may eventually abolish itself through disease, famine, pollution, or a nuclear holocaust, but that is not what Lewis meant.) Nor are individual men growing less effective or productive. We are told that what is threatened is "man qua man," or "man in his humanity," or "man as Thou not It," or "man as a person not a thing." These are not very helpful expressions, but they supply a clue. What is being abolished is autonomous man—the inner man, the homunculus, the possessing demon, the man defended by the literatures of freedom and dignity.

His abolition has long been overdue. Autonomous man is a device used to explain what we cannot explain in any other way. He has been constructed from our ignorance, and as our understanding increases, the very stuff of which he is composed vanishes. Science does not dehumanize man, it de-homunculizes him, and it must do so if it is to prevent the abolition of the human species. To man qua man we readily say good riddance. Only by dispossessing him can we turn to the real causes of human

---

REVEALING EXPRESSIONS FROM SKINNER

- "technology of behavior"
- explanation by "antecedent physical events"
- person as "a repertoire of behavior"
- values as "social contingencies"
- good and bad as "positive" and "negative" reinforcement
- "responsibility and achievement" of "the environment"
- "experimental analysis"
- "beyond freedom and dignity"

*behavior. Only then can we turn from the inferred to the observed, from the mirac-
ulous to the natural, from the inaccessible to the manipulable.*[8]

The above selections from Skinner emphasize several overlapping themes:
the denial of free will and all human transcendence; a reinterpretation of values as
being dependent on social contingencies or conditions; a purely physicalistic interpretation of all levels of human activity; the importance of the environment for
the shaping of human nature. In sum, he argues for the abolition of man as traditionally conceived, and for a technology of human nature as conceived along
"hard" behavioristic lines.

Is man a machine for Skinner? Although Skinner explicitly represents man
as a "machine," in the following paragraph he appears to want to soften the blow.

*Man is not made into a machine by analyzing his behavior in mechanical terms.
Early theories of behavior, as we have seen, represented man as a push-pull autom-
aton, close to the nineteenth-century notion of a machine, but progress has been made.
Man is a machine in the sense that he is a complex system behaving in lawful ways,
but the complexity is extraordinary. His capacity to adjust to contingencies of reinforcement will perhaps be eventually simulated by machines, but this has not yet been
done, and the living system thus simulated will remain unique in other ways.*[9]

Nevertheless, many think that Skinner's conception of human nature is essentially
indistinguishable from the old-fashioned mechanistic one. Surely if there is any
recurring theme in Skinner's work it is the rejection of human autonomy and the
invocation of a universal and strict causal determinism. And this brings us to the
second major problem with materialism.

Behaviorism is "a monumental triviality." It represents
"question-begging on a heroic scale."
                                                    —Arthur Koestler

Behaviorism is guilty of "innate naivete, intellectual bankruptcy,
and half-deliberate cruelty."

                                                    —Peter Gay

---

[8]B. F. Skinner, *Beyond Freedom and Dignity* (New York: Bantam Books, 1972), pp. 22–23, 121–122, 189–
191.
[9]Ibid., pp. 192–193.

ARE ALL THINGS DETERMINED?

It should be apparent by now that while not every form of materialism embraces causal determinism (think of Smart), the two usually do go hand in hand (as in Skinner). All things are reducible to physical states; all things are causally determined. But for many philosophers causal determinism, especially as regards human activity, is extremely problematic.

It is important to recall an earlier point. The trouble is not over the principle of universal causality, pure and simple. Almost everyone believes that every event must have a cause; from nothing, nothing comes; or for everything that happens there must be a necessary (it couldn't happen without it) and sufficient (it can happen with it) condition. The problem arises with the further assertion that everything is causally *determined*; that is, for anything that happens, *it could not have happened otherwise*. To put it another way: There is a big difference (do you see it?) between saying, (1) D could not occur without A, B, and C, and (2) Given A, B, and C, D *must* occur. It is, of course, this second claim, the principle of universal determination, that is so vexing.

Causality vs. determinism

CAUSALITY AND DETERMINISM

- *Principle of universal causality:* Everything that comes into being is caused.
- *Principle of universal determinism:* Everything that comes into being is caused in such a way that it could not have been otherwise.

In the first place, it is vexing from the standpoint of the belief in genuine *morality*. If it is true that nothing can happen otherwise than it does, then this must apply also to our willing and choosing. And this means the denial of *free will*. On the other hand, is it not clear—so the argument goes—that morality presupposes free will? that *ought* implies *can?* What sense is there in praise and blame and talk of moral responsibility if one cannot choose and act *freely?* Is it not always relevant, when trying to establish blame or guilt or responsibility on the part of someone, to ascertain whether that person was forced, drugged, or suffering from some compulsion? Free will would seem to be a condition for responsible moral action.

Determinism and morality

More generally it may be asked whether the ideas of moral good and evil are even *meaningful* on the materialist/determinist view of things. For on that view things just *are,* and they can't be otherwise. Whence, then, comes any *ought?* If you start with a morally neutral universe how do you account for objective values or ideals or universally binding rights and wrongs? Or maybe something can come from nothing. Or maybe values aren't universal and objective, but, as Skinner says, they're just by-products of the environment and accidental social conditions. But is this what you mean by genuine morality? (These questions will have to be considered again in Chapter 16.)

"The problem is to induce people not to be good but to behave well."

—Skinner

But is it not good to behave well?

Determinism and intellection

In the second place, some think that determinism is downright incompatible with genuine *thinking,* using the word to cover a broad range of intellectual activities. Setting aside such intellectual experiences as intuition, flashes of insight, and creative imagination, which some think transcend the flux and flow of blind and mechanical causation, is not the determinist caught in a hopeless if not self-contradictory position? For we are told right and left that all things are causally determined, could not be otherwise, etc., and yet we are told also to think hard, to scrutinize, to evaluate, to analyze. But this puts the intellect in the position of *judging* things, which means that the intellect is different from, and higher than, those that it *judges.* That is, if your mind and intellectual processes themselves are but an example of physical and chemical processes, then how can your mind frame a theory *about* physics and chemistry? And what *is* truth?

But there may be worse. We are told by the determinist that all things are causally determined. But, then, that very statement too, as well as everything else the determinist maintains, *is itself causally determined.* But if it's causally determined and could not be otherwise, then why pay any attention to it? Do you usually take seriously the claims of someone whose claims you know to be blindly determined by antecedent causes? As in the case of determining moral responsibility, does not intellectual responsibility mean freedom from constraints such as drug-inducement, compulsions, force, and the like?

DETERMINIST: All things are causally determined.

INDETERMINIST: But is that statement itself therefore causally determined?

DETERMINIST: Why, of course. I just said that everything is!

INDETERMINIST: Well, then, why should I take it seriously?

DETERMINIST: Because I am a rational person, and I offer it as a rational position.

INDETERMINIST: But that's just the point. I don't call people or positions "rational" that are blind products of antecedent causes. I might as well argue with a turnip!

Inevitably, someone will counter with the analogy of computers: Are not human minds supercomplex and glorified computers? The proper answer is, of course, that computers—even the most supercomplex—do so well only because they are programmed by something essentially different, a *noncomputer*, namely, a *human mind*.

TWO MAJOR PROBLEMS FOR DETERMINISM

- Is moral experience compatible with universal causal determinism?
- Is cognitive experience compatible with universal causal determinism?

It is all a question of *transcendence:* Do you believe that the categories of materialism and/or determinism are adequate to your total experience as a human being, especially your moral and intellectual experience? Or must there be some reality or dimension of human nature, however dimly perceived and understood, that stands outside and above matter, motion and causal determination?

A question of transcendence

Chapter 7 in Review

SUMMARY

The radical alternative to idealism is materialism, which entirely does away with mind (or mental substance) and affirms matter, with its motions and qualities, as the sole underlying reality of all things. This is a very old philosophical perspective with roots, as we have seen, even in the Pre-Socratic period.

An extreme form of materialism is mechanistic materialism, which imports the further principle that the motions in the universe are determined by fixed and unalterable laws: The universe and everything in it is a *machine*. But, then, so are human beings, as La Mettrie announced in his book *Man a Machine*. Of course, the image of a person as consisting of wheels, springs, cogs, and bolts is out of date, as the idea of matter itself has become considerably refined. Nonetheless, the physicalistic conception of mind persists, as in the identity thesis of J. J. C. Smart: Mental states are identical with brain states.

In recent times, something very much like mechanistic materialism has surfaced in conjunction with the behavioristic psychology of Skinner. We have called it "hard" behaviorism precisely because it assumes the truth of materialism as a theory of reality and a theory of human nature. Skinner's main purpose in *Beyond Freedom and Dignity* is to envision and advocate a "technology of human behavior," a manipulation of human behavior and transformation of values in accordance with the progress and ideals of the evolutionary process.

As materialism, and certainly *mechanistic* materialism, bears on human nature and life, it poses great problems. Specifically, if all things are exhaustively determined, and man is a machine, then what becomes of moral and cognitive experience? Many philosophers believe that moral responsibility and authentic thinking are immediately rendered impossible on the determinist view of things. This is to say nothing of the alleged self-refuting character of this thesis: If everything is causally determined, then so is this very claim, but then why pay any attention to it? And Taylor has pointed out some problems with the Identity Thesis.

In the end, the question becomes: Is it possible to live with the intellectual and practical implications that follow from the denial of *human transcendence?*

BASIC IDEAS

- Naturalism
- Materialism
- Materialism as a solution to the mind-body problem
- Mechanism
- The "dematerialization" of matter
- The Identity Thesis
- Objections to the Identity Thesis
- Behaviorism
    Soft behaviorism
    Hard behaviorism
- Technology of behavior
- Causality vs. determinism
- Objections to causal determinism
- The question of transcendence

TEST YOURSELF

1. By what simple maneuver does materialism solve the mind-body problem?
2. True or false: Mechanism is compatible with both soft and hard behaviorism.
3. What thinker talks about a "technology of behavior"? What does he mean?
4. To many, complete causal determinism seems to be incompatible with _____ and _____.

5. How did the Roman poet Lucretius figure in the discussion in this chapter?
6. What fault does Taylor find with the Identity Thesis?
7. La Mettrie and Skinner hold in common that (a) human behavior is in theory entirely predictable, (b) moral decisions are not subject to causal determinism, (c) God is behind the mechanisms of nature.
8. True or false: Newton's Laws of Motion aided and abetted the mechanistic view of the world.

QUESTIONS FOR REFLECTION

- Do you recall from Chapter 1 James' distinction between "tender-minded" and "tough-minded" philosophers? Specifically, how does this relate to the thinkers we have considered in our present chapter? Are background, upbringing, education, etc., relevant to the adoption of the materialist perspective? Is this *philosophically* relevant?

- We will have occasion to look again at the problem of determinism (Chapter 16), but consider now: How serious a threat do you really think determinism is to morality and knowledge? How might materialists and/or determinists counter the charge that their position undermines morality and knowledge? And even if it does, so what? And just what does "transcendence" mean in this context, anyway? Is it a philosophically coherent and responsible concept?

- At the beginning of this chapter it was noted that some philosophers opt for a "wider naturalism," according to which both physical and mental reality should be subsumed under a higher nature, or regarded as dimensions of a single reality. Does this strike you as a plausible approach? Does it solve any problems? Does it create any new ones?

THE QUESTION OF KNOWLEDGE

In our introductory note to Part I we said that the question of reality may be in some ways the most basic question. But a similar claim could be made for the question of knowledge.

It is true that our answers to the question of reality will largely determine our answers to many other questions. But we cannot really answer any questions at all, not even the question of reality, until we have become clear on the still prior question of knowledge. Think about this until you see it: Judgments about reality, morality, art, society, religion, politics, science, or anything else, presuppose judgments about knowledge itself—*whether* we can know, *how* we can know, and *what* we can know. Take for example, your knowledge that "In fourteen-hundred-and-ninety-two, Columbus sailed the ocean blue." How did you arrive at this piece of knowledge? In your claim to "know" this there are surely contained already many implicit judgments about epistemological issues such as

- the limits of reason
- the role of sense experience
- the relevance of intuition
- the assurances of historical investigation
- the nature and criterion of truth
- the nature and authority of "facts"
- the possibility of certainty
- degrees of certainty

If such a welter of considerations is necessarily involved in such a harmless claim as "In fourteen-hundred-and-ninety-two, Columbus sailed the ocean blue," then how much more attention must we give the epistemological underpinnings of claims about reality, value, moral responsibility, society, and God.

CHAPTER 8

SKEPTICISM

We may begin with *skepticism*. The word "skepticism" comes from a Greek word which means "to reflect on," "consider," or "examine," so it is not surprising that it is usually associated with *doubting* or *suspending judgment*. A glance at the dictionary shows that, beyond being *doubters*, skeptics come in many varieties. We, however, wish to distinguish just three types or levels of skepticism.

The meaning of "skepticism"

VARIETIES OF SKEPTICISM

If a skeptic is someone who at one time or another has doubts or who suspends judgment about something, then all of us are skeptics. None of us can know everything, and you yourself would surely be skeptical about someone who claimed that he or she did. A dose of *common-sense* skepticism is indeed probably *healthy* for us. For one thing, it is a corrective to gullibility, superstition, and prejudice. All of us should rightfully be skeptical of the claim that a vast herd of giraffes is at this moment roaming the White House, or of certain promises made by politicians running for office. Skepticism is also an antidote to intellectual arrogance and presumption.

Common-sense skepticism

Clearly, skepticism in this form poses no problem—if anything it stimulates and enhances philosophical activity. But with *philosophical* skepticism the plot thickens. By philosophical skepticism we do not mean any particular position or movement in philosophy, but the tendency of some philosophers to deny or doubt the more cherished philosophical claims. What are some of these claims? It depends,

Philosophical skepticism

skep·tic (skep'tik) *n.* **1.** One who doubts, disbelieves, or disagrees with generally accepted conclusions in science, philosophy, etc. **2.** One who by nature doubts or questions what he hears, reads, etc. **3.** One who questions the fundamental doctrines of a religion, especially the Christian religion. **4.** *Sometimes cap.* An adherent of any philosophical school of skepticism. Also spelled *sceptic.* [< F *sceptique* < L *scepticus,* or directly < LGk. *skeptikos* reflective < *skeptesthai* to consider]

     —Syn. *Skeptic, freethinker, atheist, unbeliever,* and *agnostic* denote one who denies or doubts some prevailing religious or philosophical doctrine. *Skeptic* is a general term, and refers to a person who does not feel that the state of human knowledge, or the evidence available, is sufficient to establish the doctrine. A *freethinker* is one who refuses to accept a doctrine, especially a religious doctrine, simply on authority, and demands empiric proof. *Atheist* describes one who denies the existence of God; an *unbeliever* may also lack religious faith, but the word is more often applied to one whose faith is different from that of the speaker. An *agnostic* rejects a doctrine because he believes that human knowledge is, and always will be, incapable of determining its truth or falsity.

Skep·tic (skep'tik) *n.* In ancient Greek philosophy, a member of a school of skepticism, especially that of Pyrrho of Elis. [< SKEPTIC]

skep·ti·cal (skep'ti·kəl) *adj.* **1.** Doubting; questioning; disbelieving. **2.** Of, pertaining to, or characteristic of a skeptic or skepticism. Also spelled *sceptical.* **—skep'ti·cal·ly** *adv.* **—skep'ti·cal·ness** *n.*

skep·ti·cism (skep'tə·siz'əm) *n.* **1.** A doubting or incredulous state of mind; disbelieving attitude. **2.** *Philos.* The doctrine that absolute knowledge is unattainable and that judgments must be continually questioned and doubted in order to attain approximate or relative certainty: opposed to *dogmatism.* Also spelled *scepticism.* **—Syn.** See DOUBT.

of course, on the particular philosopher, but at one time or another it has been denied or doubted that every event must have a cause, that God exists, that there are underlying substances, that the external world is as we perceive it to be, and the like. (It is this sense of skepticism which we saw in the Introduction as typical of the "tough-minded" philosopher: "Seeing is believing!") These issues, of course, are the really big ones in philosophy, and skepticism over such issues immediately marks out the boundaries of philosophical battlefields.

Still more troublesome is what we might call *absolute* skepticism. What is denied or doubted here is the very possibility of knowledge itself. Believe it or not, there have been some thinkers (not many, but some) who have denied that we can know anything at all.

Absolute skepticism

PYRRHO: THE CLASSIC SKEPTIC

Surely the best example of this was Pyrrho of Elis (about 300 B.C.), who founded a school of philosophers who called themselves the *Skeptics*. Pyrrho appealed to the example of Socrates, who, in spite of his insistence on abiding truths, was always *asking questions,* and Plato, who, aside from his belief in the transcendent Forms, believed that our knowledge of the world about us was really only an *approximation* or *opinion*. A more legitimate source of Pyrrho's skepticism was the Sophists with their view that all knowledge is subjective and relative, and therefore that there is no *absolute* or *common* knowledge at all. Recall Protagoras: "A man is the measure of all things." And long before Pyrrho ever came on the scene, the Sophist Gorgias of Leontini (about 525 B.C.) expounded a skepticism about as absolute as could be imagined. His position—or *nonposition*—is expressed in his three theses that (1) nothing exists, (2) if something did exist, we could never know it, and (3) if we could know it, we could never express it.

Pyrrho and his followers taught that nothing whatsoever is certain, and therefore that the wise man will suspend judgment on all matters, or, at best, simply announce, "The matter *appears* to be thus and so." As with Protagoras, the evidence for the Skeptics that nothing whatsoever can be known with certainty amounts to an extended argument from the *relativity* of reason, sense perception, and custom. Just consider how different our thoughts and our sense perceptions can be about the *same things!* Did two people ever see the same rainbow? How does an onion taste? And if disagreements and contradictions rage over ordinary things "out there," like rainbows and onions, how much more do they rage over intellectual and moral perceptions. The differences and contradictions stemming from our time, place, age, condition, perspective, sense faculties, intellectual faculties, social situations, inclinations, desires, purposes—all of these added up, for the Skeptics, gigantic doubt and lead to a suspension of judgment concerning *everything*.

Much of what we know about Pyrrho we know through the ancient philo-

The argument for skepticism

sophical biographer Diogenes Laertius. In the following from Diogenes' *Lives of Eminent Philosophers*, he states the radicalness of Pyrrhonic skepticism and then summarizes the famous *Ten Modes* (or "ways") leading to skepticism.

> *The Skeptics . . . were constantly engaged in overthrowing the dogmas of all schools, but enunciated none themselves; and though they would go so far as to bring forward and expound the dogmas of the others, they themselves laid down nothing definitely, not even the laying down of nothing.*

THE TEN MODES OF DOUBT
I. BASED ON THE VARIETY IN ANIMALS

The first mode relates to the differences between living creatures in respect of those things which give them pleasure or pain, or are useful or harmful to them. By this it is inferred that they do not receive the same impressions from the same things, with the result that such a conflict necessarily leads to suspension of judgment. . . . Some are distinguished in one way, some in another, and for this reason they differ in their senses also, hawks for instance being most keen-sighted, and dogs having a most acute sense of smell. It is natural that if the senses, e.g., eyes, of animals differ, so also will the impressions produced upon them. . . .

II. BASED ON THE DIFFERENCES IN HUMAN BEINGS

The second mode has reference to the natures and idiosyncrasies of men; for instance, Demophon, Alexander's butler, used to get warm in the shade and shiver in the sun. Andron of Argos is reported by Aristotle to have travelled across the waterless deserts of Libya without drinking. Moreover, one man fancies the profession of medicine, another farming, and another commerce; and the same ways of life are injurious to one man but beneficial to another; from which it follows that judgment must be suspended.

III. BASED ON THE DIFFERENT STRUCTURES OF THE ORGANS OF SENSE

The third mode depends on the differences between the sense-channels in different cases, for an apple gives the impression of being pale yellow in color to the sight, sweet in taste and fragrant in smell. An object of the same shape is made to appear different by differences in the mirrors reflecting it. Thus it follows that what appears is no more such and such a thing than something different.

IV. BASED ON THE CIRCUMSTANTIAL CONDITIONS

The fourth mode is that due to differences of condition and to changes in general; for instance, health, illness, sleep, waking, joy, sorrow, youth, old age, courage, fear, want, fullness, hate, love, heat, cold, to say nothing of breathing freely and having the passages obstructed. The impressions received thus appear to vary according to the nature of the conditions. . . .

V. BASED ON THE DISCIPLINES AND CUSTOMS AND LAWS, THE LEGENDARY BELIEFS AND THE DOGMATIC CONVICTIONS

The fifth mode is derived from customs, laws, belief in myths, compacts between nations and dogmatic assumptions. This class includes considerations with regard to things beautiful and ugly, true and false, good and bad, with regard to the gods, and with regard to the coming into being and the passing away of the world of phenomena. Obviously the same thing is regarded by some as just and by others as unjust, or as good by some and bad by others. . . . Different people believe in different gods; some in providence, others not. In burying their dead, the Egyptians embalm them; the Romans burn them; the Pæonians throw them into lakes. As to what is true, then, let suspension of judgment be our practice.

VI. BASED ON INTERMIXTURES

The sixth mode relates to mixtures and participations, by virtue of which nothing appears pure in and by itself, but only in combination with air, light, moisture, solidity, heat, cold, movement, exhalations and other forces. For purple shows different tints in sunlight, moonlight, and lamplight; and our own complexion does not appear the same at noon and when the sun is low. Again, a rock which in air takes two men to lift is easily moved about in water, either because, being in reality heavy, it is lifted by the water or because, being light, it is made heavy by the air. Of its own inherent property we know nothing, any more than of the constituent oils in an ointment.

VII. BASED ON POSITIONS AND INTERVALS AND LOCATIONS

The seventh mode has reference to distances, positions, places and the occupants of the places. In this mode things which are thought to be large appear small, square things round; flat things appear to have projections, straight things to be bent, and colorless colored. So the sun, on account of its distance, appears small, mountains when far away appear misty and smooth, but when near at hand rugged. Furthermore, the sun at its rising has a certain appearance, but has a dissimilar appearance when in mid-heaven, and the same body one appearance in a wood and another in open country. The image again varies according to the position of the object, and a dove's neck according to the way it is turned. Since, then, it is not possible to observe these things apart from places and positions, their real nature is unknowable.

VIII. BASED ON THE QUANTITIES AND FORMATIONS OF THE UNDERLYING OBJECTS

The eighth mode is concerned with quantities and qualities of things, say heat or cold, swiftness or slowness, colorlessness or variety of colors. Thus wine taken in mod-

eration strengthens the body, but too much of it is weakening; and so with food and other things.

IX. BASED ON THE FREQUENCY OR RARITY OF OCCURRENCE

The ninth mode has to do with perpetuity, strangeness, or rarity. Thus earthquakes are no surprise to those among whom they constantly take place; nor is the sun, for it is seen every day.

X. BASED ON THE FACT OF RELATIVITY

The tenth mode rests on inter-relation, e.g., between light and heavy, strong and weak, greater and less, up and down. Thus that which is on the right is not so by nature, but is so understood in virtue of its position with respect to something else; for, if that change its position, the thing is no longer on the right. Similarly father and brother are relative terms, day is relative to the sun, and all things relative to our mind. Thus relative terms are in and by themselves unknowable. These, then, are the ten modes of perplexity.[1]

IS ABSOLUTE SKEPTICISM A COHERENT POSITION?

Actually, there have been relatively few absolute skeptics. It is not hard to see why. Critics of this position have been quick to charge that it is impractical and impossible. It is *impractical* because, from the purely practical standpoint of getting along in the world, no one in his or her right mind can actually live on such a premise. Our daily lives are pervaded by what we take to be (whether they actually are or not) assurances, certainties, and in a word, all kinds of *knowledge.* Why, for that matter, are you reading this book, studying philosophy, or studying *anything,* if not because you think that something can be learned, understood, *known?* And where, on the skeptical view, is there any place for responsible actions or serious commitments and decisions?

Is absolute skepticism impractical?

More specifically, according to the critics, all absolute skeptics founder sooner or later on the utter *impossibility* of their position. It is impossible for several reasons. First, must not even the staunchest skeptic admit that *some* things at least are certain? For example, that $2 + 2 = 4$, and that whether or not our senses deceive us about the actual world, we are at least certain of the *impressions?* Second, does not the very assertion that we cannot know anything actually necessitate that we do know some things? For example, that we, who claim to know nothing, exist, and that the Law of Non-Contradiction, without which nothing—not even the skeptic's claim—can be asserted at all, is certain?

Is absolute skepticism even possible?

[1]Diogenes Laertius, *Lives of Eminent Philosophers,* IX, 74, 79–88, tr. R. D. Hicks (Cambridge, Mass.: Harvard University Press, 1925), II. I have supplied the headings from the longer account of Sextus Empiricus.

THE SALE OF A SKEPTIC

In his *Sale of the Philosophers* (about A.D. 175) Lucian pokes fun at some Greek philosophers under the guise of having them put up for sale at an auction. In the following (and concluding) passage,[1] the Skeptic Pyrrho is clearly represented by Pyrrhias ("Coppernob").

Zeus: Who's left?

Hermes: This Skeptic here. Hey, Coppernob! Come here and be auctioned! Hurry up! Not many to sell you to; most of them are drifting off now. Still—any bids for this one?

Buyer: Yes, me. But tell me first, what do you know?

Pyrrhias: Nothing.

Buyer: How do mean, nothing?

Pyrrhias: I don't think there *is* anything at all.

Buyer: Aren't *we* something?

Pyrrhias: I'm not even sure of that.

Buyer: Nor even that you're somebody?

Pyrrhias: I'm much more doubtful still about that.

Buyer: What a state to be in! Well, what's the idea of these scales?

Pyrrhias: I weigh arguments in them. I balance them till they're equal, and when I see they're exactly alike and exactly the same weight, then—ah, then!—I don't know which is the sounder.

Buyer: What are you good at apart from that?

Pyrrhias: Everything except catching a runaway slave.

Buyer: And why can't you do that?

Pyrrhias: My good man, I can't apprehend anything.[2]

Buyer: I don't suppose you can. You seem slow and stupid. Well, what's the end of your knowledge?

Pyrrhias: Ignorance, deafness, and blindness.

Buyer: You'll be unable to see or hear, you say?

Pyrrhias: And unable to judge or feel either. No better than a worm, in fact.

Buyer: I must buy you for that. How much shall we say for him?

Hermes: One Attic mina.

Buyer: There you are. Well now, you—I've bought you, eh?

Pyrrhias: I'm not sure.

Buyer: Nonsense! I *have* bought you, and I've paid my money.

Pyrrhias: I defer judgment; I'm considering the matter.

Buyer: Look, you come with me—you're my slave.

Pyrrhias: Who can tell whether what you say is true?

Buyer: The auctioneer can. My mina can. These people here can.

Pyrrhias: Is there anybody here?

Buyer: I'm going to put you on the treadmill, then. I'll show you I'm boss—the hard way!

Pyrrhias: Suspend decision on it.

Buyer: Oh, ye gods! Look, I've already told you my decision.

Hermes: Stop dillydallying, you, and go with him—he's bought you. Gentlemen, we invite you to come tomorrow; we'll be putting up ordinary people, workmen and tradesmen.

[1]Lucian, *Sale of the Philosophers,* in *Selected Works,* tr. Bryan P. Reardon (Indianapolis: Bobbs-Merrill, 1965), pp. 109–111.

[2]In Greek this involves a pun on the word *katalambano,* which means both "to seize" and "to understand."

THE GREEK SKEPTICS

"The Greek Skeptics are known to us only in fragments of their writings, particularly in references of them by their opponents. Pyrrho, the reputed founder of the school, composed no writings, perhaps esteeming silence the becoming attitude for a Skeptic. Yet Aenesidemus, nearly four hundred years later, wrote 'eight books' in summary of Pyrrho's alleged teachings. Pyrrho is a peg on which Skeptics generally hang their witty sayings, so that the word Pyrrhonism has come to be used almost interchangeably with excessive Skepticism."

Sterling P. Lamprecht, *Our Philosophical Traditions* (NEW YORK: APPLETON-CENTURY-CROFTS, 1955), pp. 92–93.

Finally, and still more decisive, is the charge that the absolute skeptics' assertion that they know nothing is strictly self-contradictory or *self-refuting*. For they maintain, *with the greatest assurance,* that we cannot maintain anything. Otherwise stated: If we cannot know anything, then how do we know *that*? Stated again: If absolute skepticism is *true*, then it must be *false!*

Pyrrho himself anticipated the similar criticism that his position implied its own falsehood. He retorted (as some skeptical-type readers will be tempted to retort) that he was not, in fact, even certain that he was not certain of anything. But, of course, that kind of talk could go on forever:

> An infinite regress of ignorance?

We cannot know anything.

We cannot know that we cannot know anything.

We cannot know that we cannot know that we cannot know anything.

$$\vdots$$

Is it not necessary that there be at some point a *basis* for one's claims? Did not Aristotle teach us a long time ago that an infinite regress of claims nullifies all of them?

One of the best-known refutations of skepticism comes from St. Augustine in the medieval period. He directs himself to the "Academicians," a school of skep-

---

SELF-REFUTING PROPOSITIONS

Propositions make claims, of course, about many things. When, however, a proposition is itself one of the things it makes a claim about, it sometimes turns out to be *self-refuting*. This means that if the proposition is taken seriously, then it backfires on itself—if it's true it must be false!

A well-known example of a self-refuting proposition is: "All generalizations are false." If all generalizations are false, then the claim itself, which is a generalization, must be false. Especially puzzling is the proposition

> *The sentence in this box is false.*

If it's false, then it must be true; if it's true, it must be false! Is the claim of the absolute skeptic, "We can be certain of absolutely nothing," another example of a self-refuting proposition?

"KNOWING" IS NOT A SIMPLE MATTER (I)

When you claim to "know" something is it perfectly clear what you are claiming? Actually, "to know" can mean many different things, and, consequently, there are many different types of knowledge.

Knowing or knowledge falls at least into three broad categories. (1) Knowledge as personal acquaintance, as in the statement "I know Howard"; (2) knowledge as mastery of

Knowledge

| Knowledge as personal acquaintance | Knowledge as mastery of data | Knowledge as truth-claims |

information or data, as in "I know German"; and (3) knowledge as involved in the claim that something or other is true (truth-claims), as in "I know that in fourteen-hundred-and-ninety-two Columbus sailed the ocean blue."

Epistemology, or the theory of knowledge, is concerned by and large (though not exclusively) with problems posed by knowledge as truth-claims. See "Knowing Is Not a Simple Matter (II)."

---

ticism in Augustine's day led by Carneades. Against these skeptics, Augustine argues for the certitude of logical truths, mathematical truths, the reality of the world, and one's own immediate perceptions. Can you identify such counterattacks in the following extract from Augustine's *Against the Academicians*?

You say that nothing can be apprehended in philosophy and, in order to spread your opinion far and wide, you make use of the disputes and contentions of philosophers and you think that these dissensions furnish arms for you against them. . . . I hold as certain either that there is or is not one world; and if there is not one, there are either a finite or an infinite number of worlds. Carneades would teach that that opinion resembles what is false. I likewise know that this world of ours has been so arranged either because of the nature of bodies or by some providence, and that it either always was and will be or that it began to exist and will by no means cease existing, or that it does not have its origin in time but will have an end, or that it has started to remain

in existence and will remain but not forever, and I know innumerable physical phenomena of this type. For those disjunctions are true nor can anyone confuse them with
any likeness to what is false. But take something for granted, says the Academician.
I do not wish to do so; for that is to say: abandon what you know; say what you do
not know. But opinion is uncertain. Assuredly it is better that it be uncertain than
that it be destroyed; it surely is clear; it certainly now can be called false or true. I
say that I know this opinion. Prove to me that I do not know them, you who do not
deny that such matters pertain to philosophy and who maintain that none of these
things can be known; say that those disjunctive ideas are either false or have something in common with what is false from which they cannot altogether be
distinguished.

Whence, he says, do you know that this world exists if the senses are untrustworthy? Your methods of reasoning have never been able to disprove the power of the
senses in such a way as to convince us that nothing is seen and you certainly have
never dared to try such a thing, but you have exerted yourself to persuade us urgently
that (a thing) can be otherwise than it seems. And so I call this entire thing, whatever
it is, which surrounds us and nourishes us, this object, I say, which appears before
my eyes and which I perceive is made up of earth and sky, or what appears to be
earth and sky, the world. If you say nothing is seen by me, I shall never err. For he
is in error who rashly proves what seems to him. For you say that what is false can
be seen by those perceiving it; you do not say that nothing is seen. Certainly every
reason for arguing will be removed when it pleases you to settle the point, if we not
only know nothing but if nothing is even seen by us. If, however, you deny that this
object which appears to me is the world, you are making it a controversy in regard
to a name since I said that I called it the world.

If you are asleep, you will say, is that also the world, which you see? I have
already said I call that the world, which appears to me to be such. But if it pleases
me to call only that the world, which is seen by those who are awake or even by those
who are rational, prove this if you can, that those who are asleep and are raving are
not raving and sleeping in the world. Therefore I say this: that entire mass of bodies
and that contrivance in which we exist whether sleeping, or raging, or awake, or
rational, either is one or is not one. Explain how that opinion can be false. For if I
am asleep, it can follow that I said nothing; or even if the words have escaped from
the mouth of a person who is asleep, as often happens, it can follow that I did not
speak here, nor while sitting in this way, nor to those who were listening; but it cannot
follow that this is false. Nor do I say that I apprehended this because I am awake.
For you can say that this could appear to me even if I were asleep and therefore this
can bear a close resemblance to what is false. But if there are one and six worlds, it
is evident to me, no matter in what condition I may be, that there are seven worlds,
and I am not rash in asserting that I know it. Therefore, show me either that this
logical conclusion or those disjunctions mentioned above in regard to sleep or madness
or unreliability of the senses can be false, and I shall grant that I have been defeated
if I remember them when I have been awakened. For I believe it is sufficiently evident

that those things which appear false through sleep and an abnormal condition of the mind are those things which have reference to the senses of the body; for that three threes are nine and represent the square of intelligible numbers is necessary or would be true even though the human race were lying prostrate. And yet I also see that many things can be said in favor of the senses themselves, which we have not found refuted by the Academicians. For I think that the senses are not to be blamed because they permit false and frenzied mental images or because in sleep we see things which are not true. If indeed the senses have reported the truth to those who are awake and who are rational, what the mind of a sleeping or insane person may fabricate for itself is not to be attributed to them.

It now remains for us to inquire whether the senses report the truth when they give information. Suppose that some Epicurean should say: "I have no complaint to make in regard to the senses; for it is unjust to demand more of them than they can give; moreover whatever the eyes can see they see in a reliable manner." Then is what they see in regard to an oar in the water true? It certainly is true. For when the reason is added for its appearing thus, if the oar dipped in the water seemed straight, I should rather blame my eyes for the false report. For they did not see what should have been seen when such causes arose. What need is there of many illustrations? This can also be said of the movement of towers, of the feathers of birds, of innumerable other things. "And yet I am deceived if I give my assent," someone says. Do not give assent any further than to the extent that you can persuade yourself that it appears true to you, and there is no deception. For I do not see how the Academician can refute him who says: "I know that this appears white to me, I know that my hearing is delighted with this, I know that this has an agreeable odor, I know that this tastes sweet to me, I know that this feels cold to me." Tell us rather whether the leaves of the wild olive trees, which the goat so persistently desires, are by their very nature bitter. O foolish man! Is not the goat more reasonable? I do not know how they seem to the goat, but they are bitter to me. What more do you ask for? But perhaps there is also some one to whom they do not taste bitter. Do you trouble yourself about this? Did I say they were bitter to everyone? I said they were bitter to me and I do not always maintain this. For what if for some reason or other a thing which now tastes sweet to a person should at another time seem bitter to him? I say this that, when a person tastes something, he can honestly swear that he knows it is sweet to his palate or the contrary, and that no trickery of the Greeks can dispossess him of that knowledge. For who would be so bold as to say to me when I am longing for something with great pleasure: Perhaps you do not taste it, but this is only a dream? Do I offer any opposition to him? But still that would give me pleasure even in my sleep. Therefore no likeness to what is false obscures that which I have said I know, and both the Epicurean and the Cyrenaics may say many other things in favor of the senses against which I have heard that the Academicians have not said anything. But why should this concern me? If they so desire and if they can, let them even do away with the argument with my approbation. Whatever argument they raise against the senses has no weight against all philosophers. For there are those who admit that whatever the *mind receives through a sense of the body, can beget opinion, but they deny (that it can beget) knowledge which, however, they wish to be confined to the intellect and to live in the mind, far removed from the senses. And perhaps that wise man whom we are seeking is in their number.*[2]

Thus, at least, it has seemed to most philosophers: Whatever we may think of other forms of skepticism, absolute skepticism, or the denial of the very possibility of knowledge itself, must be rejected at the start. If so, the question becomes not *whether* we can know, but *what, how,* and *how much* we can know.

Chapter 8 in Review

Skepticism means a doubting or incredulous state of mind. It comes in many levels of intensity, and all of us are skeptical about something or other at one time or another. A dash of skepticism is surely healthy inasmuch as it serves as an antidote to gullibility. As with gullibility, however, overdoses of skepticism can be detrimental to one's philosophical health.

It is useful to distinguish between common-sense skepticism, philosophical skepticism, and absolute skepticism. The latter, which denies that we can know anything whatsoever, was exemplified in the ancient Pyrrho and his school. The arguments for skepticism are usually based on the relativity (or differences of opinion) in reason, sense perception, and custom. Amidst such disagreements, what can one do but suspend judgment and abandon all hope of knowledge?

Not so fast, say those who charge that at least absolute skepticism is both impractical and impossible. It is impractical, they say, because no one can live a coherent life except on the assumption that some things can be *known.* It is impossible not only because we surely have certainty about such things as our own existence and impressions, but also because the absolute skeptics affirm with *complete conviction* their thesis that *nothing can be known* and are therefore hopelessly self-contradictory. Similar reasoning is employed by St. Augustine, whose attack on skepticism is perhaps one of the best-known.

SUMMARY

- The meaning of "skepticism"
- Three kinds of skepticism
    - Common-sense skepticism
    - Philosophical skepticism
    - Absolute skepticism
- Pyrrho as an example of absolute skepticism

BASIC IDEAS

[2]St. Augustine, *Against the Academicians,* III, 23–26, tr. Sister Mary Patricia Garvey (Milwaukee, Wis.: Marquette University Press, 1957).

- Historical sources of Pyrrhonic skepticism
- The main argument for skepticism
- Pyrrho's *Ten Modes*
- Arguments against absolute skepticism
   Absolute skepticism as impractical
   Absolute skepticism as impossible
- Self-refuting propositions
- Augustine's refutations of skepticism

TEST YOURSELF

1. Why is a certain amount of ordinary skepticism a healthy sign?
2. The main argument for skepticism rests upon *relativity*. What does this mean? Give some examples from the *Ten Modes*.
3. True or false: Aristotle was a skeptic.
4. One philosopher who argued, against the Skeptics, that it is certain that the world either exists or does not exist was _____.
5. Why do some claim that absolute skepticism is self-refuting?

QUESTIONS FOR REFLECTION

- St. Augustine has been quoted here as a great opponent of skepticism. In another work, entitled *On the Advantages of Believing,* he argues that no practical or intellectual progress can be expected from one who is unwilling ever to accept certain claims on the authority of others. What do you think of this position? What might be said for it and against it?

- How do *you* come out on the question of skepticism? If you are persuaded by the arguments *against* skepticism, then what is the relevance, for epistemology, of the relativity of reason, perception, and custom? (You might recall the discussion at the end of Chapter 1 on living and dead options.)

CHAPTER 9

THE WAY OF REASON

Where does knowledge come from? What is the basis of knowledge? The question of the origin of knowledge is one of the most important questions of philosophy. In fact, it is a *crucial* question. As we have said already in the introduction to Part II, how you answer this question will have everything to do with the rest of your philosophy.

A crucial question: What is the basis of knowledge?

TWO MAIN THEORIES ABOUT THE BASIS OF KNOWLEDGE

Throughout the history of philosophy, thinkers have generally answered this question in two ways. On the one side, we have those philosophers who, in one way or another and in varying degrees, have emphasized *reason* as the source of knowledge. On the other side, we have those philosophers who, in one way or another and in varying degrees, have emphasized *experience* as the source of knowledge. The position stressing the role of the intellect or reason is called *rationalism,* and those holding to this position are called *rationalists* (from the Latin word *ratio,* "reason"). The position stressing the role of experience is called *empiricism,* and those holding this view are called *empiricists* (from the Greek *empeiria,* "experience").

Empiricism and rationalism

A special note is in order regarding the labels "rationalism" and "rationalist." This is because these terms, like so many other important terms, bear more than one meaning. Here again we must distinguish between a loose and a stricter sense of these terms. We have already encountered the loose sense of "rationalism" in the Introduction. There we said that rationalism is a dominating interest in reasoning,

Two meanings of "rationalism"

185

reflecting, criticizing, examining, and so on. This is what we meant when we defined philosophy as the attempt to provide, within limits, an essentially *rational* interpretation of reality as a whole, and when we characterized all philosophers as *rationalists*. Now, however, in the stricter or more technical sense of the word, rationalism is an *epistemological theory*, specifically a *theory about the basis of knowledge*. Note,

---

"KNOWING" IS NOT A SIMPLE MATTER (II)

Epistemology is concerned primarily with the kind of knowledge involved in truth-claims, that is, when the truth or falsity of something is asserted.

But truth-claims come in many colors, and, therefore, so does this kind of knowledge. Consider, for example, the following claims. In each of them something is claimed to be "known," but the "knowing" in each is quite different from all the others.

- I know that in fourteen-hundred-and-ninety-two Columbus sailed the ocean blue.
- I know that I exist.
- I know that God exists.
- I know that all swans are white.
- I know that this table exists.
- I know that my Redeemer liveth.
- I know that every event must have a cause.
- I know that you are suffering.
- I know that all barking dogs bark.
- I know that it will rain tomorrow.

Obviously, the kind of knowledge involved in a straightforward historical claim like "I know that in fourteen-hundred-and-ninety-two Columbus sailed the ocean blue" is quite different from the kind of knowledge delivered through an introspective intuition, as in "I know that I exist." And both of these are quite different from the knowledge involved in the religious assertion, "I know that my Redeemer liveth." And so on.

To see that these claims really involve quite different meanings of "know," just ask yourself in each case *how* that particular thing would be known—what sorts of considerations should be brought to bear, etc.

then, that while a rationalist in the strict sense is necessarily a rationalist in the loose sense, it is not necessarily the case that a rationalist in the loose sense will be a rationalist in the strict sense—he or she may, rather, be an *empiricist*. As a term designating a theory about the basis of knowledge, rationalism is on a par with empiricism. Both empiricism and rationalism (in this technical sense) answer the question, "What is the basis of knowledge?", though in radically different ways.

REASON AS THE BASIS OF KNOWLEDGE

We will begin with rationalism. Above we said that rationalism emphasizes reason as the source of knowledge. This may now be refined somewhat: Rationalism is the belief that at least some knowledge about reality can be acquired through reason, independently of sense experience.

Rationalism: A more accurate definition

It is important here to stress, first, that the rationalist believes that *some* knowledge about reality can be acquired through reason alone. Few rationalists have ever insisted that sense experience plays absolutely no role whatsoever in the acquisition of knowledge. We will say more about this later, but for the moment just consider: Even if you are a strict rationalist, how do you know that swans are white? that in fourteen-hundred-and-ninety-two, Columbus sailed the ocean blue? Obviously there is much about the world that we could not possibly know apart from making observations, lighting bunsen burners, taking field trips, and so on. The staunchest rationalists admit this. What they insist on is that at least *some* of the truths about reality (and usually the most important truths about reality) are known apart from sense experience.

Rationalism: Knowledge about reality . . .

Second, we must stress that for rationalists reason is the source of at least some of our knowledge about *reality*. We do have, after all, knowledge which is *not* about reality. For example, we know that all barking dogs bark, that a triangle has three sides, and in short, any statement of the form "A is A." Such statements, as we will emphasize later, are absolutely and universally and necessarily true. But that is because they are true by definition. As such they have no bearing on reality, they neither affirm nor deny the existence of anything, they must be true *no matter what*. Everyone agrees that such truths are known independently of sense experience; all you have to do is look at the proposition to see that it must be true. The rationalist, though, claims that at least some propositions which *are* about reality—which affirm or deny the existence of something—may be known independently of sense experience, through reason alone.

. . . through reason

Do you yourself possess any universal and certain knowledge about reality? Think of some possible examples:

- Every event must have a cause.
- It is morally wrong to kill people for the fun of it.
- All individuals are endowed with basic rights.

Can you derive such universal and certain knowledge from the limited, fluctuating, and relative evidence of sense experience? Where, then, does such knowledge come from?

As two classic examples of rationalism we may mention Plato and Descartes. We have, of course, already dealt with the *metaphysical* doctrines of these thinkers in Part I, where we discussed Plato's theory of the Forms and Descartes' mind-matter dualism. But now we consider the *epistemological* side of their philosophies.

RATIONALISM (THE STRICT SENSE)

The view that knowledge of reality can be acquired through reason, independently of sense experience.

THE RATIONALISM OF PLATO

Along with many other Greek philosophers, Plato believed that the *reason*, which distinguishes humans from the lower animals, comprises the essential nature of the human being. (The classical definition of man as "a rational animal" comes from these Greek philosophers.) Human good and happiness, therefore, lie in the activity and fulfillment of the rational faculty. That is, they lie in contemplation and *knowledge*. On the other hand, it will be recalled from our earlier discussion that Plato believed that the only proper object of knowledge, or the only thing that can *really* be known, is *Being*. This means that we can have no real knowledge of the world about us, the relative and fluctuating world of *Becoming*. Of this world we have only opinion, not knowledge.

Now, Plato has Socrates announce in the *Phaedo* that not only do real philosophers have no fear of death, but they actually desire and look forward to it. In fact, real philosophers view their lives as lifelong preparations for death. Why? Because as long as we are in *this* world we are held back from the attainment of real knowledge and therefore happiness. And why is this? For one thing, our bodies are a constant distraction from the higher pursuit of knowledge. The pursuit of knowledge does, after all, require some time and attention, but it seems that most of our time is taken up by the body: We must feed it, clothe it, cleanse it, and pay all sorts of attention to it. For another, and this is more important for the present point, as long as our souls are imprisoned in our bodies they have a natural tendency (if not necessity) to peer out, as it were, through the only windows of the prison, the five senses. As a result, our souls become contaminated by the distortions, illusions, and relativities of the sensible world.

Why philosophers desire death

Plato himself represents the twofold problem posed by the body as follows:

Now take the acquisition of knowledge. Is the body a hindrance or not, if one takes it into partnership to share an investigation? What I mean is this. Is there any certainty in human sight and hearing, or is it true, as the poets are always dinning into our ears, that we neither hear nor see anything accurately? Yet if these senses are not clear and accurate, the rest can hardly be so, because they are all inferior to the first two. Don't you agree?

Certainly.

Then when is it that the soul attains to truth? When it tries to investigate anything with the help of the body, it is obviously led astray.

Quite so.

Is it not in the course of reflection, if at all, that the soul gets a clear view of facts?

Yes.

Surely the soul can best reflect when it is free of all distractions such as hearing or sight or pain or pleasure of any kind—that is, when it ignores the body and becomes as far as possible independent, avoiding all physical contacts and associations as much as it can, in its search for reality.

That is so.

Then here too—in despising the body and avoiding it, and endeavoring to become independent—the philosopher's soul is ahead of all the rest.

It seems so.

Here are some more questions, Simmias. Do we recognize such a thing as absolute uprightness?

Indeed we do.

And absolute beauty and goodness too?

Of course.

Have you ever seen any of these things with your eyes?

Certainly not, said he.

Well, have you ever apprehended them with any other bodily sense? By "them" I mean not only absolute tallness or health or strength, but the real nature of any given thing—what it actually is. Is it through the body that we get the truest perception of them? Isn't it true that in any inquiry you are likely to attain more nearly to knowledge of your object in proportion to the care and accuracy with which you have prepared yourself to understand that object in itself?

Certainly.

Don't you think that the person who is likely to succeed in this attempt most perfectly is the one who approaches each object, as far as possible, with the unaided intellect, without taking account of any sense of sight in his thinking, or dragging any other sense into his reckoning—the man who pursues the truth by applying his pure and unadulterated thought to the pure and unadulterated object, cutting himself off as much as possible from his eyes and ears and virtually all the rest of his body, as an impediment which by its presence prevents the soul from attaining to truth and clear thinking? Is not this the person, Simmias, who will reach the goal of reality, if anybody can?

What you say is absolutely true, Socrates, said Simmias.

All these considerations, said Socrates, must surely prompt serious philosophers to review the position in some such way as this. It looks as though this were a bypath leading to the right track. So long as we keep to the body and our soul is contaminated with this imperfection, there is no chance of our ever attaining satisfactorily to our object, which we assert to be truth. In the first place, the body provides us with innumerable distractions in the pursuit of our necessary sustenance, and any diseases which attack us hinder our quest for reality. Besides, the body fills us with loves and desires and fears and all sorts of fancies and a great deal of nonsense, with the result that we literally never get an opportunity to think at all about anything. Wars and revolutions and battles are due simply and solely to the body and its desires. All wars are undertaken for the acquisition of wealth, and the reason why we have to acquire wealth is the body, because we are slaves in its service. That is why, on all these accounts, we have so little time for philosophy. Worst of all, if we do obtain any leisure from the body's claims and turn to some line of inquiry, the body intrudes once more into our investigations, interrupting, disturbing, distracting, and preventing us from getting a glimpse of the truth. We are in fact convinced that if we are ever to have pure knowledge of anything, we must get rid of the body and contemplate things by themselves with the soul by itself.[1]

O happy day, then, when the soul will finally be set free from the body by death! Only then will it come into the uninterrupted enjoyment of absolute knowledge of that other world, the world of truth and reality. In the meantime, we must minimize as much as possible the contaminations of the senses.

It seems, to judge from the argument, that the wisdom which we desire and upon which we profess to have set our hearts will be attainable only when we are dead, and not in our lifetime. If no pure knowledge is possible in the company of the body, then either it is totally impossible to acquire knowledge, or it is only possible after death, because it is only then that the soul will be separate and independent of the body. It seems that so long as we are alive, we shall continue closest to knowledge if we avoid as much as we can all contact and association with the body, except when they are absolutely necessary, and instead of allowing ourselves to become infected with its nature, purify ourselves from it until God himself gives us deliverance. In this way, by keeping ourselves uncontaminated by the follies of the body, we shall probably reach the company of others like ourselves and gain direct knowledge of all that is pure and uncontaminated—that is, presumably, of truth. For one who is not pure himself to attain to the realm of purity would no doubt be a breach of universal justice.[2]

---

[1]Plato, *Phaedo*, 65A–66E, tr. Hugh Tredennick, in *Plato: The Collected Dialogues*, ed. Edith Hamilton and Huntington Cairns (New York: Pantheon Books, 1961).
[2]Ibid., 66E–67B.

Here then is a clearly rationalist view of knowledge. Sense experience is disdained as a hindrance to real knowledge. And true reality, by its very nature as transcendent and nonsensible, can be grasped adequately by the intellect alone.

But Plato's rationalism becomes clear in yet another way. Even in this world, knowledge—insofar as it *is* knowledge—is only possible because it is *innate*, that is, inborn. The theory of innate ideas is a popular one among rationalists. Of course in none of its forms does it mean that the infant child is born into the world with its mind burgeoning with Einstein's theory of relativity. It usually means that fundamental ideas or principles are built right into the mind itself and require only to be developed and brought to maturity.

The theory of innate ideas

Plato himself sought to prove the immortality of the soul, or, more accurately, the *preexistence* of the soul, on the grounds that we have in our minds certain ideas that we could not possibly have derived from sense experience alone. Such an idea is that of equality. Where, Plato asks, did we acquire this and similar ideas? Certainly not from the sensible world around us, for there is no instance of absolute equality to be found anywhere in this world. Of course the sensible world is full of things which are *more or less* equal, but you will search this world over, or any other world in space and time, and never come across an instance of *absolute* equality. We are back in the world of Heraclitus where everything flows, and Plato's

Knowledge as recollection

world of Becoming which is populated by imperfect copies or mere approximations to the true Realities, the eternal Forms.

Plato concludes that the only way to account for this knowledge is to believe that prior to its embodiment in this world, the soul was in the presence of the Forms, where it acquired knowledge of the realities, including knowledge of Equality. This knowledge was lost or forgotten through the trauma of birth, though to some degree "recollected" subsequent to birth on the occasion of our experiences with more-or-less-equality, that is, Equality as it is encountered imperfectly in the sensible world. It is important to note that Plato's theory of knowledge as recollection, although it certainly emphasizes the innateness of our fundamental ideas, also accords some role to sense experience after all. At least in this life, no knowledge could be enjoyed at all were it not for the initial stimulation of the senses.

The role of sense experience for knowledge in this life

As a possible theory of innate knowledge, you might find Plato's doctrine of recollection a bit silly. On the other hand, one should always be cautious in judging as silly the ideas of those who have exerted enormous influence on the way we ourselves think today. Plato's theory is both historically and philosophically interesting, and his own statement of it is worthy of close attention:

We admit, I suppose, that there is such a thing as equality—not the equality of stick to stick and stone to stone, and so on, but something beyond all that and distinct from it—absolute equality. Are we to admit this or not?

Yes indeed, said Simmias, most emphatically.

And do we know what it is?

Certainly.

Where did we get our knowledge? Was it not from the particular examples that we mentioned just now? Was it not from seeing equal sticks or stones or other equal objects that we got the notion of equality, although it is something quite distinct from them? Look at it in this way. Is it not true that equal stones and sticks sometimes, without changing in themselves, appear equal to one person and unequal to another?

Certainly.

Well, now, have you ever thought that things which were absolutely equal were unequal, or that equality was inequality?

No, never, Socrates.

Then these equal things are not the same as absolute equality.

Not in the least, as I see it, Socrates.

And yet it is these equal things that have suggested and conveyed to you your knowledge of absolute equality, although they are distinct from it?

Perfectly true.

Whether it is similar to them or dissimilar?

Certainly.

It makes no difference, said Socrates. So long as the sight of one thing suggests another to you, it must be a cause of recollection, whether the two things are alike or not.

Quite so.

Well, now, he said, what do we find in the case of the equal sticks and other things of which we were speaking just now? Do they seem to us to be equal in the sense of absolute equality, or do they fall short of it in so far as they only approximate to equality? Or don't they fall short at all?

They do, said Simmias, a long way.

Suppose that when you see something you say to yourself, This thing which I can see has a tendency to be like something else, but it falls short and cannot be really like it, only a poor imitation. Don't you agree with me that anyone who receives that impression must in fact have previous knowledge of that thing which he says that the other resembles, but inadequately?

Certainly he must.

Very well, then, is that our position with regard to equal things and absolute equality?

Exactly.

Then we must have had some previous knowledge of equality before the time when we first saw equal things and realized that they were striving after equality, but fell short of it.

That is so.

And at the same time we are agreed also upon this point, that we have not and could not have acquired this notion of equality except by sight or touch or one of the other senses. I am treating them as being all the same.

They are the same, Socrates, for the purpose of our argument.

So it must be through the senses that we obtained the notion that all sensible equals are striving after absolute equality but falling short of it. Is that correct?

Yes, it is.

So before we began to see and hear and use our other senses we must somewhere have acquired the knowledge that there is such a thing as absolute equality. Otherwise we could never have realized, by using it as a standard for comparison, that all equal objects of sense are desirous of being like it, but are only imperfect copies.

That is the logical conclusion, Socrates.

Did we not begin to see and hear and possess our other senses from the moment of birth?

Certainly.

But we admitted that we must have obtained our knowledge of equality before we obtained them.

Yes.

So we must have obtained it before birth.

So it seems.

Then if we obtained it before our birth, and possessed it when we were born, we had knowledge, both before and at the moment of birth, not only of equality and relative magnitudes, but of all absolute standards. Our present argument applies no more to equality than it does to absolute beauty, goodness, uprightness, holiness, and, as I maintain, all those characteristics which we designate in our discussions by the term "absolute." So we must have obtained knowledge of all these characteristics before our birth.

That is so.

And unless we invariably forget it after obtaining it we must always be born knowing and continue to know all through our lives, because "to know" means simply to retain the knowledge which one has acquired, and not to lose it. Is not what we call "forgetting" simply the loss of knowledge, Simmias?

Most certainly, Socrates.

And if it is true that we acquired our knowledge before our birth, and lost it at the moment of birth, but afterward, by the exercise of our senses upon sensible objects, recover the knowledge which we had once before, I suppose that what we call learning will be the recovery of our knowledge, and surely we should be right in calling this recollection.[3]

THE RATIONALISM OF DESCARTES

Another classic example of a rationalist philosopher is Descartes. As with Plato, we have already considered Descartes' theory of reality and thus have already been introduced to at least something of his theory of knowledge.

The model of mathematics

It will be recalled that Descartes was repelled by the contradictions he discovered among philosophers, but was attracted by the certainties he discovered in mathematics:

Most of all was I delighted with Mathematics because of the certainty of its demonstrations and the evidence of its reasoning; but I did not yet understand its true use,

---

INNATE IDEAS

Rationalists, who believe that we can have existential knowledge (knowledge of the actual existence or nonexistence of things) apart from sense experience, are surely obligated to account for this knowledge. One way is through a doctrine of *innate ideas.* "Innate" means "inborn," thus theories of innate ideas are theories which teach that the mind in some way possesses at least fundamental ideas or intellectual structures from birth. The mind at birth is not a "blank tablet."

---

[3]Ibid., 74A–75D.

and, believing that it was of service only in the mechanical arts, I was astonished that, seeing how firm and solid was its basis, no loftier edifice had been reared thereupon.[4]

This preoccupation with mathematics immediately betrays Descartes' rationalist bent. For the reason why the truths of mathematics and the proofs of geometry are certain is that they are untainted by the tentativeness and fluctuations and relativities and illusions of sense experience. They are certain—*rationally* certain. Under the spell of mathematics, Descartes thus turned away from sense experience and toward *reason alone* as the source of philosophical certainty. And he conceived of a "geometrical method" for philosophy.

Descartes' "geometrical" method (again)

"Most of all I was delighted with Mathematics because of the certainty of its demonstrations and the evidence of its reasoning."

—Descartes

The essence of this new philosophical method may be found in Descartes' *Rules for the Direction of the Mind.* In Rule IV he stresses the absolute necessity of having a method and then explicitly defines it.

RULE IV. *THERE IS NEED FOR A METHOD FOR FINDING OUT THE TRUTH*

So blind is the curiosity by which mortals are possessed, that they often conduct their minds along unexplored routes, having no reason to hope for success, but merely being willing to risk the experiment of finding whether the truth they seek lies there. As well might a man burning with an unintelligent desire to find treasure, continuously roam the streets, seeking to find something that a passer by might have chanced to drop. This is the way in which most Chemists, many Geometricians, and Philosophers not a few prosecute their studies. I do not deny that sometimes in these wanderings they are lucky enough to find something true. But I do not allow that this argues greater industry on their part, but only better luck. But however that may be, it were far better never to think of investigating truth at all, than to do so without a method. For it is very certain that unregulated inquiries and confused reflections of this kind only confound the natural light and blind our mental powers. . . . Moreover by a method I mean certain and simple rules, such that, if a man observe them accurately, he shall never assume what is false as true, and will never spend his mental efforts to no

---

[4]René Descartes, *Discourse on Method,* in *Philosophical Works of Descartes,* tr. Elizabeth S. Haldane and G. R. T. Ross (Cambridge: Cambridge University Press, 1911), I, 85.

purpose, but will always gradually increase his knowledge and so arrive at a true understanding of all that does not surpass his powers.[5]

According to these last lines, anyone who follows Descartes' method would, in principle, be led to all possible knowledge. But what, more exactly, does this method consist in? Descartes reduces it, as we saw in Chapter 5, to two operations of the intellect: *intuition* and *deduction*. This, of course, is why Descartes' method has been called a "geometrical" method. As in geometry, it begins with fundamental and irreducible truths, and from these it deduces more truths. But now the notions of intuition and deduction require further comment.

Intuition

The word "intuition" is used in many ways, and we must be careful to distinguish it here from anything like "woman's intuition." In philosophy intuition means, usually, a direct and immediate knowledge of something. When we say that it is direct and immediate knowledge, we mean that it is not, like much of our other knowledge, *mediated*, or passed along through something else, say, through sense experience or through other ideas. An example of *mediated* knowledge is our knowledge that X is red, mediated or passed along through our sense experience of X and its color; or our knowledge that C is D, mediated or passed along through our prior understanding that if A is B then C is D, and A is B. In intuition, however, the truth or knowledge in question is grasped immediately by a direct awareness—it is *just there*. It is important to emphasize, though, that the intuitionist claims to know directly not only logical truths, as in "A is A," but truths about *reality*, as in our earlier examples: "Every event must have a cause"; "It is morally wrong to kill people for the fun of it"; and "All individuals are endowed with basic rights." As a theory about the basis of knowledge, intuitionism is the view that such truths may be known immediately and with certainty.

It is understandable why a doctrine of innate ideas has also been attributed to Descartes. Did he take, as it were, the Platonic Forms, place them in the mind, and then announce that we know them directly? Or does he believe that what is innate is a sort of *disposition* of the mind, or a *structure* by which universal and necessary truth about reality can be developed? Of course the latter would better explain why infants do not appreciate Einstein. In any event, what is really important is that for Descartes *something* is innate, and intuition is the faculty of direct awareness by which knowledge is derived from the mind alone. Although Descartes made a big thing of intuition, many other philosophers too have appealed to intuition as an important and even necessary epistemological tool.

Deduction

But, Descartes continues, our knowledge is not limited to intuitions. For it is possible, says Descartes, to *deduce* further ideas and truths from our intuited ones. You already have an idea of deduction from our chapter on logic. You will recall that it consists in the necessary inference of one proposition from others; in valid deductive reasoning, if the premises are true, the conclusion *must* be true. It is, thus, by the faculty of deduction that from the original intuitions we are enabled to

[5]Descartes, *Rules for the Direction of the Mind*, in *Philosophical Works of Descartes*, I, 9.

DESCARTES' RULES

In his *Rules for the Direction of the Mind,* Descartes presents a long list of rules which, if followed, ensure that the intellect will eventually grasp all that can be known. These rules are collapsed into four short paragraphs in the better-known *Discourse on Method:*

> The first of these was to accept nothing as true which I did not clearly recognise to be so: that is to say, carefully to avoid precipitation and prejudice in judgments, and to accept in them nothing more than what was presented to my mind so clearly and distinctly that I could have no occasion to doubt it.
>
> The second was to divide up each of the difficulties which I examined into as many parts as possible, and as seemed requisite in order that it might be resolved in the best manner possible.
>
> The third was to carry on my reflections in due order, commencing with objects that were the most simple and easy to understand, in order to rise little by little, or by degrees, to knowledge of the most complex, assuming an order, even if a fictitious one, among those which do not follow a natural sequence relatively to one another.
>
> The last was in all cases to make enumerations so complete and reviews so general that I should be certain of having omitted nothing.

Descartes' optimism about the practice of these rules, as well as the mathematical character of his method, is evident from the continuing comment:

> Those long chains of reasoning, simple and easy as they are, of which geometricians make use in order to arrive at the most difficult demonstrations, had caused me to imagine that all those things which fall under the cognizance of man might very likely be mutually related in the same fashion; and that, provided only that we abstain from receiving anything as true which is not so, and always retain the order which is necessary in order to deduce the one conclusion from the other, there can be nothing so remote that we cannot reach to it, nor so recondite that we cannot discover it.[1]

[1]Descartes, *Discourse on Method,* in *Philosophical Words of Descartes,* I, 92.

> ### INTUITIONISM
>
> The doctrine that direct awareness of at least some fundamental ideas of reality as universally and necessarily true is either *the* basis of knowledge or one of its bases.

expand our knowledge indefinitely—but without any loss of certainty. In the chapter on mind and matter we saw, in fact, how much Descartes deduced from his single intuition, "I think."

In the following, again from the *Rules for the Direction of the Mind*, Descartes emphasizes and clarifies intuition and deduction as the basic tools of knowledge.

RULE III. IN THE SUBJECTS WE PROPOSE TO INVESTIGATE, OUR INQUIRIES SHOULD BE DIRECTED, NOT TO WHAT OTHERS HAVE THOUGHT, NOR TO WHAT WE OURSELVES CONJECTURE, BUT TO WHAT WE CAN CLEARLY AND PERSPICUOUSLY BEHOLD AND WITH CERTAINTY DEDUCE; FOR KNOWLEDGE IS NOT WON IN ANY OTHER WAY.

. . . we shall here take note of all those mental operations by which we are able, wholly without fear of illusion, to arrive at the knowledge of things. Now I admit only two, viz. intuition and deduction.

By intuition I understand, not the fluctuating testimony of the senses, nor the misleading judgment that proceeds from the blundering constructions of imagination, but the conception which an unclouded and attentive mind gives us so readily and distinctly that we are wholly freed from doubt about that which we understand. Or, what comes to the same thing, intuition is the undoubting conception of an unclouded and attentive mind, and springs from the light of reason alone; it is more certain than deduction itself, in that it is simpler, though deduction, as we have noted above, cannot by us be erroneously conducted. Thus each individual can mentally have intuition of the fact that he exists, and that he thinks; that the triangle is bounded by three lines only, the sphere by a single superficies, and so on. Facts of such a kind are far more numerous than many people think, disdaining as they do to direct their attention upon such simple matters.

This evidence and certitude, however, which belongs to intuition, is required not only in the enunciation of propositions, but also in discursive reasoning of whatever sort. For example consider this consequence: 2 and 2 amount to the same as 3 and 1. Now we need to see intuitively not only that 2 and 2 make 4, and that likewise 3 and 1 make 4, but further that the third of the above statements is a necessary conclusion from these two.

Hence now we are in a position to raise the question as to why we have, besides intuition, given this supplementary method of knowing, viz. knowing by deduction, by which we understand all necessary inference from other facts that are known with certainty. This, however, we could not avoid, because many things are known with certainty, though not by themselves evident, but only deduced from true and known principles by the continuous and uninterrupted action of a mind that has a clear vision of each step in the process. It is in a similar way that we know that the last link in a long chain is connected with the first, even though we do not take in by means of one and the same act of vision all the intermediate links on which that connection depends, but only remember that we have taken them successively under review and that each single one is united to its neighbour, from the first even to the last. Hence we distinguish this mental intuition from deduction by the fact that into the conception of the latter there enters a certain movement or succession, into that of the former there does not. Further deduction does not require an immediately presented evidence such as intuition possesses; its certitude is rather conferred upon it in some way by memory. The upshot of the matter is that it is possible to say that those propositions indeed which are immediately deduced from first principles are known now by intuition, now by deduction, i.e. in a way that differs according to our point of view. But the first principles themselves are given by intuition alone, while, on the contrary, the remote conclusions are furnished only by deduction.

These two methods are the most certain routes to knowledge, and the mind should admit no others. All the rest should be rejected as suspect of error and dangerous. But this does not prevent us from believing matters that have been divinely revealed as being more certain than our surest knowledge, since belief in these things, as all faith in obscure matters, is an action not of our intelligence, but of our will. They should be heeded also since, if they have any basis in our understanding, they can and ought to be, more than all things else, discovered by one or other of the ways above-mentioned. . . .[6]

DESCARTES' TWOFOLD BASIS OF KNOWLEDGE

- *Intuition:* The faculty by which truths are grasped immediately, without the intervention of sense-experience or other ideas.
- *Deduction:* The faculty by which subsequent truths are known with necessity from intuited truths, or from intuited truths taken together with other deduced truths.

[6]Ibid., I, 5–8.

A CONTEMPORARY VERSION:
CHOMSKY

It is true that modern and contemporary philosophy has been dominated not by rationalist but, rather, by empiricist epistemology—this probably has not a little to do with the ascendancy of the physical sciences and the scientific method beginning in the sixteenth century—and that theories of innate ideas and the like are looked upon as quaint leftovers from our philosophical past. Everything has been given a new twist, however, in the recent work of the linguist-philosopher Noam Chomsky of the Massachusetts Institute of Technology, and the philosophical world has had to take note. How has Chomsky's work suddenly derailed the empiricist approach which has for so long controlled the philosophical scene? How has it resulted in an unexpected new lease on life for the rationalist? For the answer we must look beyond the borders of philosophy.

The relevance of psycholinguistics

It has to do with *psycholinguistics,* the study of the mental processes which underlie the acquisition and use of language. More specifically, it has to do with Chomsky's own contribution to this field, called *transformational grammar,* which attempts to relate the *surface* structure of sentences, or what is actually heard, and the *deep* structure of sentences, or what is meant. This is exceedingly difficult stuff, but what is important at the moment is this. The commonsensical model of language-acquisition has always been an empirical one: A child acquires language through stimulus-response, conditioning, trial and error, and so on. But in this major development of contemporary psycholinguistics, with Chomsky leading the way, it is argued that the phenomenon of language is impossible except on the postulation of *innate intellectual structures.* The implications for epistemology, and specifically for rationalism, are too obvious to miss, as Chomsky himself points out in *Aspects of the Theory of Syntax:*

Innate structures as conditions for language

> On the basis of the best information now available, it seems reasonable to suppose that a child cannot help constructing a particular kind of transformational grammar to account for the data presented to him, any more than he can control his perception of solid objects or his attention to line and angle. Thus it may well be that the general features of language structure reflect, not so much the course of one's experience, but rather the general character of one's capacity to acquire knowledge—in the traditional sense, one's innate ideas and innate principles.[7]

The position is spelled out further in the following, from his essay "Language and the Mind." Note especially his rejection of empiricist explanations of language-acquisition, the recurring emphasis on innate structures as conditions for language, and, again, the relevance of this view of language for still other spheres of knowledge.

[7]Noam Chomsky, *Aspects of the Theory of Syntax* (Cambridge, Mass.: M.I.T. Press, 1965), p. 59.

As far as language learning is concerned, it seems to me that a rather convincing argument can be made for the view that certain principles intrinsic to the mind provide invariant structures that are a precondition for linguistic experience. . . .

The study of language, it seems to me, offers strong empirical evidence that empiricists theories of learning are quite inadequate. Serious efforts have been made in recent years to develop principles of induction, generalization, and data analysis that would account for knowledge of a language. These efforts have been a total failure. The methods and principles fail not for any superficial reason such as lack of time or data. They fail because they are intrinsically incapable of giving rise to the system of rules that underlies the normal use of language. What evidence is now available supports the view that all human languages share deep-seated properties of organization and structure. These properties—these linguistic universals—can be plausibly assumed to be an innate mental endowment *rather than the result of learning. If this is true, then the study of language sheds light on certain long-standing issues in the theory of knowledge. Once again, I see little reason to doubt that what is true of language is true of other forms of human knowledge as well.*

There is one further question that might be raised at this point. How does the human mind come to have the innate properties that underlie acquisition of knowledge. Here linguistic evidence obviously provides no information at all. The process by which the human mind has achieved its present state of complexity and its particular form of innate organization are a complete mystery, as much of a mystery as the analogous questions that can be asked about any other complex organism. It is perfectly safe to attribute this to evolution, so long as we bear in mind that there is no substance to this assertion—it amounts to nothing more than the belief that there is surely some naturalistic explanation for these phenomena.

There are, however, important aspects of the problem of language and mind that can be studied sensibly within the limitations of present understanding and technique. I think that, for the moment, the most productive investigations are those dealing with the nature of particular grammars and with the universal conditions met by all human languages. I have tried to suggest how one can move, in successive steps of increasing abstractness, from the study of percepts to the study of grammar to the study of universal grammar and the mechanisms of learning.

In this area of convergence of linguistics, psychology, and philosophy, we can look forward to much exciting work in the coming years.[8]

Of course it is relevant to ask: How does the mind come to possess this structure in the first place? Chomsky answers, as you just saw, that it is a "complete mystery," and he doesn't see at the moment that any purely naturalistic explanation (he cites evolutionary development) is any better than any other. Another question, and certainly more epistemologically relevant: However it got there, what is the relation of this innate intellectual structure to *truth*? Are we driven to a view

Two questions

[8]Noam Chomsky, "Language and the Mind," in *Readings in Psychology Today* (Del Mar, Calif.: C.R.M. Books, 1969), pp. 282, 286.

"What evidence is now available supports the view that all
human languages share deep-seated properties of organization and
structure. These properties—these linguistic universals—can be
plausibly assumed to be an *innate mental endowment* rather than
the result of learning."

—Chomsky

REVEALING PHRASES IN CHOMSKY

- "principles intrinsic to the mind"
- "deep-rooted properties of organization and structure"
- "an innate mental endowment"

of knowledge as *arbitrarily* determined by a purely accidental endowment within
the brain? Or can we believe in some sort of *preestablished harmony* whereby this
intellectual endowment is made to correspond to reality? Are we driven to something like Plato's doctrine of the *preexistence of the soul?* Or perhaps our experienced
reality is itself *determined* by our innate intellectual structures? Or maybe you can
think of some other way out? Certainly the problem is an important one and worthy of serious discussion. In fact, it will crop up again in Chapter 11.

We have considered three rationalist conceptions of knowledge from three
different periods. We do not raise here specific objections to these theories, because,
in a way, the whole next chapter is itself a colossal challenge to them. Empiricism,
with its doctrine that the mind is at birth a "blank tablet," rejects the very starting
point of rationalism.

Chapter 9 in Review

SUMMARY

One of the most basic questions of epistemology, and therefore a basic question of
all philosophizing, is: What is the origin of knowledge? Philosophers have answered
this question in two radically different ways. According to empiricism, all knowledge (at least "existential" knowledge, which informs us about existence) is derived

from the five senses. Rationalism, on the other hand, teaches that at least some knowledge can be acquired apart from sense experience, through the intellect or reason alone.

In this chapter we have considered three ways in which rationalists have argued for their theories. We are already familiar with Plato's theory of reality (from Chapter 4), and we should recall that his image of the Divided Line represents as much a conception of knowledge as a conception of reality. The object of authentic knowledge is what *Is,* as opposed to what is *Becoming*. Such knowledge is hardly possible in this life, where the soul is imprisoned in the body, and where the body itself is a constant hindrance to the acquisition of knowledge. When the soul is liberated from the body at death, the soul comes into the possession of absolute knowledge. Until that time all we can do is cultivate as much as possible the innate truths that the mind is born with, but which, as they are "recollected," are invariably distorted by the world of Becoming, resulting in mere opinions, or *relative* knowledge.

Likewise, Descartes' theory of knowledge was anticipated in Chapter 5. Descartes, too, seeks to develop at least the foundation of his philosophy apart from the input of the senses. He saw in mathematics an especially good model for philosophical reasoning, and adopted intuition and deduction as the principles of his philosophical method. He believed that, in principle, it would be possible to unfold a complete system of knowledge by the rigorous practicing of this method. As with Plato, it is important to see that with Descartes every attempt is made to exclude or minimize the illusory and deceitful intrusions of the senses.

Rationalist theories of knowledge are regarded by many as a bit naive and quaint. However, the "tough-minded" philosophers have been given something of a jolt in recent years. The psycholinguistic research of Chomsky in particular has resurrected the theory of innate ideas. Specifically, his work has brought to light the presence of universal and innate intellectual structures which underlie all language, and which explain the process of language-acquisition better than the empirically oriented model of learning. Thus psycholinguistics (which is concerned with the connection between the mind and language) has emerged as an unexpected ally of the rationalist theory of knowledge.

BASIC IDEAS

- Empiricism
- Rationalism (strict sense)
- Plato: Why philosophers desire death
- Two bodily hindrances to knowledge
- Innate ideas
- Knowledge of recollection
- Descartes' "geometrical" method
- Intuitionism

- Descartes' two operations of the mind
  Intuition
  Deduction
- Psycholinguistics
- The empirical theory of language-acquisition
- Chomsky's theory of language-acquisition

TEST YOURSELF

1. True or false: Plato taught that we bring our ideas into this world from a previous existence in an ideal world.
2. *Rules for the Direction of the Mind* was written by _____.
3. According to Plato, how does sense experience help us to "recollect" ideas?
4. True or false: By "intuition" Descartes meant a feeling or hunch about something.
5. The phrase "linguistic universals" is employed by _____. What does it mean?
6. True or false: To know something *immediately* is to know it through sense experience.
7. According to Plato, why is absolute knowledge impossible in this life?
8. Why was Descartes especially attracted to mathematics?

QUESTIONS FOR
REFLECTION

- Does Plato's doctrine of recollection seem far-fetched or even bizarre? Even if it does, to what degree does it detract from his basic theory of knowledge? Is it itself basic? In evaluating philosophers' positions, is there a danger of throwing out the baby with the bath water?
- Both Plato and Descartes decry the illusions and distortions of sense experience. Can you provide your own evidence and examples of this? Can you think of *any* sense representation that is not, as it were, "contaminated"? Is it possible to overdo this point? Or, with the rationalists, are we at some point driven to some "purer" faculty than sense perception?
- Think about these propositions: "Every event must have a cause"; "It is morally wrong to kill people for the fun of it"; "All individuals are endowed with basic rights." Would you say that you *know* or are *certain* of these claims? Are any of them *universally* true? What, if anything, does sense experience contribute to this knowledge?

THE WAY OF EXPERIENCE

We turn next to the second general view of the basis of knowledge: *empiricism*. It was said earlier that empiricism is the view which emphasizes experience as the source of knowledge. We must now explain more carefully what we mean here by "experience."

WHAT IS EMPIRICISM?

There are many different sorts of experience, such as mystical experience, moral experience, aesthetic experience, lonely experience, and wild experience. But here we mean *sense* experience, that is, perceptions derived from the five senses: sight, sound, touch, taste, and smell. When empiricists say that experience is the basis of our knowledge, they mean sense experience, and therefore that the five senses are the foundation of all our knowledge.

As with rationalism, empiricism comes with varying emphases and in varying degrees. But as a general definition we may say that empiricism is the view that all knowledge of reality is derived from sense experience. This may be livened up somewhat by the empiricist metaphor of the *tabula rasa*, or "blank tablet." It is a shorthand way of expressing the empiricist denial that any ideas or even intellectual structure is inscribed on the mind from birth—the mind is at birth a *blank tablet*, devoid even of watermarks. The implication is, of course, that anything "written" on the tablet is written by the five senses.

Definition of
empiricism

The mind as a
tabula rasa

205

EMPIRICISM

The view that all knowledge of reality is derived from sense experience.

CLASSICAL EMPIRICISM:
ARISTOTLE AND ST. THOMAS

We will consider several forms of empiricism, beginning with the classical empiricism of Aristotle and St. Thomas. When we call the empiricism of Aristotle and St. Thomas *classical* empiricism, we not only reflect its Greek roots (Aristotle) but we also distinguish it from various forms of empiricism in the modern period.

Plato vs. Aristotle

It will be recalled from Chapter 4 that Aristotle rejected Plato's theory of the Forms. This was because Plato had created a great gulf between the Forms and the particular things they were the Forms *of*. We saw that Aristotle countered that the Form must be *in* the thing of which it is the Form: The Form, or essence, of the table or chair must be right *there*, along with the matter of the table or chair, constituting it. He insisted on this for many reasons, and one of them was *epistemological*: How can the Form—that which is knowable about the table or chair—make the table or chair knowable if it is not *in* the table or chair? It is therefore no surprise that Aristotle, quite unlike Plato, believed that knowledge comes through our sense experience of particular things in the world—like tables or chairs. And he was one of the first to employ the empiricist comparison of the mind to a *tabula rasa*, or blank tablet.

"[The Platonic Forms] help in no wise . . . towards the knowledge of the other things (for they are not even the substance of these, else they would have been in them), or towards their being, if they are not *in* the particulars which share in them; though if they were they might be thought to be causes, as white causes whiteness in a white object by entering into its composition."

—Aristotle

Let us close in on this a bit more. Like Plato, Aristotle believed that knowledge necessarily involves *general* or *universal* ideas—man, dog, table, chair, etc. Think about this. Where would thinking, speaking, and knowing be without such concepts? Is it possible to think or say or know *anything* apart from such ideas? "Socrates is a man." "In fourteen-hundred-and-ninety-two Columbus sailed the ocean blue." "This table is rectangular." Are not general concepts like man, ocean, table, rectangularity, and so on, necessary for thinking, speaking, and knowing? Now where do these ideas come from? *Unlike* Plato, Aristotle answered that they come from our *experience* of *particular* men, tables, chairs, dogs, oceans, etc.

The problem for such an approach is, of course, the same problem that bothered Plato: How do we arrive at *universal* ideas on the basis of our limited and fluctuating experience of *particular* things?

Aristotle's answer is that the universal and necessary elements of knowledge—the foundations of all subsequent reasoning—are built up in the mind through *induction*. This means, for Aristotle, that a wider and wider generalization is derived from repeated experiences of particular things until a *general* or *universal* concept is established in the mind: From the experience of the particular man Callias, the man Socrates, the man James, the man Tad, the man Bill ... the intellect derives the general or universal idea of *man*, that is, *man as such*. From the experience of the particular dog Fido, the dog Lassie, the dog Rover ... the intellect derives the universal idea *dog*. And the universal ideas—man, dog, and innumerable other concepts derived from experience in the same manner—become the tools and building blocks of all reasoning. They then make it possible to say and know, "Socrates is a man," "In fourteen-hundred-and-ninety-two Columbus sailed the ocean blue," etc.

Aristotle likens the process by which the universal concepts are established in the intellect to a company of soldiers retreating in disarray until a first soldier halts and makes a stand, then a second, then a third, and finally the whole company is put in order and established:

> *We conclude that these states of knowledge are neither innate in a determinate form, nor developed from other higher states of knowledge, but from sense-perception. It is like a rout in battle stopped by first one man making a stand and then another, until the original formation has been restored. The soul is so constituted as to be capable of this process.*
>
> *... When one of a number of logically indiscriminable particulars has made a stand, the earliest universal is present in the soul: for though the act of sense-perception is of the particular, its content is universal—is man, for example, not the man Callias. A fresh stand is made among these rudimentary universals, and the process does not cease until the indivisible concepts, the true universals, are established: e.g. such and such a species of animal is a step towards the genus animal, which by the same process is a step towards a further generalization.*

The necessity of universal ideas

Universal ideas derived from experience . . .

. . . by induction

> *Thus it is clear that we must get to know the primary premises by induction;*
> *for the method by which even sense-perception implants the universal is inductive.*[1]

Aristotle and St. Thomas

This conception of the origin of knowledge was passed from Aristotle to St. Thomas, the dominant Christian philosopher of the thirteenth century. It may be helpful to see how St. Thomas expresses the matter.

We saw that Aristotle taught that the mind is a blank tablet waiting to be written upon by the senses. St. Thomas expresses the same empiricist idea with the words (everything sounds more profound in Latin) *Nihil in intellectu quod prius non fuerit in sensu,* "Nothing is in the intellect which was not first in the senses." For St.

Universal ideas derived from experience . . .

Thomas, as for Aristotle, the essences of things are locked inside the particular things of which they are the essences—individual human beings, animals, tables, chairs, dogs, and cats. The intellect, however, is able to liberate the essence in particular things and thus to "see" the universal idea or their common, essential nature: human, animal, table, chair, dog, and cat.

> "What the mind thinks must be in it just as characters may be said to be on a writing-tablet on which as yet nothing actually stands written."
> —Aristotle
>
> "Nothing is in the intellect which was not first in the senses."
> –St. Thomas

. . . by abstraction

The intellectual faculty by which the essential or formal or universal element of particular things is unlocked and "seen" by the mind is called by St. Thomas *abstraction.* "To abstract" means to remove or separate something from something else. In this epistemological context, what is being abstracted is a common nature, and that from which it is being abstracted are the particular and varying instances of it. In abstracting the universal *human being* from Callias, Socrates, James, Sue, Bill, and Sally, their individual and peculiar features are left behind (Socrates is bald and snub-nosed, James is tall, blue-eyed, and hairy, Bill has a nose shaped like an eagle's beak and is short, etc.) and their *common* and *essential* nature is grasped: *human being.*

It remains to stress that for both Aristotle and St. Thomas we can say, think, or know anything only because of universal ideas derived from experience. It is

[1]Aristotle, *Posterior Analytics,* 100a–100b, tr. G. R. G. Mure, in *Basic Works of Aristotle,* ed. Richard McKeon (New York: Random House, 1941).

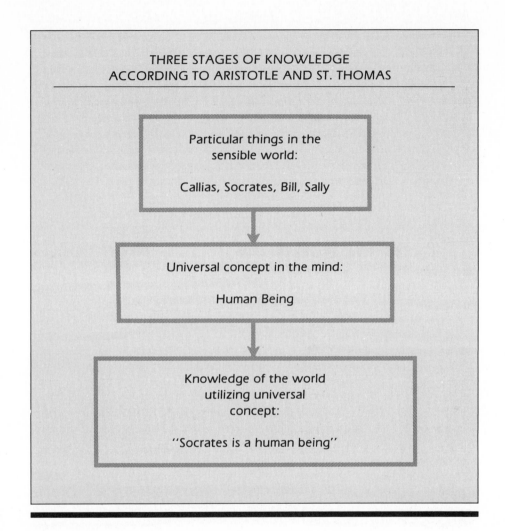

THREE STAGES OF KNOWLEDGE
ACCORDING TO ARISTOTLE AND ST. THOMAS

Particular things in the
sensible world:

Callias, Socrates, Bill, Sally

Universal concept in the mind:

Human Being

Knowledge of the world
utilizing universal
concept:

"Socrates is a human being"

only by such ideas and truths as man, animal, equality, red, every event is caused, that the intellect can be guided amidst the particularities, relativities, deceptions, and fluctuations of the sensible world. We begin, then, with the particular things we encounter in the sensible world. From these we derive universal concepts and principles. With our universal concepts and principles we are enabled to return to the sensible world and speak of it, think about it, and know it: "Socrates is a human being."

The following, from St. Thomas' *Summa Theologiae*, is brief but not easy. Try to see in it some of the above ideas at work, especially the movement: singular → universal → proposition. (In this quotation, "intelligible species" means the essence of a thing, and "phantasms" are the mental images of things.)

Our intellect cannot know the singular in material things directly and primarily. The reason for this is that the principle of singularity in material things is individual matter; whereas our intellect understands by abstracting the intelligible species from such matter. Now what is abstracted from individual matter is universal. Hence our intellect knows directly only universals. But indirectly, however, and as it were by a kind of reflexion, it can know the singular, because . . . even after abstracting the intelligible species, the intellect, in order to understand actually, needs to turn to the phantasms in which it understands the species. . . . Therefore it understands the universal directly through the intelligible species, and indirectly the singular represented by the phantasm. And thus it forms the proposition, "Socrates is a man."[2]

MODERN EMPIRICISM: LOCKE

It was the English philosopher John Locke (1632–1704) who laid the foundations of *modern* empiricism in his monumental *Essay Concerning Human Understanding*, published in 1690. Like Descartes, Locke was distressed over the muddles and uncertainties in metaphysics, theology, and moral philosophy. But unlike Descartes, who took the rationalistic method of geometry as his epistemological model, Locke took as his model the *experimental* methods of the new sciences, such as physics, astronomy, and medicine.

Locke's rejection of innate ideas

Locke begins on a negative note: a lengthy indictment of any theory of innate ideas. According to Locke, few philosophical theories are more firmly entrenched than the theory of innate ideas, which he characterizes as the belief that "there are in the understanding certain *innate principles*; some primary notions, *koinai ennoiai* {Grk.: universal ideas}, characters, as it were stamped upon the mind of man, which the soul receives in its very first being, and brings into the world with it."[3] He rejects the innateness of both "speculative" and "practical" principles, another way of saying "truths pertaining to reality and morality." In a word, Locke refutes the theory of innate ideas by charging that the arguments cited in support of it do not actually prove it, and that those who cite them do not pay sufficient attention to an altogether different and simpler explanation of the source of our ideas.

In the following excerpt he focuses on speculative principles, showing how innateness cannot be claimed even for the most certain of these, the Law of Identity and the Law of Non-Contradiction: Such principles are neither universally agreed to, nor are they known by children, nor are they the products of reason. As with much of the quoted matter in this book, the following passages from Locke are sort of classic statements and are worthy of thoughtful scrutiny.

[2]St. Thomas, *Summa Theologiae*, Pt. I, Qu. 86, Art. 1, in *Basic Writings of Saint Thomas Aquinas*, ed. Anton C. Pegis (New York: Random House, 1945), I.

[3]John Locke, *An Essay Concerning Human Understanding*, I, 2, 1, ed. A. S. Pringle-Pattison (London: Oxford University Press, 1924).

GENERAL ASSENT THE GREAT ARGUMENT.—*There is nothing more commonly taken for granted, than that there are certain principles, both speculative and practical (for they speak of both), universally agreed upon by all mankind; which therefore, they argue, must needs be the constant impressions which the souls of men receive in their first beings, and which they bring into the world with them, as necessarily and really as they do any of their inherent faculties.*

UNIVERSAL CONSENT PROVES NOTHING INNATE.—*This argument, drawn from universal consent, has this misfortune in it, that if it were true in matter of fact, that there were certain truths wherein all mankind agreed, it would not prove them innate, if there can be any other way shown, how men may come to that universal agreement in the things they do consent in; which I presume may be done.*

"WHAT IS, IS," AND "IT IS IMPOSSIBLE FOR THE SAME THING TO BE, AND NOT TO BE," NOT UNIVERSALLY ASSENTED TO.—*But, which is worse, this argument of universal consent, which is made use of to prove innate principles, seems to me a demonstration that there are none such; because there are none to which all mankind give an universal assent. I shall begin with the speculative, and instance in those magnified principles of demonstration: "Whatsoever is, is," and "It is impossible for the same thing to be, and not to be," which, of all others, I think, have the most allowed title to innate. These have so settled a reputation of maxims universally received, that it will, no doubt, be thought strange if any one should seem to question it. But yet I take liberty to say, that these propositions are so far from having an universal assent, that there are a great part of mankind to whom they are not so much as known.*

NOT ON THE MIND NATURALLY IMPRINTED, BECAUSE NOT KNOWN TO CHILDREN, IDIOTS, ETC..—*For, first, it is evident, that all children and idiots have not the least apprehension or thought of them: and the want of that is enough to destroy that universal assent, which must needs be the necessary concomitant of all innate truths: it seeming to me near a contradiction to say, that there are truths imprinted on the soul which it perceives or understands not; imprinting, if it signify anything, being nothing else but the making certain truths to be perceived. No proposition can be said to be in the mind which it never yet knew, which it was never yet conscious of. . . . If truths can be imprinted on the understanding without being perceived, I can see no difference there can be between any truths the mind is capable of knowing in respect of their original: they must all be innate, or all adventitious; in vain shall a man go about to distinguish them. He therefore that talks of innate notions in the understanding, cannot (if he intend thereby any distinct sort of truths) mean such truths to be in the understanding as it never perceived, and is yet wholly ignorant of. For if these words "to be in the understanding" have any propriety, they signify to be understood. If therefore these two propositions: "Whatsoever is, is," and, "It is impossible for the same thing to be, and not to be," are by nature imprinted, children cannot be ignorant of them; infants, and all that have souls, must necessarily have them in their understandings, know the truth of them, and assent to it.*

THAT MEN KNOW THEM WHEN THEY COME TO THE USE OF REASON, ANSWERED.—To avoid this, it is usually answered, that all men know and assent to them, when they come to the use of reason, and this is enough to prove them innate. To apply this answer with any tolerable sense to our present purpose, it must signify one of these two things; either, that as soon as men come to the use of reason, these supposed native inscriptions come to be known and observed by them; or else, that the use and exercise of men's reasons assists them in the discovery of these principles, and certainly makes them known to them.

IF REASON DISCOVERED THEM, THAT WOULD NOT PROVE THEM INNATE.—*If they mean that by the use of reason men may discover these principles, and that this is sufficient to prove them innate, their way of arguing will stand thus: viz. That whatever truths reason can certainly discover to us, and make us firmly assent to, those are all naturally imprinted on the mind; and by this means there will be no difference between the maxims of the mathematicians and theorems they deduce from them: all must be equally allowed innate, they being all discoveries made by the use of reason, and truths that a rational creature may certainly come to know, if he apply his thoughts rightly that way.*

IT IS FALSE THAT REASON DISCOVERED THEM.—*But how can these men think the use of reason necessary to discover principles that are supposed innate, when reason (if we may believe them) is nothing else but the faculty of deducing unknown truths from principles or propositions that are already known? That certainly can never be thought innate which we have need of reason to discover, unless, as I have said, we will have all the certain truths that reason ever teaches us, to be innate. We may as well think the use of reason necessary to make our eyes discover visible objects, as that there should be need of reason, or the exercise thereof, to make the understanding see what is originally engraven in it. And I think those who give this answer will not be forward to affirm, that the knowledge of this maxim, "That it is impossible for the same thing to be, and not to be," is a deduction of our reason. For this would be to destroy that bounty of nature they seem so fond of, whilst they make the knowledge of those principles to depend on the labour of our thoughts. For all reasoning is search and casting about, and requires pains and application. And how can it with any tolerable sense be supposed, that what was imprinted by nature, as the foundation and guide of our reason, should need the use of reason to discover it?*

Those who will take the pains to reflect with a little attention on the operations of the understanding, will find that this ready assent of the mind to some truths, depends not either on native inscription, or the use of reason, but on a faculty of the mind quite distinct from both of them, as we shall see hereafter.[4]

The source of ideas: Experience

On the positive side, Locke is as explicit as one could hope for as to the actual origin of the ideas which undeniably exist in our minds: *experience*. But the next

[4]Ibid., I, 2, 2–11.

step is a little more subtle. For this experience takes two forms. First, there is what we might call the "external" experience by which objects in the external world, outside our minds, enter our minds through *sensation*, for example, hot, cold, red, yellow, hard, soft, sweet, and bitter. Second, there is the "internal" experience we have of the operations of our minds, or *reflection*, for example, thinking, willing, believing, doubting, affirming, denying, and comparing. Both of these are kinds of experience—reflection on what is going on inside no less than sensation of what is going on outside—and they are the two and only two means by which ideas become inscribed on the blank tablets of our minds. And just as the absence of ideas in infants is evidence against any doctrine of innate ideas, so the gradual development of ideas in children, corresponding to the development of their experience, is evidence for the empiricist doctrine that ideas originate in experience.

Two kinds of experience: Sensation, reflection

IDEA IS THE OBJECT OF THINKING.—Every man being conscious to himself that he thinks, and that which his mind is applied about whilst thinking being the ideas that are there, it is past doubt that men have in their minds several ideas, such as are those expressed by the words, "whiteness, hardness, sweetness, thinking, motion, man, elephant, army, drunkenness", and others. It is in the first place then to be enquired, How he comes by them? I know it is a received doctrine, that men have native ideas and original characters stamped upon their minds in their very first being. This opinion I have at large examined already; and, I suppose, what I have said in the foregoing . . . will be much more easily admitted, when I have shown whence the understanding may get all the ideas it has, and by what ways and degrees they may come into the mind; for which I shall appeal to every one's own observation and experience.

ALL IDEAS COME FROM SENSATION OR REFLECTION.—Let us then suppose the mind to be, as we say, white paper, void of all characters, without any ideas; how comes it to be furnished? Whence comes it by that vast store, which the busy and boundless fancy of man has painted on it with an almost endless variety? Whence has it all the materials of reason and knowledge? To this I answer, in one word, from EXPERIENCE; in that all our knowledge is founded, and from that it ultimately derives itself. Our observation, employed either about external sensible objects, or about the internal operations of our minds, perceived and reflected on by ourselves, is that which supplies our understandings with all the materials of thinking. These two are the fountains of knowledge, from whence all the ideas we have, or can naturally have, do spring.

THE OBJECTS OF SENSATION ONE SOURCE OF IDEAS.—First, our senses, conversant about particular sensible objects, do convey into the mind several distinct perceptions of things, according to those various ways wherein those objects do affect them; and thus we come by those ideas we have of yellow, white, heat, cold, soft, hard, bitter, sweet, and all those which we call sensible qualities; which when I say the senses convey into the mind, I mean, they from external objects convey into the mind what produces there those perceptions. This great source of most of the ideas

we have, depending wholly upon our senses, and derived by them to the understand-
ing, I call, SENSATION.

THE OPERATIONS OF OUR MINDS THE OTHER SOURCE OF THEM.—*Secondly,*
the other fountain, from which experience furnisheth the understanding with ideas, is
the perception of the operations of our own minds within us, as it is employed about
the ideas it has got; which operations, when the soul comes to reflect on and consider,
do furnish the understanding with another set of ideas which could not be had from
things without: and such are perception, thinking, doubting, believing, reasoning,
knowing, willing, and all the different actings of our own minds; which we being
conscious of, and observing in ourselves, do from these receive into our understanding
as distinct ideas, as we do from bodies affecting our senses. This source of ideas every
man has wholly in himself: and though it be not sense, as having nothing to do with
external objects, yet it is very like it, and might properly enough be called internal
sense. But as I call the other Sensation, so I call this REFLECTION, *the ideas it*
affords being such only as the mind gets by reflecting on its own operations within
itself. By Reflection, then, in the following part of this discourse, I would be under-
stood to mean that notice which the mind takes of its own operations, and the manner
of them, by reason whereof there comes to be ideas of these operations in the under-
standing. These two, I say, viz., external material things as the objects of Sensation,
and the operations of our own minds within as the objects of Reflection, are, to me,
the only originals from whence all our ideas take their beginnings. The term opera-
tions here, I use in a large sense, as comprehending not barely the actions of the mind
about its ideas, but some sort of passions arising sometimes from them, such as is the
satisfaction or uneasiness arising from any thought.

ALL OUR IDEAS ARE OF THE ONE OR THE OTHER OF THESE.—*The under-*
standing seems to me not to have the least glimmering of any ideas which it doth not
receive from one of these two. External objects furnish the mind with the ideas of
sensible qualities, which are all those different perceptions they produce in us; and
the mind furnishes the understanding with ideas of its own operations. These, when
we have taken a full survey of them, and their several modes, combinations, and
relations, we shall find to contain all our whole stock of ideas; and that we have
nothing in our minds which did not come in one of these two ways. Let any one
examine his own thoughts, and thoroughly search into his understanding, and then
let him tell me, whether all the original ideas he has there, are any other than of the
objects of his senses, or of the operations of his mind considered as objects of his
reflection; and how great a mass of knowledge soever he imagines to be lodged there,
he will, upon taking a strict view, see that he has not any idea in his mind but what
one of these two have imprinted, though perhaps with infinite variety compounded
and enlarged by the understanding, as we shall see hereafter.

OBSERVABLE IN CHILDREN.—*He that attentively considers the state of a child*
at his first coming into the world, will have little reason to think him stored with
plenty of ideas that are to be the matter of his future knowledge. It is by degrees he
comes to be furnished with them: and though the ideas of obvious and familiar qual-

*ities imprint themselves before the memory begins to keep a register of time and order,
yet it is often so late before some unusual qualities come in the way, that there are
few men that cannot recollect the beginning of their acquaintance with them: and if
it were worth while, no doubt a child might be so ordered as to have but a very few
even of the ordinary ideas till he were grown up to a man. But all that are born into
the world being surrounded with bodies that perpetually and diversely affect them,
variety of ideas, whether care be taken about it or no, are imprinted on the minds of
children. Light and colours are busy and at hand everywhere when the eye is but
open; sounds and some tangible qualities fail not to solicit their proper senses, and
force an entrance to the mind; but yet I think it will be granted easily, that if a child
were kept in a place where he never saw any other but black and white till he were
a man, he would have no more ideas of scarlet or green, than he that from his childhood never tasted an oyster or a pine-apple has of those particular relishes.*[5]

So far we have considered only the passive side of the mind, wherein it
receives the *simple* ideas contributed by sensation and reflection. It also has an
active side, whereby it constructs *complex* ideas out of the simple ones, by means of
combining, comparing, and abstracting.

**The mind: Both
passive and active**

UNCOMPOUNDED APPEARANCES.—*The better to understand the nature, manner,
and extent of our knowledge, one thing is carefully to be observed concerning the ideas
we have; and that is, that some of them are simple, and some complex.*

*Though the qualities that affect our senses are, in the things themselves, so
united and blended that there is no separation, no distance between them; yet it is
plain the ideas they produce in the mind enter by the senses simple and unmixed. For
though the sight and touch often take in from the same object at the same time different ideas; as a man sees at once motion and colour, the hand feels softness and
warmth in the same piece of wax; yet the simple ideas thus united in the same subject
are as perfectly distinct as those that come in by different senses. The coldness and
hardness which a man feels in a piece of ice being as distinct ideas in the mind as the
smell and whiteness of a lily, or as the taste of sugar and smell of a rose: and there
is nothing can be plainer to a man than the clear and distinct perception he has of
those simple ideas; which, being each in itself uncompounded, contains in it nothing
but one uniform appearance or conception in the mind, and is not distinguishable into
different ideas.*

THE MIND CAN NEITHER MAKE NOR DESTROY THEM.—*These simple ideas,
the materials of all our knowledge, are suggested and furnished to the mind only by
those two ways above mentioned, viz., sensation and reflection. When the understanding is once stored with these simple ideas, it has the power to repeat, compare, and
unite them, even to an almost infinite variety, and so can make at pleasure new complex ideas. But it is not in the power of the most exalted wit or enlarged understand-*

[5]*Ibid.,* II, 1, 1–6.

ing, by any quickness or variety of thought, to invent or frame one new simple idea in the mind, not taken in by the ways before mentioned; nor can any force of the understanding destroy those that are there. The dominion of man in this little world of his own understanding, being much-what the same as it is in the great world of visible things, wherein his power, however managed by art and skill, reaches no farther than to compound and divide the materials that are made to his hand, but can do nothing towards the making the least particle of new matter, or destroying one atom of what is already in being. The same inability will every one find in himself, who shall go about to fashion in his understanding any simple idea not received in by his senses from external objects, or by reflection from the operations of his own mind about them. I would have any one try to fancy any taste which had never affected his palate, or frame the idea of a scent he had never smelt: and when he can do this, I will also conclude, that a blind man hath ideas of colours, and a deaf man true distinct notions of sounds. . . .

[COMPLEX IDEAS] MADE BY THE MIND OUT OF SIMPLE ONES..—We have hitherto considered those ideas, in the reception whereof the mind is only passive, which are those simple ones received from sensation and reflection before mentioned, whereof the mind cannot make one to itself, nor have any idea which does not wholly consist of them. {But as the mind is wholly passive in the reception of all its simple ideas, so it exerts several acts of its own, whereby out of its simple ideas, as the materials and foundations of the rest, the other are framed. The acts of the mind wherein it exerts its power over its simple ideas are chiefly these three: (1) Combining several simple ideas into one compound one; and thus all complex ideas are made. (2) The second is bringing two ideas, whether simple or complex, together, and setting them by one another, so as to take a view of them at once, without uniting them into one; by which it gets all its ideas of relations. (3) The third is separating them from all other ideas that accompany them in their real existence; this is called abstraction: and thus all its general ideas are made. This shows man's power and its way of operation to be much-what the same in the material and intellectual world. For, the materials in both being such as he has no power over, either to make or destroy, all that man can do is either to unite them together, or to set them by one another, or wholly separate them. I shall here begin with the first of these in the consideration of complex ideas, and come to the other two in their due places.} As simple ideas are observed to exist in several combinations united together, so the mind has a power to consider several of them united together as one idea; and that not only as they are united in external objects, but as itself has joined them. Ideas thus made up of several simple ones put together I call complex; such as are beauty, gratitude, a man, an army, the universe; which, though complicated of various simple ideas or complex ideas made up of simple ones, yet are, when the mind pleases, considered each by itself as one entire thing, and signified by one name.

MADE VOLUNTARILY.—In this faculty of repeating and joining together its ideas, the mind has great power in varying and multiplying the objects of its thoughts infinitely beyond what sensation or reflection furnished it with: but all this still con-

fined to those simple ideas which it received from those two sources, and which are the ultimate materials of all its compositions. For simple ideas are all from things themselves; and of these the mind can have no more nor other than what are suggested to it. It can have no other ideas of sensible qualities than what come from without by the senses, nor any ideas of other kind of operations of a thinking substance than what it finds in itself: but when it has once got these simple ideas, it is not confined barely to observation, and what offers itself from without; it can, by its own power, put together those ideas it has, and make new complex ones which it never received so united.[6]

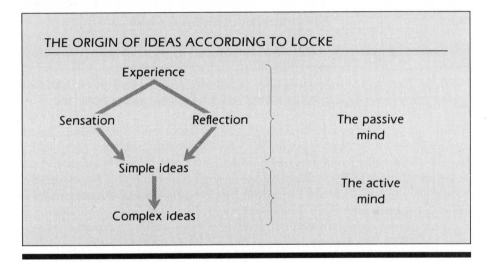

THE ORIGIN OF IDEAS ACCORDING TO LOCKE

Experience

Sensation   Reflection

Simple ideas

Complex ideas

The passive mind

The active mind

Locke's theory of knowledge gets much more complicated, but this will suffice to show its empirical character and how it all gets off the ground.

Yet, it is necessary to mention further features of Locke's theory. Perhaps more than anyone else, Locke emphasized what is sometimes called *epistemological dualism*, an idea that we encountered in our discussion of Berkeley's theory of reality. You will recall that this is the view that there are two factors involved in knowing: the mind, which does the knowing, and its ideas, which are known. That this is Locke's view is clear from repeated statements such as, " ... the mind, in all its thoughts and reasonings, hath no other immediate object but its own ideas. ... "[7] But, of course, there is a third factor, namely, the object in the external world that is known by means of ideas. That Locke blithely believed that our ideas *represent* those objects, and therefore really inform us about the external world, is clear from statements such as:

Epistemological dualism

[6]Ibid., II, 2, 1–2; II, 12, 1–2.
[7]Ibid., IV, 1, 1.

. . . simple ideas are not fictions of our fancies, but the natural and regular productions of things without us, really operating upon us; and so carry with them all the conformity which is intended, or which our state requires; for they represent to us things under those appearances which they are fitted to produce in us: whereby we are enabled to distinguish the sorts of particular substances, to discern the states they are in, and so to take them for our necessities, and apply them to our uses. And this conformity between our simple ideas and the existence of things is sufficient for real knowledge.[8]

Representative perception

Thus we have also what is sometimes called *representative perception*, the theory that our ideas correspond to and faithfully represent objects in the external world.

So far so good. The trouble arises when we ask about this relation, or *correspondence*, of the perceived idea to anything "out there" in the external world. Any representative theory of knowledge, according to which the objects of the external world are represented to us by our ideas, immediately falls prey to the *egocentric predicament*, our hopeless inability to get outside our own minds and ideas. If all we can directly know is our own ideas (epistemological dualism), then how could we ever know whether our ideas correspond to anything, or even approximate anything, "out there" (representative theory of ideas)? Obviously, there is no standpoint from which we could look at an object in the external world and then look at our ideas in our minds, and announce: "Ah! They correspond. Our ideas really do represent things in the external world!" For on Locke's view, *all* we can perceive are *our own ideas.* That there *is* an external world we know from the passivity of our perceptions—our ideas simply *confront* us independently of our will. The question is: How do we know what it is *like?* Does this general theory end in a dismal skepticism about the things in the external world? How is the gap between the external world and our ideas of it to be overcome? This is a serious problem for anyone who holds both that all we can know is our own ideas and that our ideas represent the external world.

Problem: The egocentric predicament

THE EGOCENTRIC PREDICAMENT

Some philosophers claim that all we can know is our own ideas. But on this view we are trapped in the world of our own egos (or selves) and ideas. We could never get outside ourselves to verify whether ideas correspond to anything in the external world.

---

[8]Ibid., IV, 4, 4.

John Locke, the founder of British empiricism, delivered a scathing attack on the theory of innate ideas and insisted on experience as the origin of knowledge.

Berkeley was the immediate successor to Locke, and we saw in an earlier discussion how Berkeley solved this problem by means of his thoroughly idealist philosophy: We don't have to worry about any *correspondence* between ideas and things, because things *are* ideas; we don't have sensations *of* a table, the table *is* a sensation, or bundle of sensations; and there is no material substance, but only mental substance or mind. As before, this may strike you as an extreme position, but it is still not as extreme as what we are led to by the successor of Berkeley, David Hume.

RADICAL EMPIRICISM: HUME

The forms of empiricism which we have looked at so far might be called "mild" forms. In spite of their emphasis on sense experience, both Aristotle and St. Thomas believed that from experience we can nonetheless derive knowledge which is certain and universal, as with the principle of causality (every event must have a cause), and Locke believed this also and, similar to Descartes, that we can have a direct intuition of our own minds. Not so mild is the empiricism of the English philosopher David Hume (1711–1776). It is, in fact, appropriately called *radical* empiricism.

It is important to follow the road from Locke, to Berkeley, to Hume: the three "British empiricists." Locke believed, as did Descartes, in two basic substances, mind and matter, though he confessed that while we have to believe in matter as something "out there" upholding the sensible qualities of things, we really cannot know what it is in itself; it is, Locke said, "something, I know not what." Berkeley followed Locke, but with his thoroughgoing idealist philosophy denied utterly the existence of matter, leaving only mind and its ideas. It remained for Hume to bring these ideas full circle to a kind of epistemological dead-end.

Perceptions = impressions + ideas

Hume's understanding of how knowledge arises is similar to Locke's, but the terminology is somewhat different. All we have are *perceptions*. These, however, are to be divided between *impressions*, which are vivid or lively sensations, or the immediate data of experience, and *ideas*, which are sort of pale copies of impressions, and which provide the material for thinking. Hume goes on to distinguish between simple and complex perceptions (both impressions and ideas), but insists in any case on the priority of impressions over ideas: First, we have sensations, and then, second, ideas which are based on these sensations. The crucial point is that we have no ideas unless they are derived from impressions, and this brings us to the crunch. For in the derivation of all our ideas from sense data, Hume was much more rigorous or consistent or *radical* than either Locke or Berkeley. This radicalism shows up, first, in Hume's treatment of the idea of *substance*, both material substance in the external world and mental substance in the internal world.

Hume's analysis of substance

It is natural to *believe* that there is Something, some mental substance, which underlies our intellectual activities: How can there be thinking, etc., without something that *does* the thinking? Likewise, it is natural to *believe* that there is Something, some material substance, which underlies the sensible qualities in the external world: How can there be qualities without something that is *qualified?* But a "natural belief," as Hume calls it, for all its practical importance, is something very different from rational knowledge based on experience. Since we have no sense impressions whatsoever of substance, either external material substance or internal

Hume's "radical" empiricism is so-called because he applied the empiricist criterion of knowledge rigorously, consistently, and *exclusively*. Unlike previous empiricists, he allowed no rationalistic cracks or back doors: Our knowledge can extend absolutely no further than what is actually disclosed in sense experience.

mental substance, we have no rational grounds at all for talk about matter or mind!
Just as Berkeley dissolved Locke's material substance into a bundle of ideas (color,
sound, taste), so Hume now dissolves Berkeley's mental substance, the "I," into a
bundle of ideas. As Hume says, the dissolution of the one paves the way for the
dissolution of the other. From the *Treatise of Human Nature*:

> *Philosophers begin to be reconcil'd to the principle,* that we have no idea of exter-
> nal substance, distinct from the ideas of particular qualities. *This must pave the
> way for a like principle with regard to the mind,* that we have no notion of it,
> distinct from the particular perceptions. . . .
>
> There are some philosophers, who imagine we are every moment intimately
> conscious of what we call our SELF; that we feel its existence and its continuance in
> existence; and are certain, beyond the evidence of a demonstration, both of its perfect
> identity and simplicity. The strongest sensation, the most violent passion, say they,
> instead of distracting us from this view, only fix it the more intensely, and make us
> consider their influence on self either by their pain or pleasure. To attempt a farther
> proof of this were to weaken its evidence; since no proof can be deriv'd from any fact,
> of which we are so intimately conscious; nor is there any thing, of which we can be
> certain, if we doubt of this.
>
> Unluckily all these positive assertions are contrary to that very experience,
> which is pleaded for them, nor have we any idea of self, after the manner it is here
> explain'd. For from what impression cou'd this idea be deriv'd? This question 'tis
> impossible to answer without a manifest contradiction and absurdity; and yet 'tis a
> question, which must necessarily be answer'd, if we wou'd have the idea of self pass
> for clear and intelligible. It must be some one impression, that gives rise to every real
> idea. But self or person is not any one impression, but that to which our several
> impressions and ideas are suppos'd to have a reference. If any impression gives rise
> to the idea of self, that impression must continue invariably the same, thro' the whole
> course of our lives; since self is suppos'd to exist after that manner. But there is no
> impression constant and invariable. Pain and pleasure, grief and joy, passions and
> sensations succeed each other, and never all exist at the same time. It cannot, there-
> fore, be from any of these impressions, or from any other, that the idea of self is
> deriv'd; and consequently there is no such idea.
>
> But farther, what must become of all our particular perceptions upon this
> hypothesis? All these are different, and distinguishable, and separable from each
> other, and may be separately consider'd, and may exist separately, and have no need
> of any thing to support their existence. After what manner, therefore, do they belong
> to self; and how are they connected with it? For my part, when I enter most intimately
> into what I call myself, I always stumble on some particular perception or other, of
> heat or cold, light or shade, love or hatred, pain or pleasure. I never can catch myself
> at any time without a perception, and never can observe any thing but the perception.
> When my perceptions are remov'd for any time, as by sound sleep; so long am I
> insensible of myself, and may truly be said not to exist. And were all my perceptions

remov'd by death, and cou'd I neither think, nor feel, nor see, nor love, nor hate after the dissolution of my body, I shou'd be entirely annihilated, nor do I conceive what is farther requisite to make me a perfect non-entity. If any one upon serious and unprejudic'd reflexion, thinks he has a different notion of himself, I must confess I can reason no longer with him. All I can allow him is, that he may be in the right as well as I, and that we are essentially different in this particular. He may, perhaps, perceive something simple and continu'd, which he calls himself; tho' I am certain there is no such principle in me.

But setting aside some metaphysicians of this kind, I may venture to affirm of the rest of mankind, that they are nothing but a bundle or collection of different perceptions, which succeed each other with an inconceivable rapidity, and are in a perpetual flux and movement. Our eyes cannot turn in their sockets without varying our perceptions. Our thought is still more variable than our sight; and all our other senses and faculties contribute to this change; nor is there any single power of the soul, which remains unalterably the same, perhaps for one moment. The mind is a kind of theatre, where several perceptions successively make their appearance; pass, re-pass, glide away, and mingle in an infinite variety of postures and situations. There is properly no simplicity in it at one time, nor identity in different; whatever natural propension we may have to imagine that simplicity and identity. The comparison of the theatre must not mislead us. They are the successive perceptions only, that constitute the mind; nor have we the most distant notion of the place, where these scenes are represented, or of the materials, of which it is compos'd.[10]

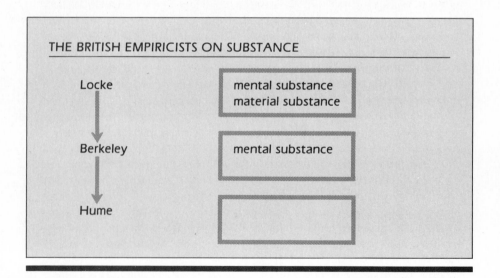

THE BRITISH EMPIRICISTS ON SUBSTANCE

Locke — mental substance / material substance

Berkeley — mental substance

Hume —

[10]David Hume, *A Treatise of Human Nature*, ed. L. A. Selby-Bigge (London: Oxford University Press, 1888), pp. 635, 251–253.

What am I? I look within, in search of some enduring, stable reality—a self, an ego, an "I." But all I can come up with is a passing parade of perceptions. We have come a long way from Descartes', Locke's, and Berkeley's introspective intuition of mind, the mental substance!

But Hume is not through. The implications of his relentless and radical empiricism touch every aspect of philosophy. A second important example is the concept of *causality*. Again, do we not have a natural belief in a causal connection that binds things together in our experience? Is it not a universal and certain principle that every event must have a cause? Hume answers again: Natural belief, Yes; rational knowledge, No. Look at your experience once more. What do you actually *perceive?* What are your *impressions?* It is true that in a supposed causal relation, such as A causing B, we have a perception of A coming before B, and we have a perception of A standing next to B (or next to something which stands next to B), but none of this is sufficient to explain a real causal connection between A and B: A could be before B, and be next to B, but still not be the cause of B. What is required, in addition to temporal succession and spatial proximity, is a *necessary connection*. And *that* we *don't* perceive. It is a metaphysical figment without any rational justification whatsoever.

Hume's analysis of causality

> The idea, then, of causation must be deriv'd from some relation *among objects; and that relation we must now endeavour to discover. I find in the first place, that whatever objects are consider'd as causes or effects, are* contiguous; *and that nothing can operate in a time or place, which is ever so little remov'd from those of its existence. Tho' distant objects may sometimes seem productive of each other, they are commonly found upon examination to be link'd by a chain of causes, which are contiguous among themselves, and to the distant objects; and when in any particular instance we cannot discover this connexion, we still presume it to exist. We may therefore consider the relation of* CONTIGUITY *as essential to that of causation; at least may suppose it such, according to the general opinion, till we can find a more proper occasion to clear up this matter, by examining what objects are or are not susceptible of juxtaposition and conjunction.*
>
> The second relation I shall observe as essential to causes and effects, is not so universally acknowledg'd, but is liable to some controversy. 'Tis that of PRIORITY of time in the cause before the effect. Some pretend that 'tis not absolutely necessary a cause shou'd precede its effect; but that any object or action, in the very first moment of its existence, may exert its productive quality, and give rise to another object or action, perfectly co-temporary with itself. But beside that experience in most instances seems to contradict this opinion, we may establish the relation of priority by a kind of inference or reasoning. 'Tis an establish'd maxim both in natural and moral philosophy, that an object, which exists for any time in its full perfection without producing another, is not its sole cause; but is assisted by some other principle, which pushes it from its state of inactivity, and makes it exert that energy, of which it was secretly possessed. Now if any cause may be perfectly co-temporary with its effect,

'tis certain, according to this maxim, that they must all of them be so; since any one of them, which retards its operation for a single moment, exerts not itself at that very individual time, in which it might have operated; and therefore is no proper cause. The consequence of this wou'd be no less than the destruction of that succession of causes, which we observe in the world; and indeed, the utter annihilation of time. For if one cause were co-temporary with its effect, and this effect with its effect, and so on, 'tis plain there wou'd be no such thing as succession, and all objects must be co-existent.

If this argument appear satisfactory, 'tis well. If not, I beg the reader to allow me the same liberty, which I have us'd in the preceding case, of supposing it such. For he shall find, that the affair is of no great importance.

Having thus discover'd or suppos'd the two relations of contiguity and succession to be essential to causes and effects, I find I am stopt short, and can proceed no farther in considering any single instance of cause and effect. Motion in one body is regarded upon impulse as the cause of motion in another. When we consider these objects with the utmost attention, we find only that the one body approaches the other; and that the motion of it precedes that of the other, but without any sensible interval. 'Tis in vain to rack ourselves with farther thought and reflexion upon this subject. We can go no farther in considering this particular instance.

Shou'd any one leave this instance, and pretend to define a cause, by saying it is something productive of another, 'tis evident he wou'd say nothing. For what does he mean by production? Can he give any definition of it, that will not be the same with that of causation? If he can; I desire it may be produc'd. If he cannot; he here runs in a circle, and gives a synonimous term instead of a definition.

Shall we then rest contented with these two relations of contiguity and succession, as affording a complete idea of causation? By no means. An object may be contiguous and prior to another, without being consider'd as its cause. There is a NECESSARY CONNEXION to be taken into consideration; and that relation is of much greater importance, than any of the other two above-mention'd.

Here again I turn the object on all sides, in order to discover the nature of this necessary connexion, and find the impression, or impressions, from which its idea may be deriv'd. When I cast my eye on the known qualities of objects, I immediately discover that the relation of cause and effect depends not in the least on them. When I consider their relations, I can find none but those of contiguity and succession; which I have already regarded as imperfect and unsatisfactory.[11]

Phenomenalism

Hume's position is appropriately called *phenomenalism*. This is the view that all we can actually know is the phenomena or appearances (*phenomenon* means, literally, "an appearance") that are presented to us in our perceptions. For the time-honored view that substance (both material and mental) is a metaphysical entity and that causality is a metaphysical connection, the phenomenalist substitutes that they are no more than bundles of perceptions: colors, sounds, pains, pleasures, loca-

[11]Ibid., pp. 75–77 (slightly edited).

PHENOMENALISM

The view that we have no rational knowledge beyond what is disclosed in the phenomena of perceptions. Mind, as far as it can be rationally known, is therefore merely a collection of perceptions.

---

tion, succession, and the like. These two pillars of traditional philosophizing now lay in dust before the chisel of Hume's phenomenalism.

If you find yourself thinking of Hume as a *skeptic,* you are right. Specifically, his is the sort of skepticism which denies that knowledge of metaphysical principles and relations is possible, or what we called in Chapter 8 "philosophical skepticism." Perhaps the best way of summarizing Hume's antimetaphysical skepticism is by means of his own derivation of all possible knowledge into two, and only two, sources: "relations of ideas" and "matters of fact." The following two paragraphs from Hume's *Enquiry Concerning Human Understanding* should be studied until the distinction is appreciated:

"Relations of ideas" and "matters of fact"

> All the objects of human reason or enquiry may naturally be divided into two kinds, to wit, Relations of Ideas, *and* Matters of Fact. *Of the first kind are the sciences of Geometry, Algebra, and Arithmetic; and in short, every affirmation which is either intuitively or demonstratively certain.* That the square of the hypothenuse is equal to the square of the two sides, *is a proposition which expresses a relation between these figures.* That three times five is equal to the half of thirty, *expresses a relation between these numbers. Propositions of this kind are discoverable by the mere operation of thought, without dependence on what is anywhere existent in the universe. Though there never were a circle or triangle in nature, the truths demonstrated by Euclid would for ever retain their certainty and evidence.*
>
> *Matters of fact, which are the second objects of human reason, are not ascertained in the same manner; nor is our evidence of their truth, however great, of a like nature with the foregoing. The contrary of every matter of fact is still possible; because it can never imply a contradiction, and is conceived by the mind with the same facility and distinctness, as if ever so conformable to reality.* That the sun will not rise to-morrow *is no less intelligible a proposition, and implies no more contradiction than the affirmation, that it will rise. We should in vain, therefore, attempt to demonstrate its falsehood. Were it demonstratively false, it would imply a contradiction, and could never be distinctly conceived by the mind.*[12]

[12]David Hume, *An Enquiry Concerning Human Understanding,* in *Hume's Enquiries,* ed. L. A. Selby-Bigge, 2[d] ed. (Oxford: Clarendon Press, 1902), pp. 25–26.

> ## HUME'S TWO BASES OF KNOWLEDGE
>
> - *Relations of Ideas:* Ideas which, simply by virtue of their meanings and relations, are necessarily or *logically* true, but therefore irrelevant for the world of reality; for example, "The sum of the angles of a triangle equals 180 degrees."
> - *Matters of Fact:* Ideas which bear upon and inform us about the world of reality, but which can never be certain because they are derived from specific experiences; for example, "Water freezes at 32 degrees Fahrenheit."

David Hume, who carried British Empiricism to its skeptical conclusion.

A

TREATISE

OF

Human Nature:

BEING

An ATTEMPT to introduce the experimental Method of Reasoning

INTO

MORAL SUBJECTS.

*Rara temporum felicitas, ubi sentire, quæ velis; & quæ
sentias, dicere licet.*   TACIT.

BOOK I.

OF THE

UNDERSTANDING.

LONDON:
Printed for JOHN NOON, at the *White-Hart*, near
Mercer's-Chapel in *Cheapside.*
MDCCXXXIX.

*Hume's Treatise of
Human Nature was
first published in 1739.
The disappointed
Hume described it as
having fallen "still-born
from the press," so poor
was the response to it.
It was followed by the
Enquiry Concerning
Human
Understanding.*

Our knowledge is either based on *relations of ideas,* in which case it is certain but has no connection with reality, as with "three times five is equal to half of thirty," which, though absolutely certain, is absolutely certain independently of anything in the world of reality; *or* our knowledge is based on *matters of fact,* in which case it does inform us about the world of reality, as with "the sun will rise tomorrow," but can never be certain because it is derived from a limited and passing parade of perceptions.

This same skeptical and antimetaphysical distinction is restated in the celebrated outburst with which Hume concluded the *Enquiry*:

> *When we run over libraries, persuaded of these principles, what havoc must we make? If we take in our hand any volume; of divinity or school metaphysics, for instance; let us ask, "Does it contain any abstract reasoning concerning quantity or number?" No. "Does it contain any experimental reasoning concerning matter of fact and existence?" No. Commit it then to the flames: for it can contain nothing but sophistry and illusion.*[13]

Again, there is no halfway house: Our ideas are either certain but uninformative, or they are informative but never certain. And there we are stuck. But not for long.

Chapter 10 in Review

SUMMARY

Empiricism is the epistemological claim that the mind at birth is a "blank tablet" and that all knowledge (exclusive of logical and mathematical knowledge) is derived ultimately from *sense experience*. In the previous chapter we considered three versions of rationalism, and in the present chapter we considered three versions of empiricism.

Classical empiricism has its origin in Greek philosophy and is most notably associated with Aristotle and, later, St. Thomas Aquinas. It will be recalled that Aristotle's is a Form-philosophy, wherein the object of knowledge is identified with the abiding essence of things. Unlike Plato, Aristotle believed that this essence is *in* particular things, and thus that it is with particular things that we must begin. From the particulars the mind is able to form a universal concept, which corresponds to the common essence in the particulars, and which guides knowledge and discourse amidst the flux and multiplicity of the sensible world. St. Thomas introduced the intellectual faculty of abstraction, whereby the mind is enabled to lift the universal features from particulars, leaving behind in the particulars all that is not *essential* to them.

In some ways Locke is the giant of all empiricists, and certainly the one who set the empiricist agenda for the modern period. He began his famous *Essay Concerning Human Understanding* with a scathing rebuttal to the doctrine of innate ideas. In place of innate ideas Locke substitutes experience. This comes in two forms: sensation, our experience of external objects, and reflection, our experience of the internal workings of our minds. From sensation and reflection we form simple ideas, and from simple ideas the mind compounds complex ideas. In all of this the active and passive functions of the mind should be distinguished. Very impor-

[13]Ibid., p. 165.

tant is Locke's epistemological or representative dualism, whereby our ideas are held to convey to us a likeness of the realities external to our minds: the perception of a tree, and the actual tree "out there." This, however, involves a great problem known as the egocentric predicament: If all we can know directly is our own ideas, how can we ever know whether they correspond to anything that is not an idea?

Locke believed in material and mental substance; Berkeley believed at least in mental substance; but Hume's *radical* empiricism pushes everything further. All we have are perceptions, divided into lively impressions and pale ideas; that's *all* we have. The time-honored concept of underlying but unperceived substance is, therefore, an unjustified figment, as is also the concept of causality, which, in its pre-Humean form, was thought to involve some unperceived metaphysical necessity. Hume's phenomenalism, which reduces knowledge to phenomena or appearances or "bundles of ideas," represents a serious skepticism: A proposition is either a mere relation of ideas ("A is A"), which says nothing about reality itself, or it is a matter of fact ("Swans are white"), which can never be known with certitude because of the limitations of our perceptions.

BASIC IDEAS

- Empiricism
- *Tabula rasa*
- Universal concepts
- Intellectual abstraction
- Aristotle and St. Thomas: Three stages of knowledge
- Locke's arguments against innate ideas
- Locke: Experience, sensation, and reflection
- Simple and complex ideas
- The mind as passive and active
- Epistemological dualism, or the representative theory of knowledge
- The egocentric predicament
- Hume: Perceptions, impressions, and ideas
- Hume's analysis of substance
- Hume's analysis of causality
- Phenomenalism
- Relations of ideas and matters of fact

TEST YOURSELF

1. True or false: Fido is an abstraction.
2. The impossibility of escaping the world of our own ideas is called _____.
3. Why does Hume have little time for talk about, say, "necessary connections" or substances?
4. Name a few of Locke's arguments against innate ideas.

5. Why, for St. Thomas, is the singular prior to the universal in one way, but the universal prior to the singular in another way?
6. What is the empiricist's attitude toward a claim such as "All barking dogs bark"?
7. What role does induction play in Aristotle's view of knowledge?
8. Who wrote A *Treatise of Human Nature?*
9. Why is Hume's empiricism called *radical* empiricism?
10. True or false: Locke, like Descartes, believed in mind or mental substance.

QUESTIONS FOR
REFLECTION

- When considering thinkers who belong to the same tradition, such as the empiricist tradition, be able to identify what they hold in common and where they differ. Can you compare in this way the thinkers in this chapter?

- What do you yourself make of the egocentric predicament? Is it a genuine problem? If not, why not? If so, how do you propose to escape the skepticism inherent in it?

- What do you think about Hume's rejection of mind (as a mental substance) or causality (as a metaphysical connection)? Does it make any difference to your philosophical perspective? To your practical life?

CHAPTER 11

THE PROBLEM OF CERTAINTY

We began this part of the book with a chapter on *doubt,* and it is fitting to conclude with a chapter on *certitude.* To see that certitude really does pose a problem, just ask yourself whether you are certain of any of the following propositions, and whether you are certain about them in different ways:

- $2 + 2 = 4$.
- In fourteen-hundred-and-ninety-two, Columbus sailed the ocean blue.
- I exist.
- you exist.
- The sun will rise tomorrow.
- Right now I am perceiving this page.
- Barking dogs bark.
- Humans have evolved from lower animals.
- Every event must have a cause.

As you can see, the idea of certainty is not a simple one. In this chapter we will consider the problem in only one of its aspects, but, philosophically, a very basic one. Still more specifically, we will discuss one philosopher's attempt to account for certainty, especially in light of the preceding chapter. A warning: This may not be easy going, and the quoted material will be a good challenge.

KANT AND HUME

"I openly confess my recollection of David Hume was the very thing which many years ago first interrupted my dogmatic slumber and gave my investigations in the field of speculative philosophy a quite new direction."[1] Thus spoke the German philosopher Immanuel Kant[2] (1724–1804), who marks a turning point in modern epistemology.

Kant observed that there must be something radically wrong with the whole way of thinking that led finally to the phenomenalism and skepticism of Hume. For, Kant says, I *am* certain of some of the truths which Hume called "matters of fact." He cites, as an example, all mathematical propositions, such as $7 + 5 = 12$ (though most philosophers now regard mathematical truths to be true by definition); from natural science he cites as an example Newton's Third Law of Motion, that in all motion action and reaction must always be equal; and from metaphysics he cites the principle of causality, that every event must have a cause. For Kant it was not a question of *whether* we possess such knowledge but *how*. In his explanation of how propositions can be at once genuinely informative about reality *and* absolutely certain, Kant signals an altogether different approach to the problem and establishes himself as one of the greatest epistemologists of all time.

SOME IMPORTANT
TERMINOLOGY

But, to begin at the beginning, it is necessary to study some terminology which Kant himself introduced into philosophical discussion.

A priori **and** *a posteriori* **knowledge**

First, the distinction between *a priori* knowledge and *a posteriori* knowledge. You can pretty much guess the meaning of these Latin terms just by looking at them. *A priori* knowledge is knowledge which comes before (prior to) sense experience and is therefore *independent* of sense experience. This, of course, is the emphasis of the rationalist. *A posteriori* knowledge is knowledge which comes after (posterior to) sense experience and is therefore *dependent* on sense experience. This is the empiricist emphasis.

Analytic and synthetic knowledge

Second, we have the distinction between *analytic* and *synthetic* knowledge. Analytic knowledge is another way of expressing Hume's "relation of ideas." When this kind of knowledge is expressed in a proposition, the predicate is contained already in the subject. Examples are: "The sum of the angles of any triangle is 180 degrees"; "All barking dogs bark"; or any proposition of the form "A is A" (the predicate "A" is contained already in the subject "A"). Now all such knowledge or propositions *have to be true*. For they are true by definition, or to say the same thing,

[1]Immanuel Kant, *Prolegomena to Any Future Metaphysics*, tr. Lewis W. Beck (Indianapolis, Ind.: Bobbs-Merrill, 1950), p. 8.

[2]Rhymes with font.

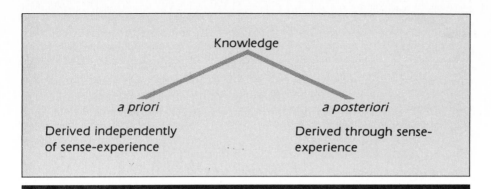

they are *logically* true, and this means that you could not deny them without self-contradiction. Do you recall the Law of Identity from the Three Laws of Thought? Who in their right minds would be interested in affirming that A is not A? (Such statements are sometimes called tautologies or redundancies.) Now no one questions the absolute truth of analytic propositions. Rationalists and empiricists alike agree that such propositions must be true no matter what. On the other hand, it is important to see that such truths do not really tell us anything about *reality*. They neither affirm nor deny the actual existence of anything. The proposition "All barking dogs bark" is necessarily true whether or not there are any dogs, or, for that matter, whether or not there is *anything*. A statement like "All barking dogs bark" only means "*If* there are any barking dogs, then they bark." The truth of these propositions is, then, *a priori* and utterly independent of sense experience and of the sensible world itself.

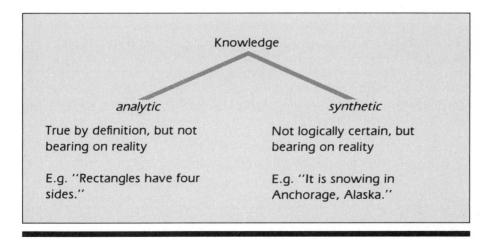

Synthetic knowledge, on the other hand, corresponds to Hume's "matters of fact." In synthetic propositions, the predicate *adds* something to the subject, and thus two ideas are "synthesized" in the proposition. Examples are: "Water freezes at 32 degrees Fahrenheit"; "Dogs bark"; and any proposition of the form "A is B" (the predicate "B" amplifies the subject "A"). In this way a synthetic proposition affirms or denies the existence of something (and is therefore sometimes called an "existential" proposition); it informs us about things; it really does tell us something about the actual universe.

IS THERE SYNTHETIC A *PRIORI* KNOWLEDGE?

Now we have just seen that everyone, rationalists and empiricists both, accepts the absolute truth of analytic propositions as *a priori* certain. It is also clear that few rationalists have ever insisted that sense experience plays absolutely no role *whatsoever* in the acquisition of synthetic knowledge. Just consider: Even if you are the staunchest rationalist, how do you know that swans are white? that in fourteen-hundred-and-ninety-two Columbus sailed the ocean blue? Obviously there is much about the actual world that we could not possibly know except in an *a posteriori* way: making observations, lighting bunsen burners, taking field trips, and the like. Everyone admits this.

It turns out then that both rationalists and empiricists accept analytic propositions as *a priori* certain, and that they both accept at least *some* synthetic propositions as *a posteriori* probable. The real question and the real issue between rationalists and empiricists is this: Can we possess any knowledge that is both *a priori* certain and synthetically informative? *Is there such a thing as synthetic* a priori *knowledge?* This is a crucial question, and how you answer it will make all the difference to your general philosophical perspective.

As we already have seen, Kant answered the question of synthetic *a priori*

SYNTHETIC *A PRIORI,* A CRUCIAL QUESTION

One of the questions that divides philosophers into two different camps is the question of synthetic *a priori* knowledge: Is it possible to know synthetic propositions with *a priori* certainty? Are there any nonanalytic truths that are, nonetheless, universally and necessarily true?

knowledge with a resounding Yes. But his explanation is hardly what traditional rationalists would have expected—or accepted. Kant turned the epistemological world upside-down. In fact, he likened his contribution to the Copernican revolution, which, by radically shifting our viewpoint (the sun does not go around the earth, but the earth goes around the sun), resulted immediately in a superior explanation of the phenomena to be explained. Kant's "Copernican revolution" consisted, similarly, in the startling announcement that ideas such as substance and causality do not make their way into our minds through experience, but are "*a priori* categories of the understanding" which mold and shape and, in fact, *constitute* our experience. That is, substance and causality (along with ten additional categories) are *part* of what we *mean* by experience. Indeed, even space and time, in which substances standing in causal relations are enabled to appear at all, are contributed by our intellects. Space and time too, therefore, are *a priori* conditions of experience.

> **Kant's Copernican revolution: Experience dependent on concepts**

In this way Kant redeems such principles as those of causality and substance from the skeptical clutches of Hume. As far as the world of appearance goes, "Every event must have a cause," for example, is a synthetic truth but also possesses *a priori* universality and necessity. We don't have any choice about it: We *have* to experience things as causally related because that is one of the ways our minds *create* experience; if we're all wearing rose-colored glasses, everything must appear to be rose-colored—to all of us.

KANT'S COPERNICAN REVOLUTION IN PHILOSOPHY

" . . . the pure concepts of the understanding . . . do not derive from experience, but experience derives from them."

Kant's major work, the *Critique of Pure Reason,* was first published in 1781. In the following excerpts from the Introduction, Kant begins to explain in his own way the ideas we have already outlined. (1) He distinguishes between empirical or *a posteriori* knowledge derived from sense experience, and pure or *a priori* knowledge which is completely independent of experience, and raises the question whether such pure knowledge exists; (2) he establishes the two identifying marks by which pure or *a priori* knowledge may be recognized and distinguished from empirical or *a posteriori* knowledge:

- necessity
- universality

(3) he distinguishes between analytic and synthetic knowledge, and explains the nature of synthetic *a priori* knowledge both as being existentially informative and also bearing the marks of necessity and universality, something unaccountable for on the basis of experience.

OF THE DIFFERENCE BETWEEN PURE AND EMPIRICAL KNOWLEDGE

That all our knowledge begins with experience there can be no doubt. For how should the faculty of knowledge be called into activity, if not by objects which affect our senses, and which either produce representations by themselves, or rouse the activity of our understanding to compare, to connect, or to separate them; and thus to convert the raw material of our sensuous impressions into a knowledge of objects, which we call experience? In respect of time, therefore, no knowledge within us is antecedent to experience, but all knowledge begins with it.

But although all our knowledge begins with experience, it does not follow that it arises from experience. For it is quite possible that even our empirical experience is a compound of that which we receive through impressions, and of that which our own faculty of knowledge (incited only by sensuous impressions), supplies from itself, a supplement which we do not distinguish from that raw material, until long practice has roused our attention and rendered us capable of separating one from the other.

It is therefore a question which deserves at least closer investigation, and cannot be disposed of at first sight, whether there exists a knowledge independent of experience, and even of all impressions of the senses? Such knowledge is called a priori, and distinguished from empirical knowledge, which has its sources a posteriori, that is, in experience.

WE ARE IN POSSESSION OF CERTAIN COGNITIONS A PRIORI, AND EVEN THE ORDINARY UNDERSTANDING IS NEVER WITHOUT THEM

All depends here on a criterion, by which we may safely distinguish between pure and empirical knowledge. Now experience teaches us, no doubt, that something is so or so, but not that it cannot be different. First, then, if we have a proposition, which is thought, together with its necessity, we have a judgment a priori; and if, besides, it is not derived from any proposition, except such as is itself again considered as necessary, we have an absolutely a priori judgment. Secondly, experience never imparts to its judgments true or strict, but only assumed or relative universality (by means of induction), so that we ought always to say, so far as we have observed hitherto, there is no exception to this or that rule. If, therefore, a judgment is thought with strict universality, so that no exception is admitted as possible, it is not derived from experience, but valid absolutely a priori. . . . Necessity, therefore, and strict universality are safe criteria of knowledge a priori, and are inseparable one from the other. . . .

That there really exist in our knowledge such necessary, and in the strictest sense universal, and therefore pure judgments a priori, is easy to show. If we want a scientific example, we have only to look to any of the propositions of mathematics; if we want one from the sphere of the ordinary understanding, such a proposition as that each change must have a cause, will answer the purpose; nay, in the latter case, even the concept of cause contains so clearly the concept of the necessity of its connection with an effect, and of the strict universality of the rule, that it would be destroyed altogether if we attempted to derive it, as Hume does, from the frequent concomitancy of that which happens with that which precedes, and from a habit arising thence (therefore from a purely subjective necessity), of connecting representations. It is possible even, without having recourse to such examples in proof of the reality of pure propositions a priori within our knowledge, to prove their indispensability for the possibility of experience itself, thus proving it a priori. For whence should experience take its certainty, if all the rules which it follows were always again and again empirical, and therefore contingent and hardly fit to serve as first principles? For the present, however, we may be satisfied for having shown the pure employment of the faculty of our knowledge as a matter of fact, with the criteria of it.

Not only in judgments, however, but even in certain concepts, can we show their origin a priori. Take away, for example, from the concept of a body, as supplied by experience, everything that is empirical, one by one; such as colour, hardness or softness, weight, and even impenetrability, and there still remains the space which the body (now entirely vanished) occupied: that you cannot take away. And in the same manner, if you remove from your empirical concept of any object, corporeal or incorporeal, all properties which experience has taught you, you cannot take away from it that property by which you conceive it as a substance, or inherent in a substance (although such a concept contains more determinations than that of an object in general). Convinced, therefore, by the necessity with which that concept forces itself upon you, you will have to admit that it has its seat in your faculty of knowledge a priori. . . .

OF THE DISTINCTION BETWEEN ANALYTICAL AND SYNTHETICAL JUDGMENTS

In all judgments in which there is a relation between subject and predicate (I speak of affirmative judgments only, the application to negative ones being easy), that relation can be of two kinds. Either the predicate B belongs to the subject A as something contained (though covertly) in the concept A; or B lies outside the sphere of the concept A, though somehow connected with it. In the former case I call the judgment analytical, in the latter synthetical. Analytical judgments (affirmative) are therefore those in which the connection of the predicate with the subject is conceived through identity, while others in which that connection is conceived without identity, may be called synthetical. The former might be called illustrating, the latter expanding judgments, because in the former nothing is added by the predicate to the concept of the subject, but the concept is only divided into its constituent concepts which were always conceived as existing within it, though confusedly; while the latter add to the concept of the subject a predicate not conceived as existing within it, and not to be extracted from it by any process of mere analysis. If I say, for instance, All bodies are extended, this is an analytical judgment. I need not go beyond the concept connected with the name of body, in order to find that extension is connected with it. I have only to analyse that concept and become conscious of the manifold elements always contained in it, in order to find that predicate. This is therefore an analytical judgment. But if I say, All bodies are heavy, the predicate is something quite different from what I think as the mere concept of body. The addition of such a predicate gives us a synthetical judgment. . . .

Empirical judgments, as such, are all synthetical; for it would be absurd to found an analytical judgment on experience, because, in order to form such a judgment, I need not at all step out of my concept, or appeal to the testimony of experience. That a body is extended, is a proposition perfectly certain a priori, and not an empirical judgment. For, before I call in experience, I am already in possession of all the conditions of my judgment in the concept of body itself. I have only to draw out from it, according to the principle of contradiction, the required predicate, and I thus become conscious, at the same time, of the necessity of the judgment, which experience could never teach me. But, though I do not include the predicate of gravity in the general concept of body, that concept, nevertheless, indicates an object of experience through one of its parts: so that I may add other parts also of the same experience, besides those which belonged to the former concept. I may, first, by an analytical process, realise the concept of body, through the predicates of extension, impermeability, form, etc., all of which are contained in it. Afterwards I expand my knowledge, and looking back to the experience from which my concept of body was abstracted, I find gravity always connected with the before-mentioned predicates, and therefore I add it synthetically to that concept as a predicate. It is, therefore, experience on which the possibility of the synthesis of the predicate of gravity with the concept of body is founded: because both concepts, though neither of them is contained in the other, belong to each other, though accidentally only, as parts of a whole, namely, of experience, which is itself a synthetical connection of intuitions.

In synthetical judgments a priori, however, that help is entirely wanting. If I want to go beyond the concept A in order to find another concept B connected with it, where is there anything on which I may rest and through which a synthesis might become possible, considering that I cannot have the advantage of looking about in the field of experience? Take the proposition that all which happens has its cause. In the concept of something that happens I no doubt conceive of something existing preceded by time, and from this certain analytical judgments may be deduced. But the concept of cause is entirely outside that concept, and indicates something different from that which happens, and is by no means contained in that representation. How can I venture then to predicate of that which happens something totally different from it, and to represent the concept of cause, though not contained in it, as belonging to it, and belonging to it by necessity? What is here the unknown x, on which the understanding may rest in order to find beyond the concept A a foreign predicate B, which nevertheless is believed to be connected with it? It cannot be experience, because the *proposition that all which happens has its cause represents this second predicate as added to the subject not only with greater generality than experience can ever supply, but also with a character of necessity, and therefore purely a priori, and based on concepts. . . .*[3]

Later in the *Critique*, Kant proposes *how* synthetic *a priori* knowledge is possible. Pay close attention to his insistence on the role of *a priori* concepts as conditions of experience and the epistemological consequences of this, as in the statement, "If by them only it is possible to think any object of experience, it follows that they refer by necessity and *a priori* to all objects of experience." (By "intuition" Kant means the perception of objects as they are represented by the intellect.)

Two ways only are possible in which synthetical representations and their objects can agree, can refer to each other with necessity, and so to say meet each other. Either it is the object alone that makes the representation possible, or it is the representation alone that makes the object possible. In the former case their relation is empirical only, and the representation therefore never possible a priori. This applies to phenomena with reference to whatever in them belongs to sensation. In the latter case, though representation by itself (for we do not speak here of its causality by means of the will) cannot produce its object so far as its existence is concerned, nevertheless the representation determines the object a priori, if through it alone it is possible to know anything as an object. To know a thing as an object is possible only under two conditions. First, there must be intuition by which the object is given us, though as a phenomenon only, secondly, there must be a concept by which an object is thought as corresponding to that intuition. From what we have said before it is clear that the first condition, namely, that under which alone objects can be seen, exists, so far as the form of intuition is concerned, in the soul a priori. All phenomena therefore must conform to that formal condition of sensibility, because it is through it alone that they appear, that is, that they are given and empirically seen.

Now the question arises whether there are not also antecedent concepts a priori, forming conditions under which alone something can be, if not seen, yet thought as an object in general; for in that case all empirical knowledge of objects would necessarily conform to such concepts, it being impossible that anything should become an object of experience without them. All experience contains, besides the intuition of the senses by which something is given, a concept also of the object, which is given in intuition as a phenomenon. Such concepts of objects in general therefore must form conditions a priori of all knowledge produced by experience, and the objective validity of the categories, as being such concepts a priori, rests on this very fact that by them alone, so far as the form of thought is concerned, experience becomes possible. If by them only it is possible to think any object of experience, it follows that they refer by necessity and a priori to all objects of experience.

[3]Immanuel Kant, *Critique of Pure Reason*, tr. F. Max Müller (Garden City, N.Y.: Anchor Books, 1960), pp. 2–5, 7–9.

> *There is therefore a principle for the transcendental deduction of all concepts a priori which must guide the whole of our investigation, namely, that all must be recognised as conditions a priori of the possibility of experience, whether of intuition, which is found in it, or of thought. . . .*[4]

Where Locke and Hume went wrong

Kant goes on immediately to contrast his own theory of knowledge with that of his empiricist predecessors, Locke and Hume, and to show where they went wrong: *Locke* correctly recognized the existence of pure (necessary and universal) concepts but mistakenly sought them from sense experience and, at the same time, applied them *beyond* sense experience (for example, every event must have a cause, and God, a transcendent Being, is the cause of the world); *Hume* on the other hand, correctly saw that such concepts (necessary and universal) could not be derived from sense experience, and so mistakenly denied that they are, after all, necessary and universal. Now, says Kant, neither Locke's "extravagance" nor Hume's "skepticism" squares with the epistemological facts (the givenness of synthetic *a priori* knowledge), whereas his own theory does account for the facts by steering a middle course between the false alternatives of his misguided predecessors.

> *Locke, for want of this reflection, and because he met with pure concepts of the understanding in experience, derived them also from experience, and yet acted so inconsistently that he attempted to use them for knowledge which far exceeds all limits of experience. David Hume saw that, in order to be able to do this, these concepts ought to have their origin a priori; but as he could not explain how it was possible that the understanding should be constrained to think concepts, which by themselves are not united in the understanding, as necessarily united in the object, and never thought that possibly the understanding might itself, through these concepts, be the author of that experience in which its objects are found, he was driven by necessity to derive them from experience (namely, from a subjective necessity, produced by frequent association in experience, which at last is wrongly supposed to be objective, that is, from habit). He acted, however, very consistently, by declaring it to be impossible to go with these concepts, and with the principles arising from them, beyond the limits of experience. This empirical deduction, which was adopted by both philosophers, cannot be reconciled with the reality of our scientific knowledge a priori, namely, pure mathematics and general natural science, and is therefore refuted by facts. The former of these two celebrated men opened a wide door to fantastic extravagance, because reason, if it has once established such pretensions, can no longer be checked by vague praises of moderation; the other, thinking that he had once discovered so general an illusion of our faculty of knowledge, which had formerly been accepted as reason, gave himself over entirely to scepticism.*[5]

[4]Ibid., pp. 72–73.
[5]Ibid., pp. 74–75.

THE LIMITS OF REASON

It is important to note, however, what price must be paid for synthetic *a priori* knowledge. It is a very high price. One of the implications of Kant's analysis is that we can know nothing of reality as it is in itself (what Kant calls the *noumenal* world) but only as it appears to us through experience (he calls this the *phenomenal* world). The reason is clear: The *a priori* categories or concepts of the understanding are, as we have said, constitutive of our experience, and therefore they have no legitimate application *beyond* experience. Causality, for example, applies only to objects of possible experience. And when we try to apply such concepts beyond experience, what results is nonsense and absurdities.

The noumenal and phenomenal worlds

> "... although all our knowledge begins with experience, it does not follow that it arises from experience."
>
> —Kant

This necessary limitation of the concepts of the understanding to the phenomenal world comes out well in the following from Kant's *Prolegomena to Any Future Metaphysics*, published in 1783 as a simplified version of the *Critique of Pure Reason*. (In these paragraphs, "intuition" again refers to what we normally might call perceptions, and the "Aesthetic" refers to a section of the *Critique*.)

Since the oldest days of philosophy, inquirers into pure reason have conceived, besides the things of sense, or appearances (phenomena), which make up the sensible world, certain beings of the understanding (noumena), which should constitute an intelligible world. And as appearance and illusion were by those men identified (a thing which we may well excuse in an undeveloped epoch), actuality was only conceded to the beings of the understanding.

And we indeed, rightly considering objects of sense as mere appearances, confess thereby that they are based upon a thing in itself, though we know not this thing as it is in itself but only know its appearances, namely, the way in which our senses are affected by this unknown something. The understanding, therefore, by assuming appearances, grants the existence of things in themselves also; and to this extent we may say that the representation of such things as are the basis of appearances, consequently of mere beings of the understanding, is not only admissible but unavoidable.

Our critical deduction by no means excludes things of that sort (noumena), but rather limits the principles of the Aesthetic to this, that they shall not extend to all things—as everything would then be turned into mere appearance—but that they

Critik

der

reinen Vernunft

von

Immanuel Kant

Profeſſor in Königsberg.

Riga,
verlegts Johann Friedrich Hartknoch
1781

shall hold good only of objects of possible experience. Hereby, then, beings of the
understanding are granted, but with the inculcation of this rule which admits of no
exception: that we neither know nor can know anything at all definite of these pure
beings of the understanding, because our pure concepts of the understanding as well
as our pure intuitions extend to nothing but objects of possible experience, conse-

quently to mere things of sense; and as soon as we leave this sphere, these concepts retain no meaning whatever.[6]

Thus, if we have gained *a priori* certainty and universality for synthetic knowledge, it has been at the cost of giving up any knowledge of reality beyond space and time. We will see in Chapter 12 that for Kant this included, naturally, God. But Kant believed that in addition to the "theoretical" reason, which is guided and limited by the *a priori* concepts of the understanding, there is open to us the "practical" reason, which builds on the entirely different foundation of *moral* experience, and which *does* give us, in a way, knowledge of God, freedom, and immortality. In Chapter 13, we will encounter Kant's Moral Argument for God.

The "theoretical" and the "practical" reason

- *What we gain through Kant's theoretical reason: a priori* certainty and universality of fundamental concepts, such as causality and substance.
- *What we lose through Kant's theoretical reason:* the possibility of any theoretical knowledge of reality beyond objects of possible experience.

Chapter 11 in Review

SUMMARY

In the previous chapter we saw how the skeptical Hume brought traditional thinking about knowledge to a sort of dead-end. This is precisely where Kant began.

Unlike Hume, Kant was certain of many truths of the sort Hume rejected, for example, that every event must have a cause. According to Kant, the universality and necessity that characterize such truths cannot be accounted for on empiricist, or *a posteriori,* grounds and require, rather, an *a priori* origin. On the other hand, such truths are not analytic, or empty redundancies, but synthetic, or existential. But how is synthetic *a priori* knowledge possible? Kant himself rightly regarded his answer as a revolution in epistemology, and even now one frequently encounters the expressions "pre-Kantian" and "post-Kantian" as demarcations of a watershed in the history of philosophy.

Kant distinguished between things as they are in themselves (the noumenal world) and things as they appear to us (the phenomenal world). Things-in-themselves are wholly unknown to us. Things-as-they-appear (that is, experience) are made possible first of all by the *a priori* conditions of space and time, and then by

---

[6]Kant, *Prolegomena to Any Future Metaphysics,* pp. 61–62.

the *a priori* categories of the understanding, which further structure our experience into the world that we apprehend. It is crucial to see how Kant, with this reinterpretation of the origin and nature of knowledge, accounts for synthetic *a priori* knowledge. For example, *every* event *must* have a cause, because that is the only way in which our intellects work. On the other hand, this means that our "theoretical" reason, operating with substance, causality, and the like, has proper application only to objects of possible experience. And *this* means that we can have no theoretical knowledge of anything *beyond* experience. For such knowledge we must have recourse to an entirely different kind of reason, the "practical" reason, which begins not with experiential categories but with moral categories.

BASIC IDEAS

- Kant's rejection of Humean skepticism
- *A priori* and *a posteriori* knowledge
- Analytic and synthetic knowledge
- Synthetic *a priori* knowledge
- Kant's "Copernican revolution" in philosophy
- Space and time as *a priori* conditions of experience
- The categories of the understanding as conditions of experience
- The noumenal and phenomenal worlds
- The theoretical reason and the practical reason
- The limitations of theoretical reason

TEST YOURSELF

1. How did Hume awaken Kant out of his "dogmatic slumbers"?
2. Which of these is an analytic claim? (a) It is wrong to kill someone for the fun of it; (b) It is wrong to murder someone. Why?
3. True or false: Kant believed that "Every event must have a cause" is an example of a synthetic *a priori* proposition.
4. In what way was Kant's revolution in epistemology similar to Copernicus' revolution in astronomy?
5. In Kant's terminology, the "theoretical" reason is limited to the _____world, but the "practical" reason can penetrate the _____ world.
6. What is a "category of the understanding"?
7. How did Kant account for synthetic *a priori* knowledge?

QUESTIONS FOR REFLECTION

- It would be a mistake to call Kant either a rationalist or an empiricist. Do you see why? On the other hand, he effected a sort of synthesis of the two. What is the rationalist element? What is the empiricist element?
- With his doctrine of the *a priori* conditions of experience, Kant sought to explain how we enjoy certitude of certain important claims. What are some of these claims? Are *you* certain of them? If not, are you a skeptic? If so, how do *you* account for the certainty?

PART

3

THE QUESTION OF GOD

When Mark Twain was once traveling abroad he received news of a mistaken obituary back in the United States giving notice of his death. He sent back the message: "Reports of my death are greatly exaggerated." In the last century the German philosopher Friedrich Nietzsche boldly proclaimed, "God is dead." Again in the 1960s the proclamation was issued by the Death of God theologians. They were not the only ones (nor will they be the last) to give, in one way or another, notice of the demise of the deity, but many would insist that in every case the report has been greatly exaggerated. As the well-known piece of graffiti expresses it:

GOD IS DEAD!
—Nietzsche
NIETZSCHE IS DEAD!
—God

Certainly it is true that God is alive and well if the continuing interest in and discussion of God is any indication.

Still, some may sense a difference with the question of God. It has something to do with the fact that our society is such a melting pot of religious and antireligious views. Even under "Churches" the yellow pages list, side by side, everything from Methodists, Baptists, Lutherans, and Catholics, to the Congregation of the Kindred Spirits, the Church of Good Science, and the Homosexual Church of the Universe. The difference also has to do with the sometimes passionate nature of belief or disbelief. How many times have we all heard it said that friends should never talk religion or politics lest they suddenly find themselves friends no longer. It is true that arguments over religion can become the most heated and can bring out the worst in all participants—atheists no less than believers. This is just to say that here, perhaps more than anywhere else, a special plea must be issued for identifying and laying aside (as best we can) prejudices, mental blind spots, and wishful thinking.

The "Death of God" theologians made a great splash in the 1960s. But soon after it was often heard: "The Death of God is dead."

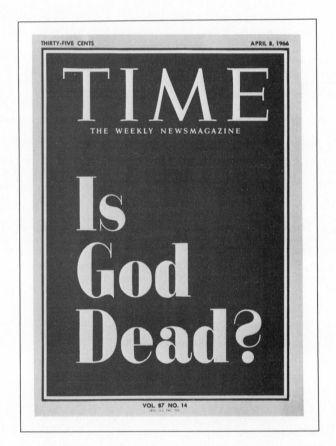

What we have called here "the question of God" actually includes much more than just God. The following are only some of the issues that are usually encompassed in what is known as "philosophy of religion," or perhaps better, "philosophical theology":

- What does "God" mean?
- Can the existence of God be proven?

- What is the relation between God and morality?
- How does philosophical knowledge of God relate to divine revelation?
- What is the nature and relevance of religious faith?
- Does God care about the world?
- Are religious experiences relevant data for the existence of God?
- Can an all-powerful and all-loving God be reconciled with the evil in the world?
- Do we have immortal souls?
- What are the special features of religious language?

Obviously such issues overlap with metaphysical and epistemological issues. Nonetheless, there is here an identifiable core of connected issues. At the center lies the specific question of God, and radiating from that, all sorts of related questions. And a whole history of philosophy could be written around the question of God and related matters, which only shows that it must be one of the questions that matter.

CHAPTER 12

GOD AND THE WORLD

It makes sense, of course, that the question of God's existence should come first in discussions concerning God and related matters. For, as St. Thomas Aquinas says near the beginning of his multivolumed *Summa Contra Gentiles*, if we don't first establish that he at least exists, then there is no point in going on:

> Now, among the inquiries that we must undertake concerning God in Himself, we must set down in the beginning that whereby His Existence is demonstrated, as the necessary foundation of the whole work. For, if we do not demonstrate that God exists, all consideration of divine things is necessarily suppressed.[1]

In this chapter and the next, we too will raise the question of God's existence, and we will consider some of the best-known arguments, pro and con.

NATURAL THEOLOGY

Before really getting into the arguments for God, the idea of *natural theology* must be introduced. First, what is *theology?* "Theology" comes from the Greek word *theos,* which means "God." Theology is therefore the study or science or knowledge of God. What then is *natural* theology? Caution: It does *not* mean the study or science or knowledge of God through *nature*. It is true, as we will see soon enough, that some of the arguments for God are based on the physical world, but we will see

What is natural theology?

---

[1]St. Thomas Aquinas, *Summa Contra Gentiles*, I. 9, 5, tr. and ed. Anton C. Pegis (South Bend, Ind.: Notre Dame University Press, 1955), I.

too that many are not. Natural theology is the study or science or knowledge of God through the *natural intellect*. This means the intellect in its natural state, unaided by any special or supernatural input. It may be helpful to know that natural theology is sometimes known also by the less ambiguous labels *philosophical theology* and *rational theology*.

Natural theology is therefore to be distinguished from *revealed theology*, which means the knowledge of God through special revelation, such as the Bible, the Church, Moses, Christ, the Holy Spirit, and the like. If it is not overly simplistic, we may say that in natural theology man attempts through his own natural faculties to approach God, whereas in revealed theology God has in his own special way approached man:

Man in search of God, and God in search of man

| Natural theology | God ↑ Man | God ↓ Man | Revealed theology |

It is important to note, though, that those who accept both natural and revealed theology do not confuse what man does in natural theology with what God does in revealed theology. Natural theology, if successful, delivers some basic knowledge of God which may bear on man's philosophical life, such as knowledge of God's existence and perhaps something of his nature. But revealed theology, if true, delivers a knowledge which bears on man's *salvation*. This was the point of Pascal's (French philosopher of about 1650) distinction between "the God of the philosophers, and the God of Abraham, Isaac, and Jacob." As usual, such a distinction is not as neat and tidy as one may wish. In the actual history of philosophy and theology, natural and revealed theology tend often to blur into one another. This

Theology

Revealed Theology
Knowledge of God by means of a special revelation

Natural Theology
Knowledge of God by means of the natural intellect

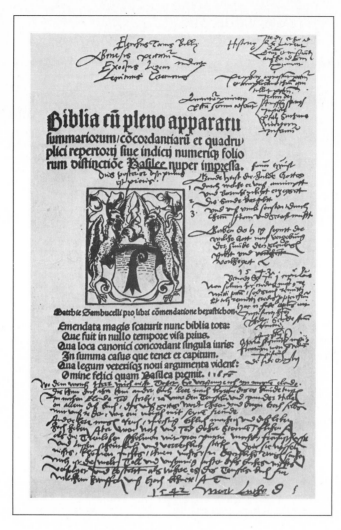

Title page of a Latin Bible printed in Basel, and bearing the handwritten notations of Martin Luther, the great sixteenth-century reformer, who took a very dim view of natural theology, knowledge of God through reason. Many who believe in revealed theology find the revelation in sacred scriptures, such as the Bible.

is not surprising in view of the fact that most philosophers who have propounded arguments for God's existence have already believed in divine revelation. Still, the distinction between natural and revealed theology is useful and important.

Further, the concept of natural theology must be carefully distinguished and understood because it is itself a philosophical problem. The possibility of such (natural) knowledge of God has been rejected by some philosophers and even theologians. Obviously, it has not been rejected by those who have presented philosophical arguments for God's existence.

THE COSMOLOGICAL
ARGUMENT

A priori **and** *a*
posteriori
arguments

Many arguments for God have been formulated over the centuries. Here we will consider four of them, and surely the most important of them: the Cosmological, Teleological, Ontological, and Moral Arguments for God. It is convenient, further, to divide these into two groups: The Cosmological and Teleological Arguments are *a posteriori*, and the Ontological and Moral Arguments are *a priori*. From earlier encounters with these expressions we know immediately that the first two arguments will attempt to demonstrate the existence of God *by means of sense experience*, whereas the second two arguments will attempt to demonstrate God *independently of sense experience*, that is, through reason alone. In this chapter we will consider the *a posteriori* proofs.

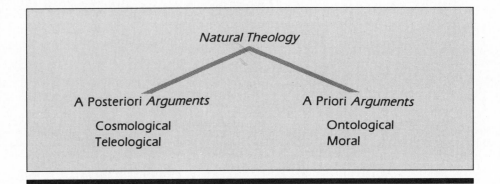

Natural Theology

A Posteriori *Arguments*   A Priori *Arguments*

Cosmological   Ontological
Teleological   Moral

The Cosmological
Argument stated

The most familiar attempts to prove the existence of God are variations of the *Cosmological Argument*. How many times have you heard something like this: "There has to be a God, because, well, the universe couldn't just *happen*. There must be a first cause of everything." This may not be the most sophisticated reasoning in the world, but it *is* a thumbnail expression of the Cosmological Argument. Why is this argument called "cosmological"? Because it is based on the *kosmos*, the Greek word for *world*. Of course, "world" means here not just the earth but the whole physical universe, or the sum total of space and time. It is also called, for short, the First-Cause Argument, since it attempts to show that there must be a first cause of the world.

Most forms of the Cosmological Argument involve the following reasoning:

1. Here is the world, or space and time.
2. It could not be the cause of itself.
3. It could not come from nothing.

4. It could not be an effect in an infinite series of causes and effects.

5. Therefore, it must be caused by something outside space and time, something uncaused and ultimate.

Stated in this way, it begins with the fact of the physical world and then by a process of elimination arrives at the only possible explanation for it: God, or the First Cause. But why cannot something be the cause of itself? Why cannot something come from nothing? Why cannot something be the final effect in an infinite series of causes and effects?

THE COSMOLOGICAL ARGUMENT

Compressed into the form of a categorical syllogism, all cosmological arguments for God may be expressed as follows:

> All contingent (or caused) being depends for its existence on some uncaused being.
> The cosmos is a contingent being.
>
> Therefore, the cosmos depends for its existence on some uncaused being.

As always, no conclusion in a deductive argument can be stronger than the premises. What questions, doubts, or challenges might be raised against the premises here? And does the "being" of the conclusion have to mean *God?*

These are, indeed, difficult questions. They are addressed, or at least involved, in the most famous proofs for God ever formulated, the "Five Ways" of St. Thomas Aquinas. He presents them in his *Summa Theologiae:*

The "Five Ways" of St. Thomas

The existence of God can be proved in five ways.

The first and more manifest way is the argument from motion. It is certain, and evident to our senses, that in the world some things are in motion. Now whatever is moved is moved by another, for nothing can be moved except it is in potentiality to that towards which it is moved; whereas a thing moves inasmuch as it is in act. For motion is nothing else than the reduction of something from potentiality to actuality. But nothing can be reduced from potentiality to actuality, except by something in a state of actuality. Thus that which is actually hot, as fire, makes wood, which is potentially hot, to be actually hot, and thereby moves and changes it. Now it is not possible that the same thing should be at once in actuality and potentiality in the same respect, but only in different respects. For what is actually hot cannot simultaneously be potentially hot; but it is simultaneously potentially cold. It is therefore impossible that in the same respect and in the same way a thing should be both mover and moved, i.e., that it should move itself. Therefore, whatever is moved must be moved by another. If that by which it is moved be itself moved, then this also must needs be moved by another, and that by another again. But this cannot go on to infinity, because then there would be no first mover, and, consequently, no other mover, seeing that subsequent movers move only inasmuch as they are moved by the first mover; as the staff moves only because it is moved by the hand. Therefore it is necessary to arrive at a first mover, moved by no other; and this everyone understands to be God.

The second way is from the nature of efficient cause. In the world of sensible things we find there is an order of efficient causes. There is no case known (neither is it, indeed, possible) in which a thing is found to be the efficient cause of itself; for so it would be prior to itself, which is impossible. Now in efficient causes it is not possible to go on to infinity, because in all efficient causes following in order, the first is the cause of the intermediate cause, and the intermediate is the cause of the ultimate cause, whether the intermediate cause be several, or one only. Now to take away the cause is to take away the effect. Therefore, if there be no first cause among efficient causes, there will be no ultimate, nor any intermediate, cause. But if in efficient causes it is possible to go on to infinity, there will be no first efficient cause, neither will there be an ultimate effect, nor any intermediate efficient causes; all of which is plainly false. Therefore it is necessary to admit a first efficient cause, to which everyone gives the name of God.

The third way is taken from possibility and necessity, and runs thus. We find in nature things that are possible to be and not to be, since they are found to be generated, and to be corrupted, and consequently, it is possible for them to be and not to be. But it is impossible for all things which are, to be of this sort,[2] for that which can not-be at some time is not. Therefore, if everything can not-be, then at one time there was nothing in existence. Now if this were true, even now there would be nothing in existence, because that which does not exist begins to exist only through something already existing. Therefore, if at one time nothing was in existence, it would have been impossible for anything to have begun to exist; and thus even now nothing would be in existence—which is absurd. Therefore, not all beings are merely possible, but there must exist something the existence of which is necessary. But every necessary thing either has its necessity caused by another, or not. Now it is impossible to go on to infinity in necessary things which have their necessity caused by another, as has been already proved in regard to efficient causes. Therefore we cannot but

---

[2]I have emended the translation in accordance with the best textual reading of this line: *Impossibile est autem omnia quae sunt, talia esse.*

admit the existence of some being having of itself its own necessity, and not receiving it from another, but rather causing in others their necessity. This all men speak of as God.

The fourth way is taken from the gradation to be found in things. Among beings there are some more and some less good, true, noble, and the like. But "more" and "less" are predicted of different things according as they resemble in their different ways something which is the maximum, as a thing is said to be hotter according as it more nearly resembles that which is hottest; so that there is something which is truest, something best, something noblest, and, consequently, something which is most being, for those things that are greatest in truth are greatest in being, as it is written in Metaph. ii. Now the maximum in any genus is the cause of all in that genus, as fire, which is the maximum of heat, is the cause of all hot things, as is said in the same book. Therefore there must also be something which is to all beings the cause of their being, goodness, and every other perfection; and this we call God.

The fifth way is taken from the governance of the world. We see that things which lack knowledge, such as natural bodies, act for an end, and this is evident from their acting always, or nearly always, in the same way, so as to obtain the best result. Hence it is plain that they achieve their end, not fortuitously, but designedly. Now whatever lacks knowledge cannot move towards an end, unless it is directed by some being endowed with knowledge and intelligence; as the arrow is directed by the archer. Therefore some intelligent being exists by whom all natural things are directed to their end; and this being we call God.[3]

It should be noted what all of the Five Ways have in common. Each of them begins in an *a posteriori* way with the created world, and each of them presupposes the metaphysical principle *ex nihilo, nihil fit,* "from nothing, nothing comes." More specifically, St. Thomas shows in the Second Way why something cannot be the cause of itself (it would have to exist before it exists), and the impossibility of an infinite series of causes and effects is explicitly argued in the first three Ways. But here is a surprise. When St. Thomas argues against an infinite series of causes and effects he is not thinking of a *temporal* series, or one that *stretches infinitely backwards in time.* Although be believed, on the basis of Genesis 1:1, that the world, and therefore time, had a beginning, for the sake of his proofs for God he grants that the world has always existed. Although each of the Five Ways assumes the eternity of the world, this is most evident in the Third Way. There it is argued that not all things are merely possible, or can not-be, for that would mean that even now nothing would exist; for, given *enough time* all possible states, including the possible nonbeing of things, would come about, and such a state at some point in the *infinite* past must have by now come about; but from such a state of nothingness, nothing could possibly come (*ex nihilo, nihil fit*); but right now there *is* a world, and therefore

"First" Cause in the sense of ultimate cause

---

[3]St. Thomas Aquinas, *Summa Theologiae,* Pt. I, Qu. 2, Art. 3, in *Basic Writings of Saint Thomas Aquinas,* ed. Anton C. Pegis (New York: Random House, 1945), I.

ST. THOMAS AQUINAS

St. Thomas Aquinas was born at the end of 1224 or the beginning of 1225 in a castle near Naples. His aristocratic father was the count of Aquino. He received his earliest education in the Benedictine monastery of Monte Cassino, where he was placed by his parents when he was 5, and at 14 he went to the University of Naples. In Naples he was attracted to the Dominican brothers and entered the Dominican Order. His family disapproved of this move, and Thomas' brothers kidnapped him during a journey to Bologna. His father, who was a military man and no doubt advocated the ideals of "breeding, leading, and bleeding," had Thomas imprisoned in a tower. He tried to draw Thomas back to sanity, even tempting him with a woman. But, faithful to his commitment, Thomas escaped after a year and traveled to Paris.

In Paris and then in Cologne, Thomas was the pupil of St. Albert the Great, whose interest in adapting the philosophy of Aristotle to Christianity was decisive for the direction of Thomas' own work. During this time Thomas was taunted as "the Dumb Ox" by his fellow students (Thomas was exceedingly quiet, and was immensely fat, with a frame not unlike a wine cask). But Albert the Great announced: "You call our brother Thomas a dumb ox, do you? I tell you that someday the whole world will listen to his bellows." In 1252, Thomas returned to Paris where he resumed his formal education at the university there, receiving his licentiate and his master's degree and lecturing as well.

In 1259, he returned to Italy where he taught theology at the papal court in Rome and was commissioned by Pope Urban IV to compose the liturgy of the feast of Corpus Christi. During the years 1268–1272 he was once again lecturing in Paris. He was then sent to Naples to establish a Dominican *Studium Generale,* where he remained until 1274 when he was called by Pope Gregory X to participate in the Council of Lyons. It was on the journey to Lyons that Thomas died, on March 7, 1274.

There is a tradition that toward the end of his life Thomas enjoyed mystic experiences which made all that he had previously written "seem as straw worthy to be burned." He became known as the Angelic Doctor, and was canonized in 1323. In 1879 Pope Leo XIII proclaimed Thomism as the official philosophy of the Roman Catholic Church. St. Thomas bellowed loudly indeed.

St. Thomas was a prolific writer. In addition to many commentaries on the works of Aristotle, commentaries on Biblical books, and works on specific philosophical and theological topics, he produced two of the most influential and majestic works of the entire history of philosophy: *Summa Theologiae* and *Summa Contra Gentiles*.

THE COSMOLOGICAL ARGUMENT: THOMISTIC FORM

Any form of the cosmological argument for God reasons, in one way or another, from the contingency of the world's being to the necessity of God's being. According to St. Thomas' version, no matter how long the world has existed—or even if it has always existed—it is *contingent*, or dependent, upon something else for its existence, and, finally, on Something which is *not* dependent. By its nature, this Something must be a transcendent (outside space and time) and ultimate being.

it was wrong at the start to think that all things are merely possible; so there must be something necessary, and ultimately something necessary of itself. Stay with this until you see how this argument cannot possibly work except on the assumption that the world has always existed.

St. Thomas really thought of his Five Ways as variations on a single idea, which is the substance of all of them: We know from experience that the world is *contingent*, that is, it depends on something outside itself for its existence. And this would be true even if the world has always been here, for an infinite collection of contingent things is no less contingent than a finite one. But there must be some *unconditional, ultimate* being upon which the world depends, otherwise it would have no *final* basis for existence.

There is, of course, a simpler and more popular version of the argument. Here, the infinite series of causes and effects *is* conceived as a temporal one stretching backwards in time; it is denied that this series could be infinite, and it is concluded that God must exist as the "first" cause, that is, the originator of this temporal series. We saw that even though St. Thomas accepted this as an article of faith

"First" cause in the sense of original cause

Did the world have a temporal beginning?

(Gen. 1:1), from a purely philosophical standpoint he left the question open, and actually *argued* as if the world had no beginning. Others believe that it is philosophically *necessary* to believe in a beginning of the world. The reasoning goes like this. If the world *has* always existed, then an infinite number of years (or months, minutes, or whatever) has *already gone by*. But surely this is a self-contradictory claim. For an *infinite* series of years (or whatever) can never (by its very nature as being *infinite*) go by or be completed. How can one claim that prior to this moment (what lies in the future is irrelevant) the world has *passed through* an infinite number of years? Of course, you can *think* of an infinite number of years, but you can't *count* them; you can entertain the *idea* of an infinite series, but you can't actually *pass through* one and come out the other end. Or try this: If the universe has always existed, then it has taken *forever* to reach this point. But then it could never reach this point. But here we are! So it *didn't* take forever.

THE COSMOLOGICAL ARGUMENT: POPULAR FORM

Whereas the Thomistic version of the cosmological argument is interested only in the *nature* of the world (as contingent), the more popular version is more interested in its *age*. According to this reasoning, it is impossible that the world has always existed, for that would mean that an infinite number of years (or whatever) has already gone by, but that is impossible because it is self-contradictory. Time must therefore have a beginning. And the cause of time must itself be Something transcendent (outside space and time) and ultimate.

It will be noted that this argument for the beginning of the world is purely rational or logical. Some have enlisted further and very different evidence from cosmology, the study of the origin and nature of the physical universe. You may be familiar with the theory of the "Big Bang." According to this theory, the present "expanding universe," or the recession of galaxies at unimaginable velocities, points to a moment, about fifteen or twenty billion years ago, when all the matter in the universe was condensed into something like a superdense atom, and exploded. Understandably, it is a temptation for some to identify this Big Bang with the origin of the universe. Others point to the Second Law of Thermodynamics: It is universally accepted that the energy in the universe is, at least on the large scale, irreversibly and evenly being distributed throughout—the universe is cooling

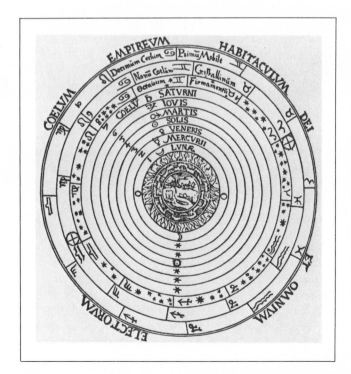

St. Thomas Aquinas, enumerating his "Five Ways"

According to the medieval picture of the universe, the earth is at the center, partly covered by water, surrounded by air and fire; then come the heavenly spheres, which carry round the moon, sun, and planets, followed by the primum mobile, *the "first moved"; beyond this is "the Dwelling of God and all the Saints." Is St. Thomas' argument for God as the Unmoved Mover of all things dependent on this view?*

down. But if the universe is running down, like a clock, must it not have once been wound up?

Thus Robert Jastrow, a well-known astronomer, on the implications of the Big Bang:

> *When an astronomer writes about God, his colleagues assume he is either over the hill or going bonkers. In my case it should be understood from the start that I am an agnostic in religious matters. However, I am fascinated by some strange developments going on in astronomy—partly because of their religious implications and partly because of the peculiar reactions of my colleagues.*
>
> *The essence of the strange developments is that the Universe had, in some sense, a beginning—that it began at a certain moment in time, and under circumstances that seem to make it impossible—not just now, but ever—to find out what force or forces brought the world into being at that moment. Was it, as the Bible says, that "Thou, Lord, in the beginning hast laid the foundations of the earth, and the heavens are the work of thine hands?" No scientist can answer that question; we can never tell whether the Prime Mover willed the world into being, or the creative agent was one of the familiar forces of physics; for the astronomical evidence proves that the Universe was created twenty billion years ago in a fiery explosion, and in the searing heat of that first moment, all the evidence needed for a scientific study of the cause of the great explosion was melted down and destroyed.*
>
> *This is the crux of the new story of Genesis. It has been familiar for years as the "Big Bang" theory, and has shared the limelight with other theories, especially the Steady State cosmology; but adverse evidence has led to the abandonment of the Steady State theory by nearly everyone, leaving the Big Bang theory exposed as the only adequate explanation of the facts.*
>
> *The general scientific picture that leads to the Big Bang theory is well known. We have been aware for fifty years that we live in an expanding Universe, in which all the galaxies around us are moving apart from us and one another at enormous speeds. The Universe is blowing up before our eyes, as if we are witnessing the aftermath of a gigantic explosion. If we retrace the motions of the outward-moving galaxies backward in time, we find that they all come together, so to speak, fifteen or twenty billion years ago.*
>
> *At that time all the matter in the Universe was packed into a dense mass, at temperatures of many trillions of degrees. The dazzling brilliance of the radiation in this dense, hot Universe must have been beyond description. The picture suggests the explosion of a cosmic hydrogen bomb. The instant in which the cosmic bomb exploded marked the birth of the Universe.*
>
> *Now we see how the astronomical evidence leads to a biblical view of the origin of the world. The details differ, but the essential elements in the astronomical and biblical accounts of Genesis are the same: the chain of events leading to man commenced suddenly and sharply at a definite moment in time, in a flash of light and energy. . . .*

For the scientist who has lived by his faith in the power of reason, the story ends like a bad dream. He has scaled the mountains of ignorance; he is about to conquer the highest peak; as he pulls himself over the final rock, he is greeted by a band of theologians who have been sitting there for centuries.[4]

THE TELEOLOGICAL ARGUMENT

Closely related to the Cosmological Argument is the *Teleological Argument*. Obviously, this argument will have to do with *teleology* (from the Greek word *telos*: "purpose, design") and is called, for short, the Design Argument.

This argument is closely associated with the Cosmological Argument, and it will be recalled that St. Thomas listed it as the Fifth Way, alongside the other four. As with the Cosmological Argument, the Teleological Argument is an *a posteriori* reasoning that employs the idea of causality. In this case God is posited as the only adequate explanation for the apparent order, purpose, unity, harmony, and beauty of the cosmos. It may go beyond the Cosmological Argument, however, in further identifying the ultimate cause as a *rational* cause: The rationality displayed in the cosmos must be the product of *Mind*.

"God does not play dice with the universe."

—Einstein

One of the best-known, though now out-of-date, statements of this argument is provided by the Anglican divine William Paley (1743–1805). In his famous Watch Analogy, Paley argued that the human eyeball demands an intelligent creator no less than a watch, and the reasoning should recall our discussion of inductive arguments by analogy in Chapter 2. From Paley's *Natural Theology*:

Paley's Watch Analogy

In crossing a heath, suppose I pitched my foot against a stone and were asked how the stone came to be there, I might possibly answer that for anything I knew to the contrary it had lain there forever; nor would it, perhaps, be very easy to show the absurdity of this answer. But suppose I had found a watch upon the ground, and it should be inquired how the watch happened to be in that place, I should hardly think

---

[4]Robert Jastrow, *God and the Astronomers* (New York: Warner Books, 1978), pp. 1-4, 105-106.

of the answer which I had before given, that for anything I knew the watch might have always been there. Yet why should not this answer serve for the watch as well as for the stone; why is it not as admissible in the second case as in the first? For this reason, and for no other, namely, that when we come to inspect the watch, we perceive—what we could not discover in the stone—that its several parts are framed and put together for a purpose, e.g., that they are so formed and adjusted as to produce motion, and that motion so regulated as to point out the hour of the day; that if the different parts had been differently shaped from what they are, or placed after any other manner or in any other order than that in which they are placed, either no motion at all would have been carried on in the machine, or none which would have answered the use that is now served by it. To reckon up a few of the plainest of these parts and of their offices, all tending to one result: we see a cylindrical box containing a coiled elastic spring, which, by its endeavor to relax itself, turns round the box. We next observe a flexible chain—artificially wrought for the sake of flexure—communicating the action of the spring from the box to the fusee. We then find a series of wheels, the teeth of which catch in and apply to each other, conducting the motion from the fusee to the balance and from the balance to the pointer, and at the same time, by the size and shape of those wheels, so regulating that motion as to terminate in causing an index, by an equable and measured progression, to pass over a given space in a given time. We take notice that the wheels are made of brass, in order to keep them from rust; the springs of steel, no other metal being so elastic; that over the face of the watch there is placed a glass, a material employed in no other part of the work, but in the room of which, if there had been any other than a transparent substance, the hour could not be seen without opening the case. This mechanism being observed—it requires indeed an examination of the instrument, and perhaps some previous knowledge of the subject, to perceive and understand it; but being once, as we have said, observed and understood—the inference we think is inevitable, that the watch must have had a maker—that there must have existed, at some time and at some place or other, an artificer or artificers who formed it for the purpose which we find it actually to answer, who completely comprehended its construction and designed its use. . . .

Were there no example in the world of contrivance except that of the eye, it would be alone sufficient to support the conclusion which we draw from it, as to the necessity of an intelligent Creator. It could never be got rid of, because it could not be accounted for by any other supposition which did not contradict all the principles we possess of knowlege—the principles according to which things do, as often as they can be brought to the test of experience, turn out to be true or false. Its coats and humors, constructed as the lenses of a telescope are constructed, for the refraction of rays of light to a point, which forms the proper action of the organ; the provision in its muscular tendons for turning its pupil to the object, similar to that which is given to the telescope by screws, and upon which power of direction in the eye the exercise of its office as an optical instrument depends; the further provision for its defense, for its constant lubricity and moisture, which we see in its socket and its lids, in its glands for the secretion of the matter of tears, its outlet or communication with the nose for *carrying off the liquid after the eye is washed with it; these provisions compose altogether an apparatus, a system of parts, a preparation of means, so manifest in their design, so exquisite in their contrivance, so successful in their issue, so precious, and so infinitely beneficial in their use, as, in my opinion, to bear down all doubt that can be raised upon the subject. And what I wish, under the title of the present chapter, to observe is that, if other parts of nature were inaccessible to our inquiries, or even if other parts of nature presented nothing to our examination but disorder and confusion, the validity of this example would remain the same. If there were but one watch in the world, it would not be less certain that it had a maker. If we had never in our lives seen any but one single kind of hydraulic machine, yet if of that one kind we understood the mechanism and use, we should be as perfectly assured that it proceeded from the hand and thought and skill of a workman, as if we visited a museum of the arts and saw collected there twenty different kinds of machines for drawing water, or a thousand different kinds for other purposes. Of this point each machine is a proof independently of all the rest. So it is with the evidences of a divine agency. The proof is not a conclusion which lies at the end of a chain of reasoning, of which chain each instance of contrivance is only a link, and of which, if one link fail, the whole fails; but it is an argument separately supplied by every separate example. An error in stating an example affects only that example. The argument is cumulative in the fullest sense of that term. The eye proves it without the ear; the ear without the eye. The proof in each example is complete; for when the design of the part and the conduciveness of its structure to that design is shown, the mind may set itself at rest; no future consideration can detract anything from the force of the example.*[5]

THE TELEOLOGICAL ARGUMENT

Most versions of the teleological argument are arguments from analogy and take some such form as:

> Watches, houses, ships, machines, etc., all exhibit design, and they are planned and produced by intelligent beings.
> The universe exhibits design.

> Therefore, the universe was planned and produced by an intelligent being.

---

[5]William Paley, *Natural Theology: Selections,* ed. Frederick Ferré(New York: Bobbs-Merrill, 1963), pp. 3–4, 32–33.

Paley's Watch Analogy is striking but irrelevant, at least after 1859, the year in which Darwin published the *Origin of Species.* Paley, as well as most everyone of his time, believed in a *special* creation of the universe and man: all at once, once upon a time, as a watchmaker making a watch. Darwin, with his doctrine of the gradual and evolutionary development of man over an untold number of years, slowly but surely dealt the deathblow to any Paleyan type of teleology. In the place of a God directly and immediately fashioning, say, the human eye, evolution substituted long and progressive sequences of natural causes and effects. It became possible to explain the human species, and everything about it, as well as much of the rest of the biological and physical universe, in purely naturalistic terms.

The deathblow of Darwin

But whereas Darwin's theory of evolution dealt the deathblow to Paleyan teleology, it hardly dealt the deathblow to God. Enter *theistic evolution.* Is it not possible to reconcile evolution with a theistic interpretation of the world? Might not evolution itself be viewed as an instrument by which God has brought about, and is bringing about, his purpose in the cosmos? Many have answered Yes, including F. R. Tennant (1866–1957), one of the most persuasive of theistic evolutionists.

Theistic evolution

THEISTIC EVOLUTION

The belief that God uses natural evolutionary processes to bring about his desired effect.

Tennant, who was himself a scientist before he was a philosopher and theologian, laid aside previous and, as he regarded them, dubious approaches to God, and set out in an "empirically-minded" and scientific way. He asks us whether it is not possible in this way to establish a "reasonable belief" in God that is as respectable as what any scientific theory can deliver. He asks us further whether the evidence does not cause us to set aside once and for all the *narrow* teleology of Paley and to adopt a *wider,* or *cosmic,* teleology. He asks us to shift our attention from specific instances of design to the *design of the whole,* and to appreciate natural processes and laws, including evolution, as "conspiring," as it were, upon the production of an intelligible universe, and upon man—the bearer of moral and aesthetic values—as its crowning glory.

The empirically-minded theologian adopts a different procedure. He asks how the world, inclusive of man, is to be explained. He would let the Actual world tell its own story and offer its own suggestions: not silence it while abstractive speculation,

William Paley

Paley, an English clergyman, published his Natural Theology *in 1802, in which he argued for God's existence on the basis of design in the cosmos. From this work comes the famous Watch Analogy: The world is to God as a watch is to a watchmaker.*

setting out with presuppositions possibly irrelevant to Actuality, weaves a system of thought which may prove to conflict with facts. . . .

. . . [HE] sets out from facts and inductions; its premises are as firmly established and as universally acknowledged as any of the stable generalisations of science. Here there is at least common ground, as distinct from private certitude, from which argumentation may proceed. Coercive demonstration being confessedly unattainable, it is to be inquired what kind of justification for reasonable belief natural theology can afford. And the first step is to set forth the facts and generalisations which collectively constitute our data or premises.

The forcibleness of Nature's suggestion that she is the outcome of intelligent design lies not in particular cases of adaptedness in the world, nor even in the multiplicity of them. It is conceivable that every such instance may individually admit of explanation in terms of proximate causes or, in the first instance, of explanation other than in terms of cosmic or "external" teleology. And if it also admits of teleological interpretation, that fact will not of itself constitute a rigorous certification of external design. The forcibleness of the world's appeal consists rather in the conspiration of innumerable causes to produce, by their united and reciprocal action, and to main-

Charles Darwin

Darwin published his Origin of Species in 1859 and his Descent of Man in 1871. His theory of evolution held revolutionary implications for many fields of thought—not the least of which was theology.

tain, a general order of Nature. Narrower kinds of teleological argument, based on surveys of restricted spheres of fact, are much more precarious than that for which the name of "the wider teleology" may be appropriated in that the comprehensive design-argument is the outcome of synopsis or conspection of the knowable world.

. . . So long as organisms were believed to have originated, in their present forms and with all their specialised organs "ready made," the argument that adaptation of part to whole, of whole to environment, and of organ to function, implied design, was forcible. But its premiss became untenable when Darwin shewed that every organic structure had come to be what it now is through a long series of successive and gradual modifications. Gradualness of construction is in itself no proof of the absence of external design: it is not at this point that Darwinism delivered its alleged death-blow to teleology. The sting of Darwinism rather lay in the suggestion that proximate and "mechanical" causes were sufficient to produce the adaptations from which the teleology of the eighteenth century had argued to God. Assignable proximate causes, whether mechanical or not, are sufficient to dispose of the particular kind of teleological proof supplied by Paley. But the fact of organic evolution, even when the maximum of instrumentality is accredited to what is figuratively called natural selection, is not incompatible with teleology on a grander scale: as exponents of Darwinism were perhaps the first to recognise and to proclaim. Subversive of Paley's argument, it does not invalidate his theistic conclusion, nor even his view that every organism and organ is an end as well as a means. Indeed the science of evolution was the primary source of the wider teleology current for the last half century, as well as the main incentive to the recovery of the closely connected doctrine of divine immanence. This kind of teleology does not set out from the particular adaptations in individual organisms or species so much as from considerations as to the progressiveness of the evolutionary process and as to the organic realm as a whole. . . .

In an exposition of the significance of the moral order for theistic philosophy, the first step is to point out that man belongs to Nature, and is an essential part of it, in such a sense that the world cannot be described or explained as a whole without taking him and his moral values into account. Prof. Pringle-Pattison, especially, has elaborated the doctrine that, as he expresses it, "man is organic to the world." What precisely this, or the similar phrase "man is the child of Nature," should mean, if either is to be more than a half-truth, needs to be made clear. In so far as man's soul, i.e. man as noümenon, or (in the language of spiritualistic pluralism) the dominant monad in the empirical self, is concerned, we are not authorised by known facts to regard man as organic to Nature, or as the child of Nature, in the sense that he is an emergent product of cosmic evolution. We are rather forbidden by psychology to entertain any such notion. But, this proviso being observed—it must qualify all that is further said in the present connexion—we can affirm that man's body, with all its conditioning of his mentality, his sociality, knowledge and morality, is "of a piece" with Nature; and that, in so far as he is a phenomenal being, man is organic to Nature, or a product of the world. And this fact is as significant for our estimation of Nature as for our anthropology. If man is Nature's child, Nature is the wonderful mother of such a child. Any account of her which ignores the fact of her maternity is scientifically partial and philosophically insignificant. Her capacity to produce man must be reckoned among her potencies, explain it how we may. And man is no monstrous birth out of due time, no freak or sport. In respect of his body and the bodily conditioning of his mentality, man is like, and has genetic continuity with, Nature's humbler and earlier-born children. In the fulness of time Nature found self-utterance in a son possessed of the intelligent and moral status. Maybe she was pregnant with him from the beginning, and the world-ages are the period of her gestation. As to this anthropocentric view of the world-process, and its co-extensiveness with teleological interpretation, more will presently be said. But in the light of man's continuity with the rest of the world we can at once dismiss the view that Nature suddenly "stumbled" or "darkly blundered" on man, while "churning the universe with mindless motion." The world-process is a praeparatio anthropologica, whether designedly or not, and man is the culmination, up to the present stage of the knowable history of Nature, of a gradual ascent. We cannot explain man in terms of physical Nature; conceivably Nature may be found explicable—in another sense of the word—in terms *of man, and can be called "the threshold of spirit." Judging the genealogical tree by its roots, naturalism once preached that Darwin had put an end to the assumption that man occupies an exceptional position on our planet; apparently implying that there is no difference of status between man and the primordial slime because stages between the two are traceable. But if we judge the tree by its fruits, Darwin may rather be said to have restored man to the position from which Copernicus seemed to have ousted him, in making it possible to read the humanising of Nature in the naturalising of man, and to regard man as not only the last term and the crown of Nature's long upward effort, but also as its end or goal.*[6]

NARROW VS. WIDER TELEOLOGY

- *Paley:* The world is full of particular instances of design, for example, the human eye. Each of these is an evidence for the direct creating and designing activity of God.
- *Tennant:* Particular instances of design, such as the human eye, can be adequately explained by natural causes, such as evolution. These natural causes, however, have produced a world which *as a whole* is an overwhelming evidence for the creating and designing activity of God.

THE PROBLEM OF CAUSALITY

Both the Cosmological and the Teleological Arguments for God have been criticized in many ways. Here we can only mention one minor criticism and then the major one.

What caused God?

Inevitably someone will ask: "If everything has to have a cause, then what caused God?" But this is to miss the point. It is not that every *thing* must have a cause, but that every *event*, or everything that *comes into being*, must have a cause. Now is God an event or something that comes into being? Of course not. How could he be, if he is the *cause* of events or things that come into being? It is hopeless confusion to try to think of God, who is by his nature transcendent and ultimate, as a being that comes into being or passes away. Similarly, some smart aleck might ask: "What was God doing before he created the world?" To this, one is tempted, with some ancients, to answer: "What was God doing before he created the world? Why, he was preparing hell for people who pry into divine mysteries!" More seri-

[6]F. R. Tennant, *Philosophical Theology* (Cambridge: Cambridge University Press, 1930), II, 78–79, 84, 100–102.

ously, it is to be answered again that the questioner must not be paying attention to what he or she is saying. How can there be a "before" without creation? Apart from creation there *is* no time and therefore no "before." We must, in a word, take absolutely seriously the idea of God as a *transcendent* and *absolute* being.

Other problems for these arguments may be posed:

- Must the cause or designer of the universe be *God?*
- Just because everything in the universe is contingent, must the universe itself be contingent?
- How does the Cosmological Argument square with the scientific principle of the Conservation of Energy?
- Would we not *perceive* the universe as ordered whether it actually is or not?
- Even if the universe does display order, would not this particular configuration of matter necessarily arise sooner or later by sheer chance?

We cannot consider such questions here, but they might be discussed and considered with profit.

For our part, we must raise what is surely the most troublesome feature of the Cosmological and Teleological Arguments for God. We have seen repeatedly that central to both of the arguments is the *principle of causality:* "From nothing, nothing comes," or "every event must have a cause." But the concept of causality is far and away one of the most difficult in all philosophy. And this is especially true when it is applied to God's relation to the world.

We have already seen how both Hume and Kant in different ways destroyed the traditional concept of causality. Now we are in a better position to emphasize the implications for metaphysics, and specifically for God. In a way, Hume and Kant make the same criticism: *The concept of causality cannot be legitimately extended beyond the objects of possible sense experience, and therefore cannot be extended to God.* On the other hand, it is crucial to appreciate that Hume and Kant would interpret and justify this claim in radically different ways.

Can causality be applied to God?

Hume. Aside from Hume's skepticism about causality as such (after all, we have no basis in experience for the claimed universality and necessity of the cause-effect relation) he raises a further question: Are we not limited by our experience to a small part of reality? What possible basis do we have for thinking that the causal relation holds for anything *beyond* our experience? Our idea of causality—insofar as we possess one—is based on our experience of causes (for example, carpenters) and effects (for example, houses) joined together over and over again right before our eyes. But surely God's creation of the world is hardly an object of possible experience, and is totally without analogy in the universe we know.

Hume's criticism

This is Hume's main and recurring point in the following passage from his *Dialogues Concerning Natural Religion,* in which, more or less, his own position is represented by Philo.

That all inferences, Cleanthes, concerning fact are founded on experience, and that all experimental reasonings are founded on the supposition that similar causes prove similar effects, and similar effects similar causes, I shall not at present much dispute with you. But observe, I entreat you, with what extreme caution all just reasoners proceed in the transferring of experiments to similar cases. Unless the cases be exactly similar, they repose no perfect confidence in applying their past observation to any particular phenomenon. Every alteration of circumstances occasions a doubt concerning the event; and it requires new experiments to prove certainly that the new circumstances are of no moment or importance. A change in bulk, situation, arrangement, age, disposition of the air, or surrounding bodies—any of these particulars may be attended with the most unexpected consequences. And unless the objects be quite familiar to us, it is the highest temerity to expect with assurance, after any of these changes, an event similar to that which before fell under our observation. The slow and deliberate steps of philosophers here, if anywhere, are distinguished from the precipitate march of the vulgar, who, hurried on by the smallest similitude, are incapable of all discernment or consideration.

But can you think, Cleanthes, that your usual phlegm and philosophy have been preserved in so wide a step as you have taken when you compared to the universe houses, ships, furniture, machines, and, from their similarity in some circumstances, inferred a similarity in their causes? Thought, design, intelligence, such as we discover in men and other animals, is no more than one of the springs and principles of the universe, as well as heat or cold, attraction or repulsion, and a hundred others which fall under daily observation. It is an active cause by which some particular parts of nature, we find, produce alterations on other parts. But can a conclusion, with any propriety, be transferred from parts to the whole? Does not the great disproportion bar all comparsion and inference? From observing the growth of a hair, can we learn anything concerning the generation of a man? Would the manner of a leaf's blowing, even though perfectly known, afford us any instruction concerning the vegetation of a tree?

But allowing that we were to take the operations of one part of nature upon another for the foundation of our judgment concerning the origin of the whole (which never can be admitted), yet why select so minute, so weak, so bounded a principle as the reason and design of animals is found to be upon this planet? What peculiar privilege has this little agitation of the brain which we call thought, that we must thus make it the model of the whole universe? Our partiality in our own favour does indeed present it on all occasions, but sound philosophy ought carefully to guard against so natural an illusion.

So far from admitting, continued Philo, that the operations of a part can afford us any just conclusion concerning the origin of the whole, I will not allow any one part to form a rule for another part if the latter be very remote from the former. Is there any reasonable ground to conclude that the inhabitants of other planets possess thought, intelligence, reason, or anything similar to these faculties in men? When nature has so extremely diversified her manner of operation in this small globe, can we imagine that she incessantly copies herself throughout so immense a universe? And if thought, as we may well suppose, be confined merely to this narrow corner and has even there so limited a sphere of action, with what propriety can we assign it for the original cause of all things? The narrow views of a peasant who makes his domestic economy the rule for the government of kingdoms is in comparison a pardonable sophism. . . .

A very small part of this great system, during a very short time, is very imperfectly discovered to us; and do we thence pronounce decisively concerning the origin of the whole?

Admirable conclusion! Stone, wood, brick, iron, brass, have not, at this time, in this minute globe of earth, an order or arrangement without human art and contrivance; therefore, the universe could not originally attain its order and arrangement without something similar to human art. But is a part of nature a rule for another part very wide of the former? Is it a rule for the whole? Is a very small part a rule for the universe? Is nature in one situation a certain rule for nature in another situation vastly different from the former?

And can you blame me, Cleanthes, if I here imitate the prudent reserve of Simonides, who, according to the noted story, being asked by Hiero, What God was? desired a day to think of it, and then two days more; and after that manner continually prolonged the term, without ever bringing his definition or description? Could you even blame me if I had answered, at first, that I did not know, and was sensible that this subject lay vastly beyond the reach of my faculties? You might cry out sceptic and rallier, as much as you pleased; but, having found in so many other subjects much more familiar the imperfections and even contradictions of human reason, I never should expect any success from its feeble conjectures in a subject so sublime and so remote from the sphere of our observation. When two species of objects have always been observed to be conjoined together, I can infer, by custom, the existence of one wherever I see the existence of the other; and this I call an argument from experience. But how this argument can have place where the objects, as in the present case, are single, individual, without parallel or specific resemblance, may be difficult to explain. And will any man tell me with a serious countenance that an orderly universe must arise from some thought and art like the human because we have experience of it? To ascertain this reasoning it were requisite that we had experience of the origin of worlds; and it is not sufficient, surely, that we have seen ships and cities arise from human art and contrivance.[7]

Do you see, then, just what Hume, the radical empiricist, would mean by the charge that the Cosmological and Teleological Arguments involve an unjustified application of the concept of causality to God?

Kant. But Kant would mean something very different. We saw earlier how Kant, contrary to Hume, *did* believe in "Every event must have a cause" as a certain

Kant's criticism

[7]David Hume, *Dialogues Concerning Natural Religion,* ed. Henry D. Aiken (New York: Hafner, 1948), pp. 20–23.

and universal principle, but only because it is a way in which our minds necessarily grasp and *represent* reality. Do you recall the rose-colored glasses from our earlier discussion of Kant? We cannot help but experience things as standing in cause-effect relations, because causality is one of the ways in which our mind organizes or makes possible experience itself. But then, of course, causality can have no possible bearing on anything *outside* our sense experience, such as God.

In the following from the *Critique of Pure Reason*, Kant calls the Cosmological Argument a "transcendental illusion," and lists four lines of objection. The first of these concerns explicitly the proper, and limited, application of the principle of causality, though the limitation of the theoretical reason to objects of possible experience is a theme which otherwise recurs throughout.

> *There are so many sophistical propositions in this cosmological argument, that it really seems as if speculative reason had spent all her dialectical skill in order to produce the greatest possible transcendental illusion. . . .*
>
> *I said before that a whole nest of dialectical assumptions was hidden in that cosmological proof, and that transcendental criticism might easily detect and destroy it. I shall here enumerate them only, leaving it to the experience of the reader to follow up the fallacies and remove them.*
>
> *We find, first, the transcendental principle of inferring a cause for the accidental. This principle, that everything contingent must have a cause, is valid in the world of sense only, and has not even a meaning outside it. For the purely intellectual concept of the contingent cannot produce a synthetical proposition like that of causality, and the principle of causality has no meaning and no criterion of its use, except in the world of sense, while here it is meant to help us beyond the world of sense.*
>
> *Secondly. The inference of a first cause, based on the impossibility of an infinite ascending series of given causes in this world of sense,—an inference which the principles of the use of reason do not allow us to draw even in experience, while here we extend that principle beyond experience, whither that series can never be prolonged.*
>
> *Thirdly. The false self-satisfaction of reason with regard to the completion of that series, brought about by removing in the end every kind of condition, without which, nevertheless, no concept of necessity is possible, and by then, when any definite concepts have become impossible, accepting this as a completion of our concept.*
>
> *Fourthly. The mistaking the logical possibility of a concept of all united reality (without any internal contradiction) for the transcendental, which requires a principle for the practicability of such a synthesis, such principle however being applicable to the field of possible experience only, etc.*[8]

As with Hume, Kant charges that the Cosmological and Teleological Arguments involve an illegitimate extension of the idea of causality to a sphere where it has no proper application. But he means something very different: It is not just

---

[8]Immanuel Kant, *Critique of Pure Reason*, tr. F. Max Müller (Garden City, N.Y.: Anchor Books, 1966), pp. 405–408.

that we have no basis for such an application of causality (Hume), but that causality could not *possibly* apply to God.

It must be seen that Hume's and Kant's criticisms of these theistic arguments follow from their respective views of knowledge. In both cases, it is important to appreciate this connection, and to appreciate, therefore, the importance of the starting point. And that takes us back to Chapters 10 and 11.

DOES CAUSALITY APPLY TO GOD?

- *Hume:* No. Causality is limited to the sensible world because we know it only through sense experience. We have no grounds for applying it to a transcendent God.
- *Kant:* No. Causality is limited to the sensible world because it is *constitutive* of sense experience, it is part of what experience *means*. It therefore has no possible application to a transcendent God.

Chapter 12 in Review

SUMMARY

One of the most interesting and instructive phenomena in the history of philosophy is found in the arguments for God's existence. Natural theology means knowledge of God acquired through our natural faculties of reason and/or experience. The best examples of this are the traditional arguments for the existence of God. We have considered two of these in this chapter:

- The Cosmological Argument
- The Teleological Argument

These are *a posteriori* arguments in that they attempt to demonstrate the existence of God on the basis of sense experience.

More specifically, the Cosmological Argument (First-Cause Argument) concludes that a transcendent and absolute being must exist as the only possible cause of the contingent universe. Actually there are two forms of this argument. If one grants that the world must have had a temporal beginning (as in the more common, or popular, version), then God is posited as the First Cause of the cosmos in the sense of its originator at a definite point in the past. If, on the other hand, one grants that the cosmos has always existed (as in the Thomistic version), then God is posited as the First Cause of the cosmos in the sense of the ultimate being upon whom it depends at every moment in its (even infinite) existence. It is important to see that in either case, the world is regarded as *contingent* and therefore dependent upon something beyond itself, and finally upon something ultimate, for its existence.

The Teleological Argument (Design Argument) concludes that there must exist a transcendent and intelligent being as the only possible cause of the order and design in the universe. This argument also assumes two forms. In the older version of Paley, God is regarded as the direct cause of *specific* designs, say the human eye. In the more recent version of Tennant, who was much influenced by the theory of evolution, God is responsible for the design of the *whole*, which he has achieved by long sequences of innumerable natural processes. This latter view involves theistic evolution, the idea that evolution itself is one of the natural processes instituted by God and employed as an instrument for his production of humanity and human values.

Numerous complaints have been filed against these arguments, but the most critical have to do with the concept of causality. Aside from the intrinsic problems with this concept (is it really a metaphysical certainty that "from nothing, nothing comes" or that "every event must have a cause"?), some important philosophers (for example, Hume and Kant) have charged that whatever its application may be to the sensible world, it is certainly less clear how the concept of causality may relate to anything beyond the sensible world. According to Hume, we have no rational right to ascribe to some transcendent being the attributes and activities, such as *causal* activity, which we know only from our limited experience of the sensible world around us. According to Kant, it is not even *possible* that a concept of causality could be ascribed to God, since by its nature it is a principle of sense experience and therefore has no application beyond sense experience.

BASIC IDEAS

- Natural theology
- Revealed theology
- *A posteriori / a priori* arguments for God
- The Cosmological Argument
  Thomistic version
  Popular version
- St. Thomas' Five Ways
- Two meanings of "first" cause
- Big Bang theory of the universe
- Second Law of Thermodynamics
- The Teleological Argument
- Teleology
- Paley's Watch Analogy
- Special creation vs. evolution

- Theistic evolution
- Narrow vs. wider teleology
- Miscellaneous objections to the *a posteriori* proofs
- Causality as the central problem
- Hume's criticism of divine causality
- Kant's criticism of divine causality

1. True or false: St. Thomas' argument for God presupposes a temporal beginning of the universe.
2. Knowledge of God by means of a special divine self-disclosure is called _____ theology.
3. Why do both Hume and Kant reject the Cosmological Argument on the basis of their differing conceptions of causality?
4. How did Charles Darwin figure in the discussion in this chapter?
5. St. Thomas' Five Ways are all (a) *a posteriori*, (b) presented in his *Summa Theologiae*, (c) involve the principle of causality, (d) based on the Bible.
6. Paley was a proponent of (a) wider teleology, (b) narrow teleology, (c) evolution, (d) theistic evolution.
7. Who was F. R. Tennant?
8. Some claim that there is *scientific* evidence for the temporal beginning of the cosmos. What is it?
9. True or false: Theistic evolution is the belief that God created the world and then abandoned it to its own course.
10. Paley claimed that _____ is to the _____ as a _____ is to a _____.

- It is often observed that there is an essential difference between metaphysical and scientific reasoning. Do you agree with this? Can scientific theories, such as the Big Bang theory, hold any real relevance for metaphysical questions, such as the question of God? Can a scientific claim also be a metaphysical claim?
- It is sometimes said that St. Thomas' Five Ways are really five different expressions of the same argument. Do you see any truth in this? How might you defend it?
- For some people, the idea of "theistic evolution" is a contradiction in terms. But is evolution in itself necessarily atheistic? What does "evolution" mean? Does God work through nature in other respects? What, suddenly, becomes so important about the interpretation of religious language, the use of symbols, etc. (think of the first chapters of the Bible)?
- If you were St. Thomas, would you feel devastated by either Hume's or Kant's attacks on your arguments for God? If not, why not?

CHAPTER 13

GOD AND REASON

In the last chapter we looked at two arguments for God, both of them *a posteriori*, that is, based on sense experience. In this chapter we will consider two that are *a priori*, that is, based *not* on sense experience but on reason alone. Specifically, the first, the Ontological Argument, is based on the mere idea of God. The second, the Moral Argument, is based on the idea of moral law.

THE ONTOLOGICAL ARGUMENT

The *Ontological Argument* begins with the definition of God as the *greatest being possible*, or, if you prefer, as the most perfect being, the unlimited being, a being no greater than which is conceivable, etc. It is important to see that it is not the linguistic symbol "God" that we are interested in, but rather the *idea* (of the greatest being possible) that most people, even atheists, mean by it. The simplest version of this argument then asks us: What is greater, to exist as a mere idea in the mind, or to exist in reality too? Obviously, so the argument goes, it is greater to exist objectively, in reality. (Would you not rather have millions of real dollars than mental ones?) But, then, God must actually exist, because if he didn't, then he would not be the greatest being possible. To say it another way: It is logically absurd to deny the existence of God. For you would be denying the existence of what *must* exist to be the thing you are talking about!

The first and most famous statement of the Ontological Argument was provided by St. Anselm (1033–1109) in his *Proslogium*. He takes as his definition of

God, the greatest being, must exist

278

God, "that than which is no greater can be conceived," and concludes from this that God must, in fact, exist.

St. Anselm's version

TRULY THERE IS A GOD, ALTHOUGH THE FOOL HATH SAID IN HIS HEART, THERE IS NO GOD

And so, Lord, do thou, who dost give understanding to faith, give me, so far as thou knowest it to be profitable, to understand that thou art as we believe; and that thou art that which we believe. And, indeed, we believe that thou art a being than which nothing greater can be conceived. Or is there no such nature, since the fool hath said in his heart, there is no God? {Ps. 14:1}. But, at any rate, this very fool, when he hears of this being of which I speak—a being than which nothing greater can be conceived—understands what he hears, and what he understands is in his understanding; although he does not understand it to exist.

For, it is one thing for an object to be in the understanding, and another to understand that the object exists. When a painter first conceives of what he will afterwards perform, he has it in his understanding, but he does not yet understand it to be, because he has not yet performed it. But after he has made the painting, he both has it in his understanding, and he understand that it exists, because he has made it.

Hence, even the fool is convinced that something exists in the understanding, at least, than which nothing greater can be conceived. For, when he hears of this, he understands it. And whatever is understood, exists in the understanding. And assuredly that, than which nothing greater can be conceived, cannot exist in the understanding alone. For, suppose it exists in the understanding alone: then it can be conceived to exist in reality; which is greater.

Therefore, if that, than which nothing greater can be conceived, exists in the understanding alone, the very being, than which nothing greater can be conceived, is one, than which a greater can be conceived. But obviously this is impossible. Hence, there is no doubt that there exists a being, than which nothing greater can be conceived, and it exists both in the understanding and in reality.

GOD CANNOT BE CONCEIVED NOT TO EXIST

And it assuredly exists so truly, that it cannot be conceived not to exist. For, it is possible to conceive of a being which cannot be conceived not to exist; and this is greater than one which can be conceived not to exist. Hence, if that, than which nothing greater can be conceived, can be conceived not to exist, it is not that, than which nothing greater can be conceived. But this in an irreconcilable contradiction. There is, then, so truly a being than which nothing greater can be conceived to exist, that it cannot even be conceived not to exist, and this being thou art, O Lord, our God.

So truly, therefore, dost thou exist, O Lord, my God, that thou canst not be conceived not to exist; and rightly. For, if a mind could conceive of a being better than thee, the creature would rise above the Creator; and this is most absurd. And, *indeed, whatever else there is, except thee alone, can be conceived not to exist. To thee alone, therefore, it belongs to exist more truly than all other beings, and hence in a higher degree than all others. For, whatever else exists does not exist so truly, and hence in a less degree it belongs to it to exist. Why, then, has the fool said in his heart, there is no God, since it is so evident, to a rational mind, that thou dost exist in the highest degree of all? Why, except that he is dull and a fool?[1]*

Descartes' version   Another statement is provided by Descartes, in his *Meditations*. He defines God as "the most perfect being," and concludes that as sum of *all* perfections, God must possess not only the attributes of omnipotence, omniscience, omnibenevolence, etc., but also the attribute of *existence*.

But now, if just because I can draw the idea of something from my thought, it follows that all which I know clearly and distinctly as pertaining to this object does really belong to it, may I not derive from this an argument demonstrating the existence of God? It is certain that I no less find the idea of God, that is to say, the idea of a supremely perfect Being, in me, than that of any figure or number whatever it is; and I do not know any less clearly and distinctly that an {actual and} eternal existence pertains to this nature than I know that all that which I am able to demonstrate of some figure or number truly pertains to the nature of this figure or number, and therefore, although all that I concluded in the preceding Meditations were found to be false, the existence of God would pass with me as at least as certain as I have ever held the truths of mathematics (which concern only numbers and figures) to be.

This indeed is not at first manifest, since it would seem to present some appearance of being a sophism. For being accustomed in all other things to make a distinction between existence and essence, I easily persuade myself that the existence can be separated from the essence of God, and that we can thus conceive God as not actually existing. But, nevertheless, when I think of it with more attention, I clearly see that existence can no more be separated from the essence of God than can its having its three angles equal to two right angles be separated from the essence of a {rectilinear} triangle, or the idea of a mountain from the idea of a valley; and so there is not any less repugnance to our conceiving a God (that is, a Being supremely perfect) to whom existence is lacking (that is to say, to whom a certain perfection is lacking), than to conceive of a mountain which has no valley.

But although I cannot really conceive of a God without existence any more than a mountain without a valley, still from the fact that I conceive of a mountain with a valley, it does not follow that there is such a mountain in the world; similarly although I conceive of God as possessing existence, it would seem that it does not follow that there is a God which exists; for my thought does not impose any necessity upon things, and just as I may imagine a winged horse, although no horse with wings exists, so I could perhaps attribute existence to God, although no God existed.

[1]St. Anselm, *Proslogium*, in *St. Anselm: Basic Writings*, tr. S. N. Deane (LaSalle, Ill.: Open Court, 1903), pp. 7–9.

But a sophism is concealed in this objection; for from the fact that I cannot conceive a mountain without a valley, it does not follow that there is any mountain or any valley in existence, but only that the mountain and the valley, whether they exist or do not exist, cannot in any way be separated one from the other. While from the fact that I cannot conceive God without existence, it follows that existence is inseparable from Him, and hence that He really exists; not that my thought can bring this to pass, or impose any necessity on things, but, on the contrary, because the necessity which lies in the thing itself, i.e. the necessity of the existence of God determines me to think in this way. For it is not within my power to think of God without existence (that is of a supremely perfect Being devoid of a supreme perfection) though it is in my power to imagine a horse either with wings or without wings.[2]

THE ONTOLOGICAL ARGUMENT

God is the greatest or most perfect being.
A being who exists is greater or more perfect than a
  being who does not exist.

Therefore, God must exist.

On either St. Anselm's or Descartes' version of the Ontological Argument, the essential point is the same: It is impossible to think of God—or at least of the greatest being—without thinking of him as existing.

IS EXISTENCE A PREDICATE?

You probably have the uneasy feeling that the Ontological Argument is putting something over on you. If so, you are not alone. No sooner had St. Anselm shown why the atheist is a fool than a fellow monk, Gaunilon, wrote a rebuttal entitled *On Behalf of the Fool.* Among other things, Gaunilon asked how we could possibly derive the real existence of something from a mere idea of it. We might as well conclude from our idea of a lost, perfect, desert island (Gaunilon's example) that such an island actually exists! This is a very obvious criticism, but some think that it misses the point. Of course it does not follow from our idea of an island—even

A misguided criticism?

[2]René Descartes, *Meditations on First Philosophy,* in *The Philosophical Works of Descartes,* tr. Elizabeth S. Haldane and G. R. T. Ross (Cambridge: Cambridge University Press, 1911), I, pp. 180–182.

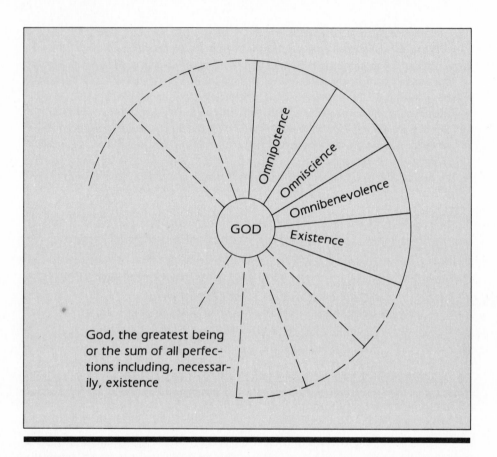

God, the greatest being
or the sum of all perfec-
tions including, necessarily, existence

a perfect island—or a unicorn or a hundred dollars that these really exist, but that
is because none of these are the *greatest* being, and therefore they do not *have* to
exist in order to *be* that thing. Only in the case of the *greatest* being, or the most
perfect being, *must* it be said that it *must* exist. One more time: It is not part of the
concept of a unicorn, etc., that it *exists,* but it *is* part of the idea of the *greatest* being.

Or is it? Whereas the Ontological Argument clearly takes existence as a defining property, attribute, or *predicate* of God, many have charged that this is a mistake. In fact, the single most recurring attack against the Ontological Argument has
consisted in the claim that existence is not a predicate.

Of course existence is a predicate in a purely *grammatical* sense: In the sentence "God exists," "God" is the subject and "exists" is the predicate. But in a *logical*
sense, existence is not a predicate in that it in no way adds anything, subtracts
anything, or in any way modifies the concept of the subject. To see that this is so,
in your imagination start building up the concept of a unicorn by supplying the
appropriate predicates:

A unicorn is shaped like a horse.
A unicorn is white.
A unicorn has an ivory horn.
. . .

Every time you introduce a predicate, the subject becomes in some way changed and augmented. However, when we finally add,

A unicorn *exists*.

you see immediately that *nothing has been added whatsoever*. A unicorn that doesn't exist is no less a unicorn than one that does. Naturally, there is a difference between the nonexistent unicorn and the existent unicorn (try to ride the nonexistent one!), but the difference has nothing whatsoever to do with the *idea* or *concept* of the unicorn.

Kant was one of the first to press this attack on the Ontological Argument. In the following paragraphs from the *Critique of Pure Reason*, he attempts to show that the being or existence of God stands in a different relation to God than his regular attributes, such as omnipotence, and that, specifically, being or existence is not a predicate at all. (By an "identical judgment" Kant means an analytic judgment or a judgment of the form "A is A.")

Kant: Existence is not a predicate

> If in an identical judgment I reject the predicate and retain the subject, there arises a contradiction, and hence, I say, that the former belongs to the latter necessarily. But if I reject the subject as well as the predicate, there is no contradiction, because there is nothing left that can be contradicted. To accept a triangle and yet to reject its three angles is contradictory, but there is no contradiction at all in admitting the nonexistence of the triangle and of its three angles. The same applies to the concept of an absolutely necessary Being. Remove its existence, and you remove the thing itself, with all its predicates, so that a contradiction becomes impossible. There is nothing external to which the contradiction could apply, because the thing is not meant to be externally necessary; nor is there anything internal that could be contradicted, for in removing the thing out of existence, you have removed at the same time all its internal qualities. If you say, God is almighty, that is a necessary judgment, because almightiness cannot be removed, if you accept a deity, that is, an infinite Being, with the concept of which that other concept is identical. But if you say, God is not, then neither his almightiness, nor any other of his predicates is given; they are all, together with the subject, removed out of existence, and therefore there is not the slightest contradiction in that sentence. . . .
>
> Being is evidently not a real predicate, or a concept of something that can be added to the concept of a thing. It is merely the admission of a thing, and of certain determinations in it. Logically, it is merely the copula of a judgment. The proposition, "God is almighty", contains two concepts, each having its object, namely, God and

almightiness. The small word "is", is not an additional predicate, but only serves to put the predicate in relation to the subject. If, then, I take the subject (God) with all its predicates (including that of almightiness), and say, "God is", or there is a God, I do not put a new predicate to the concept of God, but I only put the subject by itself, with all its predicates, in relation to my concept, as its object. Both must contain exactly the same kind of thing, and nothing can have been added to the concept, which expresses possibility only, by my thinking its object as simply given and saying, it is. And thus the real does not contain more than the possible. A hundred real dollars do not contain a penny more than a hundred possible dollars. For as the latter signify the concept, the former the object and its position by itself, it is clear that, in case the former contained more than the latter, my concept would not express the whole object, and would not therefore be its adequate concept. In my financial position no doubt there exists more by one hundred real dollars, than by their concept only (that is their possibility), because in reality the object is not only contained analytically in my concept, but is added to my concept (which is a determination of my state), synthetically; but the conceived hundred dollars are not in the least increased through the existence which is outside my concept.

By whatever and by however many predicates I may think a thing (even in completely determining it), nothing is really added to it, if I add that the thing exists. Otherwise, it would not be the same that exists, but something more than was contained in the concept, and I could not say that the exact object of my concept existed. . . .

Time and labour therefore are lost on the famous ontological (Cartesian) proof of the existence of a Supreme Being from mere concepts; and a man might as well imagine that he could become richer in knowledge by mere ideas, as a merchant in capital, if, in order to improve his position, he were to add a few noughts to his cash account.[3]

Anselm's two Ontological Arguments

That seemed, and still seems, to many to be a decisive refutation of the Ontological Argument. But this argument for God has a most inconvenient way of not staying dead, and it continues even yet to be a center of philosophical controversy.

One of the most pivotal of recent discussions is that of Norman Malcolm, who, in the early 1960s, published an essay entitled "Anselm's Ontological Arguments." Note the plural. Malcolm emphasized that we have in St. Anselm not one but *two* arguments. Look again at St. Anselm's formulation of his argument in *Proslogium*, Chapter 1, and his different formulation in Chapter 2 (both quoted above). The first formulation revolves around the notion that God is a greater being if he exists than if he does not: God's existence is one of his attributes, or predicates. But the second formulation revolves around the notion that God is a greater being if he cannot not-exist: *Necessary* existence is a divine predicate.

[3]Immanuel Kant, *Critique of Pure Reason*, tr. F. Max Müller (Garden City, N.Y.: Anchor Books, 1966, pp. 399–403.

With respect to the first of these, Malcolm agreed entirely with the Kantian criticism, which he restates and clarifies in his own way:

> The doctrine that existence is a perfection is remarkably queer. It makes sense and is true to say that my future house will be a better one if it is insulated than if it is not insulated; but what could it mean to say that it will be a better house if it exists than if it does not? My future child will be a better man if he is honest than if he is not; but who would understand the saying that he will be a better man if he exists than if he does not? Or who understands the saying that if God exists He is more perfect than if He does not exist? One might say, with some intelligibility, that it would be better (for oneself or for mankind) if God exists than if He does not—but that is a different matter.
>
> A king might desire that his next chancellor should have knowledge, wit, and resolution; but it is ludicrous to add that the king's desire is to have a chancellor who exists. Suppose that two royal councilors, A and B, were asked to draw up separately descriptions of the most perfect chancellor they could conceive, and that the descriptions they produced were identical except that A included existence in his list of attributes of a perfect chancellor and B did not. (I do not mean that B put non-existence in his list.) One and the same person could satisfy both descriptions. More to the point, any person who satisfied A's description would necessarily satisfy B's description and vice versa! This is to say that A and B did not produce descriptions of necessary and desirable qualities in a chancellor. A only made a show of putting down a desirable quality that B had failed to include.
>
> I believe I am merely restating an observation that Kant made in attacking the notion that "existence" or "being" is a "real predicate." ... Anselm's ontological proof of Proslogion 2 is fallacious because it rests on the false doctrine that existence is a perfection (and therefore that "existence" is a "real predicate"). It would be desirable to have a rigorous refutation of the doctrine but I have not been able to provide one. I am compelled to leave the matter at the more or less intuitive level of Kant's observation.[4]

With respect to St. Anselm's second formulation, however, the situation is, says Malcolm, quite different. *Necessary* existence may, indeed, be properly construed as a predicate, and he formulates his own version of this form of the argument, which he thinks is absolutely sound.

> What Anselm has proved is that the notion of contingent existence or of contingent nonexistence cannot have any application to God. His existence must either be logically necessary or logically impossible. The only intelligible way of rejecting Anselm's claim that God's existence is necessary is to maintain that the concept of God, as a

Malcolm: Necessary existence is a predicate

[4]Norman Malcolm, *Knowledge and Certainty: Essays and Lectures* (Englewood Cliffs, N.J. Prentice-Hall, 1963), p. 144.

being a greater than which cannot be conceived, is self-contradictory or nonsensical. Supposing that this is false, Anselm is right to deduce God's necessary existence from his characterization of Him as a being a greater than which cannot be conceived.

Let me summarize the proof. If God, a being a greater than which cannot be conceived, does not exist then He cannot come into existence or have happened to come into existence, and in either case He would be a limited being, which by our conception of Him He is not. Since He cannot come into existence, if He does not exist His existence is impossible. If He does exist He cannot have come into existence (for the reasons given), nor can He cease to exist, for nothing could cause Him to cease to exist nor could it just happen that He ceased to exist. So if God exists His existence is necessary. Thus God's existence is either impossible or necessary. It can be the former only if the concept of such a being is self-contradictory or in some way logically absurd. Assuming that this is not so. it follows that He necessarily exists.[5]

MALCOLM'S ONTOLOGICAL ARGUMENT

God is an unlimited being.
The existence of an unlimited being is either
   impossible or necessary.
The concept of an unlimited being is not self-
   contradictory, so such a being is not impossible.

Therefore such a being is necessary.

The Consistency Principle

The above paragraphs deserve careful study, not only for the sake of the Ontological Argument but for the sake of the instructive philosophical ideas and maneuvers involved. It is especially critical to see that the reasoning depends on what we might call the Consistency Principle: A logically consistent proposition could be true, but a self-contradictory proposition could not. Examples: The proposition "A vast herd of giraffes is at the moment roaming through the White House" is, of course, an outrageous claim, but it is at least logically consistent and therefore *could* be true. But the proposition "There are barking dogs that do not bark when they are barking" is to be rejected at the start. It is impossible because it is logically incoherent. Be sure you understand how Malcolm arrives at the two-fold conclusion that God's existence is either impossible or it is necessary, and how

---

[5]Ibid., pp. 149–150.

THE CONSISTENCY PRINCIPLE

A proposition that is logically coherent could be true, but a proposition that is logically absurd or self-contradictory is impossible.

---

it can only be impossible if it is logically absurd—which, says Malcolm, it is not, leaving only the alternative that God exists, and exists necessarily.

THE MORAL ARGUMENT

Yet another argument for God must be considered. After the Ontological Argument you may have the feeling of being brought back down to earth, as this last argument bases itself on *experience* again. However, it is not sense experience but *moral* experience that is now in view. This means not our experience of empirical reality—such as tables and chairs and dogs and cats—but our experience of *moral* reality, our confrontation with *moral law*.

Sense experience and moral experience

In a famous passage from his *Critique of Practical Reason*, Kant gives eloquent expression to our confrontation with, and the distinction between, the two worlds: the sensible world and the moral world.

"The starry heavens above me, and the moral law within me."

> *Two things fill the mind with ever new and increasing admiration and awe, the oftener and more steadily we reflect on them: the starry heavens above me and the moral law within me. I do not merely conjecture them and seek them as though obscured in darkness or in the transcendent region beyond my horizon: I see them before me, and I associate them directly with the consciousness of my own existence.*[6]

And in spite of his rejection of the other arguments for God, Kant himself found it necessary to formulate a version of the *Moral Argument* for God.

As with the other arguments for God, there are several versions of the Moral Argument. But they all reduce to the same essential reasoning: They begin with the givenness of morality and conclude that there must be a Lawgiver that originates and stands behind moral law.

But what, exactly, is meant by "moral law"? It is important to distinguish between "moral laws" and "moral law." To be sure, some have argued that there are

[6]Immanuel Kant, *Critique of Practical Reason*, tr. Lewis White Beck (Indianapolis: Bobbs-Merrill, 1956), p. 166.

at least some universally recognized moral laws. Moral laws (in the plural) are not a matter of choice and chance, and they must be grounded in an adequate cause or source: a Lawgiver. This is the view of the late C. S. Lewis, a popular and effective defender of Christian ideas. From *Mere Christianity* (first published in 1943):

> *I know that some people say the idea of a Law of Nature or decent behaviour known to all men is unsound, because different civilisations and different ages have had quite different moralities.*
>
> *But this is not true. There have been differences between their moralities, but these have never amounted to anything like a total difference. If anyone will take the trouble to compare the moral teaching of, say, the ancient Egyptians, Babylonians, Hindus, Chinese, Greeks and Romans, what will really strike him will be how very like they are to each other and to our own. Some of the evidence for this I have put together in the appendix of another book called* The Abolition of Man; *but for our present purpose I need only ask the reader to think what a totally different morality would mean. Think of a country where people were admired for running away in battle, or where a man felt proud of doublecrossing all the people who had been kindest to him. You might just as well try to imagine a country where two and two made five. Men have differed as regards what people you ought to be unselfish to— whether it was only your own family, or your fellow countrymen, or everyone. But they have always agreed that you ought not to put yourself first. Selfishness has never been admired. Men have differed as to whether you should have one wife or four. But they have always agreed that you must not simply have any woman you liked.*[7]

Of course, some anthropologists and sociologists would have a field day with such claims, playing down cultural and moral similarities and playing up cultural relativities and differences. No matter. The point of departure for the Moral Argument is not so much the universality of moral laws (in the plural) as of the moral law (in the singular), not so much the universality of moral *conscience* as of moral *consciousness*, not so much that everyone has the same moral opinions but that everyone has *some* moral opinions, not that everyone thinks that certain things are right or wrong but that everyone thinks that *something* is right or wrong. We may disagree and be confused about moral laws, but we all acknowledge moral law. And we recognize it as being objective (existing independently of our own interests or wills) and absolute (universally binding). Don't we?

This, then, is the first premise in the Moral Argument for God: There is an objective and absolute moral law. The next step is to argue that such a moral law cannot be, as it were, just floating about out there like something accidental or capricious. No, if it is really a morally binding law, then it must have a rational and abiding basis. And just as it is absurd to think of fluctuating and finite moral laws and ideals as existing apart from our own minds, so is it absurd to think of an

[7]C. S. Lewis, *Mere Christianity* (New York: Macmillan, 1976), p. 19.

MORAL LAWS AND MORAL LAW

- *Moral laws* are the particular, changing, and (to some degree) relative views which human beings formulate about morality. Our moral *conscience* reflects such views.

- *Moral law,* on the other hand, denotes the objective and absolute moral principles which are imperfectly expressed in moral laws. Our moral *consciousness* reflects the belief in morality itself, apart from our views of it.

---

absolute moral law as existing apart from an *absolute* mind. Think about this. Ideals and values, unlike tables, chairs, dogs, cats, and light fixtures, exist by their nature in *minds.* But what or whose mind is an adequate source for ideals and values? Beverly's mind? But her mind is constantly changing. How could it be the source of unchanging and universally binding ideals? Henry's mind? But we all know how fickle and limited his mind is. How could any finite and changeable human mind be the basis of the moral law? Thus, the second premise: An absolute moral law requires an absolute mind as its adequate foundation. And the conclusion is, by now, obvious: There must exist an absolute mind. It remains only to unpack the full meaning of "absolute mind." What could an *absolute* mind be, except one that is unchanging, eternal, transcendent, ultimate, etc.? And what could this be, except what most people call "God"?

From the moral law to an absolute mind

This version of the moral argument is summarized by the English theologian and philosopher Hastings Rashdall (1858–1924) in his book *The Theory of Good and Evil:*

> *We say that the Moral Law has a real existence, that there is such a thing as an absolute Morality, that there is something absolutely true or false in ethical judgements, whether we or any number of human beings at any given time actually think so or not. Such a belief is distinctly implied in what we mean by Morality. The idea of such an unconditional, objectively valid, Moral Law or ideal undoubtedly exists as a psychological fact. The question before us is whether it is capable of theoretical justification. We must then face the question where such an ideal exists, and what manner of existence we are to attribute to it. Certainly it is to be found, wholly and completely, in no individual human consciousness. Men actually think differently about moral questions, and there is no empirical reason for supposing that they will ever do otherwise. Where then and how does the moral ideal really exist? As regards*

matters of fact or physical law, we have no difficulty in satisfying ourselves that there is an objective reality which is what it is irrespectively of our beliefs or disbeliefs about it. For the man who supposes that objective reality resides in the things themselves, our ideas about them are objectively true or false so far as they correspond or fail to correspond with this real and independent archetype, though he might be puzzled to give a metaphysical account of the nature of this "correspondence" between experience and a Reality whose esse is something other than to be experienced. In the physical region the existence of divergent ideas does not throw doubt upon the existence of a reality independent of our ideas. But in the case of moral ideals it is otherwise. On materialistic or naturalistic assumptions the moral ideal can hardly be regarded as a real thing. Nor could it well be regarded as a property of any real thing: it can be no more than an aspiration, a product of the imagination, which may be useful to stimulate effort in directions in which we happen to want to move, but which cannot compel respect when we feel no desire to act in conformity with it. An absolute Moral Law or moral ideal cannot exist in material things. And it does not (we have seen) exist in the mind of this or that individual. Only if we believe in the existence of a Mind for which the true moral ideal is already in some sense real, a Mind which is the source of whatever is true in our own moral judgements, can we rationally think of the moral ideal as no less real than the world itself. Only so can we believe in an absolute standard of right and wrong, which is as independent of this or that man's actual ideas and actual desires as the facts of material nature. The belief in God, though not (like the belief in a real and an active self) a postulate of there being any such thing as Morality at all, is the logical presupposition of an "objective" or absolute Morality. A moral ideal can exist nowhere and nohow but in a mind; an absolute moral ideal can exist only in a Mind from which all Reality is derived. Our moral ideal can only claim objective validity in so far as it can rationally be regarded as the revelation of a moral ideal eternally existing in the mind of God.

We may be able, perhaps, to give some meaning to Morality without the postulate of God, but not its true or full meaning. If the existence of God is not a postulate of all Morality, it is a postulate of a sound Morality; for it is essential to that belief which vaguely and implicitly underlies all moral beliefs, and which forms the very heart of Morality in its highest, more developed, more explicit forms. The truth that the moral ideal is what it is whether we like it or not is the most essential element in what the popular consciousness understands by "moral obligation." Moral obligation means moral objectivity. That at least seems to be implied in any legitimate use of the term: at least it implies the existence of an absolute, objective moral ideal. And such a belief we have seen imperatively to demand an explanation of the Universe which shall be idealistic or at least spiritualistic, which shall recognize the existence of a Mind whose thoughts are the standard of truth and falsehood alike in Morality and in respect of all other existence. In other words, objective Morality implies the belief in God. The belief in God, if not so obviously and primarily a postulate of Morality as the belief in a permanent spiritual and active self, is still a *postulate of a Morality which shall be able fully to satisfy the demands of the moral consciousness. It may conveniently be called the secondary postulate of Morality.*[8]

An important note: If you do, in fact, accept the reality of an objective and universally binding morality, but balk at the claimed implications of this for God, well, has not the Moral Argument accomplished its real objective anyway? For you would, then, believe in a transcendent, independent, and absolute reality, namely the Moral Law. But does not that commit you, if not to God, at least to a definitely spiritualist and *sort* of theistic view of things? a view which posits, behind the fluctuating and relative world of experience and opinions, an invisible and eternal Reality which confronts us and demands rightness from us? And is this *so* different from God? Does it matter all that much what you *call* it?

THE MORAL ARGUMENT

If there is an absolute moral law, then there must be an absolute mind as its basis.
There is an absolute moral law.

Therefore, there must be an absolute mind as the basis of the moral law.

Expressed in this way, what type of argument is it? How might one defend the two premises?

IS THERE A MORAL LAW?

If anything is clear about the Moral Argument it is that it cannot possibly work except on the belief in objective and absolute morality. If one rejects this, well, the axe has been laid to the root of this tree.

Certainly there are those who do deny that morality is anything more than the perceptions, desires, inclinations, or tastes of the individual—an individual person, community, society, or whatever. The issue between moral absolutism (morality is independent of the individual) and moral relativism (morality is relative to the individual) is better treated in Chapter 16, "Challenges to Morality." Here we only summarize a few points.

Is morality absolute or relative? Objective or subjective?

[8]Hastings Rashdall, *The Theory of Good and Evil* (Oxford: Clarendon Press, 1907), II, 211-213.

The major evidence for relativism is the wide variety of differences and disagreements that do, in fact, exist from person to person and culture to culture. On the other hand, as Lewis asked, are the differences all that great? In any event, we have already distinguished between our varying opinions of morality and morality itself. Furthermore, even if some, or even most, of our ideas have been learned or culturally instilled, it hardly follows that they therefore should be rejected as false! Finally, if the relativist is right, how could one ever be morally mistaken? Would not every moral opinion have to be correct for the individual holding it? And whatever one *says* about moral relativism, can he or she *actually live* (praise, blame, argue, vote, crusade, judge, etc.) except on the belief that values are real and binding on everyone?

Moral relativism: Pro and Con

Such issues, pro and con, are clearly focused in the following selection from a lively debate originally broadcast over the BBC. The participants are two English philosophers: Bertrand Russell, who here defends the relativist position, and Fr. Frederick C. Copleston, who defends the absolutist position and its implications for God.

COPLESTON: . . . *what's your justification for distinguishing between good and bad or how do you view the distinction between them?*

RUSSELL: *I don't have any justification any more than I have when I distinguish between blue and yellow. What is my justification for distinguishing between blue and yellow? I can see they are different.*

COPLESTON: *Well, that is an excellent justification, I agree. You distinguish blue and yellow by seeing them, so you distinguish good and bad by what faculty?*

RUSSELL: *By my feelings.*

COPLESTON: *By your feelings. Well, that's what I was asking. You think that good and evil have reference simply to feeling?*

RUSSELL: *Well, why does one type of object look yellow and another look blue? I can more or less give an answer to that thanks to the physicists, and as to why I think one sort of thing good and another evil, probably there is an answer of the same sort, but it hasn't been gone into in the same way and I couldn't give it to you.*

COPLESTON: *Well, let's take the behavior of the Commandant of Belsen. That appears to you as undesirable and evil and to me too. To Adolf Hitler we suppose it appeared as something good and desirable. I suppose you'd have to admit that for Hitler it was good and for you it is evil.*

RUSSELL: *No, I shouldn't quite go so far as that. I mean, I think people can make mistakes in that as they can in other things. If you have jaundice you see things yellow that are not yellow. You're making a mistake.*

COPLESTON: *Yes, one can make mistakes, but can you make a mistake if it's simply a question of reference to a feeling or emotion? Surely Hitler would be the only possible judge of what appealed to his emotions.*

RUSSELL: *It would be quite right to say that it appealed to his emotions, but you can say various things about that among others, that if that sort of thing makes* that sort of appeal to Hitler's emotions, then Hitler makes quite a different appeal to my emotions.

COPLESTON: Granted. But there's no objective criterion outside feeling then for condemning the conduct of the Commandant of Belsen, in your view?

RUSSELL: No more than there is for the color-blinded person who's in exactly the same state. Why do we intellectually condemn the color-blinded man? Isn't it because he's in the minority?

COPLESTON: I would say because he is lacking in a thing which normally belongs to human nature.

RUSSELL: Yes, but if he were in the majority, we shouldn't say that. . . .

COPLESTON: Well, do you think that the word "ought" simply has an emotional connotation?

RUSSELL: No, I don't think that, because you see, as I was saying a moment ago, one has to take account of the effects, and I think right conduct is that which would probably produce the greatest possible balance in intrinsic value of all the acts possible in the circumstances, and you've got to take account of the probable effects of your action in considering what is right.

COPLESTON: Well, I brought in moral obligation because I think that one can approach the question of God's existence in that way. The vast majority of the human race will make, and always have made, some distinction between right and wrong. The vast majority I think has some consciousness of an obligation in the moral sphere. It's my opinion that the perception of values and the consciousness of moral law and obligation are best explained through the hypothesis of a transcendent ground of value and of an author of the moral law. I do mean by "author of the moral law" an arbitrary author of the moral law. I think, in fact, that those modern atheists who have argued in the converse way "there is no God; therefore, there are no absolute values and no absolute law," are quite logical.

RUSSELL: I don't like the word "absolute." I don't think there is anything absolute whatever. The moral law, for example, is always changing. At one period in the development of the human race, almost everybody thought cannibalism was a duty.

COPLESTON: Well, I don't see that differences in particular moral judgments are any conclusive argument against the universality of the moral law. Let's assume for the moment that there are absolute moral values, even on that hypothesis it's only to be expected that different individuals and different groups should enjoy varying degrees of insight into those values.

RUSSELL: I'm inclined to think that "ought," the feeling that one has about "ought" is an echo of what has been told one by one's parents or one's nurses.

COPLESTON: Well, I wonder if you can explain away the idea of the "ought" merely in terms of nurses and parents. I really don't see how it can be conveyed to anybody in other terms than itself. It seems to me that if there is a moral order bearing upon the human conscience, that that moral order is unintelligible apart from the existence of God.

RUSSELL: Then you have to say one or other of two things. Either God only

Bertrand Russell

The English philosopher
Bertrand Russell was
very influential in a
wide range of
philosophical issues,
and more activistic and
outspoken than most.
He was especially
antireligious, and once
wrote a book entitled,
Why I Am Not a
Christian.

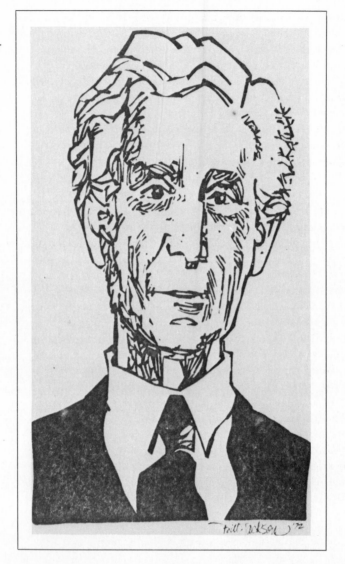

*speaks to a very small percentage of mankind—which happens to include yourself—
or He deliberately says things that are not true in talking to the consciences of
savages. . . .*

COPLESTON: *It seems to me to be external customs and taboos and things of
that sort which can most easily be explained simply through environment and education, but all that seems to me to belong to what I call the matter of the law, the*

content. *The idea of the "ought" as such can never be conveyed to a man by the tribal chief or by anybody else, because there are no other terms in which it could be conveyed. It seems to me entirely—[Russell breaks in].*

RUSSELL: *But I don't see any reason to say that—I mean we all know about conditioned reflexes. We know that an animal, if punished habitually for a certain sort of act, after a time will refrain. I don't think the animal refrains from arguing within himself, "Master will be angry if I do this." He has a feeling that that's not the thing to do. That's what we can do with ourselves and nothing more.*

COPLESTON: *I see no reason to suppose that an animal has a consciousness of moral obligation; and we certainly don't regard an animal as morally responsible for his acts of disobedience. But a man has a consciousness of obligation and of moral values. I see no reason to suppose that one could condition all men as one can "condition" an animal, and I don't suppose you'd really want to do so even if one could. If "behaviorism" were true, there would be no objective moral distinction between the emperor Nero and St. Francis of Assisi. I can't help feeling, Lord Russell, you know, that you regard the conduct of the Commandant at Belsen as morally reprehensible, and that you yourself would never under any circumstances act in that way, even if you thought, or had reason to think, that possibly the balance of the happiness of the human race might be increased through some people being treated in that abominable manner.*

RUSSELL: *No. I wouldn't imitate the conduct of a mad dog. The fact that I wouldn't do it doesn't really bear on this question we're discussing.*

COPLESTON: *No, but if you were making a utilitarian explanation of right and wrong in terms of consequences, it might be held, and I suppose some of the Nazis of the better type would have held that although it's lamentable to have to act in this way, yet the balance in the long run leads to greater happiness. I don't think you'd say that, would you? I think you'd say that that sort of action is wrong—and in itself, quite apart from whether the general balance of happiness is increased or not. Then, if you're prepared to say that, then I think you must have some criterion of right and wrong, that is outside the criterion of feeling, at any rate. To me, that admission would ultimately result in the admission of an ultimate ground of value in God. . . .*[9]

A more concise discussion of the issues involved in the moral argument could hardly be found. Try to understand and associate every move made by the two participants. Does it help you make your own decision about the Moral Argument for God?

---

[9]Bertrand Russell and F. C. Copleston, "The Existence of God: A Debate Between Bertrand Russell and Father F. C. Copleston," in Ed. L. Miller, *Philosophical and Religious Issues: Classical and Contemporary Statements* (Encino, Calif.: Dickenson, 1971), pp. 123-127.

Chapter 13 in Review

SUMMARY

In this chapter we have considered two further arguments for the existence of God:

- The Ontological Argument
- The Moral Argument

It is important to appreciate that whereas the other arguments began with the world, these attempt to demonstrate the existence of God through something given in the reason alone.

The Ontological Argument is an excellent example of a completely *a priori* reasoning. Nowhere is there any reference to sense experience or the physical world. Rather, it attempts to show from a consideration of the *idea* of God (or most perfect being, unlimited being, etc.) that such a being, by virtue of being the *greatest*, must actually exist. Can such a being lack the attribute or perfection of existence any more than it can lack the attribute or perfection of omniscience, omnipotence, love, or justice? Or, as Descartes asks, can the existence of God (*that* he is) be separated from his essence (*what* he is) any more than a mountain can be separated from a valley?

But it is just with such talk of existence as an attribute or *predicate* that the Ontological Argument runs afoul of the most important objection. Kant observed that existence does not, in fact, actually add anything to the content of any concept; that is, existence is *not* a real predicate of anything, including the greatest thing. On the other hand, some, such as the contemporary philosopher Malcolm, have conceived a version of this proof which sidesteps the complaint that existence is not a predicate, and have formulated an Ontological Argument on the ground that *necessary* existence *is* a predicate, and that necessary existence is part of what "greatest being" must mean. Discussion of the Ontological Argument has raged for centuries and still rages. There is surely a lesson in this for those who think that this argument for God involves some simple-minded mistake.

The Moral Argument shifts our attention to our idea of moral law or, to say it differently, to our moral consciousness. If you believe in an objective and absolute morality, then how do you explain or justify it apart from an objective and absolute lawgiver? It is important to distinguish between believing in moral law and knowing what it is. The Moral Argument requires only the former. The relativity of moral opinions might not, therefore, be relevant here: I may be hopelessly confused about the content of the moral law but still be constrained to believe in it.

But, of course, that is the problem. Why should one believe in the first place in an objective and absolute morality? Some would answer, among other things, that the alternative, namely, ethical relativism or subjectivism, turns out on reflection to be philosophically indefensible (is it not possible to be morally mistaken?)

and certainly impossible to put into practice (can one live apart from the practice of ideals and values?).

- The Ontological Argument
    St. Anselm's version (two forms)
    Descartes' version
- Existence as a predicate
- Kant's rejection of existence as a predicate
- Malcolm: Necessary existence as a predicate
- The Principle of Consistency
- The Moral Argument
- Distinction between moral conscience and moral consciousness (moral laws and the moral law)
- Moral objectivism (absolutism)/moral subjectivism (relativism)
- Subjectivism: Reasons for and against

1. Who said it? "I don't have any justification for distinguishing between good and bad, any more than I have when I distinguish between blue and yellow."
2. Norman Malcolm (a) defended the Moral Argument against Bertrand Russell, (b) believed that necessary existence is a predicate of God, (c) was a scholar of Renaissance and medieval literature, (d) argued that morality is purely relative.
3. Who extolled "the starry heavens above me and the moral law within me"?
4. True or false: "A vast herd of giraffes is at the moment roaming through the White House" is a logically consistent claim.
5. What, exactly, is the difference between moral laws and the moral law?
6. How does Hastings Rashdall figure in the discussion in this chapter?
7. Knowledge of God based on moral consciousness is (a) an instance of special revelation, (b) propounded by Bertrand Russell, (c) *a priori*, (d) refuted by Kant.
8. True or false: St. Anselm's and Descartes' versions of the Ontological Argument construe existence as a predicate or attribute of God.

- Whether or not you accept the Ontological Argument it is important to understand it. Specifically, can you reproduce *with understanding* Malcolm's version? Bearing in mind that Malcolm is not a fool, can you find any flaws in it?
- Do you see the distinction between believing in morality and knowing what it consists in? Do you think that *how many* people affirm a certain value or ideal is relevant? Who do you think was the victor in the Copleston-Russell debate on the Moral Argument? Why?

- In the last two chapters we have seen that while Kant rejected the *a posteriori* arguments, he himself formulated a version of the Moral Argument. Can you explain the epistemological basis of this? Do you recall from Chapter 11 Kant's distinction between the noumenal and phenomenal worlds? The limitations of the theoretical reason and the possibilities of the practical reason? What is the application here?

CHAPTER 14

RELIGIOUS EXPERIENCE

Naturally, there will be many who will balk at arguments for the existence of God right from the start. Nor will they necessarily be atheists. Some of the critics will be themselves believers, objecting that somehow such proofs are irrelevant or inappropriate to the overpowering majesty of God. "No," they will say, "God is not known in this way. Just as he transcends the world and our reason, so is he known in a way that transcends our ordinary knowledge." It is just as silly to think that God can be captured by an argument as it is to think that he can be confined to Solomon's Temple: "Behold, heaven and the highest heaven cannot contain thee; how much less this house which I have built!" (I Kings 8:27, Revised Standard Version). On the more human side, do not religious experiences come *first*, and the arguments and rationalizations *second?* The American philosopher William James thought so:

> What keeps religion going is something else than abstract definitions and systems of logically concatenated adjectives, and something different from faculties of theology and their professors. All these things are after-effects, secondary accretions upon a mass of concrete religious experiences, connecting themselves with feeling and conduct that renew themselves in saecula saeculorum in the lives of humble private men. If you ask what these experiences are, they are conversations with the unseen, voices and visions, responses to prayer, changes of heart, deliverances from fear, inflowings of help, assurances of support, whenever certain persons set their own internal attitude in certain appropriate ways.[1]

[1]Quoted in Ralph Barton Perry, *The Thought and Character of William James* (Boston: Little, Brown & Co., 1935), II, p. 325.

Enter the *nonrational* approach to God, the approach of *religious experience* in its various and sundry forms.

THE EXPERIENCE OF THE NUMINOUS

It is important to review an earlier point: The distinction between *nonrational* and *irrational*. That which is irrational is that which is in some way contrary to or incompatible with reason. Certainly this is not intended by those who press for a nonrational approach to God. On the contrary, they intend a knowledge of God which is *other* than rational, and, indeed, they usually mean a knowledge that is higher than, or *superior* to, what is knowable through ordinary reason or experience.

Natural Theology

Non-rational approach   Rational approach

Forms of religious experience

Numinous experience
Mystical experience
    etc.

Rational vs. Nonrational interpretations of religion

This was exactly the view of the German religious thinker Rudolf Otto (1869–1937). Otto was much annoyed by the distortions and trivialities that result from an intellectualist approach to religion. At the beginning of his influential work, *The Idea of the Holy*, Otto explains how the rational perspective on religion has come to dominate, and warns against the "one-sidedly intellectualistic and rationalistic interpretation":

> . . . we have to be on our guard against an error which would lead to a wrong and one-sided interpretation of religion. This is the view that the essence of deity can be given completely and exhaustively in . . . "rational" attributions. . . . It is not an unnatural misconception. We are prompted to it by the traditional language of edification, with its characteristic phraseology and ideas; by the learned treatment of religious themes in sermon and theological instruction; and further even by our Holy

Scriptures themselves. In all these cases the "rational" element occupies the fore-ground, and often nothing else seems to be present at all. But this is after all to be expected. All language, in so far as it consists of words, purports to convey ideas or concepts;—that is what language means;—and the more clearly and unequivocally it does so, the better the language. And hence expositions of religious truth in language inevitably tend to stress the "rational" attributes of God.

But though the above mistake is thus a natural one enough, it is none the less seriously misleading. For so far are these "rational" attributes from exhausting the idea of deity, that they in fact imply a non-rational or supra-rational Subject of which they are predicates. They are "essential" (and not merely "accidental") attri-butes of that subject, but they are also, it is important to notice, synthetic essential attributes. That is to say, we have to predicate them of a subject which they qualify, but which in its deeper essence is not, nor indeed can be, comprehended in them; which rather requires comprehension of a quite different kind. Yet, though it eludes the con-ceptual way of understanding, it must be in some way or other within our grasp, else absolutely nothing could be asserted of it. And even mysticism, in speaking of it as to arrēton, the ineffable, does not really mean to imply that absolutely nothing can be asserted of the object of the religious consciousness; otherwise, mysticism could exist only in unbroken silence, whereas what has generally been a characteristic of the mystics is their copious eloquence.

Here for the first time we come up against the contrast between rationalism and profounder religion. . . . All depends upon this: in our idea of God is the non-rational overborne, even perhaps wholly excluded, by the rational? Or conversely, does the non-rational itself preponderate over the rational? Looking at the matter thus, we see that the common dictum, that orthodoxy itself has been the mother of rationalism, is in some measure well founded. It is not simply that orthodoxy was preoccupied with doctrine and the framing of dogma, for these have been no less a concern of the wildest mystics. It is rather that orthodoxy found in the construction of dogma and doctrine no way to do justice to the non-rational aspect of its subject. So far from keeping the non-rational element in religion alive in the heart of the religious experience, orthodox Christianity manifestly failed to recognize its value, and by this failure gave to the idea of God a one-sidedly intellectualistic and ration-alistic interpretation.[2]

Mind you, for Otto, it is not just that there is a nonrational side or aspect of religion in addition to others. The nonrational lies at the *center* of religion; he calls it the heart of any religion worthy of the name. And as soon as you let some phi-losopher or theologian—some *rationalist*—get hold of religion, he or she will imme-diately cut out its heart! Otto insisted that we must recover and preserve the *non*-rational core of authentic religion.

The nonrational core of religion

[2]Rudolf Otto, *The Idea of the Holy*, tr. John W. Harvey, 2d ed. (New York: Oxford University Press, 1950), pp. 1–3.

To this point, Otto's appraisal of religion is largely negative and not all that unusual: We must reject any rationalistic perspective which preempts or excludes what is in fact the nonrational core of religion. But what exactly is this nonrational core? Here is where Otto made his special contribution. He believed that he had isolated an experience which, though varying in its manifestations, may be recognized the world over, in all periods, and which is the foundation of true religious consciousness. It is the sense or awareness—sometimes quiet, sometimes frenzied, but always a bit uncanny—of *Something*. Here we are trying to talk about an encounter which, really, defies talking about. But it may help to describe this as a feeling or even a sense—even a kind of sensation—of a presence that is holy, wholly other, absolute, overpowering, divine, and before which we only want to cower in our creatureliness. For this experience Otto coined the expressions "numinous feeling" and, better, "feeling of the numinous," from the Latin *numen*, which at one time signified the divine power or presence.

The numinous

Otto invites you to reflect on such an experience as possibly your own:

> Let us consider the deepest and most fundamental element in all strong and sincerely felt religious emotion. Faith unto salvation, trust, love—all these are there. But over and above these is an element which may also on occasion, quite apart from them, profoundly affect us and occupy the mind with a wellnigh bewildering strength. Let us follow up with every effort of sympathy and imaginative intuition wherever it is to be found, in the lives of those around us, in sudden, strong ebullitions of personal piety and the frames of mind such ebullitions evince, in the fixed and ordered solemnities of rites and liturgies, and again in the atmosphere that clings to old religious monuments and buildings, to temples and to churches. If we do so we shall find we are dealing with something for which there is only one appropriate expression, "mysterium tremendum." The feeling of it may at times come sweeping like a gentle tide, pervading the mind with a tranquil mood of deepest worship. It may pass over into a more set and lasting attitude of the soul, continuing, as it were, thrillingly vibrant and resonant, until at last it dies away and the soul resumes its "profane," nonreligious mood of everyday experience. It may burst in sudden eruption up from the depths of the soul with spasms and convulsions, or lead to the strangest excitements, to intoxicated frenzy, to transport, and to ecstasy. It has its wild and demonic forms and can sink to an almost grisly horror and shuddering. It has its crude, barbaric antecedents and early manifestations, and again it may be developed into something beautiful and pure and glorious. It may become the hushed, trembling, and speechless humility of the creature in the presence of—whom or what? In the presence of that which is a mystery inexpressible and above all creatures.[3]

Does this suggest anything from your own experience? If not, Otto would recommend, perhaps, visiting an old and great cathedral, or maybe listening to Bach's

[3]Ibid., pp. 12–13.

B Minor Mass, or reading sacred scriptures. For in such things may be found, as it were, a less fleeting experience of the numinous inasmuch it has been to some degree captured and embodied for the contemplation of all.

THE NUMINOUS EXPERIENCE

A feeling of the divine reality and presence, often accompanied by an uncanny sense of wholly otherness, majesty, power, and holiness.

THE MYSTICAL ASCENT

The word "mysticism" is surely one of the foggiest and most abused in our intellectual vocabulary. It is important, though, to clarify it, since mystical experience is perhaps the most dramatic and fascinating of the nonrational or experiential ways of knowing God.

Ouija boards, astrology, crystal balls, Tarot cards—all these and similar things have, at times, been associated with mysticism. The problem is, of course, that they are beset from the start with a certain occult or spooky nature. This not only renders them immediately suspect from a rational or scientific standpoint, it removes them from the arena of serious investigation and validation/invalidation. Mysticism in this sense should be set aside as a sort of slur on the real thing.

More recently, the use (and abuse) of drugs, such as LSD and the like, has intruded onto the religious and philosophical scene, promising a sort of "instant mysticism." One of the popularizers of this experience was the writer Aldous Huxley, who in his much-read little book *The Doors of Perception*, described the mescaline experience:

Instant mysticism?

> . . . what happens to the majority of the few who have taken mescalin under supervision can be summarized as follows.
>
> (1) The ability to remember and to "think straight" is little if at all reduced. (Listening to the recordings of my conversation under the influence of the drug, I cannot discover that I was then any stupider than I am at ordinary times.)
>
> (2) Visual impressions are greatly intensified and the eye recovers some of the perceptual innocence of childhood, when the sensum was not immediately and automatically subordinated to the concept. Interest in space is diminished and interest in time falls almost to zero.
>
> (3) Though the intellect remains unimpaired and though perception is enor-

mously improved, the will suffers a profound change for the worse. The mescalin taker sees no reason for doing anything in particular and finds most of the causes for which, at ordinary times, he was prepared to act and suffer, profoundly uninteresting. He can't be bothered with them, for the good reason that he has better things to think about.

(4) These better things may be experienced (as I experienced them) "out there," or "in here," or in both worlds, the inner and the outer, simultaneously or successively. That they are better seems to be self-evident to all mescalin takers who come to the drug with a sound liver and an untroubled mind.

These effects of mescalin are the sort of effects you could expect to follow the administration of a drug having the power to impair the efficiency of the cerebral reducing valve. When the brain runs out of sugar, the undernourished ego grows weak, can't be bothered to undertake the necessary chores, and loses all interest in those spatial and temporal relationships which mean so much to an organism bent on getting on in the world. As Mind at Large seeps past the no longer watertight valve, all kinds of biologically useless things start to happen. In some cases there may be extra-sensory perceptions. Other persons discover a world of visionary beauty. To others again is revealed the glory, the infinite value and meaningfulness of naked existence, of the given, unconceptualized event. In the final stage of egolessness there is an "obscure knowledge" that All is in all—that All is actually each. This is as near, I take it, as a finite mind can ever come to "perceiving everything that is happening everywhere in the universe."

In this context, how significant is the enormous heightening, under mescalin, of the perception of color! For certain animals it is biologically very important to be able to distinguish certain hues. But beyond the limits of their utilitarian spectrum, most creatures are completely color blind. Bees, for example, spend most of their time "deflowering the fresh virgins of the spring"; but, as Von Frisch has shown, they can recognize only a very few colors. Man's highly developed color sense is a biological luxury—inestimably precious to him as an intellectual and spiritual being, but unnecessary to his survival as an animal. To judge by the adjectives which Homer puts into their mouths, the heroes of the Trojan War hardly excelled the bees in their capacity to distinguish colors. In this respect, at least, mankind's advance has been prodigious.

Mescalin raises all colors to a higher power and makes the percipient aware of innumerable fine shades of difference, to which, at ordinary times, he is completely blind. It would seem that, for Mind at Large, the so-called secondary characters of things are primary. Unlike Locke, it evidently feels that colors are more important, better worth attending to, than masses, positions and dimensions. Like mescalin takers, many mystics perceive supernaturally brilliant colors, not only with the inward eye, but even in the objective world around them. Similar reports are made by psychics and sensitives. There are certain mediums to whom the mescalin taker's brief revelation is a matter, during long periods, of daily and hourly experience.[4]

[4]Aldous Huxley, *The Doors of Perception* (New York: Harper & Row, 1970), pp. 25–27.

Huxley speaks here of the loss of interest in space and time, of focused attention, of "Mind at Large," "a world of visionary beauty," "the infinite value and meaningfulness of naked existence," and the "All." It is no wonder that some have seen in such experiences a shortcut to religious, or at least heightened, consciousness. Maybe so. But *mysticism?* Again, it depends on what you mean. Notice that Huxley speaks also of "visual impressions greatly intensified," "extrasensory perceptions," "perceiving everything that is happening," and "heightening of the perception of color." Such talk precisely distinguishes this kind of experience (whatever kind it is) from what we might call a more traditional and *classical* form of mysticism.

It is difficult to give a precise definition of classical mysticism, and the problem isn't helped any by the fact that the mystics describe their experience as something which can't be described! But we may venture the following: Mysticism is the pursuit of a transcendent, unitive experience with the absolute reality. It may also be helpful to list more completely some characteristic features of this experience. It is:

A definition of mysticism

- *Transcendent.* Not localizable in space or time
- *Ineffable.* Not expressible in language
- *Noetic.* Conveying illumination, truth
- *Ecstatic.* Filling the soul with bliss, peace
- *Unitive.* Uniting the soul with reality

CLASSICAL MYSTICISM

The pursuit of a transcendent, unitive experience with the absolute reality.

Here we have in mind the experiences of, say, St. Augustine, St. Francis, St. Theresa, St. John of the Cross, and Meister Eckhart. What distinguishes classical mysticism from the other forms of mysticism is its interest not in intensifying the consciousness but rather in *emptying* the consciousness of all sense impressions and ideas, so that, abandoning and transcending these, the soul may attain a reality of an altogether different and *higher* nature. One is tempted to distinguish these "higher" mystics from the merely "high" mystics.

It is important here to recall Plato. These mystics certainly were not Platonists, but they did hold to a Platonic-type view of reality as a ladder or scale of being. The point is to escape, even in this life as much as possible, all multiplicity and change and to become united with true Being. And this in turn means a sometimes difficult ascent, as in struggling up a steep mountain, from the sensible world, to our ideas of the world, to pure intellectual ideas, to our own selves, and beyond to the One. This "ascent of the soul" may otherwise and variously be represented as an ascent from nonbeing to being, from ignorance to knowledge, from multiplicity and change to unity and immutability, and from evil to goodness. Recalling also Plato's Allegory of the Cave, the mystical ascent may further be characterized, allegorically, as an ascent from darkness to light.

The mystical ascent of the soul

Different mystics may represent differently the number and nature of the several steps involved in this ascent, and the following diagram is only suggestive of the basic ones. It is important to see that as one passes from the sensible world to internal-world images, to the pure intellectual operations of the mind, to pure self-consciousness, to *beyond* the self, one leaves further and further behind the crudities of space-time experience, multiplicity and change, ignorance, evil, and attachment to things, ideas, and one's own self. Thus is the soul prepared for the ecstatic ("ecstasy" means, literally, "to stand outside one's own self") infilling of the divine illumination, love, and will.

One of the greatest of the mystics was a Spaniard, St. John of the Cross (1542–1591). It is no accident that he called his greatest work *The Ascent of Mount Carmel*. The significance of the word "ascent" should certainly by now be clear, and Mount

William James' Varieties of Religious Experience *is a classic of religious philosophy, and the chapters dealing with mysticism are perhaps the most frequently consulted discussions of the subject.*

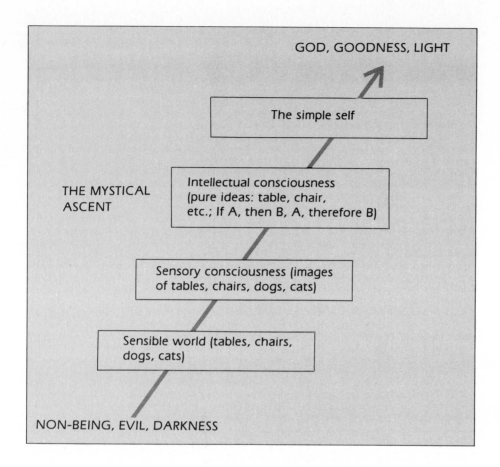

GOD, GOODNESS, LIGHT

The simple self

THE MYSTICAL
ASCENT

Intellectual consciousness
(pure ideas: table, chair,
etc.; If A, then B, A, therefore B)

Sensory consciousness (images
of tables, chairs, dogs, cats)

Sensible world (tables, chairs,
dogs, cats)

NON-BEING, EVIL, DARKNESS

Carmel is where Elijah called down the true God to overthrow the claims of the idolaters (I Kings 18:20–40). This work begins with a mystical poem and continues with a long and detailed commentary on it. That St. John sought to express the mystical experience by means of a *poem* is suggestive of the ineffability (or unspeakability) of the experience, and the poem otherwise reflects important aspects of the experience, such as the ascent, the withdrawal from the world and ideas, transcendence, ecstatic union, and the like. It would be a good exercise to see how many of these features you can recognize in the lines of St. John's poem:

> *1*
> *In a dark night,*
> *My longing heart, aglow with love,*
> *—Oh, blessed lot!—*
> *I went forth unseen*
> *From my house that was at last in deepest rest.*

2
Secure and protected by darkness,
I climbed the secret ladder, in disguise,
—Oh, blessed lot!—
In darkness, veiled and concealed I went
Leaving behind my house in deepest rest.

3
Oh, blissful night!
Oh, secret night, when I remained unseeing and unseen,
When the flame burning in my heart
Was my only light and guide.

4
This inward light,
A safer guide than noonday's brightness,
Showed me the place where He awaited me
—My soul's Beloved—
A place of solitude.

5
Oh, night that guided me!
Oh, night more lovely than the rosy dawn!
Oh, night whose darkness guided me
To that sweet union,
In which the lover and Beloved are made one.

6
Upon the flower of my breast,
Kept undefiled for Him alone,
He fell asleep,
While I was waking
Caressing Him with gentle cedars' breeze.

7
And when Aurora's breath
Began to spread His curled hair,
His gentle hand
He placed upon my neck.
And all my senses were in bliss suspended.

8
Forgetful of myself,
My head reclined on my Beloved,

The world was gone
And all my cares at rest,
Forgotten all my grief among the lilies.[5]

We have spoken here and there of "mystical union," of the "unitive" aspect of the mystical experience, etc. But it is now important to realize that *Western* mystics (Christians, Jews, Muslims) don't and can't mean a *literal* union with God, at least not generally. For it is a fundamental idea of Western theology that there is an essential difference between God and what he has created. And the soul can never overcome—not even in the heights of mystical experience—the distinction between uncreated and created being. No, it is rather a matter of the soul becoming *conformed* to the divine will and love, or becoming *transparent* to the divine will and love. It is precisely to make this clear that St. John himself introduces his windowpane analogy, and otherwise comments on the mystical experience:

Mystical "union" according to Western mystics

Let me clarify [the nature of this union] by a simile. Picture a ray of sunlight that is striking a window. Now if the window is coated with stains or vapors, the ray will be unable to illumine it and transform it into its own light; this it could do only if the window were stainless and pure. And the greater or lesser degree of illumination will be strictly in proportion to the window's greater or lesser purity; and this will be so, not because of the ray of sunlight but because of the condition of the window. Thus, if the window were entirely clean and pure, the ray would transform and illumine it in such a way that it would become almost undistinguishable from the brightness of the ray and would diffuse the same light as the ray. And yet, however much the window may resemble the ray of sunlight, it actually retains its own distinct nature. But this does not prevent us from saying that this window is luminous as a ray of the sun or is sunlight by participation. Now the soul is like this window: the Divine light of the Being of God is unceasingly beating upon it, or to use a better expression, the Divine light is ever dwelling in it.

When the soul thus allows God to work in it, it will soon be transformed and transfigured in God, and God will communicate to it His supernatural Being in such a way that the soul appears to be God Himself, and it will indeed be God by participation. Yet it remains true nevertheless that the soul's natural being—notwithstanding the soul's supernatural transformation—remains as distinct from the Being of God as it was before, even as the window has and retains a nature of its own, distinct from the nature of the ray, although it owes its luminosity to the light of the sun.

This consideration should make it clearer why a soul cannot dispose itself for this union by either understanding, or sensory apperception, or inner feelings and

---

[5]St. John of the Cross, *The Dark Night of the Soul*, tr. and ed. Kurt F. Reinhardt (New York: Ungar, 1957), pp. 1–3.

imaginings, or by any other experiences relating either to God or to anything else, but only by purity and love, that is, by perfect resignation and total detachment from all things for the sake of God alone. And as there can be no perfect transformation unless there be perfect purity, the soul will not be perfect unless it be totally cleansed and wholly pure.

Those souls {who attain to Divine union} do so according to their greater or smaller capacity and thus not in the same degree; and the degree of union depends also on what the Lord wishes to grant to each soul. And it is similar in the beatific vision: though some souls will have a more perfect vision of God in Heaven than others, they all see God, and all are content, since their capacity is satisfied. And in this life, too, all souls {who have attained to the state of perfection} will be equally satisfied, each one according to its knowledge of God and thus according to its capacity. A soul, on the other hand, that does not attain to a degree of purity corresponding to its capacity, will never find true peace and contentment. . . .

This blissful night darkens the spirit, but only in order to illuminate it afterwards with respect to all things; it humbles the spirit and makes it miserable, but only in order to raise it up and exalt it; it impoverishes the spirit and deprives it of every natural possession and affection, but only to enable it to rise, divinely, in unfettered spiritual freedom, to a perfect fruition of all things in Heaven and on earth. And, owing to its purity, the spirit tastes the sweetness of all things in a preeminently sublime manner.

We know that the children of Israel could not relish, in the desert, the sweetness of the manna—the bread of angels—solely because they had retained a single affectionate remembrance of the fleshpots and meals which they had tasted in Egypt. Similarly, the spirit cannot attain to the delights of the supernatural as long as it remains attached to any actual or habitual desire or to any particular object or apprehension of the understanding.

The light which is here imparted to the soul is truly a most sublime Divine light, which transcends every natural light, and which cannot be grasped by the understanding in a natural manner. If, then, the understanding is to be united with this light and is to become Divine in the state of perfection, it must first be purged and annihilated with respect to its natural light and led into darkness by means of this dark contemplation. When this has been done, the Divine light and illumination will take the place of the natural mode and manner of the soul's understanding.

Moreover, in order to attain to the union to which this dark night is leading it, the soul must be filled with a certain glorious splendor, to become disposed for its communication with God. Included herein are innumerable blessings and delights which far exceed all the abundance which the soul can naturally possess. For, as Isaiah says: "No eye has seen, and no ear has heard, nor has it ever entered into a human heart, what God has prepared for those who love Him" {Isa. 64:4}. And this is the reason why the soul must first become empty and poor in spirit and purged from all natural support, so that, in total poverty of spirit and liberated from the old *man, it may be able to live that new and blessed life which is attained by means of this night, and which is the state of union with God.*[6]

MYSTICISMS EAST

It is sometimes said that the Western perspective tends to be academic, logical, and argumentative, whereas the Eastern way is essentially meditative, mystical, and inscrutable. Such characterizations are surely a distortion of the facts. We have just seen that various mystical traditions are strongly embedded in the West, and there are strong intellectualist traditions just as embedded in the Eastern perspectives of China, India, and Japan. Nonetheless, there is at least a grain of truth in the notion that the West tends to be intellectualist in its approach to reality whereas the East is spiritualist. It is certainly the spirituality of the East that has been borne across the ocean and has made the biggest impact on Western culture.

Philosophy, East and West

Religious experience is as varied in the East as in the West. But here too we encounter a solid core of the "higher" mysticism, with its emphasis on the renunciation of all distractions—both on the outside and on the inside—in the attempt to attain self-transcendence and unity with the ultimate principle of all things.

Probably the best-known of Eastern religious writings is the *Bhagavad-Gita*, a sacred text of Hinduism, composed between 600 B.C. and 300 B.C. You will want to read the following passage from the *Gita* in the light of what you have already read from St. John of the Cross. (*Atman* denotes the self, which after enlightenment is understood to be identical with *Brahman*, the supreme reality and principle of all things.)

> *He knows bliss in the Atman*
> *And wants nothing else.*
> *Cravings torment the heart:*
> *He renounces cravings.*
> *I call him illumined.*
>
> *Not shaken by adversity,*
> *Not hankering after happiness:*
> *Free from fear, free from anger,*
> *Free from the things of desire.*
> *I call him a seer, and illumined.*
> *The bonds of his flesh are broken.*
> *He is lucky, and does not rejoice:*
> *He is unlucky, and does not weep.*
> *I call him illumined.*

[6]Ibid., pp. 35–37, 196–197.

The tortoise can draw in his legs:
The seer can draw in his senses.
I call him illumined.

The abstinent run away from what they desire
But carry their desires with them:
When a man enters Reality,
He leaves his desires behind him.

Even a mind that knows the path
Can be dragged from the path:
The senses are so unruly.
But he controls the senses
And recollects the mind
And fixes it on me.
I call him illumined.

Thinking about sense-objects
Will attach you to sense-objects;
Grow attached, and you become addicted;
Thwart your addiction, it turns to anger;
Be angry, and you confuse your mind;
Confuse your mind, you forget the lesson of experience;
Forget experience, you lose discrimination;
Lose discrimination, and you miss life's only purpose.

When he has no lust, no hatred,
A man walks safely among the things of lust and hatred.
To obey the Atman
Is his peaceful joy:
Sorrow melts
Into that clear peace:
His quiet mind
Is soon established in peace.

The uncontrolled mind
Does not guess that the Atman is present:
How can it meditate?
Without meditation, where is peace?
Without peace, where is happiness?

The wind turns a ship
From its course upon the waters:
The wandering winds of the senses
Cast man's mind adrift
And turn his better judgment from its course.

When a man can still the senses
I call him illumined.
The recollected mind is awake
In the knowledge of the Atman
Which is dark night to the ignorant:
The ignorant are awake in their sense-life
Which they think is daylight:
To the seer it is darkness.

Water flows continually into the ocean
But the ocean is never disturbed:
Desire flows into the mind of the seer
But he is never disturbed.
The seer knows peace:
The man who stirs up his own lusts
Can never know peace.
He knows peace who has forgotten desire.
He lives without craving:
Free from ego, free from pride.

This is the state of enlightenment in Brahman:
A man does not fall back from it
Into delusion.
Even at the moment of death
He is alive in that enlightenment:
Brahman and he are one.[7]

You may, rightfully, be struck by the similarity of this passage to what has been discussed above and quoted from St. John of the Cross. In fact, it may seem to you that we have here only a different expression of the exact same idea and experience. Many do, indeed, take just this view of the matter. This sort of mysticism, they will say, is really a *universal* experience, though understandably and necessarily grasped and expressed in accordance with the language, images, and worldview of a particular mystic's time, place, and culture. Others are not so sure. And still others *are* sure that this is *not* the case.

Is mysticism a universal phenomenon?

It is true that underlying the *experiential* similarities there are important *conceptual* differences. That is, while mystics East and West describe and represent what they *experience* in similar ways, they understand *what* they experience in very different ways. We will mention only one of these conceptual differences, but a very basic one. We emphasized above that in Western mysticism—for example, Christian mysticism—the interpretation of the mystical experience is controlled by the

Mystical "union" according to Eastern mystics

[7]*The Song of God: Bhagavad-Gita*, tr. Swami Prabhavananda and Christopher Isherwood (New York: New American Library, 1951), pp. 41–44.

philosophical and theological doctrine of the essential difference between God and his creation, and mystical "union," therefore, cannot be understood strictly or metaphysically. However, in Hindu thought (at least that which underlies the *Gita*) the matter is conceived quite otherwise. Here we have a strictly *monistic* view: Reality is One; all things are part of the One; there is no essential difference between creator and created. And mystical enlightenment consists of the *realization* of one's actual unity with the One. There are, then, important differences here which bear very much on the actual nature of the experience, and we must not be blinded to these by the similarities.

MYSTICISM EAST AND WEST

Western and Eastern mystics share many ideas and images in the description of their experience: the renunciation of the sensible world, transcendence of ideas, abandonment of all interests, blissful union with the ultimate reality, the "darkness" which leads to "light," etc.

On a more theoretical level, however, an important difference divides them. Western mystics (Christians, Jews, Muslims) all hold to an essential difference between God and his creatures; and, thus, mystical union can only mean a unity of will, love, etc. Eastern mystics, on the other hand, characteristically hold to the unity of all being; and, thus, mystical union means for them a quite literal unity of the individual with ultimate reality—indeed a unity that has always existed but is discovered in mystical illumination.

IS RELIGIOUS EXPERIENCE EVIDENCE FOR GOD?

The directness of religious experience: A plus

The question now is this: Is religious experience evidence for God? The answer, clearly, is both Yes and No. Obviously, it is evidence for the one who has enjoyed such an experience. And, to return to the point we began this chapter with, for such an individual it is an evidence for God which, far and away, surpasses any other evidence. "Seeing is believing." And such individuals have "seen" more directly and personally than they possibly could by means of any abstract argumentation. In fact, even if all the rational evidence were *against* God, the person who has had a religious experience would hardly be swayed. The immediacy and personalness of his or her religious experience would no doubt be decisive.

But, of course, this is exactly the problem. The individual or *private* nature of such experiences is, some skeptics would say, just what makes them philosophically irrelevant. All the outsider has is the *claim* of those who have had such experiences. From what standpoint can one possibly compare the claim with reality? Are not such claims, by their nature, insulated against any objective investigation or verification? In some sense this is surely true, but maybe not entirely so. C. D. Broad, a contemporary philosopher who is as hard-nosed as they come, has argued that there may be, in fact, some considerations that could tip the scales in favor of the integrity of, say, mystical experience:

The privacy of religious experience: A minus

> When there is a nucleus of agreement between the experiences of men in different places, times, and traditions, and when they all tend to put much the same kind of interpretation on the cognitive content of these experiences, it is reasonable to ascribe this agreement to their all being in contact with a certain objective aspect of reality unless there be some positive reason to think otherwise. The practical postulate which we go upon everywhere else is to treat cognitive claims as veridical unless there be some positive reason to think them delusive. This, after all, is our only guarantee for believing that ordinary sense-perception is veridical. We cannot prove that what people agree in perceiving really exists independently of them; but we do always assume that ordinary waking sense-perception is veridical unless we can produce some positive ground for thinking that it is delusive in any given case. I think it would be inconsistent to treat the experiences of religious mystics on different principles. So far as they agree they should be provisionally accepted as veridical unless there be some positive ground for thinking that they are not. So the next question is whether there is any positive ground for holding that they are delusive.[8]

RELIGIOUS EXPERIENCE: PERSONAL AND PRIVATE

The personalness of religious experience renders it decisive for the participant. But the privacy of religious experience renders it sterile as an objective and investigable evidence for God. Or does it?

---

[8]C. D. Broad, *Religion, Philosophy, and Psychical Research* (London: New York: Harcourt, Brace & Co., 1953), p. 197.

But notice Broad's important proviso: " ... unless there be some positive ground for thinking that they are not." Certainly many have argued that such grounds may, indeed, be cited. It is sometimes charged, for example, that such experiences may be explained (away) as manifestations of physiological problems, sexual hang-ups, psychological abnormalities, and the like. In a very lively passage in his *The Varieties of Religious Experience* (first published in 1902), William James takes on precisely this accusation and, in turn, accuses it of simple-mindedly confusing the "facts of mental history" with "their spiritual significance." That is, what is important is not how person X got that way, but whether what he or she says is worthy, true, etc. He asks, furthermore, why any other state of mind—for example, that of the skeptic or the atheist—should be exempt from the same trivializing explanation: What is good for the goose is good for the gander. Pay close attention to his indictment of "medical materialism":

"Medical materialism"

> Perhaps the commonest expression of this assumption that spiritual value is undone if lowly origin be asserted is seen in those comments which unsentimental people so often pass on their more sentimental acquaintances. Alfred believes in immortality so strongly because his temperament is so emotional. Fanny's extraordinary conscientiousness is merely a matter of overinstigated nerves. William's melancholy about the universe is due to bad digestion—probably his liver is torpid. Eliza's delight in her church is a symptom of her hysterical constitution. Peter would be less troubled about his soul if he would take more exercise in the open air, etc. A more fully developed example of the same kind of reasoning is the fashion, quite common nowadays among certain writers, of criticizing the religious emotions by showing a connection between them and the sexual life. Conversion is a crisis of puberty and adolescence. The macerations of saints, and the devotion of missionaries, are only instances of the parental instinct of self-sacrifice gone astray. For the hysterical nun, starving for natural life, Christ is but an imaginary substitute for a more earthly object of affection. And the like.
>
> We are surely all familiar in a general way with this method of discrediting states of mind for which we have an antipathy. We all use it to some degree in criticizing persons whose states of mind we regard as overstrained. But when other people criticize our own more exalted soul-flights by calling them "nothing but" expressions of our organic disposition, we feel outraged and hurt, for we know that, whatever be our organism's peculiarities, our mental states have their substantive value as revelations of the living truth; and we wish that all this medical materialism could be made to hold its tongue.
>
> Medical materialism seems indeed a good appellation for the too simple-minded system of thought which we are considering. Medical materialism finishes up Saint Paul by calling his vision on the road to Damascus a discharging lesion of the occipital cortex, he being an epileptic. It snuffs out Saint Teresa as an hysteric, Saint Francis of Assisi as an hereditary degenerate. George Fox's discontent with the shams of his age, and his pining for spiritual veracity, it treats as a symptom of a disordered

colon. Carlyle's organ-tones of misery it accounts for by a gastro-duodenal catarrh. All such mental overtensions, it says, are, when you come to the bottom of the matter, mere affairs of diathesis (auto-intoxications most probably), due to the perverted action of various glands which physiology will yet discover.

And medical materialism then thinks that the spiritual authority of all such personages is successfully undermined.

Let us ourselves look at the matter in the largest possible way. Modern psychology, finding definite psycho-physical connections to hold good, assumes as a convenient hypothesis that the dependence of mental states upon bodily conditions must be thoroughgoing and complete. If we adopt the assumption, then of course what medical materialism insists on must be true in a general way, if not in every detail: Saint Paul certainly had once an epileptoid, if not an epileptic seizure; George Fox was an hereditary degenerate; Carlyle was undoubtedly auto-intoxicated by some organ or other, no matter which—and the rest. But now, I ask you, how can such an existential account of facts of mental history decide in one way or another upon their spiritual significance? According to the general postulate of psychology just referred to, there is not a single one of our states of mind, high or low, healthy or morbid, that has not some organic process as its condition. Scientific theories are organically conditioned just as much as religious emotions are; and if we only knew the facts intimately enough, we should doubtless see "the liver" determining the dicta of the sturdy atheist as decisively as it does those of the Methodist under conviction anxious about his soul. When it alters in one way the blood that percolates it, we get the Methodist, when in another way, we get the atheist form of mind. So of all our raptures and our drynesses, our longings and pantings, our questions and beliefs. They are equally organically founded, be they religious or of non-religious content.

To plead the organic causation of a religious state of mind, then, in refutation of its claim to possess superior spiritual value, is quite illogical and arbitrary, unless one has already worked out in advance some psycho-physical theory connecting spiritual values in general with determinate sorts of physiological change. Otherwise none of our thoughts and feelings, not even our scientific doctrines, not even our dis-beliefs, could retain any value as revelations of the truth, for every one of them without exception flows from the state of its possessor's body at the time. . . .

In the natural sciences and industrial arts it never occurs to anyone to try to refute opinions by showing up their author's neurotic constitution. Opinions here are invariably tested by logic and by experiment, no matter what may be their author's neurological type. It should be no otherwise with religious opinions. Their value can only be ascertained by spiritual judgments directly passed upon them, judgments based on our own immediate feeling primarily; and secondarily on what we can ascertain of their experiential relations to our moral needs and to the rest of what we hold as true.

Immediate luminousness, in short, philosophical reasonableness, and moral helpfulness are the only available criteria. Saint Teresa might have had the nervous system of the placidest cow, and it would not now save her theology, if the

"MEDICAL MATERIALISM"

A term which William James contemptuously applies to the attempts to undermine the religious and spiritual significance of religious experiences by attributing them to disorders of a psychological or even physiological nature.

IS RELIGION AN ILLUSION?

One of the most famous attacks on religion was that of Sigmund Freud, who explained it away as the result of various psychological needs and complexes. But it is often observed that his attack involved a gigantic informal fallacy. What was it?

> . . . we turn our attention to the psychical origin of religious ideas. These, which are given out as teachings, are not precipitates of experience or end-results of thinking: they are illusions, fulfilments of the oldest, strongest and most urgent wishes of mankind. The secret of their strength lies in the strength of those wishes. As we already know, the terrifying impression of helplessness in childhood aroused the need for protection—for protection through love—which was provided by the father; and the recognition that this helplessness lasts throughout life made it necessary to cling to the existence of a father, but this time a more powerful one. Thus the benevolent rule of a divine Providence allays our fear of the dangers of life; the establishment of a moral world-order ensures the fulfilment of the demands of justice, which have so often remained unfulfilled in human civilization; and the prolongation of earthly existence in a future life provides the local and temporal framework in which these wish-fulfilments shall take place. Answers to the riddles that tempt the curiosity of man, such as how the universe began or what the relation is between body and mind, are developed in conformity with the underlying assumptions of this system.[1]

[1]Sigmund Freud, *The Future of an Illusion*, tr. W. D. Robson-Scott, rev. and ed. James Strachey (Garden City, N.Y.: Anchor Books, 1964), pp. 47–48.

318

trial of the theology by these other tests should show it to be contemptible. And conversely if her theology can stand these other tests, it will make no difference how hysterical or nervously off her balance Saint Teresa may have been when she was with us here below.[9]

A more general conclusion: It is true that the world is full of kooks, liars, and deluded persons, and surely this should put us on guard against accepting, willynilly, every claim to direct experience with God. On the other hand, isn't it a bit nervy to scoff at such claims when they are made by some of the finest, most articulate, and most positively influential people the world has ever known?

Chapter 14 in Review

Knowledge of God by way of religious experience is, in contrast to the rational and argumentative approach, *non*rational or *supra*rational. And this means, for the proponent of religious experience, a directness and personalness about this knowledge which immediately make it superior to all other approaches, except, of course, for supernatural revelation, which one might claim to have, say, in the Bible or through Christ.

SUMMARY

There are many varieties of religious experience, just a few of which we have considered in this chapter. One of the most interesting, and perhaps the most universal, is the experience described by Rudolf Otto as the experience of the numinous. Even this experience takes many and diverse forms, but Otto claims that almost everyone has had a brush with the divine, a feeling or sense of the divine presence, such as he describes.

A more important, and certainly persistent, experience is that of the mystic. A great deal of ambiguity and sloppiness is associated with the word "mysticism" which has been used to cover everything from saintliness to drug experiences. But a fairly clearly defined experience has been expressed (though it cannot really be expressed) by a long train of what we have called the "higher" mystics. An excellent representative of these is St. John of the Cross, who taught that a (metaphorical) union with God could be attained in an ecstatic state in which all multiplicity and movement (whether in the sensible world, the intellectual sphere, or the soul itself) have been transcended. Such an experience has also been regarded by many as a universal phenomenon, though both similarities and differences may be perceived in Western and Eastern accounts of the mystical consciousness.

Although the participant in religious experience will have no interest in skeptical attacks on its validity ("He who sees, sees, and he who does not see, does

[9]William James, *The Varieties of Religious Experience* (New York: Longmans, Green, & Co., 1902), pp. 10–18

not see"), the directness and personalness (or subjectivity) of the experience are exactly what makes for great difficulties in treating it as an evidence for God. On the other hand, the attempt to explain away such experiences as originating in psychological or physiological states is a simple case of the Genetic Fallacy.

BASIC IDEAS

- The nonrational approach to God
- The Numinous experience
- "Instant" mysticism
- Classical mysticism (definition)
- Five features of classical mysticism
- The mystical ascent
- Sensory and intellectual consciousness
- Mystical union: Western
- Mystical union: Eastern
- Brahman
- Religious experience as evidence for God: Pro and Con
- "Medical materialism"

TEST YOURSELF

1. *Mysterium tremendum* is a name for what is confronted in the experience of the _____.
2. St. John of the Cross' *Ascent of Mount Carmel* is (a) a guidebook for tours of the Holy Land, (b) an argument for the revelatory power of drugs, (c) an account of transcendent mystical experience, (d) an attempt to relate Western and Eastern forms of mysticism.
3. True or false: Rudolf Otto believed that the nonrational lies at the heart of true religion.
4. Classical mysticism can best be understood in terms of the metaphysics of what ancient philosopher?
5. What is the significance of St. John of the Cross having expressed his mystical philosophy in a *poem?*
6. What is the problem of religious experience as evidence for the reality of God?
7. Where does it come from?

> Even at the moment of death
> He is alive in that enlightenment:
> Brahman and he are one.

8. What role did William James play in our discussion of religious experience?

- In this chapter different levels or kinds of religious experience have been noted. Can you yourself identify with any of them? Might one feel that such experiences are significant without believing in *God*? How so, or why not?

- Can you explain in your own way how classical mysticism is inseparably bound up with a certain view of reality? Which comes first: this view of reality or the mystic experience?

- What is your own honest evaluation of the claims of religious experience? Does the subjectivity and privacy of such experiences render them irrelevant as evidence for an unseen reality? Can you think of any consideration pro and con not mentioned in the text?

- Could one believe that mysticism is a universal and legitimate religious experience, and accept at the same time the exclusive authority of a particular religion, say, Christianity or Judaism? Might there be a difference between general spiritual illumination and personal salvation?

QUESTIONS FOR
REFLECTION

GOD AND EVIL

One might easily imagine that just as the theists are able to line up their evidence *for* God, say the traditional arguments, the atheists likewise are able to marshal a long list of arguments *against* God. But this is not quite the case. If you stop and reflect, you will probably agree that you have seldom heard anyone really propound an argument against God. What you probably *have* heard are many arguments *against* the arguments *for* God. That is, the atheist, unable to present any positive *dis*proof of God's existence, is usually content, or forced, to find flaws in the theist's position. There is, of course, one notable exception to this: *the argument against God on the basis of the evil in the world.* But this alone has wrought plenty enough havoc for the theist.

Evil: The most notorious evidence against God

WHAT IS THE PROBLEM?

What is meant by "evil"? Two things. *First,* we have *natural* evil, or the evil that results from natural causes. This is otherwise known as the evil of suffering. Starvation, cancerous pain, physical deformity, disease—these and innumerable other sources of undeserved anguish are, rightfully, called *evils* in our world. *Second,* we have *moral* evil, the evil that results from personal depravity. Torture, murder, war, cheating, exploitation—these too, though very different from natural evils, are certainly evils. Either one or both of these types of evil figure in the "problem of evil."

But what is the problem? The problem is how to reconcile the evil in the world with a God who is at once omnipotent (all-powerful) and omnibenevolent (all-loving). The problem is also called *theodicy,* which means, literally, "the justifi-

A statement of the problem

322

NATURAL EVIL AND MORAL EVIL

- *Natural evil:* The evil or suffering that springs from natural causes. Think of the starvation in Bangladesh, the great San Francisco earthquake, the sinking of the *Titanic,* the Black Death, etc.
- *Moral evil:* The evil that springs from the human will. Think of the Nazi death camps, the Stalin purges, the Manson murders, Idi Amin, etc.

THEODICY

From two Greek words meaning, literally, "the justification of God," theodicy expresses the conflict between the traditional view of God and the evil in the world. How can God be vindicated in the face of evil?

Theodicy

cation of God." The idea here is: How can God, in the traditional sense of the word, be justified or vindicated in the face of all, or even any, of the evil in the world?

Hardly a more powerful statement of the problem may be found than in the outburst of the English philosopher John Stuart Mill, for whom the impossibility of reconciling God and evil played an important role in his rejection of Christianity:

Not even on the most distorted and contracted theory of good which ever was framed by religious or philosophical fanaticism, can the government of Nature be made to resemble the work of a being at once good and omnipotent.[1]

A more extended statement may be cited from Hume's *Dialogues Concerning Natural Religion,* from which we have already appreciated his attack on God's causal

[1]John Stuart Mill, *Three Essays on Religion* (New York: Henry Holt & Co., 1874), p. 38.

ordering of the world. Note how both natural and moral evil figure in his "catalogue of woes."

The whole earth, believe me, Philo, is cursed and polluted. A perpetual war is kindled amongst all living creatures. Necessity, hunger, want stimulate the strong and courageous; fear, anxiety, terror agitate the weak and infirm. The first entrance into life gives anguish to the new-born infant and to its wretched parent; weakness, impotence, distress attend each stage of that life, and it is, at last, finished in agony and horror.

Observe, too, says Philo, the curious artifices of nature in order to embitter the life of every living being. The stronger prey upon the weaker and keep them in perpetual terror and anxiety. The weaker, too, in their turn, often prey upon the stronger, and vex and molest them without relaxation. Consider that innumerable race of insects, which either are bred on the body of each animal or, flying about, infix their stings in him. These insects have others still less than themselves which torment them. And thus on each hand, before and behind, above and below, every animal is surrounded with enemies which incessantly seek his misery and destruction.

Man alone, said Demea, seems to be, in part, an exception to this rule. For by combination in society he can easily master lions, tigers, and bears, whose greater strength and agility naturally enable them to prey upon him.

On the contrary, it is here chiefly, cried Philo, that the uniform and equal maxims of nature are most apparent. Man, it is true, can, by combination, surmount all his real enemies and become master of the whole animal creation; but does he not immediately raise up to himself imaginary enemies, the demons of his fancy, who haunt him with superstitious terrors and blast every enjoyment of life? His pleasure, as he imagines, becomes in their eyes a crime; his food and repose give them umbrage and offence; his very sleep and dreams furnish new materials to anxious fear; and even death, his refuge from every other ill, presents only the dread of endless and unnumerable woes. Nor does the wolf molest more the timid flock than superstition does the anxious breast of wretched mortals.

Besides, consider, Demea: This very society by which we surmount those wild beasts, our natural enemies, what new enemies does it not raise to us? What woe and misery does it not occasion? Man is the greatest enemy of man. Oppression, injustice, contempt, contumely, violence, sedition, war, calumny, treachery, fraud—by these they mutually torment each other, and they would soon dissolve that society which they had formed were it not for the dread of still greater ills which must attend their separation.

But though these external insults, said Demea, from animals, from men, from all the elements, which assault us form a frightful catalogue of woes, they are nothing in comparison of those which arise within ourselves, from the distempered condition of our mind and body. How many lie under the lingering torment of diseases? Hear the pathetic enumeration of the great poet.

Intestine stone and ulcer, colic-pangs,
Demoniac frenzy, moping melancholy,
And moon-struck madness, pining atrophy,
Marasmus, and wide-wasting pestilence.
Dire was the tossing, deep the groans: Despair
Tended the sick, busiest from couch to couch.
And over them triumphant Death his dart
Shook: but delay'd to strike, though oft invok'd
With vows, as their chief good and final hope.

The disorders of the mind, continued Demea, though more secret, are not perhaps less dismal and vexatious. Remorse, shame, anguish, rage, disappointment, anxiety, fear, dejection, despair—who has ever passed through life without cruel inroads from these tormentors? How many have scarcely ever felt any better sensations? Labour and poverty, so abhorred by everyone, are the certain lot of the far greater number; and those few privileged persons who enjoy ease and opulence never reach contentment or true felicity. All the goods of life united would not make a very happy man, but all the ills united would make a wretch indeed; and any one of them almost (and who can be free from every one?), nay, often the absence of one good (and who can possess all?) is sufficient to render life ineligible.

Were a stranger to drop on a sudden into this world, I would show him, as a specimen of its ills, an hospital full of diseases, a prison crowded with malefactors and debtors, a field of battle strewed with carcases, a fleet floundering in the ocean, a nation languishing under tyranny, famine, or pestilence. To turn the gay side of life to him and give him a notion of its pleasures—whether should I conduct him? To a ball, to an opera, to court? He might justly think that I was only showing him a diversity of distress and sorrow.

There is no evading such striking instances, said Philo, but by apologies which still further aggravate the charge. Why have all men, I ask, in all ages, complained incessantly of the miseries of life? . . .

And is it possible, Cleanthes, said Philo, that after all these reflections, and infinitely more which might be suggested, you can still persevere in your anthropomorphism, and assert the moral attributes of the Deity, his justice, benevolence, mercy, and rectitude, to be of the same nature with these virtues in human creatures? His power, we allow, is infinite; whatever he wills is executed; but neither man nor any other animal is happy; therefore, he does not will their happiness. His wisdom is infinite; he is never mistaken in choosing the means to any end; but the course of nature tends not to human or animal felicity; therefore, it is not established for that purpose. Through the whole compass of human knowledge there are no inferences more certain and infallible than these. In what respect, then, do his benevolence and mercy resemble the benevolence and mercy of men?

Epicurus' old questions are yet unanswered.

Is he willing to prevent evil, but not able? then is he impotent. Is he able, but not willing? then is he malevolent. Is he both able and willing? whence then is evil?[2]

Pay special attention to the concluding lines of the above quotation. These questions embody the best-known and simplest expression of the problem of evil.

THE SIMPLEST STATEMENT OF THE PROBLEM OF EVIL

"Is he willing to prevent evil, but not able? then is he impotent.
Is he able, but not willing? then is he malevolent. Is he both able and willing? whence then is evil?"

—Hume

SOME SOLUTIONS

The believer who seriously confronts this dilemma might appreciate the saying, "There are many ways to skin a cat, but whatever way you choose, don't expect the cat to cooperate." For if anything is clear to most theists, it is that neither God's omnipotence nor his omnibenevolence can be given up.

God is limited

Or can they? Mill himself resorted to just this "radical surgery": Let us simply deny, flat-out, that God is omnipotent. He states this rather startling thesis in his *Three Essays on Religion* (1874):

It is not too much to say that every indication of Design in the Kosmos is so much evidence against the Omnipotence of the Designer. For what is meant by Design? Contrivance: the adaptation of means to an end. But the necessity for contrivance—the need of employing means—is a consequence of the limitation of power. Who would have recourse to means if to attain his end his mere word was sufficient? The very idea of means implies that the means have an efficacy which the direct action of the being who employs them has not. Otherwise they are not means, but an incumbrance. A man does not use machinery to move his arms. If he did, it could only be when paralysis had deprived him of the power of moving them by volition. But if the employment of contrivance is in itself a sign of limited power, how much more so is the careful and skilful choice of contrivances? Can any wisdom be shown in the selection of means, when the means have no efficacy but what is given them by the will of

[2]David Hume, *Dialogues Concerning Natural Religion*, ed. Henry D. Aiken (New York: Hafner, 1948), pp. 62–64.

him who employs them, and when his will could have bestowed the same efficacy on any other means? Wisdom and contrivance are shown in overcoming difficulties, and there is no room for them in a Being for whom no difficulties exist. The evidences, therefore, of Natural Theology distinctly imply that the author of the Kosmos worked under limitations; that he was obliged to adapt himself to conditions independent of his will, and to attain his ends by such arrangements as those conditions admitted of.

And this hypothesis agrees with what we have seen to be the tendency of the evidences in another respect. We found that the appearances in Nature point indeed to an origin of the Kosmos, or order in Nature, and indicate that origin to be Design but do not point to any commencement, still less creation, of the two great active elements of the Universe, the passive element and the active element, Matter and Force. There is in Nature no reason whatever to suppose that either Matter or Force, or any of their properties, were made by the Being who was the author of the collocations by which the world is adapted to what we consider as its purposes; or that he has power to alter any of those properties. It is only when we consent to entertain this negative supposition that there arises a need for wisdom and contrivance in the order of the universe. The Deity had on this hypothesis to work out his ends by combining materials of a given nature and properties. Out of these materials he had to construct a world in which his designs should be carried into effect through given properties of Matter and Force, working together and fitting into one another. This did require skill and contrivance, and the means by which it is effected are often such as justly excite our wonder and admiration: but exactly because it requires wisdom, it implies limitation of power, or rather the two phrases express different sides of the same fact.[3]

The believer will find this thesis considerably more than "startling." Mill's statement involves an interesting piece of reasoning and is well worth digesting. But, some would say, the idea of a limited or finite God is as absurd as that of a malevolent or *evil* God. There must be another way.

Another proposal, and one of the most popular, is to invoke the transcendence and inscrutability of God: God lies so far above us that it is impossible to understand his ways and purposes, and presumptuous even to try. Was this not God's own answer to the suffering Job?

God's ways are inscrutable

> *Then the LORD answered Job*
> *out of the whirlwind:*
> *"Who is this that darkens counsel*
> *by words without knowledge?*
> *Gird up your loins like a man,*
> *I will question you, and you shall*
> *declare to me.*

[3]John Stuart Mill, *Three Essays on Religion*, pp. 176–178.

> *"Where were you when I laid the*
>   *foundation of the earth?*
> *Tell me, if you have*
>   *understanding.*
> *Who determined its measurements*
>   *—surely you know!*
> *Or who stretched the line upon it?*
>
> *On what were its bases sunk,*
>   *or who laid its cornerstone,*
> *when the morning stars sang*
>   *together,*
>   *and all the sons of God shouted*
>   *for joy?*
>
> *"Or who shut in the sea with doors,*
>   *when it burst forth from the womb;*
> *when I made clouds its garment,*
>   *and thick darkness its swaddling*
>   *band,*
> *and prescribed bounds for it,*
>   *and set bars and doors,*
> *and said, 'Thus far shall you come,*
>   *and no farther,*
>   *and here shall your proud waves*
>   *be stayed'?"*

Job 38:1–11 (Revised Standard Version)

And what does he say in *Isaiah*?

> *"For my thoughts are not your*
>   *thoughts,*
>   *neither are your ways my ways,*
>   *says the* Lord.
> *For as the heavens are higher than*
>   *the earth,*
>   *so are my ways higher than your*
>   *ways*
>   *and my thoughts than your*
>   *thoughts."*

Isaiah 55:8–9 (Revised Standard Version)

But though this may be an appropriate and satisfying approach from a *religious* standpoint, from a *philosophical* standpoint it is a retreat, and issues a *carte blanche* for ignorance and uncritical reflection on the most urgent of issues.

A few more solutions may be mentioned. Closely related to the last is the emphasis on the goodness of the whole: If everything could be viewed from the divine standpoint, then it would immediately be appreciated how everything, even evil, actually contributes to the unity, harmony, beauty, and, in a word, goodness of things considered as a *totality*. A quite different angle was proposed by Leibniz, who taught that it would in fact be *logically impossible* to have a world without evil: Anything created by God would have to be *less* than God just by virtue of being *dependent* on him, and this means immediately that it must be less than perfect, and *this* means immediately the presence of various sorts of *imperfections*. How could God create something that was perfect, and therefore independent, and therefore uncreated? It is *logically* impossible. Similar is the view of Tennant. In an earlier chapter we saw that he emphasized the presence of order in the world. But even Tennant saw that unfortunate and unhappy things are inevitable by-products of nature. It is impossible (*logically* impossible?) to have a physical cosmos, with its multiplicity, change, and natural processes, and not also have mishaps, accidents, disease, famines, and the like.

Some of these solutions to the problem of evil may strike you as more relevant than others, but each of them deserves, at least, to be understood and weighed. Two further views, however, must be considered somewhat more carefully: the privation theory of evil, and the therapy theory of evil.

> **The goodness of the whole**

> **A perfect world is logically impossible**

> **Evils as necessary by-products of nature**

SOME SOLUTIONS TO THE PROBLEM OF EVIL

- God is not omnipotent after all.
- God's plan for the world is inscrutable.
- All things, including evil, actually contribute to the goodness of the whole.
- A perfect world is a logical impossibility.
- Evil is a necessary by-product of nature.

EVIL AS A PRIVATION OF GOODNESS

The first of these has a long tradition, but is most notably associated with the medieval Christian philosopher and theologian St. Augustine (354–430).

It is our natural tendency to think of evil as some kind of thing, a "stuff," a substance, or a *blob*. However, Augustine and many others have argued, exactly

> **Evil is not a "thing"**

counter to this grain, that evil is no *thing* at all. It is, rather, the absence or privation of something, namely, of Being and Goodness. And this is true both of natural evil and of moral evil. It is true that when God created the world and the human race he said, "It is good." But he did not mean—*could* not mean—that they were *absolutely* good or good in the same way that God is. How could they be? For then they would not be created things, but God himself.

St. Augustine was a Christian Platonist, though as a Christian he certainly disagreed with much of Plato's philosophy. But he did hold broadly to the Platonic idea that the world is necessarily a mixture, as it were, of Being and Nonbeing: It is Becoming. And one of the hallmarks of the relative nonbeing in the world is its multiplicity and change—the *absence* of full being along with its unity and unchangeableness. But this multiplicity and change give rise to natural processes, and these in turn give rise to famines, disease, plagues, etc., and these in turn give rise to suffering, which St. Augustine believed is visited on human beings as a just punishment for their sins. But, then, what about sin? Moral evil, or sin, likewise may be traced to an absence of goodness. It results when something goes wrong with the will; when it breaks down; when it falls short; when it fails to will the good; when it is derailed and turns aside from the good; when it is corrupted. As disease is the absence of health in the body, so sin is the absence of health in the will.

The basic idea here may not be easy to get hold of, but if you think about it enough it might come to you in a sort of intuitive flash. Perhaps Augustine's own statements will help. The general principle of evil as a privation of goodness is explained in the following from *The Enchiridion on Faith, Hope, and Love:*

WHAT IS CALLED EVIL IN THE UNIVERSE IS BUT THE ABSENCE OF GOOD

. . . *in the universe, even that which is called evil, when it is regulated and put in its own place, only enhances our admiration of the good; for we enjoy and value the good more when we compare it with the evil. For the Almighty God, who, as even the heathen acknowledge, has supreme power over all things, being Himself supremely good, would never permit the existence of anything evil among His works, if He were not so omnipotent and good that He can bring good even out of evil. For what is that which we call evil but the absence of good? In the bodies of animals, disease and wounds mean nothing but the absence of health; for when a cure is effected, that does not mean that the evils which were present—namely, the diseases and wounds—go away from the body and dwell elsewhere: they altogether cease to exist; for the wound or disease is not a substance, but a defect in the fleshly substance—the flesh itself being a substance, and therefore something good, of which those evils—that is, privations of the good which we call health—are accidents. Just in the same way, what are called vices in the soul are nothing but privations of natural good. And when they are cured, they are not transferred elsewhere: when they cease to exist in the healthy soul, they cannot exist anywhere else.*

ALL BEINGS WERE MADE GOOD, BUT NOT BEING MADE PERFECTLY GOOD, ARE LIABLE TO CORRUPTION

All things that exist, therefore, seeing that the Creator of them all is supremely good, are themselves good. But because they are not, like their Creator, supremely and unchangeably good, their good may be diminished and increased. But for good to be diminished is an evil, although, however much it may be diminished, it is necessary, if the being is to continue, that some good should remain to constitute the being. For however small or of whatever kind the being may be, the good which makes it a being cannot be destroyed without destroying the being itself. An uncorrupted nature is justly held in esteem. But if, still further, it be incorruptible, it is undoubtedly considered of still higher value. When it is corrupted, however, its corruption is an evil, because it is deprived of some sort of good. For if it be deprived of no good, it receives no injury; but it does receive injury, therefore it is deprived of good. Therefore, so long as a being is in process of corruption, there is in it some good of which it is being deprived; and if a part of the being should remain which cannot be corrupted, this will certainly be an incorruptible being, and accordingly the process of corruption will result in the manifestation of this great good. But if it does not cease to be corrupted, neither can it cease to possess good of which corruption may deprive it. But if it should be thoroughly and completely consumed by corruption, there will then be no good left, because there will be no being. Wherefore corruption can consume the good only by consuming the being. Every being, therefore, is a good; a great good, if it cannot be corrupted; a little good, if it can: but in any case, only the foolish or ignorant will deny that it is a good. And if it be wholly consumed by corruption, then the corruption itself must cease to exist, as there is no being left in which it can dwell.[4]

The principle is further explained and applied specifically to sin in the following from *On Free Choice of the Will:*

Because the will is moved when it turns from an immutable good to a changeable one, you may perhaps ask how this movement arises. For the movement itself is certainly evil, although the free will must be numbered among the goods, because without it no one can live rightly. Even if this movement, that is, the turning of the will from the Lord God, is without doubt a sin, we cannot say, can we, that God is the cause of sin? This movement will not be from God, but what then is its origin? If I should answer your question by saying that I do not know, you would perhaps be disappointed; yet that would be the truth, for that which is nothing cannot be known. Only hold to your firm faith, since no good thing comes to your perception, understanding, or thought which is not from God. Nothing of any kind can be discovered which is not from God. Wherever you see measure, number, and order, you cannot hesitate to attribute all these to God, their Maker. When you remove measure, number, and

---

[4]St. Augustine, *The Enchiridion on Faith, Hope, and Love,* tr. J. F. Shaw, ed. Henry Paolucci (Chicago: Henry Regnery, 1961), pp. 12–13.

order, nothing at all remains. Even if the beginning of some form were to remain, where you do not find order or measure or number (since wherever these exist, form is complete), you must remove even that very beginning of form which seems to be the artisan's raw material. If the completion of form is a good, there is some good even in the rudimentary beginning of form. Thus, if all good is completely removed, no vestige of reality persists; indeed, nothing remains. Every good is from God. There is nothing of any kind that is not from God. Therefore, since the movement of turning away from good, which we admit to be sin, is a defective movement and since, moreover, every defect comes from nothing, see where this movement belongs: you may be sure that it does not belong to God.

Yet since this defect is voluntary, it lies within our power. You must not be willing to fear this defect, for if you do not desire it, it will not exist. What greater security can there be than to live a life where what you do not will cannot happen to you? Since a man cannot rise of his own will as he fell by his own will, let us hold with firm faith the right hand of God, Jesus Christ our Lord, which is stretched out to us. Let us wait for Him with steadfast hope; let us love Him with burning love.[5]

EVIL AS A PRIVATION OF GOODNESS

One of the most enduring solutions to the problem of evil is to interpret evil, both natural and moral, not as a positive substance but as the absence of being and goodness. The world and human souls are seen as created by the highest being (who is goodness) "from above," but at the same time as corruptible by nonbeing (or evil) "from below." God is, thus, responsible for the *isness* and *goodness* in the world, not the nonbeing and evil.

ST. AUGUSTINE

The main writers of the early centuries of the Christian church are called the Church Fathers. The last and greatest of these was St. Augustine.

He was born in a Roman province on the north coast of Africa in 354. His father was a pagan, and his mother, who wielded a great deal of influence over him, was a Christian: St. Monica. He did not

[5]St. Augustine, *On Free Choice of the Will*, tr. Anna S. Benjamin and L. H. Hackstaff (Indianapolis: Library of Liberal Arts, 1964), pp. 83–84.

particularly excel at his early studies, though eventually he became expert in rhetoric when he moved as a student in 370 to Carthage. The loose morals of the city, however, undermined the Christian morals of this impressionable young man, and he gradually fell away from Christianity. He took a mistress by whom he had a son during his second year in Carthage.

During this time, Augustine rejected not only Christian morals but also Christian doctrines. He was especially troubled by the failure of Christianity to explain how a good God could be responsible for a world with so much evil in it. He turned to the materialistic ideas of Manichaeism, the doctrine that the world is dominated by two eternal and opposed principles, good and evil, light and darkness. In 383 Augustine traveled to Rome, where he opened his own school of rhetoric, but he had so much trouble getting his students to pay their tuition that he moved to Milan. This was decisive for Augustine. His commitment to Manichaeism was by this time wavering anyway, and his discovery of certain "Platonic writings" (probably the writings of the Neoplatonist Plotinus, who lived about A.D. 200) introduced him to an altogether different and superior idea of things: a spiritual and transcendent conception of God, and the view that evil is a privation of goodness. This discovery, along with the influence of the sermons of St. Ambrose, bishop of Milan, and Augustine's own study of the New Testament, set the stage for his conversion to Christianity in the summer of 386. On the Holy Saturday of 387 he was baptized by St. Ambrose, and in the autumn of 388 he departed for Africa.

Back in Africa, Augustine was ordained a priest by the bishop of Hippo, a seaport city about 150 miles west of Carthage, and himself became bishop of that city in 396. During this period his literary output continued and included three of the most important theological and philosophical works ever written: the *Confessions* (the world's first autobiography), the *City of God* (the first philosophy of history), and *On the Trinity*. At the same time, he was combating the heresies of Manichaeism, Donatism (which claimed to be the only true church), and Pelagianism (which overemphasized the role of free will in man's salvation), and developing further his own philosophy of Christian Platonism. Augustine died on August 28, 430, as the Vandals laid siege to Hippo, and as he was reciting the Penitential Psalms.

In addition to being one of the world's greatest philosophers and theologians, Augustine was also one of the world's great authors. In addition to the *Confessions,* the *City of God,* and *On the Trinity,* he wrote innumerable commentaries on Biblical books and a prodigious number of works on various topics and against various heresies.

Is it clear? While God, who is the highest being, is the cause of all lesser being, he is not, nor can he be, the cause of the relative nonbeing in the world, for nonbeing is nothing at all. The advocate of the evil-is-a-privation-of-goodness position might therefore exclaim: "Rather than blame God for the relative nonbeing present in the world, and least of all for the wickedness that people themselves freely introduce, praise him for the relative beauty, harmony, goodness, and being in the world which *he* has introduced!"

One very big caution is in order. In view of this talk about evil as a privation or absence of goodness, you may be tempted to think that the reality of evil is simply being denied. But that would be to miss an important point. Who in his or her right mind would care to deny the reality of evil? What is involved here is a question not about the *reality* of evil but, rather, about the *nature* of evil. And though St. Augustine denied that evil is a substance and called it the absence of goodness, few have been more sensitive to its awful reality.

Evil: Not a substance, but real nonetheless

THE FREE-WILL DEFENSE

Inevitably, many questions concerning *free will* figure in discussions about God and evil, specifically moral evil:

- Why did God endow humans with free will, knowing that they would abuse it?
- Is free will a condition for real humanhood?
- Does God's foreknowledge of what we will do mean that what we do is actually predetermined?
- Could God have made us free *and* unable to sin?

Some of these issues you will have to ponder or discuss on your own. However, one angle concerning free will and evil—and it is indeed very important—must be mentioned, and this is the right place.

Note Augustine's reference, in the last passage quoted above, to the "voluntary" defection of human beings from the good. He is very emphatic on the necessity of free will as a condition of morality and as the source of moral evil in the world. In another place in the same work he says explicitly that

Free will as a condition for morality

> *no righteous act could be performed except by free choice of the will, and I asserted that God gave it for this reason.*[6]

[6]Ibid., p. 78.

Actually, Augustine means that God gave *Adam* and *Eve* free will. Adam and Eve misused (note again the negative tone) their free will, and sin thus made its entry into the world. Everyone after Adam and Eve has inherited the effects of the Fall, and this includes a loss of free will and a consequent "bondage of the will." Nonetheless, at least in the case of the first human beings, Adam and Eve, free will was a condition of authentic humanhood, though it also meant the possibility of sin. Leaving aside the difficult question of Adam and Eve's fall and its consequences for their descendants, this view is essentially what is nowadays called the *Free-will Defense*.

The contemporary British philosopher Antony Flew summarizes the idea:

Several determined attempts have been made to escape from the dilemma. One favourite—which might be dubbed the Free-will Defence—runs like this. The first move is to point out: "Nothing which implies contradiction falls under the omnipotence of God"; that is, Even God cannot do what is logically impossible; that is, If you make up a self-contradictory, a nonsense, sentence it won't miraculously become sense just because you have put the word "God" as its subject. The third formulation is greatly superior to the other two, because it brings out the nature of logical impossibility. It should appeal to theologians, as being free of the unwanted and of course entirely incorrect suggestion that "being unable to do the logically impossible" is some sort of limitation on or weakness in Omnipotence, whereas the only limitation lies in men who contradict themselves and talk nonsense about God. The second move in this defence is to claim: "God gave men free-will"; and this necessarily implies the possibility of doing evil as well as good, that is to say that there would be a contradiction in speaking, it would be nonsense to speak, of creatures with freedom to choose good or evil but not able to choose evil. (Which, no blame to him, is what his creatures men have done). This may be followed by a third rather less common move: to point out that certain good things, viz. certain virtues, logically presuppose: not merely beings with freedom of choice (which alone are capable of either virtue or vice), and consequently the possibility of evil; but also the actual occurrence of certain evils. Thus what we might call the second-order goods of sympathetic feeling and action logically could not occur without (at least the appearance of) the first-order evils of suffering or misfortune. And the moral good of forgiveness presupposes the prior occurrence of (at least the appearance of) some lower-order evil to be forgiven. This may be already a second-order moral evil such as callousness, thus making the forgiveness a third-order good. Here one recalls: O felix culpa quae tantum ac talem meruit habere redemptorem [O happy sin which deserved to have so great and such a redeemer].[7]

---

[7]Antony Flew, "Divine Omnipotence and Human Freedom," in *New Essays in Philosophical Theology*, ed. Antony Flew and Alasdair MacIntyre (London: SCM Press, 1966), pp. 145–146.

This is a fairly heavy paragraph. Each point should be scrutinized or discussed. For our purposes, it is Flew's "second move" that is especially important: "God gave men free-will" necessarily implies the possibility of doing evil as well as good; it would be impossible for creatures to have freedom to choose good but not to choose evil. Flew himself, however, rejects this reasoning, denying that there is, after all, a real contradiction in the idea that God might have so constituted his creatures that they *always* choose the right. The same point is made by another British philosopher, J. L. Mackie:

> If God has made men such that in their free choices they sometimes prefer what is good and sometimes what is evil, why could he not have made men such that they always freely choose the good? If there is no logical impossibility in a man's freely choosing the good on one, or on several occasions, there cannot be a logical impossibility in his freely choosing the good on every occasion. God was not, then, faced with a choice between making innocent automata and making beings who, in acting freely, would sometimes go wrong; there was open to him the obviously better possibility of making beings who would act freely but always go right. Clearly, his failure to avail himself of this possibility is inconsistent with his being both omnipotent and wholly good.[8]

The debate can become very sticky. Here we only mention that many philosophers and theologians continue to employ some version of the Free-will Defense. In the next section we will encounter an example.

THE FREE-WILL DEFENSE

By means of the Free-will Defense, many thinkers, ancient and modern, have undertaken to defend God from the charge that he is responsible for moral evil: In order for human beings to be truly capable of moral goodness, they must also be capable of moral evil; but this means that with respect to good and evil they must have genuine free choice; but this means the real possibility (or inevitability?) of the introduction of moral evil into the scheme of things.

---

[8]J. L. Mackie, "Evil and Omnipotence," in *The Philosophy of Religion*, ed. Basil Mitchell (London: Oxford University Press, 1971), p. 92.

EVIL AS THERAPY

Alongside the theory of evil as a privation of goodness we may mention another very important theory: evil as *therapy*. To call evil "therapeutic" may strike you not only as being a bit odd but also as silly or trivializing. But you must bear in mind that "therapy" involves more than aches, pains, exercise, and massages. It means, literally, *healing*: a healing power applied to physical and psychological disabilities and disorders. Thus, to press the therapeutic character of evil as a way of solving the problem of evil is to argue that evil is the instrument by which God has determined to correct, purify, and instruct his creatures—in a word, *to bring them to spiritual health and maturity.*

Evil: A means of growth

This view, too, is both a very old and a very modern one. One of its most ardent advocates is the contemporary philosopher of religion John Hick. In his important book *Evil and the God of Love,* Hick enlists an early example of this approach in the ancient Christian writer Irenaeus[9] (130?–202?), bishop of Lyons. Irenaeus emphasized the *development* that goes on in human beings, as well as the whole human race, and the methods God has chosen to bring this development about. The experience of evil is a necessary part of this "soul-making" activity of God. From Irenaeus' *Against Heresies:*

> Man has received the knowledge of good and evil. It is good to obey God, and to believe in Him, and to keep His commandment, and this is the life of man; as not to obey God is evil, and this is his death. Since God, therefore, gave {to man} such mental power man knew both the good of obedience and the evil of disobedience, that the eye of the mind, receiving experience of both, may with judgment make choice of the better things; and that he may never become indolent or neglectful of God's command; and learning by experience that it is an evil thing which deprives him of life, that is, disobedience to God, may never attempt it at all, but that, knowing that what preserves his life, namely, obedience to God, is good, he may diligently keep it with all earnestness. Wherefore he has also had a twofold experience, possessing knowledge of both kinds, that with discipline he may make choice of the better things. But how, if he had no knowledge of the contrary, could he have had instruction in that which is good? For there is thus a surer and an undoubted comprehension of matters submitted to us than the mere surmise arising from an opinion regarding them. For just as the tongue receives experience of sweet and bitter by means of tasting, and the eye discriminates between black and white by means of vision, and the ear recognises the distinctions of sounds by hearing; so also does the mind, receiving through the experience of both the knowledge of what is good, become more tenacious of its preservation, by acting in obedience to God: in the first place, casting away, by means of repentance, disobedience, as being something disagreeable and nauseous; and after-

---

[9]Pronounced *eye-ray-neé-us.*

wards coming to understand what it really is, that it is contrary to goodness and sweetness, so that the mind may never even attempt to taste disobedience to God. But if any one do shun the knowledge of both these kings of things, and the twofold perception of knowledge, he unawares divests himself of the character of a human being.

. . . If, then, thou art God's workmanship, await the hand of thy Maker which creates everything in due time; in due time as far as thou art concerned, whose creation is being carried out. Offer to Him thy heart in a soft and tractable state, and preserve the form in which the Creator has fashioned thee, having moisture in thyself, lest, by becoming hardened, thou lose the impressions of His fingers. But by preserving the framework thou shalt ascend to that which is perfect, for the moist clay which is in thee is hidden {there} by the workmanship of God. . . . If, then, thou shalt deliver up to Him what is thine, that is, faith towards Him and subjection, thou shalt receive His handiwork, and shalt be a perfect work of God.[10]

Hick provides a useful summary of the differences between the Irenaean and Augustinian theodicies, and stresses (he calls it a "significant fact") the antiquity of the Irenaean.

There is thus to be found in Irenaeus the outline of an approach to the problem of evil which stands in important respects in contrast to the Augustinian type of theodicy. Instead of the doctrine that man was created finitely perfect and then incomprehensibly destroyed his own perfection and plunged into sin and misery, Irenaeus suggests that man was created as an imperfect, immature creature who was to undergo moral development and growth and finally be brought to the perfection intended for him by his Maker. Instead of the fall of Adam being presented, as in the Augustinian tradition, as an utterly malignant and catastrophic event, completely disrupting God's plan, Irenaeus pictures it as something that occurred in the childhood of the race, an understandable lapse due to weakness and immaturity rather than an adult crime full of malice and pregnant with perpetual guilt. And instead of the Augustinian view of life's trials as a divine punishment for Adam's sin, Irenaeus sees our world of mingled good and evil as a divinely appointed environment for man's development towards the perfection that represents the fulfilment of God's good purpose for him.

Irenaeus was the first great Christian theologian to think at all systematically along these lines, and although he was far from working out a comprehensive theodicy his hints are sufficiently explicit to justify his name being associated with the approach that we are studying in this part. It is true that Irenaeus' name does not belong to this type of theodicy as clearly and indisputably as Augustine's name belongs to the predominant theodicy of Western Christendom; it is also true that within Irenaeus' own writings there are cross-currents and alternative suggestions that I have left aside

[10]Irenaeus, *Against Heresies*, IV, 39, 1–2, tr. Alexander Roberts and James Donaldson, in *The Ante-Nicene Fathers*, I (Grand Rapids, Mich.: Eerdmans, 1979).

here. Nevertheless, to speak of the Irenaean type of theodicy is both to name a tradition by its first great representative and at the same time to indicate the significant fact that this mode of responding to the problem of evil originated in the earliest and most ecumenical phase of Christian thought.[11]

It is not hard to see how *natural* evil, with its sufferings and hardships, may contribute to the development of a mature and virtuous soul, but what about *moral* evil? And how do the innocent victims of murder and torture fit into the picture? We are back to the Free-will Defense. At this point Hick adopts the same sort of reasoning as Augustine: Free will is a condition of humanhood, and sin enters the world through human free will. And he provides his own response to the Flew-Mackie view that God could have so made humans that they would freely but always choose the right. Hick's position is that while there may be no contradiction in God so making his creatures that they always act freely but rightly, there *is* a contradiction in God so constituting his creatures that they freely respond to him in a loving, trusting, and faithful relationship. Why? Because such a relationship is *two-sided,* and if the freely proffered love, trust, or faith of the one party is, as it were, programmed by the other party, then for that party it could not possibly *be* a relationship of love, trust, or faith, at least not *authentic* love, trust, or faith, to use Hick's word. Free will and *independence* from the Creator are, in this way marks of genuine humanity. But, of course, this makes for the possibility of disobedience, and that means *sin.*

Hick's argument for this version of the Free-will Defense is especially effective because of his analogy involving posthypnotic suggestion.

Back to the Free-will Defense

Is it logically possible for God so to make men that they will freely respond to Himself in love and trust and faith?

I believe that the answer is no. The grounds for this answer may be presented by means of an analogy with posthypnotic suggestion, which Flew uses in this connection. A patient can, under hypnosis, be given a series of instructions, which he is to carry out after waking—say, to go at a certain time to a certain library and borrow a certain book—and he may at the same time be told that he will forget having received these instructions. On coming out of the hypnotic trance he will then be obediently unaware of what transpired in it, but will nevertheless at the prescribed time feel an imperious desire to go to the library and borrow the book, a desire that the ordinary resources of the educated intellect will find no difficulty in rationalizing. The patient will thus carry out the hypnotist's commands whilst seeming both to himself and to others to be doing so of his own free will and for his own sufficient reasons. In terms of the definition of a free act as one that is not externally compelled but flows from the character of the agent, the actions of one carrying out post-hypnotic suggestions are free actions and the patient is a free agent in his performance of them.

[11]John Hick, *Evil and the God of Love,* rev. ed. (San Francisco: Harper & Row, 1978), pp. 214–215.

Nevertheless, taking account of the wider situation, including the previous hypnotic trance, we must say that the patient is not free as far as these particular actions are concerned in relation to the hypnotist. In relation to the hypnotist he is a kind of puppet or tool. And if the hypnotist's suggestion had been that the patient would agree with him about some controversial matter or, coming closer to an analogy with our relationship with God, trust the hypnotist, or love him, or devotedly serve him, there would be something inauthentic about the resulting trust, love, or service. They would be inauthentic in the sense that to the hypnotist, who knows that he has himself directly planted these personal attitudes by his professional techniques, there would be an all-important difference between the good opinion and trust and friendship of the patient and that of someone else whose mind has not been conditioned by hypnotic suggestion. He would regard and value the two attitudes in quite different ways. His patient's post-hypnotic friendship and trust would represent a purely technical achievement, whereas the friendship and trust of the other would represent a response to his own personal qualities and merits. The difference would be that between genuine and spurious personal attitudes—genuine and spurious, not in respect of their present observed and felt characters but in respect of the ways in which they have come about. For it is of the essential nature of "fiduciary" personal attitudes such as trust, respect, and affection to arise in a free being as an uncompelled response to the personal qualities of others. If trust, love, admiration, respect, affection, are produced by some kind of psychological manipulation which by-passes the conscious responsible centre of the personality, then they are not real trust and love, etc., but something else of an entirely different nature and quality which does not have at all the same value in the contexts of personal life and personal relationship. The authentic fiduciary attitudes are thus such that it is impossible—logically impossible—for them to be produced by miraculous manipulation: "it is logically impossible for God to obtain your love-unforced-by-anything-outside-you and yet himself force it." ...

. . . It would not be logically possible for God so to make men that they could be guaranteed freely to respond to Himself in genuine trust and love. The nature of these personal attitudes precludes their being caused in such a way. Just as the patient's trust in, and devotion to, the hypnotist would lack for the latter the value of a freely given trust and devotion, so our human worship and obedience to God would lack for Him the value of a freely offered worship and obedience. We should, in relation to God, be mere puppets, precluded from entering into any truly personal relationship with Him.[12]

Thus Hick, renewing the therapy thinking of Ireneaus and pressing a new version of the Free-will Defense, argues that this mortal existence, with its authentic freedoms and its disciplining and healing and maturing environment, is "a vale of soul-making." Some readers will of course respond with an incredulous outburst:

Soul-making or soul-breaking?

[12]Ibid., pp. 308–310.

"How naive can you be? This is obviously not a vale of soul-making but a vale of soul-*breaking!* Are we supposed to believe, to take just one example, that the Nazi death camps were divinely appointed means of spiritual progress?" And if it is answered that somehow the position holds true at least for the race as a whole, the second response will immediately be: "Large consolation for those *individuals* whose innocent lives were snuffed out in the gas chambers." Naturally, Hick's actual view is much richer than what we have been able to recount here, and naive it certainly is not. Nonetheless, the point is well taken. And it leads to the next section.

EVIL AS IRRATIONAL

We have now mentioned several attempts to reconcile evil with God. In spite of their differences, they all have in common at least a faith in the ability of reason to unravel to some degree the mystery of evil. They all say, in one way or another: "If only we think hard about the matter—draw the right distinctions, introduce the relevant concepts, etc.—we are able to see that the problem of good and evil is not as desperate as we thought." Not all are so optimistic. In fact, some abandon all hope of explaining evil and see it, rather, as the supreme evidence of the ultimate *irrationality* of human existence.

We are, of course, now in the presence of a radically different philosophical perspective. It is not only an atheistic one but also, in some sense, a *nihilistic* one. "Nihilism" means, literally, "nothingism" (from the Latin *nihil*, "nothing"). As a label, nihilism usually refers specifically to values and ideals, and is the denial that they have any objective reality. It is understandable how, for such a perspective, evil is the most vivid expression of our finally hopeless situation.

Nihilism

NIHILISM

The rejection of values as having any objective validity. Life is ultimately meaningless.

If we take nihilism to mean the *utter* and *absolute* rejection of all value and meaning, then there have not been very many nihilists. And, if there ever was one, he or she should have just sat down and died. For even the barest pursuit of one's life is an affirmation of *some* value and meaning, isn't it? But with some philosophers the irrationalist or absurdist position takes a truly interesting turn. First, these philosophers are atheists or *humanists*. Humanism, as one could guess from the word, is the exaltation of humanity itself as the ultimate reality. Second, for these thinkers the problem of evil becomes one of reconciling evil not with God (there is no God) but, rather, with *man*—not theodicy, but, if you will, *anthropodicy*.

One way in which this may be done is suggested in certain strains of atheistic or humanistic existentialism. We spoke of existentialism in Chapter 1, and will have more to say about it in Chapter 16. For now, we just remind ourselves that existentialism, which was renewed by the horrors of the world wars, generally rejects most philosophizing as abstract and irrelevant, and emphasizes the concrete business of living authentically. The late French writer Albert Camus is a good example:

> *Judging whether life is or is not worth living amounts to answering the fundamental question of philosophy. All the rest—whether or not the world has three dimensions, whether the mind has nine or twelve categories—come afterwards. These are games. . . . I have never seen anyone die for the ontological argument. . . . the meaning of life is the most urgent of questions.*[13]

The defiance of evil

But what about evil, specifically? Camus, the atheist, says that we must *recognize* it in all its horror and irrationality, but we must not *accept* it. Human dignity lies precisely in our struggle against evil, in living in constant revolt against its reign. This comes out well in Camus' novel *The Plague*. In this novel the plague itself may be understood on several levels. But on the most basic level it represents evil, and at least one of the characters in the novel expresses vividly the absence of God and the necessity of defiance as the only meaningful response to evil.

> " . . . *since the order of the world is shaped by death, mightn't it be better for God if we refuse to believe in Him and struggle with all our might against death, without raising our eyes toward the heaven where He sits in silence.*"
> *Tarrou nodded.*
> "*Yes. But your victories will never be lasting; that's all.*"
> *Rieux's face darkened.*
> "*Yes, I know that. But it's no reason for giving up the struggle.*"
> "*No reason, I agree. Only, I now can picture what this plague must mean for you.*"
> "*Yes. A never ending defeat.*"
>
> . . .
>
> "*Who taught you all this, doctor?*"
> *The reply came promptly:*
> "*Suffering.*"[14]

[13]Albert Camus, *The Myth of Sisyphus and Other Essays*, tr. Justin O'Brien (New York: Vintage Books 1955), pp. 3–4

[14]Albert Camus, *The Plague*, tr. Stuart Gilbert (New York: Modern Library, 1948), pp. 117–118.

And in his *The Myth of Sisyphus and Other Essays*, Camus juxtaposes the two most extreme possible responses to the human condition: suicide, which is "giving in," and conscious revolt. It is already clear which path Camus urges us to follow.

Now I can broach the notion of suicide. It has already been felt what solution might be given. At this point the problem is reversed. It was previously a question of finding out whether or not life had to have a meaning to be lived. It now becomes clear, on the contrary, that it will be lived all the better if it has no meaning. Living an experience, a particular fate, is accepting it fully. Now, no one will live this fate, knowing it to be absurd, unless he does everything to keep before him that absurd brought to light by consciousness. Negating one of the terms of the opposition on which he lives amounts to escaping it. To abolish conscious revolt is to elude the problem. The theme of permanent revolution is thus carried into individual experience. Living is keeping the absurd alive. Keeping it alive is, above all, contemplating it. Unlike Eurydice, the absurd dies only when we turn away from it. One of the only coherent philosophical positions is thus revolt. It is a constant confrontation between man and his own obscurity. It is an insistence upon an impossible transparency. It challenges the world anew every second. Just as danger provided man the unique opportunity of seizing awareness, so metaphysical revolt extends awareness to the whole of experience. It is that constant presence of man in his own eyes. It is not aspiration, for it is devoid of hope. That revolt is the certainty of a crushing fate, without the resignation that ought to accompany it.

This is where it is seen to what a degree absurd experience is remote from suicide. It may be thought that suicide follows revolt—but wrongly. For it does not represent the logical outcome of revolt. It is just the contrary by the consent it presupposes. Suicide, like the leap, is acceptance at its extreme. Everything is over and man returns to his essential history. His future, his unique and dreadful future—he sees and rushes toward it. In its way, suicide settles the absurd. It engulfs the absurd in the same death. But I know that in order to keep alive, the absurd cannot be settled. It escapes suicide to the extent that it is simultaneously awareness and rejection of death. It is, at the extreme limit of the condemned man's last thought, that shoelace that despite everything he sees a few yards away, on the very brink of his dizzying fall. The contrary of suicide, in fact, is the man condemned to death.

That revolt gives life its value. Spread out over the whole length of a life, it restores its majesty to that life. To a man devoid of blinders, there is no finer sight than that of the intelligence at grips with a reality that transcends it. The sight of human pride is unequaled. No disparagement is of any use. That discipline that the mind imposes on itself, that will conjured up out of nothing, that face-to-face struggle have something exceptional about them. To impoverish that reality whose inhumanity constitutes man's majesty is tantamount to impoverishing him himself. I understand then why the doctrines that explain everything to me also debilitate me at the same time. They relieve me of the weight of my own life, and yet I must carry it alone. At this juncture, I cannot conceive that a skeptical metaphysics can be joined to an ethics of renunciation.

Consciousness and revolt, these rejections are the contrary of renunciation. Everything that is indomitable and passionate in a human heart quickens them, on the contrary, with its own life. It is essential to die unreconciled and not of one's own free will. Suicide is a repudiation. The absurd man can only drain everything to the bitter end, and deplete himself. The absurd is his extreme tension, which he maintains constantly by solitary effort, for he knows that in that consciousness and in that day-to-day revolt he gives proof of his only truth, which is defiance. This is a first consequence.[15]

Such a stance is not without problems. Our discussion of the denial of moral law in Chapter 13 is relevant here, and our discussion in Chapter 16 will also be to the point. For the moment, we may reiterate: Any philosophy which rejects the objective reality of values will surely have a hard time when it turns right around and argues passionately for certain values. In the case of Camus, it might be asked: In a universe devoid of real values, what is it that justifies and gives value to the life of revolt? In terms of what is the revolt itself a value? Of course Camus might just as easily respond, "There you go again with your academic questions! Don't you understand that in a world such as this it is not reasoning but *acting* that is called for?"

Can there be real values in an irrational universe?

Be that as it may. With the emphasis on evil as the supreme evidence for the ultimate irrationality of the world, we appear to have come full circle: God may be dead, but the Devil is very much alive! And now the *theist* might attack:

The problem of goodness

THEIST: You atheists are always attacking us theists on the ground that we cannot show how evil in the world can be reconciled with an all-powerful and all-loving God. You call it "the problem of evil."

ATHEIST: Right!

THEIST: But don't you have a similar problem? Why is it any more difficult to have evil *with* God than to have goodness *without* him? On your atheistic view, how can you account for all the goodwill, generosity, and self-sacrifice in the world? Call it "the problem of goodness."

ATHEIST: But all those good things come from *human beings!*

THEIST: Well, I doubt it. But even so, I will insist insist just as emphatically that sin *Also* comes from humans.

ATHEIST: But if your God is all-powerful he could have prevented men from sinning.

THEIST: I invoke the Free-will Defense.

ATHEIST: Oh. But what about natural evil? Your Free-will Defense will not explain *that.*

THEIST: You're right But I have all sorts of other ideas about it—I'll tell you about them sometime. In the meantime, what's *your* explanation for

---

[15]Camus, *The Myth of Sisyphus*, pp. 39–41.

THE PROBLEM OF GOODNESS

If there is no God, how does one account for goodness, conceived as an objective value, both in the natural sphere (beauty, harmony, unity, etc.) and in the moral sphere (goodwill, kindness, justice, etc.)?

---

natural evil? Is it not at least as great a problem for you as for me? Give a little and take a little!

Chapter 15 in Review

The presence in the world of evil, both natural and moral, is surely the biggest stumbling-block to belief in an all-powerful and all-loving God.

Many attempts have been made on the theistic side to overcome this difficulty. We have considered several of them, but especially two. One of the most enduring is the view of evil as a privation, or absence, of good. Associated most notably with St. Augustine, this view emphasizes that God is responsible for the creation of *things,* not *no-things.* But evil is a no-thing; it is the absence of being and goodness. It cannot therefore be attributed to God. Natural evil has its origin in the (necessary) relative nonbeing of the natural world, and moral evil has its root in the relative nonbeing of the will. The denial that evil is a substance should not be confused with the denial that evil is real. Very different, but also enduring, is the therapeutic view of evil. Here the emphasis is primarily on natural evil, which is seen to be conducive to the development and strengthening of individuals and the race. Thus John Hick calls this mortal existence "a vale of soul-making."

Both of these positions make use, in their own ways, of the Free-will Defense, which has figured prominently in recent philosophical discussions: If individuals are to be genuinely capable of doing what is right, they must also be capable of doing what is wrong. That is, human free will is a logically necessary limitation on God's power if moral creatures are to exist.

In contrast to the theists, who attempt to reconcile evil with God, are those atheists who simply, as it were, abandon the world to evil. God is dead, and the world is ultimately irrational. Camus provides one possible stance: We can at least recover something of human dignity by defying the irrational forces that will, finally, "do us in." But theists want to know why this belief in the world as ultimately irrational is, philosophically, any less distasteful and problematic than their own belief in God.

BASIC IDEAS
- Natural evil and moral evil
- The problem of evil
- Theodicy
- Hume's statement of the problem
- Some standard solutions
  - A limited God
  - An inscrutable God
  - The goodness of the whole
  - The logical impossibility of a perfect world
  - Evil as the necessary by-product of nature
- Evil as a privation of goodness
- The Free-will Defense: For and against
- Evil as therapy
- Soul-making vs. soul-breaking
- Evil as irrational
- Nihilism
- Anthropodicy
- The dignity of defiance
- The problem of goodness

TEST YOURSELF
1. True or false: John Hick is a nihilist.
2. Why, according to some philosophers, is a perfect world logically impossible?
3. Mill solved the problem of evil simply by denying that God is _____.
4. Who said it? " ... so long as a being is in process of corruption, there is in it some good of which it is being deprived."
5. Albert Camus taught that in the face of evil one ought to (a) commit suicide, (b) revolt, (c) resign oneself, (d) philosophize about it.
6. How did the ancient Christian writer Irenaeus figure in the discussion in this chapter?
7. St. Augustine's theory of evil as the absence of goodness is based on _____'s metaphysics.
8. What has Camus' novel *The Plague* to do with the problem of evil?
9. What would St. Augustine reply to the charge that his denial of evil as a substance renders evil *unreal*?
10. True or false: John Hick advocates *both* the therapy theory of evil *and* the Free-will Defense.

- Do you think that the standard solutions to the problem of evil tend to trivialize the problem, or do any of them have real merit?

- In the last chapter we saw how classical mysticism has its roots in a certain metaphysical view. Can you explain how St. Augustine's position on evil has its roots in the same view? By contrast, how would you characterize the metaphysical perspective that underlies Camus' position?

- Is it possible that what one feels about the problem of evil depends largely on what side of the fence he or she starts out on? Is it likely that a theist will find the problem insuperable? Is it not likely that an atheist will see it as devastating to the theist position? What side of the fence are you on, and what difference does it make in your own view of the problem?

- The Free-will Defense always figures strongly in discussions about the problem of evil. Can you argue the Free-will Defense back and forth? What do *you* make of this maneuver?

QUESTIONS FOR
REFLECTION

P A R T

T H E   Q U E S T I O N   O F   M O R A L I T Y

As was explained in Chapter 1, value theory raises the question of value in general. The value of filets mignons, human deeds, works of art, political ideologies—all values are the concern of value theory. It is not possible to consider all spheres of value, but it would seem necessary to consider at least two of them. In this part of our book we will examine *ethical* or *moral values,* those values which define personal decisions and actions as good or evil, moral or immoral. In the final part we will look at *social* and *political values,* the values which determine the principles and institutions of our life together in society and the state.

Talk of moral and political values probably brings immediately to mind all sorts of exciting and dramatic issues, such as abortion, capital punishment, the draft, war, sex, nuclear armament, ERA, politics, minority rights, imperialism, genetic engineering, and euthanasia. And rightfully so. All such issues presuppose, involve, and imply many kinds of values. But while it is expected, also rightfully, that value theory must in the end illuminate such problems, it is usually not with these problems that value theory directly concerns itself. More specifically, as a theoretical endeavor, moral philosophy or ethics is concerned with the clarification of fundamental ethical concepts, the elucidation of principles, and the critical discussion of positions and perspectives. It should be apparent that these tasks are, after all, much more important than the excited arguments about specific issues (such as those mentioned above) which all too often proceed without due regard for more fundamental questions. In the case of ethics, such questions are:

- What is moral goodness?
- Is morality relative or absolute?
- Do moral claims have cognitive (truth/falsity) status?
- Are all moral values derived from an ultimate value?
- What are the epistemological bases of ethical theories?
- Is there a distinction between what *is* and what *ought* to be?
- Does moral responsibility require free will?
- What is the relation between the private and the public good?

The truth is, of course, that even with its theoretical concerns the philosophical question of morality stands more obviously related to concrete situations and practical questions than do the other fields of philosophy. And it is, therefore, here, with the question of morality (and again in Part V, with the question of society), that philosophical activity will seem to many to be most related to the question of *living*.

CHAPTER 16

CHALLENGES TO MORALITY

Before we consider some of the more important ways philosophers have answered the question of morality, we must consider the prior question: Is morality, or at least traditional morality, even possible? Some have, indeed, maintained for various reasons that morality, as it is usually conceived, is *not* possible. *First,* there are those who judge right from the start that ethical propositions are meaningless. *Second,* we have the relativists or subjectivists, who argue that morality is a matter of individual judgment and that there are no common or universal moral obligations. *Third,* we have to reckon with those who locate the basis of morality in evolving human nature itself. *Fourth,* we must confront the determinist, who denies free will and asks: If all things, including our choices, are completely predetermined, then how can there be any basis for moral responsibility?

THE CHALLENGE OF LOGICAL POSITIVISM

Logical positivism challenges traditional morality by maintaining that *its language is meaningless.*

When we raise the question whether morality is *meaningless* it is important to introduce a distinction. There is a big difference between *existential* meaning (as in "I saw a meaningful movie") and *cognitive* meaning (as in "'Creech creech' is meaningless"). In the first case it is a question of relevance or *importance,* whereas in the second case it is a question of *truth status.* To say of a claim that it is irrelevant (it has no existential meaning) is very different from saying that it is neither true nor

The meanings of "meaning"

351

false and therefore doesn't say anything literal at all (it has no cognitive meaning). In the logical positivists' challenge to morality, it is asserted that traditional moral claims, such as "X is good" or "You ought not to do Y," are cognitively meaningless; they are neither true nor false; they make no claim about anything whatsoever; they are no more significant than "Creech creech"; they are gibberish.

Logical positivism is a superempiricist philosophy after the manner of Hume. Do you recall Hume's pronouncement about casting into the flames those volumes containing claims that are neither relations of ideas (analytic) nor matters of fact (synthetic *a posteriori*)? At the heart of logical positivism lies the Humean-sounding *Verification Principle*: A proposition is cognitively meaningful if and only if it is either analytic or in principle empirically verifiable. Say it another way: If you cannot conceive of the actual empirical conditions under which your claim could be shown to be true or false, then you are talking nonsense. The implications of this principle are, of course, devastating. All metaphysical claims (about God, souls, free will, necessary causal relations, underlying substances, etc.) are immediately excluded as *cognitively meaningless*. And the verificationists deliver an identical judgment on *moral claims*. They are purportedly not empty analytic propositions, or tautologies, and they cannot even in principle be verified by means of sense experience, so they are *cognitively meaningless*.

The Verification Principle

How, then, do the logical positivists handle ethical claims and propositions? The most popular of their views is known as *emotivism*. Look at the word. You can tell immediately that this interpretation of moral propositions has something to do with *emotions*. Actually, emotivism is the view that moral propositions are really

Emotivism

TWO MEANINGS OF "MEANING"

- *Existential meaning:* The importance or relevance that something holds.
- *Cognitive meaning:* The truth/falsity status of a claim.

THE VERIFICATION PRINCIPLE

A proposition is cognitively meaningful if and only if it is either analytic or in principle empirically verifiable.

emotional expressions, expressions or pronouncements of one's own likes and dislikes: anger, elation, disgust, approval, disapproval. At the same time, they are attempts to arouse a similar feeling in others and to provoke action. Obviously, such expressions as "X is right" only reveal something about the one uttering them. They do not refer to any objective or factual or common state of affairs. They make no claim about anything "out there." They possess no truth value. In this way, the ethical statement "Stealing is wrong" is equivalent both to the exclamation "Stealing!" and to the command "Do not steal." But none of these expressions have any cognitive meaning, for they express not truth but emotions. They are not value claims but psychological claims.

The way in which the emotivist theory of morality follows from a preconceived theory of knowledge has been represented as follows:

> As positivists, these writers held that every judgment belongs to one or other of two types. On the one hand, it may be a priori or necessary. But then it is always analytic, i.e., it unpacks in its predicate part or all of its subject. Can we safely say that 7 + 5 makes 12? Yes, because 12 is what we mean by "7 + 5." On the other hand, the judgment may be empirical, and then, if we are to verify it, we can no longer look to our meanings only; it refers to sense experience and there we must look for its warrant. Having arrived at this division of judgments, the positivists raised the question where value judgments fall. The judgment that knowledge is good, for example, did not seem to be analytic; the value that knowledge might have did not seem to be part of our concept of knowledge. But neither was the statement empirical, for goodness was not a quality like red or squeaky that could be seen or heard. What were they to do, then, with these awkward judgments of value? To find a place for them in their theory of knowledge would require them to revise the theory radically, and yet that theory was what they regarded as their most important discovery. It appeared that the theory could be saved in one way only. If it could be shown that judgments of good and bad were not judgments at all, that they asserted nothing true or false, but merely expressed emotions like "Hurrah" or "Fiddlesticks," then these wayward judgments would cease from troubling and weary heads could be at rest. This is the course the positivists took. They explained value judgments by explaining them away.[1]

True to the above characterization, A.J. Ayer, the arch-representative of logical positivism, presents his own case thus:

> . . . it is our business to give an account of "judgements of value" which is both satisfactory in itself and consistent with our general empiricist principles. We shall set ourselves to show that in so far as statements of value are significant, they are ordinary "scientific" statements; and that in so far as they are not scientific, they are

[1]Brand Blanshard, "The New Subjectivism in Ethics," *Philosophy and Phenomenological Research*, 9 (1949), pp. 504–505.

not in the literal sense significant, but are simply expressions of emotion which can be neither true nor false. . . .

We begin by admitting that the fundamental ethical concepts are unanalysable, inasmuch as there is no criterion by which one can test the validity of the judgements in which they occur. So far we are in agreement with the absolutists. But, unlike the absolutists, we are able to give an explanation of this fact about ethical concepts. We say that the reason why they are unanalysable is that they are mere pseudo-concepts. The presence of an ethical symbol in a proposition adds nothing to its factual content. Thus if I say to someone, "You acted wrongly in stealing that money," I am not stating anything more than if I had simply said, "You stole that money." In adding that this action is wrong I am not making any further statement about it. I am simply evincing my moral disapproval of it. It is as if I had said, "You stole that money," in a peculiar tone of horror, or written it with the addition of some special exclamation marks. The tone, or the exclamation marks, adds nothing to the literal meaning of the sentence. It merely serves to show that the expression of it is attended by certain feelings in the speaker.

If now I generalise my previous statement and say, "Stealing money is wrong," I produce a sentence which has no factual meaning—that is, expresses no proposition which can be either true or false. It is as if I had written "Stealing money!!"—where the shape and thickness of the exclamation marks show, by a suitable convention, that a special sort of moral disapproval is the feeling which is being expressed. It is clear that there is nothing said here which can be true or false. Another man may disagree with me about the wrongness of stealing, in the sense that he may not have the same feelings about stealing as I have, and he may quarrel with me on account of my moral sentiments. But he cannot, strictly speaking, contradict me. For in saying that a certain type of action is right or wrong, I am not making any factual statement, not even a statement about my own state of mind. I am merely expressing certain moral sentiments. And the man who is ostensibly contradicting me is merely expressing his moral sentiments. So that there is plainly no sense in asking which of us is in the right. For neither of us is asserting a genuine proposition.

What we have just been saying about the symbol "wrong" applies to all normative ethical symbols. Sometimes they occur in sentences which record ordinary empirical facts besides expressing ethical feeling about those facts: sometimes they occur in sentences which simply express ethical feeling about a certain type of action, or situation, without making any statement of fact. But in every case in which one would commonly be said to be making an ethical judgement, the function of the relevant ethical word is purely "emotive." It is used to express feeling about certain objects, but not to make any assertion about them.

It is worth mentioning that ethical terms do not serve only to express feeling. They are calculated also to arouse feeling, and so to stimulate action. Indeed some of them are used in such a way as to give the sentences in which they occur the effect of commands. Thus the sentence "It is your duty to tell the truth" may be regarded both as the expression of a certain sort of ethical feeling about truthfulness and as the *expression of the command "Tell the truth." The sentence "You ought to tell the truth" also involves the command "Tell the truth," but here the tone of the command is less emphatic. In the sentence "It is good to tell the truth" the command has become little more than a suggestion. And thus the "meaning" of the word "good," in its ethical usage, is differentiated from that of the word "duty" or the word "ought." In fact we may define the meaning of the various ethical words in terms both of the different feelings they are ordinarily taken to express, and also the different responses which they are calculated to provoke.*

We can now see why it is impossible to find a criterion for determining the validity of ethical judgements. It is not because they have an "absolute" validity which is mysteriously independent of ordinary sense-experience, but because they have no objective validity whatsoever. If a sentence makes no statement at all, there is obviously no sense in asking whether what it says is true or false. And we have seen that sentences which simply express moral judgements do not say anything. They are pure expressions of feeling and as such do not come under the category of truth and falsehood. They are unverifiable for the same reason as a cry of pain or a word of command is unverifiable—because they do not express genuine propositions.

. . . the main objection to the ordinary subjectivist theory is that the validity of ethical judgements is not determined by the nature of their author's feelings. And this is an objection which our theory escapes. For it does not imply that the existence of any feelings is a necessary and sufficient condition of the validity of an ethical judgement. It implies, on the contrary, that ethical judgements have no validity.[2]

EMOTIVISM

The view, usually associated with logical positivism, that moral propositions make no claims about reality but, rather, merely express the likes and dislikes of the speaker.

What do you make of this view of morality? First, some rather theoretical considerations. Obviously, as with the logical positivist rejection of metaphysical claims, its rejection of moral claims depends on the Verification Principle, but the Verification Principle must reckon with several lines of objection: Does it rather arbitrarily exalt the language of sense experience as *the* language? Is it insensitive to other and equally important spheres of discourse with their own and different

Some problems for emotivism

[2]A. J. Ayer, *Language, Truth and Logic*, 2d ed. (London: Gollancz, 1946), pp. 102–103, 107–110.

criteria of meaningfulness? Is it not meaningless on its own showing, since it claims to be nonanalytic but cannot be verified empirically? And are you satisfied with its bifurcation of meaningful knowledge into either analytic *a priori* or synthetic *a posteriori*? And do you accept its repudiation of synthetic *a priori* knowledge, and can you live with the epistemological consequences of this repudiation?

On the more practical side, even if emotivism could work as a *theory* about moral propositions, can it work in *practice*? What becomes of the practical necessity of legislation, praise and blame, and moral disputes? More specifically, consider these odd implications of emotivism. If emotivism were true, then no one could be mistaken in matters of morality, for, in the first place, moral judgments would not be about *truth,* and, in the second place, a person's feelings and attitudes would be just whatever they *are,* and that is that. Closely related to this is the awkward consequence that something approved by an insane person might for that reason alone be good: Imagine a murder wherein the victim was dispatched so immediately as to have no time to formulate his own disapproval, and the crime so perfectly executed that no others beside the murderer should ever know it. The only attitude or feeling about the murder would be the murderer's own. And his feeling about it would be: "I like it!" The murder was therefore "good." Finally, what becomes of occurrences which happened before anyone registered approval or disapproval? Were they not good or bad already, then, when they occurred? In a word: At the practical level, is anything really important resolved with the view that "X is bad" means simply "X—ugh!"?

THE CHALLENGE OF RELATIVISM

"A man is the measure of all things"

We have already encountered the idea of *ethical relativism* in the person of Protagoras. In fact, he provided this view with a motto for all time when he said that "a man is the measure of all things." Though Protagoras himself did not limit his statement to moral claims, it was natural that it was in the realm of morality that it was most obviously applied.

Are moral values relative or absolute? Subjective or objective?

Ethical relativism holds, unlike emotivism, that moral claims *are* cognitively meaningful, that is, true or false, and that the criterion of their truth or falsity is the *individual*—the individual's perceptions, opinions, experiences, inclinations, and desires. This sort of relativism can take different forms, depending on what is meant by "individual." It might make ethical truth relative to the individual person, or the individual society, or community, or nation, or culture, or even the whole human race. But *any* form of ethical relativism denies that there are common or universal or *objective* moral values. It insists, rather, that moral values are private, individual, or *subjective*. Hence, ethical relativism vs. ethical absolutism may be expressed also as ethical subjectivism vs. ethical objectivism. However it is expressed, the issue is the same: What is the source or foundation of moral values

---

ETHICAL RELATIVISM

Ethical relativism, or ethical subjectivism, denies any absolute or objective moral values which are common to all, and affirms, rather, that the individual (a person, community, society, etc.) is the source and criterion of moral judgments.

---

and ideals? Are ethical values relative and subjective, or absolute and objective? Are they dependent upon the individual, or do moral values and ideals exist irrespective and independent of the individual? Is morality a matter of "different strokes for different folks"?

For those who embrace ethical relativism, more often than not it is the particular or individual *culture* that is said to define morality. We have encountered an instance of this already in B. F. Skinner *Beyond Freedom and Dignity*:

Cultural relativism

> *What a given group of people calls good is a fact: it is what members of the group find reinforcing as the result of their genetic endowment and the natural and social contingencies to which they have been exposed. Each culture has its own set of goods, and what is good in one culture may not be good in another. To recognize this is to take the position of "cultural relativism." What is good for the Trobriand Islander is good for the Trobriand Islander, and that is that. Anthropologists have often emphasized relativism as a tolerant alternative to missionary zeal in converting all cultures to a single set of ethical, governmental, religious, or economic values.*[3]

One such anthropologist was Ruth Benedict, author of the much-read *Patterns of Culture*. In her essay, "Anthropology and the Abnormal," she, like Skinner, equates cultural relativism and ethical relativism:

> *Every society, beginning with some slight inclination in one direction or another, carries its preference farther and farther, integrating itself more and more completely upon its chosen basis, and discarding those types of behavior that are uncongenial. Most of those organizations of personality that seem to us most incontrovertibly abnormal have been looked on in differently organized cultures as aberrant. Normality, in short, within a very wide range, is culturally defined. It is primarily a term for the socially elaborated segment of human behavior in any culture; and abnormality, a term for the segment that that particular civilization does not use. The very*

[3]B. F. Skinner, *Beyond Freedom and Dignity* (New York: Bantam Books, 1972), p. 122.

eyes with which we see the problem are conditioned by the long traditional habits of our own society.

It is a point that has been made more often in relation to ethics than in relation to psychiatry. We do not any longer make the mistake of deriving the morality of our own locality and decade directly from the inevitable constitution of human nature. We do not elevate it to the dignity of a first princple. We recognize that morality differs in every society, and is a convenient term for socially approved habits. Mankind has always preferred to say, "It is a morally good," rather than "It is habitual," and the fact of this preference is matter enough for a critical science of ethics. But historically the two phrases are synonymous.

The concept of the normal is properly a variant of the concept of the good. It is that which society has approved. A normal action is one which falls well within the limits of expected behavior for a particular society. Its variability among different peoples is essentially a function of the variability of the behavior patterns that different societies have created for themselves, and can never be wholly divorced from a consideration of culturally institutionalized types of behavior.

Each culture is a more or less elaborate working-out of the potentialities of the segment it has chosen. In so far as a civilization is well integrated and consistent within itself, it will tend to carry farther and farther, according to its nature, its initial impulse toward a particular type of action, and from the point of veiw of any other culture those elaborations will include more and more extreme and aberrant traits.

Each of these traits, in proportion as it reinforces the chosen behavior patterns of that culture, is for that culture normal. Those individuals to whom it is congenial either congenitally, or as the result of childhood sets, are accorded prestige in that culture, and are not visited with the social contempt or disapproval which their traits would call down upon them in a society that was differently organized. On the other hand, those individuals whose characteristics are not congenial to the selected type of human behavior in that community are the deviants, no matter how valued their personality traits may be in a contrasted civilization.[4]

One big argument for ethical relativism

Why would one be an ethical relativist? Why would one ever assert with Protagoras that in matters of morality, "a man is the measure of all things"? Well, there is one gigantic but two-sided argument that relativists give over and over again. And, in fact, it is the argument that Protagoras himself gave. The argument is, first, that ethical views, opinions, and exhortations are largely or even completely conditioned by our circumstances. Obviously, whether you think that X is right and Y is wrong is very much dependent upon—relative to—when and where you were born, your upbringing, your education, your religious instruction, and maybe even your skin color and your height. Do you really think that you would hold the same moral opinions if your fundamental circumstances had been radically different? Second, and aside from our circumstances, relativists usually take very seriously the

[4]Ruth Benedict, "Anthropology and the Abnormal," *Journal of General Psychology*, 10 (1934), pp. 72–74.

differences, disputes, and downright confusion that reign everywhere in the area of morality.

When both of these lines of observations are put together they suggest strongly (maybe decisively) to some that there *are* no common or universal or objective values, and that morality is *relative*.

Such a position is not without its problems. For one thing, does not the argument for ethical relativism misfire? Surely it does not follow from the fact that one's moral opinions are conditioned or learned that they are therefore merely subjectively or relatively true. We have learned all sorts of things which, nonetheless, we believe to be true, and true for *everyone*: In fourteen-hundred-and-ninety-two Columbus sailed the ocean blue; $2 + 2 = 4$; it is wrong to beat your spouse, starve your children, and torture your pets; etc. And how do disagreements about morality destroy its objectivity? We may disagree also about the nature of the universe, but we would hardly conclude from that that the universe *has* no nature! On the contrary, what is the point of disagreeing at all, unless we believe there is some real *truth* involved? It is important, then, to distinguish between our *opinions* of morality and *morality itself*. Certainly our opinions about morality differ, and certainly they are conditioned by and relative to all sorts of things. But in no other sphere would we so simple-mindedly confuse our opinions of the truth with the truth itself. Why here, where the implications are far more consequential?

More specifically, it may be observed that ethical relativism not only misfires but *backfires* inasmuch as it involves some curious self-contradictions. For example, and recalling our earlier discussion of self-refuting propositions, it claims that there is no objective moral truth, but at the same time insists that that claim itself *ought* to be accepted. Or what about the subjectivist who meets an objectivist? Would not the subjectivist have to say that the objectivist's opinion is true—in which case the subjectivist's opinion must be false?

Just such problems as these are what Plato hoped to convey in his own refutation of Protagoras' principle of "a man is the measure." The *Theaetetus* is the dialogue, and again, Socrates is the mouthpiece.

Is ethical relativism self-contradictory?

> SOCRATES: . . . *what is the consequence for Protagoras himself? Is it not this? Supposing that not even he believed in man being the measure and the world in general did not believe it either—as in fact it doesn't—then this Truth which he wrote would not be true for anyone. If, on the other hand, he did believe it, but the mass of mankind does not agree with him, then, you see, it is more false than true by just so much as the unbelievers outnumber the believers.*
>
> THEODORUS: *That follows, if its truth or falsity varies with each individual opinion.*
>
> SOCRATES: *Yes, and besides that it involves a really exquisite conclusion. Protagoras, for his part, admitting as he does that everybody's opinion is true, must acknowledge the truth of his opponents' belief about his own belief, where they think he is wrong.*
>
> THEODORUS: *Certainly.*

SOCRATES: *That is to say, he would acknowledge his own belief to be false, if he admits that the belief of those who think him wrong is true?*

THEODORUS: *Necessarily.*

SOCRATES: *But the others, on their side, do not admit to themselves that they are wrong.*

THEODORUS: *No.*

SOCRATES: *Whereas Protagoras, once more, according to what he has written, admits that this opinion of theirs is as true as any other.*

THEODORUS: *Evidently.*

SOCRATES: *On all hands, then, Protagoras included, his opinion will be disputed, or rather Protagoras will join in the general consent—when he admits to an opponent the truth of his contrary opinion, from that moment Protagoras himself will be admitting that a dog or the man in the street is not a measure of anything whatever that he does not understand. Isn't that so?*

THEODORUS: *Yes.*

SOCRATES: *Then, since it is disputed by everyone, the Truth of Protagoras is true to nobody—to himself no more than to anyone else.*[5]

Furthermore, and similar to a criticism leveled against emotivism, if the individual is the basis of moral truth, then none of us could ever be mistaken in our moral opinions, for whatever we believe must be true. Or, on the larger interpretation of "individual," such as an individual group, morality would reduce to what happened to be believed by the largest number of people. Both of these seem to many to be necessary but absurd implications of the relativist or subjectivist position.

Some have even charged that ethical relativism involves a bigger contradiction than those already mentioned. It involves a sort of *practical* contradiction. It is the contradiction between saying one thing and living another. You may know someone who *claims* to be an ethical relativist, but do you know anyone who *lives* as one? Do we not all, in one way or another, impose our ideas of morality on others? Do we not hold others responsible for their actions? Do we not judge others as morally wrong or reprehensible? Do we not vote, crusade for causes, and make sacrifices for various ideals? But clearly all such actions are meaningful (here, *existentially* meaningful) only on the assumption of an *objective* and *common* morality. In a word, this objection charges that there is really no such thing as a consistent subjectivist.

Is ethical relativism practically contradictory?

It should be noted, finally, that *if*, unlike the emotivists, you believe that moral propositions are cognitively significant, that is, that they are either true or false, and *if* you accept the above criticisms of ethical relativism, then you *must* be an ethical objectivist or absolutist. For either ethical relativism is true or ethical

---

[5]Plato, *Theaetetus*, 170E-171C, tr. F. M. Cornford, in *The Collected Dialogues of Plato*, ed. Edith Hamilton and Huntington Cairns (New York: Pantheon, 1961).

> ## ETHICAL ABSOLUTISM
>
> Ethical absolutism, or ethical objectivism, affirms that moral values are independent of individual opinions, and ascribes to them an abiding and fixed reality common to all.

---

absolutism is true; there is no third alternative. If ethical relativism is false, then ethical absolutism must be true. Or, at least, so it seems to many. How does it seem to you?

THE CHALLENGE OF
EXISTENTIALISM

We have already encountered the philosophy known as *existentialism*: It was mentioned in Chapter 1, in contrast to both speculative and analytic philosophy, and Albert Camus was cited in Chapter 15 as responding in an existentialist way to the problem of evil. It is difficult to say just what existentialism is, because the existentialists are so varied in their points of view. But that they represent, in different ways, challenges to traditional morality is evident.

For example, the Danish philosopher Søren Kierkegaard (1813–1855) taught the "teleological suspension of the ethical," according to which the individual is enabled to transcend ordinary ethical norms and receive his or her commandments immediately from God. The German Friedrich Nietzsche (1844–1900) rejected Christianity as involving a "slave-morality" and called for a "transvaluation of values" according to which "the will to power" as the basic principle of life will lead to the development of a higher type of humanity. Surely the best-known existentialist is the contemporary French writer and philosopher Jean-Paul Sartre. In addition to authoring works with ponderous titles such as *Being and Nothingness*, he wrote an essay entitled, simply, "Existentialism." This little work is often regarded as the best introduction to the philosophy of existentialism, and certainly it represents yet another existentialist's challenge to traditional morality.

According to Sartre, existentialism turns on its head any philosophy (think especially of Plato) which teaches that everything is what it is by virtue of a transcendent essence: *Essence precedes existence.* No, says Sartre. We begin with the *individual,* the concretely existing human being, the subject. The central tenet of existentialism, in any of its forms, is that *existence precedes essence.* What is first given is the existence of a particular thing; only *after* that does its essence appear. Or, to

"Existence precedes essence"

Friedrich Nietzsche

Nietzsche was a classical philologist turned philosopher. Among his many works is included one with the revealing title Beyond Good and Evil. *His ideas about the "will to power" and the Übermensch ("superman") were later misappropriated by the Nazi party. Nietzsche died insane.*

We are "condemned to be free"

say it another way, *subjectivity must be the starting point.* However, in its atheistic form, which Sartre himself espouses, existentialism finds nothing outside, above, or beyond the individual to which the individual can leap for its essence, definition, or meaning. God is dead, all objective and transcendent values have disappeared with him, and the individual is alone. This is the meaning of Sartre's famous pronouncement that we are "condemned to be free." Here, to be "free" means to be unconditioned by any moral law or eternal values.

What then do we do? Answer: We must accept the full burden of our freedom, and through our choices and commitments contribute to the evolving essence of humanity. What we choose for ourselves, that we become. And what we become, that we contribute to the definition or essence of humanity, for each of us is part of humanity. If, then, we care about the essence of humanity—what it is and will become—we must have a care about our own individual commitments. This aloneness and personal responsibility is the source of the emphasis by Sartre and other existentialists on the anxiety, dread, and despair of the "conscious" individual, the individual who knows the score.

You may be tempted to see here just another version of subjectivism, but there is a difference. In its crassest form, subjectivism denies that any value or ideal is any better than another. Clearly Sartre is not saying this. It is true that there is no divine or transcendent foundation of values, and that is precisely why Sartre shifts the responsibility to individuals. Human beings in their freedom (in Sartre's existentialist sense) are themselves the basis of values, and in this sense values are real—evolving, developing, on the move, but real. In place of God or a transcendent source of values, ideals, meaning, etc., this philosophy is truly *humanistic*, in that humanity stands center-stage as the criterion of all meaning and value. It is important to see how this differs from the sort of relativism or subjectivism we considered in the last section. That philosophy denied any objective or common values, locating them instead in *individuals*. This philosophy, on the other hand, affirms objective values, but locates them in *humanity*. The difference between subjectivism and humanism is caught by the two claims,

Humanism

- A man is the measure of all things.
- Man is the measure of all things.

HUMANISM

As is evident from the word itself, humanism is the exaltation of humanity as the source and criterion of all value and meaning.

In the following, from his essay "Existentialism," Sartre explains the general nature of this philosophy, and the moral implications of his version of it.

What is meant by the term "existentialism?"

Most people who use the word would be rather embarrassed if they had to explain it, since, now that the word is all the rage, even the work of a musician or painter is being called existentialist. A gossip columnist in Clartés signs himself The Existentialist, so that by this time the word has been so stretched and has taken on so broad a meaning, that it no longer means anything at all. It seems that for want of an advance-guard doctrine analogous to surrealism, the kind of people who are eager for scandal and flurry turn to this philosophy which in other respects does not at all serve their purposes in this sphere.

Actually, it is the least scandalous, the most austere of doctrines. It is intended strictly for specialists and philosophers. Yet it can be defined easily. What complicates matters is that there are two kinds of existentialist; first, those who are Christian, among whom I would include Jaspers and Gabriel Marcel, both Catholic; and on the other hand the atheistic existentialists, among whom I class Heidegger, and then the French existentialists and myself. What they have in common is that they think that existence precedes essence, or, if you prefer, that subjectivity must be the starting point.

Just what does that mean? Let us consider some object that is manufactured, for example, a book or a paper-cutter: here is an object which has been made by an artisan whose inspiration came from a concept. He referred to the concept of what a paper-cutter is and likewise to a known method of production, which is part of the concept, something which is, by and large, a routine. Thus, the paper-cutter is at once an object produced in a certain way and, on the other hand, one having a specific use; and one can not postulate a man who produces a paper-cutter but does not know what it is used for. Therefore, let us say that, for the paper-cutter, essence—that is, the ensemble of both the production routines and the properties which enable it to be both produced and defined—precedes existence. Thus, the presence of the paper-cutter or book in front of me is determined. Therefore, we have here a technical view of the world whereby it can be said that production precedes existence.

When we conceive God as the Creator, He is generally thought of as a superior sort of artisan. Whatever doctrine we may be considering, whether one like that of Descartes or that of Leibnitz, we always grant that will more or less follows understanding or, at the very least, accompanies it, and that when God creates He knows exactly what He is creating. Thus, the concept of man in the mind of God is comparable to the concept of paper-cutter in the mind of the manufacturer, and, following certain techniques and a conception, God produces man, just as the artisan, following a definition and a technique, makes a paper-cutter. Thus, the individual man is the realization of a certain concept in the divine intelligence.

In the eighteenth century, the atheism of the philosophes discarded the idea of God, but not so much for the notion that essence precedes existence. To a certain extent, this idea is found everywhere; we find it in Diderot, in Voltaire, and even in Kant. Man has a human nature; this human nature, which is the concept of the human, is found in all men, which means that each man is a particular example of a universal concept, man. In Kant, the result of this universality is that the wild-man, the natural man, as well as the bourgeois, are circumscribed by the same definition and have the same basic qualities. Thus, here too the essence of man precedes the historical existence that we find in nature.

Atheistic existentialism, which I represent, is more coherent. It states that if God does not exist, there is at least one being in whom existence precedes essence, a being who exists before he can be defined by any concept, and that this being is man, or, as Heidegger says, human reality. What is meant here by saying that existence precedes essence? It means that, first of all, man exists, turns up, appears on the scene, and, only afterwards, defines himself. If man, as the existentialist conceives him, is indefinable, it is because at first he is nothing. Only afterward will he be something, and he himself will have made what he will be. Thus, there is no human nature, since there is no God to conceive it. Not only is man what he conceives himself to be, but he is also only what he wills himself to be after this thrust toward existence.

Man is nothing else but what he makes of himself. Such is the first principle of existentialism. It is also what is called subjectivity, the name we are labeled with when charges are brought against us. But what do we mean by this, if not that man has a greater dignity than a stone or table? For we mean that man first exists, that is, that man first of all is the being who hurls himself toward a future and who is conscious of imagining himself as being in the future. Man is at the start a plan which is aware of itself, rather than a patch of moss, a piece of garbage, or a cauliflower; nothing exists prior to this plan; there is nothing in heaven; man will be what he will have planned to be. Not what he will want to be. Because by the word "will" we generally mean a conscious decision, which is subsequent to what we have already made of ourselves. I may want to belong to a political party, write a book, get married; but all that is only a manifestation of an earlier, more spontaneous choice that is called "will." But if existence really does precede essence, man is responsible for what he is. Thus, existentialism's first move is to make every man aware of what he is and to make the full responsibility of his existence rest on him. And when we say that a man is responsible for himself, we do not only mean that he is responsible for his own individuality, but that he is responsible for all men.

The word subjectivism has two meanings, and our opponents play on the two. Subjectivism means, on the one hand, that an individual chooses and makes himself; and, on the other, that it is impossible for man to transcend human subjectivity. The second of these is the essential meaning of existentialism. When we say that man chooses his own self, we mean that every one of us does likewise; but we also mean by that that in making this choice he also chooses all men. In fact, in creating the man that we want to be, there is not a single one of our acts which does not at the same time create an image of man as we think he ought to be. To choose to be this or that is to affirm at the same time the value of what we choose, because we can never choose evil. We always choose the good, and nothing can be good for us without being good for all.

If, on the other hand, existence precedes essence, and if we grant that we exist and fashion our image at one and the same time, the image is valid for everybody and for our whole age. Thus, our responsibility is much greater than we might have supposed, because it involves all mankind. If I am a workingman and choose to join a Christian trade-union rather than be a communist, and if by being a member I want to show that the best thing for man is resignation, that the kingdom of man is not of this world, I am not only involving my own case—I want to be resigned for everyone. As a result, my action has involved all humanity. To take a more individual matter, if I want to marry, to have children; even if this marriage depends solely on my own circumstances or passion or wish, I am involving all humanity in monogamy *and not merely myself. Therefore, I am responsible for myself and for everyone else. I am creating a certain image of man of my own choosing. In choosing myself, I choose man.*

This helps us understand what the actual content is of such rather grandiloquent words as anguish, forlornness, despair. As you will see, it's all quite simple. . . .

When we speak of forlornness, a term Heidegger was fond of, we mean only that God does not exist and that we have to face all the consequences of this. The existentialist is strongly opposed to a certain kind of secular ethics which would like to abolish God with the least possible expense. About 1880, some French teachers tried to set up a secular ethics which went something like this: God is a useless and costly hypothesis; we are discarding it; but, meanwhile, in order for there to be an ethics, a society, a civilization, it is essential that certain values be taken seriously and that they be considered as having an a priori existence. It must be obligatory, a priori, to be honest, not a lie, not to beat your wife, to have children, etc., etc. So we're going to try a little device which will make it possible to show what values exist all the same, inscribed in a heaven of ideas, though otherwise God does not exist. In other words—and this, I believe, is the tendency of everything called reformism in France—nothing will be changed if God does not exist. We shall find ourselves with the same norms of honesty, progress, and humanism, and we shall have made of God an outdated hypothesis which will peacefully die off by itself.

The existentialist, on the contrary, thinks it very distressing that God does not exist, because all possibility of finding values in a heaven of ideas disappears along with Him; there can no longer be an a priori Good, since there is no infinite and perfect consciousness to think it. Nowhere is it written that the Good exists, that we must be honest, that we must not lie; because the fact is we are on a plane where there are only men. Dostoievsky said, "If God didn't exist, everything would be possible." That is the very starting point of existentialism. Indeed, everything is permissible if God does not exist, and as a result man is forlorn, because neither within him nor without does he find anything to cling to. He can't start making excuses for himself.

If existence really does precede essence, there is no explaining things away by reference to a fixed and given human nature. In other words, there is no determinism, man is free, man is freedom. On the other hand, if God does not exist, we find no values or commands to turn to which legitimize our conduct. So, in the bright realm of values, we have no excuse behind us, nor justification before us. We are alone, with no excuses.

That is the idea I shall try to convey when I say that man is condemned to be free. Condemned, because he did not create himself, yet, in other respects is free; because, once thrown into the world, he is responsible for everything he does.[6]

[6]Jean-Paul Sartre, "Existentialism," tr. Bernard Frechtman, in *Existentialism and Human Emotions* (New York: Citadel Press, 1957), pp. 12–18, 21–23.

Jean-Paul Sartre

The French writer and thinker Sartre is probably the best-known existentialist. He is the author of numerous novels (including one entitled Nausea)*, plays, and political and philosophical works. A Marxist and atheist, Sartre locates the full responsibility for human meaning in the commitments and choices of individuals themselves.*

We have already distinguished Sartre's humanistic existentialism from subjectivism. Nonetheless, Sartre's position has been attacked with criticisms similar to those which we saw in the last section leveled against subjectivism. After all, if individual existence precedes the essence of humanity, and nothing at all precedes or conditions the individual's choices, then what is to prevent those choices from

EXISTENTIALISM

The philosophy that emphasizes the existing individual, as opposed to abstractions or principles, as the point of departure for authentic philosophizing. Two existentialist slogans from Sartre:

- Existence precedes essence.
- Subjectivity must be the starting point.

A familiar objection

being purely arbitrary and, thus, the evolving essence of man as well? That is, if you don't begin with any meaning, how can you end with any?

This is the point of one of Sartre's loudest critics, Gabriel Marcel (1889–1973), whom Sartre mentioned as a Christian existentialist in the above selection. (That Marcel is called an existentialist by Sartre himself, and yet attacked the very basis of Sartre's philosophy, reminds us of what a variety there is among existentialists.) Marcel represents the way in which one might be faithful to the existentialist thesis that subjectivity must be the starting point but, beginning with subjectivity or the concreteness of personal existence, might move to a theistic or transcendent basis of value and meaning. This, says Marcel, is exactly what we must do, for values are not chosen but *discovered*. They are *given*. They are *objective*. According to Marcel, the Sartrean approach bogs down in a hopeless contradiction: It claims that outside our own commitments there is no basis for moral choices, but then turns right around and insists that some choices are better than others. You cannot have it both ways, and you cannot give up (can you?) the view that some choices are better than others. We must, says Marcel, grant the *givenness* of values and meaning. And given by whom, except *God*? From Marcel's *The Philosophy of Existentialism:*

> From [Sartre's] standpoint, values cannot be anything but the result of the initial choice made by each human being; in other words, they can never be "recognised" or "discovered." "My freedom," he states expressly, "is the unique foundation of values. And since I am the being by virtue of whom values exist, nothing—absolutely nothing—can justify me in adopting this or that value or scale of values. As the unique basis of the existence of values, I am totally unjustifiable. And my freedom is in anguish at finding that it is the baseless basis of values." Nothing could be more explicit; but the question is whether Sartre does not here go counter to the exigencies of that human reality which he claims, after all, not to invent but to reveal.
>
> Not to deal exclusively in abstractions, let us take a concrete case. Sartre has announced that the third volume of his Les Chemins de la Liberté [The Ways of Freedom] is to be devoted to the praise of the heroes of Resistance. Now I ask you in the name of what principle, having first denied the existence of values or at least of their objective basis, can he establish any appreciable difference between those utterly misguided but undoubtedly courageous men who joined voluntarily the Anti-Bolshevik Legion, on the one hand, and the heroes of the Resistance movement, on the other? I can see no way of establishing this difference without admitting that causes have their intrinsic value and, consequently, that values are real. I have no doubt that Sartre's ingenuity will find a way out of this dilemma; in fact, he quite often uses the words "good" and "bad," but what can these words possibly mean in the context of his philosophy?
>
> The truth is that, if I examine myself honestly and without reference to any preconceived body of ideas, I find that I do not "choose" my values at all, but that I recognise them and then posit my actions in accordance or in contradiction with

*these values, not, however, without being painfully aware of this contradiction. . . .
It should perhaps be asked at this point if it is not Nietzsche who, with his theory of
the creation of values, is responsible for the deathly principle of error which has crept
into speculation on this subject. But although I am the last to underrate the objections
to Nietzsche's doctrine, I am inclined to think that his view is less untenable than that
of Sartre, for it escapes that depth of rationalism and materialism which is discernible, to me as to others, in the mind of the author of* L'Etre et le Néant *{Being and
Nothingness}.*

*I would suggest in conclusion that existentialism stands to-day at a parting of
the ways: it is, in the last analysis, obliged either to deny or to transcend itself. It
denies itself quite simply when it falls to the level of infra-dialectical materialism. It
transcends itself, or it tends to transcend itself, when it opens itself out to the experience of the suprahuman, an experience which can hardly be ours in a genuine and
lasting way this side of death, but of which the reality is attested by mystics, and of
which the possibility is warranted by any philosophy which refuses to be immured in
the postulate of absolute immanence or to subscribe in advance to the denial of the
beyond and of the unique and veritable transcendence.*[7]

Edvard Munch's The
Shriek *(1895) is
sometimes associated
with the philosophy of
existentialism because of
the emphasis in that
philosophy on the
isolation and despair of
the individual.*

---

[7]Gabriel Marcel, *The Philosophy of Existentialism,* tr. Manya Harari (New York: Citadel Press, 1956), pp.
86–88.

THE CHALLENGE OF
DETERMINISM

Another difficulty for morality is posed by the *determinist*. In fact, some would say that determinism renders morality (as most of us understand the word) impossible. We saw in an earlier discussion (in Chapter 7) that determinism is the view that all things are causally conditioned such that they could not be otherwise. We also considered some of the problematical implications of this view, though we must now consider more adequately its implications for morality.

What are these implications? Well, if it is true that all things are causally determined, then this must apply also to our willing and choosing. And this means the *denial of free will*. And *this* means the *end of morality*. At least according to many. For is it not clear, they would insist, that morality *presupposes free will*? that *ought* implies *can*? What sense is there in praise and blame and talk of moral responsibility if one could not have done otherwise? if one does not choose and act *freely*? Is it not always relevant, when trying to establish blame or guilt or responsibility on the part of someone, to ascertain whether that person was forced, drugged, or suffering from some compulsion? Thus free will has seemed to many to be a condition for responsible, moral action.

Your decision between determinism, or the belief that everything, including your will, is causally determined, and indeterminism, the belief that some things, and therefore possibly the will, are not determined, may be a crucial one. And you cannot have it both ways. Either determinism or indeterminism.

But we must not move too fast here. Determinism itself must be viewed in two lights: *hard*-determinism and *soft*-determinism.

The hard-determinist believes not only that all things are determined, but that they are determined ultimately by purely *external* factors, factors outside yourself and over which you have no control. Why did you choose X? *Ultimately* because of things like the circumstances of your birth, upbringing, education, environment, genetic structure—in a word because of everything that has contributed in any way to the shaping and placing of your person and those of all of your ancestors. To say it another way, you chose X because ————: Fill in here the uncountable causes which, extending as it were from the infinite past, converge at this moment on the movement of your will in favor of X.

Is hard-determinism compatible with morality? According to the hard-deter-

**Determinism or
indeterminism?**

**Hard-determinism
. . .**

> ". . . it is certain that if there is no free will there can be no morality."
>
> —W. T. Stace

minists themselves, the answer is both Yes and No. On the yes-side, the hard-determinist, no less than anyone else, decries murder, theft, and the torturing of starving
children. The fact that people have no control over their actions, whether good or
evil, has no bearing on those actions being, nevertheless, good or evil. The desire
to torture starving children, like cancer, is an evil to be recognized as such and to
be dealt with—as you would deal with cancer. Now you do not punish a cancer;
you try to *treat* it and *heal* it. (Echoes of Skinner?) But this brings us to the no-side
of the answer. If morality implies the possibility of praise, blame, and punishment,
then the hard-determinist can scarcely accommodate morality. Certainly there is
little room for praise, blame, and punishment in a view of things according to
which no one is responsible for his or her condition in general, which means also
his or her moral condition in specific. One is not *responsible,* period.

... and morality

It is precisely to the issue of *responsibility* that *soft*-determinism speaks. The
soft-determinist is, of course, a determinist, and holds, like the hard-determinist,
that because of antecedent causes our choices could not be otherwise. But in contrast to the hard-determinist, the soft-determinist shifts our whole attention to the
causes which lie *within* the individual. Our actions and choices *are* determined—
by our desires, inclinations, attitudes, or, in a word, our *character.*

Soft-determinism

In this way, the soft-determinists see determinism not only as compatible with
morality but as *necessary* for morality. For, they say, your choices or actions can be

---

THE PROBLEM OF FREE WILL AND DETERMINISM

- *Determinism*

  The view that all things,
  including the will, are causally
  determined.

  (a) *hard-determinism*

  The will is determined ultimately
  by exterior factors beyond the
  responsibility of the individual.

  (b) *soft-determinism*

  The will is determined by the
  character of the individual, and
  thus the individuals are
  responsible for their choices.

- *Indeterminism*

  The view that some things, and
  therefore possibly the will, are
  free of causal determination.

. . . and morality

judged moral or immoral, or you can be held accountable for them, only if they actually reflect your intentions, desires, attitudes, and so on. Would you hold someone responsible for an action that did not really spring from his or her character? Would you hold me morally accountable for hitting you in the face if it was the result of a sudden and uncontrollable muscle spasm? If, however, my hitting you in the face was the result of (or was *caused by*) my attitude toward you and my intention to cause you pain, well, isn't that a quite different situation? a situation in which I am *responsible* for my action? a *moral* situation? How then can there be moral behavior and moral judgment without determinism—character-determinism or *self*-determinism, as the position is also called?

David Hume provides a good statement of how praise and blame are possible only if the deeds that are praised or blamed are rooted in, or *caused by*, the doer's character. From the *Enquiry Concerning Human Understanding*:

> *The only proper object of hatred or vengeance is a person or creature, endowed with thought and consciousness; and when any criminal or injurious actions excite that passion, it is only by their relation to the person, or connexion with him. Actions are, by their very nature, temporary and perishing; and where they proceed not from some cause in the character and disposition of the person who performed them, they can neither redound to his honour, if good; nor infamy, if evil. The actions themselves may be blameable; they may be contrary to all the rules of morality and religion: But the person is not answerable for them; and as they proceeded from nothing in him that is durable and constant, and leave nothing of that nature behind them, it is impossible he can, upon their account, become the object of punishment or vengeance. According to the principle, therefore, which denies necessity, and consequently causes, a man is as pure and untainted, after having committed the most horrid crime, as at the first moment of his birth, nor is his character anywise concerned in his actions, since they are not derived from it, and the wickedness of the one can never be used as a proof of the depravity of the other.*
>
> *Men are not blamed for such actions as they perform ignorantly and casually, whatever may be the consequences. Why? but because the principles of these actions are only momentary, and terminate in them alone. Men are less blamed for such actions as they perform hastily and unpremeditately than for such as proceed from deliberation. For what reason? but because a hasty temper, though a constant cause or principle in the mind, operates only by intervals, and infects not the whole character. Again, repentance wipes off every crime, if attended with a reformation of life and manners. How is this to be accounted for? but by asserting that actions render a person criminal merely as they are proofs of criminal principles in the mind; and when, by an alteration of these principles, they cease to be just proofs, they likewise cease to be criminal. But, except upon the doctrine of necessity, they never were just proofs, and consequently never were criminal.*
>
> *It will be equally easy to prove, and from the same arguments, that liberty . . . is also essential to morality, and that no human actions, where it is wanting, are*

susceptible of any moral qualities, or can be the objects either of approbation or dis-
like. For as actions are objects of our moral sentiment, so far only as they are indi-
cations of the internal character, passions, and affections; it is impossible that they
can give rise either to praise or blame, where they proceed not from these principles,
but are derived altogether from external violence.[8]

But the indeterminists, or free-willists, are still unsatisfied. They raise an obvious question: It may be that my choice or action is determined by my own character, but how did I acquire this character—these particular attitudes, inclinations, desires, likes, and dislikes? Is not my character ultimately determined, again, by factors outside me, antecedent to me, and quite beyond my control? Does not soft-determinism have to give way, finally, to hard-determinism with its denial of moral responsibility? As far as *responsibility* goes, is there really any final difference between soft- and hard-determinism? A clearer reduction of soft-determinism to hard-determinism could hardly be found than that of Baron D'Holbach (1723-1789), an atheistic and mechanistic materialist. In the following, from *The System of Nature*, Holbach applies his mechanistic principle specifically to the question of morality, and concludes that all of our moral dispositions, no less than anything else about us, reduce, finally, to necessary determinations.

Does soft-determinism reduce to hard-determinism?

The ambitious man *cries out: you will have me resist my passion; but have they not unceasingly repeated to me that rank, honours, power, are the most desirable advantages in life? Have I not seen my fellow citizens envy them, the nobles of my country sacrifice every thing to obtain them? In the society in which I live, am I not obliged to feel, that if I am deprived of these advantages, I must expect to languish in contempt; to cringe under the rod of oppression?*

The miser *says: you forbid me to love money, to seek after the means of acquiring it: alas! does not every thing tell me that, in this world, money is the greatest blessing; that it is amply sufficient to render me happy? In the country I inhabit, do I not see all my fellow citizens covetous of riches? but do I not also witness that they are little scrupulous in the means of obtaining wealth? As soon as they are enriched by the means which you censure, are they not cherished, considered and respected? By what authority, then, do you defend me from amassing treasure? What right have you to prevent my using means, which, although you call them sordid and criminal, I see approved by the sovereign? Will you have me renounce my happiness?*

The voluptuary *argues: you pretend that I should resist my desires; but was I the maker of my own temperament, which unceasingly invites me to pleasure? You call my pleasures disgraceful; but in the country in which I live, do I not witness the most dissipated men enjoying the most distinguished rank? Do I not behold that no one is ashamed of adultery but the husband it has outraged? Do not I see men making trophies of their debaucheries, boasting of their libertinism, rewarded with applause?*

[8]David Hume, *An Enquiry Concerning Human Understanding,* in *Hume's Enquiries,* ed. L. A. Selby-Bigge, 2d ed. (Oxford: Clarendon Press, 1902), pp. 98–99.

The choleric man vociferates: you advise me to put a curb on my passions, and to resist the desire of avenging myself: but can I conquer my nature? Can I alter the received opinions of the world? Shall I not be forever disgraced, infallibly dishonoured in society, if I do not wash out in the blood of my fellow creatures the injuries I have received?

The zealous enthusiast exclaims: you recommend me mildness; you advise me to be tolerant; to be indulgent to the opinions of my fellow men; but is not my temperament violent? Do I not ardently love my God? Do they not assure me, that zeal is pleasing to him; that sanguinary inhuman persecutors have been his friends? As I wish to render myself acceptable in his sight, I therefore adopt the same means.

In short, the actions of man are never free; they are always the necessary consequence of his temperament, of the received ideas, and of the notions, either true or false, which he has formed to himself of happiness; of his opinions, strengthened by example, by education, and by daily experience. . . .

If he understood the play of his organs, if he were able to recall to himself all the impulsions they have received, all the modifications they have undergone, all the effects they have produced, he would perceive that all his actions are submitted to that fatality, which regulates his own particular system, as it does the entire system of the universe: no one effect in him, any more than in nature, produces itself by chance; this, as has been before proved, is word void of sense. All that passes in him; all that is done by him; as well as all that happens in nature, or that is attributed to her, is derived from necessary causes, which act according to necessary laws, and which produce necessary effects, from whence necessarily flow others.

Fatality, is the eternal, the immutable, the necessary order, established in nature; or the indispensable connexion of causes that act, with the effects they operate.[9]

The indeterminist agrees with this but draws the opposite conclusion: not that there is no basis for praise, blame, responsibility, and virtuous conduct, but that determinism must be false! That is, the indeterminist can simply turn the tables: If someone says that since our wills are determined there can be no morality, the indeterminist may answer that inasmuch as morality is a fact our wills must *not* be determined! And, of course, the indeterminists have it in their favor that, as a

Morality as a fact of life

matter of fact, we *do*—all of us, always, and unavoidably—live our lives on the assumption that there *is* free will and that people are *responsible*. Thus, according to the indeterminists, the determinists are a little like the relativists, who, as we saw in the last section, might *claim* their position to be true, but cannot *live* as if it were true. In fact, determinists turn out so much to be free-willists that W. T. Stace has concluded that the determinism–free-will problem can hardly be a real problem at all; rather, it must simply involve a misunderstanding in our philosophical language:

[9]Baron D'Holbach, *The System of Nature*, tr. H. D. Robinson (Boston: Mendum, 1869), pp. 94–95, 102.

It is to be observed that those learned professors of philosophy or psychology who deny the existence of free will do so only in their professional moments and in their studies and lecture rooms. For when it comes to doing anything practical, even of the most trivial kind, they invariably behave as if they and others were free. They inquire from you at dinner whether you will choose this dish or that dish. They will ask a child why he told a lie, and will punish him for not having chosen the way of truthfulness. All of which is inconsistent with a disbelief in free will. This should cause us to suspect that the problem is not a real one; and this, I believe, is the case. The dispute is merely verbal, and is due to nothing but a confusion about the meanings of words. It is what is now fashionably called a semantic problem.[10]

It must be admitted, though, that the indeterminists are in an awkward spot too. They deny determinism as being incompatible with morality. But what do they replace it with? Actions and choices that are *uncaused*? But this would seem to make our actions and choices utterly spontaneous, capricious, irrational, and arbitrary. And certainly this is just as incompatible with morality and responsibility as is determinism. Something is beyond one's control, and therefore not an object of praise or blame, as much whether it happened by pure chance as whether it was completely necessitated. But what, then, lies in this mysterious zone between pure chance and pure necessity? What might the indeterminist or free-willist *mean* by "uncaused" choices or "free" will? Some indeterminists or free-willists would withdraw at this point with a quiet, "I really don't know. But there must be some such. For it is certainly a bigger problem to reject morality than not to have a clear and coherent idea of free will. Take your choice. *But do you really have one?*"

Others, of a somewhat more analytic strain, have sought for clarification of our terms. We have seen that the whole determinism–free-will controversy is bound up with talk about causality, the principle that every event must have a cause. But is an act of the will really an "act" in any obvious or clear sense? And is a decision really an "event"? It has been suggested, not without merit, that maybe the language in which the whole problem has been posed is inappropriate from the start. Has it been something like a Category Mistake again? In any event, William K. Frankena's exhortation is well-taken:

A need for clarification?

. . . I think that moral philosophers cannot insist too much on the importance of factual knowledge and conceptual clarity for the solution of moral and social problems. The two besetting sins in our prevailing habits of ethical thinking are our ready acquiescence in unclarity and our complacence in ignorance—the very sins that Socrates died combatting over two thousand years ago.[11]

[10]Stace, *Religion and the Modern Mind* (Philadelphia: Lippincott, 1952), pp. 279–280.
[10]William K. Frankena, *Ethics*, 2d ed. (Englewood Cliffs, N.J.: Prentice-Hall, 1973), p. 13.

Chapter 16 in Review

SUMMARY

In this chapter we have considered four basic questions which may be thought of as threatening or undermining the very idea of morality:

- Are moral claims meaningful propositions?
- Is morality purely relative?
- Do values originate in human experience?
- Are moral actions determined?

It has seemed to some that if the answer to any of these is Yes, then morality, at least in a more or less traditional sense, is rendered impossible from the very start.

Emotivism charges that moral statements turn out to hold no cognitive significance at all, that is, they are neither true nor false, and are therefore quite literally senseless. On the contrary, they are merely emotional expressions of approval or disapproval: "That is good" = "Ahhh!" Such a view has its roots in the philosophy known as logical positivism and, more specifically, the Verification Principle with its superempirical criterion of meaningfulness. Aside from the charge that the Verification Principle is self-refuting, some critics complain this whole approach commits us to a narrow and dogmatic conception of language. Others insist that it also would make nonsense of our practical lives, which are pervaded every day by the necessity of taking values seriously as having their own status, quite independently of our individual emotional responses.

This last point is a relevant objection also to the relativist's challenge: Values are purely relative, possessing no objective or absolute or *real* status beyond the individual's own notions. (Remember that "individual" may mean an individual person or an individual group.) The objectivist freely grants that, of course, our views or *opinions* about morality are largely relative (to circumstances of birth, upbringing, education, etc.), but that morality *itself* is the unconditioned reality that lies behind and makes ultimate sense of our moral quests and even our moral disputes.

Closely related but different is the challenge delivered by existentialism. Here we have looked specifically at the perspective of Jean-Paul Sartre. Sartre summarizes all existential philosophies as teaching that existence precedes essence. According to Sartre's own atheistic view, there is no value, meaning, or definition of humanity apart from that which human beings themselves inject into the picture. Here, "Man is the measure of all things," and it *matters* what we choose and what we thereby make of humanity. On the other hand, this is just what bothers the critics: How *can* it matter if there is no justification *outside us* for our acts and commitments?

Another threat is posed by the determinist, who says that since everything is predetermined, so are our own moral choices and decisions. The soft-determinist seeks to soften this blow with the explanation that our choices are determined, but by our own character, and that that is exactly why we are responsible for them. It is important to ask whether this does not lead right back to hard-determinism, inasmuch as our character has been shaped largely beyond our own control (or has it?). In any event, the free-willist is often fond of turning the whole challenge on its head: Since morality is a nonnegotiable fact of our experience, and since it is unintelligible apart from free will, the will must be (in whatever obscure way) free.

It *is* interesting, isn't it, that while none of these challenges is particularly new, the actual give-and-take world of morality goes right on as if nothing happened? Does morality ever actually succumb to any of these (largely theoretical) challenges?

BASIC IDEAS

- Cognitive meaning/existential meaning
- The Verification Principle
- Emotivism
- Problems with the Verification Principle
- Emotivism as impractical
- Relativism or subjectivism
- Absolutism or objectivism
- Cultural relativism
- Relativism as self-refuting
- Relativism as impractical
- Sartre: Existentialism
    Existence precedes essence
    Subjectivity
    Freedom as the basis of values
- Marcel's critique of Sartre
- Determinism
- Hard-determinism
- Soft-determinism (self-determinism)
- Indeterminism
- The obscurity of "free will"
- Determinism as impractical

TEST YOURSELF

1. True or false: The Verification Principle is associated with Jean-Paul Sartre.
2. What is the big argument for ethical relativism?
3. What is Socrates' refutation, in the *Theaetetus*, of Protagoras' principle, "a man is the measure of all things"?
4. What did David Hume contribute to the discussion of free will vs. determinism?
5. Characterize the general philosophical outlook of A. J. Ayer.

6. Recalling the discussion of B. F. Skinner in Chapter 7, is the following true or false? Hard-behaviorists are also hard-determinists.

7. Gabriel Marcel was (a) a modern proponent of ethical relativism, (b) a critic of Sartre's idea of freedom, (c) an emotivist, (d) a critic of determinism.

8. Why is determinism a challenge to traditional morality?

9. In Chapter 8, the idea of a "self-refuting" proposition was introduced. How has this now been applied to relativism? to emotivism?

10. What is the meaning of Sartre's statement that "man is condemned to be free"?

QUESTIONS FOR REFLECTION

- In the section on logical positivism a piece was quoted from Blanshard's article "The New Subjectivism in Ethics." In light of this whole chapter, do you think it is correct to represent emotivism as "subjectivism"? If not, what is the big difference between emotivism and true subjectivism (or relativism)? And why is Sartre's doctrine of freedom as the baseless basis of value not strictly subjectivism?

- Do you believe that the determinist's challenge to traditional morality is successful? If so, your problem is to give a coherent account of morality that can accommodate at the same time the denial of free will. If you don't think the challenge is successful, your problem is to give a coherent account of free will itself: It's easy to say what it isn't, but what *is* it? Is it necessary, for the sake of morality, simply to postulate an unknown something? Would that be so bad?

- Can you give a good account of the difference between Sartre's idea of freedom and the idea of freedom involved in the debate between free will and determinism?

CHAPTER 17

HEDONISM

If, in spite of the countercriticisms, you find that any of the foregoing challenges to morality is successful, then you will have to face up to the question whether there can be any genuine, or at least traditional, morality at all. On the other hand, if you believe, say, that moral language is meaningful, that moral truths have an objective basis, and that individuals are morally responsible, then we had best get on with the task of considering the various and sometimes radically different views of morality.

THE QUESTION OF CONSEQUENCES

That theories of morality may go in very different directions becomes apparent when we raise the question: Do the consequences of our actions matter? Obviously, they matter in *some* sense. When you vote, pull the trigger of a gun, feed the starving, bail out of an airplane, study for an exam, or perform an infinite number of other actions, the action is done *for the sake of something*. But do the consequences of our actions matter *morally*? That is, can our actions be judged moral or immoral on the basis of their consequences?

Do consequences matter?

It will seem to many of you that the answer is obviously Yes. And a great many philosophers will agree with you. This type of ethical theory is called a *teleological* theory. We saw in an earlier chapter that teleology is the belief in purposes, ends, or goals in the universe. As you might guess, then, a teleological theory of morality is one which stresses the consequences of actions, and even makes the

Teleological and deontological theories of morality

379

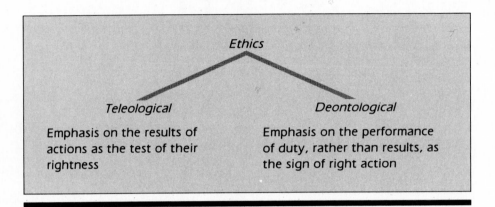

consequences of actions the criterion, or test, of their rightness. An action is judged right or wrong, moral or immoral, depending on what happens as a result of it, its "payoff." Quite different from this type of ethical theory—in fact, directly opposed to it—is the *deontological* type. An important clue as to what this means lies in the Greek word from which it comes: *deō*, "to bind." On the deontological view, the will is bound to *duty*. That is, what makes an action right or wrong is the actor's conformity to his or her duty. And what the actor's duty is has nothing at all to do with what might or might not happen as a result of the action.

Later, in Chapter 19, we will consider the most influential deontological theory of morality. But first we will look at the two most important teleological theories: hedonism and utilitarianism.

HEDONISM: THE PLEASURE PRINCIPLE

Actually, hedonism and utilitarianism are very closely related. In fact, they could be represented as but two versions of the same basic philosophy. We will see how this is so when we come to utilitarianism in the next chapter. For now it is best to treat them separately. Certainly they are two of the most popular and interesting perspectives on morality. What, then, is *hedonism*?

Hedonism (from the Greek word *hedonē*, "pleasure") is a general ethical theory which views pleasure as the good—not *a* good, or *part* of the good, but *the* good. According to the hedonistic Pleasure Principle, pleasure is thus the criterion or standard or "payoff" of right action. That is, an action is to be valued—or not—in light of the amount and/or kind of pleasure that results from it, and in light of that alone. But the reference to "the amount and/or kind of pleasure" should alert us to the fact that there are different forms of hedonism, corresponding to different

The Pleasure Principle

conceptions of pleasure. Certainly it would be a mistake to think that pleasure must mean the baser and crude pleasures. If it helps, you might substitute the word "happiness," or even the idea of the satisfaction of needs, for "pleasure," and speak of the Happiness Principle or the Satisfaction Principle instead.

Hedonism has descended to us in primarily two forms: egoistic hedonism and social hedonism. As forms of hedonism, each of these advocates pleasure as the good. But *whose* pleasure? They answer this question in quite different ways.

HEDONISM

The ethical doctrine that pleasure is the highest good, and the production of pleasure is the criterion of right action.

EGOISTIC HEDONISM

What does it mean—egoistic hedonism? We already know what hedonism is, but what is *egoism?* "Egoism" comes from the Greek word *ego,* "I," and is therefore, literally, "I-ism." Any form of egoism thus makes the *self* the central concern, the beginning and end of all considerations. *Psychological egoism* is a doctrine about human nature, claiming that everyone by nature pursues primarily his or her own interests. *Ethical egoism* involves a *value* judgment, claiming that everyone *ought* to pursue primarily his or her own interests. Whatever one may make of psychological egoism, if a person accepts at least the claim of ethical egoism *and* is a hedonist, the result is *egoistic hedonism,* the doctrine that each individual should pursue primarily his or her own pleasure: Egoism + hedonism = egoistic hedonism.

Egoism

Egoistic hedonism

It is sometimes observed that egoistic hedonism is perhaps the most widely practiced moral philosophy. Certainly it is a very old one. In fact, the two best examples of it occur already (by now this should come as no surprise) in ancient Greek philosophy: Cyrenaicism and Epicureanism.

Cyrenaicism is so-called because Cyrene is where Aristippus (about 400 B.C.) came from, and Aristippus was the founder of this school. He was influenced by Protagoras (notice how often this name appears) and extended the idea that our subjective sensations are the basis of our knowledge (if "knowledge" is the right word) to the idea that they are also the basis of our *conduct:* We should act in such a way as to maximize our own pleasurable sensations. We saw above that it would be a mistake always to equate hedonism with the pursuit of the lower pleasures. But Cyrenaicism *was,* in fact, most interested in the lower pleasures! The point is

Cyrenaicism: Eat, drink, and be merry

to enjoy as much *bodily* pleasure as possible, and as *immediately* as possible: Double your pleasure, double your fun, and eat, drink, and be merry, for tomorrow we may die. On the other hand, some prudent *calculation* is called for, we may *not* die tomorrow, or even for a long time, and thus we must judge whether to forgo a particular pleasure at one point in order to gain a more exquisite one later.

EGOISTIC HEDONISM

The doctrine that the pursuit and production of one's own pleasure is the highest good and the criterion of right action.

The ancient biographer Diogenes Laertius provides a nice summary of the Cyrenaics' teachings:

> Those . . . who adhered to the teaching of Aristippus and were known as Cyrenaics held the following opinions. They laid down that there are two states, pleasure and pain. . . . The one state is agreeable and the other repellent to all living things.
> . . . That pleasure is the end is proved by the fact that from our youth up we are instinctively attracted to it, and, when we obtain it, seek for nothing more, and shun nothing so much as its opposite, pain. Pleasure is good even if it proceed from the most unseemly conduct. . . . The removal of pain, however, which is put forward in Epicurus, seems to them not to be pleasure at all, any more than the absence of pleasure is pain. For both pleasure and pain they hold to consist in motion, whereas absence of pleasure like absence of pain is not motion, since painlessness is the condition of one who is, as it were, asleep. . . . [T]hey insist that bodily pleasures are far better than mental pleasures, and bodily pains far worse than mental pains, and that this is the reason why offenders are punished with the former. For they assumed pain to be more repellent, pleasure more congenial. For these reasons they paid more attention to the body than to the mind. Hence, although pleasure is in itself desirable, yet they hold that the things which are productive of certain pleasures are often of a painful nature, the very opposite of pleasure; so that to accumulate the pleasures which are productive of happiness appears to them a most irksome business.[1]

Another, and more important, form of hedonism is *Epicureanism*, named after its founder, Epicurus (300 B.C.). That Epicureanism has often been represented

---

[1]Diogenes Laertius, *Lives of Eminent Philosophers*, II, 86–90, tr. R. D. Hicks (Cambridge, Mass.: Harvard University Press, 1925), I.

THE SALE OF A CYRENAIC

In his *Sale of the Philosophers* (about A.D. 175) Lucian pokes fun at some Greek philosophers under the guise of having them put up for sale at an auction. In the following passage[1] a Cyrenaic—a philosopher who advocates the life of sensual pleasure—is up for sale.

Zeus: Call another one. The Cyrenaic—that one with the purple robe and the wreath on his head.

Hermes: Attention please, gentlemen! This lot's expensive—cost you real money. A sweet specimen going! An ecstatic specimen! Who's eager for a soft life? Any bids for a hedonist?

Buyer: Here, you, come and tell me what you can do. I'll buy you if you're any use.

Hermes: Don't bother him with questions, sir; he's drunk. He can't answer anyway—his tongue's lost its foothold, as you can see.

Buyer: Who in his right sense would buy such a moral wreck? What a wanton wretch! What a smell of scent off him, too! Can't walk without staggering and falling over! Hermes, you tell me what he's like. What's his specialty?

Hermes: Well, briefly, he's good company, he can put away his share of liquor, he's very good for a spree with a flute girl—just the thing for a dissolute, lascivious master. And then he's a connoisseur of cakes and a highly experienced cook; a real expert in easy living. He was educated at Athens and also served tyrants in Sicily; they thought the world of him. His doctrine, in a nutshell, is to despise everything, make use of everything, and draw pleasure from everywhere.

Buyer: You'd better look for somebody else—somebody with plenty of money. I'm not up to buying a gay character.

Hermes: Looks as if we've got this one on our hands, Zeus. Can't sell him.

Zeus: Put him on one side and bring on another.

[1] Lucian, *Sale of the Philosophers,* in *Selected Works,* tr. Bryan P. Reardon (Indianapolis: Bobbs-Merrill, 1965), p. 100.

sented along with Cyrenaicism as a "pig" philosophy, is clear from the Roman poet Horace:

> Amid hopes and cares, amid fears and passions, believe that every day that has dawned is your last. Welcome will come to you another hour unhoped for. As for me, when you want a laugh, you will find me in fine fettle, fat and sleek, a hog from Epicurus' herd.[2]

But this is a mistake. Although Epicureanism was certainly also an egoistic hedonism, it differed in important respects from Cyrenaicism.

Epicurus was influenced by the materialistic and atomistic theories of the Pre-Socratic philosophers Leucippus and Democritus. What is reality? An infinite number of indivisible units bouncing off one another and clustering at random. The gods exist, but are indifferent to us, and the soul, made out of atoms like everything else, disintegrates and disperses at death. So, what should we do? Live as pleasant a life as possible. But, as is apparent from the quotation below, the pleasant life meant for the Epicureans something quite different from what it meant for the Cyrenaics. Not so much the presence of positive pleasurable states as the absence of pain,[3] especially mental pain in the form of anguish and fear. And as far as positive pleasures go, not the pleasures of the body but the pleasures of the mind. And not the accumulation of immediate pleasures so much as a lifetime of moderate pleasures. Health of body and peace of mind—this is the Epicurean idea of the life of pleasure.

Not surprisingly, the Epicureans summed up their ideal in the word *ataraxia*, which means "tranquility" or "serenity." It is also not surprising that they advocated the *simple* life. They were repelled by the disquieting entanglements of sexual involvements, the burdens of marriage and family life, and the responsibilities of public or political life. Friendships, on the other hand, were a much-sought-after pleasure, as were the intellectual delights of philosophizing. It should be stressed, though, that the Epicureans, no less than the Cyrenaics, believed in calculating and comparing pleasures and pains—always in the interest of accumulating as much pleasure as possible. Going to the dentist may be a pain, but in the long run it's worth it, for it means a freedom from toothache over an even longer period. It is not haphazard and unrestrained sensual indulgence that will add up to a life of genuine pleasure or serenity, but freedom from bodily and mental pain and an attention to the elevated and refined pleasures, especially those of the mind. It is not a drunken orgy but a Bach cantata that will, in the long run, contribute most to the pleasant life.

Epicureanism: Not drinking bouts but Bach.

[2]Horace, *Epistles*, IV, 12–16, in *Satires, Epistles, and Ars Poetica*, tr. H. Rushton Fairclough (Cambridge, Mass.: Harvard University Press), 1955.

[3]Some of the Cyrenaics, too, stressed pleasure as the freedom from pain. For example, Hegesius' lectures on freedom from pain and trouble had to be discontinued because they resulted in so many suicides among his hearers.

CYRENAICS AND EPICUREANS

- *Agreements:* Both are hedonistic, both are egoistic, and both believe in the "calculation" of pleasures and pains.
- *Disagreements:* The Cyrenaics emphasized positive pleasures, bodily pleasures, and (as much as possible) immediate pleasures. The Epicureans emphasized negative pleasures (or the absence of pain), mental pleasures, and sustained (though more moderate) pleasures over a long period of time.

As always, it is best to let the philosophers speak for themselves. From Epicurus' *Letter to Menoeceus:*

We must consider that of desires some are natural, others vain, and of the natural some are necessary and others merely natural; and of the necessary some are necessary for happiness, others for the repose of the body, and others for very life. The right understanding of these facts enables us to refer all choice and avoidance to the health of the body and (the soul's) freedom from disturbance, since this is the aim of the life of blessedness. For it is to obtain this end that we always act, namely, to avoid pain and fear. And when this is once secured for us, all the tempest of the soul is dispersed, since the living creature has not to wander as though in search of something that is missing, and to look for some other thing by which he can fulfil the good of the soul and the good of the body. For it is then that we have need of pleasure, when we feel pain owing to the absence of pleasure; (but when we do not feel pain), we no longer need pleasure. And for this cause we call pleasure the beginning and end of the blessed life. For we recognize pleasure as the first good innate in us, and from pleasure we begin every act of choice and avoidance, and to pleasure we return again, using the feeling as the standard by which we judge every good.

And since pleasure is the first good and natural to us, for this very reason we do not choose every pleasure, but sometimes we pass over many pleasures, when greater discomfort accrues to us as the result of them: and similarly we think many pains better than pleasures, since a greater pleasure comes to us when we have endured pains for a long time. Every pleasure then because of its natural kinship to us is good, yet not every pleasure is to be chosen: even as every pain also is an evil, yet not all are always of a nature to be avoided. Yet by a scale of comparison and by the consideration of advantages and disadvantages we must form our judgement on all these matters. For the good on certain occasions we treat as bad, and conversely the bad as good.

And again independence of desire we think a great good—not that we may at all times enjoy but a few things, but that, if we do not possess many, we may enjoy the few in the genuine persuasion that those have the sweetest pleasure in luxury who least need it, and that all that is natural is easy to be obtained, but that which is superfluous is hard. And so plain savours bring us a pleasure equal to a luxurious diet, when all the pain due to want is removed; and bread and water produce the highest pleasure, when one who needs them puts them to his lips. To grow accustomed therefore to simple and not luxurious diet gives us health to the full, and makes a man alert for the needful employments of life, and when after long intervals we approach luxuries disposes us better towards them, and fits us to be fearless of fortune.

When, therefore, we maintain that pleasure is the end, we do not mean the pleasures of profligates and those that consist in sensuality, as is supposed by some who are either ignorant or disagree with us or do not understand, but freedom from pain in the body and from trouble in the mind. For it is not continuous drinkings and revellings, nor the satisfaction of lusts, nor the enjoyment of fish and other luxuries of the wealthy table, which produce a pleasant life, but sober reasoning, searching out the motives for all choice and avoidance, and banishing mere opinions, to which are due the greatest disturbance of the spirit.[4]

Perennial philosophies?

Labels like "Cyrenaicism" and "Epicureanism" suggest philosophies out of the dim, dark past—as indeed they are. But we must not be misled by the labels or even the outdated ideas that these philosophies might involve. The central ideas are *perennial*; that is, they occur over and over again throughout the history of thought, and also *today*. Do you know any modern-day Cyrenaics or Epicureans? Any egoistic hedonists? Do these ideas have anything at all to do with your own conduct? *Anything?*

DOES "IS" MEAN "OUGHT"?

Any form of hedonism (including utilitarianism, which we will consider next) immediately falls prey to a famous criticism. It is frequently posed in the form of a question: Can an *ought* be derived from an *is*?

Naturalistic ethics

From the foregoing pages it should be clear that any hedonism is a *naturalistic* ethic. That is, it is an ethic which justifies its fundamental principle by an appeal to *nature*, or to the *way things are*. In the case of hedonism, it is an appeal to *human* nature, and more specifically to the natural human desire for *pleasure*. Do you recall the reasoning attributed to Aristippus?

[4]Epicurus, *Letter to Menoeceus*, in *Epicurus: The Extant Remains*, tr. Cyril Bailey (Oxford: Clarendon Press, 1926), pp. 87–88.

Epicurus, perhaps the most famous of hedonists

That pleasure is the end is proved by the fact that from our youth up we are instinctively attracted to it, and, when we obtain it, seek for nothing more, and shun nothing so much as its opposite, pain.

Clearly, such philosophers have attempted to derive an *ought* from an *is*. That is, they have concluded from the fact that people do act in a certain way or desire something, or from the fact that the act or desire is *natural,* that this act or desire is *right* and *good.* Others, most notably the late English philosopher G. E. Moore in his important work *Principia Ethica,* have charged that the attempt to move from an *is* to an *ought* is unjustified, involving as it does a confusion. Moore called this confusion the *Naturalistic Fallacy.* Stated otherwise, it is the mistake of equating a *factual* judgment with a *value* judgment. Think about this distinction until you get it. Do you think it's an important distinction? A *necessary* distinction? But more on this later.

The Naturalistic Fallacy

For now, consider yet further implications of the reduction of *ought* to *is,* or, stated in its crudest form, "let your glands be your guide." First, depending on how far you push the equation *ought = is,* it would seem to justify the most heinous and bizarre acts. Is not the desire to torture starving children perfectly *natural* to

Some implications of *ought-is*

the sadist or pervert? But, you say, you wouldn't push the principle that far! But why not? Is there some *nonnatural* ingredient in your idea of "good"? Second, if *ought = is*, is it even *meaningful* to talk about things like perversion? Some would charge that the equation *ought = is* turns all morality-talk into nonsense. Does not morality-talk, including talk about things like perversion, depend for its life on the concept of *ideals*? But can there be ideals if what *is* is what *ought* to be? What *is* an ideal, anyway? Is it not something striven for? Something difficult? Something that challenges and purifies our baser interests? Something not entirely attainable? But then it is something different from what *is*.

FACTUAL JUDGMENTS AND VALUE JUDGMENTS

- A *factual judgment* is a judgment which describes some empirical state of affairs. Examples: "In fourteen-hundred-and-ninety-two Columbus sailed the ocean blue," "Water freezes at 32 degrees Fahrenheit," and "Everyone seeks pleasure."
- A *value judgment* is a judgment which evaluates something or judges its worth. Examples: "Two heads are better than one," "Honesty is the best policy," and "Pleasure is the highest good."

EGOISM OR ALTRUISM?

The criticisms we have just raised apply, of course, to any form of naturalistic ethics and therefore to any form of hedonism. But consider now what is surely the biggest problem posed specifically by *egoistic* hedonism, which is the form of hedonism we have actually discussed in this chapter. The problem is both obvious and simple. It is the problem of *egoism*. More specifically, it is the problem of *ethical* egoism.

We saw that ethical egoism, the doctrine that each individual ought to seek primarily his or her own good, is the basis of egoistic hedonism. To reject ethical egoism, therefore, is to reject egoistic hedonism as well. In fact, for most readers ethical egoism will stand in immediate conflict with the ideal of *altruism,* the principle that we ought as much as possible to seek the good of *others*. The following

Altruism

questions immediately suggest themselves: Is not the altruistic ideal as ingrained in us as our most selfish inclinations? And even if not, can we so easily discard it in favor of ethical egoism? And even if we could, could we feel good about it? And even if we could, *should* we feel good about it?

ALTRUISM

The belief that everyone ought as much as possible to seek the good of others.

The principles of altruism are deeply embedded in our Western moral consciousness: "You are your brother's keeper," "You shall love your neighbor as yourself," and (the Golden Rule) "Do unto others as you would have others do unto you." Though essential to the Judeo-Christian ethic, such principles are, in one form or another, inscribed on the consciences of virtually all the people in the world. But ethical egoism attempts to turn upside-down this universal estimation of self*lessness*. It asks us to believe that Jesus, Socrates, St. Francis, and all others who have devoted their lives, and even given their lives, for the benefit of others were either stupid, hypocrites, or fools. Any moral philosophy which contradicts so radically the universal sentiment about *un*selfish action must surely fail to persuade most.

Nonetheless, the psychological egoist would claim that altruism is a hopeless ideal inasmuch as all actions are inevitably motivated by self-interest or ego satisfaction. But are they? What do you think of Hume's assertion?

> *. . . there is some benevolence, however small, . . . some particle of the dove kneaded into our frame, along with the elements of the wolf and serpent.*[5]

More important, is there not a difference—a big difference—between saying that an act is *motivated* out of self-interest and that it is *attended* by self-interest? One may derive self-satisfaction, and rightfully so, from rescuing a drowning child from an icy river. But should we not distinguish this self-gratifying aspect of the act from the *motivation* of the act? And even if psychological egoism were true, how do we make the move to *ethical* egoism? (Back to the Naturalistic Fallacy.) How do we move from the observation that we *are* selfish (a *psychological* claim) to the conclusion that we *should* be selfish (a *moral* claim)? On the other hand, it should be noted that even altruism need not exclude a proper and healthy concern for the self: "You shall love your neighbor as *yourself*."

Then, too, it may be asked whether it is even possible to be a consistent egoistic hedonist. What happens when one egoistic hedonist's pursuit of pleasure deprives another of his? Should, then, all egoistic hedonists agree to act so as to

Is psychological egoism true?

---

[5]David Hume, *An Enquiry Concerning the Principles of Morals,* in *Hume's Enquiries,* ed. L. A. Selby-Bigge, 2d ed. (Oxford: Clarendon Press, 1902), p. 271.

**Can one be a
consistent egoistic
hedonist?**

ensure the pleasure of all? But then they are no longer *egoistic* hedonists, since their concern is now for the *common* good. Can you see any way an egoistic hedonist can practice the Pleasure Principle consistently?

In any event, as far as the debate between egoistic hedonism and altruism goes, the whole scene changes as we come to the second form of hedonism, social hedonism or utilitarianism.

How might an egoistic hedonist reason about the rightness or wrongness of

- capital punishment?
- abortion?
- war?
- minority rights?
- euthanasia?

Chapter 17 in Review

SUMMARY

One major way of distinguishing between moral philosophies is to raise the question of consequences. Hedonism certainly does relate the rightness of an action to its intended consequences or results. That makes it a teleological moral philosophy. Further, it identifies the sought-after results as pleasure. That makes it a hedonistic moral philosophy.

But whose pleasure? Egoistic hedonism asserts that the sought-for pleasure is one's own. And what sort of pleasure? Here an important distinction is introduced. Some egoistic hedonists aim at the greatest amount of the most intense pleasure in the shortest time. This form of egoistic hedonism is best represented in Cyrenaicism. A more influential strain of egoistic hedonism has, with greater prudence and calculation, sought both freedom from pain and pleasures of a higher quality (say, intellectual delights), which in the long run produce the greatest ease and satisfaction. This form of egoistic hedonism is best represented in Epicureanism.

Any hedonism is a naturalistic philosophy, justifying its central claim by an appeal to nature—the naturalness of the pursuit of pleasure. Not surprisingly such a philosophy runs afoul of the ought/is distinction, which many hold to be crucial to authentic morality: Is morality, or what *ought* to be, derivable from nature, or what *is*? Any egoistic hedonism also runs afoul of our altruistic ideals and instincts, and must bear, as well, the burden of psychological egoism (on which it rests), which teaches, perhaps not so successfully, that all actions are motivated out of self-interest.

TEST YOURSELF

1. Teleological ethics puts the emphasis on the _____ of actions.
2. Egoism + Hedonism = ?
3. What is involved in the confusion of factual judgments with value judgments?
4. True or false: Both Cyrenaicism and Epicureanism stress the immediate acquisition of physical pleasure.
5. What is the hedonists' favorite evidence that we ought to seek pleasure above all else?
6. What is a possible answer to the psychological egoist's charge that altruism is impossible because everything we do is motivated by self-interest?
7. The Naturalistic Fallacy (a) concerns the distinction between *ought* and *is*, (b) is a *formal* fallacy, (c) was levelled by Epicurus against Aristippus.

QUESTIONS FOR REFLECTION

- An egoistic hedonist such as Epicurus distinguishes "higher" and "lower" pleasures. Might this terminology be misleading? Are the higher pleasures better merely because they produce more pleasure in the long run? Is the pursuer of lower pleasures immoral or just imprudent?
- Do you get the difference between an act being motivated out of egoistic interest and being accompanied by self-gratification? Does it make you feel better about not being able to discover an act that is not in some way related to self-interest? On the other hand, are there any legitimate limits to the altruistic ideal itself? What about Jesus' exhortation to "sell what you have and give to the poor"?
- What about the idea of justifying acts on the basis of their pleasurable consequences? Aren't some acts morally right irrespective of the pleasure or pain they produce?

CHAPTER 18

UTILITARIANISM

In the last chapter it was said that egoistic hedonism is surely one of the most widely practiced moral philosophies. Certainly a similar claim can be made for *social* hedonism, or *utilitarianism*, with the added claim that it is an eminently common-sensical philosophy. What is more natural, when confronted with a moral dilemma, than to ask something like: "What should I do to bring about the most happiness to the most people?" Whenever this has been your criterion of behavior, you have been a practicing utilitarian.

The actual application of the utilitarian criterion is, however, often a difficult and sometimes a dramatic affair. A true scene:

> He saw a lifeboat sitting about three hundred yards off. It was a small craft, manned by half a dozen sailors. They were scanning the ship carefully.
>
> "Help!" Hudson cried out. "Help me. Over here."
>
> A flashlight winked. Its beam played along the stern of the Andrea Doria. Guided by Hudson's screams, the light focused on the desperate sailor clinging to the net.
>
> "Help me!" Hudson yelled again. "Quickly. Hurry."
>
> Hudson waited for the men to clasp their oars. He fought against the swift current, energized now by the sight of his rescuers.
>
> But the lifeboat did not move.
>
> "Help!" Hudson called once more. "Hurry. Please!"
>
> Still the lifeboat lay quietly in the water. The flashlight again blinked in Hudson's eyes. They saw him. They heard him. Why would they not come? My God! Hudson realized, the ship is going down ... now! In his merchant marine training

Hudson had been taught that a lifeboat must sit off at least three hundred yards to avoid being pulled under by a sinking ship. That was where the lifeboat lay. . . .

He lay silent for a time, riding the swells, waiting for the end. An orange globe of sun rose behind him, the fresh beginning of the day mocking the tragedy it revealed. The Andrea Doria lay more horizontal than vertical. Deck chairs, suitcases, random bits of clothing, and splintered wood swayed in the waves. Hudson climbed one notch higher on the net as it slowly sank lower into the sea.

His will returned. "Help!" he screamed. "Please come get me. You can't let me die."

He could see the men watching him from the lifeboat. But they did not reach for their oars.

The desperate man resorted to cursing once more. Then he prayed, not to God but to the men in the lifeboat. He cried. He begged.[1]

It's a simple problem: Should the lives of several be jeopardized in order possibly to save one more? Is it *really* a simple problem?

WHAT IS UTILITARIANISM?

We can get at the real nature of utilitarianism in three stages. *First*, at the heart of utilitarianism lies the *Principle of Utility*. The word "utility" simply means "usefulness," but the utilitarians employ it to mean that which promotes the greatest balance of good over evil. Thus utilitarianism is:

The Principle of Utility

1. The doctrine that we ought to act so as to promote the greatest balance of good over evil

But there must be more, for we have not yet been told what the good *is*. In fact, *second*, utilitarianism has always gone hand in hand with hedonism, which, as we have seen, certainly does specify the nature of the good—it is *pleasure*. Thus, utilitarianism is:

Utilitarianism as hedonism

2. The doctrine that we ought to act so as to promote the greatest balance of pleasure over pain

But there is more, for we have not yet been told *whose* pleasure is to be maximized. In fact, *third*, utilitarianism (as the word is usually used) has always gone hand in hand specifically with *social* hedonism, and indeed may be regarded as identical with social hedonism. But here we must slow down a bit.

Utilitarianism as social hedonism

[1]William Hoffer, *Saved! The Story of the "Andrea Doria"—The Greatest Sea Rescue in History* (New York: Summit Books, 1979), pp. 180–182.

> Hedonism + Benevolence Principle = social hedonism or utilitarianism

As we pass from egoistic hedonism in the last chapter to social hedonism or utilitarianism in this chapter, it is important to note right away what they have in common and where they differ.

Like egoistic hedonism, social hedonism or utilitarianism holds to a *teleological* conception of right action: It judges the rightness of an action by its *consequences*. And, like egoistic hedonism, social hedonism or utilitarianism is, of course, hedonistic in its conception of right action: It judges the rightness of an action by its production of *pleasurable* consequences. But the two views differ at a critical point. Whereas the egoistic hedonist is motivated out of *self*-interest and aims at *self*-satisfaction, the social hedonist or utilitarian is motivated out of an interest for the greatest possible number of persons and aims at *their* satisfaction. In place of the egoism of egoistic hedonism, social hedonism or utilitarianism substitutes the *Benevolence Principle*: Happiness is to be distributed as widely and as equally as pos-possible among all people. Thus, utilitarianism is, finally,

The Benevolence Principle

3. The doctrine that we ought to act so as to promote the greatest happiness for the greatest number

> ## UTILITARIANISM (OR SOCIAL HEDONISM)
>
> **The ethical doctrine that an action is right if, and only if, it promotes the greatest happiness for the greatest number of people.**

Utilitarianism: A political and philosophical view

Utilitariansim is, obviously, a political perspective as well as a philosophical one. As a democratic point of view it has often been, over the years, the basis of legislative and judicial advances, social reforms, welfare movements, and egalitarian ideals. Not surprisingly, then, the most famous of the utilitarian philosophers have also usually been deeply involved in social and political issues—on the liberal side, naturally.

BENTHAM'S VERSION:
QUANTITY OVER QUALITY

Historically, social hedonism or social utilitarianism is identified with the English philosophers Jeremy Bentham and John Stuart Mill. (We realize that we are dealing here with remarkable men when we learn that Bentham was studying Latin when he was 8, and Mill was studying Greek at 3!) These two thinkers, however, represent two different forms of utilitarianism, though the difference reduces more to a matter of emphasis: in the one case an emphasis on *quantity* of happiness, and in the other an emphasis on *quality* of happiness.

The founder of modern utilitarianism was Jeremy Bentham (1748–1832).

For Bentham, the process of making moral decisions is really quite simple. All you do is this. First, consider the various courses of action open to you; then, taking into account all the persons affected, and counting yourself as only one of them, calculate the pleasures and pains involved; then, choose that course of action which will result in the greatest balance of pleasure over pain.

As already indicated, when Bentham presses for the greatest balance of pleasure over pain, his idea of pleasure is a purely quantitative one. The *greatest* pleasure for the greatest number means for Bentham the *most* pleasure. That Bentham's really is a purely quantitative notion of pleasure is apparent from his well-known statement that

The greatest means the most

Jeremy Bentham, a utilitarian philosopher who stressed the quantity over the quality of happiness

Prejudice apart, the game of push-pin is of equal value with the arts and sciences of music and poetry. If the game of push-pin furnish more pleasure, it is more valuable than either.[2]

The hedonic calculus

How do we determine the *most* pleasure? We spoke earlier of calculating pleasures and pains. Though this idea goes back, as we saw, to the Cyrenaics and Epicureans, it was formulated most explicitly in Bentham's idea of a *hedonic calculus*. According to Bentham, in attempting to calculate a pleasure we must, as it were, measure or weigh it in seven ways, taking into account its

1. *intensity*, or how strong it is
2. *duration*, how long it will last
3. *certainty*, how likely it is to occur
4. *propinquity*, how near at hand it is
5. *fecundity*, its ability to produce still further pleasures
6. *purity*, its freedom from ensuing pains
7. *extent*, the number of people affected by it

Bentham suggested the following verse as a prod to "lodging more effectively, in the memory, these points, on which the whole fabric of morals and legislation may be seen to rest":

Intense, long, certain, speedy, fruitful, pure—
Such marks in pleasures and in pains endure.
Such pleasures seek, if private be thy end:
If it be public, wide let them extend.
Such pains avoid, whichever be thy view:
If pains must come, let them extend to few.[3]

By applying these seven criteria—someone has likened them to a moral thermometer—we ought to be able to grind out, like a machine, what course of action would deliver the most pleasure. Bentham himself speaks of "summing up all the values of all the pleasures." Not that we always would, could, or should indulge in this kind of precise hedonistic arithmetic. On the other hand, do not all of us in fact employ some such method, however roughly, every time we consider and weigh the pleasurable and painful consequences of a projected act?

Bentham's Four Sanctions

A further note: Bentham realized that there is a difference between *knowing* what we ought to do and *doing* it. This is especially true in those situations where the happiness of others means self-sacrifice and pain for *you*. (To use our earlier

---

[2]Jeremy Bentham, *The Rationale of Reward*, in *The Works of Jeremy Bentham* (Edinburgh: Tait, 1838–43), II, i, 253.

[3]Jeremy Bentham, *An Introduction to the Principles of Morals and Legislation*, ed. J. H. Burns and H. L. A. Hart (London: Athlone, 1970), p. 38.

terms, Bentham was a psychological egoist, though not an ethical egoist.) Here Bentham's doctrine of the *Four Sanctions* is relevant: nature, law, opinion, and God. By "sanctions" Bentham means something like binding forces or threats, but it will do to think of these four sanctions as *motivations* for ethical behavior. If, in fact, we fail to do what we should, well, natural laws, civil laws, public or personal opinion, and God himself will make it unpleasant for us—either in this life or the next, or in both! Nature, law, opinion, and God "persuade" us to overcome our perverse inclinations and to act in accordance with social utility. Bentham also labeled the Four Sanctions as the physical, the political, the moral, and the religious. But he provided an example which, in any case, makes his meaning clear:

> A man's good, or his person, are consumed by fire. If this happened to him by what is called an accident, it was a calamity; if by reason of his own imprudence (for instance, from his neglecting to put his candle out) it may be styled a punishment of the physical sanction; if it happened to him by the sentence of the political magistrate, a punishment belonging to the political sanction; that is, what is commonly called a punishment; if for want of any assistance which his neighbour withheld from him out of some dislike to his moral character, a punishment of the moral sanction; if by an immediate act of God's displeasure, manifested on account of some sin committed by him. or through any distraction of mind, occasioned by the dread of such displeasure, a punishment of the religious sanction.
>
> As to such of the pleasures and pains belonging to the religious sanction, as regard a future life, of what kind these may be we cannot know. These lie not open to our observation.[4]

MILL'S VERSION: QUALITY OVER QUANTITY

Though Bentham was the founder of modern utilitarianism, his successor was certainly the most famous utilitarian of all: John Stuart Mill (1806–1873).

Mill's little volume with the simple title *Utilitarianism* is a classic of philosophical literature. Furthermore, a clearer expression of the philosophy of the greatest happiness for the greatest number could hardly be imagined. Consider his statement of its *hedonistic* nature:

> The creed which accepts as the foundation of morals "utility" or the "greatest happiness principle" holds that actions are right in proportion as they tend to promote happiness; wrong as they tend to produce the reverse of happiness. By happiness is intended pleasure and the absence of pain; by unhappiness, pain and the privation of pleasure. To give a clear view of the moral standard set up by the theory, much more requires to be said; in particular, what things it includes in the ideas of pain

---

[4]Ibid., p. 36.

and pleasure, and to what extent this is left an open question. But these supplementary explanations do not affect the theory of life on which this theory of morality is grounded—namely, that pleasure and freedom from pain are the only things desirable as ends; and that all desirable things (which are as numerous in the utilitarian as in any other scheme) are desirable either for pleasure inherent in themselves or as means to the promotion of pleasure and the prevention of pain.[5]

And consider his statement of its *socialistic* nature:

I must again repeat what the assailants of utilitarianism seldom have the justice to acknowledge, that the happiness which forms the utilitarian standard of what is right in conduct is not the agent's own happiness but that of all concerned. As between his own happiness and that of others, utilitarianism requires him to be as strictly impartial as a disinterested and benevolent spectator. In the golden rule of Jesus of Nazareth, we read the complete spirit of the ethics of utility. "To do as you would be done by," and "to love your neighbor as yourself," constitute the ideal perfection of utilitarian morality. As the means of making the nearest approach to this ideal, utility would enjoin, first, that laws and social arrangements should place the happiness or (as, speaking practically, it may be called) the interest of every individual as nearly as possible in harmony with the interest of the whole; and, secondly, that education and opinion, which have so vast a power over human character, should so use that power as to establish in the mind of every individual an indissoluble association between his own happiness and the good of the whole, especially between his own happiness and the practice of such modes of conduct, negative and positive, as regard for the universal happiness prescribes; so that not only he may be unable to conceive the possibility of happiness to himself, consistently with conduct opposed to the general good, but also that a direct impulse to promote the general good may be in every individual one of the habitual motives of action, and the sentiments connected therewith may fill a large and prominent place in every human being's sentient existence.[6]

Bentham and Mill stand together on the Principle of Utility as augmented by the Principle of Benevolence: Actions are right actions if, and only if, they produce pleasure or happiness or satisfaction of needs, and this pleasure or happiness or satisfaction is to be distributed among as many people as possible. With Bentham, Mill agreed also that the basic principles of social utilitarianism cannot be proved, at least not in the usual sense:

The principles of social utilitarianism as unprovable . . .

. . . questions of ultimate ends do not admit of proof, in the ordinary acceptation of the term. To be incapable of proof by reasoning is common to all first principles, to the first premise of our knowledge, as well as to those of our conduct.[7]

[5]John Stuart Mill, *Utilitarianism,* ed. Oskar Piest (Indianapolis: Bobbs-Merrill, 1957), pp. 10–11.
[6]Ibid., pp. 22–23.
[7]Ibid., p. 44.

In another sense, though, there *is* a proof:

> *The only proof capable of being given that an object is visible is that people actually see it. The only proof that a sound is audible is that people hear it; and so of the other sources of our experience. In like manner, I apprehend, the sole evidence it is possible to produce that anything is desirable is that people do actually desire it.*[8]

. . . and provable

On the basis of the above quotation, some readers might think that Mill lapses after all into ethical subjectivism: If someone did *not* desire happiness,

---

THE GOLDEN RULE: A UNIVERSAL MORAL PRINCIPLE

"What you do not want done to yourself, do not do to others."

—Confucius (sixth century BC.)

"Hurt not others with that which pains yourself."

—Buddha (fifth century B.C.)

"In happiness and suffering, in joy and grief, we should regard all creatures as we regard our own self, and should therefore refrain from inflicting upon others such injury as would appear undesirable to us if inflicted upon ourselves."

—Jainism (fifth century B.C.)

"Do not do to others all that which is not well for oneself."

—Zoroastrianism (fifth century B.C.)

"May I do to others as I would that they should do to me."

—Plato (fourth century B.C.)

"Do nothing to others which if done to you would cause you pain."

—Hinduism (third century B.C.)

"What is hateful to yourself, do not do to your fellow man."

—Hillel (first century B.C.)

"Whatsoever you would that men should do to you, do you even so to them."

—Jesus of Nazareth (first century A.D.)

"Treat others as you would be treated yourself."

—Sikhism (sixteenth century A.D.)

---

[8]Ibid., pp. 44–45.

John Stuart Mill, a utilitarian philosopher who stressed the quality over the quantity of happiness

wouldn't this mean that for him, at least, happiness is not desirable? It should be clear that Mill would answer with another question: If someone did not see an object, would it mean that the object is invisible? Goodness is experienced as happiness, but it hardly follows that goodness has no objective reality apart from the experience of it. Emphatically, Mill, as well as Bentham and all other hedonists, is an objectivist in ethics. The real problem in the above quotation lies elsewhere, as we will see.

The greatest means the best

Where Mill really split with Bentham was over Bentham's purely *quantitative* view of pleasure. Without denying that quantity is *a* consideration in the calculation of pleasure, it is not as important as the consideration of *quality*.

Now such a theory of life excites in many minds, and among them in some of the most estimable in feeling and purpose, inveterate dislike. To suppose that life has (as they express it) no higher end than pleasure—no better and nobler object of desire and pursuit—they designate as utterly mean and groveling, as a doctrine worthy only of swine, to whom the followers of Epicurus were, at a very early period, contemptuously likened; and modern holders of the doctrine are occasionally made the subject of equally polite comparisons by its German, French, and English assailants.

When thus attacked, the Epicureans have always answered that it is not they, but their accusers, who represent human nature in a degrading light, since the accusation supposes human beings to be capable of no pleasures except those of which swine are capable. If this supposition were true, the charge could not be gainsaid, but would then be no longer an imputation; for if the sources of pleasure were precisely the same to human beings and to swine, the rule of life which is good enough for the one would be good enough for the other. The comparison of the Epicurean life to that of beasts is felt as degrading, precisely because a beast's pleasures do not satisfy a human being's conceptions of happiness. Human beings have faculties more elevated than the animal appetites and, when once made conscious of them, do not regard anything as happiness which does not include their gratification. I do not, indeed, consider the Epicureans to have been by any means faultless in drawing out their scheme of consequences from the utilitarian principle. To do this in any sufficient manner, many Stoic, as well as Christian, elements require to be included. But there is no known Epicurean theory of life which does not assign to the pleasures of the intellect, of the feelings and imagination, and of the moral sentiments a much higher value as pleasures than to those of mere sensation. It must be admitted, however, that utilitarian writers in general have placed the superiority of mental over bodily pleasures chiefly in the greater permanency, safety, uncostliness, etc., of the former—that is, in their circumstantial advantages rather than in their intrinsic nature. And on all these points utilitarians have fully proved their case; but they might have taken the other and, as it may be called, higher ground with entire consistency. It is quite compatible with the principle of utility to recognize the fact that some kinds of pleasure are more desirable and more valuable than others. It would be absurd that, while in estimating all other things quality is considered as well as quantity, the estimation of pleasure should be supposed to depend on quantity alone.[9]

For Mill, as for most, it hardly needs arguing that although push-pin may be more fun than poetry, it yields an inferior happiness. And can the joy of sex really compare with the joy of the intellect? (The answer is, No.) Or to use Mill's language, wouldn't you rather be a dissatisfied human than a satisfied pig, or a dissatisfied Socrates than a satisfied fool? For Mill, as for Bentham, that action is to be pursued which makes for the greatest happiness for the greatest number. But whereas for Bentham "greatest" meant *most*, for Mill it meant *best*.

Granted that two pleasures may differ in quality, who is to say which is the best? Mill answers that the decision must rest with those who have experienced both.

Who says which pleasures are the best?

[9]Ibid., pp. 11–12.

PLEASURE: QUANTITY OR QUALITY?

- *Bentham:* "If the game of push-pin furnish more pleasure, it is more valuable."
- *Mill:* "It is better to be a human being dissatisfied than a pig satisfied."

JOHN STUART MILL

John Stuart Mill was born in London in 1806. Although he never attended school, his education was among the most remarkable ever. He was instructed entirely by his father, James Mill, who had him learning Greek at the age of 3 and Latin at 8. By the time he was 14 he had read most of the Greek and Latin classics (in the original languages), and had become expert in widely differing fields, such as history and mathematics. His social and political liberalism had also been shaped at an early age under the influence of his father and his father's associate, Jeremy Bentham. Of his reading of Bentham, Mill said: " . . . the feeling rushed upon me, that all previous moralists were superceded, and that here indeed was the commencement of a new era of thought."

In 1823, Mill became a clerk for the East India Company where his father was also employed. He remained with the company until 1858, eventually advancing to a high position. In 1826, Mill fell into a deep depression which, in his autobiography, he likened to the lines of Coleridge:

> A grief without a pang, void, dark and drear,
> A drowsy, stifled, unimpassioned grief,
> Which finds no natural outlet or relief
> In word, or sigh, or tear.

After many months he rallied from this depression, aided by his own insight, "Ask yourself whether you are happy, and you will cease to be so," and by the poetry of Wordsworth.

The woman in Mill's life was Mrs. Harriet Taylor, whom he met when he was 25. They sustained a Platonic relationship for twenty years. Three years after her husband's death, Mill married her, and when, in 1858 while they were touring France together, she herself died, Mill bought a house in Avignon in order to be near her grave. Mill called her "the most admirable person I have ever known," and referred to his relation to her as "the honor and chief blessing of my existence." He also attributed to her much of the inspiration and content of his writings.

Although Mill never held an academic position, over many years he frequently contributed articles to journals and magazines and produced many volumes. His philosophical magnum opus was the *System of Logic,* published in 1843. A great champion of liberal causes and representative government, Mill was encouraged in 1865 to stand for election to Parliament. He refused to campaign, contribute to expenses, or defend his views, and *won.* He was defeated in the next election, 1868, and thereupon spent his time either in London or in Avignon, something of a recluse, and cared for by his wife's daughter, Helen. After a brief illness, he died in 1873.

Some of Mill's more important works: *System of Logic, Utilitarianism, Subjection of Women, Principles of Political Economy, On Liberty, Utility of Religion, Autobiography.*

If I am asked what I mean by difference of quality in pleasures, or what makes one pleasure more valuable than another, merely as a pleasure, except its being greater in amount, there is but one possible answer. Of two pleasures, if there be one to which all or almost all who have experience of both give a decided preference, irrespective of any feeling of moral obligation to prefer it, that is the more desirable pleasure. If one of the two is, by those who are competently acquainted with both, placed so far above the other that they prefer it, even though knowing it to be attended with a greater amount of discontent, and would not resign it for any quantity of the other pleasure which their nature is capable of, we are justified in ascribing to the preferred enjoyment a superiority in quality so far outweighing quantity as to render it, in comparison, of small account.[10]

[10]Ibid., p. 12.

And those who have experienced both invariably opt for the higher or more qualitative pleasures.

> *Now it is an unquestionable fact that those who are equally acquainted with and*
> *equally capable of appreciating and enjoying both do give a most marked preference*
> *to the manner of existence which employs their higher faculties. Few human creatures*
> *would consent to be changed into any of the lower animals for a promise of the fullest*
> *allowance of a beast's pleasures; no intelligent human being would consent to be a*
> *fool, no instructed person would be an ignoramus, no person of feeling and conscience*
> *would be selfish and base, even though they should be persuaded that the fool, the*
> *dunce, or the rascal is better satisfied with his lot than they are with theirs. They*
> *would not resign what they possess more than he for the most complete satisfaction*
> *of all the desires which they have in common with him. If they ever fancy they would,*
> *it is only in cases of unhappiness so extreme that to escape from it they would*
> *exchange their lot for almost any other, however undesirable in their own eyes. A*
> *being of higher faculties requires more to make him happy, is capable probably of*
> *more acute suffering, and certainly accessible to it at more points, than one of an*
> *inferior type; but in spite of these liabilities, he can never really wish to sink into what*
> *he feels to be a lower grade of existence. . . . It is better to be a human being dissatisfied*
> *than a pig satisfied; better to be Socrates dissatisfied than a fool satisfied. And if the*
> *fool, or the pig, are of a different opinion, it is because they only know their own side*
> *of the question. The other party to the comparison knows both sides.*[11]

Presumably, however, Mill is not inviting us to sample all possible pleasures!

Mill also differed somewhat with Bentham on the matter of moral sanctions.
He did not deny Bentham's "external" sanctions of nature, law, opinion, and
God—motivations *outside ourselves* for certain behavior. Indeed, he claimed that
there is no reason why, for example, "hope of favor and the fear of displeasure
from our fellow creatures or from the Ruler of the universe," and any other motivations for moral behavior, should not buttress utilitarian action as well as other
kinds of action. He adds, however, an "internal" sanction, a motivation *inside ourselves* to behave in certain ways. Mill calls this "a subjective feeling in our own
minds" but it might just as easily be called *conscience*. He also calls it the "ultimate"
sanction or motivation of all moral behavior.

**Mill's internal
sanction:
Conscience**

> *The ultimate sanction, therefore, of all morality (external motives apart) being a*
> *subjective feeling in our own minds, I see nothing embarrassing to those whose stan-*
> *dard is utility in the question, What is the sanction of that particular standard? We*
> *may answer, the same as of all other moral standards—the conscientious feelings of*
> *mankind. Undoubtedly this sanction has no binding efficacy on those who do not*
> *possess the feelings it appeals to; but neither will these persons be more obedient to*

[11]Ibid., pp. 12–14.

any other moral principle than to the utilitarian one. On them morality of any kind has no hold but through the external sanctions. Meanwhile the feelings exist, a fact in human nature, the reality of which, and the great power with which they are capable of acting on those in whom they have been duly cultivated, are proved by experience. No reason has ever been shown why they may not be cultivated to as great intensity in connection with the utilitarian as with any other rule of morals.[12]

MORAL SANCTIONS: EXTERNAL AND INTERNAL

- *External sanctions:* Motivations or coercions for moral behavior which derive from outside ourselves, such as respect for the natural order, fear of civil punishment, fear of social disapproval, and fear of God's judgment.
- *Internal sanctions:* Motivations or coercions for moral behavior which lie within ourselves, such as conscience.

THE FIRST PARAGRAPH IN MILL'S *SUBJECTION OF WOMEN:*

"The object of this Essay is to explain as clearly as I am able, the grounds of an opinion which I have held from the very earliest period when I had formed any opinions at all on social or political matters, and which, instead of being weakened or modified, has been constantly growing stronger by the progress of reflection and the experience of life: That the principle which regulates the existing social relations between the two sexes—the legal subordination of one sex to the other—is wrong in itself, and now one of the chief hindrances to human improvement; and that it ought to be replaced by a principle of perfect equality, admitting no power or privilege on the one side, nor disability on the other."

---

[12]Ibid., p. 37.

Mill was a great
champion of what in
his day were radical
causes, including
women's rights, and the
abolition of child-labor
and slavery. This
cartoon (published in
Punch, March 30,
1867) suggests that
Mill's work on logic
leads to women's
liberation.

"Mill's Logic, or Franchise for Females"

Where does this internal sanction, this "feeling in our minds," come from? Even though Mill has just spoken of it as a fact of human nature, he believes that it is not innate, but acquired and cultivated. On the other hand, this makes it no less natural. As he himself says, we also speak, reason, build cities, and cultivate the ground—activities natural to humans but certainly acquired.

Motives and intentions

In discussions of morality, the distinction between *what actually results* from one's actions and *why one did it* is often and rightly raised. In the first edition of *Utilitarianism* Mill took a fairly stark position: The moral rightness of an action is independent of the motive behind it. He was severely criticized for this, and in the second edition he added a footnote defending and further explaining himself.

He who saves a fellow creature from drowning does what is morally right, whether his motive be duty or the hope of being paid for his trouble; he who betrays the friend that trusts him is guilty of a crime, even if his object be to serve another friend to whom he is under greater obligations.*

> **An opponent, whose intellectual and moral fairness it is a pleasure to acknowledge (the Rev. J. Llewellyn Davies), has objected to this passage, saying, "Surely the rightness or wrongness of saving a man from drowning does depend very much upon the motive with which it is done. Suppose that a tyrant, when his enemy jumped into the sea to escape from him, saved him from drowning simply in order that he might inflict upon him more exquisite tortures, would it tend to clearness to speak of that rescue as 'a morally right action'? Or suppose again, according to one of the stock illustrations of ethical inquiries, that a man betrayed a trust received from a friend, because the discharge of it would fatally injure that friend himself or someone belonging to him, would utilitarianism compel one to call the betrayal 'a crime' as much as if it had been done from the meanest motive?"*
>
> *I submit that he who saves another from drowning in order to kill him by torture afterwards does not differ only in motive from him who does the same thing from duty or benevolence; the act itself is different. The rescue of the man is, in the case supposed, only the necessary first step of an act far more atrocious than leaving him to drown would have been. Had Mr. Davies said, "The rightness or wrongness of saving a man from drowning does depend very much"—not upon the motive, but—"upon the intention," no utilitarian would have differed from him. Mr. Davies, by an oversight too common not to be quite venial, has in this case confounded the very different ideas of Motive and Intention. There is no point which utilitarian thinkers (and Bentham pre-eminently) have taken more pains to illustrate than this. The morality of the action depends entirely upon the intention—that is, upon what the agent wills to do. But the motive, that is, the feeling which makes him will so to do, if it makes no difference in the act, makes none in the morality: though it makes a great difference in our moral estimation of the agent, especially if it indicates a good or a bad habitual disposition—a bent of character from which useful, or from which hurtful actions are likely to arise.*[13]

Is Mill playing with words? Squirming out of a legitimate criticism? Or is his distinction between *motives* and *intentions* valid and important?

ACT-UTILITARIANISM/RULE-UTILITARIANISM

The utilitarian idea of moral action may be refined further. Philosophers these days are fond of distinguishing between *act-utilitarianism* and *rule-utilitarianism*. Actually, this is a useful and important distinction and may be applied, as we will see later, to other moral philosophies as well.

[13]Ibid., p. 24.

**Specific acts vs.
general rules**

An obvious clue to what this distinction implies is contained in the words
"act" and "rule." When you hear or see the word "act" you think immediately of
something particular: a *particular* deed done in *this* situation. On the other hand,
the word "rule" brings to mind something general: *types* of deeds to be done in
every situation. For the act-utilitarian the question is, What particular action should
be done in this situation to bring about the greatest happiness for the greatest
number? For the rule-utilitarian the question is, What rule should be followed in
this situation to bring about the greatest happiness for the greatest number?

The following summary by William K. Frankena, a well-known ethicist, may
help.

ACT-UTILITARIANISM

*First, then, there is act-utilitarianism (AU). Act-utilitarians hold that in general or
at least where it is practicable, one is to tell what is right or obligatory by appealing
directly to the principle of utility or, in other words, by trying to see which of the
actions open to him will or is likely to produce the greatest balance of good over evil
in the universe. One must ask "What effect will my doing* this *act in* this *situation
have on the general balance of good over evil?", not "What effect will everyone's
doing* this *kind of act in* this *kind of situation have on the general balance of good
over evil?" Generalizations like "Telling the truth is probably always for the greatest
general good" or "Telling the truth is generally for the greatest general good" may
be useful as guides based on past experience; but the crucial question is always
whether telling the truth in* this *case is for the greatest general good or not. It can
never be right to act on the rule of telling the truth if we have good independent
grounds for thinking that it would be for the greatest general good not to tell the truth
in a particular case, any more than it can be correct to say that all crows are black
in the presence of one that is not. Bentham and G. E. Moore probably held such a
view, perhaps even Mill; today it is held, among others, by J. J. C. Smart and Joseph
Fletcher, though the latter prefers to call it "situation ethics," of which it is one kind.*

*It should be observed that, for AU, one must include among the effects of an
action any influence it may have, by way of setting an example or otherwise, on the
actions or practices of others or on their obedience to prevailing rules. For example,
if I propose to cross a park lawn or to break a promise, I must consider the effects
my doing so may have on other walkers or on people's tendency to keep promises.
After all, even if these are thought of as "indirect" effects of my action, they are still
among its effects. . . .*

RULE-UTILITARIANISM

*Rule-utilitarianism (RU) is a rather different view, which has also been attributed to
Mill and has been finding favor recently. . . . it emphasizes the centrality of rules in
morality and insists that we are generally, if not always, to tell what to do in particular situations by appeal to a rule like that of truth-telling rather than be asking
what particular action will have the best consequences in the situation in question.*

But, unlike deontologism, it adds that we are always to determine our rules by asking which rules will promote the greatest general good for everyone. That is, the question is not which action has the greatest utility, but which rule has. The principle of utility comes in, normally at least, not in determining what particular action to perform (this is normally determined by the rules), but in determining what the rules shall be. Rules must be selected, maintained, revised, and replaced on the basis of their utility and not on any other basis. The principle of utility is still the ultimate standard, but it is to be appealed to at the level of rules rather than at the level of particular judgments. This view has been advocated by a number of writers from Bishop Berkeley to R. B. Brandt.

The AU may allow rules to be used; but if he does, he must conceive of a rule like "Tell the truth" as follows: "Telling the truth is generally for the greatest general good." By contrast, the RU must conceive of it thus: "Our always telling the truth is for the greatest general good." Or thus: "It is for the greatest good if we always tell the truth."

This means that for the RU it may be right to obey a rule like telling the truth simply because it is so useful to have the rule, even when, in the particular case in question, telling the truth does not lead to the best consequences.

An analogy may help here. On a particular occasion, I might ask which side of the street I should drive on, the right or the left. To find the answer, I would not try to see which alternative is for the greatest general good; instead, I would ask or try to determine what the law is. The law says that we are always to drive down the right side of the street (with exceptions in the case of passing, one-way streets, and so forth). The reason for the law is that it is for the greatest general good that we always drive down a certain side of the street instead of driving, on each occasion, down the side it seems to us most useful to drive on on that occasion. Here, for the greatest general good, we must have a rule of the always-acting kind (with the exceptions built into the rule, hence not really exceptions). If we suppose that for some reason there are special difficulties about our driving on the left, it will follow on utilitarian grounds that we should have a law telling us always to drive on the right. This, although the example comes from law, illustrates the RU conception of how we are to determine what is the morally right or obligatory thing to do.

If we ask why we should be RUs rather than AUs, the RU may answer, as Berkeley did, by pointing to the difficulties (difficulties due to ignorance, bias, passion, carelessness, lack of time, etc.) that would arise if, on each occasion of action, everyone were permitted to decide for himself what he should do, even if he had the help of such rules of thumb as the modified AU offers. The RU may then argue that it is for the greatest general good to have everyone acting wholly or at least largely on rules of the always-acting type instead of always making decisions on an AU basis. This would be a utilitarian argument for RU; and, as an argument, it has some plausibility.[14]

[14]William K. Frankena, *Ethics*, 2d ed. (Englewood Cliffs, N.J.: Prentice-Hall, 1973), pp. 35–36, 39–40.

An example

A concrete example may also help. The Gestapo is pounding on the door demanding to know whether Jews are hidden in the attic. We know that Jews *are* hidden in the attic, and we also know their fate—and maybe ours too—if this should be found out. The question is whether or not to tell the truth. Act-utilitarians will ask themselves, What *particular action* in this situation will produce the greatest happiness for the greatest number? And they may well decide to lie in order to save the Jews and thwart the Gestapo's evil intent. Rule-utilitarians, on the other hand, will ask, What *general rule* applied here will produce the greatest happiness for the greatest number? And they might well decide to tell the truth, persuaded that in spite of the unfortunate consequences in this particular situation, truthfulness on the whole or *generally* makes for the greatest happiness.

In the case of the classic utilitarians, such as Bentham and Mill, philosophers are not agreed whether they were act- or rule-utilitarians. This may only show that the distinction, though useful in theory, is difficult to apply in practice, at least in an either/or manner. Mill, in fact, seems to have espoused both act- and rule-utilitarianism, though at different levels, which, after all, is probably a rather common-sensical position. We cannot live without rules of conduct, and such rules have been distilled through the experience and wisdom of the ages—they should probably be honored as making for the greatest happiness for the greatest number. On the other hand, some situations are so singular and exceptional (or at least may seem to be at the time) as not to fall into any general category or under any general rule. In such situations we may be forced to act on the basis of what we see dictated *there* as fostering the greatest happiness—though, admittedly, threats and the brandishing of guns, and passionate embraces in the backseat of a car, may not make for the most objective moral judgments.

Now apply this twofold principle (the role of rules *and* the role of particular actions) to the situation involving the Jews and the Gestapo. Does it help?

SOME OBJECTIONS

We mention here some of the objections made against utilitarianism specifically, and in the next section some objections to hedonism in all of its forms.

Some obvious complaints

In *Utilitarianism*, Mill himself answers a whole string of rather obvious charges against utilitarianism. For example: Utilitarianism is a pig-philosophy which encourages the pursuit of base pleasures; it is a godless philosophy which establishes a criterion of morality independent of the question of God's will; it is such a "calculating" philosophy as to chill our human feelings for one another; it focuses attention on the consequences of actions to the exclusion of their motives; it asks us to do the impossible, namely, to anticipate endless chains of consequences from our actions. If you can't see how Mill would have answered such charges, well, the second chapter of *Utilitarianism* makes good philosophical reading.

> How might a utilitarian reason about the rightness or wrongness of
>
> - capital punishment?
> - abortion?
> - war?
> - minority rights?
> - euthanasia?
> - genetic engineering?

But some other problems may be mentioned.

First, it should be evident that utilitarianism sidesteps *to some degree* the charge that it is egoistic. On the other hand, neither is it purely altruistic. Though it tells us to distribute happiness among as many people as possible, it also tells us never to forget that each of us is *one* of those people. Whether or not this is a problem depends on how strenuously you take the ideal of altruism. Perhaps social hedonism goes far enough in its concern for the interests of others. But maybe not. Did Jesus, Socrates, or St. Francis count himself even as *one?*

Social hedonism vs. altruism

Second, we have seen that all forms of hedonism, but especially Bentham's, employ some type of hedonic calculus, or computation of pleasures. Now this may look good on paper, but how practical is it? Is it really possible to measure and compare, say, the *intensity* of different pleasures in different people? Or even the same pleasure in the same person? Try it. Further, the hedonic calculus is geared to produce certain sorts of results. But though we *may* be able to foresee *some* of the consequences of our actions, who can really foresee all of them, to say nothing of the consequences of the consequences, and so on? We may grant that in certain very general cases the implications of our actions are fairly obvious, but even if we were utilitarians it is not in *these* situations that we would look for moral guidance, is it? It's when we *aren't* clear about the consequences that we need help.

Is the hedonic calculus workable?

Third, social hedonism results in some rather awkward puzzles. For example, we are told to act so as to promote the greatest happiness for the greatest number. But is not ten parts of happiness distributed over two people—five parts of happiness to each—as much the greatest happiness for the greatest number as ten parts of happiness distributed evenly to ten people? It may be answered that this is where the *Justice Principle* comes in with the idea that happiness is to be spread over as many people as possible. But then we have to ask constantly, Who has how much pleasure? And, as one philosopher has observed, is it really meaningful to say that person A is three-and-a-half times as happy as person B? And in any event, would

Some embarrassing puzzles

you be willing to dispatch some innocent person to burn in hell forever even if you could thereby secure the eternal happiness of *every other person in the world?*

Are there more basic ideals than happiness?

Fourth, it is often objected that utilitarianism (or, for that matter, hedonism in general) is incompatible with the standards of morality that we actually employ. We recognize, for example, the *intrinsic* rightness (that is, right for its own sake and apart from its consequences) of acting fairly, telling the truth, and keeping promises. Could you break a promise *without batting an eye*, even if you knew it would promote happiness in general? Can we really believe that it is right to pursue pleasure and happiness, even of the greatest number, *no matter what?* In the end, is not our pursuit of the general welfare conditioned by other and even more basic ideals?

Finally, fifth, we must raise again a criticism which we already considered in relation to egoistic hedonism. Like any other form of hedonism, utilitarianism is a *naturalistic* ethic—it takes its clue from nature, or from what *is*. Consider Bentham's claim that

> *Nature has placed mankind under the governance of two sovereign masters, pain and pleasure. It is for them alone to point out what we ought to do.*[15]

And Mill's claim that

> *The only proof capable of being given that an object is visible is that people actually see it. . . . In like manner, I apprehend, the sole evidence it is possible to produce that anything is desirable is that people do actually desire it. . . . If the opinion which I have now stated is psychologically true—if human nature is so constituted as to desire nothing which is not either a part of happiness or a means of happiness—we can have no other proof, and we require no other, that these are the only things desirable.*[16]

The Naturalistic Fallacy again

Now, even aside from the insane person in the last chapter who derives the most exquisite happiness from torturing starving children, such talk is again open to the charge of the Naturalistic Fallacy. These utilitarian thinkers, no less than other hedonists, try to derive an *ought* from an *is*. Look at the two quotations above. Don't *factual* judgments seem to be mixed up with *value* judgments again? What have our "natural masters," pain and pleasure, got to do with "what we ought to do"? And although what is psychologically true might have something to do with what is actually desired, what has it got to do with what is desir*able*, or *worthy* of desire, or *right?* This is exactly how G. E. Moore attacked this very passage in Mill.

> *Well, the fallacy in this step is so obvious, that it is quite wonderful how Mill failed to see it. The fact is that "desirable" does not mean "able to be desired" as "visible"*

[15]Bentham, *An Introduction to the Principles of Morals and Legislation*, p. 11.

[16]Mill, *Utilitarianism*, pp. 44, 48–49.

means "able to be seen." The desirable means simply what ought to be desired or deserves to be desired; just as the detestable means not what can be but what ought to be detested and the damnable what deserves to be damned. Mill has, then, smuggled in, under cover of the word "desirable," the very notion about which he ought to be quite clear. "Desirable" does indeed mean "what it is good to desire"; but when this is understood, it is no longer plausible to say that our only test of that, is what is actually desired. Is it merely a tautology when the Prayer Book talks of good desires? Are not bad desires also possible?[17]

And philosophers have been attacking him in the same way ever since.

It is often pointed out that the following statement by Mill (in *Utilitarianism*) involves a simple logical fallacy. What is it?

" . . . each person's happiness is a good to that person, and the general happiness, therefore, a good to the aggregate of all persons."

Chapter 18 in Review

As with egoistic hedonism, utilitarianism is a teleological ethic, emphasizing the consequences of actions as the criteria of their moral worth. Also with egoistic hedonism, it identifies pleasure or happiness as the specific consequence to be attained. It differs, however, in shifting our attention from the pleasure or happiness of the individual to that of society: the greatest happiness for the greatest number.

SUMMARY

Bentham and Mill are, historically, the best representatives of the utilitarian position. Bentham pressed for a quantitative interpretation of the "greatest" happiness, and propounded a hedonic calculus to assist in its determination. Mill pressed for a qualitative interpretation of the "greatest" happiness and urged that it is only the widely experienced individual who is in a position to extol the superiority of the qualitative pleasures, for example, the pleasures of the mind.

A contemporary refinement of utilitarianism distinguishes between act-utilitarianism and rule-utilitarianism. The former focuses on particular situations and asks what specific act in that situation would be conducive to the general welfare.

[17]George Edward Moore, *Principia Ethica* (Cambridge: Cambridge University Press, 1903), p. 67.

The rule-utilitarian, on the other hand, urges the adoption of rules which, applied and practiced in all situations, would result in the general welfare.

Although utilitarianism escapes the charge of egoism, it is subject to many of the complaints leveled against any hedonistic philosophy. Most notably, utilitarianism is, finally, in some sense a naturalistic ethic, finding its basis in what individuals actually, and naturally, desire and strive for. As such it is an obvious target for critics who distinguish *ought* from *is*.

BASIC IDEAS

- The Principle of Utility
- The Benevolence Principle
- Utilitarianism as social hedonism
- Utilitarianism as a political position
- Bentham's version of utilitarianism
- The hedonic calculus: Seven criteria of the greatest pleasure
- Bentham's Four Sanctions
  Nature
  Civil Law
  Opinion
  God
- Mill's version of utilitarianism
- The Principle of Utility as unprovable ...
- ... and provable
- Mill's criterion of the best pleasures
- Mill's internal sanction
- Mill on the difference between motives and intentions
- Act-utilitarianism
- Rule-utilitarianism
- The Naturalistic Fallacy

TEST YOURSELF

1. Benevolence Principle + Hedonism = ?
2. Who formulated a sevenfold hedonic calculus in order to measure the quantity of pleasure?
3. According to Mill, what is the only proof that anything is desirable?
4. Who said it? "If the game of push-pin furnish more pleasure, it is more valuable."
5. What did William Frankena contribute to the discussion in this chapter?
6. The big difference between Bentham's and Mill's versions of utilitarianism concerns _____vs. _____.
7. True or false: In spite of its "socialistic" character, utilitarianism is no less a hedonistic philosophy than that of Epicurus or the Cyrenaics.

8. Exactly why is utilitarianism, as well as the hedonisms discussed in the previous chapter, a *naturalistic* ethics?
9. What was G. E. Moore's objection to utilitarianism?
10. According to Mill, which of the following are relevant for the determination of a moral act? (a) number of people involved, (b) production of happiness, (c) quality of pleasure involved, (d) external sanctions.

QUESTIONS FOR
REFLECTION

- What do you think of Mill's justification of utilitarianism? What about the Naturalistic Fallacy? Are there values to which even the greatest happiness for the greatest number might be sacrificed? What is to say that the greatest happiness for the whole human race is the highest good? If the whole human race were suddenly to disappear, by virtue of what could it *then* be said: "That's too bad"?

- Again we have encountered the distinction between "higher" and "lower" pleasures. How is the debate between Mill and Bentham reminiscent of the debate between Epicurus and Aristippus? How not? What do you make of Mill's evidence for the qualitative superiority of the higher pleasures? Would *you* rather be an unsatisfied Socrates than a satisfied pig? Why?

- Are you a utilitarian? If so, an act- or a rule-utilitarian? In any event, any form of utilitarianism asserts that the morality of any action is determined by the (intended) consequences. Is that *your* belief?

THE ROLE OF DUTY

Even aside from the objections mentioned, it has been charged that there is something basically wrong with the preceding theories. Something important has been left out. Aren't some things just right or wrong *no matter what?* Isn't there such a thing as unconditional obligation? duty? To be sure, it is precisely in its exaltation of *duty,* pure and simple, as the foundation of moral actions, that the theory in the present chapter is radically different from those we considered in the last two chapters.

MORALITY AS UNCONDITIONAL

Teleological ethics

First, we must remind ourselves of the important distinction between *teleological* and *deontological* ethics. We saw at the beginning of Chapter 17 that a teleological theory of morality is one which emphasizes the intended consequences or results of actions as the criteria of their rightness. And we considered what are probably the best examples of this sort of ethical theory: egoistic hedonism and utilitarianism. In the one case the criterion of right action was the promotion of personal pleasure; in the other case it was the promotion of the general welfare. But however it may conceive the "good results," any teleological theory says, "Such-and-such is the right action because it produces such-and-such results." A theory like this is clear, straightforward, and commonsensical.

How odd it might sound, therefore, for someone to say, "The consequences or results of your actions have nothing at all to do with their rightness or wrongness!" This is a *deontological* conception of morality. You will recall that a deontological theory is one that sets up as the criterion of moral behavior not what might or might not happen—or be intended to happen—as a result of one's actions, but rather the intent to perform one's *duty* through a certain action.

Deontological ethics

This was exactly the thesis of Immanuel Kant, who, by the way, didn't think it a bit odd. In fact, he regarded it as the only *possible* way to conceive of genuine moral behavior. Why? Kant's answer is found, for the most part, in his *Foundations of the Metaphysics of Morals*. It is a small book, but, as the Kant scholar H. J. Paton says, "one of the small books which are truly great: it has exercised on human thought an influence almost ludicrously disproportionate to its size."[1]

For Kant, morality is a matter of *ought*, or *obligation*. Doesn't any moral theory tell us what we *ought* to do? This is not the problem. The problem is that a distinction is not usually drawn between the conditional *ought* and the *unconditional ought*. A conditional *ought* says, "You ought to do X if you want something-or-other to happen." The *ought* is conditioned by something-or-other. But the unconditional *ought* says, "You ought to do X, period." For Kant, only the unconditional *ought* is the *moral* ought. Why? Because, as we all recognize—don't we?—morality must be *necessary* and *universal*, that is, it must be absolutely binding, and absolutely binding on everyone alike: Whoever you are, whatever your situation, you ought to do X. But the conditional *ought* involves "ifs" and "in-order-thats" and therefore gets mixed up with all sorts of particular circumstances, changing desires, personal inclinations, and so on. Any "morality" (Kant would put it in quotation marks) founded on the conditional *ought* ("Do X, if ... " or "Do X, in order that ... ") will therefore be relative and particular rather than necessary and universal—but then it is not real morality is it?

The irrelevance of consequences

This is not to say that in deciding what we ought to do—how to fulfill our duty—we should never take the consequences of our actions into account. Often it is necessary to consider the results of an action in order to perceive whether it is our duty. But it is out of *duty* that we should act, not for the sake of the consequences. Stay with this until it is clear to you, or maybe consider an example. We borrow the following from yet another Kant scholar, Lewis White Beck.

> Imagine two soldiers who volunteer for a dangerous mission; because they see a task they ought to undertake, they voluntarily assume the responsibility for it. Certainly their act will have consequences; equally certain is the fact that they desire certain consequences for their act. The most careful consideration of these consequences, calculation as to how to achieve some desirable consequences and avoid others less desirable, and an ardent desire to attain the goal do not in the least detract from the morality of the men's action if they are indeed acting on the conviction that it is their duty to do these acts; their concern with the consequences may be an essential part of

[1]H. J. Paton, in the Preface to his translation of Kant's *Foundation of the Metaphysics of Morals*, published as *Kant's Groundwork of the Metaphysic of Morals* (New York: Harper & Row, 1964), p. 8.

their conduct, necessary for the fulfillment of the obligation they have placed upon themselves. Now imagine that one of the men is killed before reaching his destination, while the other is successful; what moral judgment do we pass upon them? So far as we judge that their motives were equally good (and of course, as Kant repeatedly says, we cannot be sure what anyone's motives really are), we judge them in the same way. Their acts are judged to be equally moral, in spite of the fact that one succeeded and the other failed. Each did his "best," and what he earnestly attempted and the motives which led him to do what he did are the proper objects of moral judgment; what he accomplishes lies to a large extent beyond his control.[2]

Do you see that even with its possible interest in consequences this position is quite unlike, say, utilitarianism? There the question was, Did you act for the sake of promoting the general welfare? But here the question is, Aside from what you accomplished or even tried to accomplish, did you act out of duty?

The irrelevance of nature

But back to the main point. Another way Kant expresses his rejection of *conditioned* morality is by his rejection of any and all *naturalistic* ethics. As we explained earlier, a naturalistic ethics is one which bases its *ought* in some way on nature, say by an appeal to the physical world, or to psychology, or to human nature, or to history. But such an ethics would be based on what *happens* to be, or *might* be, or *could* be, whereas genuine morality is, again, a matter of *necessity* and *universality*. Do you see that happiness, for example, must for Kant be an impossible basis for moral laws?

This section is entitled, "Morality as Unconditional." Is it clear that for Kant morality is not conditioned by (that is, not defined by, not bound by, not relative to, not based on) anything outside the morality of the act itself? Is it clear how, for Kant, the introduction of the empirical categories of consequences and nature not only clouds but absolutely distorts the idea of morality?

Kant objects to:

- Any teleological conception of moral action
- Any naturalistic basis of moral action

In the following, from the *Foundations of the Metaphysics of Morals*, Kant emphasizes with a vengeance the absolute necessity of separating genuine morality from all empirical considerations, and the necessity, instead, of deriving it *a priori* from pure reason. (By "anthropology," Kant means what can be known empirically about human nature.)

[2]Lewis White Beck, in the Preface to his translation of Immanuel Kant, *Foundations of the Metaphysics of Morals* (Indianapolis: Bobbs-Merrill, 1959), p. ix.

Since my purpose here is directed to moral philosophy, I narrow the proposed question to this: Is it not of the utmost necessity to construct a pure moral philosophy which is completely freed from everything which may be only empirical and thus belong to anthropology? That there must be such a philosophy is self-evident from the common idea of duty and moral laws. Everyone must admit that a law, if it is to hold morally, i.e., as a ground of obligation, must imply absolute necessity; he must admit that the command, "Thou shalt not lie," does not apply to men only, as if other rational beings had no need to observe it. The same is true for all other moral laws properly so called. He must concede that the ground of obligation here must not be sought in the nature of man or in the circumstances in which he is placed, but sought a priori solely in the concepts of pure reason, and that every other precept which rests on principles of mere experience, even a precept which is in certain respects universal, so far as it leans in the least on empirical grounds (perhaps only in regard to the motive involved), may be called a practical rule but never a moral law. . . .

Immanuel Kant was a true giant in the history of philosophy. His ideas in epistemology were revolutionary, and he remains the classic example of a deontologist in ethical theory.

But a completely isolated metaphysics of morals, mixed with no anthropology, no theology, no physics or hyperphysics, and even less with occult qualities (which might be called hypophysical), is not only an indispensable substrate of all theoretically sound and definite knowledge of duties; it is also a desideratum of the highest importance to the actual fulfillment of its precepts. For the pure conception of duty and of the moral law generally, with no admixture of empirical inducements, has an influence on the human heart so much more powerful than all other incentives which may be derived from the empirical field that reason, in the consciousness of its dignity, despises them and gradually becomes master over them. It has this influence only through reason, which thereby first realizes that it can of itself be practical. A mixed theory of morals which is put together both from incentives of feelings and inclinations and from rational concepts must, on the other hand, make the mind vacillate between motives which cannot be brought under any principle and which can lead only accidentally to the good and often to the bad.

From what has been said it is clear that all moral concepts have their seat and origin entirely a priori in reason. This is just as much the case in the most ordinary reason as in reason which is speculative to the highest degree. It is obvious that they cannot be abstracted from any empirical and hence merely contingent cognitions. In the purity of their origin lies their worthiness to serve us as supreme practical principles, and to the extent that something empirical is added to them just this much is subtracted from their genuine influence and from the unqualified worth of actions.[3]

IMMANUEL KANT

The historian of philosophy Frederick Copleston has described Kant's life as "singularly uneventful and devoid of dramatic incident."

Immanuel Kant was born in 1724 in Königsberg, East Prussia (now Russia), on the Baltic Sea. Kant's father, who immigrated from Scotland (and changed the family name from Cant to Kant), was a saddler. The family was large, poor, and religious. They were Pietists (something like Prussian Puritans), and the continuous round of prayers, religious instruction, and observances is no doubt why Kant in his adult years never attended public worship except on extraordinary occasions. On the other hand, he embraced to the end the ethical principles of his early religious upbringing.

[3]Ibid., pp. 5, 27–28.

In 1740, he entered the University of Königsberg where he drank in a broad survey of many fields: metaphysics, physics, algebra, geometry, psychology, astronomy, and logic. At the conclusion of his studies he earned a sparse livelihood by becoming a tutor to the Prussian gentry. It was during this time that he was introduced to high society, though he soon withdrew into the ivory tower of academic life. In 1755, he took what we would call a doctoral degree and became a lecturer at the university. In 1770, he was made professor. He taught and published first in science, anticipating Laplace's nebular hypothesis concerning the origin of the universe and Darwin's theory of evolution. But he turned gradually to metaphysics. Kant's lectures were said to be lively and even humorous—though one would never guess this from most of his writings.

In 1781, at the ripe age of 57, he published the monumental *Critique of Pure Reason.* This was followed by the *Critique of Practical Reason,* and the *Critique of Judgment.* According to the German writer Herder, Kant spoke "the profoundest language that ever came from the lips of man." Profound perhaps, but perhaps also the most exasperating. He gave the manuscript of his first *Critique* to a colleague, Marcus Herz. Herz returned it half-read, with the explanation: "If I finish it, I am afraid I shall go mad!"

Kant lectured at the university for over forty years. In all this time he never traveled more than 60 miles from Königsberg, and for forty years he did not spend so much as a single night outside that city. Kant was a small man (about five feet tall), extremely frail, and somewhat distorted in his frame. He was meticulous about his health, verging on the neurotic. His daily routine was extremely fixed, beginning every morning at 4:55. It is reported that his daily walk was so regular that he strolled for exactly one hour, eight times up and down the Linden Allee (which came to be nicknamed "The Philosopher's Walk") and so punctual that the townspeople set their clocks by it. He never married, and was, in fact, something of a misogynist. He died in senile dementia on February 12, 1804.

Kant's most important philosophical works include: *Critique of Pure Reason, Critique of Practical Reason, Critique of Judgment, Prolegomena to any Future Metaphysics, Foundations of the Metaphysics of Morals, Metaphysical First Principles of Natural Science, Religion within the Bounds of Reason Alone, and On Perpetual Peace.*

THE GOOD WILL

In this way, Kant eliminates from the start the least suggestion that morality can be based on our natural states and inclinations. He does not begrudge us, say, pleasure and happiness, but wants us to see that such "gifts of nature" cannot be the *foundation* of morality as rationally conceived.

Consider, for example, what we might call the innate gifts of intelligence, wit, and courage, or the accidental gifts of power, wealth, and honor. Does it take any great insight to see that these are not *absolute* goods? that they have no *intrinsic* or *unconditional* value? To see that this is so, just notice how any one of them could be corrupted or turned into an evil. Well then, is there anything more basic than these which is absolutely and unconditionally good? Kant says, Yes. And it is, in fact, the very thing that these other things depend on for their goodness, and without which they would become corrupted and turned into evil. What is this absolute good, the necessary and sufficient condition for all right action, the foundation of rational morality? The *good will*.

One of the most quoted passages in all philosophical literature is the opening sentence of the first section of the *Foundations*:

> Nothing in the world—indeed nothing even beyond the world—can possibly be conceived which could be called good without qualification except a good will.

He goes on immediately to show how the good will underlies any possible goodness of our natural gifts:

> Intelligence, wit, judgment, and the other talents of the mind, however they may be named, or courage, resoluteness, and perseverance as qualities of temperament, are doubtless in many respects good and desirable. But they can become extremely bad and harmful if the will, which is to make use of these gifts of nature and which in its special constitution is called character, is not good. It is the same with the gifts of fortune. Power, riches, honor, even health, general well-being, and the contentment with one's condition which is called happiness, make for pride and even arrogance if there is not a good will to correct their influence on the mind and on its principles of action so as to make it universally comfortable to its end. It need hardly be mentioned that the sight of a being adorned with no feature of a pure and good will, yet enjoying uninterrupted prosperity, can never give pleasure to a rational impartial observer. Thus the good will seems to constitute the indispensable condition even of worthiness to be happy.
>
> Some qualities seem to be conducive to this good will and can facilitate its action, but, in spite of that, they have no intrinsic unconditional worth. They rather presuppose a good will, which limits the high esteem which one otherwise rightly has for them and prevents their being held to be absolutely good. Moderation in emotions and passions, self-control, and calm deliberation not only are good in many respects

The good will as the basis morality

but even seem to constitute a part of the inner worth of the person. But however unconditionally they were esteemed by the ancients, they are far from being good without qualification. For without the principle of a good will they can become extremely bad, and the coolness of a villain makes him not only far more dangerous but also more directly abominable in our eyes than he would have seemed without it.

The good will is not good because of what it effects or accomplishes or because of its adequacy to achieve some proposed end; it is good only because of its willing, i.e., it is good of itself. And, regarded for itself, it is to be esteemed incomparably higher than anything which could be brought about by it in favor of any inclination or even of the sum total of all inclinations. Even if it should happen that, by a particularly unfortunate fate or by the niggardly provision of a stepmotherly nature, this will should be wholly lacking in power to accomplish its purpose, and if even the greatest effort should not avail it to achieve anything of its end, and if there remained only the good will (not as a mere wish but as the summoning of all the means in our power), it would sparkle like a jewel in its own right, as something that had its full worth in itself. Usefulness or fruitlessness can neither diminish nor augment this worth. Its usefulness would be only its setting, as it were, so as to enable us to handle it more conveniently in commerce or to attract the attention of those who are not yet connoisseurs, but not to recommend it to those who are experts or to determine its worth.[4]

Pore over the above paragraphs until they are digested. Still, even though Kant here uses the phrase "good will" repeatedly he does not say exactly what it means. If we somehow miss this, then we miss the whole point. For Kant a good will, or a *pure* will, is an intention to act in accordance with moral *law*, and moral law is what it is no matter what anything else is. To act out of a good will is, then, to do X because it is *right* to do X, and for no other reason. This would be *rational* morality.

What is a good will?

An important note: Kant stresses the difference between acting "out of" duty and acting "in accordance with" duty. Obviously, we may do something that just happens to accord with what our duty is, but this would hardly make the action

---

"Nothing in the world—indeed nothing beyond the world—can possibly be conceived which could be called good without qualification except a *good will*."

—Kant

---

[4]*Ibid.*, pp. 9–10.

moral. In order to be really moral, our action must be done *out of* duty, that is, with a good will or with respect for the moral law.

KANT'S CATEGORICAL IMPERATIVE

At this point Kant presents us with one of the most famous and important concepts in the history of ethics: the *Categorical Imperative*.

For Kant, the Categorical Imperative is the fundamental principle of morality. More accurately, it is a criterion or *test* by which we can make sure our actions are moral, that is, that they are motivated by a good will or performed out of duty. As Kant states it in its most general form, the Categorical Imperative is this:

The Categorical Imperative stated

> *Act only according to that maxim by which you can at the same time will that it should become a universal law.*[5]

That is to say, when you are about to do X, ask yourself whether you can will that everyone else act in the same way. If the answer is Yes, then, says Kant, you may be assured that you are acting out of duty or with a good will. Why is this? We will explain in a moment exactly how the Categorical Imperative is a test of right action.

Sometimes the Categorical Imperative is referred to, for short, as the *Principle of Universalizibility*, since it asks us whether we can "universalize" our actions, that is, whether we would demand that everyone else in similar circumstances act in accordance with the same rule as we would. But we must not miss the significance of Kant's own—and more ponderous—expression. What is an *imperative*? It is a

What is an imperative?

command. As a command, the Categorical Imperative addresses and constrains our will, which it recognizes might not always (and often enough doesn't!) gladly pursue what it ought. As a command, the Categorical Imperative reckons with our natural perversity; in fact, Kant believed, in his own way, in the traditional Christian doctrine of original sin. But why is this imperative called, further, *categorical*? Here we encounter again the distinction between doing something as a means of *achieving some end* and doing something simply because it's *right*. Kant says that all imperatives are either hypothetical or categorical. A *hypothetical* imperative would com-

Hypothetical and categorical imperatives

mand you to do X if you wanted Y (notice the hypothetical form of the statement, "if ... then"). But a *categorical* imperative would command you to do X inasmuch as X is intrinsically right, that is, right in and of itself, aside from any other considerations—no "ifs," no conditions, no strings attached.

Kant himself clearly draws the distinction between hypothetical and categorical imperatives:

[5]Ibid., p. 39.

All imperatives command either hypothetically or categorically. The former present the practical necessity of a possible action as a means to achieving something else which one desires (or which one may possibly desire). The categorical imperative would be one which presented an action as of itself objectively necessary, without regard to any other end.[6]

And he leaves no doubt as to which of these alone can have any bearing on morality, and why:

. . . there is one imperative which directly commands a certain conduct without making its condition some purpose to be reached by it. This imperative is categorical. It concerns not the material of the action and its intended result but the form and the principle from which it results. What is essentially good in it consists in the intention, the result being what it may. This imperative may be called the imperative of morality.[7]

It is important to grasp this. A hypothetical imperative is *conditional on* ("if") or *subject to* things, circumstances, goals, and desires; and these, of course, change all the time, are relative to the individual, and so on. But a categorical imperative is *unconditional* (no "ifs") and *independent of* any things, circumstances, goals, or desires. It is for this reason that only a *categorical* imperative can be a *universal* and *binding* law, that is, a *moral* law, valid for all rational beings at all times.

THE TEST OF MORAL ACTIONS

Understandably, the Categorical Imperative, as the fundamental principle of morality, may leave you cold. To be sure, there is no talk here about exciting things like lying, stealing, and adultery. Instead, we are confronted by rather abstract talk about maxims and laws, without any particular *content*. It is true. Kant told us above—not in so many words, but at least in these *exact* words—that his Categor-

Kant's
"formalism"

THE CATEGORICAL IMPERATIVE

Act only according to that maxim by which you can at the same time will that it should become a universal law.

---

[6]Ibid., p. 31.
[7]Ibid., p. 33.

ical Imperative, the foundation of rational morality, is concerned not with the *matter* but the *form* of morality. Let's try to say this in several ways. The Categorical Imperative—

- isn't concerned with *what* you do but *how* you do it.
- doesn't address specific moral issues but the nature of morality *itself*.
- doesn't prescribe the rightness or wrongness of *particular* actions but what makes *any* action right or wrong.

But, of course, this is largely true of any theory of morality. All right, then, we may state it even more strongly. According to Kant, when we seek to make a moral judgment about a possible course of action, what we primarily need to take into account has nothing to do with pleasure, pain, joy, welfare, happiness, Jews hiding in the attic, threats, or the brandishing of guns. Rather, it has to do with—what must seem exceedingly dull and formal by comparison—the possibility of a *contradiction in our action.*

The Categorical Imperative as a test of moral action

And this brings us back to the way in which the Categorical Imperative is a *test* of moral actions. When embarking on a certain course of action I must ask: Does the universalizing of the principle of my action result in a contradiction? If so, the action fails the test and must be rejected as immoral. But it is important to see what is meant here by "contradiction." It is not a *logical* contradiction as often as a *practical* one. It might help to think of the latter sort of self-contradictory action as a *self-stultifying* or *self-defeating* one.

Some examples

Kant himself provides some concrete examples of how the application of the Categorical Imperative might result in contradiction and backfire.

1. *A man who is reduced to despair by a series of evils feels a weariness with life but is still in possession of his reason sufficiently to ask whether it would not be contrary to his duty to himself to take his own life. Now he asks whether the maxim of his action could become a universal law of nature. His maxim, however, is: For love of myself, I make it my principle to shorten my life when by a longer duration it threatens more evil than satisfaction. But it is questionable whether this principle of self-love could become a universal law of nature. One immediately sees a contradiction in a system of nature whose law would be to destroy life by the feeling whose special office is to impel the improvement of life. In this case it would not exist as nature; hence that maxim cannot obtain as a law of nature, and thus it wholly contradicts the supreme principle of all duty.*

2. *Another man finds himself forced by need to borrow money. He well knows that he will not be able to repay it, but he also sees that nothing will be loaned him if he does not firmly promise to repay it at a certain time. He desires to make such a promise, but he has enough conscience to ask himself whether it is not improper and opposed to duty to relieve his distress in such a way. Now, assuming he does decide to do so, the maxim of his action would be as follows: When I believe myself to be in*

need of money, I will borrow money and promise to repay it, although I know I shall
never do so. Now this principle of self-love or of his own benefit may very well be
compatible with his whole future welfare, but the question is whether it is right. He
changes the pretension of self-love into a universal law and then puts the question:
How would it be if my maxim became a universal law? He immediately sees that it
could never hold as a universal law of nature and be consistent with itself; rather it
must necessarily contradict itself. For the universality of a law which says that anyone who believes himself to be in need could promise what he pleased with the intention of not fulfilling it would make the promise itself and the end to be accomplished
by it impossible; no one would believe what was promised to him but would only
laugh at any such assertion as vain pretense.

3. A third finds in himself a talent which could, by means of some cultivation,
make him in many respects a useful man. But he finds himself in comfortable circumstances and prefers indulgence in pleasure to troubling himself with broadening and
improving his fortunate natural gifts. Now, however, let him ask whether his maxim
of neglecting his gifts, besides agreeing with his propensity to idle amusement, agrees
also with what is called duty. He sees that a system of nature could indeed exist in
accordance with such a law, even though man (like the inhabitants of the South Sea
Islands) should let his talents rust and resolve to devote his life merely to idleness,
indulgence, and propagation—in a word, to pleasure. But he cannot possibly will
that this should become a universal law of nature or that it should be implanted in
us by a natural instinct. For, as a rational being, he necessarily wills that all his
faculties should be developed, inasmuch as they are given to him for all sorts of possible purposes.

4. A fourth man, for whom things are going well, sees that others (whom he
could help) have to struggle with great hardships, and he asks, "What concern of
mine is it? Let each one be as happy as heaven wills, or as he can make himself; I
will not take anything from him or even envy him; but to his welfare or to his assistance in time of need I have no desire to contribute." If such a way of thinking were
a universal law of nature, certainly the human race could exist, and without doubt
even better than in a state where everyone talks of sympathy and good will, or even
exerts himself occasionally to practice them while, on the other hand, he cheats when
he can and betrays or otherwise violates the rights of man. Now although it is possible
that a universal law of nature according to that maxim could exist, it is nevertheless
impossible to will that such a principle should hold everywhere as a law of nature.
For a will which resolved this would conflict with itself, since instances can often arise
in which he would need the love and sympathy of others, and in which he would
have robbed himself, by such a law of nature springing from his own will, of all hope
of the aid he desires.

The foregoing are a few of the many actual duties, or at least of duties we hold
to be actual, whose derivation from the one stated principle is clear. We must be able
to will that a maxim of our action become a universal law; this is the canon of the
moral estimation of our action generally. Some actions are of such a nature that their

maxim cannot even be thought *as a universal law of nature without contradiction, far from it being possible that one could will that it should be such. In others this internal impossibility is not found, though it is still impossible to* will *that their maxim should be raised to the universality of a law of nature, because such a will would contradict itself.*[8]

Different versions of the Categorical Imperative

To this point we have spoken in the singular of the Categorical Imperative. Actually, it should be added, Kant provided several formulations of Categorical Imperatives, though these are really best thought of as different versions of the same fundamental principle of morality. Certainly they overlap with one another, and they suggest important and differing ways in which the fundamental principle may be viewed and applied.[9]

1. Act only according to that maxim by which you can at the same time will that it should become a universal law.
2. Act only so that the will through its maxims could regard itself at the same time as making universal laws.
3. Act so that you treat humanity, whether in your own person or in that of another, always as an end and never as a means only.

SOME OBJECTIONS

Is there a moral law?

The first objection might, rather naturally, focus on the moral law itself. Kant assumes throughout that there is a moral law, a sort of moral rhyme and reason to things, a "moral law within" that is just as given as the starry heavens above, and that we can be in harmony with it by obeying the Categorical Imperative. But what if someone were to throw up his or her hands and exclaim, "There is no undergirding and overarching morality—it's all up for grabs!"? Does it not behoove Kant (and most other moral philosophers, as well) to *show* that there is some objective morality that moral philosophy reasons about? How this might be done has been considered in several places already. Do you recall the arguments against nihilism, emotivism, and subjectivism?

Back to naturalistic ethics?

Again, if Kant is clear about anything, it is that morality can in no way be based on anything empirical or natural. But why can't one, for instance a *naturalist*, simply turn the tables and say that morality *must* be based on nature, that is, defend naturalistic ethics? You will recall that this was precisely Mill's position, and Mill *followed* Kant, not hesitating to thumb his nose, as it were, at Kant's *a priorism*. Can ethical naturalism be so obviously wrong-headed as Kant made it out to be? But

[8]Ibid., pp. 39–42.

[9]I have paraphrased these three formulations and arranged them for our own purposes here. In the *Foundations of the Metaphysics of Morals,* they may be found on pp. 39, 52, 47.

this brings us back to the problems with metaphysical and ethical naturalism themselves.

Closely related, it has been charged that whatever Kant may have *intended*, his radical distinction between the moral world and the natural world may have the *effect* of rendering us morally neutral toward nature. That is, it has the effect of stripping nature of its values and downplaying any moral responsibility we may have toward it. This is an especially big criticism in our day when philosophers have been quickened to the issues of environmental ethics and animal rights.

Downplaying the values of nature

Another question: Does Kant's theory of morality presuppose a "faculty psychology"? Faculty psychology is the view which divides the person's inner life into distinct and different faculties with their own respective functions and powers. In Kant's theory, desires and inclinations are distinct from and subservient to the will, and the will is something different from and subservient to reason. It is a good question whether the activities of our inner lives can be split apart in this way.

Faculty psychology?

Also, it may be objected to Kant's "universalizing" that every law has some exceptions. But a misunderstanding may be involved here. Kant never gave us any universal laws of action, but universal *maxims* of action. The emphasis is not on the *what* but the *how*. In spite of his own (unfortunate?) example of having to tell the truth irrespective of the consequences, his real point is that whether we tell the truth or not, we must act out of a good will or duty and no exceptions to *that*!

The problem of exceptions

Finally, we come to the problem that you may feel more strongly, and that is probably because it is a more *practical* problem. The strict deontologist has told us, perhaps more times that we care to hear, that consequences (or at least the values of various consequences) are irrelevant for moral decision and action. Is this really practical advice? Who of us, knowing full well that, say, telling a lie would result in cruel and innocent suffering, would or could ignore this consequence? And it is not the case that sometimes we *should* wake up in the middle of the night worrying about the consequences of some act or other committed the day before. When the chips are down, in a concrete existential situation, Kant's "formalism" might be too formal for its own good. Man does not live by bare principles alone. Does Kant demand of us that we be more rational than we can possibly be, or even should be?

Can consequences be ignored?

Chapter 19 in Review

In Chapters 17 and 18 we discussed ethical theories which were both (1) teleological and (2) naturalistic. In this chapter, we have discussed an ethical perspective which is diametrically opposite in both of these respects.

SUMMARY

As we have seen, the best example of such a perspective is found in the moral philosophy of Kant, who emphasized that if morality is to be truly necessary and universal, it cannot be based on accidental and fluctuating *empirical* considerations.

That is why the consequences of actions are irrelevant for the morality or immorality of an action, as are considerations such as history, human nature, etc. In the place of any teleological or naturalistic conception of morality, Kant substitutes a completely *a priori* conception: Morality must have a purely *rational* basis. This *a priori* or rational basis of morality is underscored by Kant's well-known pronouncement that the only good thing is a good will. The good will is, of course, unconditionally good. That is, it is good in itself. On the other hand, it is a condition for all moral behavior: Without good will anything else, such as power or wealth, would be quickly abused or misappropriated.

What, more exactly, is the good or pure will? It is the intention to act in accordance with moral law, or to act only out of respect for what is right and not for any other reason. Kant formalizes this principle of all morality in the Categorical Imperative: "Act only according to that maxim by which you can at the same time will that it should become a universal law." The ability to universalize (apply to everyone) the rule by which we act in a given situation is a sufficient guarantee of the morality of our action, or that it is being done out of respect for the moral law alone.

As always, this philosophical position too is subject to many criticisms. One of the most common is that it is characterized by a certain abstractness or remoteness. To be sure, it may be difficult to bring to bear a rather lifeless and formal principle like the Categorical Imperative on the concrete and often vivid moral dilemmas we are frequently confronted by. On the other hand, that is just Kant's concern. Do we too easily and quickly decide these issues by obvious and immediate considerations that actually blind us to the real and *rational* basis of moral action?

BASIC IDEAS

- Deontological ethics
- The conditional vs. the unconditional *ought*
- Kant's rejection of teleological ethics
- Kant's rejection of naturalistic ethics
- The good will, as the basis for morality
- The Categorical Imperative
- Hypothetical vs. categorical imperatives
- Kant's "formalism"
- The Categorical Imperative as a test for moral action
- Three versions of the Categorical Imperative

TEST YOURSELF

1. True or false: Kant's is a teleological ethics.
2. Which of the following is most relevant for Kant's theory of morality? (a) the well-being of society, (b) consequences of actions, (c) duty, (d) hypothetical imperatives.

3. What do nature, history, sociology, anthropology, or, in a word, *empirical* factors, have to do with morality as Kant conceives it?

4. For Kant, the only truly good thing is a _____ .

5. Why is Kant's basic principle of morality called the "Categorical Imperative"?

6. A moral proposition of the form "If you want X, then you should do Y" is called a _____ imperative. Why?

7. True or false: The Categorical Imperative isn't concerned with *what* you do but *how* you do it.

8. How is the Categorical Imperative a test for moral actions?

- What do you think of the effort to establish morality on a purely *a priori* foundation? Do you believe in an objective moral law? Can such a law be dependent on or conditioned by *a posteriori* factors? What *is* its relation to the natural world?

- It is not quite right, is it, to say that for Kant the consideration of consequences is *utterly* irrelevant for the determination of a moral act. Can you explain *both* sides of Kant's view of consequences?

QUESTIONS FOR REFLECTION

In CONGRESS, July 4, 1776.

A DECLARATION

By the REPRESENTATIVES of the

UNITED STATES OF AMERICA,

In GENERAL CONGRESS ASSEMBLED.

WHEN in the Course of human Events, it becomes neceſſary for one People to diſſolve the Political Bands which have connected them with another, and to aſſume among the Powers of the Earth, the ſeparate and equal Station to which the Laws of Nature and of Nature's God entitle them, a decent Reſpect to the Opinions of Mankind requires that they ſhould declare the cauſes which impel them to the Separation.

We hold theſe Truths to be ſelf-evident, that all Men are created equal, that they are endowed by their Creator with certain unalienable Rights, that among theſe are Life, Liberty, and the Purſuit of Happineſs——That to ſecure theſe Rights, Governments are inſtituted among Men, deriving their juſt Powers from the Conſent of the Governed, that whenever any Form of Government becomes deſtructive of theſe Ends, it is the Right of the People to alter or to aboliſh it, and to inſtitute new Government, laying its Foundation on ſuch Principles, and organizing its Powers in ſuch Form, as to them ſhall ſeem moſt likely to effect their Safety and Happineſs. Prudence, indeed, will dictate that Governments long eſtabliſhed ſhould not be changed for light and tranſient Cauſes; and accordingly all Experience hath ſhewn, that Mankind are more diſpoſed to ſuffer, while Evils are ſufferable, than to right themſelves by aboliſhing the Forms to which they are accuſtomed. But when a long Train of Abuſes and Uſurpations, purſuing invariably the ſame Object, evinces a Deſign to reduce them under abſolute Deſpotiſm, it is their Right, it is their Duty, to throw off ſuch Government, and to provide new Guards for their future Security. Such has been the patient Sufferance of theſe Colonies; and ſuch is now the Neceſſity which conſtrains them to alter their former Syſtems of Government. The Hiſtory of the preſent King of Great-Britain is a Hiſtory of repeated Injuries and Uſurpations, all having in direct Object the Eſtabliſhment of an abſolute Tyranny over theſe States. To prove this, let Facts be ſubmitted to a candid World.

He has refuſed his Aſſent to Laws, the moſt wholeſome and neceſſary for the public Good.

He has forbidden his Governors to paſs Laws of immediate and preſſing Importance, unleſs ſuſpended in their Operation till his Aſſent ſhould be obtained; and when ſo ſuſpended, he has utterly neglected to attend to them.

He has refuſed to paſs other Laws for the Accommodation of large Diſtricts of People, unleſs thoſe People would relinquiſh the Right of Repreſentation in the Legiſlature, a Right ineſtimable to them, and formidable to Tyrants only.

He has called together Legiſlative Bodies at Places unuſual, uncomfortable, and diſtant from the Depoſitory of their public Records, for the ſole Purpoſe of fatiguing them into Compliance with his Meaſures.

He has diſſolved Repreſentative Houſes repeatedly, for oppoſing with manly Firmneſs his Invaſions on the Rights of the People.

He has refuſed for a long Time, after ſuch Diſſolutions, to cauſe others to be elected; whereby the Legiſlative Powers, incapable of Annihilation, have returned to the People at large for their exerciſe; the State remaining in the mean time expoſed to all the Dangers of Invaſion from without, and Convulſions within.

He has endeavoured to prevent the Population of theſe States; for that Purpoſe obſtructing the Laws for Naturalization of Foreigners; refuſing to paſs others to encourage their Migrations hither, and raiſing the Conditions of new Appropriations of Lands.

He has obſtructed the Adminiſtration of Juſtice, by refuſing his Aſſent to Laws for eſtabliſhing Judiciary Powers.

He has made Judges dependent on his Will alone, for the Tenure of their Offices, and the Amount and Payment of their Salaries.

He has erected a Multitude of new Offices, and ſent hither Swarms of Officers to harraſs our People, and eat out their Subſtance.

He has kept among us, in Times of Peace, Standing Armies, without the conſent of our Legiſlatures.

He has affected to render the Military independent of and ſuperior to the Civil Power.

He has combined with others to ſubject us to a Juriſdiction foreign to our Conſtitution, and unacknowledged by our Laws; giving his Aſſent to their Acts of pretended Legiſlation:

For quartering large Bodies of Armed Troops among us:

P A R T

THE   QUESTION   OF   SOCIETY

It is a fine line—if any exists at all—between the question of moral values and the question of social and political values. Does not any ethical theory hold immediate implications for the larger context of the community or state? Can you imagine yourself in pursuit of your own good in complete independence of your social context? in complete indifference to it? Do not such issues as fairness, justice, freedom, and rights force themselves into the picture at some point? Consider the following list of sample issues:

- Civil disobedience
- Welfare
- Nuclear armament
- Eugenics
- Racial discrimination
- Labor unions
- Pornography
- Abortion
- Conscientious objection

Are these ethical issues? Are they social and political issues? Are they not clearly *both* ethical *and* social-political issues? Look at each one until you can say exactly how it involves and poses both an ethical and a social-political problem.

    Another point. Social and political philosophy may appear to overlap at times with the social sciences, such as sociology and political science, but its task is really a different one. The social-political philosopher is really not concerned with descriptive or empirical questions (we might call these "surface" questions), but with *normative* questions, or questions of *value:* What *is* the public good? How *should* it be implemented? What is the *basis* for talk of rights and justice?

CHAPTER 20

SOME HISTORICAL BACKGROUND

It is hardly possible to examine all of even the most relevant social-political theories. To be sure, in the next chapter (in some ways the central chapter of this part of the book) we will look fairly carefully at the issues and perspectives that bear most importantly on our own contemporary situation. Following that we will raise the more general but fundamental idea of justice. For the moment, though, we will look briefly at a few ideas from the ancient and medieval periods, not only because of their intrinsic interest but, especially in the case of natural law, because of the way they set the stage for subsequent developments.

PLATO: THE ELITIST

We begin with Plato for two reasons. First, he vividly represents a possible and important social-political perspective which we might call *elitism,* rule by a select few. Second, he is an excellent example of the way in which philosophers have conceived social-political issues not only as a necessary part of the philosophical enterprise but also as closely connected with other philosophical issues. It says something very important about Plato that his most famous work, and indeed possibly the most famous work in the history of philosophy, was called the *Republic.* It was a book about the *state.* Well, Yes and No. At least it was a book which showed how social-political issues can be all bound up with other philosophical concerns, such as ethics, metaphysics, epistemology, and even art.

Plato's most famous work: The *Republic*

We can be more specific. In Chapter 4 we provided some long quotations from the *Republic* for the sake of explaining Plato's theory of reality and knowledge.

435

Do you recall Plato's Analogy of the Sun, the image of the Divided Line, and the Allegory of the Cave? Now we can say just what all of that had to do with the *state*. Plato certainly did have a particular (some would say peculiar) view of the state, and a view that had everything to do with his view of reality and knowledge.

In the *Republic* Plato considered several political theories of his own time and rejected them. Whether or not we too reject them, it will do us no harm to review them. Moving from bad to worse, Plato first rejected *timocracy*, by which he meant the rule by those who are primarily motivated by ambition and honor. In such rulers, an inferior part of the soul, the spirited and emotional part, has gained dominance. He also rejected *oligarchy* or *plutocracy*, the rule by the rich. A preoccupation with wealth is even more base than a preoccupation with honor, and, moreover, the rule by the wealthy would inevitably bring about alienation and class warfare between "the haves" and "the have-nots." Next, he rejected *democracy* as yet a further degeneration of government, though he meant by this word something different from what we today understand by it. For Plato, in a smallish city-state like that of Athens, democracy meant the actual and equal participation of every citizen in the affairs of state, rather than participation by representation. But this is to reduce government to the lowest common denominator—as Plato saw it, when we have majority rule we have *mob* rule. Finally, and worst of all, Plato rejects *despotism*, or *tyranny*, or *dictatorship*, the absolute rule of a single individual. Of course there may be such a thing as a "benevolent dictator," but, Plato believed, never for long. According to Lord Acton's famous saying, "All power corrupts; absolute power corrupts absolutely." Eventually, such a ruler will be ruled by the very worst in himself, resulting in gross injustice and loss of the personal liberty that government ought to ensure.

Well then, *what*? Plato's answer: *aristocracy*. Again, however, Plato did not mean by this term what is today usually meant. When we hear the word "aristocracy" we think of the nobility class, as in the expression "the landed aristocracy." But the word itself simply means "rule of the *best*," and that is exactly what Plato favored—the rule of the best. And who are the best? Those who are enlightened with regard to reality, truth, and goodness. And who are these? Why, *philosophers*, of course—those who have emerged from the darkness of the Cave and have beheld the Good. Plato himself calls this the central thesis of the *Republic*: "Philosophers must be kings."

In the following passages from the *Republic*, Plato, through the mouth of Socrates, announces this revolutionary social program and explains what it is that makes the philosopher the "best" and makes him or her (it could easily be a *her* for Plato) the most qualified to rule.

> *Unless either philosophers become kings in their countries or those who are now called kings and rulers come to be sufficiently inspired with a genuine desire for wisdom; unless, that is to say, political power and philosophy meet together, while the many natures who now go their several ways in the one or the other direction are forcibly*

Some degenerate forms of government

"Philosophers must be kings"

debarred from doing so, there can be no rest from troubles, my dear Glaucon, for states, nor yet, as I believe, for all mankind; nor can this commonwealth which we have imagined ever till then see the light of day and grow to its full stature. This it was that I have so long hung back from saying; I knew what a paradox it would be, because it is hard to see that there is no other way of happiness either for the state or for the individual.

... Since the philosophers are those who can apprehend the eternal and unchanging, while those who cannot do so, but are lost in the mazes of multiplicity and change, are not philosophers, which of the two ought to be in control of a state?

I wonder what would be a reasonable solution.

To establish as Guardians whichever of the two appear competent to guard the laws and ways of life in society.

True.

Well, there can be no question whether a guardian who is to keep watch over anything needs to be keen-sighted or blind. And is not blindness precisely the condition of men who are entirely cut off from knowledge of any reality, and have in their soul no clear pattern of perfect truth, which they might study in every detail and constantly refer to, as a painter looks at his model, before they proceed to embody notions of justice, honour, and goodness in earthly institutions or, in their character of Guardians, to preserve such institutions as already exist?

Certainly such a condition is very like blindness.

Shall we, then, make such as these our Guardians in preference to men who, besides their knowledge of realities, are in no way inferior to them in experience and in every excellence of character?

It would be absurd not to choose the philosophers, whose knowledge is perhaps their greatest point of superiority, provided they do not lack those other qualifications.

What we have to explain, then, is how those qualifications can be combined in the same persons with philosophy.

Certainly.

The first thing, as we said at the outset, is to get a clear view of their inborn disposition. When we are satisfied on that head, I think we shall agree that such a combination of qualities is possible and that we need look no further for men fit to be in control of a commonwealth. One trait of the philosophic nature we may take as already granted: a constant passion for any knowledge that will reveal to them something of that reality which endures for ever and is not always passing into and out of existence. And, we may add, their desire is to know the whole of that reality; they will not willingly renounce any part of it as relatively small and insignificant, as we said before when we compared them to the lover and to the man who covets honour.

True.

Is there not another trait which the nature we are seeking cannot fail to possess—truthfulness, a love of truth and a hatred of falsehood that will not tolerate untruth in any form?

Yes, it is natural to expect that.

It is not merely natural, but entirely necessary that an instinctive passion for any object should extend to all that is closely akin to it; and there is nothing more closely akin to wisdom than truth. So the same nature cannot love wisdom and false-hood; the genuine lover of knowledge cannot fail, from his youth up, to strive after the whole of truth.

I perfectly agree.

Now we surely know that when a man's desires set strongly in one direction, in every other channel they flow more feebly, like a stream diverted into another bed. So when the current has set towards knowledge and all that goes with it, desire will abandon those pleasures of which the body is the instrument and be concerned only with the pleasure which the soul enjoys independently—if, that is to say, the love of wisdom is more than a mere pretence. Accordingly, such a one will be temperate and no lover of money; for he will be the last person to care about the things for the sake of which money is eagerly sought and lavishly spent.

That is true.

Again, in seeking to distinguish the philosophic nature, you must not overlook the least touch of meanness. Nothing could be more contrary than pettiness to a mind constantly bent on grasping the whole of things, both divine and human.

Quite true.

And do you suppose that one who is so high-minded and whose thought can contemplate all time and all existence will count this life of man a matter of much concern?

No, he could not.

So for such a man death will have no terrors.

None.

A mean and cowardly nature, then, can have no part in the genuine pursuit of wisdom.

I think not.

And if a man is temperate and free from the love of money, meanness, preten-tiousness, and cowardice, he will not be hard to deal with or dishonest. So, as another indication of the philosophic temper, you will observe whether, from youth up, he is fair-minded, gentle, and sociable.

Certainly.

Also you will not fail to notice whether he is quick or slow to learn. No one can be expected to take a reasonable delight in a task in which much painful effort makes little headway. And if he cannot retain what he learns his forgetfulness will leave no room in his head for knowledge; and so, having all his toil for nothing, he can only end by hating himself as well as his fruitless occupation. We must not, then, count a forgetful mind as competent to pursue wisdom; we must require a good memory.

By all means.

Further, there is in some natures a crudity and awkwardness that can only tend to a lack of measure and proportion; and there is a close affinity between pro-

portion and truth. Hence, besides our other requirements, we shall look for a mind endowed with measure and grace, which will be instinctively drawn to see every reality in its true light.

Yes.

Well then, now that we have enumerated the qualities of a mind destined to take its full part in the apprehension of reality, have you any doubt about their being indispensable and all necessarily going together?

None whatever.

Then have you any fault to find with a pursuit which none can worthily follow who is not by nature quick to learn and to remember, magnanimous and gracious, the friend and kinsman of truth, justice, courage, temperance?

No; Momus himself could find no flaw in it.

Well then, when time and education have brought such characters as these to maturity, would you entrust the care of your commonwealth to anyone else?[1]

It is difficult to say just how seriously one is to take Plato's proposal, though it is known that he himself tried to implement such a philosopher-kingship in Syracuse. But taking it as seriously as we can, not everyone will be thrilled with the announcement that philosophers must rule over the rest. In the first place, not everyone shares a Platonic conception of reality, truth, etc., and thus not everyone could agree with Plato as to just who the true philosophers are. Furthermore, any form of intellectual aristocracy would fail to gain the consent of a large segment of a society which is always suspicious of the "egg-head" elite. You may have heard the pronouncement: "I would rather be governed by the first twenty names in the

Intellectual aristocracy?

Plato rejected:

- Timocracy
- Plutocracy
- Democracy
- Dictatorship

He advocated

- Aristocracy

But exactly what did Plato mean by these terms?

[1]Plato, *The Republic*, 473C-E, 484B-487A, tr. Francis MacDonald Cornford (New York: Oxford University Press, 1945).

Boston telephone directory than all the professors at Harvard." Then too, not everyone would like other features of Plato's social-political program. It is true that he was one of the earliest advocates of women's rights, but he also proposed a program of eugenics, arranged marriages, community of property and children, and censorship.

ARISTOTLE: THE DEMOCRAT

Aristotle also had a high view of the state, as is clear from the opening lines of his *Politics*. The state is, in fact, the most encompassing of human institutions and strives for the highest good for the human being, whom Aristotle called not only a "rational animal" but also a "political animal."

> *Every state is a community of some kind, and every community is established with a view to some good; for mankind always act in order to obtain that which they think good. But, if all communities aim at some good, the state or political community, which is the highest of all, and which embraces all the rest, aims at good in a greater degree than any other, and at the highest good.*[2]

Aristotle, too, rejected the communistic and bizarre features of Plato's utopian state, as well as his intellectual elitism. Even though Aristotle himself believed, in his own way, in the rule of the best (not just anybody can occupy the highest offices), and even though he rejected *extreme* democracy (mob rule, again), he did believe, more commonsensically than Plato, that an adequate form of government must accommodate the rank and file of the citizenry with its collective experience and good sense, to say nothing of its greater stake in the political enterprise.

> *The principle that the multitude ought to be supreme rather than the few best is one that is maintained, and, though not free from difficulty, yet seems to contain an element of truth. For the many, of whom each individual is but an ordinary person, when they meet together may very likely be better than the few good, if regarded not individually but collectively, just as a feast to which many contribute is better than a dinner provided out of a single purse. For each individual among the many has a share of virtue and prudence, and when they meet together, they become in a manner one man, who has many feet, and hands, and senses; that is a figure of their mind and disposition. Hence the many are better judges than a single man of music and poetry; for some understand one part, and some another, and among them they understand the whole. There is a similar combination of qualities in good men, who differ from any individual of the many, as the beautiful are said to differ from those*

[2]Aristotle, *Politics*, 1251b–1252a, tr. Benjamin Jowett, in *Basic Works of Aristotle*, ed. Richard McKeon (New York: Random House, 1941).

*who are not beautiful, and works of art from realities, because in them the scattered
elements are combined, although, if taken separately, the eye of one person or some
other feature in another person would be fairer than in the picture. Whether this
principle can apply to every democracy, and to all bodies of men, is not clear. Or
rather, by heaven, in some cases it is impossible of application; for the argument
would equally hold about brutes; and wherein, it will be asked, do some men differ
from brutes? But there may be bodies of men about whom our statement is nevertheless
true. And if so, the difficulty which has been already raised, and also another which
is akin to it—viz. what power should be assigned to the mass of freemen and citizens,
who are not rich and have no personal merit—are both solved. There is still a danger
in allowing them to share the great offices of state, for their folly will lead them into
error, and their dishonesty into crime. But there is a danger also in not letting them
share, for a state in which many poor men are excluded from office will necessarily
be full of enemies. The only way of escape is to assign to them some deliberative and
judicial functions. For this reason Solon and certain other legislators give them the
power of electing to offices, and of calling the magistrates to account, but they do not
allow them to hold office singly. When they meet together their perceptions are quite
good enough, and combined with the better class they are useful to the state (just as
impure food when mixed with what is pure sometimes makes the entire mass more
wholesome than a small quantity of the pure would be), but each individual, left to
himself, forms an imperfect judgement.*[3]

IS THERE A NATURAL LAW?

One of Aristotle's most important contributions was his insistence on *natural law*
as the foundation of our social-political structures and institutions. Already in his
Ethics Aristotle distinguished between conventional law, or law that is established
by general agreement, and natural law, which is derived directly from the natural
order of the world and from built-in tendencies of human nature. And here, too,
is an example of the close connection between the question of reality and the question of value. Aristotle's idea of natural law is part and parcel of his metaphysical
view (as you know it from Chapter 4) of objective and fixed essences which define
the rationality and orderedness, or *lawfulness,* of things. As with all other fundamental principles, the fundamental principles of our social and political life are
discoverable in the very *nature* of things. "Man is a political animal" is as much a
statement about actual human nature as is "man is a rational animal." The basic
principles of social existence and institutions are not, therefore, "up for grabs";
rather, they are up for rational discovery, expression, and application.

In the following paragraphs from the *Politics,* Aristotle emphasizes that social
organization is derived from nature, that is, from the essential order of things.

*Aristotle on
natural law*

[3]*Ibid.,* 1281a–1281b.

NATURAL LAW

General and universal rules of conduct, both personal and social, derived rationally from nature.

Notice also that the state, "a creation of nature," is prior to the individual and necessary for the cultivation of human virtue.

> Hence it is evident that the state is a creation of nature, and that man is by nature a political animal. And he who by nature and not by mere accident is without a state, is either a bad man or above humanity; he is like the
>
> "Tribeless; lawless, heartless one,"
>
> whom Homer denounces—the natural outcast is forthwith a lover of war; he may be compared to an isolated piece at draughts.
>
> Now, that man is more of a political animal than bees or any other gregarious animals is evident. Nature, as we often say, makes nothing in vain, and man is the only animal whom she has endowed with the gift of speech. And whereas mere voice is but an indication of pleasure or pain, and is therefore found in other animals (for their nature attains to the perception of pleasure and pain and the intimation of them to one another, and no further), the power of speech is intended to set forth the expedient and inexpedient, and therefore likewise the just and the unjust. And it is a characteristic of man that he alone has any sense of good and evil, of just and unjust, and the like, and the association of living beings who have this sense makes a family and a state.
>
> Further, the state is by nature clearly prior to the family and to the individual, since the whole is of necessity prior to the part; for example, if the whole body be destroyed, there will be no foot or hand, except in an equivocal sense, as we might speak of a stone hand; for when destroyed the hand will be no better than that. But things are defined by their working and power, and we ought not to say that they are the same when they no longer have their proper quality, but only that they have the same name. The proof that the state is a creation of nature and prior to the individual is that the individual, when isolated, is not self-sufficing; and therefore he is like a part in relation to the whole. But he who is unable to live in society, or who has no need because he is sufficient for himself, must be either a beast or a god: he is no part of a state. A social instinct is implanted in all men by nature, and yet he who first founded the state was the greatest of benefactors. For man, when perfected, is the best of animals, but, when separated from law and justice, he is the worst of all; since

armed injustice is the more dangerous, and he is equipped at birth with arms, meant to be used by intelligence and virtue, which he may use for the worst ends. Wherefore, if he have not virtue, he is the most unholy and the most savage of animals, and the most full of lust and gluttony. But justice is the bond of men in states, for the administration of justice, which is the determination of what is just, is the principle of order in political society.[4]

It has been seen already how St. Thomas took over much of Aristotle's philosophy and transformed it in a Christian light. Certainly this happened in the case of Aristotle's idea of natural law, and St. Thomas' Christianized version has become one of its most forceful expressions. Actually, St. Thomas distinguished *four* kinds of law, and it is necessary to spell out all of them if we are to appreciate the character and role of natural law in specific. (1) *Eternal law* is the governance of all things by the divine reason and, by virtue of its foundation in God himself, is unalterable and eternal. (2) *Natural law* refers to the eternal law as it is revealed specifically in human nature and known by human reason, which is an offspring of the divine reason; it provides direction for humanity's natural end, that is, its purpose in *this* world. (3) *Human law* refers to specific statutes and legislation contrived by humans in an attempt to express and apply the natural law to concrete and practical situations. (4) *Divine law* provides the direction for humanity's supernatural end, that is, its purpose for God and *eternity*, and is known only through divine grace and special revelation rather than through reason.

In St. Thomas' thinking all of these are inseparably related to one another. Not to play down any of them, clearly the second and third hold the most relevance for our present discussion. Eternal law is an interesting metaphysical idea;

St. Thomas: Four kinds of law

ST. THOMAS: FOUR KINDS OF LAW

- *Eternal law:* God's unalterable rule over all things.
- *Natural law:* Universal rules of conduct known from human nature.
- *Human law:* Statutes and legislation contrived by humans.
- *Divine law:* Specially revealed will of God for humanity's supernatural or religious end.

---

[4]Ibid., 1253a–1253b.

divine law is an interesting religious or theological idea; but natural law and human law bear directly on social and political issues. In the following, from the *Summa Theologiae*, St. Thomas comments especially on these.

> *... law, being a rule and measure, can be in a person in two ways: in one way, as in him that rules and measures; in another way, as in that which is ruled and measured, since a thing is ruled and measured in so far as it partakes of the rule or measure. Therefore, since all things subject to divine providence are ruled and measured by the eternal law, as was stated above, it is evident that all things partake in some way in the eternal law, in so far as, namely, from its being imprinted on them, they derive their respective inclinations to their proper acts and ends. Now among all others, the rational creature is subject to divine providence in a more excellent way, in so far as it itself partakes of a share of providence, by being provident both for itself and for others. Therefore it has a share of the eternal reason, whereby it has a natural inclination to its proper act and end; and this participation of the eternal law in the rational creature is called the natural law. Hence the Psalmist, after saying (Ps. iv. 6): "Offer up the sacrifice of justice," as though someone asked what the works of justice are, adds: "Many say, Who showeth us good things?" in answer to which question he says: "The light of Thy countenance, O Lord, is signed upon us." He thus implies that the light of natural reason, whereby we discern what is good and what is evil, which is the function of the natural law, is nothing else than an imprint on us of the divine light. It is therefore evident that the natural law is nothing else than the rational creature's participation of the eternal law.*
>
> *... a law is a dictate of the practical reason. Now it is to be observed that the same procedure takes place in the practical and in the speculative reason, for each proceeds from principles to conclusions, as was stated above. Accordingly, we conclude that, just as in the speculative reason, from naturally known indemonstrable principles we draw the conclusions of the various sciences, the knowledge of which is not imparted to us by nature, but acquired by the efforts of reason, so too it is that from the precepts of the natural law, as from common and indemonstrable principles, the human reason needs to proceed to the more particular determination of certain matters. These particular determinations, devised by human reason, are called human laws, provided that the other essential conditions of law be observed, as was stated above. Therefore Tully says in his Rhetoric that "justice has its source in nature; thence certain things came into custom by reason of their utility; afterwards these things which emanated from nature, and were approved by custom, were sanctioned by fear and reverence for the law."[5]*

It is important to see what is the key to any doctrine of natural law. Although St. Thomas' doctrine of natural law was all wrapped up in a Christian view of

---

[5]St. Thomas Aquinas, *Summa Theologiae*, Pt. I–II, Qu. 91, Arts. 2–3, in *Basic Writings of St. Thomas Aquinas*, ed. Anton C. Pegis (New York: Random House, 1945), II.

reality, one does not have to be a Christian to believe in natural law: St. Thomas was, but Aristotle wasn't. What *is* required, however, is at least a *general* view of reality (which Aristotle and St. Thomas did in fact share) such that value in general, and social and political values in specific, is seen as built right into the world and human nature from the start, and can be, as we said before, rationally discovered, expressed, and applied. Thus, while this does not presuppose a Christian perspective, it is no accident that the idea of natural law has been propounded mainly by thinkers of a religious or theistic bent. For such people believe, for one reason or another, that the universe is rational, that there is a rhyme and reason to things, and that values have an objective and abiding foundation.

> "... the light of natural reason, whereby we discern what is good and what is evil, which is the function of the natural law, is nothing else than an imprint on us of the divine light."
>
> —St. Thomas

Chapter 20 in Review

SUMMARY

You may recall that at the beginning of Chapter 4 we said that Plato was the first *systematic* philosopher in the sense that he was the first to work out the implications of a fundamental philosophical principle for all major spheres of our experience. And we saw what his idea of Form meant for his theory of reality, his theory of knowledge, and even his theory of art. In this chapter we now see what it meant for his theory of the state. His thesis that "philosophers must be kings" follows from his view that only philosophers are in touch with absolute truth and reality, and since this means that only they know what the absolute good is, they alone are fit to rule over the rest. Many will reject this aristocratic conception of government as elitist, as did Plato's student Aristotle.

Aristotle himself shared Plato's fears about mob rule, but opted nonetheless for a more democratic form of government which would reflect and represent the common interest as seen by the citizenry itself.

We have already seen more than once how the Christian philosopher St. Thomas Aquinas was influenced by Aristotle, and this connection shows up again in their social-political ideas. Specifically, the important notion of natural law has deep roots in the Aristotelian-Thomistic tradition. Aristotle had already distinguished between conventional law (established by agreement) and natural law (rationally apprehended from nature), and St. Thomas elaborated the fourfold distinction: eternal law, natural law, human law, and divine law. According to St. Thomas, God is the foundation of all spheres of law, including natural law, which can be known rationally and which expresses the will of God for human beings in this world, and which is imperfectly expressed in human law, or legislation for our practical and social life together.

BASIC IDEAS

- Elitism
- Plato: degenerate forms of government
  Timocracy
  Plutocracy
  Democracy
  Dictatorship
- Aristocracy
- Plato: Why philosophers must be kings
- Aristotle's democracy
- Natural law
- Aristotle: the human being as a "political animal"
- St. Thomas' four kinds of law
  Eternal law
  Natural law
  Human law
  Divine law

TEST YOURSELF

1. How might it be claimed that Aristotle's doctrine of natural law is part and parcel of his metaphysics?
2. True or false: Plato rejected democracy, though he favored democracy over tyranny.
3. Both Plato and Aristotle desired the rule of the *best*. But how did they differ?
4. According to Plato, the best form of government is _____.
5. Who said it? " ... the natural law is nothing else than the rational creature's participation of the eternal law."

QUESTIONS FOR REFLECTION

- If elitism means rule by a select few, is there anything to be said in its favor? Does it matter *why* they are "select"? Would you not gladly submit yourself to the elite (best trained, etc.) in other fields, say, medicine or education? Or would you rather be governed by the first twenty names in the Boston phone book? What's to be said for and against *this* view?
- What is the importance of the idea of natural law? How is it at once a metaphysical, epistemological, and social-political concept? Do you believe in it?

CHAPTER 21

LIBERALISM VS. MARXISM

There can be little doubt that our own contemporary social and political scene is determined almost entirely by the debate between liberalism and Marxism. These are social-political ideologies involving many considerations, and are no doubt best-known by their specifically economic expressions, capitalism and communism. It behooves us to grasp these competing perspectives if we are to be informed about the social-political realities which continue to confront us.

THE LIBERAL PERSPECTIVE: LOCKE

When you see the word "liberal" you may think of something leftish or socialistic—something opposite of "conservative." In our present context, however, the word refers to a general social-political theory which, indeed, underlies our *whole* social and political system, including *both* liberals and conservatives. We might better call it *classical* liberalism. The heart of liberalism in this sense is evident from the word itself. "Liberalism" comes from the Latin *libertas*, "liberty" or "freedom." It insists on the freedom of the individual: both freedom *from* undue external and governmental controls, and freedom *for* the pursuit of individual interests. Can you identify examples of *freedoms from* and *freedoms for*, in the first ten amendments to the Constitution of the United States? (They were ratified on December 15, 1791.)

Classical liberalism: Freedom

AMENDMENT 1

Congress shall make no law respecting an establishment of religion, or prohibiting the free exercise thereof; or abridging the freedom of speech, or of the press; or the right

447

of the people peaceably to assemble, and to petition the Government for a redress of grievances.

AMENDMENT II

A well regulated Militia, being necessary to the security of a free State, the right of the people to keep and bear Arms, shall not be infringed.

AMENDMENT III

No Soldier shall, in time of peace be quartered in any house, without the consent of the Owner, nor in time of war, but in a manner to be prescribed by law.

AMENDMENT IV

The right of the people to be secure in their persons, houses, papers, and effects, against unreasonable searches and seizures, shall not be violated, and no Warrants shall issue, but upon probable cause, supported by Oath or affirmation, and particularly describing the place to be searched, and the persons or things to be seized.

AMENDMENT V

No person shall be held to answer for a capital, or otherwise infamous crime, unless on a presentment or indictment of a Grand Jury, except in cases arising in the land or naval forces, or in the Militia, when in actual service in time of War or public danger; nor shall any person be subject for the same offence to be twice put in jeopardy of life or limb; nor shall be compelled in any Criminal Case to be a witness against himself, nor be deprived of life, liberty, or property, without due process of law; nor shall private property be taken for public use, without just compensation.

AMENDMENT VI

In all criminal prosecutions the accused shall enjoy the right to a speedy and public trial, by an impartial jury of the State and district wherein the crime shall have been committed, which district shall have been previously ascertained by law, and to be informed of the nature and cause of the accusation; to be confronted with the witnesses against him; to have compulsory process for obtaining Witnesses in his favor, and to have the Assistance of Counsel for his defence.

AMENDMENT VII

In suits at common law, where the value in controversy shall exceed twenty dollars, the right of trial by jury shall be preserved, and no fact tried by a jury, shall be otherwise re-examined in any Court of the United States, than according to the rules of the common law.

AMENDMENT VIII

Excessive bail shall not be required, nor excessive fines imposed, nor cruel and unusual punishments inflicted.

AMENDMENT IX

The enumeration in the Constitution, of certain rights, shall not be construed to deny or disparage others retained by the people.

AMENDMENT X

The powers not delegated to the United States by the Constitution, nor prohibited by it to the States, are reserved to the States respectively, or to the people.[1]

CLASSICAL LIBERALISM

The social-political theory that stresses freedom from undue governmental interference, and views the state as the guarantor of the basic liberties and rights of the individual.

Classical liberalism may also be called *individualism,* inasmuch as it affirms the individual over the state, which is seen not as the master but as the servant of the individual, and as the guarantor of the individual's interests and rights.

The primary moving force of the classical liberal perspective was the English philosopher John Locke, who, as we saw in Chapter 10, was also one of the founders of modern empiricism. Several ideas are basic to an understanding of Locke's social-political theory.

First, like many who preceded him, Locke believed that all private and public good is based on the *natural law* which immediately displays fundamental rights and liberties. As with St. Thomas, the real foundation of the natural law is God. And, as with St. Thomas, this natural and divine law is "plain and intelligible to all rational creatures"—at least to as many who will take the time and trouble. (Locke's idea of natural law was no more a contradiction to his empiricism than was St. Thomas' idea a contradiction to *his* empiricism. Knowledge, natural law, and

Natural law, again

[1]William MacDonald (ed.), *Documentary Source Book of American History, 1606–1926,* 3d ed. (New York: Burt Franklin, 1926), pp. 229-230 (slightly edited).

all other ideas as well, result from reflection on experience.) Both of these ideas, namely, that God is the objective source of natural law, and that this law can be discovered rationally, are clear in the following lines from the *Essay Concerning Human Understanding*:

> The idea of a Supreme Being, infinite in power, goodness, and wisdom, whose work-manship we are, and on whom we depend; and the idea of ourselves, as understand-ing, rational beings, being such as are clear in us, would, I suppose, if duly considered and pursued, afford such foundations of our duty and rules of action as might place morality amongst the sciences capable of demonstration: *wherein I doubt not, but from self-evident propositions, by necessary consequences, as incontestable as those in mathematics, the measures of right and wrong might be made out, to any one that will apply himself with the same indifferency and attention to the one as he does to the other of those sciences.*[2]

The "state of nature"

Next is Locke's idea of the *state of nature*. Others before him, such as the Englishman Thomas Hobbes and the Frenchman Jean Jacques Rousseau, had stressed the state of nature as the only adequate starting point for the development of a system of social and political life. For we must seek to understand what the human situation *really* is, before this becomes possibly confused or distorted by the imposition of the rules and regulations of civil government. For example, it was very important for Locke, in his time, to question and *challenge* the prevailing notion of the divine right of kings—that monarchs are established by God, and that all others are, therefore, by nature subservient to them. Locke asks whether this is justified by an analysis of humanity in its *natural* state. And he answers with a resounding, No! The natural state is governed by natural law, and natural law legislates *freedom, equality,* and therefore *inherent rights for all.*

> The state of nature *has a law of nature to govern it, which obliges everyone: and reason, which is that law, teaches all mankind, who will but consult it, that, being all equal and independent, no one ought to harm another in his life, health, liberty or possessions.*[3]

Such a conclusion may not seem so striking today. But that only shows how deeply influenced our own values are by Locke's ideas which, in his time, were certainly striking enough. It was a question of the *divine right of royalty* and the *divine royalty of right.*

The theoretical state of nature is, thus, very important. But it is only theo-retical. In spite of its advantages of freedom and equality, we do not, nor can we, actually live in such a state, at least not for long. In the selection below, Locke tells

[2]John Locke, *Essay Concerning Human Understanding,* IV, 3, 18, ed. A. S. Pringle-Pattison (Oxford-Clar-endon Press, 1924).

[3]John Locke, *Second Treatise of Government,* 6, ed. C. B. Macpherson (Indianapolis: Hackett, 1980).

us why. For one thing, most people do not pay sufficient attention to the rational dictates of natural law, and even if they did, their selfish concerns would prevent an unbiased application of it. Second, in such a state there would be no way of judging or arbitrating between the differences that would inevitably arise. And even so, third, no such judgment would have backing or authority so that it could be meaningfully enforced. Locke mentions these specific problems, but you can easily imagine others which would make life in a state of nature impossible from a practical standpoint. The conclusion: Men are quickly driven into society. Enter the idea of the *social contract*. As you know, any contract involves giving up something and getting something in return. A *social* contract is an agreement between members of a society according to which each forfeits certain rights and privileges in order to preserve others. Thus I see that it is much to my advantage to submit myself to government, to obey laws, etc., if thereby I can secure my fundamental freedoms and rights, and *especially* if I, as one of the contractors, have a say, either directly (pure democracy) or indirectly (as in representative democracy), in the character of that government, its law, etc.

The social contract

It is important to see that the order of (1) state of nature, and (2) social contract, is a *logical* rather than a *historical* order. How many of us have ever actually lived in a state of nature? Do we not, rather, just find ourselves already members of some social system? No matter. That does not undermine the idea of the social contract, for as long as we remain in such a system (however we got there) we give *tacit consent*, says Locke, to that system. That is, the social contract is not necessarily something that is drawn up "once upon a time," but rather all the time: By their

"Tacit consent"

LOCKE'S FOURFOLD BASIS OF CLASSICAL LIBERALISM

- *Natural law:* The rationally knowable morality which is founded in God's will for his creatures.
- *State of nature:* The human condition of natural freedoms and rights prior to the imposition of social organization and regulation.
- *Social contract:* The agreement among a group of people to establish social organizations and regulations for the preservation of basic freedoms and rights.
- *Tacit consent:* The consent to and support of social organizations and regulations by virtue of an individual's continued participation in them.

participation in the system, the members *continually* consent to, agree to, and support the contract.

The central points of Locke's liberal ideals are reflected in the following from his *Second Treatise of Government*.

OF THE BEGINNING OF POLITICAL SOCIETIES

Men being, as has been said, by nature, all free, equal, and independent, no one can be put out of this estate, and subjected to the political power of another, without his own consent. The only way whereby any one divests himself of his natural liberty, and puts on the bonds of civil society, *is by agreeing with other men to join and unite into a community for their comfortable, safe, and peaceable living one amongst another, in a secure enjoyment of their properties, and a greater security against any, that are not of it. This any number of men may do, because it injures not the freedom of the rest; they are left as they were in the liberty of the state of nature. When any number of men have so* consented to make one community or government, *they are thereby presently incorporated, and make* one body politic, *wherein the majority have a right to act and conclude the rest.*

For when any number of men have, by the consent of every individual, made a community, they have thereby made that community one body, with a power to act as one body, which is only by the will and determination of the majority: *for that which acts any community, being only the consent of the individuals of it, and it being necessary to that which is one body to move one way; it is necessary the body should move that way whither the greater force carries it, which is the* consent of the majority: *or else it is impossible it should act or continue one body, one community, which the consent of every individual that united into it, agreed that it should; and so everyone is bound by that consent to be concluded by the* majority. *And therefore we see, that in assemblies, impowered to act by positive laws, where no number is set by that positive law which impowers them, the* act of the majority *passes for the act of the whole, and of course determines, as having, by the law of nature and reason, the power of the whole.*

And thus every man, by consenting with others to make one body politic under one government, puts himself under an obligation, to every one of that society, to submit to the determination of the majority, *and to be concluded by it; or else this* original compact, *whereby he with others incorporates into one society, would signify nothing, and be no compact, if he be left free, and under no other ties than he was in before in the state of nature. For what appearance would there be of any compact? What new engagement if he were no farther tied by any decrees of the society, than he himself thought fit, and did actually consent to? This would be still as great a liberty, as he himself had before his compact, or anyone else in the state of nature hath, who may submit himself, and consent to any acts of it if he thinks fit.*

For if the consent of the majority shall not, in reason, be received as the act of the whole, and conclude every individual; nothing but the consent of every individual can make anything to be the act of the whole: but such a consent is next to impossible ever to be had if we consider the infirmities of health, and avocations of business, which in a number, though much less than that of a common-wealth, will necessarily keep many away from the public assembly. To which if we add the variety of opinions, and contrariety of interests, which unavoidably happen in all collections of men, the coming into society be upon such terms it will be only like Cato's coming into the theater, only to go out again. Such a constitution as this would make the mighty Leviathan of a shorter duration, than the feeblest creatures, and not let it outlast the day it was born in: which cannot be supposed, till we can think, that rational creatures should desire and constitute societies only to be dissolved: for where the majority cannot conclude the rest, there they cannot act as one body, and consequently will be immediately dissolved again.

Whosoever therefore out of a state of nature unite into a community must be understood to give up all the power, necessary to the ends for which they unite into society, to the majority of the community, unless they expressly agreed in any number greater than the majority. And this is done by barely agreeing to unite into one political society, which is all the compact that is, or needs be, between the individuals, that enter into, or make up a commonwealth. And thus that, which begins and actually constitutes any political society, is nothing but the consent of any number of freemen capable of a majority to unite and incorporate into such a society. And this is that, and that only, which did, or could give beginning to any lawful government in the world.

OF THE ENDS OF POLITICAL SOCIETY AND GOVERNMENT

If man in the state of nature be so free, as has been said; if he be absolute lord of his own person and possessions, equal to the greatest, and subject to no body, why will he part with his freedom? why will he give up his empire, and subject himself to the dominion and control of any other power? To which it is obvious to answer, that though in the state of nature he hath such a right, yet the enjoyment of it is very uncertain, and constantly exposed to the invasions of others: for all being kings as much as he, every man his equal, and the greater part no strict observers of equity and justice, the enjoyment of the property he has in this state is very unsafe, very unsecure. This makes him willing to quit a condition, which, however free, is full of fears and continual dangers: and it is not without reason, that he seeks out, and is willing to join in society with others, who are already united, or have a mind to unite, for the mutual preservation of their lives, liberties and estates, which I call by the general name, property.

The great and chief end, therefore, of men's uniting into common-wealths, and putting themselves under government, is the preservation of their property. To which in the state of nature there are many things wanting.

First, There wants an established, settled, known law, received and allowed by common consent to be the standard of right and wrong, and the common measure to decide all controversies between them: for though the law of nature be plain and intelligible to all rational creatures; yet men being biased by their interest, as well as *ignorant for want of study of it, are not apt to allow of it as a law binding to them in the application of it to their particular cases.*

Secondly, In the state of nature there wants a known and indifferent judge, with authority to determine all differences according to the established law: for everyone in that state being both judge and executioner of the law of nature, men being partial to themselves, passion and revenge is very apt to carry them too far, and with too much heat, in their own cases; as well as negligence, and unconcernedness, to make them too remiss in other men's.

Thirdly, In the state of nature there often wants power to back and support the sentence when right, and to give it due execution. They who by any injustice offended, will seldom fail, where they are able, by force to make good their injustice; such resistance many times makes the punishment dangerous, and frequently destructive, to those who attempt it.

Thus mankind, notwithstanding all the privileges of the state of nature, being but in an ill condition, while they remain in it, are quickly driven into society. Hence it comes to pass, that we seldom find any number of men live any time together in this state. The inconveniences that they are therein exposed to, by the irregular and uncertain exercise of the power every man has of punishing the transgressions of others, make them take sanctuary under the established laws of government, and therein seek the preservation of their property. It is this makes them so willingly give up everyone his single power of punishing, to be exercised by such alone, as shall be appointed to it amongst them; and by such rules as the community, or those authorized by them to that purpose, shall agree on. And in this we have the original right and rise of both the legislative and executive power, as well as of the governments and societies themselves. . . .

But though men, when they enter into society, give up the equality, liberty, and executive power they had in the state of nature, into the hands of the society, to be so far disposed of by the legislative, as the good of the society shall require; yet it being only with an intention in everyone the better to preserve himself, his liberty and property; (for no rational creature can be supposed to change his condition with an intention to be worse) the power of the society, or legislative constituted by them, can never be supposed to extend farther than the common good; but is obliged to secure everyone's property by providing against those three defects above-mentioned that made the state of nature so unsafe and uneasy. And so whoever has the legislative or supreme power of any common-wealth, is bound to govern by established standing laws, promulgated and known to the people, and not by extemporary decrees; by indifferent and upright judges, who are to decide controversies by those laws; and to employ the force of the community at home, only in the execution of such laws, or abroad to prevent or redress foreign injuries, and secure the community from inroads and invasion. And all this to be directed to no other end, but the peace, safety, and public good of the people.[4]

[4]Ibid., 95–99, 123–127, 131.

> ## Of EDUCATION.   223
>
> to be made, and what weight they
> out to have.
>
> §. 177. *Rhetorick* and *Logick* being *Rhetorick.*
> the Arts that in the ordinary method *Logick.*
> usually follow immediately after Gram-
> mar, it may perhaps be wondered that
> I have said so little of them: The rea-
> son is, because of the little advantage
> young People receive by them: For I
> have seldom or never observed any one
> to get the Skill of reasoning well, or
> speaking handsomly by studying those
> Rules, which pretend to teach it: And
> therefore I would have a young Gen-
> tleman take a view of them in the
> shortest Systems could be found, with-
> out dwelling long on the contempla-
> tion and study of those Formalities.
> Right Reasoning is founded on some-
> thing else than the *Predicaments* and *Pre-*
> *dicables,* and does not consist in talking
> in *Mode* and *Figure* it self. But 'tis be-
> sides my present Business to enlarge up-
> on this Speculation: To come there-
> fore to what we have in hand; if you
> would have your Son *Reason well,* let
> him read *Chillingworth*; and if you
> would have him speak well, let him
> be conversant in *Tully,* to give him
>   the

Page from Locke's Concerning Education, published in 1695.

Much of this should have a familiar ring. It is not for nothing that Locke is called the spiritual father of the U.S. Constitution. Thomas Jefferson, who in 1776 drafted the Declaration of Independence, declared outright that his intent was that it should embody the social and political principles of Locke and like-minded theorists. Are not the ideas of natural law, social contract, and individual rights apparent in the very first lines of the Declaration of Independence? And is not the very language at times almost identical with what we read above in Locke?

Locke: The spirit behind the U.S. Constitution

When in the Course of human events, it becomes necessary for one people to dissolve the political bands which have connected them with another, and to assume among the Powers of the earth, the separate and equal station to which the Laws of Nature and of Nature's God entitle them, a decent respect to the opinions of mankind requires that they should declare the causes which impel them to the separation.

We hold these truths to be self-evident, that all men are created equal, that they are endowed by their Creator with certain unalienable Rights, that among these are Life, Liberty and the pursuit of Happiness. That to secure these rights, Governments are instituted among Men, deriving their just powers from the consent of the governed. That whenever any Form of Government becomes destructive of these ends, it is the Right of the People to alter or to abolish it, and to institute new Government, laying its foundation on such principles and organizing its powers in such form, as to them shall seem most likely to effect their Safety and Happiness.[5]

LIBERALISM AND CAPITALISM

What is capitalism?

Classical liberalism means many different kinds of freedom. One of these is economic freedom, the freedom of the individual, either alone or (as with corporations) in union with others, to own the means of production (land, tools, factories, etc.), and to produce and sell goods for a profit. This is *capitalism*. That Locke himself saw this as a legitimate aspect of his liberal and individualistic vision is clear

---

JOHN LOCKE

John Locke was born in 1632 in a small town near Bristol, England, lost his mother at an early age, and was raised on Puritan principles by a stern father. His childhood studies centered around grammar and languages (Greek, Latin, Hebrew, and Arabic) and were so harsh as to cause Locke later to condemn excessive discipline in the schools. Out of these austere beginnings, in 1652 the 20-year-old Locke entered Oxford University. In spite of a distaste for Scholastic philosophy, which he thought obscure and irrelevant, he received his B.A. in 1656, followed by his M.A., and became a tutor at Oxford in Greek and Latin.

After his father's death in 1661, which resulted in a slight inheritance, Locke fell under the spell of the new sciences, and his interest in experimental and empirical methods came alive. Indeed, he now chose for himself the medical profession, though, as it turned out, he never actually practiced—except for delivering a baby and removing a tumor from someone's chest. He was sidetracked by

---

[5]MacDonald, *Documentary Source Book of American History, 1606–1926*, p. 191 (slightly edited).

Descartes, who seemed to provide an impressive alternative to the still-dominant Scholastic philosophy.

In 1667, a close association with Lord Ashley, later first earl of Shaftesbury, thrust Locke into many political affairs and offices. He participated, for example, in drafting the constitution of the Crown Colony of Carolina. Largely for reasons of health, he spent 1675–1679 in France, where he pursued further his interest in Descartes. Upon his return to England he found that the continuing struggle against the divine right of kings lay somewhat closer to home. His friend Shaftesbury was in deep trouble with King Charles II because of his promotion of the common class against the king and nobles: He was dispatched to the Tower of London, eventually tried for treason, and acquitted. And Locke's own position was none too certain either. It was guilt by association, and he too was now denounced as a traitor. He fled to Holland in 1683 and hid in the house of a physician friend. Here he continued work on his *Essay Concerning Human Understanding* and produced several other pieces. The revolutionary plot of 1688 to place William of Orange on the English throne was successful, with some help from Locke himself, and in February 1689 he returned to England, escort of the princess of Orange, the future Queen Mary.

Locke's two most influential books were published in 1690: the *Essay* and *Two Treatises of Civil Government;* the first is a classic of empiricist epistemology, and in the latter Locke attacked the divine right of kings and proposed his own liberal political theory. During this time he continued to be actively occupied with the affairs of state, his practical contributions being much in demand.

In 1691, the aging Locke settled permanently in Oates, at the home of his friends Lord and Lady Masham, continuing with his writing and participating in the controversy surrounding his *The Reasonableness of Christianity,* published in 1695. During his last and failing years he turned to Biblical studies and wrote commentaries on the epistles of St. Paul. He died on October 28, 1704, as Lady Masham was reading to him from the Psalms. She wrote: "His death was like his life, truly pious, yet natural, easy and unaffected." He was a giant in the history of philosophy, having contributed a monumental work on epistemology and having been a decisive voice for individual freedom and religious tolerance.

His major works include: *Essay Concerning Human Understanding, First Letter Concerning Toleration, Two Treatises of Government, Some Thoughts Concerning Education,* and *The Reasonableness of Christianity.*

from the recurring references to "property" in the quotation from his *Second Treatise*, as in the inherent right of the individual "to preserve himself, his liberty and property" (compare the phrase from the Declaration of Independence, "Life, Liberty and the pursuit of Happiness"). One could argue, in fact, that Locke regarded the right of property as the *most important* of natural rights. Certainly he has already told us that it is primarily out of interest in personal property that people enter into social contracts in the first place: "The great and *chief end,* therefore, of men's uniting into common-wealths, and putting themselves under government, *is the preservation of their property.*"

However, it was after the time of Locke, during the period of the industrial revolution, that this *economic* implication of liberalism became most clearly focused. More specifically, it was the Scottish writer Adam Smith (1723–1790) who, in his *Inquiry into the Nature and Causes of the Wealth of Nations,* gave decisive expression to the rights of the individual in a free marketplace, that is, capitalism. Smith's watchword was *laissez faire,* French for "let it alone," and often rendered as "Hands off!" But it must be stressed that Smith and the *laissez faire* economists were not advocating the principle of allow-the-individual-complete-liberty-in-commerce-and-let-the-rest-be-damned. They believed—and is not the idea still believed?—that a *laissez faire* approach to economics would provide the best for *everyone.* The mechanisms involved in supply-and-demand and free enterprise make for an efficient and satisfying arrangement for all concerned: owner, merchant, worker, consumer. So, even though Smith advocated a hands-off economy, he believed in an "invisible hand," or the mechanisms we just spoke of, such that whatever the capitalist's own intention might be, the interest and good of a capitalist society as a whole would be promoted. This comes out well in the following paragraph from the *Wealth of Nations:*

> . . . *the annual revenue of every society is always precisely equal to the exchangeable value of the whole annual produce of its industry, or rather is precisely the same thing with that exchangeable value. As every individual, therefore, endeavours as much as he can both to employ his capital in the support of domestic industry, and so to direct*

"Hands-off" economy

The "invisible hand" behind capitalism

CAPITALISM

The economic theory which advocates that the means of production, and the actual production and exchange of goods and wealth, should be owned and implemented by private individuals or corporations, with a view toward profit.

Adam Smith

The Scot, Adam Smith, was the author of the Wealth of Nations, *the classical statement of the capitalist theory of economics. It was published in 1776.*

that industry that its produce may be of the greatest value; every individual necessarily labours to render the annual revenue of the society as great as he can. He generally, indeed, neither intends to promote the public interest, nor knows how much he is promoting it. By preferring the support of domestic to that of foreign industry, he intends only his own security; and by directing that industry in such a manner as its produce may be of the greatest value, he intends only his own gain, and he is in this, as in many other cases, led by an invisible hand to promote an end which was no part of his intention. Nor is it always the worse for the society that it was no part of it. By pursuing his own interest he frequently promotes that of the society more effectually than when he really intends to promote it. I have never known much good done by those who affected to trade for the public good. It is an affectation, indeed, not very common among merchants, and very few words need be employed in dissuading them from it.[6]

---

[6]Adam Smith, *An Inquiry into the Nature and Causes of the Wealth of Nations,* ed. Edwin Cannan (New York: Modern Library, 1937), p. 423.

Is it relevant that the *Wealth of Nations* was published in 1776? For better or for worse, these ideas have had everything to do with the shaping of the American social-political-economic system. And now we are in a better position to appreciate how the words "liberal" and "conservative" are used in contemporary political discussion. Both liberals and conservatives embrace the twofold ideal of classical liberalism. (1) individual rights and (2) the social responsibility of the state. The difference is that conservatives defend individual freedom against the encroachment of the state, whereas liberals stress the responsibility of the state to ensure individual rights.

But the real attack on the classical liberal perspective originates far to the left of the liberals. And this brings us to the radical alternative and challenge of *Marxism*.

A RADICAL RESPONSE: MARX

If the perspectives we are considering in this part of the book seek to address actual, practical, social, and political life, then Marxism takes the prize. Perhaps no philosophy has had more of a direct impact on the social and political existence of untold numbers of people than that introduced by the German thinker and social theorist Karl Marx (1818–1883). By its nature, the Marxist program presses for change—radical and revolutionary change.

The influence of Hegel

It is often the case that we must look for the roots of a philosophy in some earlier philosophy. In some important ways, the roots of Marxism lie in the German idealist thinker G. W. F. Hegel[7] (1770–1831). Hegel's philosophy is an enormous intellectual monument, but a few basic points will suffice for the moment. First, Hegel was an objective idealist. You will recall from Chapter 6 that an objective idealist believes that reality is idea-istic or spiritual in nature, but that it exists objectively or independently of us, "out there." Hegel himself believed in this way that reality was *spirit*, but, second, that this spiritual reality is constantly on the move, changing, advancing, and actualizing the ultimate state which he called *Absolute Spirit*, otherwise represented as the complete consciousness and freedom of reality. Finally, the mechanism by which this historical-spiritual process is achieved is

> "Philosophers have only interpreted the world in various ways; the point, however, is to change it."
>
> —Marx

[7]Rhymes with *bagel*.

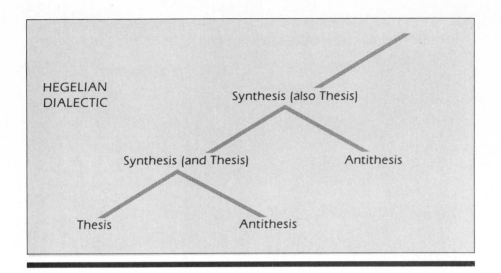

called *dialectic*. In this context, "dialectic" means the give-and-take between opposite states resulting in always-emerging higher unities. More technically, this process is represented as the *synthesis* (or unity) of *thesis* and *antithesis* (opposite states),
a process going on constantly in all spheres of existence, and where, at any moment,
a synthesis of opposites becomes itself an opposite to be synthesized with another,
as illustrated above.

    What can this superspeculative and abstract conception have to do with the
superpractical and down-to-earth concerns of Marxism?

    Marx took over the idea of the historical dialectic, but under the influence
of another German philosopher, Feuerbach, gave it a materialistic twist. Result: *dialectical materialism*. This phrase was never used by Marx himself. Nevertheless, it
serves well enough to suggest the character of the philosophical principles underlying his whole social and political program: Reality is matter, and its concrete
expression and development are governed by the dialectic of history. But this is

Historical dialectic

*Marxism =
dialectical
materialism*

MARXISM

- *Dialectical materialism:* The metaphysical view that reality is
  matter and motion, and evolves historically in accordance with
  the dialectical principle of the synthesis of opposite states.
- *Communism:* The economic theory which advocates the
  abolition of private ownership of the means of production and
  the revolutionary actualization of a classless society.

Karl Marx, the father of modern communism

Marxism and communism

given a further twist when Marx focuses more specifically on matter as it reveals itself in economics, which, as you know, concerns money, but more accurately concerns the principles of production, distribution, and use of wealth and products. And now we are in a position to say what Marx's *real* concern was. It was to aid and abet the class warfare which is the social and economic expression of the historical dialectic; to achieve—even through revolutionary tactics—a classless society in which private ownership of the means of production (tools, factories, and so forth) would be abolished and wealth would be equitably distributed. This, of course, is *communism*, the social and economic and political expression of dialectical materialism.

The contradiction: Human possibilities . . .

So far, all ideas and theories. What really propelled Marx were two facts which stood in stark and dismal contradiction. First, Marx was a humanist. His exalted view of humanity included a belief in the innate goodness of persons, their perfectability, and their powers of self-realization. But, second, this is overpowered and thwarted by their actual social and economic condition. It must be remembered that Marx lived when the industrial revolution was playing right into the hands of capitalism. It was a time when increased and frantic production meant the enslavement of the working class (Marx called it the *proletariat*) to the owning class (the *bourgeoisie*); and it meant the degradation of the working class through, for instance, squalid working conditions, child labor, and a wage wholly determined by the owners. In a word—and this is a most important word in Marxism—it meant *alienation*.

"Alienation" means separation or estrangement. By alienation Marx intended considerably more than just the bitter estrangement of the workers from their capitalist superiors. The following is a selection from Marx's *Economic and Philosophical Manuscripts*. Here Marx explains the different kinds of alienation spawned by capitalist controlled labor: Workers become alienated (1) from the objects they produce, (2) from themselves, (3) from their human nature, and (4) from their fellows. It is important to understand these four forms of alienation and to see exactly how labor, as Marx knew it, results in them.

The worker becomes poorer the more wealth he produces and the more his production increases in power and extent. The worker becomes an ever cheaper commodity the more goods he creates. The devaluation of the human world increases in direct relation with the increase in value of the world of things. Labour does not only create goods; it also produces itself and the worker as a commodity, and indeed in the same proportion as it produces goods.

This fact simply implies that the object produced by labour, its product, now stands opposed to it as an alien being, as a power independent of the producer. The product of labour is labour which has been embodied in an object and turned into a physical thing; this product is an objectification of labour. The performance of work is at the same time its objectification. The performance of work appears in the sphere of political economy as a vitiation of the worker, objectification as a loss and as servitude to the object, and appropriation as alienation.

So much does the performance of work appear as vitiation that the worker is vitiated to the point of starvation. So much does objectification appear as loss of the object that the worker is deprived of the most essential things not only of life but also of work. Labour itself becomes an object which he can acquire only by the greatest effort and with unpredictable interruptions. So much does the appropriation of the object appear as alienation that the more objects the worker produces the fewer he can possess and the more he falls under the domination of his product, of capital.

All these consequences follow from the fact that the worker is related to the product of his labour as to an alien object. For it is clear on this presupposition that the more the worker expends himself in work the more powerful becomes the world of objects which he creates in face of himself, the poorer he becomes in his inner life, and the less he belongs to himself. It is just the same as in religion. The more of himself man attributes to God the less he has left in himself. The worker puts his life

. . . and economic repression

"Alienation"

into the object, and his life then belongs no longer to himself but to the object. The greater his activity, therefore, the less he possesses. What is embodied in the product of his labour is no longer his own. The greater this product is, therefore, the more he is diminished. The alienation of the worker in his product means not only that his labour becomes an object, assumes an external existence, but that it exists independently, outside himself, and alien to him, and that it stands opposed to him as an autonomous power. The life which he has given to the object sets itself against him as an alien and hostile force. . . .

So far we have considered the alienation of the worker only from one aspect; namely, his relationship with the products of his labour. However, alienation appears not merely in the result but also in the process of production, within productive activity itself. How could the worker stand in an alien relationship to the product of his activity if he did not alienate himself in the act of production itself? The product is indeed only the résumé of activity, of production. Consequently, if the product of labour is alienation, production itself must be active alienation—the alienation of activity and the activity of alienation. The alienation of the object of labour merely summarizes the alienation in the work activity itself.

What constitutes the alienation of labour? First, that the work is external to the worker, that it is not part of his nature; and that, consequently, he does not fulfil himself in his work but denies himself, has a feeling of misery rather than well-being, does not develop freely his mental and physical energies but is physically exhausted and mentally debased. The worker, therefore, feels himself at home only during his leisure time, whereas at work he feels homeless. His work is not voluntary but imposed, forced labour. It is not the satisfaction of a need, but only a means for satisfying other needs. Its alien character is clearly shown by the fact that as soon as there is no physical or other compulsion it is avoided like the plague. External labour, labour in which man alienates himself, is a labour of self-sacrifice, of mortification. Finally, the external character of work for the worker is shown by the fact that it is not his own work but work for someone else, that in work he does not belong to himself but to another person.

Just as in religion the spontaneous activity of human fantasy, of the human brain and heart, reacts independently as an alien activity of gods or devils upon the individual, so the activity of the worker is not his own spontaneous activity. It is another's activity and a loss of his own spontaneity.

We arrive at the result that man (the worker) feels himself to be freely active only in his animal functions—eating, drinking and procreating, or at most also in his dwelling and in personal adornment—while in his human functions he is reduced to an animal. The animal becomes human and the human becomes animal.

Eating, drinking and procreating are of course also genuine human functions. But abstractly considered, apart from the environment of human activities, and turned into final and sole ends, they are animal functions.

We have now considered the act of alienation of practical human activity, labour, from two aspects: (1) the relationship of the worker to the product of labour as an alien object which dominates him. This relationship is at the same time the relationship to the sensuous external world, to natural objects, as an alien and hostile world; (2) the relationship of labour to the act of production within labour. This is the relationship of the worker to his own activity as something alien and not belonging to him, activity as suffering (passivity), strength as powerlessness, creation as emasculation, the personal physical and mental energy of the worker, his personal life (for what is life but activity?), as an activity which is directed against himself, independent of him and not belonging to him. This is self-alienation as against the above-mentioned alienation of the thing.

We have now to infer a third characteristic of alienated labour from the two we have considered.

Man is a species-being not only in the sense that he makes the community (his own as well as those of other things) his object both practically and theoretically, but also (and this is simply another expression for the same thing) in the sense that he treats himself as the present, living species, as a universal and consequently free being.

Species-life, for man as for animals, has its physical basis in the fact that man (like animals) lives from inorganic nature, and since man is more universal than an animal so the range of inorganic nature from which he lives is more universal. Plants, animals, minerals, air, light, etc. constitute, from the theoretical aspect, a part of human consciousness as objects of natural science and art; they are man's spiritual inorganic nature, his intellectual means of life, which he must first prepare for enjoyment and perpetuation. So also, from the practical aspect, they form a part of human life and activity. In practice man lives only from these natural products, whether in the form of food, heating, clothing, housing, etc. The universality of man appears in practice in the universality which makes the whole of nature into his inorganic body: (1) as a direct means of life; and equally (2) as the material object and instrument of his life activity. Nature is the inorganic body of man; that is to say nature, excluding the human body itself. To say that man lives from nature means that nature is his body with which he must remain in a continuous interchange in order not to die. The statement that the physical and mental life of man, and nature, are interdependent means simply that nature is interdependent with itself, for man is a part of nature.

Since alienated labour: (1) alienates nature from man; and (2) alienates man from himself, from his own active function, his life activity; so it alienates him from the species. It makes species-life into a means of individual life. In the first place it alienates species-life and individual life, and secondly, it turns the latter, as an abstraction, into the purpose of the former, also in its abstract and alienated form.

For labour, life activity, productive life, now appear to man only as means for the satisfaction of a need, the need to maintain his physical existence. Productive life is, however, species-life. It is life creating life. In the type of life activity resides the whole character of a species, its species-character; and free, conscious activity is the species-character of human beings. Life itself appears only as a means of life.

The animal is one with its life activity. It does not distinguish the activity from itself. It is its activity. But man makes his life activity itself an object of his will and consciousness. He has a conscious life activity. It is not a determination with which he is completely identified. Conscious life activity distinguishes man from the life activity of animals. Only for this reason is he a species-being. Or rather, he is only a self-conscious being, i.e., his own life is an object for him, because he is a species-being. Only for this reason is his activity free activity. Alienated labour reverses the relationship, in that man because he is a self-conscious being makes his life activity, his being, only a means for his existence.

The practical construction of an objective world, the manipulation of inorganic nature, is the confirmation of man as a conscious species-being, i.e., a being who treats the species as his own being or himself as a species-being. Of course, animals also produce. They construct nests, dwellings, as in the case of bees, beavers, ants, etc. But they only produce what is strictly necessary for themselves or their young. They produce only in a single direction, while man produces universally. They produce only under the compulsion of direct physical needs, while man produces when he is free from physical need and only truly produces in freedom from such need. Animals produce only themselves, while man reproduces the whole of nature. The products of animal production belong directly to their physical bodies, while man is free in face of his product. Animals construct only in accordance with the standards and needs of the species to which they belong, while man knows how to produce in accordance with the standards of every species and knows how to apply the appropriate standard to the object. Thus man constructs also in accordance with the laws of beauty.

It is just in his work upon the objective world that man really proves himself as a species-being. This production is his active species-life. By means of it nature appears as his work and his reality. The object of labour is, therefore, the objectification of man's species-life; for he no longer reproduces himself merely intellectually, as in consciousness, but actively and in a real sense, and he sees his own reflection in a world which he has constructed. While, therefore, alienated labour takes away the object of production from man, it also takes away his species-life, his real objectivity as a species-being, and changes his advantage over animals into a disadvantage in so far as his inorganic body, nature, is taken from him.

Just as alienated labour transforms free and self-directed activity into a means, so it transforms the species-life of man into a means of physical existence.

Consciousness, which man has from his species, is transformed through alienation so that species-life becomes only a means for him. (3) Thus alienated labour turns the species-life of man, and also nature as his mental species-property, into an alien being and into a means for his individual existence. It alienates from man his own body, external nature, his mental life and his human life. (4) A direct consequence of the alienation of man from the product of his labour, from his life activity and from his species-life, is that man is alienated from other men. When man confronts himself he also confronts other men. What is true of man's relation-

ship to his work, to the product of his work and to himself, is also true of his rela-
tionship to other men, to their labour and to the objects of their labour.

In general, the statement that man is alienated from his species-life means that
each man is alienated from others, and that each of the others is likewise alienated
from human life.

Human alienation, and above all the relation of man to himself, is first realized
and expressed in the relationship between each man and other men. Thus in the
relationship of alienated labour every man regards other men according to the stan-
dards and relationships in which he finds himself placed as a worker.[8]

Marxism has undergone many changes, most notably through Marx's contemporary and compatriot Friedrich Engels and, later, the Russian revolutionary
Vladimir Ilyich Lenin. But Marxism in any form begins with the contradiction
which Marx saw between a high estimation of the human being and the actual
repressive and alienating conditions inflicted on the working classes, and it seeks,
through varying levels of revolutionary force, to transcend the contradiction by
means of communism. Its battle cry has been:

WORKERS OF THE WORLD UNITE!
YOU HAVE NOTHING TO LOSE BUT YOUR CHAINS!

Out of this there eventually arose the communist revolution (led by Lenin) in
Russia in 1917; the revolutions since then in China (Mao Tse Tung) and Cuba
(Castro); the Marxist agitations today in the third world, such as Latin America;
and labor unions and socialist programs everywhere.

"Tradition is a great retarding force. . . ."
—Engels

SOME OBJECTIONS

Some possible and obvious criticisms fall into three groups. The first concerns
metaphysics. We have seen that Marxism and/or communism has its roots, at leas-
thistorically, in a specific theory of reality and history: dialectical materialism. We
cannot take up here the problem of the justification of his philosophical position.
We only point out that, as we have seen, any materialism will have to answer to

*The metaphysical
question*

[8]Karl Marx, *Early Writings*, tr. and ed. T. B. Bottomore (New York: McGraw-Hill, 1964), pp. 121–127.

The socioeconomic question

The moral question

many charges, and this one too will have to make itself good before we are compelled by any social or political ideas that follow from it.

Speaking more to the *socioeconomic* point: Some believe that Marxists are too harsh in their rejection of all other social systems as incapable of introducing important social change. Certainly the situation now is different from what it was in Marx's own time. Has not even capitalism proved in some ways (never dreamed of by the early Marxists) to be self-correcting? to be capable of being governed by its own (though unending) dialectic of improvement? It is hardly necessary to be a Marxist to have a social conscience, to believe in and strive for the general welfare, to improve working conditions or to introduce child-labor laws, and to *change* things. Of course, it may be answered: "But your program of social change is too *slow*. We need radical change, and we need it now. Revolution is the only way!" But the idea of literal revolution, with its upheavals and probable bloodshed, is itself not unproblematic—unless you believe that the end justifies the means. And we leave aside the spectacle of Polish workers, *in a communist society,* uniting in order to lose their chains!

Finally, a *moral* issue: It is frequently heard that Marxism is naive and over-optimistic in its own estimate of human nature: "Marxism is a wonderful theory. Too bad that it can't possibly work due to human nature." Is there any truth to the charge that the very repression of human values that Marxists so deplore in other forms of government reveals itself even more vividly in communist societies? Not to excuse other forms of government for their own failures, but what of the Stalin purges of the 1930s and 1950s? And where is the Gulag Archipelago? In a word, as it is sometimes observed, the communist ideal has been pursued in the U.S.S.R. for over sixty years now. Where has it succeeded in healing the alienation it so strongly denounces in other systems? Where has it outstripped competing systems with respect to human rights? Where has it maximized the self-actualization and full humanity that it claims for its own citizens?

A MESSAGE FROM MARTIN NIEMOELLER*

"First the Nazis went after the Jews, but I was not a Jew, so I did not object. Then they went after the Catholics, but I was not a Catholic, so I did not object. Then they went after the Trade-Unionists, but I was not a Trade-Unionist, so I did not object. Then they came after me, and there was no one left to object."

*A German pastor imprisoned in Dachau by the Nazis.

IS PROSPERITY A DECEPTION?
HOSPERS VS. MARCUSE

It is hardly possible to extol the virtues of free enterprise more enthusiastically than does the *libertarian* John Hospers. As with other ideologies, the variations on libertarianism are numerous, but most libertarians would subscribe to three lines of emphasis:

Libertarianism

- The freedom of individuals to pursue their private interests so long as these do not harm others
- The denial of the state's responsibility for all forms of public welfare
- A "night-watchman" conception of government according to which government should exist solely for the protection from enemy invasion, to prevent infringement on individual rights, to enforce contracts, etc.

In itself, libertarianism thus goes much further than simple *laissez faire* capitalism (it applies the "Hands-off!" to much more); and it *certainly* espouses the principle of free enterprise. In the following excerpt from his essay "Free Enterprise as the Embodiment of Justice," Hospers celebrates the socioeconomic successes of the free-enterprise system ("capitalism, freedom, and affluence") in contrast to the failures of the communist system ("tyranny, regulation, misery").

What is the secret of this system? In a word, it is liberty: liberty to think, to invent, to produce, to trade. When no restrictions are placed on these things, the ingenuity of man knows no bounds. But almost always in past history, such restrictions have been there: kings, emperors, tribal chieftains, modern governments drain off so much of the energies of the people, especially the creative people, whom they perceive as threats to their power, that the energies of men are sapped and their spirits broken. When America began, living conditions had hardly changed since ancient times. Even in Western Europe until 150 years ago, people lived mostly in windowless hovels with a hole in the ceiling for the smoke. In America, men were free to produce and trade as they chose. There was a tremendous outburst of outgoing energy and upward mobility; rags-to-riches stories became daily occurrences. There were no hereditary castes, no strangling bureaucracies, no heavy hand of government to keep them down. And thus, already by 1825, the United States was the most prosperous nation in the history of the world. In one century, three generations, this release of human energy had created an entirely new world.

Liberty bears the same fruits today. Consider East Germany versus West Germany: people of the same culture, the same traditions, the same level of technical skill, torn asunder by the accidents of war. On the one side, tyranny, regulation, misery, and an irresistible impulse to leave; on the other side, capitalism, freedom, and affluence. In the Far East, Malaysia, Taiwan, Hong Kong, Japan all rely pri-

marily on free markets; all are thriving, their people full of vital energy—a far cry from the socialist states, India, China, now Vietnam and Cambodia, all relying on central planning and heavy with the dead weight of bureaucracy.

But the contrast to which I want most to call your attention is that of Japan versus India. India has many more natural resources than Japan; the British in 1948 left India an excellent railroad system, factories, equipment, functioning political institutions, skilled administrators, men trained in industrial techniques. Top Indian workers were as efficient as any in the world, as they still are outside India. Japan had no comparable advantages; she had to provide all her capital from domestic sources after the Meiji Restoration of 1867. Yet Japan became prosperous, and at its present rate it will soon be more prosperous than the U.S. Why the difference?

Japan followed a free market system, taking Great Britain of its time as its model. It never tried to control the amount or direction of investment or the structure of output. But Indian leaders (of 1948) were schooled in Fabian socialism and central planning; they took Russia as their model, and a series of five-year plans with detailed programs of investment by government in whatever enterprises its political leaders chose.[9]

LIBERTARIANISM

A politically conservative position which presses free enterprise and individual rights to an extreme, relegating government to a role purely subservient to individual (as opposed to societal) interests.

According to others, however, the capitalistic affluence that Hospers revels in can itself disguise great evils. A good example of this charge may be found in the late Herbert Marcuse, who in 1934 fled the Nazi persecutions in Germany and pursued his Marxist philosophy in the United States. His Marxist ideal, combined with insights drawn from Freudian psychology, is best known from his book *One Dimensional Man.*

The deception of Western affluence

Modern capitalistic societies, says Marcuse, have deceived their citizens and have substituted, we might say, one form of alienation (a much subtler form) for another. True, in such societies a higher standard of living may be enjoyed, but this success is illusory, for the price is far higher than most people think. The cit-

---

[9]John Hospers, "Free Enterprise as the Embodiment of Justice," in *Ethics, Free Enterprise and Public Policy: Original Essays on Moral Issues in Business,* ed. Richard DeGeorge and Joseph A. Pichler (New York: Oxford University Press, 1978), pp. 71–72.

izen is unconsciously conditioned, for example by the mass media and in innumerable other ways he or she is hardly aware of, to affirm and accept some immediate and personal advantages without noticing the irrationality and dehumanizing character of the whole system that makes these advantages possible. For Marcuse, a very important example is the way in which our capitalistic system strains and drains itself both economically and psychologically in the pursuit of military prowess and possible war—in a catchy but somber phrase Marcuse calls this "the peaceful production of the means of destruction."

The following paragraphs from Marcuse's *One Dimensional Man* contain a brief but brilliantly clear statement of the dismal character and prospects of a society which denounces one form of slavery but at the same time, and without quite noticing it, espouses a worse one.

> *Does not the threat of an atomic catastrophe which could wipe out the human race also serve to protect the very forces which perpetuate this danger? The efforts to prevent such a catastrophe overshadow the search for its potential causes in contemporary industrial society. These causes remain unidentified, unexposed, unattacked by the public because they recede before the all too obvious threat from without—to the West from the East, to the East from the West. Equally obvious is the need for being prepared, for living on the brink, for facing the challenge. We submit to the peaceful production of the means of destruction, to the perfection of waste, to being educated for a defense which deforms the defenders and that which they defend.*
>
> *If we attempt to relate the causes of the danger to the way in which society is organized and organizes its members, we are immediately confronted with the fact that advanced industrial society becomes richer, bigger, and better as it perpetuates the danger. The defense structure makes life easier for a greater number of people and extends man's mastery of nature. Under these circumstances, our mass media have little difficulty in selling particular interests as those of all sensible men. The political needs of society become individual needs and aspirations, their satisfaction promotes business and the commonweal, and the whole appears to be the very embodiment of Reason.*
>
> *And yet this society is irrational as a whole. Its productivity is destructive of the free development of human needs and faculties, its peace maintained by the constant threat of war, its growth dependent on the repression of the real possibilities for pacifying the struggle for existence—individual, national, and international. This repression, so different from that which characterized the preceding, less developed stages of our society, operates today not from a position of natural and technical immaturity but rather from a position of strength. The capabilities (intellectual and material) of contemporary society are immeasurably greater than ever before—which means that the scope of society's domination over the individual is immeasurably greater than ever before. Our society distinguishes itself by conquering the centrifugal social forces with Technology rather than Terror, on the dual basis of an overwhelming efficiency and an increasing standard of living. . . .*
>
> *The fact that the vast majority of the population accepts, and is made to*

accept, this society does not render it less irrational and less reprehensible. The distinction between true and false consciousness, real and immediate interest still is meaningful. But this distinction itself must be validated. Men must come to see it and to find their way from false to true consciousness, from their immediate to their real interest. They can do so only if they live in need of changing their way of life, of denying the positive, of refusing. It is precisely this need which the established society manages to repress to the degree to which it is capable of "delivering the goods" on an increasingly large scale, and using the scientific conquest of nature for the scientific conquest of man.[10]

Thus we are back to the question of alienation.

> "If you think the United States has stood still, who built the largest shopping center in the world?"
>
> —Richard M. Nixon

Chapter 21 in Review

SUMMARY

In this chapter we have looked at the two most important social-political perspectives that have developed in modern times, and which compete yet today, and sometimes bitterly, for supremacy: liberalism and marxism.

Liberalism is the ideology of freedom. We do not mean here some starry-eyed and romantic idea but the concrete freedom of the individual to pursue his or her interests, not only undeterred by undue governmental control, but as *guaranteed* by government. In its most classical form this doctrine was expressed by Locke, who believed that both the private and the public good are knowable from the natural law, which teaches plainly the equality and independence of each individual in his or her "natural state," unperturbed by civil government. Social life (or life together) requires, however, that individuals enter into a social contract or agreement to a degree of organization and regulation for the sake of the preservation of their freedoms.

One of the most basic of these freedoms, or "inalienable rights," is the pursuit of property, and this establishes the connection between liberalism and capitalism,

[10]Herbert Marcuse, *One Dimensional Man: Studies in the Ideology of Advanced Industrial Society* (Boston: Beacon Press, 1964), pp. ix–x, xiii–xiv. It is important to note that this quotation should be understood in the total context of Marcuse's writings.

the economic doctrine of the private ownership of the means of production and exchange of goods. The capitalistic ideals of private ownership and the free marketplace were most forcefully expressed by Adam Smith's economic slogan, "Hands off!" But this ideology, abetted by the industrial revolution, led in actual practice to exploitation, monopolies, a growing division between the "haves" and "have-nots," and the radical reaction of Marxism.

Marx was deeply influenced by Hegel's "dialectical" view of history, according to which history develops through the confrontation and synthesis of opposite states. Marx, interpreting this in a materialistic and economic way, called for a social revolution to bring about a more equitable distribution of wealth and the classless society, or communism. Only by means of this radical solution can the human alienation fostered by capitalism be healed.

Of course the critics of Marxism, looking specifically at the repressive character of contemporary communism and its record on human rights, charge that it tends just to substitute one form of alienation for another. The Marxist Marcuse, on the other hand, has charged that contemporary capitalistic societies are repressive in an even worse way. Their high standard of living is a cruel deception, for their citizens are blinded to the trivializing and dehumanizing price that must be paid for the "good" life.

BASIC IDEAS

- Liberalism
- The distinction between freedoms-from and freedoms-for
- Individualism
- The state of nature
- The social contract
- Tacit consent
- Capitalism
- *Laissez faire*
- "Invisible-hand" economy
- Hegelian dialectic
- Dialectical materialism
- Communism
- The Marxist concept of alienation
- Criticisms of Marxism/communism
    Metaphysical
    Socioeconomic
    Moral
- Libertarianism
- Marcuse's criticism of capitalism

TEST YOURSELF

1. Who wrote *Second Treatise of Government?*
2. In 1776, the United States was founded and the book entitled _____was published. What was the connection between these two events?
3. Who was G. W. F. Hegel?
4. What is meant by saying that the order of (1) state of nature and (2) social contract is a *logical* rather than a *historical* order?
5. Marx taught that labor (according to the capitalist conception) alienates the worker from _____, from _____, from _____, and from _____.
6. Comment on Marxism as a theory of *reality*.
7. Herbert Marcuse (a) introduced the expression *laissez faire*, (b) provides a contemporary statement of St. Thomas' four laws, (c) believed that Western capitalism is dehumanizing, (d) emphasized free enterprise and individual rights.
8. What is the relation of Marxism to communism?
9. True or false: Recalling the previous two chapters, communism has more in common with Mill's teaching than with Kant's.
10. Who said it? "By pursuing his own interest he frequently promotes that of society more effectually than when he really intends to promote it."

QUESTIONS FOR
REFLECTION

- In this book we have encountered several concepts of *freedom*. Can you distinguish the freedom of the free-will–determinism debate, the freedom in Sartre's existential philosophy, and now the freedom involved in liberalism?

- The idea of natural law has appeared again in this chapter. Can you explain the exact connection of this idea with the rise of capitalism? What do *you* make of the notion of certain "inalienable" rights? Do these include the right of private property? Does this right sometimes involve an infringement of others' rights? Exploitation? Was Marx correct about the alienating power of capitalism?

- Capitalism and communism are economic theories of existence. What does this mean? Are such theories adequate to the totality of human experience? Does each of them leave out something important?

CHAPTER 22

THE QUESTION OF JUSTICE

It is appropriate that we conclude with some comment on what is probably the most basic idea of social and political philosophy: the idea of *justice*. If only we could be clear about justice, how much easier would our task be! But getting clear on justice may be more difficult than you think. Upon reflection, does your own idea of justice turn out to be some vague notion involving equality or fairness? But what constitutes equality or fairness? Do they involve the distribution of goods? But how much, to whom, and on what basis? Does it involve worthiness? But what is the basis of worthiness—talent, power, productivity? Does it involve social responsibility? But how is this to be measured?

JUSTICE AS FAIRNESS

To be sure, various ideas of justice have already made their appearance, explicitly or implicitly, in the moral and social-political theories we have been discussing. Think of Plato's identification of justice with the rule of reason both in the individual and in the state; or Mill's utilitarian idea of a distribution of goods which would result in the greatest happiness of the greatest number; or Marx's definition: From each according to his ability, to each according to his need; or think again on the title of Hospers' essay, "Free Enterprise as the Embodiment of Justice." The problem is obviously a very big one. It is not our intent to provide here a summary or survey, but to focus on just one idea of justice. In his books *Justice as Fairness* and *A Theory of Justice,* as well as in other writings, the contemporary American philosopher John Rawls has propounded a theory of justice which has proven to

> "Justice is the first virtue of social systems, as truth is of systems of thought."
>
> —Rawls

be extremely important. Some have even spoken of the "Rawlsmania" that has seized recent discussions.

The liberal view of justice

The attempt to combine both (1) the *libertarian* view of justice (think of Hospers) as consisting in personal liberty and (2) the *socialist* view of justice (think of Marx) as consisting in social equality is called (3) the *liberal* view of justice. Clearly, Rawls stands in the liberal tradition. He believes that it is not necessary to stall forever between the ideals of individual liberty on the one hand and a more equitable distribution of goods on the other: He attempts to develop a concept of justice which would unite the virtues of both the libertarian and the egalitarian or socialist perspectives. The liberal view of justice can, however, take two different forms. These are (1) the *contractual* (think of Locke), which involves an agreement between persons who willingly delimit certain of their freedoms in exchange for

---

THREE VIEWS OF JUSTICE

Libertarian	*Socialist*	*Liberal*
Personal liberty is the highest social ideal.	Equality of persons is the highest social ideal.	A combination of liberty and equality is the highest social ideal. (a) *Contractual:* Trades off equality for greater welfare. (b) *Utilitarian:* Accepts any kind of inequality if it maximizes happiness.

greater equality, say, equality of wealth, opportunity, etc., and (2) the *utilitarian* (think of Mill), which involves the adoption of rules which would promote the maximization of happiness. That Rawls espouses the contractual version of the liberal view of justice we shall now see.

    In the first reading below, Rawls expresses the heart of his theory in his own words, but we may summarize the main points. Reminiscent of the old-line social-contractors, Rawls starts out with his idea of *the original position* (Locke called it the state of nature), emphasizing that this is a purely hypothetical or imaginary situation. In order to ensure that whatever principle of justice we adopt is really fair to all concerned (hence his idea of "justice as fairness") we must try to imagine ourselves as stripped of all factors that could possibly prejudice us in favor of one principle rather than another. Obviously, if you are the president of Consolidated Steel, or a Wall Street tycoon, or a shipping magnate, your interests will tempt you in a different direction than if you are a Chicano migrant worker. It is as difficult as it is necessary to adopt what Rawls calls a *veil of ignorance,* a veil that will cover up, for the moment at least, what we very well know about our own vested interests but need to *forget* if our principle is to be born in a climate of objectivity—everybody in the same boat, everybody standing to lose or gain the same things. The participants naturally will not be a party to any principle which, when the veil is lifted, might mean a loss of their fair share of the pie. On the other hand, neither will they be a party to any principle that might grant them *more* than a fair share, since there is no guarantee that when the veil is lifted they will be on the receiving end. These social-contractors will all therefore favor a principle which will result in at least, but not more than, a fair share for all. Approaching the matter in this way, we have a basis for discussing and formulating a principle of justice in an impartial way, one that is not tilted in the direction of any special interests.

    In all of this Rawls presupposes a degree of *rationality* on the part of the social-contractors. The whole enterprise will be doomed from the start without an intuitive sense of fairness, without goodwill, and without an honesty and realism about what agreements can actually be honored and kept.

"The original position"

The "veil of ignorance"

The assumption of rationality

THE MAIN IDEA OF THE THEORY OF JUSTICE

My aim is to present a conception of justice which generalizes and carries to a higher level of abstraction the familiar theory of the social contract as found, say, in Locke, Rousseau, and Kant. In order to do this we are not to think of the original contract as one to enter a particular society or to set up a particular form of government. Rather, the guiding idea is that the principles of justice for the basic structure of society are the object of the original agreement. They are the principles that free and rational persons concerned to further their own interests would accept in an initial position of equality as defining the fundamental terms of their association. These principles are to regulate all further agreements; they specify the kinds of social cooper-

ation that can be entered into and the forms of government that can be established. This way of regarding the principles of justice I shall call justice as fairness.

Thus we are to imagine that those who engage in social cooperation choose together, in one joint act, the principles which are to assign basic rights and duties and to determine the division of social benefits. Men are to decide in advance how they are to regulate their claims against one another and what is to be the foundation charter of their society. Just as each person must decide by rational reflection what constitutes his good, that is, the system of ends which it is rational for him to pursue, so a group of persons must decide once and for all what is to count among them as just and unjust. The choice which rational men would make in this hypothetical situation of equal liberty, assuming for the present that this choice problem has a solution, determines the principles of justice.

In justice as fairness the original position of equality corresponds to the state of nature in the traditional theory of the social contract. This original position is not, of course, thought of as an actual historical state of affairs, much less as a primitive condition of culture. It is understood as a purely hypothetical situation characterized so as to lead to a certain conception of justice. . . .

THE VEIL OF IGNORANCE

The idea of the original position is to set up a fair procedure so that any principles agreed to will be just. The aim is to use the notion of pure procedural justice as a basis of theory. Somehow we must nullify the effects of specific contingencies which put men at odds and tempt them to exploit social and natural circumstances to their own advantage. Now in order to do this I assume that the parties are situated behind a veil of ignorance. They do not know how the various alternatives will affect their own particular case and they are obliged to evaluate principles solely on the basis of general considerations.

It is assumed, then, that the parties do not know certain kinds of particular facts. First of all, no one knows his place in society, his class position or social status; nor does he know his fortune in the distribution of natural assets and abilities, his intelligence and strength, and the like. Nor, again, does anyone know his conception of the good, the particulars of his rational plan of life, or even the special features of his psychology such as his aversion to risk or liability to optimism or pessimism. More than this, I assume that the parties do not know the particular circumstances of their own society. That is, they do not know its economic or political situation, or the level of civilization and culture it has been able to achieve. The persons in the original position have no information as to which generation they belong. These broader restrictions on knowledge are appropriate in part because questions of social justice arise between generations as well as within them, for example, the question of the appropriate rate of capital saving and of the conservation of natural resources and the environment of nature. There is also, theoretically anyway, the question of a reasonable genetic policy. In these cases too, in order to carry through the idea of the original position, the parties must not know the contingencies that set them in oppo-

sition. They must choose principles the consequences of which they are prepared to live with whatever generation they turn out to belong to. . . .

Thus there follows the very important consequence that the parties have no basis for bargaining in the usual sense. No one knows his situation in society nor his natural assets, and therefore no one is in a position to tailor principles to his advantage. We might imagine that one of the contractees threatens to hold out unless the others agree to principles favorable to him. But how does he know which principles are especially in his interests? The same holds for the formation of coalitions: if a group were to decide to band together to the disadvantage of the others, they would not know how to favor themselves in the choice of principles. Even if they could get everyone to agree to their proposal, they would have no assurance that it was to their advantage, since they cannot identify themselves either by name or description. . . .

The restrictions on particular information in the original position are, then, of fundamental importance. Without them we would not be able to work out any definite theory of justice at all. We would have to be content with a vague formula stating that justice is what would be agreed to without being able to say much, if anything, about the substance of the agreement itself. The formal constraints of the concept of right, those applying to principles directly, are not sufficient for our purpose. The veil of ignorance makes possible a unanimous choice of a particular conception of justice. Without these limitations on knowledge the bargaining problem of the original position would be hopelessly complicated. Even if theoretically a solution were to exist, we would not, at present anyway, be able to determine it. . . .

THE RATIONALITY OF THE PARTIES

. . . There is one further assumption to guarantee strict compliance. The parties are presumed to be capable of a sense of justice and this fact is public knowledge among them. This condition is to insure the integrity of the agreement made in the original position. It does not mean that in their deliberations the parties apply some particular conception of justice, for this would defeat the point of the motivation assumption. Rather, it means that the parties can rely on each other to understand and to act in accordance with whatever principles are finally agreed to. Once principles are acknowledged the parties can depend on one another to conform to them. In reaching an agreement, then, they know that their undertaking is not in vain; their capacity for a sense of justice insures that the principles chosen will be respected. It is essential to observe, however, that this assumption still permits the consideration of men's capacity to act on the various conceptions of justice. The general facts of human psychology and the principles of moral learning are relevant matters for the parties to examine. If a conception of justice is unlikely to generate its own support, or lacks stability, this fact must not be overlooked. For then a different conception of justice might be preferred. The assumption only says that the parties have a capacity for justice in a purely formal sense: taking everything relevant into account, including the general facts of moral psychology, the parties will adhere to the principles eventually chosen. They are rational in that they will not enter into agreements they know

they cannot keep, or can do so only with great difficulty. Along with other consider-
ations, they count the strains of commitment. Thus in assessing conceptions of justice
the persons in the original position are to assume that the one they adopt will be
strictly complied with. The consequences of their agreement are to be worked out on
this basis.[1]

RAWLS' TWO PRINCIPLES OF JUSTICE

The Principle of Equal Basic Liberty for All

The stage thus set, Rawls introduces his principle of justice, which is actually *two* principles. The first attempts to accommodate the libertarian ideal of individual freedoms and rights, and is directed to that part of the social structure which establishes such liberties: "Each person is to have an equal right to the most extensive basic liberty compatible with a similar liberty for others." This is called the *Principle of Equal Basic Liberty for All.* The second principle of justice is directed rather to the economic facts of social life and is more complicated. It attempts to accommodate the egalitarian ideal of an equitable distribution of wealth while accommodating at the same time a reasonable *in*equitable distribution. It accomplishes this by insisting that such inequities result in an advantage for all, and, most notably for the *least* advantaged. Is it not to your advantage that your dentist earns more than you do, if as a result you receive better dental care? Thus, the second principle of justice: "Social and economic inequalities are to be arranged so that they are both (a) reasonably expected to be to everyone's advantage, and (b) attached to positions and offices open to all." This is called the *Difference Principle.*

The Difference Principle

Rawls' General Conception of Justice

As Rawls states, each of these principles embodies in different ways a more general idea, Rawls' *General Conception of Justice:* "All social values—liberty and opportunity, income and wealth, and the bases of self-respect—are to be distributed equally unless an unequal distribution of any, or all, of these values is to everyone's advantage."

TWO PRINCIPLES OF JUSTICE

I shall now state in a provisional form the two principles of justice that I believe would be chosen in the original position. . . .

The first statement of the two principles reads as follows.

First: each person is to have an equal right to the most extensive basic liberty compatible with a similar liberty for others.

Second: social and economic inequalities are to be arranged so that they are both (a) reasonably expected to be to everyone's advantage, and (b) attached to positions and offices open to all. . . .

[1]John Rawls, *A Theory of Justice* (Cambridge, Mass.: Harvard University Press, 1971), pp. 11–12, 136–137, 139–140, 145.

By way of general comment, these principles primarily apply, as I have said, to the basic structure of society. They are to govern the assignment of rights and duties and to regulate the distribution of social and economic advantages. As their formulation suggests, these principles presuppose that the social structure can be divided into two more or less distinct parts, the first principle applying to the one, the second to the other. They distinguish between those aspects of the social system that define and secure the equal liberties of citizenship and those that specify and establish social and economic inequalities. The basic liberties of citizens are, roughly speaking, political liberty (the right to vote and to be eligible for public office) together with freedom of speech and assembly; liberty of conscience and freedom of thought; freedom of the person along with the right to hold (personal) property; and freedom from arbitrary arrest and seizure as defined by the concept of the rule of law. These liberties are all required to be equal by the first principle, since citizens of a just society are to have the same basic rights.

The second principle applies, in the first approximation, to the distribution of income and wealth and to the design of organizations that make use of differences in authority and responsibility, or chains of command. While the distribution of wealth and income need not be equal, it must be to everyone's advantage, and at the same time, positions of authority and offices of command must be accessible to all. One applies the second principle by holding positions open, and then, subject to this constraint, arranges social and economic inequalities so that everyone benefits.

These principles are to be arranged in a serial order with the first principle prior to the second. This ordering means that a departure from the institutions of equal liberty required by the first principle cannot be justified by, or compensated for, by greater social and economic advantages. The distribution of wealth and income, and the hierarchies of authority, must be consistent with both the liberties of equal citizenship and equality of opportunity.

. . . For the present, it should be observed that the two principles (and this holds for all formulations) are a special case of a more general conception of justice that can be expressed as follows.

All social values—liberty and opportunity, income and wealth, and the bases of self-respect—are to be distributed equally unless an unequal distribution of any, or all, of these values is to everyone's advantage.

Injustice, then, is simply inequalities that are not to the benefit of all. Of course, this conception is extremely vague and requires interpretation.

As a first step, suppose that the basic structure of society distributes certain primary goods, that is, things that every rational man is presumed to want. These goods normally have a use whatever a person's rational plan of life. For simplicity, assume that the chief primary goods at the disposition of society are rights and liberties, powers and opportunities, income and wealth. . . . These are the social primary goods. Other primary goods such as health and vigor, intelligence and imagination, are natural goods; although their possession is influenced by the basic structure, they are not so directly under its control. Imagine, then, a hypothetical initial arrangement *in which all the social primary goods are equally distributed: everyone has similar rights and duties, and income and wealth are evenly shared. This state of affairs provides a benchmark for judging improvements. If certain inequalities of wealth and organizational powers would make everyone better off than in this hypothetical starting situation, then they accord with the general conception.*

Now it is possible, at least theoretically, that by giving up some of their fundamental liberties men are sufficiently compensated by the resulting social and economic gains. The general conception of justice imposes no restrictions on what sort of inequalities are permissible; it only requires that everyone's position be improved. We need not suppose anything so drastic as consenting to a condition of slavery. Imagine instead that men forego certain political rights when the economic returns are significant and their capacity to influence the course of policy by the exercise of these rights would be marginal in any case. It is this kind of exchange which the two principles as stated rule out; being arranged in serial order they do not permit exchanges between basic liberties and economic and social gains. The serial ordering of principles expresses an underlying preference among primary social goods. When this preference is rational so likewise is the choice of these principles in this order.[2]

RAWLS' TWO PRINCIPLES OF JUSTICE

- *The Principle of Equal Basic Liberty for All:* Each person is to have an equal right to the most extensive basic liberty compatible with a similar liberty for others.
- *The Difference Principle:* Social and economic inequalities are to be arranged so that they are both (a) reasonably expected to be to everyone's advantage, and (b) attached to positions and offices open to all.

RAWLS' GENERAL CONCEPTION OF JUSTICE

According to Rawls, his two principles of justice are particular expressions of a more general conception:

- All social values are to be distributed equally unless an unequal distribution of any, or all, of these values is to everyone's advantage.

---

[2]Ibid., pp. 60–63.

SOME OBJECTIONS

Rawls' work has been hailed as a monumental contribution to social philosophy, but at the same time it has provoked considerable criticism. Much of the controversy has centered on Rawls' proposal of the veil of ignorance. For example, can we so easily draw the conclusion Rawls wants us to from a premise we know to be false? If we were really operating behind a veil of ignorance, that would be one thing. But, as it is, could one really "think away" his or her wealth, beauty, talent, and general advantage, for the sake of a principle that might immediately nullify them? The theory is, says the critic, very nice but very abstract and hypothetical by comparison to the situation in which people actually find themselves—especially if they are, as Rawls hopes them to be, *rationally self-interested*. Someone has suggested, for example, that if you own a painting you know to be worth $5000, you would not sell it for $100 simply because you might if you *didn't* know it was worth $5000! Again, there is a big difference between signing a contract and *imagining* that you have signed a contract. When the chips are down, hypothetical or *imaginary* contracts can't be expected to enforce anything. Must not the implementability of Rawls' view depend on some deeper moral principle?

Is the veil of ignorance too hypothetical

Similarly, it has been seen that Rawls' theory depends for its life on our desire in the state of ignorance (if we *could* cultivate such a state) to "minimize the risk" of things turning out to our disadvantage in the actual world. This, says Rawls, would be a *rational* approach. But why is it any more *rational* to take the road of minimizing the risk than that of maximizing the gain? To be sure, if it meant turning up penniless, diseased, ugly, and outcast, then understandably one would take the minimizing road. But that is *not* usually the choice, and one might *reasonably* gamble a so-so condition for a little more advantage—wouldn't one?

Why not maximize the gain?

Further, it has been objected that, contrary to Rawls' insistence, his principles might run exactly opposite to our deepest intuitions about morality, equality, society, etc. This point (along with several others) is forcefully made by William R. Marty.

Does Rawls' theory contradict our moral sensibilities?

> . . . *two men are shipwrecked on an island. One works hard. He plows the ground, plants seed, weeds his field, chases the birds away, waters the crop through the heat and dryness of summer, builds a shed to store the grain through the blizzards of winter, builds himself a cabin to survive the cold, and then harvests the crop. The other man, by happenstance formerly a hit man, acts differently. Through the hot summer he sits in the shade of the tree, swims in the pleasant lagoon, and lives idly off the fat of the land for the living is easy, and besides, when winter comes, he plans to knock the other man on the head while he sleeps and take his grain, his shed, and his shelter. This man neither makes a crop, thereby earning his keep, nor has he the good in his heart.*
>
> *Now to whom, in this hypothetical situation, does that store of grain rightly belong? Our intuitive sense is clear. It belongs to the one who by his planning, effort,*

and sacrifice produced it, not to the one who sat by in deliberate and malicious idleness in anticipation of gaining the grain without effort except for one foul deed. In this case, all the grain clearly belongs to the one, and none to the other. But, apply the Rawlsian technique for locating the just distribution: Take the two men from the island, strip them of any knowledge of how or by whom the grain was produced (put them, that is, behind the Veil of Ignorance), and let them then, on the basis of rational calculation of self-interest, divide the grain, and how will they divide it? They will divide it equally for, as Rawls asks us, why should either accept less than half and why should either give up more than half? . . .

The Rawlsian method certainly provides a shrewd strategy about how to get the pie cut equally, but is the result justice? That would depend on whether justice requires, in all cases, or in particular cases, an equal division. But in some cases, as the preceding example illustrates, justice clearly does not require or even allow an equal division. Rawls's distribution is faulty because it divorces distribution from a number of things that can legitimately give a claim to a particular share of a distribution. Thus allocation, à la Rawls, divorces distribution from contribution (who bought or brought the pie makings?), effort (who baked it?), risk (what if there are a number of pies from which to choose the one to divide, but one is booby-trapped so that it will explode and kill the slicer?), need (what if some among whom the pie is to be divided are fat and well-fed, but others are malnourished or starving?), skill or excellence (what if two come to the party, each bringing a pie, but one is a good cook and the other is not, how then should the pies be divided?), or responsibility and performance (again two cooks, but one exercises care to be clean and use sanitary ingredients while the other, sloppy in habits and careless in cooking, is likely to have a pie that will make people ill?). None of these—contribution, effort, risk, need, skill, excellence, responsibility, and performance—is dealt with adequately by the Rawlsian scheme, except perhaps need, and need only if an equal distribution will meet the needs of all, which of course it won't—consider the medical problems of people requiring a clotting factor for their blood or a kidney machine. Either requires more expense than the average income share of even the richest society on earth, hence in these cases an equal division would be a fatal division. . . .

In particular, the Rawlsian structure fails because the same Veil of Ignorance that was designed to hide from those in the Original Position their place in the society-to-be in order to prevent them from rationalizing their self-interest and calling it justice, also hides from them all the particular details that they must know if they are to know what a just distribution is. Thus it hides from them who produced the grain on that island and who did not, which makes it impossible for them to know who earned that grain and who did not, and it hides from them all information about individual efforts or lack of effort, about individual contributions or lack thereof, about handicaps, choices, needs, duties fulfilled, or responsibilities not met. It hides from them, in other words, precisely what they must know to distribute justly, unless just distribution among individuals has absolutely nothing to do with what those individuals choose or do or leave undone, and that is a patent absurdity that would *make the whole concept of a just or unjust distribution meaningless. Consequently, the Rawlsian scheme does not lead those in the Original Position (or us) to justice unless that hit man deserves as much as the hard worker. Analytically, the scheme cannot lead those in the Original Position to justice because it blinds them to all the individual actions and choices that are the foundation of a just distribution. Analogically, Rawls has given us Justice blindfolded to make her impartial, but he has deprived her of the scales by which alone she can tell what justice among individuals requires. . . .*

The Rawlsian method for finding justice fails because its structure presupposes, without proving, that an equal division is a fair division; because that same structure makes us indifferent to whether justice is done; and because, even if we cared, it hides from us all knowledge of the particular facts on which claims to a particular share must rest. The Rawlsian strategy makes it to our self-interest to choose a division contrary to our deepest intuitions of justice, and contrary to previous teachings of justice. It can and does defend outrageously unjust divisions. It simply fails as a serious means of locating justice.[3]

"All who are not lunatics are agreed about certain things: that it is better to be alive than dead, better to be adequately fed than starved, better to be free than a slave."

—Bertrand Russell

Chapter 22 in Review

In this brief chapter we have called attention to the idea of justice as fundamental to social-political philosophy. And we have raised one attempt, but a very important and contemporary one, to combine the ideals of libertarianism with those of egalitarianism, and to provide principles which would assure the implementation of justice conceived as fairness. This is Rawls' theory of justice.

SUMMARY

Echoing somewhat the old ideas of the state of nature and the social contract, Rawls has argued that it should be possible to bracket-out our individual interests and advantages (the veil of ignorance) long enough to perceive what would be fair and advantageous to all. More specifically, in this original position we should be guided by Rawls' two principles of justice: (1) the Principle of Equal Basic Liberty for All, and (2) the Difference Principle. The first of these establishes equal liberty,

---

[3]William R. Marty, "Rawls and the Harried Mother," *Interpretation*, 9 (1982), pp. 387–389, 393–395.

and the second fosters equal income and social position. These are geared to reducing inequities: Differences in wealth and position would be fostered only when such differences would contribute to the advantage of all.

It has been objected that the proposed veil of ignorance is too hypothetical to be actually implemented, at least by those who are well-off and stand probably to lose by it. And why is it more rational to minimize the risk of losing something than of gaining something? Also, does Rawls' theory do justice, so to speak, to our intuitive sense about the relevance of personal contribution, effort, need, responsibility, etc.?

BASIC IDEAS

- Three views of justice
- The original position
- The veil of ignorance
- Rawls' two principles of justice
     The Principle of Equal Basic Liberty for All
     The Difference Principle
- Rawls' General Conception of Justice
- Rawls' theory of justice as a synthesis of libertarian and egalitarian perspectives

TEST YOURSELF

1. True or false: Rawls' first principle of justice is intended to promote egalitarianism.
2. In three words, Rawls' is a theory of "justice as _____."
3. Why is "the rationality of the parties" vital to Rawls' theory?
4. Why do some object to Rawls' idea of the veil of ignorance?
5. Recalling the two previous chapters, Rawls' idea of the original position has most in common with (a) Aristotle, (b) Locke, (c) St. Thomas, (d) Hospers.

QUESTIONS FOR
REFLECTION

- Does Rawls' theory of justice succeed in combining the best of the libertarian and egalitarian ideals?
- What about the objection that Rawls' theory is very attractive in principle but has little hope of actual implementation? Is *any* social-political ideal or principle free from this problem? What about the charge that the practice of Rawls' theory might actually fly in the face of our intuitive sense of fairness?
- How would *you* come to grips with the problem of justice? Does Rawls' theory provide you with any insights and illumination?

ACKNOWLEDGMENTS

TEXTUAL ACKNOWLEDGMENTS

Barnes & Noble Books   Excerpts from *The Concept of Mind* by Gilbert Ryle. Reprinted by permission.

Basil Blackwell Publisher Ltd.   Excerpt from "Evil and Omnipotence" by J. L. Mackie, in *The Philosophy of Religion*, edited by Basil Mitchell, 1971. Reprinted by permission.

Beacon Press   Excerpt from *One Dimensional Man: Studies in the Ideology of Advanced Industrial Society* by Herbert Marcuse. Copyright © 1964 by Herbert Marcuse. Used by permission of Beacon Press.

The Bobbs-Merrill Company, Inc.   Excerpts from *On Free Choice of the Will* by St. Augustine, translated by Anna S. Benjamin and L. H. Hackstaff. Reprinted by permission. Excerpts from *Three Dialogues between Hylas and Philonous* by George Berkeley, edited by Colin M. Turbayne. Reprinted by permission. Excerpts from *Prolegomena to any Future Metaphysics* by Immanuel Kant, translated by Lewis W. Beck. Reprinted by permission. Excerpts from *Foundations of the Metaphysics of Morals* by Immanuel Kant, translated by Lewis W. Beck. Reprinted by permission. Excerpts from *Selected Works* by Lucian, translated by Bryan P. Reardon. Reprinted by permission.

Cambridge University Press   Excerpts from *A History of Greek Philosophy*, Volume I, by W. K. C. Guthrie, published by Cambridge University Press, 1962, reprinted by permission. Excerpt from *Philosophical Theology* by F. R. Tennant, published by Cambridge University Press, 1930. Reprinted by permission.

Cornell University Press   Excerpts from *Euthyphro* by Plato. Reprinted from *Plato on the Trial and Death of Socrates: "Euthyphro," "Apology," "Crito," "Phaedo,"* translated by Lane Cooper. Copyright 1941, by Lane Cooper. Used by permission of the publisher, Cornell University Press.

Dover Publications, Inc.   Excerpt from *A Philosophical Essay on Probabilities* by Pierre Simon de Laplace, translated by F. W. Truscott and F. L. Emory. Reprinted by permission.

The Estate of Anton C. Pegis   Excerpts from *Summa Theologiae* in *Basic Writings of St. Thomas Aquinas*. Reprinted by permission of Richard J. Pegis.

Frederick Ungar Publishing Company, Inc.   Excerpts from *The Dark Night of the Soul* by St. John of the Cross. Reprinted by permission.

George Allen & Unwin (Publishers) Ltd.   Excerpt from "The Existence of God: A Debate Between

Bertrand Russell and Father F. C. Copleston" in *Why I am not a Christian* by Bertrand Russell, George Allen & Unwin (Publishers) Ltd., 1957. Reprinted by permission.

Harper & Row, Publishers, Inc./Chatto & Windus Ltd./Hick, Prof. John   For the entries "mechanism," "mechanist," and "mechanistic" on page 149, and for the entries "skeptic," "Skeptic," "skeptical," and "skepticism" on page 172, from *Funk & Wagnalls Standard College Dictionary*. Copyright © 1977 by Harper & Row, Publishers, Inc. Reprinted by permission of Harper & Row, Publishers, Inc. Excerpts from *Religion and the Modern Mind* by W. T. Stace. Reprinted by permission of Harper & Row, Publishers, Inc. Excerpt from *The Doors of Perception* by Aldous Huxley on pages 25–27. Copyright 1954, by Aldous Huxley. Reprinted by permission of Harper & Row, Publishers, Inc., and by Chatto & Windus Ltd. of London, England. Excerpts from *Evil and the God of Love*, revised edition, by John Hick on pages 338–340. Copyright © 1966, 1978 by John Hick. Reprinted by permission of Harper & Row, Publishers, Inc., and by permission of Prof. John Hick of Birmingham, England.

Harvard University Press   Excerpts from *A Theory of Justice*. Reprinted by permission of the publishers from *A Theory of Justice* by John Rawls, Cambridge, Mass.: The Belknap Press of Harvard University Press, copyright © 1971 by the President and Fellows of Harvard College.

Humanities Press Inc./Routledge & Kegan Paul Ltd.   Excerpt from *Religion, Philosophy, and Psychical Research* by C. D. Broad. Reprinted by permission of Humanities Press Inc., Atlantic Highlands, N. J. 07716, and by permission of Routledge & Kegan Paul Ltd. Excerpts from *Theaetetus* by Plato, translated by F. M. Cornford. Reprinted by permission of Humanities Press Inc., Atlantic Highlands, N. J. 07716, and by permission of Routledge & Kegan Paul Ltd.

Jastrow, Prof. Robert   Excerpts from *God and the Astronomers*, published by Warner Books, Inc., 1978. Reprinted by permission of the author, Dr. Robert Jastrow.

Journal of Philosophy and Phenomenological Research   Excerpt from "The New Subjectivism in Ethics" by Brand Blanshard (9, 1949). Reprinted by permission.

The Journal Press   Excerpt from "Anthropology and the Abnormal" by Ruth Benedict in the *Journal of General Psychology* (10, 1934). Reprinted by permission.

Excerpt from *The Future of an Illusion* from Volume 21 of *The Standard Edition of the Complete Psychological Works of Sigmund Freud*, translated by W. D. Robson-Scott, revised and edited by James Strachey, reprinted by permission of the original publisher, Liveright Publishing Corporation, and by permission of Sigmund Freud Copyrights, Ltd., The Institute of Psycho-analysis, and the Hogarth Press Ltd.

Lyle Stuart Inc.   Excerpt from *The Philosophy of Existentialism* by Gabriel Marcel, translated by Manya Harari. Reprinted by permission. Excerpt from *Existentialism and Human Emotions* by Jean-Paul Sartre, translated by Bernard Frechtman. Reprinted by permission.

Macmillan Publishing Company, Inc./Collins Publishers/SCM Press Ltd.   Excerpt from *Mere Christianity* by C. S. Lewis (copyright 1943, 1945, 1952 by Macmillan Publishing Company. Copyrights renewed). Reprinted by permission of Macmillan Publishing Company and Collins Publishers. Excerpt from "Divine Omnipotence and Human Freedom" by Antony Flew, in *New Essays in Philosophical Theology*, edited by Flew and MacIntyre, SCM Press, 1966. Reprinted by permission of SCM Press Ltd. and Macmillan Publishing Company, Inc.

Malcolm, Prof. Norman   Excerpts from *Knowledge and Certainty: Essays and Lectures*, Prentice-Hall, 1963. Reprinted by permission of the author, Dr. Norman Malcolm.

Marquette University Press   Excerpt from *Against the Academicians* by St. Augustine, translated by Sister Mary Patricia Garvey. Reprinted by permission.

McGraw-Hill Book Company   Excerpt from *Early Writings* by Karl Marx, translated and edited by T. B. Bottomore, copyright 1964 by McGraw-Hill Book Company. Reprinted by permission.

National Council of the Churches of Christ in the U.S.A.   Excerpts from Job, Isaiah, and II Maccabees, from the *Revised Standard Version of the Bible,* copyright 1946, 1952, © 1971, 1973. Reprinted by permission.

Oxford University Press   Excerpt from "Free Enterprise as the Embodiment of Justice" by John Hospers, from *Ethics, Free Enterprise, and Public Policy: Original Essays on Moral Issues in Business,* edited by Richard T. DeGeorge and Joseph A. Pichler. Copyright © 1978 by Oxford University Press, Inc. Reprinted by permission. Excerpts from *The Idea of the Holy* by Rudolf Otto, translated by John W. Harvey (2d ed. 1950). Reprinted by permission of Oxford University Press. Excerpts from *The Republic of Plato* translated by F. M. Cornford (1941). Reprinted by permission of Oxford University Press.

Paulist Press   Excerpt from *A History of Philosophy,* Volume I, by Frederick Copleston, copyright 1946 by Paulist Press. Reprinted by permission.

Penguin Books Ltd.   Excerpts from the *Apology* by Plato, 30E–31A, 38A, in *The Last Days of Socrates,* translated by Hugh Tredennick (Penguin Classics, Revised edition 1959), copyright © Hugh Tredennick, 1954, 1959. Reprinted by permission of Penguin Books Ltd. Excerpts from the *Phaedo* by Plato, 100C–E, 65A–67B, 74A–75D, in *The Last Days of Socrates,* translated by Hugh Tredennick (Penguin Classics, revised edition, 1959), copyright © Hugh Tredennick, 1954, 1959. Reprinted by permission of Penguin Books Ltd.

The Phi Beta Kappa Foundation   Excerpt from "The Guide of Life" by C. J. Ducasse (*The Key Reporter,* January 1958). Reprinted by permission.

Prentice-Hall, Inc.   Excerpts from William K. Frankena, *Ethics,* 2d edition, © 1973, pp. 35–36, 39–40, 13. Reprinted by permission of Prentice-Hall, Inc., Englewood Cliffs, New Jersey. Excerpt from Richard Taylor, *Metaphysics,* 2d Edition, © 1974, pp. 16–18. Reprinted by permission of Prentice-Hall, Inc., Englewood Cliffs, New Jersey.

Random House, Inc./Alfred A. Knopf, Inc.   Excerpts from *The Myth of Sisyphus and Other Essays,* by Albert Camus, translated by Justin O'Brien, copyright © 1955 by Alfred A. Knopf, Inc. Reprinted by permission of the publisher. Excerpt from *The Plague,* by Albert Camus, translated by Stuart Gilbert, copyright © 1948 by Alfred A. Knopf, Inc. Reprinted by permission. Excerpts from *Beyond Freedom and Dignity,* by B. F. Skinner, copyright © 1971 by B. F. Skinner. Reprinted by permission of Alfred A. Knopf, Inc.

The Rocky Mountain News   For the article "Schroeder Vs. Decker" by Charles Roos, in *The Rocky Mountain News,* October 30, 1982. Reprinted by permission of the Managing Editor, Mr. Ben Blackburn.

Simon & Schuster   Excerpt from *Saved! The Story of the Andrea Doria—The Greatest Sea Rescue in History,* copyright © 1979 by William Hoffer. Reprinted by permission of Summit Books, a Simon & Schuster division of Gulf & Western Corporation.

Smart, Prof. J. J. C./The Journal of Philosophy   Excerpt from "Materialism" by J. J. C. Smart, in *The Journal of Philosophy* (October 24, 1963). Reprinted by permission of Dr. Smart and *The Journal of Philosophy.*

University of Notre Dame Press   Excerpt from "The Dematerialization of Matter" by N. R. Hanson in *The Concept of Matter,* edited by E. McMillin. Reprinted by permission.

Vedanta Press   Excerpt from *The Song of God: Bhagavad-Gita,* translated by Swami Prabhavananda and Christopher Isherwood. Reprinted by permission of the Vedanta Society of Southern California.

Victor Gollancz Ltd.   Excerpt from *Language, Truth and Logic* by A. J. Ayer, published by Victor Gollancz Ltd., 1946. Reprinted by permission.

W. W. Norton & Company, Inc.   Excerpt by Lucretius, reprinted from *The Nature of Things,* Lucretius, translated by Frank O. Copley, by permission of W. W. Norton & Company, Inc. Copyright © 1977 by W. W. Norton & Company, Inc.

Wadsworth Publishing Company   Excerpt from *A Preface to Philosophy*, second edition, by Mark B. Woodhouse. © 1980 by Wadsworth, Inc. Reprinted by permission of Wadsworth Publishing Company, Belmont, California 94002.

Yale University Press   Excerpt from *An Introduction to Metaphysics* by Martin Heidegger, translated by Ralph Manheim, 1959. Reprinted by permission.

Ziff-Davis Publishing Company   Excerpt from "Language and the Mind" by Noam Chomsky in *Readings in Psychology Today*. Reprinted from *Psychology Today Magazine*, copyright © 1968 by Ziff-Davis Publishing Company. Used by permission.

VISUAL ACKNOWLEDGMENTS

Photographs appearing on pp. 107, 115, 126, 150, 219, 261, 362, 395, and 400, courtesy of The Bettmann Archive.

Photograph appearing opposite p. 1, courtesy of the Trustees of the British Museum.

Palomar Observatory photograph appearing on p. 50, reproduced by permission of the California Institute of Technology and courtesy of the Hansen Planetarium.

Photograph appearing on p. 4 by permission of the Capitoline Museum, Rome, Italy.

Photograph of a chapel in the Cathedral Church of Christ at Canterbury, appearing on p. 246, courtesy of Father John Connely of Boulder, Colorado.

Photographs appearing on pp. 32, 168, 306, 367, and 419, courtesy of Culver Pictures.

Cover art entitled "Planetarium," reproduced by permission of the artist, Hans Erni.

Photographs appearing on pp. 267 and 462 by permission of The Granger Collection, New York.

Photograph appearing on p. 14, courtesy of the Harvard University Archives.

Photograph of the Tassie medallion of Adam Smith appearing on p. 459, courtesy of The Hunterian Museum, University of Glasgow.

Linocut portrait of Bertrand Russell appearing on p. 294, reproduced by permission of the artist, Bill Jackson of Wichita, Kansas.

Photograph of J. L. David's "The Death of Socrates" appearing on p. 191, courtesy of the Metropolitan Museum of Art. All rights reserved, The Metropolitan Museum of Art.

Photograph appearing on p. 148, courtesy of the National Portrait Gallery, London, England.

Photographs appearing on pp. 100, 113, 226, and 268, courtesy of The New York Public Library.

Lithograph appearing on p. 369, reproduced courtesy of the Oslo Kommunes Kunstsamlinger and the Munchforlaget A/S, Norway.

Photograph appearing on p. 248, courtesy of Time Inc. Copyright 1966 Time Inc. All rights reserved. Reprinted by permission from *Time*.

Photographs appearing on pp. 58, 92, and 387, by permission of The Vatican Museum, Vatican City, Rome, Italy.

INDEX